Praise for Africa's Top Wildlife Countries

"Africa is an incredibly diverse and changing place. Lodges and camps come and go on the safari circuit, emerging destinations like Mozambique and Ethiopia offer new wildlife experiences, and tried and true countries like Kenya, Tanzania and Botswana continue to redefine the classic safari. The 7th edition of Mark Nolting's book stays ahead of the curve with valuable insights and information to help you plan your own unique safari."

— COSTAS CHRIST
GLOBAL TRAVEL EDITOR, NATIONAL GEOGRAPHIC ADVENTURE

"A trip to Africa is for most the trip of a lifetime. *Africa's Top Wildlife Countries* is an incredible guide that provides a wealth of information on everything you will need to help you best prepare for the adventure. It is full of wonderful tips on everything from where to stay, times to go, and the incredible wildlife that you can expect to see. Mark Nolting has taken his many years of experience in Africa and provided a resource that will be invaluable to anyone planning this dream vacation and hoping to get the most out of what this great continent has to offer. Don't go on safari before reading this book!"

— RON MAGILL
COMMUNICATIONS & MEDIA MIAMI METROZOO

"Every safari to Africa is both a physical and spiritual journey, and each is rewarding. But knowledge of the very finest African safari destinations is actually like a small secret jewel. When a safari is perfect it will be even greater than you can imagine, and literally alter they way you view life forever after. Mark's book is an honest and revealing analysis of the best. Beyond that you must choose. But once armed with this precious insight, at least you can focus on that journey with confidence, because no venture into Africa is to be taken lightly. You are visiting the roots of mankind, in our place or origin. You are reaching deep into a place of instincts and even exploring the euphoria of being close to your animalistic self. You will come back changed. And you will have fun changing. But while Africa's part of the bargain is to give you that exposure, that experience of a lifetime, as a traveler your part to play is in a dual responsibility of being open to our cultures and to be as informed as you can be. This book is the best single way to prepare for that."

— DERECK JOUBERT
EXPLORER IN RESIDENCE AT THE NATIONAL GEOGRAPHIC SOCIETY,
CONSERVATIONIST, FILMMAKER

D0054489

"Africa's Top Wildlife Countries was my key reference book ten years ago when I first started traveling in Africa. It was a first rate, no nonsense resource then and it just keeps getting better with each edition. The book contains detailed information about each country and what it offers; it is content rich and very well organized, making it very easy to use as a planning guide. Nolting's book covers all the things that matter most when traveling to Africa; where to go, when are the best times, what you will see, what activities are available in each country. Everything you need to know to plan your African Safari is covered in this fantastic book!"

— **GENE ECKHART** – PROFESSIONAL PHOTOGRAPHER AND AUTHOR OF "MOUNTAIN GORILLAS: BIOLOGY, CONSERVATION AND COEXISTENCE"

"Africa's Top Wildlife Countries is my main reference book for traveling to Africa…and has been for more than a decade. It told me about places I'd only heard of…and many I had NEVER heard of. To this day, I have used the book as a reference for planning almost a dozen 'trips of a lifetime' to Africa…and I plan to keep going on more!!"

— **ABBY LAZAR**
JAMESVILLE, NY

"I started traveling to Africa in 1993. Upon returning to New York from my second trip, I picked up a copy of *Africa's Top Wildlife Countries* and read it cover to cover as I knew I was hooked on the experience and could not wait to go again. I was very impressed with the depth of knowledge and information imparted in the book, and have used the last several editions to help me plan the 15 trips I have taken to Africa since!"

— **IVA SPITZER**
NEW YORK, NY

"When I decided to plan a trip of a lifetime to Africa, I started with National Geographic to find a travel reference they recommended. This is how I found the book *Africa's Top Wildlife Countries*. This book was an amazing resource for someone who had no idea where they wanted to go within the continent of Africa…I just knew I wanted to go to Africa! Through reading the book and contacting Mark Nolting directly at The Africa Adventure Company, I was not only able to make my decision to travel to East Africa but also make the necessary preparations for the trip."

— **JAMI GRAHAM**
TAMPA, FL

7th Edition

AFRICA's
Top Wildlife Countries

Botswana, Kenya, Namibia, Rwanda, South Africa, Tanzania,
Uganda, Zambia & Zimbabwe

also including Burundi, Congo, Ethiopia, Lesotho, Malawi, Mozambique,
Swaziland, Mauritius & Seychelles Islands

Mark W. Nolting

Africa's Top Wildlife Countries
(Seventh Edition, completely revised and updated)
    Copyright: 2009 by Mark Nolting
    ISBN: 978-0-939895-12-0
    Edited by: Alison V. H. Nolting and Sarah Taylor
    Cover and Interior Design by: 1106 Design
    Maps and Illustrations by Duncan Butchart
    Published by: Global Travel Publishers, Inc.

Enquiries should be addressed to: Global Travel Publishers, Inc. 5353 N. Federal Highway, Suite 300, Ft. Lauderdale, FL 33308, U.S.A., Telephone (954) 491-8877 or (800) 882-9453, Facsimile (954) 491-9060. Email safaribooks@aol.com

PUBLISHER'S NOTE: Although every effort has been made to ensure the correctness of the information in this book, the author, editor and publisher do not assume, and hereby disclaim, any liability to any party for any loss or damage caused by errors, omissions, misleading information or any potential travel problem caused by information in this guide, even if such errors or omission are a result of negligence, accident or any other cause.

Publisher's Cataloging-in-Publication
(Provided by Quality Books, Inc.)

Nolting, Mark, 1951–
    Africa's top wildlife countries : Botswana, Kenya,
    Namibia, Rwanda, South Africa, Tanzania, Uganda, Zambia
    & Zimbabwe : also including Burundi, Congo, Ethiopia,
    Lesotho, Malawi, Mozambique, Swaziland, Mauritius &
    Seychelles Islands / Mark W. Nolting. — 7th ed.,
    completely rev. and updated.
        p. cm.
        Includes index.
        ISBN-13: 978-0-939895-12-0
        ISBN-10: 0-939895-12-9

    1. Wildlife watching—Africa, Sub-Saharan—
    Guidebooks. 2. Safaris—Africa, Sub-Saharan—
    Guidebooks. 3. National parks and reserves—Africa,
    Sub-Saharan—Guidebooks. 4. Africa, Sub-Saharan—
    Guidebooks. I. Title.

QL337.S78N65 2009   916.704'33
                               QBI08-600237

Printed in the United States of America
Distributed by Publishers Group West

Printed on recycled paper

. . . .

Foreword

Dear Safarier:

You are about to plan the adventure of a lifetime! If this is your first safari or your twentieth, there is one thing we can guarantee — Africa will inspire you! It is impossible to not be touched in some way by the magic of Africa. The sights and sounds will leave you breathless and the people you'll encounter will leave an imprint on your spirit.

Over the past three decades I have had the privilege of exploring Africa on countless safaris. Having seen the need for an easy-to-use comprehensive travel guide covering all the top wildlife regions, I authored this guidebook — now in its 7th edition. Having spent hours of preparation for each of my earlier safaris, and carrying with me several heavy resource books on mammals, reptiles, birds and trees, as well as maps, phrase books and a diary, the idea of consolidating all this into one book was formed, and I authored the *African Safari Journal* — now available in it's 5th edition.

Why do so many people wish to go to Africa, and why do so many return time and time again after experiencing a well-planned safari? One of the main allures of Africa is that you can find adventure there. When you go on a game-viewing activity, you never know what you're going to see or what is going to happen. Every safari is exciting.

With so many changes taking place in the realm of travel, it is imperative to book your safari with a company whose expertise and passion are in sync with your own. From my very first safari I had a dream to establish a safari company unlike any other. From that dream, The Africa Adventure Company was born in 1986. For the past several years we have been honored to have been selected as one of Conde Nast *Traveler's* Top Specialists in the World. As a company we have steered clear of the cookie cutter itineraries and focused on what we love the most, remote Africa. My passion has always been to have people experience the "real Africa". If you have traveled on one of our trips you know what I am referring to; small out-of-the way camps, top notch guiding, incredible game viewing and memories to last a lifetime.

Africa is going through its own evolution of eco-conservation. More and more of the continent's wildlife is becoming threatened. We may be the last generation to see Africa in its true glory — huge herds of wildlife and tribal cultures living unaffected lifestyles. Going on a photographic safari is a donation, in itself, toward conserving African wildlife and habitats. A safari could be the most enjoyable and rewarding environmental contribution you will ever make and there is no better time to venture to Africa than the present!

Sincerely,

Mark W. Nolting, President, Africa Adventure Company

The
Africa Adventure
Company

The Africa Adventure Company
5353 N. Federal Highway, Suite 300
Ft. Lauderdale, FL 33308
Tel: 800-882-WILD (9453)
Tel: 954-491-8877
Fax: 954-491-9060
Email: safari@AfricanAdventure.com
Website: *www.AfricanAdventure.com*

An invitation

Before booking your trip to Africa, contact us at
The Africa Adventure Company
to discuss the many safari options we have to offer.
Call today — my expert staff and I would love to
assist you in planning your safari!

See pages 726–728 for additional details

OTHER BOOKS BY MARK W. NOLTING

AFRICAN SAFARI JOURNAL...
The African Safari Journal is the perfect book to take on safari
as it is a wildlife/botany guide, trip organizer, safari directory,
phrasebook, safari diary, map directory and wildlife checklist
all in one! (See pages 720–721 for details.)

Contents

Contents

Call of the Wild

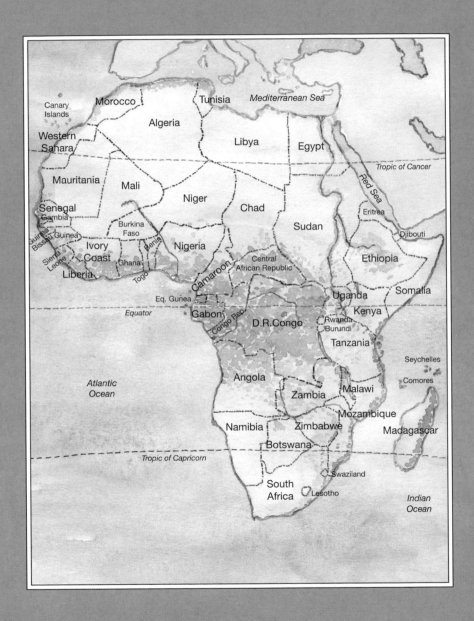

CALL OF THE WILD

A visit to Africa allows you to experience nature at its finest — almost devoid of human interference. The continent pulses to a natural rhythm of life that has remained basically unchanged since the beginning of time.

At our deepest roots, the African continent communicates with our souls. Travelers return home, not only with exciting stories and adventures to share with friends and family, but with a better understanding of nature, a feeling of accomplishment, increased self-confidence and broader horizons from having ventured where few have gone. Here's the kind of adventure about which many dream but few experience!

Having visited Africa once, you will want to return again and again to the peace, tranquility and adventure it has to offer. In this book, I invite you to explore the reasons for this ceaseless pull as we journey to some of the most fascinating places on earth.

Feature films like *The Serengeti* (Imax), *Out of Africa*, *African Queen* and *Gorillas in the Mist*, along with countless documentaries, have kindled in the hearts of many people the flame of desire for travel to Africa. Paging through oversized coffee table books like *Africa* and *Eyes Over Africa* (by Michael Poliza) also makes the thought of traveling in Africa almost irresistible.

The time to visit Africa is now. Despite a network of large wildlife reserves, Africa's poverty threatens natural habitats and the wildlife they contain, as people look for ways to get ahead. Only viable ecotourism initiatives — where local communities reap benefits from foreign income generated by lodges and entry fees to parks — can provide an alternative to short-term poaching, the growing of subsistence crops on marginal land, or selling out to

Elephants communicate with one another over long distances with subsonic "infra sounds"

multinational companies that transform entire landscapes into sterile monocultures. Most of Africa's people cherish their rich cultural background, yet they also yearn for material development. The challenge is to make room for both. Many of the localities featured in this book will provide you with an opportunity to see wildlife in abundance and also to meet people whose ancestors have been co-existing with nature for thousands of years. But the pressure is on, and the time to go is now, while Africa can still deliver all that it promises — and more!

Africa has such a tremendous variety of attractions that most everyone can find something fascinating to do. In addition to fabulous wildlife, the continent boasts one of the world's largest waterfalls (Victoria Falls), the world's longest river (the Nile), the world's largest inland delta (the Okavango), the world's largest intact volcanic caldera (Ngorongoro), the world's highest mountain that is not part of a range (Mt. Kilimanjaro) and beautiful cities like Cape Town. Africa is also home to some of the world's last and largest animal migrations. Accommodations ranging from comfortable to opulent have made Africa extremely inviting to even the most discerning traveler and the adventurer as well.

Africa is huge. It is the second largest continent on earth, covering over 20% of the planet's land surface. More than three times the size of the United States, it is also larger than Europe, the United States and China combined. No wonder it has so much to offer!

African Facts at a Glance

Area: 11,635,000-square-miles (30,420,000-km^2)

Approximate size: More than three times the size of the United States; larger than Europe, the United States and China combined; the second largest continent, covering 20% of the world's land surface

Population: 625,000,000 (approx.)

Largest waterfall: Victoria Falls (the world's largest waterfall by volume), twice the height of Niagara Falls and one-and-a-half times as wide

Longest river: Nile River (world's longest), 4,160 miles (6,710 km)

Largest crater: Ngorongoro Crater (largest intact caldera/crater in the world), 12 miles (19 km) wide with its rim rising 1,200 to 1,600 feet (366 to 488 m) off its expansive 102-square-mile (264-km^2) floor

Highest mountain: Mt. Kilimanjaro (highest mountain in the world not part of a range), 19,340 feet (5,895 m)

Largest lake: Lake Victoria (world's third largest), 26,828-square-miles (69,485-km^2)

Largest freshwater oasis: Okavango Delta (Botswana), over 6,000-square-miles (15,000-km^2)

Largest desert: Sahara (world's largest), larger than the continental United States

Largest land mammal: Elephant (world's largest), over 15,000 pounds (6,800 kg)

Largest bird: Ostrich (world's largest), over 8 feet (2.5 m) tall

Deepest lake: Lake Tanganyika (world's second deepest), over 4,700 feet (1,433 m)

Longest lake: Lake Tanganyika (world's longest), 446 miles (714 km)

Longest rift valley: The Great Rift Valley, a 5,900 mile (9,500 km) gash from the Red Sea to Lake Malawi, with 30 active volcanoes

Most species of fish: Lake Malawi (500 species)

Tallest people: The Dinka of southern Sudan (world's tallest) generally reach on average 5'11" (180 cm)

Shortest people: The pygmies of the Congo (world's shortest) reach only 4'11" (125 cm)

Eastern and Southern Africa World Heritage Sites

The United Nations Educational, Scientific and Cultural Organization (UNESCO) has a focused goal to protect and embrace the past for future generations to enjoy. World Heritage sites are chosen based on their unique and diverse natural and cultural legacy. The preservation of these sites around the world is considered to be an outstanding value to humanity.

Below is a list of Eastern and Southern Africa World Heritage Sites:

Botswana
Tsodilo Hills

Ethiopia
Simien National Park
Rock-Hewn Churches, Lalibela
Fasil Ghebbi, Gondar Region
Aksum
Lower Valley of the Awash
Lower Valley of the Omo
Tiya
Harar Jugol, the Fortified Historic
    Town

Kenya
Lake Turkana National Park
Mt. Kenya National Park / Natural
    Forest
Lamu Old Town

Malawi
Lake Malawi National Park
Chongoni Rock Art Area

Mauritius
Aapravasi Ghat

Mozambique
Ilha de Mozambique

Namibia
Twyfelfontein

Seychelles
Aldabra Atoll
Vallee de Mai Nature Reserve

South Africa
Fossil Hominid Sites of
    Sterkfontein, Swartkrans,
    Kromdraai and Environs
Greater St. Lucia Wetland Park
Robben Island
uKhahlamba/Drakensberg Park
Mapungubwe Cultural Landscape
Cape Floral Region Protected Area
Vredefort Dome
Richtersveld Cultural and
    Botanical Landscape

Tanzania
Ngorongoro Conservation Area
Ruins of Kikwa Kisiwani and
    Ruins of Songo Mnara
Serengeti National Park
Selous Game Reserve
Kilimanjaro National Park
Stone Town of Zanzibar
Kondoa Rock-Art-Sites

Uganda
Bwindi Impenetrable National
    Park
Ruwenzori Mountains National
    Park
Tombs of Buganda Kings at Kasubi

Zambia
Mosi-oa-Tunya / Victoria Falls

Zimbabwe
Mana Pools National Park, Sapi
    and Chewore Safari Areas
Great Zimbabwe National
    Monument
Khami Ruins National Monument
Mosi-oa-Tunya / Victoria Falls
Matobo Hills

HOW TO USE THIS BOOK

Africa's Top Wildlife Countries highlights and compares wildlife reserves and other major attractions in the continent's best game viewing countries.

Most people travel to Africa to see the large and spectacular wildlife, unique to this fascinating continent, in its natural surroundings. In addition to lion, elephant, rhino, buffalo, hippo and giraffe, there is an amazing array of other large and small mammals, as well as spectacular birds and a tapestry of compelling cultures.

The finest safaris are not only those that provide the thrill of seeing the big mammals, but also explore the whole ecosystem and capture the true spirit of the African wilderness — making your visit an exciting and educational experience. The combination of unforgettable adventures, great food, service, accommodations and meeting interesting people is the perfect formula for the trip of a lifetime!

This book makes planning your adventure of a lifetime easy. It is based on over 30 years of my first-hand travel experience in Africa, on trip reports from my staff and literally thousands of clients we have sent on safari. This guidebook is designed to help you decide the best place or places to go in Africa, to do what you want to do, when you want to do it, in a manner of travel that suits you.

The most social of the cat family, a pride of lions typically consist of related females and their offspring

With so much conflicting information available on the Internet, many people become quickly confused. In this book I have simplified the travel planning process by rating the safari accommodations and focusing on accommodations, parks and reserves that would be of greatest interest to international travelers.

Using the easy-to-read **When's The Best Time To Go For Game Viewing** chart (see inside front cover), you can conveniently choose the specific reserves and country(ies) that are best to visit during your vacation period. From the **What Wildlife Is Best Seen Where** chart (see inside back cover), you can easily locate the major reserves that have an abundance of the animals you wish to see most. From the **Safari Activities** chart (see page 46), you can choose the reserves that offer the safari options that interest you most. From the **Temperature and Rainfall charts** (see pages 87–88), you can decide how best to dress for safari and have an idea of what weather to expect.

Also included are **Safari Tips, Photography Tips, Birdwatching Tips, Packing Lists** and **What to Wear — What to Take, and a Visa/Vaccination chart** to better prepare you and to enhance your enjoyment while on safari.

The **Safari Glossary** (see pages 659–661) contains words commonly used on safari and defines words used throughout the book. English is the major language in most of the countries covered in this guide, so language is, in fact, not a problem for English-speaking visitors.

The **Safari Resource Directory** (see pages 633–672) provides a veritable gold mine of difficult-to-find information and sources on Africa. The **Suggested Reading List** (see pages 664–672) includes over 200 publications on the wildlife, cultures, landscapes and history of sub-Saharan Africa.

The **nine top safari countries** are divided between Southern Africa and East and Central Africa, and, in general, appear in their order of desirability as safari destinations. The most important safari countries are **Botswana, Zimbabwe, Zambia, Namibia** and **South Africa** in Southern Africa and **Tanzania, Kenya, Uganda** and **Rwanda** in East Africa. Following the top wildlife countries are chapters on the island paradise countries of **Mauritius** and the **Seychelles**. Also included are chapters on seven neighboring countries including the emerging destinations of **Ethiopia** and **Mozambique**.

To get the most out of this book, first read through this introduction ("Call of the Wild"). Next, read the chapter or chapters on the countries that you feel offer the kind of experience you are looking for in Africa. Then call us at The Africa Adventure Company (toll-free 1-800-882-9453 in the United States and Canada or 954-491-8877 from other countries) or email us (safari@ AfricanAdventure.com) to discuss your thoughts, or visit us on our website *www.AfricanAdventure.com* and complete a safari questionnaire. We will match the experience you are looking for with a fabulous safari program — putting you on track to experience the safari of a lifetime!

WHAT IS A SAFARI LIKE?

What is a safari like? For one thing, exciting beyond words! What is a typical day on safari? Most safaris are centered on guests participating in two or three activities per day, such as morning and afternoon game drives in four-wheel-drive (4wd) vehicles or minivans. A game drive consists of having your guide drive you around a park or reserve in search of wildlife. Your guide helps you to interpret and understand what you are seeing in the bush.

Most activities last two to five hours and are conducted when the wildlife is most active: early in the morning (often before breakfast), just after breakfast, in the late afternoon and at night (where allowed by park authorities). Midday activities might include spending time in a "hide" observing wildlife, lazing around the swimming pool, reading, visiting a local village or school, birdwatching or viewing game as it passes by your tent or lodge, or taking a siesta (nap). After an exhilarating day on safari, many guests return to revel in the day's adventures over exquisite European or Pan-African cuisine in lodges and camps that range from comfortable to extremely luxurious with private swimming pools and butler service.

The kind and quality of experience you may have on safari vary greatly from country to country, and even from park to park within the same country. For instance, going on safari in East Africa (Kenya, Tanzania, Uganda and Rwanda) is generally different from going on safari in Southern Africa (Botswana, Zimbabwe, Zambia, Namibia and South Africa).

Zebras live in small family groups led by one dominant stallion

Simply watching wildlife from a vehicle anywhere in Africa is an experience in itself. However, more and more people prefer to personally participate more in the adventure — to experience more from the safari than simply watching animals. How can that be accomplished? By choosing a safari that includes parks that allow you to participate in activities that make you a more integral part of the safari, like walking, boating and canoeing. Choose smaller camps and lodges that are unfenced where wildlife is allowed to walk freely about the grounds.

Depending on the park or reserve, safari activities might include day game drives, night game drives, walks, boat safaris, canoeing, kayaking, white-water rafting, ballooning, hiking, mountain climbing, fishing, horseback riding, African elephant-back riding — the options are almost endless. See "Safari Activities" (pages 45–57) and the **Safari Activities Chart** (page 46) which follow.

In terms of the long-term future of Africa's wildlife reserves, it is important to consider selecting a lodge destination from which local people benefit in tangible ways. To be guided by or to meet happy people from various cultures and to learn about their customs will greatly enhance your trip to Africa.

Another excellent way to get the most out of your adventure is to have a **private safari** arranged for you. Why? A private safari immediately becomes *your* safari. You do not have to bow to the wishes of the majority of the group or a strictly set itinerary of group departures. With your guide, you are basically

A vulture and wild dog go nose to nose

free to explore your own interests, spend as much time as you want photographing particular animals, and generally do things at a pace that suits you.

In some cases, for an extra charge you can book a private vehicle for your party when on a flying safari or on a group driving safari. I highly recommend this option as it allows you greater flexibility as to how you spend your time during the day.

To gain a better understanding of what you might experience on safari, I suggest you read the trip reports in "**Bush Tails**" (see pages 676–695).

DISPELLING MYTHS ABOUT TRAVEL ON THE "DARK CONTINENT"

Many prospective travelers to Africa seem to think that, if they go on an African safari, they may have to stay in mud or grass huts or little pup tents, eat strange foods and have dozens of vaccinations. Nothing could be further from the truth!

Almost all of the top parks and reserves covered in this guide have deluxe or first class (Class A+, A or A/B by our grading system) lodges or camps (with en suite bathrooms) that serve excellent food, specifically designed to cater to the discerning traveler's needs. Going on safari can be a very comfortable, fun-filled adventure!

Many prospective travelers to Africa have voiced their fear of being overwhelmed by mosquitoes and other insects or the fear of encountering snakes on safari. However, most travelers return pleasantly surprised, having found that insects or snakes are a greater problem in their own neighborhoods than on safari. For example, on my last several safaris I do not think I had one mosquito bite!

The fact is that most safaris do not take place in the jungle, but on open savannah during the dry season, when the insect populations are at a minimum. In addition, the best time to go on safari, for most of the countries, is during their winter, when insect levels are low and when many snakes hibernate. Also, many parks are located over 3,000 feet (915 m) in altitude, resulting in cool to cold nights, further reducing the presence of any pests. In any case, except for walking safaris, most all of your time in the bush will be spent in the safety of a vehicle or boat. Although some vaccinations are recommended, they are actually not required for travel to many of the top wildlife areas.

Language

English is widely spoken in all the countries featured in this book except Burundi and the Congo, where French is the international language.

The *African Safari Journal* (see pages 720–721) has words and phrases in French, KiSwahili (Kenya, Tanzania), Shona (Zimbabwe), Setswana (Botswana)

A male lion wades through the Okavango Delta in search of prey

and Zulu (Southern Africa), along with illustrations of 311 mammals, birds, reptiles, insects and trees. Your guide will love it if you start naming the animals you spot in his native language!

Green Travel

About 15 years ago, the terms "ecotour" and "ecotourism" hit the travel industry like cholesterol hit the food industry. Many new companies sprang up to claim that their new ecotours were environmentally friendly and implying that they had pioneered this type of travel.

More recently, "Green Travel" has been the mantra boasted by new safari camps and lodges hitting the scene. This is in fact an exciting trend in the travel industry, which has taken upon itself to be a world leader in this movement. What potential safariers need to realize is that some properties and safari operators went "Green" a decade or more ago — but have not gotten involved in hype — and deserve a lot of praise for doing so.

Travelers are becoming more and more interested in visiting properties that protect the environment as well as ensure that the local people benefit from their visits. So what does "Going Green" mean? Green travel has a very low impact on the environment. Travelers take photos and leave little more than footprints. True ecotourism ensures that the local people, who are living adjacent to parks

The Carbon Cycle and Climate Change

Carbon emissions and carbon credits are at the forefront of today's environ-mental issues. How does this relate to travel to Africa? What follows is a well-writ-ten treatise on the subject by Wilderness Safaris, a well-respected safari company managing approximately 60 safari camps and lodges in Southern Africa, and con-sidered one of the world leaders in "Green" tourism and conservation:

Life on Earth is based on carbon — it is a key element of all living matter and is released and re-absorbed in a continual process known as the Carbon Cycle. This cycle basically sees an ongoing exchange of carbon dioxide (CO_2) between the atmosphere and the Earth. This natural exchange is sustainable and healthy, as the carbon dioxide in the Earth's atmosphere helps to trap the heat of the sun, thus regulating the Earth's temperatures to create an environment that is comfortably warm and suitable for life. So how does the cycle work?

- Plants absorb carbon dioxide in the process of photosynthesis and then release it once plants decay back into the atmosphere.
- The ocean also exchanges carbon with the atmosphere at similar levels, with dissolved carbon dioxide being utilized in photosynthesis by marine organisms.

Thus, the carbon cycle is an age-old and natural process that is part of the reason we are able to survive on Earth at all.

However, since the Industrial Revolution, increased levels of carbon dioxide have been released into the atmosphere. This has mainly been as a result of the burning of fossil fuels and the subsequent release of so-called greenhouse gases such as carbon dioxide (but including others such as methane) that have been implicated in global warming. For example, pre-industrial carbon dioxide levels have risen by more than a third!

In short, the release of carbon into the atmosphere now occurs at a rate that outstrips the ability of the planet to re-absorb it. This increase in rates of release is exacerbated by a decreased capacity for absorption as a result of deforestation and other factors. In other words, the world's carbon sinks, or absorption points — places like the Amazon or Congo — that are essential parts of the world's carbon cycle, are being destroyed and impacted on in a way that affects not only local biodiversity but also global climate. Put bluntly, if carbon emissions continue to increase at this rate, climate change is the potentially catastrophic inevitability.

"Global warming" is the term used for the resulting climate change — not only because of the increase of carbon dioxide (and other gases) in our atmosphere but also because the increase itself causes more water to evaporate from the ocean and enter the atmosphere, in turn increasing the temperature a little more.

Given that intercontinental transportation is a major contributor to carbon emis-sions we also believe that this is an issue that needs to be taken seriously by the ecotourism industry and its guests.

Rather than simply pay offset fees to projects that claim to offer carbon sequestra-tion or absorption we believe it is important to understand the fundamentals of the car-bon cycle and the intrinsic value of ecotourism within this cycle as a carbon sink. What we would like to emphasize is that it is exactly this kind of travel (Green or Eco-Travel) that allows the continued existence of vitally important carbon sinks. The success of businesses like ours in all parts of the world will play an important role in the preserva-tion of the world's wilderness areas that we believe will ultimately save humankind.

The Skeleton Coast, Namibia — the oldest and most fascinating desert in the world

and reserves, benefit directly from tourism in such a way that they have a positive incentive to preserve wildlife and the environment.

A safari that includes visits to the right camps and lodges is in itself a contribution toward the preservation of wildlife and wildlife areas and an economic benefit and incentive for the local people to protect their environment, which in turn helps ensure these areas will remain intact and viable "carbon sinks" for generations to come. Taking the right safari could be one of the best donations to the "Green" movement you could make! Please contact The Africa Adventure Company for the most current list of "Green Properties".

The Evolution of Ecotourism
By Costas Christ

Africa was ecotourism's early staging ground. It was in Kenya in the late 1970s that pioneer efforts to link tourism and community-based conservation first got underway in Amboseli National Park. The international conservation community was beginning to realize that the battle to save endangered species would only succeed if local people who lived closest to protected areas and rare wildlife became partners and stakeholders in conservation. That would happen if they benefited directly from protecting nature, and the link in the chain was tourism — today among the largest industries on Earth, and one of the few economic opportunities for developing nations in Africa. The key was creating a new vision for tourism that was committed to tangible benefits to local communities and successful wildlife conservation.

While nature travel to Africa boomed in the 1980s, the tenets of what was to become **ecotourism** were slow to take root. In 1991, when a small group of scientists, conservationists and tour operators from Africa and around the world gathered in a farm house outside of Washington D.C. for the inaugural meeting of The International Ecotourism Society, our first task was to define what, exactly, ecotourism was. We decided on this: "Responsible travel to natural areas that conserves the environment and improves the wellbeing of local people." None of us, however, knew of a real working model of it anywhere.

Today, there are literally hundreds of successful ecotourism models around the world that have helped to bring back species from the verge of extinction and protect their natural habitat. The question before us, is no longer does ecotourism work, but rather just how far can we take it to reach its full potential. Ecotourism has helped to save the Mountain Gorillas of Uganda and Rwanda and protect the rare desert-adapted black rhino in Namibia. It was the reason 11,000 square miles of pristine rainforest in Africa were turned into 13 new national parks in Gabon, and it has put more than a million acres of Samburu and Maasai communal lands into a biodiversity conservation zone in Kenya's northern rangelands.

The principles that were first associated with ecotourism have now given rise to what is being called sustainable tourism — taking the same principles and practices of environmentally sensitive operations, direct social and economic benefits to local communities, and safeguarding natural and cultural heritage — and bringing them into the mainstream tourism industry — from downtown city hotels, to big national park lodges, to sun and sea beach resorts. All of this comes under the general umbrella term of "**Green Travel**". And it is the most significant transformation of tourism in the history of modern travel.

Many people still confuse ecotourism with nature travel — they are not the same thing.

If you and I were to go on a wildlife safari to Tanzania, and we stayed in a nice lodge, saw lots of interesting animals, enjoyed good food, and took wonderful photographs, we would have had a great nature tour. But when that same safari is directly supporting the protection of wildlife, engaged in "leave no trace" practices, contributing to the social and economic wellbe ing of local villagers, then it is transformed into ecotourism. In that sense, ecotourism is really a set of principles and practices that, when applied to nature and adventure travel, create a new opportunity for saving wild places and empowering local people to advance their own lives.

When we take a vacation, our travel choice makes a big difference. By letting tour operators know that we care about the environment when we travel, by following responsible behavior around wildlife in national parks and reserves, and by staying in lodges and camps that are committed to conservation, sourcing locally for their restaurants and handicrafts for gift shops, and employing local people under fair wages and benefits, we are each doing our part to make tourism a powerful opportunity for saving the natural and cultural heritage of our planet. Taking an ecotourism trip to Africa is an investment in protecting this incredible continent's amazing wildlife for future generations, while having the vacation of a lifetime.

— *Costas Christ is the Global Travel Editor for National Geographic Adventure and an internationally recognized ecotourism expert. He lived and worked for 12 years in East Africa.*

Safaris can be customized to most every traveler's unique needs and desires

Security

Concerns over security for the last few years have become less of an issue for most travelers. Finally, travelers are realizing that most of the top wildlife countries are huge (larger than the state of Texas), and that they need only be concerned with security in the areas in which they are traveling, not every crack and corner of the countries they are visiting.

The question should be "Is travel *for tourists* in the specific wildlife reserves and areas you wish to travel to safe?" For instance, I consider the neighborhood I live in "safe". However, there are parts of my city not three miles away that I would not like to risk driving through at night.

Please keep in mind that the people of these African countries covered in this guide welcome tourists with open arms! Kenya's 2007 elections caused some rioting primarily in the western area of the country far from any tourist areas, and in the slums outside Nairobi, where no tourists venture. There were thousands of tourists on any given day in Kenya during the riots, and I am not aware of any of them being negatively affected by it. When you are in the wildlife reserves, the only people you will encounter are the staff who are serving you.

Following the 2007 election, the U.S. Ambassador to Kenya, Michael E. Ranneberger, sent out an open letter that included the following:

"Dear Fellow Citizens:

I'm sure many of you have been following recent events in Kenya, specifically the crisis triggered by the sharply disputed results of elections held in late December. ... I urge you to read the U.S. State Department's Travel Warning for Kenya, available at *www.state.gov*... It does not recommend against travel to Kenya. It is similar to travel warnings issued for several dozen other countries, many of which are also close friends of the U.S. ... **I hope you'll consider visiting Kenya as a tourist or businessperson** in 2008... I hope to see you here soon! I assure you that we will do our utmost to provide appropriate support and assistance for your engagement in Kenya. Karibu Kenya"

Zimbabwe has had political and economic issues for the last decade. Over this period we have sent thousands of travelers to Victoria Falls, Hwange, Matusadona and Mana Pools National Parks, and I am not aware of any of them having any negative experiences regarding security. Even several months after the June 2008 elections no tourists were bothered. Quite the contrary, travelers report being openly welcomed and have felt greatly appreciated by the staff in the camps, and were handsomely rewarded by great game viewing in uncrowded parks at bargain rates. Victoria Falls is located on the border with Zambia and Botswana, and is far from any major cities and potential strife. Business is, in fact, good there and many of the top hotels are full in high season.

Please keep in mind that on many safaris, guests actually fly directly from one reserve to another, and the only people they encounter are other guests and the staff and guides in the safari camps and lodges at which they are staying. Driving safaris are most commonly using well-traveled roads, and the guides are in frequent contact with each other and their offices by radio and/or cellphone.

If you hear news of possible security issues, pay attention to where in the country there are concerns; most of the top safari countries in this book are huge and the area of concern could be hundreds of miles from where you are visiting.

There is little to be worried about when it comes to terrorism while on safari. Safari camps and lodges cater to people from all over the world and are, in almost all cases, owned by non-American or non-British companies. One of the safest places in the world has to be in the African bush!

Related female lions greet each other with a nuzzle

Bespoke Travel

"Bespoke Travel" is the relatively new buzz word in the travel industry to describe customized, tailor-made adventures. These elite adventures are for travelers who want to focus on unique and exclusive experiences. Many new tour companies on the scene imply that they have "invented" this level of travel, however this has been our (Africa Adventure Company) specialty for 22 years. We call upon our own expertise and valuable contacts in Africa to make those one-in-a-lifetime dreams come true.

CHOOSING ACCOMMODATIONS

There is a great variety of styles and levels of comfort in accommodation available in the major cities and while on safari; and they range from simple bungalows to extravagant suites with private swimming pools. Options include hotels, lodges, small camps with chalets or bungalows, houseboats, villas, fixed tented camps and mobile tented camps.

The type of accommodation included in a tour of Africa will have a major influence on the type of experience and adventures you will have on safari.

An important factor to consider when choosing accommodations or a tour is the size of the lodge or camp. In general, guests receive more personal attention at smaller camps and lodges than at larger ones. Large properties tend to stick to a set schedule, while smaller properties are often more willing to amend their schedules according to the preferences of their guests. However, larger accommodations tend to be less expensive, which makes tours using the larger ones more affordable.

Many larger lodges and permanent tented camps (especially in East Africa) are surrounded by electrical fences, allowing guests to move about as they please without fear of bumping into elephant and other dangerous wildlife. Travelers (including myself) who enjoy having wildlife roaming about camp should seek properties that are not fenced; these lodges and camps are best for travelers who want to experience nature at close quarters.

Many properties in Kenya and Tanzania have 50 to 200 beds (while some have under 20 beds), whereas most camps in Botswana, Namibia, South Africa, Zambia and Zimbabwe generally have 6 to 24 beds.

I feel that the most important element in choosing accommodations for a safari is *location, location, location*. If wildlife is your main focus, then the question should be: "What accommodations are located in areas that will provide the best game viewing — and even more specifically — game viewing of the species you wish to see most, and offer the activities (day and night game drives, walks motor boat excursions, canoe safaris, etc.) that interest you most?"

Game viewing can be dramatically better (or worse) from one property to the next — from properties that may be literally just a few miles (kilometers) apart. Permanent tented camps in Botswana's Okavango Delta and lodges in the private reserves near Kruger National Park (South Africa) are prime examples of this.

Through personal experience and having read literally thousands of trip reports from past clients, one area can have several times the wildlife concentrations of another area nearby. However, if you look up these properties on the Internet, they all boast to having spectacular game! This is why I suggest booking your safari with a true African expert who receives *frequent and recent* reports from visitors to camps and lodges, as they will know the properties that offer the best game experience and that offer the food, service and accommodation level that suits your interest.

Great photographers can make any camp or lodge look extremely appealing in brochures and on websites. But what is the property really like? How well do the management and staff treat their guests? Is the food really as good as they boast? Again, this is where an African expert can best assist with first-hand experience.

The web is also full of sites where guests boast or complain about properties they have visited. I frankly suggest taking these reports with a grain of salt, as it is just too easy for lodge, hotel and property owners and staff to write up bogus "outstanding" reports. In any case, the reports may be "old news" if new management or owners have been put into place and have turned a property around.

The acacia tree is the embodiment of Africa

Descriptions of most properties are easy to find on the Web. The discerning reader, however, should look for sites where independent experts have written descriptions of the hotels, safari camps and lodges — and not the properties themselves. I invite you to visit our website *www.AfricanAdventure.com* and check out our descriptions as they have been written by our expert staff; keep in mind that we do not own any properties in Africa so we are free to speak our minds!

Hotels and Hotel Classifications

Many large African cities such as Nairobi (Kenya), Johannesburg and Cape Town (South Africa) have 4- and 5-star (first class and deluxe) hotels that are comparable to lodging anywhere in the world, with air-conditioning and en suite facilities, swimming pools and one or more excellent restaurants and bars, and superb service.

Hotels are categorized as Deluxe, First Class and Tourist Class. The phrases "en suite facilities," "facilities en suite" and "en suite rooms" mean bathrooms (toilet and basin plus shower and/or bathtub) are connected to the sleeping rooms/tents. "Private facilities" means that bathrooms are exclusive to guests but are not connected to the sleeping rooms/tents. "Separate facilities" means that bathrooms are separate from the sleeping quarters, and may, in some cases, be shared by guests from more than one room/tent.

DELUXE: An excellent hotel, rooms with en suite bathroom (toilet plus shower and/or bathtub), air-conditioning, one or more restaurants that serve very good food, and that feature a swimming pool, bars, lounges, room service — all the amenities of a four- or five-star international hotel.

FIRST CLASS: A very comfortable hotel, rooms with en suite facilities, air-conditioning, at least one restaurant and bar, and most have a swimming pool.

TOURIST CLASS: A comfortable hotel with simple rooms with en suite facilities, most with air-conditioning, a restaurant and bar, and most with a swimming pool.

Lodges and Camps

Lodges that range from comfortable to deluxe (many have swimming pools) are located in or near most parks and reserves. Many lodges and camps are located in wildlife areas 3,000 feet (915 m) or more above sea level, so air-conditioning often is not necessary.

There is often confusion over the term "camp." A camp refers to lodging in chalets, bungalows or tents found in a remote location. Camps range from very basic to extremely plush. Deluxe camps often have better service and food, and most certainly a truer safari atmosphere, than large lodges and hotels.

A showdown between lioness and buffalo

Permanent tented camps (sometimes also called fixed tented camps) are camps that are not moved. Aside from generally having better food and service than lodges, guests of permanent tented camps have more of a "safari" experience. They are less isolated from the environment than those who stay in a lodge, and can, for instance, hear the sounds of the wild from inside their tent because the walls are made of canvas. Mobile tented camps are discussed below under "Types of Safaris."

Lodge and Camp Classifications

Lodges and tented camps are classified as Class A+ to F. Accommodations have been primarily graded on facilities, food and service. However, the overall experience, including quality of the guides and management as well as the location of the properties and quality of game viewing, have also, in some cases, been taken into account. For instance, a lodge that might be rated "A+" for accommodations but is in just a fair or a relatively poor game-viewing area might be rated "A".

Keep in mind that a lower-class accommodation may be preferable over a higher-class one if the lower-class option offers better guides and management, a better location (better wildlife) and/or preferable activities.

Over the last several years the overall quality of safari accommodations in Africa has increased dramatically. As the "bar" has been raised, many accommodations that for instance were rated "A" in the last edition of this book may be rated "A/B" in this edition — in spite of the fact that the accommodations may have undergone significant improvements.

CLASS A+: An extremely luxurious lodge or permanent tented camp (five-star) with superb cuisine and excellent service, virtually all with swimming pools, and many with private "plunge" pools (small swimming pools) for each chalet or tent. Lodges and chalets are air-conditioned, while the tents may be air-conditioned or fan-cooled.

CLASS A: A deluxe lodge or tented camp, almost all with swimming pools, excellent food and service, large nicely appointed rooms or tents with en suite facilities, comfortable beds and tasteful decor; the lodges have air-conditioning and the tents are usually fan-cooled.

CLASS A/B: An excellent lodge or tented camp with very good food and service, en suite bathrooms, and many have swimming pools. The rooms/tents are of good size but perhaps not as large as "Class A" properties.

CLASS B: A comfortable lodge or camp with good food and service, en suite bathrooms, and many have swimming pools.

CLASS B/C: Most often, a "Class B" property is one that is very rustic or somewhat inconsistent in the quality of accommodation, food and service, most with en suite bathrooms.

CLASS C: A simple lodge with en suite or private bathrooms; a tented camp, chalet or bungalow with en suite, private or shared facilities and fair food and service; or a "Class B" structure with fair to poor food or service.

CLASS D: A basic lodge or tented camp (lodges, chalets, bungalows and tents seldom have en suite or private bathrooms) or a "Class C" structure with poor food or service. There may be a restaurant, or it may be "self-catering."

A sampling of "Pan-African cuisine"

CLASS F: A very basic lodge or tented camp with separate bathrooms; often self-catering (no restaurant).

Food On Safari

Excellent cuisine, along with interesting local dishes, is served in the top hotels, lodges, camps and restaurants. Many of the more expensive lodges now produce a combination of "Pan-African cuisine" — innovative recipes and ingredients from across the continent, and international fare. Restaurants serving cuisine from all over the world may be found in the larger cities in Africa.

Most international travelers are impressed with the quality of the food and drink served on their safari. The fresh air will give you a healthy appetite. Typical meals include:

Breakfast — Usually fruit and cereal, eggs, bacon and sausage, toast and preserves, tea and coffee.

Lunch — Assorted cold meats and salads with cheeses and bread, and perhaps a warm dish (ie. quiche).

Dinner — Normally three courses, with an appetizer or soup, main entree and vegetables, and a dessert. Class A+ (and some Class A) lodges and camps usually serve four or more courses.

Some safari camps and lodges will provide a light breakfast of tea, coffee, rusks (hard biscuits traditionally served in southern Africa), and cereal in the early morning. Brunch is served at about 11:00 a.m. and follows a game drive or other activity. Tea, coffee, cake and biscuits (cookies) are served at about 3:30 p.m. Following the afternoon game activity, guests return to the lodge for a delicious dinner.

TYPES OF SAFARIS

Lodge and Permanent Tented Camp Safaris

Lodge safaris are simply safaris that use lodges or permanent tented camps as accommodations. Some safaris mix lodges with tented camps or camps with chalets or bungalows, providing a greater range of experiences for their guests.

Mobile Tented Camp Safaris

Private and group mobile tented camp safaris are, in my opinion, one of the best ways to experience the bush and a great way of getting off the beaten track.

Seeing hippo grazing by your tent at night or elephant walking through your camp by day is an experience not to be missed! When on safari with a professional guide, this is not as dangerous as it might sound. Animals will not try to enter a closed tent unless tempted by the smell of food. If you keep the tent flaps closed at night and you don't have food in your tent, you are generally just as safe as if you were staying in a bungalow or chalet. Tanzania, Zimbabwe and Botswana are excellent countries for mobile tented safaris; Kenya, Zambia and Namibia are also good destinations for this type of safari.

Mobile tented safaris range from deluxe to first class, midrange, limited participation and participation safaris. You may join a group departure or have a private safari, depending on your interests and budget. **Warning:** some tour operators advertise their mobile tented camp safaris as "luxury" when they actually operate them on a first class or even a midrange level (ie. small tents with shower and toilet tents separate from the sleeping tents). Be sure to be perfectly clear as to what services they provide!

Top: Deluxe mobile camping in Tanzania
Bottom: Enjoying a moment of solitude in Moremi Game Reserve, Botswana

Deluxe Mobile Tented Camp Safaris

Deluxe mobile tented camp safaris are the epitome of mobile safaris. The sleeping tents are large (approx. 12-by-16 ft./4-by-5 m in floor area or larger) and have en suite bush or safari (bucket) showers and bush or safari (short-drop) toilets. Food and service are excellent. Camp attendants take care of everything, including the delivery of hot water for your shower. Campsites are private and usually set in remote areas of parks and reserves, providing a true *Out of Africa* experience. For a party of four, the cost generally ranges from $500 to $1,000 per person per day.

First Class Mobile Tented Camp Safaris

These are similar to deluxe safaris except that the tents are a little smaller (approx. 8-by-12 ft./2.5-by-3.5 m), yet very comfortable; less expensive cutlery and crockery may be used, there are not quite as many staff, and there is usually a bush shower (hot water) and bush toilet tent attached to the back of each sleeping tent. The food and service is still very good, and private campsites are used. For a party of four, the cost is around $400 to $500 per person per day, depending on the country and season.

Midrange Mobile Tented Camp Safaris

Comfortable (and less expensive) midrange mobile tented safaris are available in a number of countries. Like deluxe and first class mobile tented safaris a camp staff takes care of all the chores. The difference is that the tents are smaller (approx. 8-by-8 ft./2.5-by-2.5 m) but are still high enough in which to stand. The food and service are good, and guests from one to three sleeping tents may share one separate toilet tent and one separate shower tent (with hot water). Private or group campsites may be used. For a party of four, the cost is usually around $300 to $400 per person per day.

Limited Participation Mobile Tented Camp Safaris

On these safaris, the guide usually has one camp attendant to do the heavy work, while guests are expected to assist in some camp chores. Bow-type nylon tents (approx. 8-by-8 ft./2.5-by-2.5 m) are often used, and you usually camp in group campsites. Rates are usually around $200 to $250 per person per day.

Full Participation Mobile Tented Camp Safaris

On full participation mobile tented safaris, participants are required to help with all of the camp chores. Group campsites with basic (if any) facilities are often used.

Reputed to have a bad temper, a black rhino stands its ground

The only advantage is price. Participation camping safaris are almost always less expensive than lodge safaris. However, these are recommended for only hardy travelers with previous camping experience or with a sense of adventure. Many operators have minimum and maximum age limits for their safaris. Hot showers are usually available most nights, but not all. The cost is usually under $150 per person per day. The problem with these low-end safaris is that the guiding is often marginal at best, greatly compromising the quality of the experience.

Guided Driving or Mobile Safaris

Driving safaris are simply safaris in which guests are driven by their driver/guide from reserve to reserve. You generally have the same guide throughout the safari, who should have very good knowledge of all the parks and reserves to be visited.

Driving safaris are usually less expensive than flying safaris (see below). However, travelers should take into account the amount of time it takes to get from reserve to reserve, the quality of the roads and whether or not there will be something enroute that will be of interest to them, and compare that to the cost of doing some or all flying on their safari.

Flying Safaris

Flying safaris are safaris in which guests are flown to or near the wildlife reserves that are to be visited. They are then usually picked up at the airport or airstrip upon arrival and driven to their camp or lodge — which is often a game drive in itself.

Guides and vehicles are based at the camps and lodges at which guests will be staying. A real advantage is that the resident guides should have intimate knowledge of the area because they are usually based in the same camp for the season.

This type of safari is very popular in Botswana, Zimbabwe, Zambia, Namibia, South Africa, Kenya and Tanzania. Time that would normally be spent on the road driving between the parks and reserves may instead be spent game viewing — the primary reason why most people travel to Africa in the first place!

Fly/Drive Safaris

As the name implies, these safaris are a combination of some driving and some flying. The general idea is to fly over areas that are not interesting to drive or that you have already covered on the ground, and drive through the areas that have the most to offer. This is an excellent option in northern Tanzania, for instance, where safariers may be driven from Arusha to Tarangire, Lake Manyara, Ngorongoro Crater and the Serengeti, and then fly back to Arusha instead of driving the same route back. Other popular fly/drive options are available in northern Botswana (small group mobile safaris) and Uganda.

Group Safaris

Group safaris are, in many cases, a more cost-effective way of experiencing the bush than private safaris (see below). Group safaris usually have scheduled departure dates. The key for group safaris in Africa is to be sure the group size is small. Group size should be limited, in my opinion, to 12 or fewer passengers, whereas a maximum of six to eight is preferable.

It never ceases to amaze me the number of tour operators that tout that their maximum group size is limited to only 16, 24 or 30 members. With such large groups, passengers in the lead vehicle see game, while those in the vehicles that follow eat dust. A great deal of time is wasted getting under way and time schedules are very inflexible. Large group tours may be fine for Europe or Asia, but they have no place in the African bush!

Private Safaris

For those who wish to avoid groups, a private safari is highly recommended for several reasons.

An itinerary can be specially designed according to the kind of experience YOU want, visiting the parks and reserves YOU wish to see most, and traveling on dates that suit YOU best.

You may spend your time doing what you want to do rather than having to compromise with the group. If you wish, you may socialize with other travelers at mealtimes and still have the flexibility to do what you want on your game activities.

For instance, if you find a leopard up a tree with a kill, you may stay five minutes or five hours at that location — it's up to you!

What few people realize is that, in many cases, a private safari need not cost more than one with a large group. In fact, I have sent many couples and small groups on private safaris for not much more (and sometimes less) than the cost of group safaris from other tour operators who offer the same or often inferior itineraries. If you find that difficult to believe, call, email or write us with what you have in mind, and we'll be happy to send you an itinerary (see pages 726–728).

Specialist Guided Safaris

A specialist guide is a seasoned naturalist with extensive experience and excellent communication skills — one of the top guides in the region.

How significant is your guide on safari? There is a maxim in the Safari Industry that "a very good guide will take your safari to the next level, and make it 'spectacular'". Using enthusiasm, insight, knowledge, and patience, an expert guide will make your vacation not just a safari, but also an unparalleled trip of a lifetime. The additional experience gained by having one of the top guides in Africa lead your safari is almost priceless.

Your safari guide will spend anywhere from 8 to 15 hours with you per day, basically every waking moment. He or she will become your protector, teacher, fireside storyteller, and most of all, friend. It is very easy for any guide to point out the animals, however an outstanding guide will reveal to you the extraordinary spirit of Africa and what it has to offer.

A specialist guide in Zimbabwe is trained to take guests close to big game

Some specialist guides are great overall naturalists, while others may be experts in particular subjects, such as elephants, predators, birds, botany, nature photography, anthropology, archaeology, etc.

I feel it is a great idea (budget permitting) for a specialist guide to accompany travelers, especially on flying safaris (from one safari camp to another), as it adds continuity of a consistent high level of guiding throughout the safari; they are generally much more experienced than guides that are based at the safari camps and lodges themselves, and are in most cases very entertaining as well. We at The Africa Adventure Company in fact offer this upgrade option to many of our clients!

For a better idea of what a specialist guide can contribute to a safari I suggest you obtain the video "As Close As You Dare" by Becci and Mark Crowe (2007) Crowe World Media. Please see page 672 for details.

Honeymoon Safaris

There is no more romantic setting for a honeymoon than an African safari. Most honeymooners begin with a few days to relax and recover from the wedding in a five-star hotel or beach resort — then it's off on safari!

Honeymoon safaris, like all safaris, can include as plush or rustic accommodations, as you wish. Most camps and small lodges have a "honeymoon tent" or "honeymoon suite" on the premises to ensure maximum privacy. Please keep in mind that most tented camps and small lodges have two single beds per room/tent, so be sure to let them know you are indeed honeymooners.

The epitome of a honeymoon safari, in my opinion, is to have a private vehicle and guide, and preferably spend at least a few nights in a private mobile tented camp. Tenting is truly the *Out of Africa* experience! A few nights mobile camping could be combined with time in more luxurious permanent tented camps and/or lodges — according to the honeymooner's tastes.

My romantic honeymoon included visiting Victoria Falls and Hwange National Park (Zimbabwe), a private reserve near Kruger National Park, Rovos Rail and Cape Town (South Africa), and the Seychelles. What an exciting way to begin a life together!

Family Safaris

More and more parents and grandparents are taking their children and grandchildren on safari. Seeing nature in all its abundance as a child is an experience that cannot be underestimated. As of this writing, our son Miles is 14 years old, and has been on eight safaris; Nicholas is 11 and has been on six safaris. We have thoroughly enjoyed experiencing Africa through their eyes.

Top: Teenagers are all smiles on safari
Bottom: Family reunions are a great way to experience a safari

Needless to say, the kids have also had a wonderful time filled with exploration and adventure!

In most cases, the best option for families is a private safari with your own vehicle(s) and guide(s). You may travel at your own pace and choose camps and lodges that offer amenities, like swimming pools, that will provide the kids with some playtime as well as help them burn off some of that endless energy they seem to possess. In addition, visits to local schools and villages can provide insights into how children of their own age live in the countries you are visiting — and will hopefully make them more thankful for what they have!

Most guides, camp and lodge staff love to have children visit, and they go out of their way to make kids and the parents feel welcome. Be sure to plan into your trips some activities that your children enjoy.

Many camps and lodges have special children's programs where they are cared for and taken on their own adventures — allowing the parents to go on game drives alone or giving them the opportunity to participate in activities like walking in the bush where young children are not allowed. On a recent trip our two boys had the time of their lives as they were taken out target practicing and were taught how to drive a land rover!

Many of the smaller camps and lodges in Africa have minimum age restrictions (usually ranging from 7 to 16 years of age) while most of the larger camps and lodges have no restrictions at all. Some camps and lodges have minimum age restrictions (12 or 16 years old) for activities offered, such as walks in the bush with professional guides and canoeing. However, if, for instance, your family or group takes over the entire lodge, camp or canoe safari departure, or if you do a private mobile safari, you can, in some instances, get around the minimum age requirements. As some safari camps and lodges cater to a maximum of 6 to 20 guests, taking over a camp may be easier than you think. Just try to book your safari well in advance to ensure availability.

For anyone wishing to travel only in malarial-free areas with their children, some reserves to consider are Madikwe, Shamwari, Addo Elephant National Park, Kwandwe, Welgevonden Game Reserve, and Marakele National Park in South Africa. Please keep in mind that malarial prophylaxes (pills or syrup) are available for children and adults alike.

Cultural Safaris/Off the Map Travel

As the world becomes more modernized, the opportunity to go "back in time" visiting remote tribes is becoming rarer by the day.

Some of the safaris I personally treasure the most are ones I have taken "off the map" — visiting remote, "primitive" tribes that have had little interaction with the western world. Ethiopia stands out as the country with the richest history and opportunity for such adventures. Located in southern Ethiopia, Omo River Valley is home to some of the most primitive tribes on earth. Isolated from the rest of the world for centuries, the distinct groups still follow their own customs. Lalibela features twelfth century rock-hewn churches that are used daily by the local people. Visiting these churches during services provides an opportunity to witness "living history" and is a very moving experience.

Other cultural highlights include spending time with bushmen while they hunt with their bows and arrows and with the women "gatherers" and with the Datoka (Mgadi) tribe in Tanzania, remote Samburu, Maasai and Gabra tribes in Kenya, the bushmen of Botswana and Namibia, and the Himba and Herero of Namibia.

If spending some or all of your trip immersed in the local cultures is of interest to you, please read "Cultural History and Cultures of Sub-Sahara Africa" pages 100–107. If this type of travel interests you, my advice is to go now!

Villa Safaris

Villa rentals are common-place in Europe and are often favored by travelers who look for a bit more independence on their vacation. The idea has expanded in Africa and now you can find villas or small safari camps that can be taken over on an exclusive basis in some of the most pristine game viewing regions in East and southern Africa. A private guide and vehicle, butler, chef and the privacy and freedom to dictate each day are just some of the reasons why villas are the perfect answer for family and friends traveling together.

Top: Little Mombo's main lounge area
Middle: Little Ongava can be reserved on an exclusive basis for small parties
Bottom: Selous Private Camp, Lake Nzerakera

A customized safari could include stays at a number of villas in different reserves. South Africa, Kenya and Tanzania have the most villas from which to choose. Some of the top villas and small camps to consider include:

Botswana: Little Mombo (Moremi GR) and Zibadianja (Linyanti)

Zambia: Luangwa House and Robin's House (South Luangwa NP), Chongwe River House (Lower Zambezi NP), Kapinga Camp (Kafue NP) and Chuma Houses (Mosi-Oa-Tunya National Park)

Namibia: Little Ongava (Ongava GR)

South Africa: Londolozi Private Granite Suites (Sabi Sands GR), Royal Malewane Royal and Malewane Suites (Thornybush GR), Koro Lodge (Cederberg), Uplands Homestead and Melton Manor (Kwandwe), Mount Anderson Ranch, Royal Madikwe (Madikwe GR), Tarkuni (Tswalu Kalahari Reserve), Getty House and Phinda Zuka Lodge (Phinda GR)

Tanzania: A 4 bedroom villa at Sasakwa Lodge (Grumeti Reserves) and Kiba Point and Selous Private Camp (Selous)

Kenya: The Sanctuary at Ol Lentille, Loisaba House and Loisaba Cottage, Laragai House and Ol Malo House (Laikipia), Ngarie Niti (Lewa Downs) and Alfajiri (the coast)

Rwanda: Jack Hanna's Guesthouse (Parc des Volcans)

Self-Drive Safaris

In Africa, self-drive safaris are a viable option for general sightseeing in countries such as South Africa and Namibia that have excellent road systems. However, self-drive safaris into wildlife parks and reserves are, in general, not a good idea for several reasons.

One major disadvantage of a self-drive safari is that you miss the information and experience that a professional driver/guide can provide. A good guide is also an excellent wildlife spotter and knows when and where to look for the animals you want to see most. In many cases, he or she can communicate with other guides to find out where the wildlife has most recently been seen. This also leaves you free to concentrate on photography and game viewing instead of worrying about the road, and it eliminates the anxiety of the possibility of getting lost.

Self-drive safaris, especially ones requiring 4wd vehicles, are most often more expensive than joining a group safari. Gas (petrol) is generally a lot more expensive that it is in North America. Vehicle rental costs are also high, and the driving is often on the left side of the road.

Finally, self-drive safaris by people without extensive experience in the bush can be dangerous. Lack of knowledge about wildlife and the bush can result in life-threatening situations.

An International Driver's License is required by some of the countries covered in this book. Contact the tourist offices, consulates, or embassies of the countries in which you wish to drive for any additional requirements.

Overland Safaris

Overland safaris may cover several countries and last from around six weeks to nine months. Participants take care of all the chores and sleep in small pup tents. In addition to the initial cost of the trip, travelers must contribute to a "food kitty". The trip leader is generally hired for his mechanical skills and often knows little if anything about wildlife. In any case these safaris are primarily about getting from point A to point B, and have little wildlife orientation. Because many of these safaris originate in Europe, where they load up with supplies, only a small amount of the money spent for the safari reaches the local people. A lack of local infusion of funds places this type of safari very low on the ecotourism scale.

SAFARI ACTIVITIES

Africa can be experienced in many exciting ways. What follows are a number of types of safari activities. For additional information, refer to the country or countries mentioned.

Game Drives

The type of vehicle used on game drives varies from country to country.

Open vehicles usually have two or three rows of elevated seats behind the driver's seat. There are no side or rear windows or permanent roof, which provides you with unobstructed views in all directions and a feeling of being part of the environment instead of on the outside looking in. This is the type of vehicle

SAFARI ACTIVITIES

Vehicles • Night Game Drives • Walking Safaris • Boat Safaris • Canoe Safaris

Country	Park or Reserve	Vehicle Type Allowed			Night Drives	Walking Safaris	Boat Safaris	Canoe (C) Mokoro (M)
		Open	Hatches	Closed				
Southern Africa								
Botswana	Chobe							
	Moremi							M, 2
	Okavango Delta						2	M, 2
	Linyanti/Selinda/Kwando						2	C, 2
	Savute (S.W. Chobe)							
	Central Kalahari							
	Tuli							
Zimbabwe	Hwange				1, 2			
	Mana Pools				1		1	C
	Matusadona				1			C
Zambia	S. & N. Luangwa							
	Lower Zambezi							C, 2
	Kafue					5	2	
Namibia	Etosha	6	6		1	1		
South Africa	Kruger N.P.	5			1, 5	1, 5		
	Pvt. Reserves near and within Kruger							
	Kwandwe/Shamwari							
	Phinda							
East & Central Africa								
Tanzania	Arusha							C
	Lake Manyara	3			2			
	Tarangire	3			1	1, 2		
	Ngorongoro					4		
	Serengeti	3			1	1		
	Selous							
	Ruaha							
	Katavi							
	Mahale/Gombe							
Kenya	Maasai Mara	3			1	1		
	Laikipia Reserves							
	Samburu					1		
	Ol Donyo Waus/Campi ya Kanzi							
	Amboseli/Lake Nakuru							
Uganda	Bwindi							
	Queen Elizabeth						4	
	Kibale							
	Murchison							
Rwanda	Volcanoes							

1: Activity is conducted on the outskirts of the park or reserve.
2: Activity is conducted at a few camps within the reserve.
3: Open vehicles are used by some camps in the reserve.
4: Activity is conducted in certain areas of the park reserve.
5: Activity is conducted by National Parks.
6: Licensed tour operators only.

most often used for viewing wildlife by safari camps in southern Africa. Open vehicles are used in Botswana, Zambia, Zimbabwe, southern Tanzania, South Africa and some reserves in northern Tanzania, Kenya, and Namibia.

In 4wd vehicles with roof hatches or pop-top roofs, riders may stand up through the hatch for game viewing and photography. Ensuring that window seats are guaranteed for every passenger (a maximum of 6 or 7 passengers) is imperative. These vehicles are primarily used in Kenya, Tanzania and Uganda. Roof-hatch vehicles in these countries are generally more practical than open vehicles, because reserves in these countries usually get some rainfall 12 months of the year. On driving safaris in eastern and southern Africa, roof-hatch vehicles are often preferred because they offer more protection from rain, sun, wind and dust.

Wildlife viewing, and especially photography, is more difficult where closed vehicles are required (i.e. in national parks in South Africa).

Night Game Drives

Many African animals, including most of the big cats, are most active after dark, and night game drives open up a whole new world of adventure.

Top: Elephants undisturbed by an open safari vehicle
Bottom: A 4wd vehicle in East Africa allows game viewing through the open hatch

Much of the actual hunting by lion and leopard happens after nightfall; therefore, night drives probably provide your best chance to observe these powerful cats feeding or even making a kill. Vehicles are typically driven by your guide, and an assistant (tracker) handles a powerful spotlight. By driving slowly and shining the beam into the surrounding bush, the eyes of animals are reflected back, and it is then possible to stop and take a closer look. When an infra-red filter is used on the beam, most animals behave in a completely natural manner (providing the occupants of the vehicle keep quiet and still) and marvelous views can be enjoyed.

Leopard, lion, hyena, bushbabies, porcupine, aardvark, genets, civets and honey badgers would be among the highlights of a night game drive, with nocturnal birds, such as owls and nightjars, adding to the experience. Night drives are conducted in national parks in Zambia and Malawi, and in private concessions or private reserves in Botswana, Kenya, Namibia, Tanzania, South Africa and Zimbabwe.

Walking Safaris

Walking safaris put you in closest touch with nature. Suddenly your senses come alive — every sight, sound and smell becomes intensely meaningful. Could that flash of bronze in the dense brush ahead be a lion? I wonder how long ago these rhino tracks were made? Can that herd of elephant ahead see or smell us approaching?

Accompanied by an armed wildlife expert or Professional Guide, walking safaris last anywhere from a few hours to several days. The bush can be examined up close and at a slower pace, allowing for more attention to its fascinating detail than a safari by vehicle. Participants can often approach game quite closely, depending on the direction of the wind and the cover available.

The excitement of tracking rhino and lion on foot, crawling among a pack of African wild dog or being mock-charged by a young bull elephant is beyond words. Guides do not usually bring guests closer to wildlife than is comfortable for them. Zimbabwe, followed by Zambia, are the best countries to visit for those looking for this type of adventure. Walking is also available in some parts of Botswana, Namibia, Tanzania, Kenya, Uganda, Rwanda and South Africa. To better understand the excitement of a walking safari, I suggest you obtain the video *As Close As You Dare* (2007) Crowe World Media. Please see page 672 for details.

A Professional Guide and his clients approach a herd of buffalo

Boat/Canoe/Kayak/ Mokoro Safaris

Wildlife viewing by boat, canoe, kayak or mokoro from rivers or lakes often allows you to approach wildlife as close or even closer than by vehicle. Game viewing and birdwatching by boat is available in:

- Chobe National Park, Linyanti, Selinda, Kwando and the Okavango Delta (Botswana)
- Along the shores of Lake Kariba including Matusadona National Park, and on the Zambezi River upstream from Victoria Falls and downstream from the Kariba Dam, including areas adjacent to Mana Pools National Park (Zimbabwe)
- Upstream from Victoria Falls and along Lower Zambezi National Park (Zambia)
- Kunene River and the Caprivi region (Namibia)
- Liwonde National Park (Malawi)
- In KwaZulu-Natal at reserves like Phinda on the fringe of Lake St. Lucia (South Africa)
- On the Rufiji River and some lakes in the Selous Game Reserve (Tanzania)
- On the Kazinga Channel in Queen Elizabeth National Park, on the Victoria Nile in Murchison Falls National Park and on Lake Mburo in Lake Mburo National Park (Uganda)

Canoe safaris are, in my opinion, one of the most exciting ways of experiencing the bush. Paddling or silently drifting past herds of elephant frolicking on the river's edge, and watching herds of buffalo and other game cross the river channels in front of you are a few examples of what you may encounter.

Canoe safaris from three to nine days are operated along the Zambezi River below Kariba Dam on both the Zimbabwe and Zambia sides of the river. Wildlife is best in the area along Mana Pools National Park (Zimbabwe) and Lower Zambezi National Park (Zambia). Of all African adventures, this is definitely one of my favorites. Motorboats are not allowed along Mana Pools National Park; however, they are allowed along the Lower Zambezi National Park. Mana Pools is, in my opinion, by far the best place in Africa (if not the world) for canoe safaris.

Short excursions are also available upstream from Victoria Falls (Zimbabwe and Zambia), along Matusadona National Park (Zimbabwe) and Kafue National Park (Zambia). One- to three-day kayak safaris are operated along Zambezi River in Zambezi National Park upstream from Victoria Falls, Zimbabwe.

Mokoro safaris from a few hours to several days in length are available in the Okavango Delta (Botswana). A mokoro is a flat-bottomed, dugout canoe used in the watery wilderness of the Okavango Delta. Although these craft may appear unstable, there is no better way to experience the beauty and tranquility of this spectacular wetland. Experienced polers pilot the mokoro through channels of papyrus and floating fields of water lilies, each with two passengers aboard.

Canoeing is one of the greatest adventures in Africa

Photographic (Photo) Safaris

The term "photo safari" generally means any kind of safari except hunting safaris.

In its strictest sense, a photo safari is a safari during which you are escorted by a professional wildlife photographer. These safaris are mainly about learning wildlife photography and getting the best photos possible. These are recommended only for the serious shutterbug.

The best option by far for the serious photographer is to have a private vehicle and guide (see "Private Safaris" pages 39–40). Group safaris generally move too quickly from place to place, allowing insufficient time to get the best shots. For additional information, please contact *The Africa Adventure Company* for details. See pages 726–728.

Balloon Safaris

At 5:30 in the morning, we were awakened by steaming hot coffee and tea brought to our bedsides by our private tent keeper. We were off at 6:00 for a short night game drive to where the hot-air balloons were being filled. Moments later, we lifted above the plains of the Serengeti Plains for the ride of a lifetime.

Silently viewing game from the perfect vantage point, we brushed the tops of giant acacia trees for close-up views of birds' nests and baboons. Most animals took little notice, but somehow the hippos knew we were there. Maybe it was our shadow or the occasional firing of the burners necessary to keep us aloft.

Our pilot was entertaining and knowledgeable of the ecosystem we flew over, and pointed out a variety of large birds flying along side us and plains game, as well as a cheetah. We had the opportunity to see part of the Great

Serengeti Migration from the air — an awesome sight indeed!

Our return to earth was an event in itself. About an hour after lift-off, our pilot made a perfect crash landing. By the way, most landings are "crash landings," so just follow your pilot's instructions and join in the fun.

Minutes later, a champagne breakfast appeared on the open savannah within clear view of herds of wildebeest, buffalo and zebra. Our return to camp was another exciting game drive, only a little bumpier than the trip out.

A scenic hot air balloon over the Serengeti plains

Hot-air balloon safaris are available in Kenya in the Maasai Mara Game Reserve, at Taita Hills near Tsavo West National Park, in Serengeti National Park (Seronera area and the Western Corridor) and the Selous (Tanzania), near Namib-Naukluft National Park (Namibia) and in Pilanesberg Nature Reserve and Hazyview in Mpumalanga (South Africa).

Gorilla Safaris

Gorilla trekking is one of the most exciting adventures you can have on the "dark continent" and is certainly one of the most exciting experiences of my life.

Mountain Gorillas now number about 300 individuals that live in the cool, forested heights of the Virunga Volcanoes, which straddle three countries — Rwanda, Uganda and the Democratic Republic of the Congo. This is the region in which renowned but controversial primatologist Dian Fossey undertook her studies.

Because the respective governments of Rwanda and Uganda do value the great apes for the foreign currency that they attract, efforts to conserve the remaining gorillas and provide opportunities to view them are extremely good. Correspondingly, security for tourists traveling to these areas is superb.

About 19 miles (30 km) to the north of the Virunga Mountains is Uganda's Bwindi Impenetrable National Park, which provides a refuge for an additional 300+ mountain gorillas.

Gorillas are perhaps the most charismatic of all animals, and a close encounter with a free-ranging family in their forest home will never be forgotten. A typical experience involves a hard, uphill slog through thick vegetation in the company of two guides, several porters and an armed guard or two. Habituated family groups are located, and you'll then sit quietly and watch as they feed and go about their business.

Mountain gorillas are one of the most critically endangered mammals on the planet

Due to the threat of their contracting potentially fatal human diseases, visitors are encouraged to keep a fair distance from them, and the maximum group size is limited to 8 visitors.

Given the physical exertion required, gorilla trekking is recommended only for safariers in good hiking condition. Nevertheless, a large and growing number of people have been inspired to visit these peaceful relatives of mankind, and permits are at a premium in terms of both cost and availability.

Gorillas are currently best seen in Bwindi Impenetrable Forest (Uganda) and Parc des Volcans in Rwanda. At the time of this writing, gorilla trekking in the Congo is not recommended, due to lack of security. Permits as of this writing cost $500.00 per visit, which provides funds for conservation. Permits for gorilla trekking are limited and gorilla safaris should be booked well in advance.

Chimpanzee Trekking

Chimpanzee trekking, like gorilla trekking, can be exciting beyond words. Chimp trekking is best in Mahale Mountains National Park and Gombe Stream

National Park (Tanzania), Kibale Forest National Park (Uganda) and Nyungwe Forest Reserve (Rwanda). Watching the interactions of members of a troop of chimpanzees around you at close quarters is very entertaining!

White-Water Rafting

For white-water enthusiasts and newcomers alike, the Zambezi River (Zambia/Zimbabwe) below Victoria Falls is one of the most challenging rivers in the world. Some rapids are "Class Five" — the highest class runable. Rafting safaris from one to eight days are available. No previous experience is required. Just hang on and have the time of your life! Jinja (Uganda) has established itself as one of the continent's premier destinations for adventure sports and outdoor enthusiasts with Class Five white water rafting and kayaking on the River Nile. Occasionally, rafting trips are offered on the Omo River in Ethiopia.

Elephant-Back Safaris

For years only available in Asia, elephant-back is a fabulous way to explore the bush. Clients may ride well-trained African elephants, which are much larger than Indian elephants, in the Okavango Delta (Botswana), near Victoria Falls and Livingstone (Zambia) and Kapama Game Reserve (South Africa). Getting "up close and personal" with these amazingly intelligent mammals is both heartwarming and exciting.

Horseback Safaris

Game viewing by horseback is yet another intriguing way to experience the bush. Horseback safaris for the avid horseman from 5 to 10 days in length are conducted in the Okavango Delta (Botswana), for several days in length in the Tuli Block (Botswana) and at Ol Donyo Waus and the Mara plains (Kenya). These safaris are for only serious riders who can canter and who would enjoy spending six or more hours in the saddle each day.

Half and full-day safaris for the amateur or serious rider with less time are available at Victoria Falls (Zambia and Zimbabwe), the Tuli Block (Botswana), Ol Donyo Wuas, Ol Lintille, Loisaba and Borana (Kenya), the Grumeti Reserves (Tanzania),

Horseback riding at locations like Ol Donyo Wuas in Kenya offer guests an exciting way to approach wildlife

Maputaland Coastal Forest Reserve, the Waterberg region and Cape Town (South Africa), and soon to be offered at Lake Mburo National Park (Uganda).

Camel Safaris

Camel safaris allow access to remote desert areas which in many cases are difficult for 4wd vehicles to reach. Guests do some riding but primarily walking on multi-day trips escorted by Samburu or other tribesmen, with overnights in fly camps. This is a fabulous family safari as families can spend quality bonding time together. Camel excursions for a few hours in length are available from a number of safari camps and lodges in the Laikipia and Samburu areas of northern Kenya.

Train Safaris

Two of the most luxurious trains in the world — Rovos Rail and the Blue Train, offer excursions primarily in South Africa but also to Namibia, Zimbabwe and Tanzania. See the chapter on South Africa for details.

Quad Biking Safaris

Quad bike safaris are a fabulous way to explore primarily the desert regions of Africa. Riding up and down 600 foot (183 m) sand dunes in the Namib Desert near Swakpmund and visiting remote Himba tribes along the Kunene River and exploring the surrounding deserts in the Kaokoland in Namibia are high on my list, as well as exploring the Makgadikgadi Pans in Botswana.

Mountain Biking

Ever thought of game viewing by mountain bike? Well then pack your bags and head for Mashatu Game Reserve in eastern Botswana, where your guide rides ahead of you with a rifle strapped on his back and leads you through the bush were you may see elephant and lots of other big game. Mountain biking in the bush is also available from some camps near Tarangire National Park and near Lake Manyara National Park (Tanzania).

Mountain Climbing

Africa has mountains to challenge the tenderfoot and the expert alike. Mt. Kilimanjaro (Tanzania), 19,340 feet (5,895 m) in altitude, is the highest mountain in Africa, followed by Mt. Kenya at 17,058 feet (5,199 m). The Ruwenzoris, or "Mountains of the Moon" (Uganda/Congo), are the highest mountain chain in Africa, rising to 16,762 feet (5,109 m). All of these mountains lie within a few degrees of the equator yet are snowcapped year-round. Hiking through fascinating and unique Afro-alpine vegetation found on all of these mountains gives you the feeling of being on another planet. With over 30,000 climbers a year, Mt. Kilimanjaro is by far the most popular of the three peaks.

Scuba Diving and Snorkeling

Kenya, Tanzania, South Africa, Mozambique, Mauritius and the Seychelles offer excellent coral reef diving in the warm waters of the Indian Ocean. Lake Malawi and Lake Tanganyika offer a fascinating freshwater dive experience.

The Malindi-Watamu Marine National Reserve is probably the best choice in Kenya, Pemba Island in Tanzania, and the Quirimbas Archipelago and the Bazaruto Archipelago in Mozambique.

The northern Natal coast of South Africa has excellent coral reefs, while the Southern Cape offers the ultimate underwater thrill of cage diving with great white sharks! Mauritius and the Seychelles offer numerous coral reefs and a variety of fabulous dive options.

Snorkeling off North Island, Seychelles

Fishing

Africa has some very fine fishing to offer — from excellent deep-sea fishing off the east coast of the continent to great inland lakes that boast some of the largest freshwater fish in the world.

The best areas for **deep-sea fishing** are found off the coast of Kenya and Tanzania and in the Mozambique Channel, where blue, black & striped marlin, yellowfin tuna, sailfish, wahoo, kingfish, barracuda and other species may be caught by day and broadbill swordfish by night.

The best fishing season for the coast of Kenya and northern Tanzania is October to March, when the pelagic fish are biting. **Sailfish** are good all year round — just keep in mind that the ocean can be rough April to August. Sailfish are the most often caught of the billfish, and are especially challenging when fished on fly tackle. **Black marlin** come close to shore and are often encountered in very shallow water, while **Stripped marlin** tend to run offshore in cleaner water. Fighting a jumping **blue marlin** is possibly the ultimate thrill. **Broadbill swordfish**, possibly the strongest fighter in the ocean, are fished on overnight expeditions where the sea floor plunges to depths between 1,500 and 2,000 feet (609 m). **Tiger, mako,** and **hammerhead sharks** species are often caught; other species include **bull** sharks and **white-tip** sharks.

The Seychelles and Mauritius also offer very good fishing. The Seychelles, in fact, is considered one of the top bonefishing destinations in the world (especially the island of Alphonse)!

Freshwater fishing for tigerfish (great fighters) or Nile Perch (often weighing over 100 lbs./45 kg) as well as other species across the continent can be very exciting. While fishing, you may watch elephant cross a channel, listen to hippo grunting and watch a variety of kingfishers and herons fly by — adding another dimension to the sport that can be found nowhere else in the world!

Nile Perch, the largest freshwater species in Africa, can attain a weight of well over 200 pounds (90 kg). These giants, like huge bass, are fished for in a similar way and fight in a similar style. They will jump, run and fight in the most spectacular manner. Most anglers fish with a 40-pound rig and large "crankbaits," and some have even caught them on fly. Nile Perch have been introduced to many large lakes in Central and East Africa, including Lake Victoria, Lake Turkana, Lake Tanganyika and Murchison Falls National Park (Uganda).

Possibly the best freshwater fighting fish in the world, the **tigerfish**, comes in two varieties: the regular tigerfish and the goliath tigerfish. Many different methods are used to catch this fearsome toothed, aggressive fish, ranging from cast and retrieve of spinners and lures, trawling spinners and lures, drifting with live bait, drifting with fish fillets and fly-fishing. Possibly the most exciting thing about tigerfishing is the high-speed strike and the manner in which they leap and jump out of the water when hooked. Classic places for tigerfishing (and game viewing at the same time) are Lower Zambezi National Park (Zambia), Mana Pools National Park (Zimbabwe) on the mighty Zambezi River, and Matusadona National Park (Zimbabwe) on Lake Kariba. Other great spots include the Okavango Delta and the Chobe River in Botswana.

Goliath tigerfish occur farther north on the Congo River and many of the lakes in that region, including Lake Tanganyika. Tigerfish attain a weight of up to 25 pounds (11 kg), though this is rare and one can expect more around the 5 to 10 pound (2.3 to 4.5 kg) mark, while the goliath tigerfish can get well over 100 pounds (45 kg), but is a lot harder to catch.

There are no natural **trout** in Africa; however, many dams, lakes and rivers have been stocked over the years and can provide some very entertaining fishing. The best areas in Africa for trout are the Eastern Highlands of Zimbabwe, the Drakensberg foothills and high-altitude grasslands east of Johannesburg in South Africa, and the Kenyan Highlands, where they are fished with many of the classic British flies.

Most often, tackle will be provided, which saves you the trouble of carrying the stuff halfway around the world only to find it unsuitable. The exception to this is fly-fishing, where you probably will need to bring your own equipment.

Most freshwater fishing requires a license, which can usually be obtained from your hotel, lodge or camp for a small fee.

Birdwatching

If you are not already a keen birdwatcher, there is a good chance that you will be converted before the end of your safari. Birdwatching in Africa is almost beyond belief. Some countries have recorded over 1,000 different species and some parks over 500. The strident, sometimes beautiful calls of many birds will form a continual "soundtrack" to your African safari, add to the atmosphere and provide lasting memories.

The wonderful thing about birds is that they are present just about everywhere, all the time. The surroundings of camps and lodges are always good localities for birdwatching because a variety of species have become used to the presence of people, and many birds will appear on the scene if you simply sit quietly on your veranda. Game drives are constantly punctuated by views of large or colorful birds, and, if you take the time, numerous less-dramatic species.

Most reserves in Africa are simply heaven for birdwatchers. The best times for birdwatching are often the opposite of the best times for big game viewing. Birdwatching, however, is good year-round in many regions. For additional information, please see "Birdwatching Tips" on pages 69–71.

Star Gazing

Breathtaking views of the night sky are a typical feature of clear nights in African wilderness areas. A cloudless night provides a glorious opportunity to become familiar with several interesting constellations and noteworthy stars, as well as up to five planets. One or more of the planets Venus, Jupiter or Mars will be visible at any given time. The Milky Way is quite astounding when viewed through binoculars! For maps of the summer and winter skies of the southern hemisphere, obtain a copy of the *African Safari Journal*.

Other Safari Activities

Additional options for the special-interest traveler include anthropology, archaeology, art and backpacking.

COMBINING EAST AND SOUTHERN AFRICA WITH OTHER WORLD DESTINATIONS

There are many areas in the world that interest travelers and many of these different destinations combine well with an Africa safari. All the different air connections make combining an Africa safari with another destination a simple matter. Many travelers stop off in Europe either before or after a safari, as there are so many flights to Africa via London, Amsterdam, etc.

Buffalo herds typically number in the hundreds but can be as large as a thousand strong

A great combination is Egypt or **Egypt** and **Jordan** — especially in the cooler months of November to May, with east Africa or even southern Africa as there are daily flights out of Cairo heading south. We send many guests on trips visiting the pyramids, Sphinx and other attractions in Cairo and on Nile cruises, as well as to Jordan to see Petra and other sites (see *www.AfricanAdventure.com*). **Dubai** is also becoming very popular as a stopover before or after a safari.

If you have time, consider combining **Australia** and/or **New Zealand** with Africa, as you can conveniently fly from Johannesburg (South Africa) directly into Perth or Sydney (Australia). From Sydney and Perth there are direct flights into Auckland in New Zealand. I recommend using our sister company, the DownUnder Adventure Company (800-882-9453; 954-491-8877, *www.safaridownunder.com*) to plan the Australia/New Zealand part of the trip, and our Africa Adventure Company for the Africa portion. This way, as our safari consultants, who are all under one roof, can work directly with you and each other, to ensure that your arrangements are superbly coordinated! Please see pages 722–725 for additional details.

As many people plan their African safari during the cooler and drier months of June to September this works out well with adding on time in Australia as being in the southern hemisphere it is also cooler during this time of year. This is also the best time to visit the Great Barrier Reef in the tropical northern part

An "alpha" female is the only member of a wild dog pack to give birth

of Australia as the dry season runs from May to October and you therefore avoid the worst of the humidity and the monsoonal downpours.

For those planning their African safari toward the end of the year, or early in the year, continuing on to New Zealand works very well as it is warmer from September to May with the warmer and more settled weather being from February to late April. A good example would be to visit Botswana during the green season (January through March) then continue on to New Zealand where you would have a much better chance of experiencing warm and settled weather. Winter in New Zealand is June to August, which is a popular time for visitors seeking snow activities in the South Island.

For those planning on visiting both Africa and **India**, there are direct flights from Nairobi (Kenya) and Johannesburg (South Africa) to Mumbai (India).

Combining **South America** with Africa also works well as there are flights from Sao Paulo (Brazil) to Johannesburg and from Buenos Aires (Argentina) to Cape Town and Johannesburg (South Africa).

Cost of a Safari

When first-time travelers to Africa start looking at safari programs, they often feel that safaris are "expensive". What they soon realize is that most safari programs include all meals and game activities while in the safari camps and lodges, road and charter flight transfers, taxes, park fees and in some cases, laundry and drinks. I like to compare this to a ski vacation, where the accommodation and flights are booked in advance and may seem quite reasonable — but after you add up the credit card bills that follow for the ski lift tickets, rental car, ski rentals and all your meals, you then have a fair comparison with the relative cost of a safari.

The cost per day is most dependent upon how comfortably you wish to travel (the level of accommodation), the remoteness of the safari, type of transportation used, the quality of the guides, whether you're on a private safari or on a group tour, and the countries involved. Deluxe accommodations and transportation are normally more expensive in countries off the beaten track than in the more popular tourism spots.

For example, deluxe (Class A) safari camps in Botswana are often more expensive that Class A lodges in Kenya. Camps in Botswana, Zambia, Namibia and Zimbabwe cater to smaller groups and are generally situated in more remote locations, and charter aircraft are often used to reach them — making safaris to these areas more expensive than a driving safari using lodges.

As in Europe and other parts of the world, general-interest tours cost less than tours with more unique itineraries. Getting off the beaten track may dip a bit more into the wallet, but many travelers find the expense well worth it!

When comparing safaris, it is important to note what is included and not included. Some companies use what I consider a sales ploy by listing a relatively attractive price for a safari in their brochures or on the Internet, and then separately listing charter flight costs and park fees — which can increase the overall cost of the safari by another 30%; let the buyer beware! Most often, if you add up all those costs, you may find that they are in fact not offering value for money compared to safaris offered by other companies.

Some tour companies market "bare-bones" trips at attractive prices, but then charge extra for many "activities", drinks, laundry, breakfast and other meals, etc. The idea is to "hook" prospective safariers on the cheap price, and then try to "upsell" them on add-ons — most of which should have been included in the cost of the safari in the first place!

Be sure to note if taxes and breakfast are included when comparing costs for hotels — as most rates advertised on the Internet do not include either. This again can easily make a difference of 20 to 35% on the price. Also keep in mind that the advertised cost of accommodations at some safari camps or lodges often does not include game drives and other activities and park fees — only room and board, while others may be more comprehensive in what they include.

For current value-packed small group tours and tailor-made itineraries, please contact The Africa Adventure Company (see pages 726–728).

Leopards are the most adaptable of Africa's large predators and are able to survive in virtually any habitat

Booking a Safari

When choosing a safari company to book your safari, there are a number of issues that should be considered:

- Are the safari camps, lodges and hotels and the tour operators they use minimizing their impact on the environment and working toward the preservation of wildlife?

- Are real benefits received by the local communities in which they operate — giving the local people an economic incentive to preserve wildlife and the environment?

- Does the company offer the "type" of safari that best fits what you are looking for? Many tour companies cater to "niche" markets. Even though the company may come highly recommended to you, it may not be the best company for the experience for which you are looking.

- Does the person or persons working for the company with which you are speaking have extensive personal experience traveling in the areas you intend visiting? For instance, someone who knows South Africa well may not be qualified to give advice on Kenya or Tanzania, or vice-versa.

- If you are considering a group tour, how large is the group? I am still amazed at companies that boast that they offer tours limited to "only" 16 or 24 or 28 travelers. In my opinion, any group over 12 is ridiculously large for Africa (6 to 10 is preferable) unless it is a private group of family or friends. These groups for instance are constantly delayed by having to wait for the slow ones in the party, and this among other issues can reach a boiling point for some of the party after several days. I have encountered a number of these groups on safari, and I must say that many of them looked pretty miserable. Smaller groups are much more flexible — and fun!

- Does the tour operator have an in-house air department? Air schedules within Africa change, and having the same company book your land and your air arrangements is the safest way to go. If there are any changes in your air schedule, the operator is notified and they can then assist in getting you back on track. If your air is purchased elsewhere, then that company probably has little obligation or interest in helping you — and you may very well be left to fend for yourself.

- Does the company offer tours to Africa only, or do they offer tours to other destinations, as well? I suggest you look more seriously at companies that either offer Africa only, or for which Africa is their primary destination. Go with a company that focuses its attention and resources on the continent you wish to visit.

- Will the operator provide you with references of clients who have recently traveled with them? This may give you a better idea of the quality of the operation, and also may give you some insight into the experience you might have on a similar safari.

- Are you enjoying working with the tour operator? Planning a safari should be enlightening, educational and fun!

- How qualified are the guides they use on safari? A good guide is absolutely crucial to the success of your African experience.

- Is the tour company you have contracted providing you with a number of safari destinations and accommodation options from which to choose? Most people that love their African adventures rave about the excellent guides they had and the fact that their accommodations matched or exceeded their expectations.

- How long has the company been in business? Companies for instance that have been in business since 1990 have weathered two Gulf Wars, September 11th and other events that have bankrupted a number of companies. This says a lot for the financial stability of a company — as well as the expertise of the management and long-standing staff members.

- Does the company take credit cards for deposits as well as final payments on land and air arrangements? I am still amazed at the number of companies (some quite well-known) that do not take credit cards.

- Does the company have liability insurance (i.e. at least $3,000,000). Many small tour operators do not have insurance. The costs of defending against a single lawsuit could put an uninsured company into bankruptcy.

I cannot tell you the number of distraught people that call our offices yearly, asking us if we can quickly put together a safari for them because they have bought non-refundable air tickets and their tour operator with whom they booked direct within Africa has "disappeared" with their money and will not return emails or calls.

Another issue to consider is reliability and safety. For instance, many companies offering tours to international guests in Kenya and Tanzania are not licensed or bonded and have no insurance. What does this mean to you? As they are not licensed, they do not have to have their vehicles inspected and are generally using the oldest vehicles available to keep their costs down — resulting in more breakdowns (perhaps with little or no backup), and making travel in their vehicles downright dangerous. They fear little or no recourse if they do not perform as contracted. The temptation may be lower price. The old adage "If it is too good to be true, then it probably isn't" — can certainly apply here. So why take the risk?

Interestingly, many top tour operators and camp and lodge owners in Africa do not take direct bookings. They simply do not have the time or staff to answer the many questions that potential safariers have before as well as after they have booked a trip. They wisely concentrate on what they do best — and that is providing a great experience for their guests once they arrive. In many cases where properties do take direct bookings, travelers can actually

A male lion's mane, unique among cats, makes him appear larger and more intimidating

book for less with a tour operator overseas that is doing substantial business with them.

A safari is all about experiencing Africa — and it is quality people assisting you by booking the right safari for you and quality people maximizing that experience on the ground that counts.

Safari Tips

While on safari, you will enjoy the attention and input of one or more guides whose job is to make sure that you have a safe, enjoyable and enlightening experience. Although you will be in capable hands, the more you know before setting off, the more you will get out of the experience.

- Background reading is perhaps the most important, although speaking to somebody who has been to the area you intend to visit can be invaluable. The *African Safari Journal* (see pages 720–721) is aimed at providing you with an advance overview, as well as being a guide and field book to record your observations. As such, it should be a constant companion on your travels.

- Your desire to visit Africa may well have been triggered by *National Geographic* documentaries or *Animal Planet*. This is all very well, but you should not expect to see everything in the way in which these films depict. The best wildlife films take years to create, and involve weeks or months of waiting for action to happen. Part of enjoying your safari is having a realistic expectation, and you should always remember that wildlife is just that, it's wild! With the exception of the most common birds and herbivorous mammals, nothing can be guaranteed on safari — and that, really, is the thrill of it. It is the anticipation and chance which makes getting up early each morning, and driving around each bend in the road, so enthralling.

- It is vital to develop a good relationship with your guide from the outset. Bear in mind that he or she will not only know the area and its wildlife, but also the best ways to reveal this to you. Make sure that you state your expectations clearly from the word go, and don't be shy to get involved in each day's routine. If you have seen enough lions for one day, for example, let your guide know that they should perhaps just park at a scenic lookout so that you can enjoy the space and serenity of the wilderness.

- Rather than spending your whole safari charging about looking only for big game, aim to get an understanding and appreciation for the whole ecosystem, of which termites and fig trees play as big a role as elephants and lions. Developing an interest in birds, reptiles and trees means that you'll have a captivating experience at all times. Perhaps the saddest thing to come across on safari is someone who has spent all day in the bush and says that he has "seen nothing!"

- Sensitivity toward wildlife is paramount. Your guide will know the correct distance to approach each individual species without causing stress, but in the rare instances where this may not be so, it is up to you to dictate the distance. The most enthralling wildlife encounters are often those in which the animals that you are viewing are unaware or unafraid.

- Being on safari generally puts you at less risk than you would be when traveling on busy roads in your own neighborhood, but many animals are potentially dangerous and some simple precautions are advisable. A good guide will naturally avert any risky situations, but as already mentioned, respecting animals' space by not attempting to get too close is paramount. Almost all large mammals are frightened of humans, and generally run or move off when confronted with the upright form of a person. This can never be taken for granted, however, and you should not be tempted to leave the safety of a safari vehicle to approach an animal. It is equally important to remain seated while in open safari vehicles, because lions, for example, appear to regard safari vehicles as one entity, rather than a collection of edible primates! Many of the best wildlife lodges are not fenced and allow free movement of all wildlife, so you can expect to be escorted to and from your room or tent after dinner by an armed guard. Most large mammals may explore lodge surroundings after dark, but typically keep well clear during daylight hours. Exceptions include impala, bushbuck and some other herbivores which realize that the lodge offers protection from predators. Opportunistic vervet monkeys, and sometimes baboons, frequently raid kitchens and table fruit. Monkeys can become aggressive once they are accustomed to handouts, so the golden rule is to never feed them, or any other animal.

- Naturally, most people will want a record of their safari, so tips on photography are provided below.

- Read the "Safari Glossary" to become familiar with the terminology used in the bush. Once on safari, you will notice that when you ask people what animals they saw on their game drive, they might reply, "elephant, lion, leopard and oryx," when in fact they saw several members of each species. This use of the singular form, when more than one of that species was seen, is common. However, one exception to this rule is saying *crocs for crocodile*. This form of "Safariese" will be used throughout this guide to help separate you from the amateur.

- Put your valuables in a room safe or safety deposit box at your lodge or hotel.

- Do not call out to a person, signaling with an index finger. This is insulting to most Africans. Instead, use four fingers with your palm facing downward.

- During daytime game viewing activities, wear colors that blend in with your surroundings (brown, tan, light green or khaki). Do not wear perfume or cologne while game viewing. Wildlife can detect unnatural smells for miles

During the Great Serengeti Migration of wildebeest, zebras join the herd to reach optimal grazing areas

and unnatural colors for hundreds of yards (meters), making close approaches difficult.

- The very few tourists who get hurt on safari are almost always those travelers who ignore the laws of nature and most probably the advice and warnings of their guides. Common sense is the rule.
- Do not wade or swim in rivers, lakes or streams unless you know for certain they are free of crocodiles, hippos and bilharzia (a snail-borne disease). Fast-moving areas of rivers are often free of bilharzia, but can still be a bit risky. Bilharzia, fortunately, is not the dreaded disease that it once was; if detected early it can be easily cured.
- Do not walk along the banks of rivers near dawn, dusk or at night. Those who do so may inadvertently cut off a hippo's path to its water hole, and the hippo may charge.
- Malaria is present in almost all the parks and reserves covered in this guide. Malarial prophylaxis (pills) should be taken and must be prescribed by a physician in the USA but are available without prescription in many countries. Because most malaria-carrying mosquitoes come out from dusk until dawn, during this period you should use mosquito repellent and wear long pants and long-sleeve shirt or blouse, shoes (not sandals) and socks. For further information see the section on "Health" in the "Resource Directory" section of this book.
- Because of the abundance of thorns and sharp twigs, wear closed-toed shoes or boots at night and also during the day if venturing out into the bush. Bring a flashlight and always have it with you at night.

- Don't venture out of your lodge or camp without your guide, especially at night, dawn or dusk. Remember that wildlife is not confined to the parks and reserves in many countries, and, in fact, roams freely in and around many camps and lodges.
- Resist the temptation to jog or walk alone in national parks, reserves or other areas where wildlife exists. To lion and other carnivores, we are just "meat on the hoof" like any other animal — only much slower and less capable of defending ourselves.

Photographic Tips

Most people will want to record their experiences on safari with photographs or video. In recent years, digital technology has advanced to such an extent that traditional 35mm cameras which use rolls of film have become almost extinct. There are some people who still use film cameras effectively, but they are in the minority.

Choosing a Camera

There are two basic kinds of digital camera (as there are conventional film cameras). One kind with a built-in lens (comparable to the old "instamatic") and the other kind with detachable lens. When choosing a digital camera, it is

A unique perspective for a photographer during a walking safari

important to select a model which takes images of 4 MB, or larger, as this will enable clear prints to be made up to 8" × 10" format. For photographing wildlife, it is important to be able to zoom close to your subject, so you'll need a minimum of 10x "optical zoom", or — in the case of digital SLR — a lens of at least 300mm. Larger magnifications will be required for photographing birds. Many cameras now have "image stabilization" technology and this can be very valuable when shooting from vehicles on safari.

Choosing a Camcorder (Video Camera)

As with digital cameras, the variety of camcorders on the market is not only bewildering, but constantly changing as technology advances. Most appropriate for use on safari are mini digital video (DV) camcorders which are small and lightweight. Some of these camcorders record onto miniDV tapes, but miniDVD and HDD (directly onto hard disc drive) are increasingly popular. Many camcorders have optical zoom of 20x or more which is ideal for shooting wildlife, but don't be fooled by high "digital zoom" statistics as these exaggerated magnifications produce images which are highly pixellated (broken up into small squares) and unsatisfactory. Some digital camcorders are also able to take still photographs, but the quality is never as good as with a dedicated still camera.

Lighting

The quality of any still photograph (or movie clip) is dependent upon lighting. For this reason, the best wildlife photographs are taken in the early morning or late afternoon when sunlight comes at an angle. In the middle of the day, sunlight comes from directly overhead which creates hard black shadows on and around your subject matter.

Composition

Choosing where to place your subject in the viewfinder of your camera is known as composition. This is a vital aspect of photography and separates great images from ordinary ones. Things to avoid are chopping off part of your subject (for example, feet), zooming in too tightly or placing your subject in the very center of your frame. It is much more pleasing on the eye if an animal is pictured off center and thus "looking in" to a space. Likewise, placing the horizon of your landscape pictures in the bottom or top third of the frame (depending on whether the sky or foreground is of more interest), rather than in the very center, will create a more interesting perspective

Camera Shake

As already mentioned, some camera lenses now have "image stabilization" technology. Blurred photographs are caused mostly by camera shake, which is the result of not holding the camera firmly, or not selecting the correct exposure options and thus using long shutter speeds. The use of a tripod is hard to beat but this is not very practical on a safari. Some travelers will extend one leg of a tripod or use a monopod. Alternately, use a soft "beanbag". Simply pack a small cloth bag in your travel kit and then fill it with dry beans (or rice) when you get to Africa. This will then provide you with a flexible yet solid support for your camera. In the absence of a tripod or beanbag, a rolled-up jacket or sweater placed on a seat or window ledge will provide decent support.

Vehicle vibrations are a major cause of blurred images, so ask your guide to turn off the vehicle engine for special shots.

Batteries and Data Cards

It is obviously necessary to have all the required battery chargers for your equipment when you travel. An electrical adaptor will also be important for connecting to local power supplies. Even the most remote safari camps usually have a generator capable of charging batteries. Consider taking two batteries for each camera, so that you always have a backup.

Data cards vary in size from 1GB to 8GB or more. Take two or three cards and consider copying the data (i.e. your images) onto a compact disc (some safari camps do this) to enable you to delete them to free up space. Some travelers now carry iPods, or even a laptop for copying image files onto; these instruments also allow you to better preview and edit photographs or video clips on the spot

It is wise to store cameras and lenses in plastic ziplock bags to protect them from dust and humidity

Birdwatching Tips

Many guides are avid birders and are only too delighted to have interested guests to show around. If your guide is not a keen birdwatcher and you are, you obviously need to let him know to ensure that you do not rush after large mammals all the time.

As many birdwatchers know, the number of species counted on a safari will depend directly on the number of habitats visited. This means that if you are a serious *twitcher* and want to log as many new "ticks" as possible, you should move a great deal throughout the safari. Africa, with its varying landscapes, lends itself well to this and in most cases you can visit two or three habitats while staying in the same camp. As mentioned before, some birding trips will take you to areas with less game and more birds — such as some of the forest areas, so a balance is important.

If you are a serious birder, it is very important to let your agent or tour operator know about it. Many companies have one or two guides who are

The powerful talons of a fish eagle grab its prey

particularly knowledgeable and, with prior notice, a private birding guide can be booked for your safari.

A lot of birding is very close range, so a close-focusing pair of binoculars is an important asset. A minimum of 8-power and preferably 10-power (10-by-40) works well for birds, as the finer details are important for identification. For the ultra keen, a spotting scope and tripod will definitely come in handy — especially for waders and bird life around lakeshores — but carrying this equipment can be cumbersome so it is recommended for only the specialist.

Checklists are fun to document what you see so don't forget a reliable pencil or pen in your backpack. Many people take a small dictaphone to record sightings and then translate them to a written list each evening in the camp. This saves fumbling around with complicated checklists while the guide is rattling off all those new and exciting species!

A woodland kingfisher feeds on lizards, beetles and other insects

If you are keen on photographing birds, a minimum of a 400mm lens, with a beanbag for the vehicle and a tripod for the land, should be used. See the previous section on "Photographic Tips" (pages 67–69) for more information.

There are several excellent illustrated field guides and references to the birds of Africa. The best identification guides are *Newman's Birds of Southern Africa* by Kenneth Newman (Struik); *Sasol Field Guide to Birds of Southern Africa* (Struik); *Birds of Kenya and Northern Tanzania* by Zimmerman, Turner and Pearson (A&C Black); and *Field Guide to the Birds of East Africa* by Terry Stevenson and John Fanshawe (Academic Press). The compact *Illustrated Checklist:*

Flamingos' breeding activity is synchronized with rainfall

Birds of Southern Africa by von Perlo (Collins) is useful in that it covers Zambia and Malawi, as well as the region south of the Zambezi River. For visitors to Seychelles, Mauritius or Madagascar, the *Birds of the Indian Ocean Islands* by Sinclair and Langrand (Struik) is indispensable.

Among the groups of birds best represented in Africa are the herons (22 species), plovers (30), storks (8), bustards (21), francolins (36), eagles (23), vultures (11), doves (41), sandgrouse (12), turacos (23), barbets (44), hornbills (25), kingfishers (14) and shrikes (79).

Some of the most spectacular bird sights are the vast flocks of flamingos on East Africa's Rift Valley lakes, the hundreds of vultures which gather at the remains of kills, the breeding colonies of carmine bee-eaters on the Zambezi River, and the comical hornbills that often approach to within arm's reach. Add to this the world's largest bird (the ostrich), the world's heaviest flying bird (the kori bustard), jewel-like sunbirds, iridescent starlings and dazzling rollers, and you'll have an idea of what awaits you!

Between the months of November and March, Africa is visited by an estimated five million migratory birds from Europe and Asia. Among these are swallows, storks, kestrels, waders and warblers. At the same time, the majority of Africa's resident birds are breeding so they are most vociferous, and may often be seen at their nests or with young. It follows that this is the best time to visit if you are specifically interested in birds, but a trip at any time of year may yield sightings of hundreds of different species.

What To Wear — What To Take

Countries close to the equator (Kenya, Tanzania, Uganda, Rwanda and Burundi) have small differences in seasonal temperatures, with June to August being the coolest time of the year; the main factor affecting temperature is altitude.

Countries in southern Africa (Botswana, Zambia, Zimbabwe, Namibia, South Africa, Swaziland, Lesotho and Malawi) have more pronounced seasons, often cool to cold (sometimes freezing) in winter (June to August) and warm to hot in summer (October to February).

There can be a great difference between day and night temperatures. The thing to remember is to layer your clothing! The temperatures start out cool in the early morning for the game drives. Consider wearing khaki pants, a t-shirt with a long sleeve button down shirt (like an oxford cloth), a fleece and then a windbreaker jacket over that. By 9:00 a.m. you often begin to peel off the layers. If you have the pants that zip into shorts, these would be perfect (unless you want protection from the sun which is quite strong). You will take off the jacket and most likely the fleece and perhaps the long sleeve shirt and will be left with t-shirt and shorts. This will be comfortable attire until the afternoon game drive when you will start out wearing the shorts but will want to bring the long sleeve garments and pant attachments when the sun starts to drop (unless you need the protection from the sun). This way, you will be layering back on as you see fit when the temperature starts dropping again.

Casual clothing is usually worn by day. Dresses for ladies and coats and ties for men are only required in a few top restaurants in Kenya, South Africa and Zimbabwe. In some restaurants, gentlemen's coats are available on request.

Bring at least one camera and a lot of film memory cards, binoculars, sun block, electric converter and adapter, a copy of the *African Safari Journal*, alarm clock, insect repellent, brown- khaki- or green-cotton clothing, including at least two pairs of long pants and two long-sleeve shirts, wide-brimmed hat, rain gear, good walking shoes, flashlight and extra batteries, two pairs of sunglasses, two pairs of prescription glasses (one for contact-lens wearers) and a copy of the prescription, medical summary from your doctor if medical problems exist, Band-aids (plasters), motion-sickness tablets, medicine for traveler's diarrhea, anti-malarial prophylaxis (malaria pills), decongestant tablets, laxative, headache tablets, throat lozenges, antacid, and antibiotic ointment.

Bring along a comfortable pair of walking shoes. If you are going on walking safaris, be sure to have a pair of earth-colored boots (not white tennis shoes!) for your walks.

Each person going on safari should definitely have his or her own pair of binoculars. I am amazed at the number of Africa travelers who have paid thousands of dollars each for a game viewing safari, yet take with them a poor-quality pair of binoculars which limits the enjoyment of the primary function of the trip. If your budget will allow, I suggest spending from $350 to $900 or more for a medium- to high-quality pair of binoculars that could be used on subsequent Africa safaris and safaris to other continents, and which can possibly provide you with a lifetime of use. I recommend binoculars with 8 to 10 power, and 30 mm to 44 mm diameter optics (i.e. 8 × 30, 10 × 42, etc.), and suggest you consider Steiner binoculars as they offer high quality at reasonable prices. Swarowski, Zeiss, Leitz and Leica are the top-of-the-line brands and generally cost in the $1,200–$2,000 range, depending on the power and field of vision.

Leave your dress watch at home and buy an inexpensive (under U.S. $50) waterproof watch with a light and alarm. Do not wear or bring any camouflage clothing; in many countries this is reserved for the military.

To receive a catalog of valuable books, maps, binoculars and safari clothing, see pages 726–728.

SUGGESTED PACKING LIST

WOMEN'S CLOTHING
- ❏ Sandals or lightweight shoes
- ❏ Walking shoes or lightweight hiking shoes (not white for walking safaris)
- ❏ Wide-brimmed hat
- ❏ Windbreaker
- ❏ Sweater or fleece
- ❏ 3 pr. safari* pants
- ❏ 3 pr. safari* shorts
- ❏ 5 pr. safari/sport socks
- ❏ 3 short-sleeve safari* shirts
- ❏ 3 long-sleeve safari* shirts
- ❏ Swimsuit/cover-up
- ❏ 1 pr. casual slacks or skirt
- ❏ 1 or 2 blouses
- ❏ Belts
- ❏ 6 sets underwear
- ❏ 3 bras

OPTIONAL
- ❏ 1 cocktail dress

- ❏ 1 pr. dress shoes and nylons/panty hose
- ❏ 1 sports bra (for rough roads)

MEN'S CLOTHING
- ❏ Sandals or lightweight shoes
- ❏ Walking shoes or lightweight hiking shoes (not white for walking safaris)
- ❏ Wide-brimmed hat
- ❏ Windbreaker
- ❏ Sweater or fleece
- ❏ 3 pr. safari* pants
- ❏ 3 pr. safari* shorts
- ❏ 5 pr. safari/sports socks
- ❏ 3 short-sleeve safari* shirts
- ❏ 3 long-sleeve safari* shirts
- ❏ Swim trunks
- ❏ 1 pr. casual slacks
- ❏ 1 sports shirt
- ❏ 6 sets underwear
- ❏ Belts

* Any comfortable cotton clothing for safari should be neutral in color *(tan, brown, light green, khaki)*. Evening wear can be any color you like!

- ❏ Large handkerchief

OPTIONAL
- ❏ 1 pr. dress slacks, shoes and dress socks
- ❏ 1 dress shirt/jacket/tie

TOILETRIES AND FIRST AID
- ❏ Anti-malaria pills (prescription)
- ❏ Vitamins
- ❏ Aspirin/Tylenol/Advil
- ❏ Motion sickness pills
- ❏ Decongestant
- ❏ Throat lozenges
- ❏ Laxative
- ❏ Anti-diarrhea medicine
- ❏ Antacid
- ❏ Antibiotic
- ❏ Cortisone cream
- ❏ Antibiotic ointment
- ❏ Anti-fungal cream or powder

SUNDRIES
- ❏ Passport (with visas, if needed)
- ❏ International Certificates of Vaccination
- ❏ Air tickets/vouchers
- ❏ Money pouch
- ❏ Credit cards
- ❏ Traveler's checks
- ❏ Personal checks
- ❏ Insurance cards
- ❏ Pocket calculator
- ❏ Sunglasses/guard
- ❏ Spare prescription glasses/contacts
- ❏ Copy of prescription(s)
- ❏ Eyeglass case
- ❏ Travel alarm clock
- ❏ Small flashlight (torch) and extra batteries

- ❏ Prescription drugs
- ❏ Medical summary from your doctor (if needed)
- ❏ Medical alert bracelet or necklace
- ❏ Band-Aids (plasters)
- ❏ Thermometer
- ❏ Insect repellent
- ❏ Sunscreen/sun block
- ❏ Shampoo (small container)
- ❏ Conditioner (small container)
- ❏ Deodorant
- ❏ Toothpaste
- ❏ Toothbrush
- ❏ Hairbrush/comb
- ❏ Razor
- ❏ Q-tips/cotton balls
- ❏ Nail clipper
- ❏ Emery boards
- ❏ Makeup
- ❏ Tweezers
- ❏ Binoculars
- ❏ Sewing kit
- ❏ Small scissors
- ❏ Tissues (travel packs)
- ❏ Handiwipes (individual)
- ❏ Anti-bacterial soap
- ❏ Laundry soap (for washing delicates)
- ❏ Large ziplock bags for damp laundry
- ❏ Copy of the *African Safari Journal*
- ❏ Maps
- ❏ Business cards
- ❏ Pens
- ❏ Deck of cards
- ❏ Reading materials
- ❏ Decaffeinated coffee/herbal tea
- ❏ Sugar substitute

CAMERA EQUIPMENT
- ❏ Lenses
- ❏ Digital memory cards/Film
- ❏ Camera bag or backpack
- ❏ Lens cleaning fluid
- ❏ Lens tissue/brush
- ❏ Extra camera batteries
- ❏ Flash
- ❏ Flash batteries
- ❏ Battery charger and adapters
- ❏ Ziploc bags for lenses and camera body
- ❏ Beanbag, small tripod or monopod
- ❏ Extra video camera batteries
- ❏ Video charger
- ❏ Outlet adapters (3-prong square and round plugs)
- ❏ Cigarette lighter charger (optional)

GIFTS & TRADES
- ❏ T-shirts
- ❏ Pens
- ❏ Inexpensive watches
- ❏ Postcards from your area/state
- ❏ Children's magazines and books
- ❏ Small acrylic mirrors
- ❏ Balloons
- ❏ School supplies

OTHER

- ❏ _____
- ❏ _____
- ❏ _____
- ❏ _____

- ❏ _____
- ❏ _____
- ❏ _____
- ❏ _____

Cheetah, the fastest land mammal, favor open habitat to search for prey

AFRICAN ECOSYSTEMS

Africa is a continent of incredible diversity. Straddling the equator, and stretching beyond both the tropic of Cancer and Capricorn, almost every conceivable landscape and climate is present on the giant landmass. From snow-capped peaks to parched deserts, and from dripping rainforests to expansive savannahs, each habitat has its own particular community of plants and animals. No other parts of the world contain as much unaltered habitat, and nowhere are large mammals still so numerous and widespread. All African countries have extensive networks of protected areas and — in many cases — these are actually increasing in size as nature-based tourism becomes an ever more important component of local economies. Nevertheless, Africa's wild places face innumerable threats and challenges as human populations increase, and development goes unchecked. The impact of man-induced climate change is of growing concern here, as it is around the world.

Leopards are solitary — and in typical cat fashion — come together only to mate

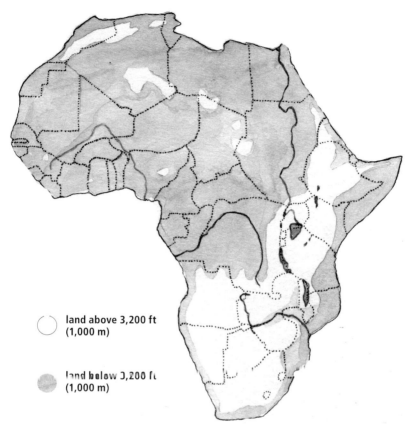

land above 3,200 ft
(1,000 m)

land below 3,200 ft
(1,000 m)

Altitude above sea level is a major factor in terms of Africa's climate, as it determines the vegetation types and distribution of wildlife, as well as the patterns of human settlement. The continent can be divided into "high" and "low" regions, with the land above 3,200 feet being more temperate even on the equator. European colonists chose to establish settlements on the higher plateaus, where wheat, tea and livestock such as cattle and sheep were able to thrive. Malaria and most livestock diseases are prolific in hot lowlands, so these areas were spared from much development and still contain some extensive wilderness areas. The Congo Basin and most of west Africa is a steamy wet lowland, while the majority of countries of east and southern Africa enjoy the benefits of both temperate and tropical or subtropical climates. The southern African highveld plateau experiences bitterly cold night temperatures during winter (May to August), while towns that are at high altitude such as Nairobi experience cool nights throughout much of the year.

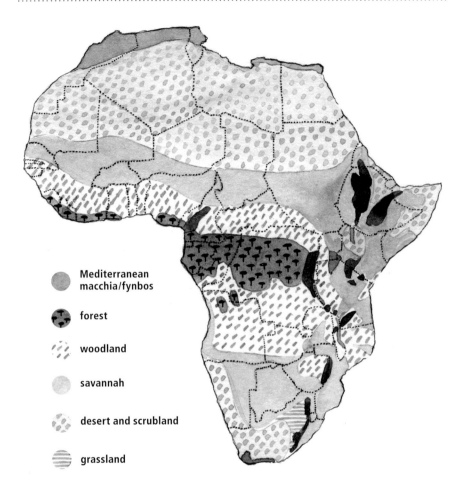

Mediterranean macchia/fynbos

forest

woodland

savannah

desert and scrubland

grassland

Africa can be divided into several broad categories of landscape which are a result of climate (particularly rainfall), altitude, topography and soils, all of which are interlinked. Geographers refer to these landscapes as vegetation zones (or biomes), and they include well-known types such as forest, desert and grassland. In most cases, these and other vegetation zones do not have well defined boundaries but merge into adjacent habitats to create zones of transition. On the following pages, the more conspicuous vegetation types, and their characteristic wildlife, are briefly described.

Savannah

The African landscape so often depicted in films — and imagined by travelers — is a park-like vista of grassland dotted with flat-topped trees. This is the savannah, a mosaic of woodland and grassland. The ratio of trees to grass, and the dominant species of trees is determined by rainfall and soil type. This is the dominant habitat in most of the large wildlife reserves in East and southern Africa, with thorny acacia trees being conspicuous. Seasonal grass fires are an important mechanism in the maintenance of savannah ecosystems, as they

encourage grass growth and limit the spread of woody plants. Large herbivores including giraffe, elephant, zebra, buffalo and wildebeest favor the savannah which also supports the highest density of lions and other large predators. Bird diversity is great with eagles, vultures, bustards, rollers, hornbills, larks, shrikes, starlings and weavers among the conspicuous families.

Woodland

Woodland generally occurs in higher rainfall areas but often merges with savannah. Trees are taller and more closely spaced, sometimes with their canopies touching. Much of southern Tanzania, Zambia and Zimbabwe is blanketed in moist *miombo woodland,* while swathes of dry *mopane woodland* occur in northern Botswana and the low-lying parts of Zimbabwe and northeastern South Africa. Browsing herbivores such as kudu live in woodlands, while roan and sable favor grassy clearings. African elephant may be seasonally abundant in mopane woodland. Birds such as woodpeckers, cuckoos, turacos, tits, orioles, warblers and sunbirds are well represented in woodlands.

Scrublands and Semidesert

In low rainfall areas such as the Kalahari and northern Kenya, short thorny trees and shrubs (particularly acacia and commiphora) are interspersed with hardy grasses. Termite mounds may be a conspicuous feature of these landscapes. Bands of taller trees occur along seasonal streams (drainage lines) where they typically tap into an underground water supply. Aloes, euphorbias and other succulents may occur on well-drained slopes. These landscapes are transformed after good rainfall and typically explode with life for short periods. Gazelles, oryx, cheetah, bat-eared fox and black-backed jackal are often resident, while gerbils and other rodents can be seasonally abundant. Bustards, sandgrouse and larks are typical birds, while eagles, goshawks, falcons and other raptors are often conspicuous.

Desert

Africa has two true deserts. The Sahara is undoubtedly the world's most famous but it is not known for its wildlife and is not dealt with here. In contrast, the Namib Desert (after which the country of Namibia is named) is an extraordinary wilderness with a host of unique arid-adapted plants and animals. Deserts are characterized by extremely low annual rainfall, although brief periods of bounty follow uncharacteristic thunderstorms. Large mammals are few and mostly nomadic, but a variety of interesting arid-adapted birds and reptiles are present.

Forest

Forest may be defined as an area with total tree cover where tree canopies interlock. There are several kinds of forest in Africa, ranging from equatorial/lowland rain forest, coastal forest, temperate montane forest and bands of riverine forest in savannah habitats. The temperate montane forests of Rwanda and Uganda are home to mountain gorillas, while chimpanzees and various other primates occur in forest pockets of Uganda and Tanzania. African elephant, buffalo and various species of duiker are typical forest mammals. A large number of bird species are restricted to forests of one kind or another throughout Africa; some are canopy feeders while others skulk on the forest floor. The

Congo Basin is the second largest rainforest on the planet, after the Amazon. Lowland forests contain hardwood trees attractive to loggers and extensive areas have been cleared or are currently under threat.

High Altitude Grassland

On the highveld plateau of South Africa, a prarie-like grassland once dominated the landscape but intensive agriculture and coal mining have now reduced this to a fragment of its former extent and many grassland specialist species are now endangered. Indigenous trees are largely absent due to winter frosts and regular fires, but hardy alien species such as eucalyptus and weeping willow are now conspicuous. The upland regions of Ethiopia, Kenya, Malawi and Tanzania have smaller but usually more pristine areas of high altitude grassland. Large mammals are few but birds are abundant and conspicuous.

Rivers, Lakes and Wetlands

Africa has several major rivers, including the north-flowing Nile — the world's longest — which empties into the Mediterranean. The Congo River is second only to the Amazon in terms of volume as it drains west into the Atlantic. The Zambezi, Limpopo, Ruvuma, Rufiji, Galana and Tana are the major river systems draining southern and eastern Africa into the Indian Ocean. These rivers are all fed by smaller tributaries, many of which are seasonal. All of these waterbodies are essential for people and wildlife but many are threatened by inappropriate agriculture, deforestation and erosion of catchments and the impacts of global warming. A chain of great lakes occurs in the two arms of the Rift Valley, and the world's third largest — Lake Victoria — is sandwiched in between. Botswana's Okavango Delta is formed by the river of the same name spilling out into the Kalahari Basin; the Rufiji and Zambezi Deltas are important coastal wetlands. Hippo are restricted to rivers and wetlands, while elephant, buffalo and many other large mammals are water dependent. A vast array of birds including pelicans, flamingos, storks, herons, ducks, geese, cormorants, kingfishers, jacanas, plovers and migratory sandpipers inhabit wetlands of various types.

Coast and Reefs

The shore and seas off Africa's coast support diverse wildlife communities in habitats ranging from kelp beds and coral reefs, to mangroves and pristine beaches. The deep pelagic waters beyond the continental shelf are home to whales, dolphins, sea turtles and great white sharks, as well as birds such as albatrosses, petrels and shearwaters.

There is a vast difference between the east and west coasts of the continent. The cold Benguela current sweeps north from the Antarctic to bring cool, nutrient rich water to the western Cape and Namibia, with large numbers of fur seals and gannets thriving in the productive waters which are, however, threatened by commercial fishing fleets. In contrast, the Indian Ocean is warmed by equatorial waters, with coral reefs off the Kenyan, Tanzanian and Mozambican coasts, and palm-fringed islands such as Zanzibar and Seychelles. Fish and other wildlife have been heavily harvested along this tropical coast which has been exploited and fought over by traders, settlers and locals for centuries. Fortunately, marine reserves in Kenya, Tanzania and South Africa protect extensive areas.

A few days on an island or beach is a perfect way to end an African safari, with the splendour of a healthy coral reef surpassing most terrestrial habitats in terms of diversity and color.

The animals listed in the **Animals by Habitat and Diet** chart (see page 89) are classified according to the habitat where most of their time is spent — their most dominant habitat. The animals are listed in order of size by weight.

The major parks and reserves listed in the **Major Wildlife Areas By Habitat** charts (see pages 90–91) are classified according to their most dominant habitats.

Many of these wildlife areas are composed of more than one habitat, so consult the text of this book for in-depth descriptions. Keep in mind that savannah and forest animals may visit wetland habitats to drink and that many forest animals are more easily seen on the open savannah.

A well-rounded safari includes visits to several types of habitats and parks, which gives the visitor an overall picture of wildlife and ecosystems.

Use the **What Wildlife Is Best Seen Where** chart (see the inside back cover) as a guide in finding the major parks and reserves that are most likely to have the animals you are most interested in seeing on safari.

When's The Best Time To Go?

The **When's The Best Time To Go For Game Viewing** chart (see the inside front cover) shows, at a glance, when you should go to see the greatest numbers or concentration of large mammals in the countries, parks and

Sociable and inquisitive, a wild dog pack is intrigued by a different sort of mammal

reserves of your choice. Alternatively, the chart shows the best places to go in the month(s) in which you are planning to take your vacation. In other words, how to be in the right place at the right time!

For example, your vacation is in February and your primary interest is game viewing on a photographic safari. Find the countries on the chart in which game viewing is "excellent" or "good," in February. Turn to the respective country chapters for additional information and choose the ones that intrigue you the most. In this example, for instance, northern Tanzania would be an excellent choice. Use this chart as a general guideline because conditions vary from year to year. Timing can make a world of difference!

In most cases, the best game viewing, as exhibited on the chart, also corresponds to the dry season. Wildlife concentrates around water holes and rivers, and the vegetation is less dense than in the wet season, making game easier to find.

Generally speaking, game viewing is best (game is most concentrated) in Kenya and Tanzania mid-December to March and June to mid-November, while the best game viewing in Zimbabwe, Zambia and South Africa is June to October. Good game viewing in Botswana, top private reserves in South Africa, northern Tanzania and parts of Kenya can be found year-round.

There are, however, parks and reserves that are actually better outside of the dry season. In Botswana, there are a number of reserves including the Central Kalahari Game Reserve, Magadikgadi Pans National Park and Nxai Pan National Park as well as several concession areas in the Okavango Delta that are better in the green season, November to April. In the Okavango Delta, flood waters have receded by November, exposing large floodplains of fresh grass that attracts antelope from the surrounding woodlands — that in turn attract lion, leopard and other carnivores out into the open. And as Okavango Delta camp rates at this time are about one-third less than high season, there is an additional attraction for visitors that normally could not afford high season rates — or who simply prefer being able to stay longer in the bush.

Many travelers are now, in fact, discovering that traveling during low season actually fits their interests better than in high season. During the green season, the land is often luxuriously green and the air clear. The rainy season for the top wildlife countries usually involves occasional thundershowers followed by clear skies — not continuous downpours for days on end. People interested in scenery or who have dust allergies may want to plan their visits shortly after the rains are predicted to have started or soon after the rains are predicted to have stopped. Game may be a bit more difficult to find, but there are usually fewer travelers in the parks and reserves, which adds to the overall quality of the safari.

Many camps and lodges offer low-season rates, making travel during those times economically attractive. The low season in Kenya and Tanzania for most camps and lodges is April and May (except for Easter), while in Botswana the "Green Season" (offering the lowest rates) is generally December to March and the low season is April through May, (and June for some camps and lodges). South Africa's high season is September to April for hotels and many safari camps and lodges as that is the time many Europeans travel to get out of the cold winter. Interestingly enough, December through March is the rainy season yet some of the camp and lodge rates are often higher than in the dry season when game viewing is better!

Another advantage of traveling during the low season, especially if you visit the more popular parks and reserves in Kenya and Tanzania, is that there will be fewer tourists. In fact, one of my favorite times to visit this part of Africa is in November.

The best "Green Season" parks and reserves to visit in southern Africa (December to March) are the Okavango Delta, Moremi, Savute, Central Kalahari, Makgadikgadi, Nxai Pans (Botswana), Hwange (Zimbabwe), all regions of Namibia (except Etosha), and the private reserves near Kruger NP and the Cape Provinces in South Africa, and for East Africa (April, May and November) the Serengeti, and Ngorongoro Crater (Tanzania) and the Maasi Mara (Kenya).

In summary, the best time for you to go may be a combination of the best time to see the wildlife that interests you most (large mammals vs. birds), the relative costs involved (low or high season), and when you can get vacation time.

The **Temperature and Rainfall Charts** (see pages 87–88) give average high and low temperatures and average rainfall for each month of the year for a number of locations. Keep in mind that these are average temperatures; you should expect variations of at least 7 to 10°F (5 to 7°C) from the averages listed on the chart. Also keep in mind that at higher altitudes you should expect cooler temperatures. This is why many parks and reserves in Africa can be warm during the day and cool to cold at night. The most common packing mistake safariers make is not bringing enough warm layers of clothing!

Even though mid-day temperatures may be high, humidity levels are usually low as most reserves are located in semi-arid regions and/or at altitudes over 3,300 feet (1,000 m) above sea level.

AVERAGE MONTHLY TEMPERATURES
MIN/MAX IN FAHRENHEIT

CITY	JAN	FEB	MAR	APR	MAY	JUN	JUL	AUG	SEP	OCT	NOV	DEC
EAST AFRICA												
Dar-Es-Salaam	77/88	76/87	76/89	74/87	72/85	68/85	66/84	66/84	68/84	68/86	73/87	76/88
Dodoma	66/86	66/85	64/84	64/84	62/83	57/82	57/79	57/81	59/85	63/88	64/89	65/88
Kigoma	67/81	68/82	68/82	67/82	68/83	67/82	63/83	65/85	67/86	69/85	68/81	67/80
Nairobi	55/78	56/80	58/78	58/76	56/73	54/70	51/70	52/71	53/76	55/77	56/74	55/75
Mombasa	75/88	76/88	77/89	76/87	75/84	74/83	71/81	71/81	72/83	74/85	75/86	76/87
Kampala	65/84	65/83	64/82	64/81	63/79	63/78	63/78	62/78	63/81	63/82	62/81	62/81
Kabale	49/76	50/76	50/75	51/74	51/73	50/73	48/75	49/75	50/76	51/75	50/73	50/73
Kigali	43/68	48/68	46/68	43/68	41/68	37/68	41/68	39/70	37/70	48/68	37/68	39/68
Bujumbura	66/83	66/83	66/83	66/83	66/83	65/85	64/85	65/87	67/89	68/87	67/83	67/83
SOUTHERN AFRICA												
Harare	61/79	61/79	59/79	56/79	50/75	45/71	45/71	47/75	54/80	58/84	60/82	61/79
Victoria Falls	65/85	64/85	62/85	57/84	49/81	43/76	42/77	47/82	55/89	62/91	64/90	64/86
Hwange	64/85	64/84	62/85	56/83	47/80	42/76	40/76	45/81	54/88	61/90	64/89	64/85
Kariba	71/88	71/88	69/88	65/87	58/84	53/80	52/79	57/84	67/91	74/95	74/93	72/89
Mana Pools	71/89	71/89	70/89	67/88	62/85	57/81	56/81	59/86	66/92	73/97	74/95	72/91
Bulawayo	61/82	61/81	60/80	57/80	50/75	46/70	46/71	49/75	55/82	59/86	61/85	61/83
Maun	66/90	66/88	64/88	57/88	48/82	43/77	43/77	48/82	55/91	64/95	66/93	66/90
Lusaka	63/78	63/79	62/79	59/79	55/78	50/73	49/73	53/77	59/84	64/88	64/85	63/81
S. Luangwa	68/90	68/88	66/90	64/90	66/88	54/86	52/84	54/86	59/95	68/104	72/99	72/91
Windhoek	63/86	63/84	59/81	55/77	48/72	45/68	45/68	46/73	54/79	57/84	61/84	63/88
Swakopmund	54/77	54/73	54/73	59/77	59/77	64/82	59/82	59/82	54/77	54/77	54/77	54/77
Johannesburg	59/79	57/77	55/75	52/72	46/66	41/61	41/61	45/66	48/72	54/75	55/77	57/77
Durban	70/82	70/82	68/82	63/79	55/75	50/73	50/73	54/73	59/73	63/75	64/77	68/81
Cape Town	61/79	59/79	57/77	54/73	50/68	46/64	45/63	45/64	46/66	50/70	55/75	59/77

AVERAGE MONTHLY TEMPERATURES
MIN/MAX IN CENTIGRADE

CITY	JAN	FEB	MAR	APR	MAY	JUN	JUL	AUG	SEP	OCT	NOV	DEC
EAST AFRICA												
Dar-es-Salaam	25/32	25/32	24/32	23/31	22/29	20/29	19/28	19/28	19/28	21/29	23/31	24/31
Dodoma	18/29	18/29	18/28	18/28	16/28	15/27	13/27	14/27	15/29	17/31	18/31	18/31
Kigoma	19/27	20/27	20/27	19/27	19/28	188/29	17/28	18/29	19/30	21/29	20/27	19/26
Nairobi	12/25	13/26	14/25	14/24	13/22	12/21	11/21	11/21	11/24	14/25	13/24	13/24
Mombasa	24/32	24/32	25/32	24/31	23/28	23/28	22/27	22/27	22/28	23/29	24/29	24/30
Kampala	18/28	18/28	18/27	18/26	25/17	26/18	26/18	26/17	27/17	27/17	27/17	27/17
Kabale	9/24	11/24	11/24	11/24	11/23	10/23	9/23	10/23	10/24	11/24	11/24	10/24
Kigali					No Numbers							
Bujumbura	19/28	19/28	19/28	19/28	19/28	18/29	18/29	18/31	19/32	20/31	19/29	19/29
SOUTHERN AFRICA												
Harare	17/27	17/27	15/27	13/27	10/24	8/22	7/22	8/24	12/27	14/29	16/28	16/27
Bulawayo	17/28	17/28	16/27	14/27	10/24	8/22	8/22	10/24	12/28	15/30	16/31	16/29
Victoria Falls	18/29	17/29	17/29	14/29	9/27	5/24	7/27	12/31	16/32	18/32	18/31	18/30
Hwange	18/29	18/29	17/29	14/29	9/27	5/24	5/25	7/27	12/31	16/32	18/32	18/30
Kariba	22/31	21/31	21/31	19/31	15/29	12/27	11/26	14/29	19/33	23/35	24/34	22/32
Mana Pools	22/32	21/32	21/32	20/31	17/29	14/27	13/27	15/30	19/34	23/36	23/35	22/33
Maun	19/32	19/31	18/31	14/31	9/28	6/25	6/25	9/28	13/33	18/35	19/34	19/34
Lusaka	17/26	17/26	17/26	15/26	13/25	10/24	10/23	12/25	15/30	18/31	18/30	17/28
S. Luangwa	20/32	20/31	19/32	18/32	19/31	12/30	11/29	12/30	15/35	20/40	22/37	22/33
Windhoek	17/30	17/29	15/27	13/25	9/22	7/20	7/20	8/23	12/26	14/29	16/29	17/31
Swakopmund	12/25	12/23	12/23	15/25	15/25	18/28	15/28	15/28	12/25	12/25	12/25	12/25
Johannesburg	15/26	14/25	13/24	11/22	8/19	5/16	5/16	7/19	9/22	12/24	13/25	14/25
Durban	21/28	21/28	20/28	17/26	13/24	10/23	10/23	12/23	15/23	17/24	18/25	20/27
Cape Town	16/26	15/26	14/25	12/23	10/20	8/18	7/17	7/18	8/19	10/21	13/24	15/25

AVERAGE MONTHLY RAINFALL IN INCHES

EAST AFRICA											
CITY	JAN	FEB	MAR	APR	MAY	JUN	JUL	AUG	SEP	OCT	NOV	DEC
Dar-es-Salaam	2.6	2.6	5.1	11.4	7.4	1.3	1.2	1.0	1.2	1.6	2.9	3.6
Dodoma	6.0	4.3	5.4	1.9	0.2	0	0	0	0	0.2	0.9	3.6
Kigoma	4.8	5.0	5.9	5.1	1.7	0.2	0.1	0.2	0.7	1.9	5.6	5.3
Nairobi	1.5	2.5	4.9	8.3	6.2	1.8	0.7	0.9	1.3	2.2	4.3	3.4
Mombasa	1.1	0.8	2.4	7.7	12.7	4.7	3.5	2.6	2.6	3.4	3.8	2.4
Kampala	1.8	2.4	5.1	6.9	5.8	2.9	1.8	3.4	3.6	3.8	4.8	3.9
Kabale	2.4	3.8	5.2	4.9	3.6	1.2	0.8	2.4	3.7	3.9	4.4	3.4
Kigali	3.5	3.5	4.1	6.5	4.9	1.0	.3	.8	2.4	3.9	3.9	3.5
Bujumbura	3.7	4.4	4.8	4.9	2.3	0.4	0.3	0.4	1.5	2.5	3.9	4.4
SOUTHERN AFRICA												
Harare	7.7	7.1	4.5	1.2	0.5	0.2	0	0.1	0.3	1.2	3.8	6.4
Bulawayo	5.6	4.4	3.3	0.8	0.4	0.1	0	0	0.2	0.8	3.3	4.9
Victoria Falls	6.6	5	2.8	1.0	0.1	0	0	0	0.7	1.1	2.5	6.8
Hwange	5.7	5.1	2.3	0.8	0.1	0	0	0	0.1	0.8	2.2	5.0
Kariba	7.5	6.2	4.4	1.2	0.2	0	0	0	0	0.7	2.9	6.9
Mana Pools	8.7	7.1	4.2	1.0	0.2	0	0	0	0	0.5	2.3	9.1
Maun	4.3	3.2	2.8	1.0	0.3	0.1	0	0	0	1.2	2.0	3.8
Lusaka	9.1	7.6	5.7	0.7	0.2	0	0	0	0	0.4	3.6	5.9
S. Luangwa	7.7	11.3	5.6	3.6	0	0	0	0	0	2.0	4.3	4.3
Windhoek	1.7	2.0	2.2	1.1	0.2	0.1	0.1	0.1	0.1	0.4	0.9	1.0
Swakopmund	0.5	0.5	0.5	0.4	0.4	0.4	0.3	0.4	0.4	0.6	0.6	0.4
Johannesburg	4.5	3.8	2.9	2.5	0.9	0.3	0.3	0.2	0.1	2.7	4.6	4.3
Durban	5.1	4.5	5.3	4.2	2.0	1.2	1.4	1.7	2.4	3.9	4.5	4.6
Cape Town	0.6	0.7	0.7	2.0	3.5	3.3	3.5	3.1	2.0	1.4	0.5	0.6

AVERAGE MONTHLY RAINFALL IN MILLIMETERS

EAST AFRICA											
CITY	JAN	FEB	MAR	APR	MAY	JUN	JUL	AUG	SEP	OCT	NOV	DEC
Dar-es-Salaam	66	66	130	292	188	33	33	26	31	42	74	91
Dodoma	152	110	138	49	5	0	0	0	0	5	24	92
Kigoma	123	128	150	130	44	5	3	5	19	28	143	135
Nairobi	39	65	125	211	158	47	15	24	32	53	110	87
Mombasa	25	19	65	197	320	120	90	65	65	87	98	62
Kampala	47	61	130	175	148	73	45	85	90	96	122	99
Kabale	58	97	130	125	92	28	20	58	98	99	110	87
Kigali	90	90	105	165	125	25	7	20	60	100	100	90
Bujumbura	95	110	121	125	56	11	5	11	37	65	100	115
SOUTHERN AFRICA												
Harare	196	179	118	28	14	3	0	3	5	28	97	163
Bulawayo	143	110	85	19	10	3	0	0	5	20	81	123
Victoria Falls	168	126	70	24	3	1	0	0	2	27	64	174
Hwange	145	129	57	20	3	0	0	0	2	21	56	127
Kariba	192	158	113	30	4	1	1	0	1	18	74	175
Mana Pools	221	181	107	26	4	0	0	0	1	13	59	231
Maun	110	80	70	25	7	3	0	0	0	30	50	95
Lusaka	232	192	144	18	3	0	0	0	0	11	92	150
S. Luangwa	195	287	141	91	0	0	0	0	0	50	108	110
Windhoek	43	53	56	28	5	3	3	3	3	10	23	26
Swakopmund	12	15	12	10	10	10	7	9	11	15	16	11
Johannesburg	112	96	74	61	23	8	8	5	3	69	117	109
Durban	130	114	135	107	54	31	36	43	61	99	114	117
Cape Town	15	18	18	50	90	85	90	80	50	36	13	15

Animals By Habitat And Diet

The animals listed below are classified according to the habitat where most of their time is spent. The animals are listed in order of size by weight.

SAVANNAH/SAVANNAH WOODLAND		
GRAZERS	BROWSERS	CARNIVORES
White Rhino	Elephant	Lion
Eland	Giraffe	Hyena (three species)
Zebra	Nyala	Cheetah
Roan Antelope	Bushbuck	African Wild Dog
Gemsbok (Oryx)	Gerenuk	Jackal (three species)
Topi	Duiker, Grey	Serval
Hartebeest	Dikdik	Bat-Eared Fox
Wildebeest		Mongoose (many species)
Tsessebe		Genet (two species)
Warthog		Caracal
Reedbuck		
Grant's Gazelle	Grant's Gazelle	
Impala	Impala	
Springbok	Springbok	
Thomson's Gazelle	Thomson's Gazelle	
Klipspringer	Klipspringer	
Steenbok	Steenbok	

FOREST		
OMNIVORES	BROWSERS	CARNIVORES
Gorilla	Elephant	Leopard
Chimpanzee	Colobus Monkey	Serval
Syke's Monkey	Bongo	Genet
	Bushbuck	
	Duiker (several species)	

WETLANDS	
BROWSERS	CARNIVORES
Hippopotamus	Crocodile
Buffalo	Otter
Sitatunga	

SCRUBLANDS, SEMIDESERTS AND DESERTS
See savannah grazers, browsers and carnivores above

Major Wildlife Areas By Habitat
P–Primary Habitat S–Secondary Habitat (R)–Riverine (L)–Lake
East and Central Africa

COUNTRY	WILDLIFE AREA	WOODLAND/ SAVANNAH	FOREST	WETLAND
Tanzania	Arusha (N.P.)		P	S
	Lake Manyara	S	S	P (L)
	Ngorongoro Crater	P	S	S (L)
	Serengeti	P		S (R)
	Tarangire	P		S (R)
	Mt. Kilimanjaro		P	
	Selous	P		S (R)
	Ruaha	P		S (R)
	Mikumi	P		
	Gombe Stream		P	S (L)
	Mahale Mountains		P	S (L)
Kenya	Nairobi (N.P.)	P		
	Amboseli	P		S
	Tsavo	P		
	Maasai Mara	P		S (R)
	Mt. Elgon		P	
	Aberdare		P	
	Mt. Kenya		P	
	Meru	P	S	
	Lake Navaisha			P (L)
	Lake Nakuru			P (L)
	Lake Bogoria			P (L)
	Lake Baringo			P (L)
	Samburu	P		S (R)
	Lewa Downs	P		
	Laikipia	P		
Uganda	Murchison Falls	P	S	S (R)
	Queen Elizabeth N.P.	P	S	S(L)
	Bwindi		P	
	Kibale Forest		P	
Rwanda	Volcano N.P.		P	
Congo	Virunga (Rwindi area)	P		S (L)
	Virunga (other areas)	S	P	
	Kahuzi-Biega		P	

Major Wildlife Areas By Habitat
P–Primary Habitat S–Secondary Habitat (R)–Riverine (L)–Lake
Southern Africa

COUNTRY	WILDLIFE AREA	WOODLAND/ SAVANNAH	FOREST	WETLAND	DESERT
	Okavango Delta	S		P	
	Moremi	P		S	
	Linyanti/Selinda/Kwando	S		P	
Botswana	Savute	P			
	Chobe	P		S(R)	
	Makgadikgadi	S		P	
	Nxai Pan	S	P		
	Kalahari Desert	S			P
	Hwange	P			
	Matusadona	S		P (L)	
Zimbabwe	Mana Pools	S		P (R)	
	Matobo Hills	P			
	Chizarira	P			
	Ghonorhezo	P			
	South Luangwa	P		S(R)	
	North Luangwa	P		S(R)	
Zambia	Lower Zambezi	S		P(R)	
	Kafue	P		S	
	Lochinvar	S		P	
Malawi	Liwonde	S		P	
	Etosha	P			S
	East Caprivi	P		S	
Namibia	Damaraland	P			
	Skeleton Coast	P			
	Namib-Naukluft	P			
	Kruger	P		S(R)	
	Private Reserves (Kruger)	P			
South Africa	Hluhluwe Umfolozi	P			
	St. Lucia	S	S	P(L)	
	Phinda	P	S	S(R)	
	Kgalagadi Transfrontier Pk.	S			P

HISTORY OF SAFARI

The word "safari" is an Arabic verb which means "to make a journey" — this word was infused into the Swahili language where it refers to an expedition or voyage, and subsequently into the English language.

The modern safari has its origin in the expeditions of European hunters and naturalists who traveled to hitherto uncharted parts of the continent in search of unusual animals for scientific description or as trophies during the early part of the nineteenth century. Among the better known explorers and hunters of the 1800s were William Burchell, Cornwallis Harris and Frederick Courtney Selous. Although Selous was undoubtedly in pursuit of macho adventure, thrill and bounty, he eventually proposed that wanton destruction of large mammals ought to be tempered with the British concept of "sportsmanship". This was in contrast to the African hunters armed by Arab merchants, and the Boer settlers in South Africa, who had set about decimating virtually all large mammals. Within a few decades of the publication of Selous's famous book *A Hunter's Wanderings in Africa* the first game control laws were established in most African countries which, in the early part of the twentieth century, were European colonies. It is perhaps fitting that one of Africa's largest protected areas — the Selous Game Reserve in Tanzania — should be so named, although many conservationists remain horrified at the number of rhino and other animals Selous "bagged" over the years.

It was Kenya and other parts of East Africa that attracted a growing number of American and European trophy hunters. The extravagant and glamorous expeditions of Theodore Roosevelt and others became legendary, as did the often eccentric antics of the foreign and colonial participants. Hunting safari outfitting companies such as Kerr & Downey sprung up to service the industry, and professional hunters became established. Needless to say, overland safaris relied heavily upon unheralded gun bearers and porters until the introduction of motorized transport.

By the 1970s, the idea of a safari based on looking at and photographing game — as opposed to shooting and skinning — had become established. In many national parks and other protected areas, overland safaris were organized, tented camps erected and lodges constructed. Over time, these tours and facilities have become increasingly sophisticated both in terms of the guided interpretation, and the quality of meals, accommodation and transportation which may rival a five-star luxury hotel.

Interestingly, many of the best wildlife-watching experiences still rely on the very same acute observational skills of trackers and patient naturalists upon which the early explorers were dependent. Another thing that has not changed about the safari is the marvelous sense of adventure and wondrous anticipation that comes with every walk or drive in Africa's wild places.

A leopard cub remains with its mother for a year before venturing out alone

CONSERVATION IN AFRICA

Africa is blessed with some of the most extensive wilderness areas on planet Earth — the Serengeti, Okavango and Congo Basin are among the most spectacular. A look at any map will show that a large proportion of land has been set aside as national parks or game reserves in many countries, with Botswana (39%) and Tanzania (15%) among those with the greatest percentage of land devoted to wildlife.

In most cases, these national parks were founded by colonial governments prior to 1960; although there are some notable exceptions such as in Uganda where three new national parks were established in 1993. Many of the national parks were initially set aside as hunting reserves for settlers. Rural people, most of whom were dependent upon wildlife for their sustenance, were deliberately excluded. It was because wildlife was primarily seen as something to pursue, hunt and kill that the word "game" (as in "fair game") came into use, and that is why wildlife reserves are still today known as game reserves (even though hunting is prohibited). In time, hunting came to an end in the national parks, because the wildlife resource was seen to be finite, and a "conservation" ethic took root.

In most cases, the early national parks were run along military lines, and local people who attempted to capture "game" were regarded as the enemy — poachers to be punished and jailed. This approach to national parks undoubtedly safeguarded large areas of wild land (for which modern-day conservationists can be grateful), but, at the same time, it alienated local communities who came to regard the reserves — and sometimes even the animals themselves — as symbols of repression.

To the credit of many African nations, the sanctity of most national parks has remained intact since the wave of independence during the 1960s — sometimes in the face of great pressure from rural communities. But while the boundaries of the parks were unchanged, the animals within were subjected to intensive hunting, either for food or for skin, horn and ivory. In numerous instances the poaching (for it was still illegal) involved the very staff who were charged with the responsibility of safeguarding the wildlife.

The 1970s and 1980s were decades of decimation in many African parks, because human populations grew and global marketplaces for rhino horn and elephant tusks opened up. Corruption, often at a high level, facilitated the illegal export of wildlife products to the Far East and elsewhere. At this time, too, the parks and reserves became ever more isolated as agriculture and settlements encroached upon the boundaries of protected areas.

In the 1990s, conservation philosophy in Africa swung toward initiatives that brought communities and wildlife closer together. Two things had become obvious. First, even the largest national parks contained only portions of ecosystems; many species extended their range beyond the boundaries. Second, a protectionist approach dictated to local people by governments or enthusiastic foreign environmentalists would have very little chance of succeeding in the absence of any real incentives.

While the borders of most national parks remain intact, innovative community-based programs encourage local people to develop sustainable resource utilization in adjoining areas. This concept serves to maintain natural ecosystems beyond the borders of protected areas, as opposed to the establishment of marginal farming activities that generally destroy or displace all wildlife.

Non-consumptive utilization, such as ecotourism, provides jobs and financial returns to communities, while the harvesting of thatching grass, honey, wood and wildlife, such as antelope and fish, provides direct sustenance. In some regions, trophy hunting, regulated by government permits, brings large sums of cash into communities. In essence, these programs set out to

The Nile crocodile is the largest and most dangerous reptile in Africa

restore ownership and responsibility for wildlife to the local people. In areas of low seasonal rainfall (much of East and southern Africa) the financial returns from wildlife have proven to exceed most forms of agriculture or livestock farming.

Perhaps the most interesting development in recent years are the so-called transfrontier initiatives, such as Peace Parks, which link existing protected areas across national boundaries. These potentially massive areas not only allow for greater expansion of wildlife but also provide developing countries with growth points for ecotourism and stimulate greater economic cooperation between neighbors.

There can be little doubt that ecotourism has made a significant contribution to the conservation of wildlife in Africa, through job creation and the stimulation of local economies. Another important benefit is that many young African people have been reconnected to the wildlife that their grandparents interacted with and depended upon, because they have become skilled and articulate guides, hosts and hostesses.

At the start of the new millennium, there is much to be positive about for the future of African wildlife. As many governments recognize the value of ecotourism, many rural people are deriving real benefits from sustainable resource use, and protected areas are actually increasing in size. But conservation is not just about elephants and other large mammals — it is about the land itself. Much still has to be achieved outside of Africa's savannah biome, because rainforests, temperate grasslands and specialized ecosystems, such as mangroves, shrink daily and rare, geographically isolated species face extinction.

TRANSFRONTIER CONSERVATION AREAS IN AFRICA

The creation of transfrontier conservation areas is an extremely important and exciting movement toward the preservation of both plant and animal species in Africa.

The vision for conserving biodiversity by the creation of TFCA (Trans Frontier Conservation Areas) throughout Africa has it's roots in southern Africa, where several nations have already formed transfrontier parks. The best known and among the oldest of these is the Kgalagadi Transfrontier Park situated between South Africa and Botswana, which is being managed as a single entity, both for wildlife and tourism. It is largely through the success of this park that the conservation planners and politicians have been driven on to create further parks and conservation areas between countries. Transfrontier conservation areas have been accepted as being viable, sustainable, and politically acceptable to most nations, as they have been shown to benefit society, the local communities and biodiversity conservation of wildlife.

The Transfrontier Conservation Areas map that follows features the protected areas of south central Africa, along with numbered areas envisaged for TFCA development. These are but the major TFCA areas, as there are a number of smaller projects also being considered. Private and public land is constantly being developed by communities and private landowners into conservancies under wildlife utilization as the environmental and economic benefits are realized. Therefore this is an ongoing and growing initiative, which will actually increase the area of land under wildlife in Africa into the future. The major areas are listed as follows.

1) Ais-Ais/Richtersveld Transfrontier Park
The total area of the park is 2,402-square-miles (6,222-km²), of which 31% is in South Africa and the remainder (69%) is in Namibia. This rugged, semi-desert area was established on August 1, 2003 and features the Fish River Canyon at the core.

2) Kgalagadi Transfrontier Park
Situated between South Africa and Botswana, this 14,668-square-mile (37,991-km²) park is a highly successful collaboration for management of southern Kgalagadi biomes. This huge area can be freely traversed from either country, but for the Botswana side a serious 4wd vehicle is required. Depending on the season the game and birds viewing along the Nossop River is outstanding, featuring lion, cheetah, oryx, springbuck, wildebeest, ostrich and a host of other desert specialists.

3) Limpopo-Shashe Transfrontier Conservation Area
This proposed area embodies unique features from three countries (Botswana, South Africa and Zimbabwe) that will combine a strong wildlife and conservation component to a historical and cultural theme that dates back to the dinosaurs and more recently to an African kingdom that predates Great Zimbabwe. The area is to include 521-square-miles (1,350-km²) in Botswana, 1,881-square-miles (4,872-km²) in South Africa and 370-square-miles (960-km²) in Zimbabwe, and has its center on the Limpopo/Shashe river confluence. The owners and stakeholders consist of private owners in all three countries, state land in South Africa, communal lands and government owned safari hunting area in Zimbabwe. The well known Tuli Game Reserve of Botswana with its large numbers of elephant and lion is included as is the Mapungubwe Cultural Landscape in South Africa. This exciting and diverse area offers a wide range of opportunities for visitors and once complete may be extended eastward toward the Great Limpopo complex.

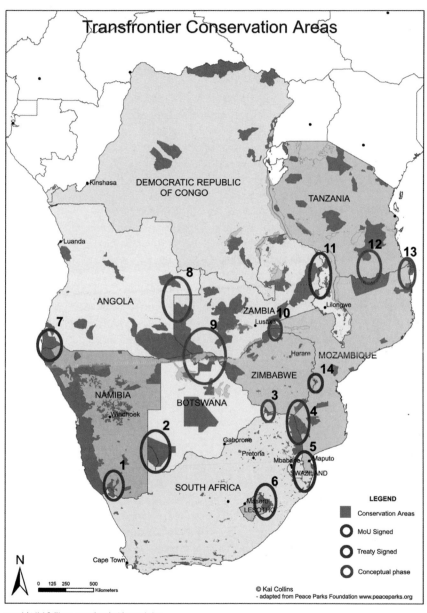

Transfrontier Conservation Areas

DEMOCRATIC REPUBLIC
OF CONGO

Kinshasa

TANZANIA

Luanda

11

12

13

8

ANGOLA

ZAMBIA

10

9

Lilongwe

7

Lusaka

Harare

MOZAMBIQUE

ZIMBABWE

14

NAMIBIA

BOTSWANA

3

4

Windhoek

2

Gaborone

5

Pretoria

Mbabane

Maputo

SWAZILAND

1

SOUTH AFRICA

6

Maseru

LESOTHO

Cape Town

N

0 125 250   500
                Kilometers

LEGEND

Conservation Areas

MoU Signed

Treaty Signed

Conceptual phase

© Kai Collins
- adapted from Peace Parks Foundation www.peaceparks.org

4) Great Limpopo Transfrontier Conservation Area
This is a much publicized area which is already partially in existence, with further land developments and corridors planned. The main part of this TFCA is Kruger National Park in South Africa, with other components being the Coutada 16 block in Mozambique and the Gonarezhou National Park in Zimbabwe which will be linked by a corridor. The end result could be a 15,445-square-mile (40,000-km^2) area allowing for free movement of large numbers of elephant, buffalo and many other species. A long-term vision proposes linkages with the St. Lucia Game Reserve in South Africa by way of the Lebombo Mountains, Maputo Elephant Reserve, Tembe Elephant Reserve and the Ndumo Reserve. This is an important conservation area in the envisaged wildlife management of the "bushveld" biome of southern Africa.

5) Lebombo Transfrontier Reserve and Resource Area
Between South Africa, Mozambique and Swaziland, these relatively small areas could link together creating opportunities for biodiversity and resource use. As mentioned, long-term linkages with the Great Limpopo may be a possibility.

6) Maluti/Drakensberg Development Area
Between South Africa and Lesotho, this small transfrontier area protects the biodiversity of the Drakensberg highlands including important water sources and habitats for endangered bearded vultures and other species.

7) Iona/Skeleton Coast Transfrontier Conservation Area
An extremely remote conservation area with components within Angola and Namibia and the Kunene River running through the center, this area has unique geological and faunal features found nowhere else in the world.

8) Liuwa Plains/Kameia Transfrontier Conservation Area
The Liuwa Plains in Zambia, although little known among tourists, is well know among conservationists for large floodplains and huge numbers of migratory wildebeest and other species. Historically, these plains shared much movement of wildlife with the Kameia area in Angola during wet and dry seasons. Unfortunately, during the troubles in Angola, much wildlife was decimated and animals were forced to stay largely on the Zambian side. With the cessation of hostilities in Angola, this TFCA could return the area to its former natural state.

9) Kavango Zambezi Transfrontier Conservation Area
Also known as the KAZA TFCA, the vision for this area for which a memorandum of understanding has been signed by the governments involved, will bring

into existence one of the largest conservation areas on Earth. Joining parts of Botswana, Namibia, Angola, Zambia and Zimbabwe, and containing the largest populations of African elephant on earth (some 250,000+) along with a huge range of other mammals, plants and over 500 bird species, the KAZA TFCA should become the economic and conservation focus for the entire region.

The internationally important conservation areas including the Chobe National Park, Hwange National Park, Kafue National Park, Victoria Falls and the world's largest protected wetland, the Okavango Delta, all occur within this mega conservation area. The addition of huge and unused areas within southeastern Angola have the potential to increase the elephant carrying capacity by at least another 50%.

Already internationally recognized as one of the best wildlife safari areas in Africa, the addition of corridors and community conservation areas will make this a world class tourism destination and offer economic opportunities for thousands of remote dwelling people.

10) Lower Zambezi/Mana Pools Transfrontier Conservation Area
With the mighty Zambezi River as the centerpiece, these two wild and unspoiled areas would combine habitats on both banks of the river and bring benefits to both countries as well as the wildlife, especially elephant, which move between them. The future potential for corridor linkages with the Luangwa valley areas further into Zambia will enhance the biodiversity and tourism potential of the whole area.

11) Malawi/Zambia Transfrontier Conservation Area
The unique flora of the Malawi and Zambian highlands on the common boundary between the two has long been an attraction to the area. Conservationists and visitors alike marvel at the beauty and floristic diversity of this highland kingdom situated in the heart of Africa. The ability to enter the Nyika Plateau National Park unhindered from either country will not only assist tourism, but allow for movement of wildlife and conservationists.

12) Niassa/Selous Transfrontier Conservation Area
The inclusion of southern hunting blocks of the Selous (Tanzania) into the corridor linking these two mighty reserves should see this becoming another of the greatest conservation areas in the world. Both the Selous and Niassa (Mozambique) areas are renowned for the truly wild experience offered to visitors and the diversity of wildlife is also magnificent.

13) Mnazi Bay/Quirimbas Transfrontier Marine Conservation Area
The combination of two marine conservation areas along the Indian Ocean coast including parts of Mozambique and Tanzania makes this an important

and sufficiently large area to ensure the biodiversity of those two areas is preserved. The success of the management of this reserve could lead to further reserves being planned and promulgated.

14) Chimanimani Transfrontier Conservation Area
This is another highland area of great natural beauty and biodiversity, situated on the border between Mozambique and Zimbabwe. The combination will allow for the protection of flora and important water catchments of the area.

CULTURAL HISTORY AND CULTURES OF SUB-SAHARA AFRICA

For millions of years East Africa has been the cradle of mankind, and yet at the dawn of modern man, some 100,000 years ago, our total population was probably no more than ten thousand individuals. Within that small population was an individual whom scientists and genealogists refer to as "Scientific Adam", the biological forefather of most of us. We should view him as the very first modern man. He and his extended family unit were possibly the first individuals to develop complex thinking and language and with that newfound tool they were ready to take on the rest of the world with one of evolution's strongest weapons — speech, thinking and the ability to reason among one another.

A female Mursi's body adornment includes of a large clay lip plate

Of this very small population, a handful of families migrated northeastward and 60,000 years ago eventually crossed the land bridge between Africa and the Middle East. Some individuals followed the south Asian coastline eastward and within a few thousand years that gene pool had colonized the isolated continent of Australia. Others branched northward into Western Europe (first inhabited about 40,000 years ago), and eventually east across central Asia, the Baring Straits and onto the Americas as recently as 15,000 years ago. In essence, 98% of modern man's genetic material remained in Africa, while all the races of the rest of the world potentially relate back to the handful of individuals who left Africa in that initial exodus. Genealogists studying these migrations have discovered that the genetic variation of a population of 2,000 individuals on the Indian Ocean Island of Pate, near Lamu in Kenya, is greater than most countries in Europe, Asian and Americas with populations of hundreds of millions!

The remaining population of modern man was sparsely distributed across the African continent and for the next 50,000 years, five distinct populations grew in relative isolation from one another, and with them an equal number of distinct complex languages, as distinct from one another as English and Chinese. The origin of language is therefore today an important, but not exclusive indicator to understanding ethnic origin.

The **Nilotic** speakers originated in the north central African savannahs, the **Bantu** speakers of the west African rainforests, **Cushites** from the horn of Africa, **Hamitic** languages in the central highlands and the click-speaking **Koishans** were the original inhabitants of central, east and southern Africa.

Modern day English is very different from the English spoken only 300 years ago, which is as a result of so much interference from other languages. English contains approximately 30 distinct sounds — whereas Koishans with their "click languages" contain as many as 100 distinct sounds — a reflection of age without change. There are approximately 30 click languages spoken in the world today of which all but one are endemic to Africa.

Some 10,000 years ago further climatic changes and the domestication of livestock started large scale migrations across the continent. Bantu speakers who were generally agriculturalists started moving eastward, the Cushitic people from the horn of Africa southwestward, and more recently in only the last thousand years as northern Africa's desertification started, the heavily pastoralist Nilotic communities started their migrations southward down the Nile Valley in search of new grazing lands. During this process some groups interacted with one another, shared genetic material, exchanged various cultural values, beliefs and means of adornment. This was the birth of tribal individualism that expanded into some 400 or more distinct tribal groups across the continent. The concept of pure isolation of different tribes is not entirely accurate; trade, intermarriage and exchanging of ideas was and still is widespread.

Tall, slim and slender, the **Maasai** and **Samburu** are probably the most well known Nilots in East Africa, who migrated down the Nile Valley to Kenya and northern Tanzania from what is today the Sudan about 1,000 years ago. They are nomadic cattle and goat herders, and for them cattle is the most important social, economic, and political factor. Cattle are a sign of wealth and social standing, as well as a food source from a mixture of milk and blood tapped from a cow's jugular vein. The **Maasai** traditional homeland is southern Kenya and northern Tanzania in an area that has the most visited game parks and reserves, and are therefore the most frequently encountered by visiting tourists.

A Maasai displays the artistry of their African beadwork

Considering this exposure to western tourists, they still maintain remarkable facets of their original cultural identity.

The **Samburu** are closely related to the Maasai, speaking the same language (*Maa*) and follow many similar traditions. With their traditional homeland around Maralal in north central Kenya, the majority of their population are well away from the main areas of tourist and government influence. Like the Maasai, their morani (warriors) prefer red blankets and use red ochre to decorate their heads, and the women wear beaded jewelry. They also tend cattle and goats, but it is cattle which is the center of Samburu social, political, and economic life. The Samburu are still nomadic people and when pasture becomes scarce in this semi-arid land, they pack up their manyattas (small settlements) on camels and move to better pastures.

Both the Maasai and Samburu operate an age set system which among the Samburu is still very traditional. Male children are first known as *Nkeria* (child), are then trusted as a shepherd of the family goats and sheep and take the name *Layeni*. On circumcision (borne without a flinch lest the family name be disgraced) they become *Lmurran*, before finally achieving the status of *Lpayan* — an elder and responsible member of the tribe ready and able to participate in the decision making process. Armed only with a classical looking spear known as a *Mpere* and short stabbing sword and the *rungu* or club, defending himself only with a buffalo of giraffe hide shield, a Samburu warrior is renowned for bravery across northern Kenya.

Also of **Nilotic** origin are the **Mursi** and **Surma** (Ethiopia), where the women practice some of the most

The Mursi tribe is just one of the many unique cultures present in Ethiopia

profound forms of body adornment in the world today — inserting a seven inch diameter clay plate into their lower lips. When a young girl reaches the age of 15 or 16 a small incision is made into the girl's bottom lip, using a small knife, the front teeth of the lower jaw are removed, and a disc of locally-derived baked clay is inserted into the incision. As the girl ages, and the bottom lip stretches with the weight of the plate, the smaller discs are removed and replaced with ever-larger discs, further stretching the lip until it becomes so distended that the lip (with the plate removed) can sometimes be pulled right over the head. The discs are removed at mealtimes to allow for eating and drinking.

Various anthropological studies have been made to determine the cultural significance of the lip plates, including the idea that the lip plate prevents the entry of evil spirits into the body via the mouth, and the idea that the practice was instituted to mar the appearance and hence put off slave traders looking for unblemished girls. However, the prevalent philosophy is that the size of the lip plate is representative of the wearer's family's wealth, and thus is indicative of her bride price.

Mursi are very superstitious. If one asks a Mursi (or any other Nilotic tribesman) how many head of cattle he possesses, he invariably replies, "more than ten". According to an ancient tribal superstition, knowing the exact number of one's herd brings disaster to it. When not tending their livestock and crops or hunting game, they pass their time playing *gadaba*, an ancient game of chance also known by it's Arabic name of *mangala* (*Mankala*) or *mbao* in Kenya and Tanzania. It is one of the world's oldest games (similar in concept to backgammon) and is known to have almost 700 set's of rules — is that one for each tribe?

Among the Mursi and Surma, a single-combat sport of physical skill known as "Donga" or "stick fighting" has evolved into something of an art form that allows young men to take part in competitions of strength and masculinity, earn honor among their peers and win the hands of girls in marriage without serious risk of death. Often as many as 50 unmarried men will compete from two age sets between 16 and 32 years of age. The

A San woman from Tsumkwe in Namibia

ultimate winner is borne away on a platform of poles to a group of girls who will decide among themselves which one of them will ask for his hand in marriage. Donga stick fights take place at the end of the rainy season and continue for a 3-month period. Each week, chosen villages come together and the top fighters from each village challenge each other.

The Khoisan's or **Bushmen** are short in stature and of a yellowish/brown color, often living a hunter gathering lifestyle. Their language contains a variety of distinct clicks. These are the very earliest of cultures of Africa, responsible for the ancient rock paintings found in the Kalahari and south. Rock paintings in Tanzania have been found where this ethnic group resides today, such as the Sandawe Rock Art sites of Kondoa. The **Hadzape** (or Hadzabe) live around the Lake Eyasi area in northern Tanzania's Rift Valley, and are comprised of only a few hundred people. Although simplistic in explanation, the Khoisan's and especially the Hadzape are genetically more similar to Scientific Adam than any community elsewhere on the planet.

Top: The Karo display ornate body art and body scarification to express beauty
Bottom: A young member of the Hamar Koke tribe participates in the "bullah" ceremony

Short and muscular, with broad faces, the **Hamites** are best represented by the **Hamar Koke**, who are a large agro-pastoralist tribe with a population of around 15, 000 to 20,000 in southern Ethiopia between Lakes Stephanie and Turkana. Both men and women are stunningly beautiful with their long braided hair, and very proud of the welts and scars that mark their lower backs. The scars are a symbol of a woman's strength, love and devotion to their men. They are extremely superstitious and believe that evil and bad luck exist in certain unholy or impure things. The intestines of a goat or cow are read at the birth of each child to determine its fate. In addition, a child born out of wedlock is given away or left to die and one of the mother's front upper teeth is removed. In fact, infanticide is relatively common in Hamar and **Karo** societies. Otherwise, the family would risk crop failure, drought or ill health.

The Hamar have an elaborate age-set system marking the periodic rites of passage from one age grade to another, most likely adopted and modified to suit their needs after millennia of interaction with the Nilotic tribes. Hairstyles and bodily scarifications are used to mark the stages. The most important ceremony is the "**bullah**" or "jumping of the bulls", when a boy becomes engaged and is about to pass into adulthood. This is a complicated ceremony witnessed by several hundred invited guests in which the *"Maz"*, or recently initiated men must take a running leap onto the back of the first bull, then run across the backs of some 15 or more lined up in a row, without falling, back and forth, 4 times. While he is running, his young female cousins and sisters are ritualistically whipped by the *Maz* to encourage him. They don't show the pain they must feel and they say they're proud of the huge scars that result. Successfully done, the initiate is then allowed to join the *Maz*. If he falls, he is considered completely unworthy and the embarrassment of failure will stay with him for the rest of his life. At the end of the leap, he is blessed and sent off with the *Maz* who shave his head and make him one of their number. His kinsmen and neighbors decamp for a huge dance which is also a chance for large-scale flirting. The girls get to choose who they want to dance with and indicate their chosen partner by kicking him on the leg.

The **Bantu** people comprise at least 95% of the population of East Africa. Some examples of the Bantu tribes are the **Chagga** on the slopes of Mt. Kilimanjaro, the **Kikuyu** (or Gikuyu) who's homeland is around Mt. Kenya. For the Kikuyu, land ownership is the most important social, political, religious, and economic factor. They have a complex system of land ownership that revolves around close relatives. The importance of land brought them into conflict with the colonial government when white settlers and farmers occupied their traditional lands. Today, Kikuyu farmers produce most of the fresh produce that is consumed in Nairobi as well as coffee and tea for export. Many Kikuyu have also been successful in economic and commercial endeavors.

Traditionally, the Kikuyu were governed by a council of elders based on clans. The **Akamba** (or Ukambani), also of Bantu origin, migrated into their present homeland which is east of Nairobi toward Tsavo National Park about 200 years ago. Like many other ethnic groups, the Akamba have a series of age sets, and the men are initiated into adulthood at around age 12. Elders were responsible for administrative and judicial functions as well as overseeing religious rituals and observances.

The **Zulu**, **Xhosa** and **Himba** of southern Africa are all Bantu pastoralist people. Dancing and singing is very much a part of the lifestyle of the Zulu people, and each dance formation or movement symbolizes an event or happening within the clan.

The **Himba** inhabit the Kaokoland area of Namibia and are actually descendants of a group of **Herero** herders who fled into the remote northwest after coming into conflict with other tribes. The Himba have clung to their traditions more than most tribes. Their houses are just simple cone-shaped structures made with sticks covered in mud and dung from where they maintain their traditional beliefs of ancestor worship. They are truly striking people to look at, as both men and women cover their bodies with a mixture of rancid butter, ash and ochre to protect them from the sun and give them their "signature" deep red color. Their hair is long and plaited into beautifully intricate designs. You can identify the marital status of a Himba woman by the way she wears her hair. Likewise, a married man wears his hair in a turban-like fashion to denote his social position.

Cushitic speaking people in Kenya include the Somali, Boran, Dassenech, Gabbra and Rendille. The **Gabbra** are a striking tribe also following a traditional age-set system, common among the Northern nomads, known as the Gada system of passing through distinct age groups every seven years. Each age group elects two leaders or "Hayu" to act as their representatives at meetings known as "Dabela", convened by the tribal elders. The Gabbra calendar consists of a remarkably accurate 365 days but no leap year. Their religious worship is intended to create "Nagaya" (peace in its most holistic sense) through appeal to "Waqa" — the god of rain and peace. They are a warrior nation whose traditional enemies come from the south — the Samburu whom they term "Korre". As a tribute to bravery, a warrior who has killed an enemy will be awarded a large ivory ring or Arbora, worn with pride on his arm. With no written language the continued existence of these tribal customs is a tribute to these hardy and resilient people who live very much beyond the confines of the modern world in possibly the harshest desert environment on the continent.

A Dassanech child stands along the Omo River

Although the **Dassanech** consider themselves cushitic pastoralists, they also practice flood retreat cultivation on the vast expanses of the Omo Delta in southern Ethiopia. The Dassanech tribe is not strictly defined by ethnicity, as anyone — man or woman — will be admitted, as long as they agree to be circumcised and live by the culture of the Dassanech. So over the centuries, the tribe has absorbed a wide range of different peoples ousted from neighboring communities, creating a melting pot of ethnic origin.

The Dassanech build their houses from long branches, using leather sheets as cover. Close to the houses one finds high sturdy platforms that are sorghum stores, keeping the grain off the ground and protecting it from flooding, mice and rodents. The men share the tidy colorful and tightly wound mud hairstyle akin to Kenya's neighboring Turkana tribe (who are Nilotic in origin).

Many of the Dassanech men are spectacularly scarified — depicting the numbers of enemy killed in battle. Scarification is a practice of cutting the skin into hundreds of small flaps in artistic patterns across the body with a sharp blade, then rubbing fire ash into the wound to create a permanent raised welt. Known for their very colorful dowry ceremony, the Dassanech men wear ceremonial cheetah and leopard skins with ostrich plume headdresses. The ceremony culminates with an evocative dance, and goats and sheep are handed over in partial payment of the bride dowry.

Nowhere in the world is as well endowed with such distinct traditional tribal cultures as East Africa. Here all 5 of Africa's linguistic groups intermingle and cultural integrity is still largely intact for what may be the last generation of adventure travelers to immerse themselves. Imagine the fact that the very first jewelry on the planet appeared at 8000 BC made from flat beads of carved ostrich shells, and the Turkana and Pokot of northwest Kenya wear the same jewelry to this day.

As elements of the modern world are slowly penetrating every crack and corner of the globe, anyone interested in experiencing these fascinating cultures should travel there as soon as possible!

Top: A distinguished gentleman from Lalibela, Ethiopia
Bottom: One of the many unique scenes in Lalibela

Southern Africa

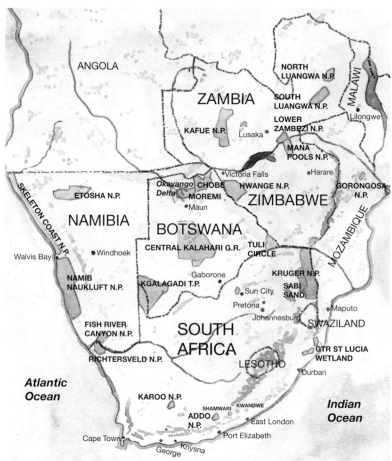

Botswana

Botswana

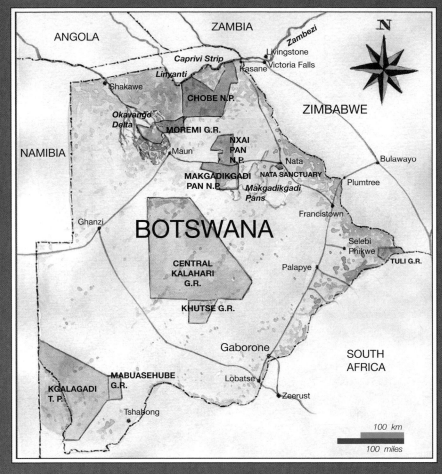

Botswana is dominated by the great Kalahari Desert which is actually a varied landscape of grasslands, bush scrub and savannah. In the far northwest, the Okavango River spills out onto the deep Kalahari sands to create the magical Okavango Delta — one of the continent's great wilderness regions. At some 224,606-square-miles (581,730-km²) Botswana is about the size of Texas (or France). The average elevation is around 3,200 feet (1,000 m) above sea level. Botswana's population numbers some 1.6 million, with the great majority living in the southeast, including the capital city of Gaborone. Setswana and English are the official languages. Currency is the Pula.

Botswana
Country Highlights

- Botswana is considered by many experts as the top wildlife country in Southern Africa
- Enjoy a mokoro ride through the crystal clear waterways of the Okavango Delta
- The magic of possibly seeing the big cats (leopard, cheetah and lion) surrounded by Botswana's epic scenery
- The mysteries of the Kalahari, from the famous Bushmen to spending time with habituated meerkats
- Spending several nights (if not your whole safari) in one of Botswana's world-class permanent tented or mobile tented camps
- The elephant herds of Chobe and the Linyanti/Selinda/Kwando region, numbering several hundred strong

Best Parks and Reserves to Visit — Best Times to Go

Best Parks and Reserves to Visit	Best Times to Go
Moremi and the Okavango Delta	May to November in some regions; Year-round in others
Linyanti/Selinda/Kwando region	May to October
Chobe	June to October
Savute, Central Kalahari GR	December to April

• *Please note that Botswana has become a year-round destination!*

Best Accommodations
Mombo and Little Mombo, Kings Pool, Jao, Vumbura Plains, Zibadianja, Selinda Camp, Jack's Camp, Chief's Camp, Khwai River Lodge and Chobe Chilwero

BOTSWANA

In recent years, Botswana has earned a reputation as perhaps the finest safari destination in Africa. Very little of the country has been developed in any way, and the small population of less than two million people is concentrated in the southeastern part of the country. The vast northern region of the Okavango Delta and the contiguous conservation areas of Moremi, Kwando, Linyanti, Selinda, Savute and Chobe, along with nearby Nxai Pan, Makgadikgadi Pans and the Central Kalahari Game Reserve, are some of the greatest wildernesses on the planet.

The best-selling book, *The Cry of the Kalahari* by Mark and Delia Owens (Houghton Mifflin), and the hilarious feature films, *The Gods Must Be Crazy (I and II)*, feature stories in National Geographic, numerous documentaries on television and the production of many beautiful books have all helped Botswana to gain international recognition as a top safari destination.

More than four-fifths of the country is covered by the sands of the Kalahari, scrub savannah and grasslands. The land is basically flat with a mean elevation of 3,280 feet (1,000 m).

The Kalahari Desert is not a barren desert of rolling sand dunes as one might imagine. It contains grasslands, bush, shrub and tree savannah, dry riverbeds and occasional rocky outcrops.

The "Pula" is not only Botswana's unit of currency, but also the Setswana word for rain, which is so critical to this country's wealth and survival. The rainy season is December to March, with the heaviest rains usually occurring in January and February. Winter brings almost cloudless skies. January (summer) temperatures range from an average maximum of 92°F (33°C) to an average minimum of 64°F (18°C). July (winter) temperatures range from an average maximum of 72°F (22°C) to an average minimum of 42°F (6°C). Frost sometimes occurs in midwinter.

The Sotho-Tswana group of people comprise well over half of the country's population, and they all speak the Setswana language. English is spoken by most of the people, especially the youth. Cattle are their most important symbol of wealth and prestige. Ancestor worship was the chief form of religion until missionaries arrived in 1816 and converted large numbers of Batswana to Christianity.

The San, Basarwa or bushmen, were the first inhabitants of the area and may have come to southern Africa 30,000 years ago. Bechuanaland became a protectorate of the British Empire on September 30, 1885, and became the independent country of Botswana on September 30, 1966.

Today, very few of the people dress in their traditional costume, except for special celebrations. However, for many Batswana, tribal customs are still important in day-to-day life.

Botswana has a multi-party democracy and is one of the most economically successful and politically stable countries on the continent. Botswana's greatest foreign exchange earners are diamonds, tourism, cattle (there are three times as many cattle in Botswana as there are people) and copper-nickel matte.

🐾 WILDLIFE AND WILDLIFE AREAS

As far as wildlife is concerned, Botswana has been one of Africa's best-kept secrets. It is not surprising, though, because the country has set aside nearly 40% of its land area for wildlife. National parks and game reserves cover 17% of the country's area — one of the highest percentages of any country in the world. In addition, another 22% of the country has been set aside as wildlife management areas. These wildlife management areas adjoin the national parks and game reserves and form the core around which the safari industry operates. Most of the 22% of the wildlife land is leased out by the authorities to safari companies. In turn, they have created wonderful, private reserves

The intensity of a wild dog on the hunt

A leopard cub's hypnotic stare

(or concession areas as they are known locally) that have incredible wildlife-viewing opportunities. These private reserves are what make Botswana's tourism what it is today. Visitors are able to get away from crowds, as numbers are strictly regulated, and guests are able to enjoy probably the highest ratio of wildlife acreage per visitor anywhere in Africa.

Botswana's combination of great game, uncrowded reserves, excellent small camps (most cater to 24 or fewer guests) and the use of open vehicles for day and night game viewing is difficult to beat.

The five main reserve areas most often visited by international tourists are all in the far northern reaches of the country. They are the Okavango Delta, Moremi Game Reserve (within the Okavango Delta), Linyanti/Selinda/Kwando region, the Savute (southwestern part of Chobe National Park), and the Chobe River region in the northeastern part of Chobe National Park near Kasane. Chobe National Park (northeastern section) is the only one of these regions that may be crowded.

The Linyanti/Selinda/Kwando region, and the majority of the Okavango Delta outside of Moremi Game Reserve, has been divided into private concession areas that feature limited numbers of camps, which can be visited by a limited number of guests. Only guests staying at the camps within each respective concession are allowed in these areas, guaranteeing exclusivity. Night game drives and limited, off-road driving are allowed in most of these areas, because the rules governing these concession areas are not as restrictive as in the national parks and game reserves. Game viewing in many of these concessions is, in fact, as good or better than game viewing in some of the reserves themselves.

Because the five regions are each distinct in character, if time allows, a well-rounded wildlife safari to Botswana should include two to three days in three or more of these areas, along with possibly a few days in the Makgadikgadi Pans, Nxai Pan or Central Kalahari Game Reserve.

Chobe National Park, Moremi Game Reserve, the Okavango Delta, and the Linyanti/Selinda/Kwando region rank among the best wildlife areas in Africa. The Okavango Delta is the largest inland delta in the world. This "water in the desert" phenomenon has created a unique and fascinating ecosystem that is well worth exploring.

Generally speaking, game viewing for the Okavango Delta, Moremi, Linyanti, Chobe and Savute is good all year, although large numbers of elephant concentrate around the waterways and marshlands in the dryer months of April through November.

The rainy season is predominantly December to March and usually consists of occasional short thundershowers. More and more travelers are preferring to travel at this time of the year, as the bush is luxuriantly green and lush with little dust in the air. You may have to work a little harder at finding game in some areas, but there is still plenty to see, and as the safari camp and lodge rates are significantly lower than in high season, visitors can afford to stay a lot longer — easily making up the difference in game seen! Another advantage is that there are fewer travelers in most of the camps — allowing for more personal attention.

Many areas of Botswana including parts of the Okavango Delta, the Savute, Nxai Pan National Park, Makgadikgadi Pans National Park and the Central Kalahari Game Reserve are, in fact, better to visit during this period than in the dry (high) season. Game viewing in Nxai Pan is best

Top: Cheetah keep a watchful eye over the plains
Bottom: White rhino have been reintroduced to Moremi Game Reserve

in the wet summer season (November to April), and Makgadikgadi Pans and Central Kalahari Game Reserve are best December to April. Reserves in the south are, at times, excellent, but they are season dependent.

Calving season throughout the country is November to February, during the summer months. The abundance of young animals (babies) make for wonderful photographic opportunities from mid-November or December through March. The sight of warthog piglets and impala lambs, only a few days to a few months old, will charm even the most stoic safarier.

The rut, or season when impala males fight for dominance, provides plenty of action from April to May.

Fishing for tigerfish, bream, barbel and pike is very good, especially September to December (fishing is not allowed in the Moremi Game Reserve area of the Okavango).

Many camps are accessed only by small aircraft, which allows visitors to minimize the time spent on roads between reserves and maximize the time viewing wildlife and enjoying the variety of other activities Botswana has to offer. Game activities are conducted by resident guides in the camps. Specialist guides may be booked to travel with you — adding a consistent high level of guiding throughout your safari.

Game viewing by air is usually quite fruitful. On one flight from the Savute to the Okavango Delta, we spotted four large herds of elephant, among numerous

One of the large herds of buffalo near Selinda Camp

other species. Most charter flights have baggage limits of 44 pounds (20 kg) per person (unless you decide to "purchase" an extra seat on the plane for your extra luggage), so bring only what you need, and pack it in only soft-sided bags. Free laundry service and amenities are available at all of the better camps.

Group and private luxury, first-class (full-service) and budget (participatory) mobile tented safaris are generally less expensive per day than flying safaris, and they are another excellent way to experience the reserves. I highly recommend small group and private luxury mobile camp safaris here, especially as the guides are generally excellent, and stay with you (as guides do with the other levels of mobile safaris) throughout the safari.

The Wildlife Department runs the parks. Driving in the parks is currently not allowed at night, but it is allowed in the private concession areas. However, it is expected — in the near future — that professionally licensed guides will be allowed to conduct night game drives in Moremi. Camping is allowed at designated spots.

NORTH AND CENTRAL

Maun

Maun is the safari center of the country's most important tourist region. Many travelers fly into Maun to join their safari; others begin their safari at Victoria Falls (Zimbabwe), Livingstone (Zambia) or Kasane, Botswana, and end up in Maun. Very few international travelers actually stay in Maun; instead they fly in and connect directly to a safari camp.

ACCOMMODATION — TOURIST CLASS: • **Motsentsela Tree Lodge** is a small lodge situated on a 500-acre (200-hectare) farm just 10 miles (15 km) south of Maun airport on the western border of a farm on the Thamalakane River, consisting of 7 large Meru-style tents plus two honeymoon suites each with private facilities, catering for a maximum of eighteen guests.• **Riley's Hotel** has air-conditioned rooms with en suite facilities and a popular bar and restaurant. • **Island Safari Lodge** is located 9 miles (14 km) north of Maun on the western bank of the Thamalakane River and has brick-and-thatch bungalows with private facilities, campsites, swimming pool, bar and restaurant.

The Okavango Delta

The Okavango, covering over 6,000-square-miles (15,000-km^2), is a natural mosaic of palm-fringed islands, open savannah, flowing rivers, crystal-clear lagoons and floodplains sprinkled with water lilies, and gigantic baobab and jackalberry trees.

Okavango Delta

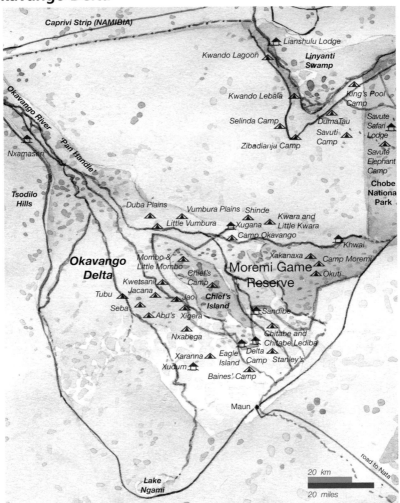

The Okavango River originates in the central African highlands, located in Angola which is about 600 miles (1,000 km) northwest of Botswana, then it fans out into the Kalahari Desert to create a vast system of thousands of waterways, separated by innumerable islands, and it eventually disappears into the Kalahari sands.

The opportunities to explore and experience the wonder of this inland delta and enjoy the primordial silence, unusual flora, bird life, hippo, crocs, and excellent fishing, are well worth the visit.

A view of the Okavango Delta from the air

Game viewing for the larger land mammal species is excellent in many parts of the Delta. Large herds of buffalo, elephant, giraffe and a variety of antelope are often seen. Lion, leopard, cheetah and other predators are also frequently encountered.

Crocodiles are most heavily concentrated in the larger waterways and in the northern part of the Delta and the panhandle, where there is permanent, deep water. However, crocs are found throughout the Delta.

The Okavango, an ornithologist's and botanist's dream come true, is beautifully presented in Okavango — *Africa's Last Eden* by Frans Lanting (Hale Publishers), *Running Wild* by John McNutt and Lesley Boggs (Southern Book Publishers), *Okavango: Sea of Land, Land of Water* by Peter Johnson and Anthony Bannister (Struik Publishers), *Okavango: Jewel of the Kalahari* by Karen Ross (Macmillan Publishing), *Okavango — Africa's Wetland Wilderness* by Adrian Bailey (Struik Publishers) and *Okavango River — The Flow of a Lifeline* by John Mendelsohn and Selma el Obeid (Struik Publishers).

Mother Nature must have smiled on this region, for the waters are highest during the peak of the dry season. It takes six months for the rainy season floodwaters to travel from their source in the Angolan highlands to the Delta. Flying into the Delta gives you an overall perspective of the region and is an adventure in itself. Game can be easily spotted and photographed from the air.

Top: Mobile camping in the heart
of Moremi
Middle: Giraffes silhouetted at
sunset
Bottom: A Cessna Caravan flying
over the Delta between camps

A 150-mile- (240-km) long buffalo fence has been constructed along the southern and western edges of the Delta to keep cattle from moving into the pristine natural areas. The villages and their cattle are to the west and south of the fence; therefore, little game is found on the Maun (southern) side.

Calling the Okavango a "swamp" is a misnomer, since the waters are very clear and are continually moving. The clarity is mainly due to the fact that the waters carry little sediment. There is only about a 203 foot (63 m) drop in altitude over 150 miles (240 km) from the upper to the lower Delta. In addition, the larger stands of papyrus in both the panhandle and in the north act as a large filtration plant, filtering out impurities and helping to keep the waters crystal clear. Very little bilharzia (a snail-borne disease) exists in the area; the only real problem region is around Maun, where the waters can become stagnant.

Activities in the Delta include mokoro (dugout canoe) and modern canoe excursions, motorized boat game safaris, day and night vehicle game drives, nature walks on islands, bird watching, and fishing on request. Motor boats allow you to visit more distant attractions, and must be used for fishing or where the water is too deep to pole a mokoro or canoe. Where there is access by land, a 4wd vehicle is necessary.

The best way to experience the majesty of the Okavango Delta waterways is by mokoro. Traveling by

Mokoro ride in the Okavango Delta

mokoro allows you to become a part of the environment. Sitting inches from the waterline, thoughts of hippos or crocodiles overturning your boat cross your mind but soon pass with assurances from your guide and the peacefulness of the pristine environment.

Patterns of gold are created by the reflection of papyrus on the still waters of the narrow channels during early morning and late afternoon. You sometimes pass through channels that can appear to be narrower than the boat itself. Silence is broken only by the ngashi (boatman's pole) penetrating and leaving the water, by the cries of countless birds and by the movement of game along the Delta's banks. Tiny frogs chime to an unknown melody. At sunset, clouds reflect in the waters and create the illusion of floating in the sky. Life slows to a regenerative pace. This relaxed form of adventure and exploration is difficult to match anywhere in the world. On one occasion, I tried poling our canoe across a small lagoon. My guide was right, it's definitely not as easy as it looks!

Guided excursions, ranging in length from a few hours to a full day, using mekoro (plural for mokoro), canoes or small motor boats, are offered by many camps in the Delta. Canoes are larger and therefore a little more comfortable, but mekoro harmonize better with the natural surroundings. To minimize cutting the large trees in the Delta, many camps use specially built fiberglass mekoro, which look and move like the real thing — without a cost to the woodlands. Mokoro trips for two or more days, during which you camp on remote islands in the Delta, are possible when booked in advance.

On one mokoro trip, we spotted an elusive sitatunga antelope running through the reeds. Sitatunga are rare, shy, solitary antelope that are not often seen, and a real highlight if spotted.

The islands in the Delta are created by many natural geological forces. Another of the causes for islands are termites, whose mounds have been built up over the eons. Because of the cement-like quality of termite mounds, the soil is sometimes dug up and used to build elevated paths in camps and even air-strips. Meanwhile, diamond prospectors inspect termite mounds closely. Since soil is brought up from quite a depth, it provides them with easily accessible core samples.

High speed excitement

During a day game drive in the Jao Concession, we witnessed one of the most incredible sightings — a leopard stalking and killing a red lechwe antelope. As the leopard held on to the lechwe's neck, the antelope fought and tossed the leopard about for several minutes, until the lechwe finally succumbed. Later that day we spotted five lion, giraffe, a variety of other species — and hundreds of red lechwe — the ones that got away!

On yet another day game drive in the Delta, we saw a pride of 19 lion on a buffalo kill. On a night drive, we also observed an aardwolf and a large spotted genet, along with other general game. The next morning, by mokoro, we saw large herds of red lechwe, a hippo out of water, and myriad bird species. I had forgotten how relaxing it was!

That afternoon, on the way to the boat station, we spotted two leopards. As we approached them, the leopard ran off, and we found a reedbuck kill they had abandoned. We then went by motorboat to an island for sundowners (drinks and snacks), and we traveled through channels surrounded by thick papyrus and reeds. From the looks of it, this could have been Tarzan and Jane's island.

We returned to the dock and headed off on a night drive to the location of the previous leopard sighting. Just as we drove up, we saw two leopard cubs run up a tree followed closely by their mother, who was chased about 20 feet up the tree by a female lion! The mother leopard came down the tree two more times, and was again chased up the tree by the lioness — seemingly to tease the lioness who had stolen their kill! The following morning on a game drive we saw three giraffe, two cheetah males, a pride of four lion, wattled crane, lilac-breasted roller, tawny eagle, fish eagle and bateleur eagles.

One of the real highlights of any safari is to sight African wild dogs, and the northern regions of Botswana are one of Africa's last refuges for this rare and endangered animal.

As might be expected of an inland delta, the Okavango is a haven for birds and a huge attraction for birdwatchers from around the world. There is a bewildering variety of aquatic and terrestrial species, and the Okavango boasts the highest concentration of African fish eagles on the continent. There are good numbers of the elusive and awe-inspiring Pel's fishing owl and the seasonally breeding African skimmers. On numerous occasions our

The giraffe is the tallest member of the animal kingdom

guide waved a fish in the air and called to a fish eagle perched high in a tree over a half-mile away, then tossed the fish into the water about 30 feet (9 m) from the boat. Like magic, the eagle dived down at full speed and plucked the fish from the water. You must be fast with a camera to catch that on film!

Large, mixed aggregations of waterfowl are common during the dry winter months, when the Angolan floodwaters fill up the seasonal wetlands. It is not uncommon to see five or six species of heron alongside four or five varieties of stork, with ducks, waders, cormorants and kingfishers — all gathered in the shallows or surrounding vegetation. The beautiful African pygmy goose, lesser jacana, slaty egret, wattled crane and the goliath heron are among the most sought-after birds.

It is not only waterfowl that populate the Okavango Delta, for the surrounding savannah and riverine woodlands provide ideal habitats for a host of hornbills, parrots, woodpeckers, rollers, shrikes, plovers, waxbills, weavers and bee-eaters, among others. Northern Botswana (and, indeed, the whole country) is renowned as a stronghold for birds of prey, with substantial populations of martial eagle, bateleur, tawny eagle, white-headed vulture, to name just a few.

Bird species we spotted on a recent visit included the coppery-tailed coucal, purple heron, striped kingfisher, Meyer's parrot, black-collared barbet, yellow-fronted tinker barbet, hamerkop, red-billed woodhoopoe, saddle-billed stork, Dickinson's kestrel, lesser spotted eagle, grey lourie, carmine bee-eater (they are migrants that are found in the Okavango from late August to March), slaty egret (a real birder's highlight!), little egret, reed cormorant, wattled crane, green-backed heron, goliath heron, blacksmith plover, pied kingfisher, yellow-billed kite,

Top: A colorful
malachite kingfisher
Bottom: Southern
carmine bee-eater

western banded snake eagle, African darter, African jacana and numerous fish eagles.

Coasting along one afternoon in a small motorboat, we drove right by an 8-foot (2.4-m) long crocodile. We went back for a closer look and discovered it was fast asleep. We maneuvered the boat within 5 feet (1.5 m) of it, and it still didn't wake up — and I'm glad it didn't!

Fishing is best in the northwestern part of the Delta. The best time of the year for catching tigerfish is September to November. For barbel, the best time is from the end of September through October, when the fish are running (a feeding frenzy). Overall, the best time for fishing is September to December.

Horseback safaris, possibly the finest in Africa, last from 5 to 10 days. Four to six hours a day are spent in the saddle. Afternoons are often spent walking, swimming, fishing or on mokoro trips. Only experienced riders are allowed, because they must be able to confidently canter alongside herds of game, including zebra, giraffe and antelope. Accommodations are usually in mobile tented camps.

An elephant-back safari (on an African elephant) is a unique way of experiencing the bush. Guests can fly to Abu's Camp for a three-day safari, during which they join the lead elephant along with several other adults and youngsters. Another option is Stanley's and Baines' Camps, where guests may walk for a few hours with trained elephants.

If you wish to visit Tsodilo Hills (see below) to see the rock paintings, consider making reservations in advance. By booking in advance, you can fly from your camp in the Okavango to the Tsodilo Hills airstrip and then be driven to the hills.

One issue to consider when visiting the Okavango Delta is the water levels and how they can affect a camp, its access and your activities. Each year the Okavango presents a different scenario to its inhabitants and its visitors. The changes are caused by the varying yearly rainfall in central Africa. The annual flood is an eagerly awaited event, and the levels of the incoming water have an enormous impact on the region. A safari camp, after a low flood, may be surrounded by huge, open grassland savannahs. The next year, that same camp may be surrounded by water as the result of an extremely high flood, and the game viewing areas will have moved. This is all part of the fun of traveling to the Okavango. It's a dynamic and constantly changing system!

When the floods arrive, much of the savannah is submerged — forcing the wildlife to concentrate on fewer and smaller islands. The area covered by game drives may be reduced; however, the drives are often more productive.

An elephant-back safari at Abu's Camp

ACCOMMODATION — CLASS A+: • **Jao Camp,** one of the most luxurious camps in Botswana, is located in a private concession area west of the Moremi Game Reserve. This beautiful camp has 9 large tented rooms (including 1 "family tent") with a lounge area and en suite bathrooms, all under a thatched roof. Each room has an outdoor shower and a "sala" with mattresses under thatch, for great midday siestas. Jao has two plunge pools, an outdoor boma, an exercise room and spa featuring a variety of massage therapies. Activities include day and night game drives in open vehicles, boat game drives (usually May to October, depending on water levels), mokoro (dugout canoe) trips to explore the crystal-clear channels, islands and waterways, and walks. Guests staying for three or more nights may spend one night under the stars in a fly camp. • **Vumbura Plains Camp** is a premier luxury camp with 14 tents (divided into 2 separate camps of 7 tents each), with private plunge pools and huge decks, linked by raised boardwalks to the dining, lounge and bar areas. Vumbura Plains is located in the northern part of the Delta. Day and night game viewing by vehicle, mokoro excursions, walks, boat game drives and fishing are offered.

CLASS A: • **Abu's Camp** is a 10-bed, deluxe tented camp with en suite facilities. Elephant-back safaris, mokoro rides, walks and vehicular game drives are offered. Guests stay at the camp for either 3 or 6 nights. • **Duba Plains** accommodates a maximum of 12 guests in luxury tents with en suite bathroom facilities, including inside and outside showers, and is located in a remote region of the Delta. Game drives and walks are offered. There is a pool and a hide overlooking a waterhole at the back of the camp. One of Africa's highest concentrations of lion exist there, feeding off of the large herds of buffalo in the area. • **Kwetsani Camp** is a 10-bed luxury tented camp, located in the same private concession area as Jao. The camp is raised on stilts beneath the shady

Top: The stunning view from Jao's pool deck
Middle: A decadent bedroom at Kwetsani Camp
Bottom: A game viewing vehicle in Botswana

canopy that overlooks the expansive plains. The 5 spacious tented "treehouse" chalets are built under thatch roofs, and all have en suite facilities, including a shower, flush toilet, basin and outdoor shower. Guests staying 3 or more nights may spend 1 night in a fly camp (highly recommended).
• **Little Vumbura Camp** offers a private location in the northern area of the Delta that borders Moremi. It has been completely renovated and has 6 large, luxury tented rooms (including 1 family tent), each with full en suite facilities and outdoor shower. The main dining area has a decked lounge and a pool. It offers both water and land activities, including boat game drives, game viewing by mokoro, day and night game drives, and walks.
• **Xaranna Tented Camp** is a new camp located on the edge of the Okavango Delta, featuring 12 refined tents each with en suite bathroom, sala and private plunge pool with sweeping views across the delta. Activities include boating, mekoros as well as morning and night game drives.
• **Xudum Delta Lodge**, located in the same concession as Xaranna, is also new and offers 12 suites with large bathtubs, outdoor showers and private plunge pools. Activities include boating, mekoros as well as day and night game drives. • **Eagle Island Camp** is situated on the island of Xaxaba in the Delta, west of Chief's Island, and has 11 air-conditioned luxury tents with thatched roofs. Each tent is set on raised wooden decks overlooking the floodplain with en suite facilities.

April through October, activities include mokoro rides, motorized boats, and sundowner cruises. December through March, morning, afternoon and night game drives are offered. Walks are available year round and helicopter game-viewing flights are also offered. • **Nxabega Okavango Safari Camp** has 9 beautifully furnished East-African-style tents with en suite facilities. Activities include game drives, walks and mokoro rides. • **Stanley's Camp,** located to the south of the Moremi Game Reserve, consists of 8 tents raised up on a boardwalk and offers day and night game drives, guided walks and mokoro excursions (water levels permitting). For an additional fee, guests may spend time walking with trained elephants. • **Baines' Camp** is located in the same concession as Stanley's Camp and features 5 well appointed rooms set on elevated platforms in the tree line. The main area features an oversize deck for outdoor dining and views over the permanent water of the lagoon, as well as a swimming pool. Activities include game drives, mokoro safaris, as well as walks with an armed guide. An educational elephant interaction offered at Stanley's Camp is available to guests at Baines'.

The interior of a tent at Tubu Tree Camp

• **Tubu Tree Camp,** situated in the Jao Concession, is a treehouse-style tented safari camp built on raised wooden platforms. The camp sleeps a maximum of 10 guests in 5 large, comfortable tents, each with small, private decks, en suite bathroom facilities and private outdoor shower. Activities include day and night game drives in open 4wd vehicles, as well as walks with an armed guide. When the Okavango's annual flood is at its highest (normally May to late September), boating, fishing and mokoro trips are also offered.

CLASS A/B:• **Camp Okavango** is a tented camp in the eastern Delta accommodating 24 guests in East-African-style tents with private facilities located down a private walkway behind each tent. • **Jacana Camp** is a small (10-bedded) camp set in the Jao Concession, and is primarily a water camp that offers mokoro excursions, boat game drives and escorted walks. Day and night game drives are generally possible by vehicle September through May, when the water levels are lower. • **Shinde Island Camp** has 8 deluxe tents (16 beds) with private facilities situated a few feet behind each tent, and a small swimming pool. Activities include mokoro trips, boat rides, fishing, walks and game drives. • **Xugana Island Lodge** has 8 reed chalets (16 beds) built on stilts, with en suite facilities and a swimming pool. Xugana offers boat rides, mokoro trips, walks and fishing. • **Seba Camp** is a new camp situated in the Okavango on an island facing west. Each of the 8 guest tents has an en suite bathroom with dual basins, toilet and shower as well as an outdoor shower. Activities include limited game drives, night drives, boating, mokoros, walks and general birding around the camp.

CLASS B: • **Nxamaseri Camp,** located in the panhandle of the Delta, is one of the top fishing camps in the Okavango. Guests also enjoy boat game drives and mekoro trips. • **Delta Camp** has 8 reed chalets with en suite facilities. Walks and mekoro excursions are offered.

Tsodilo Hills

Over 2,700 bushmen paintings are scattered through the rocky outcrops of Tsodilo Hills, one of the last places in Botswana where bushmen may be found. The largest of the four hills rises 1,000 feet (305 m) above the surrounding plain. Archaeological evidence indicates that these hills may have been inhabited as long as 30,000 years ago.

Located west of the Okavango Delta, Tsodilo Hills is accessible by a flight from Maun (or from safari camps in northern Botswana) to the Tsodilo Hills airstrip, where a guide must be pre-arranged to drive you to the sites. Alternatively, Tsodilo is a very long and rough day's ride from Maun by 4wd vehicle. There are no facilities, so travelers must fly in just for the day, or be totally self-sufficient. Unfortunately, the bushman experience has become touristy, so don't expect to see Bushmen living as they did thousands of years ago. However, the rock paintings are worth a visit. Because water is scarce in this area, be sensitive and do not drink in the presence of Bushmen.

ACCOMMODATION: None.

Moremi Game Reserve

Moremi is the most diversified of all the Botswana parks, in terms of wildlife and scenery, and many people feel it is the most beautiful. Located in the northeastern part of the Okavango Delta, Moremi contains over 1,160-square-miles (3,000-km^2) of permanent swamps, islands, floodplains, forests and dry land. The park's boundaries have been recently extended to the west and northwest, significantly enlarging its size.

One of the reasons Moremi is so unique is that it (as well as some other parts of the northern Delta) receives the richest deposits of sediment from the annual floods. This produces the most nutritious grasses that attract large herds of antelope, which in turn attract large numbers of predators.

In the floodplains, reedbuck, common waterbuck, red lechwe, tsessebe, ostrich, sable and roan antelope, crocodile, hippo and otter can be found. In the riparian forest, you may spot elephant, greater kudu, southern giraffe, impala, buffalo and Burchell's zebra, along with such predators as lion, leopard, ratel (honey badger), spotted hyena and cheetah.

Lechwe feed on the rich grasses of the Moremi Reserve

Bat-eared fox, black-backed and side-striped jackals are often seen in the riparian forest, as well as in the floodplain. Seldom-seen species include pangolin, aardvark, porcupine and hedgehog.

The reserve has a large wild dog population, as creatively presented in the book *Running Wild: Dispelling the Myths of the African Wild Dog* by John McNutt and Lesley Boggs, with photography by Helene Heldring and Dave Hamman (Russel Friedman Books).

Game viewing is excellent during the drier months of May to November when the bush has thinned out, making wildlife sightings a bit easier. In parts of Moremi, game viewing is, in fact, excellent year-round.

During a visit in 2001, I was honored to witness four white rhino being released into the wild at Mombo Camp. The release was part of a grand, ongoing plan to repopulate both black and white rhino species into the wild in Botswana and in collaboration with Wilderness Safaris and the Botswana Governments. At the ceremony, Lt. General Khama, Vice President of Botswana (currently the President of Botswana), spoke of the importance of the reintroduction of rhino to wildlife conservation and to the people of Botswana. As a result of further introductions and a healthy breeding population, the national herd has grown to 41 rhino (including four black rhino). You now have a chance of seeing the "Big Five" (lion, leopard, elephant, buffalo and rhino) once more on safari in Botswana!

Botswana and South Africa have an agreement to swap roan antelope from Botswana for white rhino from South Africa. Such efforts will form viable breeding nuclei to repopulate rhino throughout northern Botswana.

Other wildlife sightings during my last visit in November included over 30 lion, including a pair mating, 10 spotted hyena, cheetah, slender mongoose, giraffe, red lechwe, impala, tsessebe, large herds of elephant, and warthog piglets and impala calves only a day or two old!

One of the most hilarious sightings I have experienced was several juvenile lions confronting a water monitor. A lion would cautiously approach the

Prides are usually lorded over by two or three adult males, which are often related (brothers)

monitor, and then beat a hasty retreat the second the monitor made a quick move. The monitor eventually walked away unharmed!

We enjoyed the fascinating sight of a male dung beetle rolling a huge ball of dung with the female riding on it. Once he got it to the right place, he buried the female along with the dung.

During a morning game drive on another visit, we saw two herds of sable antelope, elephant, greater kudu, tsessebe, impala and Burchell's zebra. That

The delicate markings of a female bushbuck

same afternoon and evening we saw a variety of game, including leopard, seven lion, cheetah, bat-eared fox, and several species of antelope. The following afternoon we found leopard, and later a cheetah with her two cubs stalking a male impala. We also found two male cheetahs and a mother leopard with her two cubs.

In a single day we spotted leopard, three honey badgers, side-striped and black-backed jackal and a lioness that had chased a warthog into its hole and then dug it out for the kill. The lioness then kept going back to the hole, digging a bit deeper each time. Just as she moved a few feet away from the hole, a warthog shot out like a rocket and ran to safety.

On another game drive we saw giraffe, greater kudu, wildebeest, black-backed jackal and wattled cranes. Our group also spotted seven lion on a buffalo kill: three adult male, a female and three juveniles.

Elephant and buffalo are the only large animals that migrate. After the rains have begun, they move northward to the area between Moremi and the Kwando-Linyanti River systems. Other wildlife may move to the periphery of, or just outside, the reserve.

Moremi is also an ornithologist's delight. Fish eagles, kingfishers and bee-eaters abound. Other birds commonly seen include parrots, shrikes, egrets, jacanas, pelicans, bateleur eagles, hornbills, herons, saddle-billed storks, yellow-billed oxpeckers, wattled cranes, reed cormorants, spur-winged geese, long-tailed shrikes and flocks of thousands of red-billed quelea, which group together in the form of a sphere like a great spotted flying ball.

With the onset of the floods in May or June, waterfowl follow the progression of the floodwaters as they flow through the region.

Under new park rules, which are expected to be in place in the near future, night game drives and escorted walks with an armed guide may be allowed in Moremi.

Moremi is open year-round; however, some areas may be temporarily closed due to heavy rains or floods. Four-wheel-drive vehicles are necessary. The South Gate is about 62 miles (100 km) north of Maun

ACCOMMODATION IN MOREMI GAME RESERVE — CLASS A+: • **Little Mombo** is an exclusive, luxury tented camp with only 3 tents (6 beds) set on decks, with en suite bathrooms, indoor and outdoor showers, private salas (lounging areas), separate lounge/dining room and plunge pool. Morning and afternoon game drives are conducted in open vehicles. The camp is connected to Mombo Camp by a raised walkway. • **Mombo Camp** is a luxury tented camp with 9 large tents (18 beds total) set on decks with en suite facilities, indoor and outdoor showers, a swimming pool and a gym. These two camps (along with Jao Camp, Vumbura Plains, Kings Pool and Zibadianja) have set the highest standard for luxury and service of all permanent tented camps in southern Africa. Both camps are situated in the reserve near the northern tip of Chief's Island, where the savannah meets the Okavango, in what is considered by

Mombo Camp's welcoming fire pit and deck

Top: The ultimate in al fresco dining at Chief's Camp
Middle: Game viewing from Chitabe's pool
Bottom: An eventful game drive in Moremi

many to be the best game viewing area in southern Africa. Big game is plentiful year-round in this area. Activities include day and early evening game drives (up to a half hour after sunset). Night game drives are expected to be allowed from both camps soon.

CLASS A: • **Chief's Camp,** located on the western side of Chief's Island (9 miles/15 km south of Mombo), was completely refurbished in 2007 and has 12 luxury tents with private viewing decks, en suite bathrooms, and a swimming pool. The private viewing decks are large and include hammocks and loungers with views over the seasonal flood plains. A beauty treatment room and zen garden have recently been added. • **Xigera Camp** is situated within the Moremi Game Reserve on a large island in the Delta. The camp has 10 luxury tented rooms with en suite facilities. Activities include mokoro rides, walks and game viewing by vehicle and by boat.

CLASS A/B: • **Xakanaxa Camp** is a 12 tented camp with en suite facilities. The camp is located within the park, overlooking the Xakanaxa Lagoon. Game drives and boat trips are offered. • **Camp Moremi** is a 22-bed tented camp located overlooking Xakanaxa Lagoon within the reserve. Private facilities are situated a short walk down a secluded pathway behind each tent. Game drives are offered.

CLASS B/C: • **Camp Okuti,** located within the reserve, has brick-and-thatch chalets with en suite facilities.

ACCOMMODATION ON THE PERIPHERY OF MOREMI GAME RESERVE — CLASS A: • **Chitabe Camp,** located on a private concession bordered by Moremi Game Reserve on 3 sides, has 8 luxury tents set on wooden decks, with en suite facilities and an additional outside shower. Day and night game drives, morning walks, and extended walking safaris with over-nights on tree platforms are offered. There are a number of hides in the area. • **Chitabe Lediba,** located in the same private concession area as Chitabe Camp, has 5 luxury tents with en suite facilities. Activities include day and night game drives and walks. • **Khwai River Lodge,** situated outside the reserve and overlooking the Khwai floodplains, has 14 air-conditioned tents (28 beds) under thatch with en suite facilities, mini-bars and private viewing decks with ham-mocks. The camp has a gym and spa facility plus swimming pool. Day and night game drives, guided walks along Khwai River and cultural visits to village are offered. • **Sandibe Lodge,** also located on a private concession surrounded by Moremi Game Reserve on three sides, has 8 thatched cottages with en suite facilities. Activities include day and night game drives, escorted walks, mokoro trips and boat game drives.

Tall palms welcome guests to Chitabe Lediba

CLASS A/B: • **Kwara Camp,** situated just north of the reserve, has 8 tents (16 beds) with en suite facilities and offers day and night game drives, walks, mokoro rides, fishing and evening boat cruises. • **Little Kwara Camp** is next to Kwara Camp and has 5 tents with en suite facilities. It also offers day and night game drives, walks, mokoro rides, fishing and evening boat cruises.

CAMPING: • **South Gate Campsite** is located just outside the South Gate and has only toilet facilities. • **Third Bridge** is Moremi's most popular campsite and can be very crowded in peak season. This camp has only long-drop toilets. Water is available from the river. • **Xaxanaka** has no facilities. • **North Gate** campsite is situated just inside the reserve and has showers, toilet facilities and water. Because all of these campsites (and the permanent tented camps and lodges) are not fenced, beware of lion and other wild animals.

Linyanti, Selinda and Kwando

The Linyanti, Selinda and Kwando concession areas, situated northeast of the Okavango Delta and northwest of the Savute marshes within Chobe National Park, are home to many crocodile, hippo, sitatunga, lechwe, south-ern giraffe, elephant, buffalo, lion, wild dog (with good chances of seeing

Linyanti, Selinda and Kwando Concession Areas

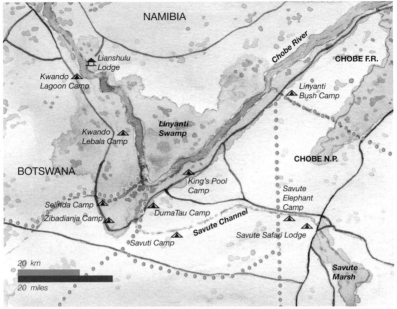

them) and spotted hyena. The region is, in essence, a mini "Okavango Delta" with a lot of big game. During the dry season this is, in fact, big elephant country with literally thousands in the region.

The Savute (Savuti) Channel, which had been dry for decades, as of this writing is flowing more than it has in over 25 years, bringing much needed water inland to this arid environment. The part of the channel within Chobe National Park is called "Savute," and the area outside of the park is called "Savuti."

On a recent visit we had an excellent leopard sighting, took a boat game drive and canoed among herds of elephant crossing the river channels, and we even walked up to a large bull elephant. On a night drive we saw lesser bushbaby, African wild cat, hyena, a pride of lion on a giraffe kill, a caracal that had killed a cattle egret, a giant eagle owl and a white-faced owl.

On another visit we saw large herds of elephant, zebra, several prides of lion, buffalo and bat-eared fox, along with a variety of other game. We stopped by a lagoon for a cool drink, and we watched two elephant playing in the water with the sun setting behind them. On a night game drive we saw 6 African wild dog on a greater kudu kill, a pride of 13 lion, leopard, serval, and a very vocal and aggressive confrontation between two adult female hyena and a subadult — the likes of which I have never seen!

Stirring things up in the Linyanti Reserve

The Kwando and Linyanti Rivers form the region's border with Namibia. The Kwando River flows southeast and then meets the southern end of the Great Rift Valley. This causes the river to flow northeast, and at this point its name changes to the Linyanti River and later to the Chobe River, which eventually meets the Zambezi River.

This region is prolific in bird life. Big game is most concentrated in this region during the dry season (May to November). Game viewing for the rest of the year is also quite good except for elephant and zebra that migrate out of the area. Much of the rest of the game including the predators, remain in the region.

ACCOMMODATION — CLASS A+:
• **Zibadianja Camp,** located on the Selinda Concession, is an ultra-exclusive luxurious 8-bed tented camp (which can be booked on a private basis if it's a group of 6 guests) with en suite facilities, sumptuous tents and vast decks overlooking the floodplains of the Zibadianja Lagoon.
• **Kings Pool Camp,** located on the Linyanti Concession overlooking a

A luxurious tent at Zibadianja Camp

Top: Selinda Camp is tucked away in the trees
Bottom: The tents at DumaTau are surrounded by lush vegetation

lagoon, has 9 ultra-luxurious tents set on raised decks, en suite facilities, indoor and outdoor showers, gym and a plunge pool. The camp is set on a small lagoon that is often full of hippo. Day and night vehicle game drives, boat game drives on a double-decker houseboat (water levels permitting), and walks are offered. The hides are a great attraction at Kings Pool. There is a hide within the camp, and guests enjoy great viewing around midday. There are also a number of hides in the bush, including a seasonal underground hide where guests can enjoy viewing animals at water level (great for photography).

CLASS A: • **Selinda Camp** is a 16-bedded tented camp with en suite facilities, set on the Selinda Concession. Activities include day and night game drives by vehicle, boat game drives (water levels permitting — usually July to October), morning walks and walking safaris for up to 6 guests and lasting two to three days. • **DumaTau** is a 20-bed tented camp with en suite facilities, indoor and outdoor showers, family tent and plunge pool. It is located within the Linyanti Concession close to the source of the Savuti Channel and overlooks an enormous lagoon. DumaTau offers day and night vehicle game drives, boat game viewing excursions and walks. • **Savuti Camp,** located on the Savuti Channel about 10 miles (17 km) from its source within the Linyanti Concession, has 7 standard tents plus 1 family tent, each with en suite facilities. A number of waterholes and hides are located along the channel. A waterhole in front of camp is a magnet for game in the dry season. Day and night game drives are offered.

CLASS A/B: • **Kwando Lebala Camp,** also located in the Kwando Concession, is situated on vast open plains and has 8 luxury tents (16 beds) under thatch with en suite facilities. Day and night game drives are offered. The Kwando Concession is a great area to see wild dog. • **Linyanti Bush Camp** is a small, intimate 12-bedded tented camp located in a concession area within the Chobe Forest Reserve. The Meru-style tents are en suite and include a bedroom and living area. The main area is elevated on a wooden decking giving you the full view of the dramatic Linyanti swamp. Activities include day and night game drives, walking and hides. • **Lianshulu Lodge** — see page 256 in the Namibia chapter.

CLASS B: • **Kwando Lagoon Camp** is set on the banks of the Kwando River within the Kwando Concession and has 8 tents (16 beds) under thatch, with en suite facilities. Day and night vehicle game drives, boat excursions, walks and fishing are offered.

Savute (Chobe National Park)

Savute is an arid region located in the southern part of Chobe National Park. The landscape ranges from sandveld to mopane forest, acacia savannah, marshlands (always dry) to rocky outcrops. The Savute Channel connects the grasslands or marshlands of the interior with the Linyanti River. The Savute River is flowing for the first time in many years, but has not yet reached the park areas, and the marshlands are still currently dry. The Savute Channel changes its spelling as it arrives within Chobe National Park.

Outside of the Chobe it is called the Savuti, and within the park it is known as the Savute.

The Savute, like the northern part of Chobe National Park, is famous for its lions and its bull elephant herds. The area is also home to eland, kudu, roan

Elephants in search of a water hole

antelope, sable antelope, waterbuck, tsessebe, giraffe, wildebeest, impala and many other antelope, along with numerous predators, including leopard, cheetah, wild dog, spotted hyena, black-backed jackal and bat-eared fox.

The Savute region is affected by the seasons, and is at its best in the wet season (November to March), or during the early dry season (April to May). When the rains fall, from November to April, the plains become green and large herds of zebra and tsessebe are present. From July to October it is typically dusty and dry, and bull elephants dominate the small, man-made waterholes.

To secure access to a permanent water source, most antelope, along with breeding herds of elephant, migrate to and settle around the Linyanti Swamps (the Linyanti/Selinda/Kwando Region) from May to October. Burchell's zebra migrate from the Mababe Depression, which is south of the Savute Marsh, northward to the Linyanti Swamps in May, and they return to the Mababe Depression in November.

Bird watching is best during the green season (November to April). Large flocks of dazzling carmine bee-eaters hawk insects, and large gatherings of white and Abdim's storks patrol the plains for grasshoppers. The world's heaviest flying bird — the kori bustard — is a common and conspicuous inhabitant of the area. Rollers, kestrels, plovers, sandgrouse, coursers, queleas and doves are among the other prominent groups.

On a morning drive down the dry Savute Channel, we stopped for tea and watched a herd of 15 giraffe and a large herd of zebra cross the channel. There were many elephant in the area, and we were amazed by how many juvenile bateleurs we saw. We saw lion and bat-eared fox on numerous occasions.

On another game drive we spotted impala, 5 greater kudu, warthog, elephant, 2 black-backed jackals, steenbok, about 50 tsessebe, a herd of blue wildebeest, 12 bat-eared fox, tawny eagle, yellow-billed hornbill and kori bustard. We followed vultures to a warthog kill, where we found only part of the carcass remaining. A large male lion was lying in the bush nearby.

Sometimes, during the dry season, 20 to 40 lone elephant bulls can simultaneously gather at a water hole. Females tend to stick close to permanent sources of water, which are found to the west along the Linyanti River or up north along the Chobe River.

A few bushmen paintings may be found in this region. Four-wheel-drive vehicles are necessary for the Savute.

ACCOMMODATION — CLASS A: • **Savute Elephant Camp** is located within the park and has 12 luxury en suite air-conditioned tents with thatched roofs set on raised wooden decks overlooking the Savute Channel. The camp has a fireplace and lounge area, library and a swimming pool which overlooks a water hole. Morning and afternoon game drives are offered.

CLASS A/B: • **Savute Safari Lodge,** situated within the park on the banks of the Savute Channel, has 12 Swedish-style wood-and-thatch chalets with en suite bathrooms. The lounge, dining area and plunge pool overlook the channel. Day game drives are conducted.

CAMPING: A National Parks Campsite is located near Savute Elephant Camp. The site is very sandy, and there is little shade. Toilet and shower facilities are not always operational. Beware of wild animals.

Chobe National Park (Chobe River/Northern Region)

Famous for its large herds of elephant, Chobe National Park covers about 4,250-square-miles (11,000-km²) and is beautifully depicted in *Chobe — Africa's Untamed Wilderness* by Daryl and Sharna Balfour (Southern Book Publishers).

The park is situated only about 50 miles (80 km) from Victoria Falls (Zimbabwe and Zambia) and the Chobe River forms its northern and north-western boundaries. Across the river is Namibia's Caprivi Strip. Bird life is prolific, especially in the riverine areas.

The four main regions of the park are along the Chobe River in the northeast near Kasane, the Corridor around Ngwezumba and Nogatsaa, a portion of the Linyanti Swamps in the northwest, and the Savute (discussed above) in the west. This is the only park in Botswana that receives large numbers of tourists.

Northern Chobe is famous for its huge elephant and buffalo populations, which number in the thousands. Lion are often seen. Game viewing by boat along the Chobe River can be spectacular, especially May to November in the dry season. Often large herds of elephant and a variety of other wildlife come down to the river to drink. On my last three visits we witnessed herds of 50 to 100 elephant swimming across the river at sunset. Mothers were assisting several babies in the herd to make it across. Once they reached the riverbank, the herds had dust baths and wandered off into the bush. This is an excellent park for game viewing by boat!

On a recent vehicle game drive we saw over 100 elephant, a pride of lion, greater kudu, hippo, sable antelope, fish eagles and crocs. Game viewing is actually very good during the mid-day at this park, as well as in the mornings and late afternoons. Animals can be seen making their way to the river to drink and may be seen along the river's edge at close range by both boat and vehicle.

Game viewing on the Chobe River

Chobe National Park

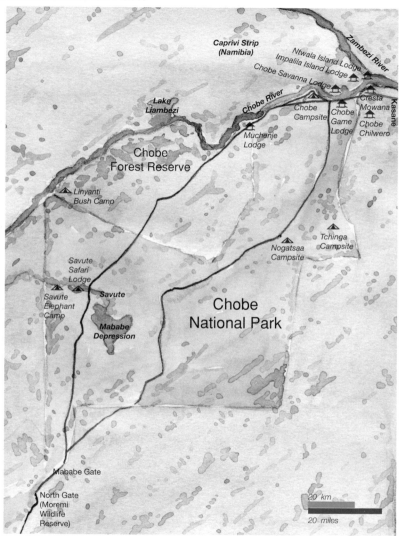

Along the River Road between the entrance gate from Kasane and Chobe Game Lodge, you are likely to see numerous hippo, red lechwe, puku, common waterbuck, warthog and guinea fowl. Driving from the lodge toward the old Serondela Campsite, you can usually see giraffe, impala, zebra and occasionally kudu and Chobe bushbuck. Large monitor lizards are commonly seen.

The hot and dry Corridor (Ngwezumba to Nogatsaa) is one of the few areas in the country where oribi (a delicate long-necked antelope) is found. Gemsbok, eland, ostrich and steenbok are sometimes seen. Prevalent species include giraffe, elephant, and roan and sable antelope. The large populations of both resident and migratory elephant have inflicted severe damage on the riverine forest along the Chobe River, virtually eliminating the band of evergreen trees within the national park. Opinions vary as to whether this is a natural phenomenon or a result of too many elephants being hemmed in. As a consequence of the elephant browsing pressure, species dependent upon dense cover such as the Chobe bushbuck and narina trogon, have become extremely rare.

One of the great highlights of the Chobe River is the breeding colonies (with up to 1,000 birds per colony) of carmine bee-eaters, which are active during September and early October. These magnificent birds — dressed in pink and turquoise — provide a truly breathtaking spectacle. Other species found along the river are the rare rock pratincoles, African skimmer and large, mobile flocks of open-billed stork and spur-winged geese.

4wd vehicles are necessary for most of the park. Vehicles are restricted to the roads. Some guests stay in accommodations across the Chobe River in Namibia.

ACCOMMODATION—NORTHERN CHOBE — CLASS A+: • **Chobe Chilwero Camp** has 15 luxurious air-conditioned cottages with mini-bars, en suite facilities, balcony and outdoor shower. The property boasts a wine cellar, business center, library, wood burning pizza oven and full-fledged spa. Located on an escarpment, the views extend all the way to Namibia's Caprivi Strip and the Chobe River. Game viewing is by vehicle and boat.

Chobe Chilwero's luxurious accommodations

CLASS A: • **Ntwala Island Lodge** offers 4 ultra luxurious suites with en suite facilities, private plunge pools fringed by white sand and viewing deck, outdoor bath as well as private sala. Access is by boat transfer from the Kasane area. Game viewing is by private boat.

CLASS A/B: • **Muchenje Safari Lodge** is situated on an escarpment edge, located outside the western boundary of Chobe National Park on the Chobe River. The camp consists of 10 thatched chalets (20 guests) with en suite facilities, lounge/dining room, viewing deck overlooking the Chobe floodplain and swimming pool. Activities include morning and night game drives, boat trips, bush walks and cultural visits to a nearby village. This area is not crowded, making it all the more attractive. • **Chobe Savanna Lodge,** located on the Namibian banks of the Chobe River and overlooking the national park, has 12 stone-and-thatch cottages with private decks, air-conditioning, mini bars, en suite bathrooms and swimming pool. Activities include early morning or evening game drives, sunset cruises, fishing and guided nature walks. • **Chobe Game Lodge** is a beautifully decorated, Moorish-style lodge, with 96 beds, set on the banks of the Chobe River within the park. The lodge has a large swimming pool and beautifully kept, spacious grounds. All rooms are air-conditioned and have en suite facilities, and the 4 luxury suites have private swimming pools. Sundowner cruises and day game drives are offered. • **The Nguni Voyager** is a luxurious **houseboat** with 5 comfortable cabins, lounge, bar, jacuzzi and viewing decks. Each room has its own private tender boat and guide to enable exclusive water-based activities (no land based activities are offered). The houseboat moors in secluded spots along the river at night giving guests a new location and change of scenery daily. • **Cresta Mowana Lodge** is located 5 miles (8 km) east of the park. All 111 rooms have en suite facilities. Game drives by vehicle and by boat are offered.

CLASS B: • **Impalila Island Lodge,** situated on an island across from Chobe National Park in Namibia, has 8 elevated chalets with en suite facilities and swimming pool. Access is by boat transfer from the Kasane area. Activities offered are mostly water based, including mokoro trips, boat game drives and fishing. • **Chobe Safari Lodge** has recently undergone extensive renovation and rooms consist of a large living room, private facilities, and guests enjoy a swimming pool and boats for hire.

CLASS C: • **Kubu Lodge** has wood-and-thatch chalets with en suite facilities, a swimming pool and spacious lawns. It is a 10-minute drive from the Chobe National Park gate.

CAMPING: The public campsites in Northern Chobe, Savute and Nogatsaa have toilets and showers, while the campsite at Tjinga has only a water tank. Ihaha, the new site for the public campsites in Northern Chobe (moved from Serondela), is often very crowded. The camps are accessible by 2wd vehicles and are close to Kasane. Beware of wild animals, including baboons, which may raid tents for food.

Kasane

Kasane is a small town only a few miles northeast of Chobe National Park about a two-hour drive from Victoria Falls (Zimbabwe and Zambia). Many tourists are driven here from Victoria Falls and, after clearing customs at the border, begin their Botswana safari.

ACCOMMODATION — See "Chobe National Park" above.

CAMPING: Sites are available at Chobe Safari Lodge and Kubu Lodge.

Nxai Pan National Park

Nxai Pan National Park, well known for its huge springbok population, covers over 810-square-miles (2,100-km²) and is located north of the Maun-Nata road in Northern Botswana.

The Nxai Pan is a fossil lake bed about 15-square-miles (40-km²) in size; it is covered with grass during the rains. The landscape is dotted with baobab and acacia trees. Kgama-Kgama Pan is second to Nxai Pan in size.

In addition to southern giraffe, wildlife includes gemsbok, eland, greater kudu, blue wildebeest, red hartebeest, springbok, steenbok, brown and spotted hyena, cheetah and other predators. During the rains, elephant and buffalo may also be seen. After the first rains have fallen (December through April), game viewing can be good. Bird life is excellent during the rains.

Gemsbok are often found in Nxai Pan National Park

Baines' Baobabs, situated in the park not far from the Maun-Nata road, were immortalized by the famous painter Thomas Baines in 1862. His painting, titled "The Sleeping Five," is of five baobabs, one of which is growing on its side. Seldom are baobab trees found growing so closely together. Baines' Baobabs were later painted by Prince Charles.

This park is seldom visited by international travelers because there are no permanent, fully catered camps. A 4wd vehicle is necessary.

ACCOMMODATION: None as of this writing. However, a permanent tented camp is expected to be built here in the near future.

CAMPING: There are two campsites, one of which has an ablution block. Water is usually available at both sites.

Makgadikgadi Pans National Park

Makgadikgadi Pans National Park includes a portion of the 4,600-square-mile (12,000-km²) Makgadikgadi Pans, which is the size of Portugal. The pans are nearly devoid of human habitation and give one a feeling of true isolation.

Once one of the world's largest prehistoric lakes, the Makgadikgadi Pans are now barren salt plains fringed with grasslands and isolated "land islands" of vegetation, baobab and palm trees. Scattered Stone Age tools have been found. Engravings left by explorers David Livingstone and Frederick Selous in the trunks of ancient baobab trees mark their passage through the region so many years ago.

The reserve itself covers about 1,550-square-miles (3,900-km²). It is located south of the Maun-Nata road in northern Botswana and borders Nxai Pan National Park to the north. Large herds of blue wildebeest, zebra, springbok, gemsbok and thousands of flamingos may be seen December to May. Other wildlife includes hyena, suricate and meerkat. A 4wd vehicle is highly recommended.

Top: A bushman of the Kalahari
Bottom: Celebrities of the Kalahari – the meerkats

Quad bike excursions are offered during the dry season (usually May to November) and are a fun way to experience the vastness of these pans. One evening we drove several miles (kilometers) from camp, turned off the engines and experienced the most "deafening" silence and brightest stars imaginable.

A highlight of my last visit was spending time with a troop of habituated meerkats — voted by the British as the cutest animal species in the world. Guided by one of the researchers, you sit closely to them, and walk with them as they hunt for food. Don't be surprised if one climbs on you to get a better view!

A highlight of my first visit many years ago was that I was able to see my first brown hyena. A den has been located near Jack's and San Camp, and the hyena have become habituated to human presence. This has to be one of the best places to see them in all of Africa!

ACCOMMODATION — CLASS A:
• **Jack's Camp** is a classic camp (20 beds) in the '40s safari style. The tents have beautiful en suite bathrooms with indoor/outdoor showers, flush toilets and hot and cold running water. A brand new pool has been built under a tent, guaranteeing a cool respite from the hot sun. Activities include day and night game drives, riding quad motorbikes on the pans (in the dry season), game walks with bushmen trackers, visiting habituated troops of meerkats and lectures by resident researchers.

CLASS A/B: • **San Camp,** a 12-bed tented camp with en suite facilities, is set right on the edge of the pans and offers the same activities as Jack's Camp. The camp was completely

Jack's Camp offers guests classic style

rebuilt in 2008 and each tent offers hot and cold running water, flush toilets and swing beds on the verandahs. The guides at both camps have university degrees in zoology, biology, anthropology or similar subjects. Adventurous 2-night/3-day Kubu Island quad-bike trips are also offered. • **Leroo La Tau** overlooks the western border of Makgadikgadi National Park and consists of 7 Meru-style tents on raised decks with en suite facilities. The camp overlooks a waterhole, and the main activity is watching the wildlife dramas that unfold right in front of the lodge. Activities include guided walks, limited morning and night game drives and cultural excursions to the nearby village.

ACCOMMODATION NEAR THE RESERVE: CLASS B & C — • **Planet Baobab** offers either traditional painted mud huts with en suite facilities or grass huts and campsites with shared facilities plus a pool for guests to enjoy. Cultural safaris and overnight fly camps to view fossil plates are offered. The Kalahari Surf Club offers a Pan experience — guests camp on the edge of the saltpans and take quad bike trips across the pans and escorted walks.

CAMPING: There are two camping areas with limited facilities. Travelers must be totally self-sufficient.

Nata Bird Sanctuary

The recently established Nata Bird Sanctuary is set on the eastern fringe of the Makgadikgadi Pans and provides a chance to view the aggregations of lesser and greater flamingos, white pelican, avocet, African spoonbill and other birds, which arrive here seasonally. Information on how to access the sanctuary and what birds might be present can be obtained at Nata Lodge. Thousands of flamingos may breed at Makgadikgadi but this is a highly unpredictable event and viewing is limited, because even the best-intentioned human observers can cause great disturbance, even nest desertion, by these sensitive birds.

ACCOMMODATION: CLASS C: • **Nata Lodge**, located just off the Nata/Francistown Road, has chalets and tents with en suite facilities.

Central Kalahari Game Reserve

This 20,000-square-mile (52,000-km²) reserve, one of the largest in the world, covers a portion of the Kalahari Desert. It is an area of enormity, epic landscapes, wooded dunes and petrified river valleys. Wildlife is not abundant in the dry season, but the area becomes alive after brief rain showers and is at its peak from December through April as herbivores with their newborn young (followed by predators) gravitate into the petrified river systems.

With arguably the best cheetah populations within Botswana, the Central Kalahari Game Reserve is also home to the black-maned lions, good populations of meerkats, brown hyena, lynx, leopard, Cape fox, bat eared fox, black backed jackals, eland, red hartebeest, honey badger, steenbuck, oryx, springbuck and blue wildebeest. Even wild dogs are resident in the Kalahari, albeit at lower concentrations than the Okavango Delta and Linyanti.

Perhaps the best part of this gigantic reserve, from a visitor's perspective, is the **Deception Valley** area where American researchers Mark and Delia Owens were based during their work on the brown hyena. This drainage line is in a hauntingly remote location, populated with mostly nomadic wildlife and thin vegetation.

Travelers are encouraged to stay within the park, as this is where the key experience is. Kalahari Plains, one of the new concessions, is located in the Okwa Valley and is one of the most remote dry river systems in the park. A permanent waterhole and access to the interdunal system, including the pans provide a more annual game experience.

ACCOMMODATION — CLASS A/B: • **Kalahari Plains Camp** is a new tented camp located within the reserve with 10 tents with en suite facilities. Activities include guided walks and game drives on a private game viewing area as well as access to the famous Deception Valley. Optional excursions to visit local bushmen are also offered. • **Deception Valley Lodge,** located outside of the northern periphery of the reserve, has 5 large units with en suite facilities and outside showers. Walks with bushmen guides offer an opportunity to learn about their hunting and survival skills, culture and crafts. Afternoon and night drives are available.

CAMPING: No facilities. Travelers must on an organized mobile camping safari, or be self-sufficient and use 4wd vehicles.

Khutse Game Reserve

The Khutse Game Reserve shares its northern boundary with the Central Kalahari Game Reserve and is the closest reserve to Gaborone. Khutse covers 965-square-miles (2,500-km²) of gently rolling savannah and pans (over 50) and is best known for its bird life.

Lion, leopard, cheetah and antelope have adapted to the arid environment. However, wildlife is seasonal and numbers depend on the rains. If there has been little rain, game is usually scarce. The best time to visit is after the rainy season has begun, usually December through April.

Khutse is a 5-hour drive (136 miles/220 km) from Gaborone via Molepolole. The route is not well marked. Four-wheel-drive vehicles are essential.

ACCOMMODATION: None.

CAMPING: There is one public campsite with toilets. Water is available at the gate.

THE SOUTH

Gaborone

Gaborone, phonetically pronounced "Hab oh roni," is the capital of Botswana. In the center of town is the main shopping and commercial center — the Mall. Other than some shopping, there is little of interest for the international traveler, with the exception of the **National Museum**.

ACCOMMODATION — FIRST CLASS: • **Grand Palm Hotel** has 152 air-conditioned rooms, 3 restaurants, outdoor heated pool, fitness center, lighted tennis courts and business center. • **The Gaborone Sun** is located 1.5 miles (2 km) from the city center. This 203-room, air-conditioned hotel has a swimming pool, tennis and squash courts and casino. • **The President Hotel** is an air-conditioned hotel centrally located in the Mall.

Top: This region of Botswana hosts large herds of elephant
Middle: A spectacular view of the Mashatu Game Reserve
Bottom: A thrill offered to guests at Mashatu is game viewing on mountain bikes

Northern Tuli Game Reserve

In the remote southeastern corner of Botswana, at the confluence of the Limpopo and Shashe Rivers, and at the junction of the borders of Botswana, South Africa and Zimbabwe, lies an area of approximately 180,000-acres (72,000-hectares). It is known historically as the Tuli enclave — a diverse wilderness of open grassland, mopane veld, riverine forest, semi-arid bush savannah, marshland, and sandstone outcrops.

A unique feature of this region is the history, both natural and culturally that dates back 80 million years. Dinosaur footprints and fossilized dinosaur skeletons compliment the cultural history of Mapungubwe and Mmamagwa, two African kingdoms that predate Great Zimbabwe and Tulamela. The formation of the Limpopo-Shashe Transfrontier Conservation area involving Botswana, South Africa and Zimbabwe with a focus on wildlife and cultural history is nearing completion and is set to be a tourism drawing card for those visitors seeking a more adventurous safari.

Because the properties within the reserve are privately owned, they are generally less restricted than the private concession areas, reserves and national parks in Botswana, and may conduct activities such as off-road driving, walking with armed rangers, night game drives, horseback riding and mountain biking. This is a great reserve for the active traveler!

Leopard are often seen in the Tuli Game Reserve

The Tuli is home to large herds of elephant, as well as lion, cheetah, eland, impala, wildebeest, giraffe and zebra. Bat-eared fox, African wild cat, hyena, jackal and leopard may be seen searching for prey. Wild dog have been reintroduced to the area and are expected to thrive in this wildlife rich region of Botswana. The introduction of black rhino is also expected to take place soon.

This reserve has to be one of the best kept secrets in Africa for game viewing — a real "sleeper". During my last visit with my family we saw 6 leopard (5 of which we saw during the full light of day), cheetah, lion, large herds of elephant, porcupine, and lots of other game in just 2 days. In addition to game drives we went game viewing by mountain bike, escorted by an armed guide with a rifle strapped over his shoulder.

The region is a 5.5-hour drive from Johannesburg and a 6-hour drive from Gaborone. Alternatively, a scheduled flight and air or road transfer can be arranged into the Limpopo Valley Airfield, which is situated within the Nothern Tuli Game Reserve. You may also fly by scheduled air charter from Johannesburg.

Mashatu Main Camp

ACCOMMODATION — CLASS A:
• **Nitani,** located in the northwest of the reserve on the banks of the Majale River, is family-owned and has 5 thatched en suite chalets built on platforms with private swimming pools. In addition to the traditional safari, the camp offers a full spa facility and specializes in star gazing with a state-of-the-art telescope and knowledgeable guides in attendance. Hot air ballooning is available from the camp.
• **Mashatu Main Camp,** located on the Mashatu Game Reserve, was completely renovated in 2003 and accommodates a maximum of 28 guests in 14 air-conditioned suites featuring en suite "his" and "her" bathrooms. The property has a floodlit waterhole and a swimming pool. Game viewing, for which the camp is renowned, is conducted in open 4wd vehicles, on mountain bikes, on foot and on horseback. Fly camping is also offered. Mashatu Game Reserve, the largest and most diverse of the properties in the reserve with 70,000 acres (28,000 hectares) of privately owned land, is managed and owned by the same company that owns MalaMala Game Reserve in South Africa.

CLASS A/B: • **Tuli Safari Lodge,** situated on the banks of the Limpopo River, has 10 thatched chalets with en suite facilities and swimming pool. • **Mashatu Tented Camp,** set in a remote northern area of the Mashatu Game Reserve, accommodates up to 16 guests in eight fan-cooled tents, with en suite facilities and plunge pool. Guests explore the reserve in 4wd vehicles, on foot, with mountain bikes and on horseback.

Mashatu Tented Camp's lounge

CLASS C: • **Tuli Wilderness Trails,** located on a 24,710-acre (10,000-hectare) concession within the reserve, offers professionally guided walking wilderness trails and accommodates guests in 3 distinct bush camps with self- or full-catering accommodations.

Mabuasehube Game Reserve

Mabuasehube is an extremely remote reserve in southwestern Botswana. Mabuasehube is about 695-square-miles (1,800-km²) in size and shares its western border with Kgalagadi Transfrontier Park. The park has 6 large pans and sand dunes over 100 feet (30 m) high.

The best time to visit is during and just after the rainy season begins (December to April), when a variety of arid-adapted animals can be seen. Springbok are present in good numbers, while gemsbok, eland and red hartebeest are sparse, but are likely to be seen. This is an excellent locality for the elusive brown hyena, and impressive Kalahari lions are invariably present. Other interesting mammals seen here are the Cape fox, honey badger, aardwolf and aardvark. Among the many interesting birds here are the secretary bird, kori bustard, black-breasted snake eagle, crimson-breasted shrike and the swallow-tailed bee-eater. The huge communal nests of the sociable weaver are a feature of this pristine landscape. At sunset the sandveld comes alive to the clicking sound of barking geckos, calling from their burrow entrances.

Mabuasehube is 333 miles (533 km) from Gaborone. A 4wd vehicle is needed, and the drive takes at least 11 hours.

ACCOMMODATION: None.

CAMPING: No facilities. Water may be available at the Game Scouts Camp.

Kgalagadi Transfronteir Park

See "Kgalagadi Transfrontier Park" in the chapter on South Africa for details.

Zimbabwe

Zimbabwe

Zimbabwe is a scenic land consisting of a central plateau which drops down to the Zambezi and Limpopo River valleys in the north and south respectively. The average altitude is about 3,300 feet (1,000 m) on the plateau, rising to 8,000 feet (2,440 m) in the Eastern Highlands. The plateau is dominated by *brachystegia* (miombo) woodland, with acacia and mopane savanna in the larger valleys. A mosaic of grassland and forest occurs in the Eastern Highlands. With an area of 150,872-square-miles (390,759-km²), Zimbabwe is about the size of California (or Great Britain). The population is estimated at 11.5 million, with the capital of Harare having some 2 million inhabitants. Shona, Ndebele and English are the main languages. Currency is the Zimbabwean dollar.

Zimbabwe
Country Highlights

- You would be missing out on one of the greatest African adventures if you did not take a walking safari while in Zimbabwe. The guides are ranked as the best on the continent.
- This destination is my top pick for excitement as you have the opportunity to really be "in the adventure" by walking or canoeing up to big game.
- Experience some of the best game viewing by vehicle on the continent with opportunities to see difficult-to-find wild dog in Mana Pools, black rhino in Matusadona and huge herds of elephants in Hwange.
- Canoeing in Mana Pools is another of my favorite adventures that I recommend! Your canoe drifts silently past giant bull elephants, herds of buffalo, even a lion coming down to the Zambezi River. Hippos and crocs provide natural obstacles. A delightful dinner and mobile camp wait at the end of a great day.
- During the down time between game drives and walks in Hwange, visitors have the opportunity to sit in one of the numerous hides to see the animals from a totally different perspective.
- A visit to Victoria Falls, not only to see the falls but to take an elephant back safari or try a day of white water rafting down the Zambezi River — Class 5 rapids. A wild ride!

Best Parks and Reserves to Visit   **Best Times to Go**

Best Parks and Reserves to Visit	Best Times to Go
Hwange	Year round (best during June to October)
Matusadona	May to October
Mana Pools	July to October but also good May and June

Best Accommodations

Pamushana, Makalolo and Little Makalolo, Vundu Camp, Victoria Falls Hotel, Victoria Falls Safari Lodge, The Stanley and Livingstone, Matetsi Safari Lodge and Matetsi Water Lodge

ZIMBABWE

Thought by some to be the land of King Solomon's mines, Zimbabwe (previously called Rhodesia) is a country blessed with beautiful and varied landscapes, and excellent game parks. This is the best country in Africa for walking safaris and canoe safaris.

Most of Zimbabwe consists of a central plateau, 3,000 to 4,000 feet (915 to 1,220 m) above sea level. The highveld, or high plateau, stretches from southwest to northeast from 4,000 to 5,000 feet (1,220 to 1,525 m) with a mountainous region along the eastern border from 6,000 to 8,000 feet (1,830 to 2,440 m) in altitude.

The northern border is formed by the mighty Zambezi River, while the Limpopo River creates the division between Zimbabwe and South Africa in the south. The spectacular Victoria Falls were created by a fracture in the Zambezi Valley, which is an extension of the Great Rift Valley.

Zimbabwe is a land-locked country, but it is rich in biological diversity due to its proximity to the temperate south, tropical north and semi-arid west. Much of the country is a highland plateau at about 3,300 feet (1,000 m) above sea level on one of the world's oldest granite formations. In the north and south, the Zambezi and Limpopo River valleys, respectively, create hot lowlands as well as international boundaries. The granite shield forms the main watershed of the country, with numerous spectacular rock formations. This plateau is dominated by miombo woodland, but is also ideal farming country, so much of the natural vegetation has been replaced.

The so-called Eastern Highlands are a chain of sandstone and basalt mountains, characterized by a cooler, wetter climate. The highest peaks rise above 6,500 feet (2,000 m). Temperate forests occur in patches from Nyanga to Chimanimani, and sub-tropical forests are found in the humid lowlands of the Honde, Burma and Rusitu valleys, which enter Mozambique. In the western part of the country, on the border with Botswana, deep Kalahari sands dominate in places and create yet another unique environment for wildlife.

The climate is moderate on the central plateau, but hot in the low-lying Zambezi and Limpopo valleys. Seasons are reversed from the northern hemisphere. Winter days (May to August) are generally dry and sunny with day temperatures averaging 59–68°F (15–20°C). Summer daytime temperatures average 77–86°F (25–30°C), and October is the hottest month. The rainy season is December through March.

The major ethnic groups are the Mashona and Ndebele. About fifty percent of the population is syncretic (part Christian and part traditional beliefs), twenty-five percent Christian, twenty-four percent traditional and one percent Hindu and Muslim. Twenty-five percent of the population lives in urban areas, with half of that twenty-five percent residing in the cities of Harare and nearby Chitungwiza. English is understood by a majority of the population.

In the first century, the region was inhabited by hunters related to the San Bushmen. Cecil Rhodes and the British South Africa Company took control

Canoeing on the Zambezi River offers new thrills to the safarier

in 1890, and the area was named Southern Rhodesia, which became a British colony in 1923. Prime Minister Ian Smith and the white minority declared unilateral independence from Britain on November 11, 1965. Zimbabwe officially became independent on April 18, 1980, with Robert Mugabe as president.

Main foreign exchange earners are tobacco, minerals, agriculture and tourism.

Zimbabwe has had more than its share of political and economic woes during the last few years. Tourists that have traveled Victoria Falls, Hwange, Matusadona and Mana Pools have been handsomely rewarded with excellent wildlife viewing and guiding in uncrowded parks.

By visiting the parks, tourists are supporting camps and lodges that in turn provide fuel and transportation for National Park anti-poaching units. These teams protect this great natural resource for the future which has the potential of attracting tens of thousands of tourists once the political climate changes. Park fees paid by tourists go directly to the national parks to help fund them. In addition, tourists are providing jobs for Africans working in the camps, many of whom are supporting an average of over 10 family members living in villages. If there is one wildlife country in Africa where the people and the wildlife populations stand to benefit more from tourism — Zimbabwe is it!

🐾 WILDLIFE AND WILDLIFE AREAS

Adventurers wishing to do more than view wildlife from a vehicle should seriously consider a safari in Zimbabwe. It offers the greatest variety of methods of wildlife viewing in Africa, including day and night game drives in open vehicles, game viewing by motorboat, walking, backpacking, canoeing, kayaking and travel by houseboat.

As mentioned earlier, the country is situated at the junction of three major climatic zones (temperate south, tropical northeast and semi-arid west), and there is a resultant diversity of wildlife. All of Africa's big-game species are here, as well as over 660 bird species and an amazing variety of reptiles, frogs and invertebrates. Plant life is equally impressive, from Afro-alpine proteas in the east to tropical baobabs in the hot valleys of the north and south. The distinctive miombo woodlands (dominated by *Brachystegia* trees) are characterized by a unique variety of plants and associated wildlife.

Zimbabwe offers excellent and well-maintained parks and reserves. The country's three premier reserves, which also rate among the best in Africa, are Hwange, Mana Pools and Matusadona National Parks.

Hwange National Park is famous for its huge elephant population (over 25,000) and numerous large pans. Matusadona National Park, located along the southern shores of beautiful Lake Kariba, has enormous buffalo and elephant populations, and is one of the best parks in Africa to track black rhino on foot. During the dry season, Mana Pools on the Zambezi River has one of the highest concentrations of wildlife of any park on the continent.

Many of the safari camps cater to only 10 to 16 guests and offer personalized service, comfortable accommodations and superb guiding. The professional guiding standards in Zimbabwe are, in fact, the highest of any country on the continent.

Instead of driving to the reserves, virtually all international visitors fly to the parks, taking advantage of scheduled charter flights connecting Victoria Falls, Hwange, Matusadona and Mana Pools. There are also private mobile tented safaris available in Hwange and Mana Pools.

Game viewing is by open vehicle,

Top: Tracking lion in Matusadona with a specialist guide
Bottom: A colorful sunset reflecting on a pod of hippos

and walking is allowed with a licensed Professional Guide who carries a high-caliber rifle at all times. Night game drives are conducted in some areas adjacent to the reserves and on some private concessions within the reserves.

THE WEST

Victoria Falls National Park

Dr. David Livingstone became the first European man to see Victoria Falls on November 16, 1855, and named them after the British queen of his day. In his journal he wrote, "Scenes so lovely must have been gazed upon by angels in flight."

Victoria Falls is approximately 5,600 feet (1,700 m) wide, twice the height of Niagara Falls, and one and one-half times as wide. It is divided into five separate waterfalls: Devil's Cataract, Main Falls, Horseshoe Falls, Rainbow Falls and Eastern Cataract, ranging in height from 200 to 355 feet (61 to 108 m).

Peak floodwaters usually occur around mid-April when 150 million gallons (625 million liters) per minute crash onto the rocks below, spraying water up to 1,650 feet (500 m) in the air. During March and April, so much water is falling that the spray makes it difficult to see the falls. May to February is actually a better time to see them, but keep in mind that they are spectacular any time of the year.

Victoria Falls and the Zambezi River form the border between Zambia and Zimbabwe. The banks of the 1,675-mile- (2,700-km) long Zambezi River, the fourth largest river in Africa and the only major river in Africa to flow into the Indian Ocean, are lined with thick riverine forest.

A rainbow over the falls can often be seen during the day and a lunar rainbow within a two- to four-night period over a full moon.

Top: Victoria Falls's double rainbow
Bottom: Known as "The Smoke that Thunders" (Mosi-oa-Tunya)

Fortunately, the area around the falls has not been commercialized on the Zimbabwe side, and there are unobstructed views from many vantage points, which are connected by paved paths. An entry fee (currently US$ 20.00) is required. Be prepared to get wet as you walk through a luxuriant rain forest surrounding the falls, a result of the continuous spray. A path called the Chain Walk descends from near Livingstone's statue into the gorge of the Devil's Cataract, which provides an excellent vantage point.

Victoria Falls can also be viewed from Zambia. Zambian visas for day visits are generally available at the border for most nationalities (the border crossing can take up to a few hours so please allow plenty of time). Generally speaking, the falls are more impressive on the Zimbabwean side — especially July to December.

Mammals that can be seen in close proximity to the falls include

Victoria Falls

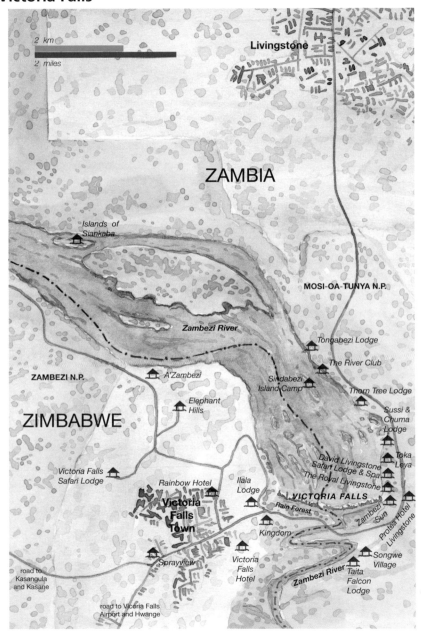

Livingstone

2 km

2 miles

ZAMBIA

Islands of
Siankaba

MOSI-OA-TUNYA N.P.

Zambezi River

Tongabezi Lodge

The River Club

ZAMBEZI N.P.

A'Zambezi

Sindabezi
Island Camp

Thorn Tree Lodge

ZIMBABWE

Elephant
Hills

Sussi &
Chuma
Lodge

David Livingstone
Safari Lodge & Spa

Toka
Leya

Victoria Falls
Safari Lodge

Rainbow Hotel

Ilala
Lodge

The Royal Livingstone

Victoria
Falls
Town

VICTORIA FALLS

Rain Forest

Protea Hotel
Livingstone

Kingdom

Sprayview

Victoria
Falls
Hotel

Songwe
Village

road to
Kasangula
and Kasane

Zambezi River

Taita
Falcon
Lodge

road to Victoria Falls
Airport and Hwange

Northwestern Zimbabwe

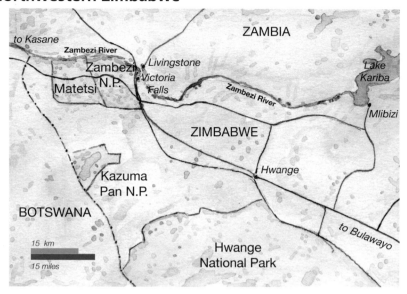

the beautifully marked bushbuck, vervet monkey and banded mongoose. Birds to look out for include the noisy trumpeter hornbill, green pigeon and Schalow's turaco, which feed on figs, and the rock pratincole, reed cormorant and giant kingfisher that may be found in the rapids above the falls. One of Africa's rarest birds of prey, the diminutive Taita falcon, is frequently seen on the cliffs below the falls, alongside peregrine falcon, augur buzzard and Verreaux's (black) eagle.

The **Zambezi Nature Sanctuary** has crocodiles up to 14 feet (4.3 m) in length and weighing close to 1,000 pounds (450 kg). The **Craft Village** in the middle of town has living quarters and other structures representing the traditional Zimbabwean life of the country's major tribes, and it features the best African dance show in town. Tribal dancing may also be seen at the Boma Restaurant near the Victoria Falls Safari Lodge. **Big Tree** is a giant baobab over 50 feet (15 m) in circumference, 65 feet (20 m) high and 1,000 to 1,500 years old.

Sundowner cruises operate above the falls, where hippo may be spotted and elephant and other wildlife may be seen coming to the shore to drink.

The **"Flight of Angels,"** a flight over the falls by helicopter (best choice) or in a small plane, is highly recommended to acquire a feeling for the true majesty of the falls. Game-viewing flights, upstream from the falls along the Zambezi River and over Victoria Falls National Park, are also available. It is best to reserve seats in advance.

One of the world's highest commercially run **bungee jumps** (over 300 feet (100 m) is operated on the bridge crossing the Zambezi River. Even more exciting is the **Gorge Swing** — a 200 foot (70 m) free-fall, ending in a swing across the Zambezi Gorge.

Canoeing and kayaking safaris are a great way to explore the upper Zambezi, from near Kazungula to just above Victoria Falls. Adventurers pass numerous hippo, crocs, elephant and other wildlife as they paddle two-man kayaks or canoes on safaris rang-

Not to be missed — an elephant back safari at Victoria Falls

ing from a half-day to four days in length. No previous kayaking or canoeing experience is necessary. Accommodation is in tents with separate bush shower and toilet facilities.

Half- and full-day **horseback rides** around the Victoria Falls area are available for novice and experienced riders, while multi-day horseback safaris are available only for experienced riders. Morning and afternoon **elephant back safaris** (African elephants) provide another interesting way to experience the bush and to view some game, and they are less expensive than those offered in Botswana.

The upper Zambezi River offers one of the most exciting and challenging **white-water rafting** trips in the world. There are numerous fifth-class rapids, which are the highest class runable, and these can be experienced either with a professional oarsman at the helm or in a raft with everyone paddling. No experience is required; just hang on and enjoy the ride! The 1-day trip is rated as the wildest commercially run 1-day trip in the world. For some travelers, this trip is a highlight of their safari. For the even more adventurous, there is **boogie boarding** on the rapids. This is often done in conjunction with a half or full day of white-water rafting.

Around 8:30 a.m., rafters walk down into the gorge to the river's edge where the rafting safari begins. Rafts with up to 8 paddlers, or up to 8 riders and 1 oarsperson, disappear from sight as they drop into deep holes and crash into waves over 12 feet (3.5 m) high, and they are further dwarfed by sheer cliffs that often rise hundreds of feet on both sides of the canyon.

Each group is usually accompanied by a professional kayaker who helps "rescue" those who have fallen out of the rafts. At the end of the trip, rafters have to climb back out of the gorge to the top of the escarpment, about

Top: Victoria Falls Safari Lodge
overlooks a water hole
Middle: The entrance to Victoria
Falls Safari Lodge
Bottom: The colonial elegance of the
Victoria Falls Hotel

700 feet (213 m) above. For most people, this is the most difficult part of the excursion.

The 1-day trips are operated from approximately mid-May to January, and the overnight, 2.5 and 5 day trips are operated July to January, depending on water levels.

ACCOMMODATION — DELUXE: • **Victoria Falls Safari Lodge**, located a 5-minute drive from the falls, has 72 stylishly decorated air-conditioned rooms and suites with private facilities, and a swimming pool. The lodge is built under thatch and overlooks a floodlit water hole where wildlife may be seen coming to drink. Optional excursions including nature trails, bird and game hides, and game walks with a professional guide are offered. A complimentary hourly shuttle service is available to Victoria Falls town and to the entrance to the falls. • **Victoria Falls Hotel** was refurbished in 2008 and has maintained much of its colonial elegance, including its graceful architecture, spacious terraces and colorful gardens, and it is only a 10-minute walk from Victoria Falls. The hotel has 181 air-conditioned rooms and suites with en suite facilities, swimming pool and tennis courts. From the hotel you can see the bridge and the Zambezi Gorge.

FIRST CLASS: • **Ilala Lodge**, a small, 35-room thatched lodge with en suite facilities and a swimming pool, is located within walking distance to the falls. • **Elephant Hills Hotel** is a large hotel located about 15 minutes out of town. It has a golf course, casino and swimming pool.

TOURIST CLASS: • **The Kingdom Hotel** is only a 10-minute walk from the falls and has 294 air-conditioned rooms with en suite facilities, that are separated in 2 and 3-story units, a casino, food court and swimming pool. This is a good hotel for families.

• **Sprayview Hotel** is a budget hotel with rooms with en suite facilities located a little more than a mile (2 km) from the falls. • **Rainbow Hotel** is located near Victoria Falls village and has 88 air-conditioned rooms with private facilities and a swimming pool. • **The A-Zambezi River Lodge**, one of the largest buildings under traditional thatch on the continent, is located 1.5 miles (2.5 km) from town on the banks of the Zambezi River. The lodge has a swimming pool and 83 air-conditioned rooms with en suite facilities, and provides complimentary scheduled transfers to the town and the falls.

CLASS D, F AND CAMPING: • **Victoria Falls Rest** and **Caravan Park** have self-catering cottages, a small hostel, camping and trailer (caravan) sites, swimming pool and restaurant.

ACCOMMODATION NEAR VICTORIA FALLS — CLASS A: • **The Stanley and Livingstone**, situated on a 6,075-acre (2,430-hectare) private estate a 10-minute drive from the falls, has 16 suites with private facilities. A raised patio overlooks nearby waterholes. • **Matetsi Safari Lodge** and • **Matetsi Water Lodge** are situated on a private game reserve about a 45-minute drive from Victoria Falls. Matetsi Water Lodge has 3 riverside camps, each with 6 air-conditioned en suite bedrooms, fan-cooled living rooms and private splash pools. Matetsi Safari Lodge consists of a tented camp with 12 air-conditioned luxury tents. Day and night game drives, walks, boat cruises, fishing and canoeing are offered. (At the time of this writing the lodge is closed for refurbishment.)

CLASS A/B: • **Imbabala Camp**, located on private land on the banks of the Zambezi River only a mile (2 km) from the Botswana border, has 8 en suite individual chalets (1 family chalet sleeps 4 people) and a swimming pool. The camp has recently been totally upgraded and refurbished. Day and night game drives by vehicle, boat game viewing excursions, birding walks and fishing are offered.

CLASS A/B: • **Gorges Lodge**, located 15 miles (24 km) from Victoria Falls, overlooks the Zambezi Gorge and has 6 single and 4 double-story rooms with en suite facilities and a swimming pool. • **Masuwe Lodge** is a 20-bed tented lodge located 4 miles (7 km) from Victoria Falls on a private game concession that adjoins Zambezi National Park.

CLASS D: See "Zambezi National Park."

Zambezi National Park

Victoria Falls National Park includes Victoria Falls as well as the 216-square-mile (560-km²) Zambezi National Park. The park is located west of the falls and extends for 25 miles (40 km) along the Zambezi River.

Zambezi National Park is well known for its abundance of sable antelope, among other species, such as elephant, zebra, eland, buffalo, giraffe, lion, kudu and waterbuck. Noteworthy birds include collared palm thrush, white-breasted cuckooshrike, racquet-tailed roller, African finfoot, Schalow's turaco, Pel's fishing owl and rock pratincole.

Day game drives, walks, canoeing and kayaking are offered from Victoria Falls. Fishing for tigerfish and tilapia is good. There are 30 sites along the river for picnicking and fishing (beware of crocodiles). Since the game reserve does not have all-weather roads, parts of it are usually closed during the rains from November 1 to May 1.

ACCOMMODATION — CLASS D: • **Zambezi National Park Lodges**, scenically situated on the banks of the Zambezi, consist of 15 self-service lodges, each catering to a maximum of 6 people.

Kazuma Pan National Park

Located north of Hwange National Park in the Matetsi Safari Area, Kazuma Pan National Park is a small park (121-square-miles/313-km²) that has a series of pans that flood in the rainy season. The eastern part of the park is wooded, with more water and a greater variety and concentration of wildlife than the western side of the park, which is predominantly grasslands. Lion and cheetah may be seen.

This is an outstanding park for birdwatchers during the rainy season, when large aggregations of ducks, geese, storks, ibises, herons and egrets forage in the seasonal wetlands.

The park is open to campers who are self-contained. Walking is allowed with a professionally licensed guide. As there are no facilities, visitors generally stay in mobile tented camps with their own private guides.

Hwange National Park

Hwange (previously called Wankie), Zimbabwe's largest national park, is famous for its large herds of elephant and buffalo, and thriving population of both black and white rhino. Other predominant species include buffalo, giraffe, zebra, wildebeest, lion, wild dog and bat-eared fox. This is one of the best parks on the continent to see sable antelope.

Hwange National Park

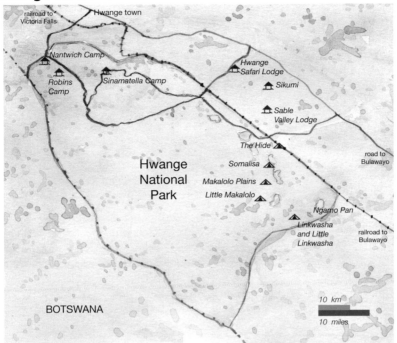

Hwange is slightly larger than the state of Connecticut, covering 5,656-square-miles (14,651-km²). The park is located in the northwest corner of the country, just west of the main road between Bulawayo and Victoria Falls. Hwange boasts over 100 species of mammals and 400 species of birds.

The park ranges from semi-desert in the south to a plateau in the north. The northern part of Hwange is mudstone and basalt, and the southern part is Kalahari sand veld. The park has an average altitude of 3,300 feet (1,000 m). Winter nights can drop to below freezing, and summer days can be over 100°F (38°C), while average temperatures range from 65 to 83°F (18 to 28°C).

There are no rivers and only a few streams in the north of the park, but waterholes (fed by wells) provide sources of water year-round for wildlife. During the dry season, these permanent water holes (pans) provide a spectacular stage for guests to view wildlife performing day-to-day scenes of survival.

Generally, there are no seasonal animal migrations. The best time to see the highest concentrations of wildlife is during the dry season, from June to October, when the game concentrates around the waterholes. Game viewing is very good in May, November and December, and good January through April.

During the "Green Season" from January to March, game in most of the park is widely dispersed in the mopane woodland. However, due to a sustained management program over the last 10 years, game viewing has become increasingly better in the "Green Season", making the Makalolo/Somalisa region of the park a year-round destination.

An estimated population of 28,000 elephants lives in Hwange, although these animals move freely to the north and west into Botswana. Nevertheless, the browsing pressure of these great pachyderms is a threat to the extensive hardwood forests upon which other wildlife is dependent. Birdwatching is excellent, and numerous Kalahari-sand specialists are present in good numbers. Kori bustard, Bradfield's hornbill, crimson-breasted bushshrike, swallow-tailed bee-eater and scaly-feathered finch are all abundant. Hwange is an important refuge for birds of prey, with bateleur, martial eagle and white-headed vulture among the species that enjoy sanctuary here.

The **wilderness area** of Hwange in the southeastern part of the park is absolutely superb for seeing a great variety of game and is much less crowded than the **"Main Camp" area**. Safari camps in this private area include Makalolo, Little Makalolo, Linkwasha, Little Linkwasha and Somalisa. The combination of great game and exclusivity make this the best region in Hwange for an overall wildlife experience.

Top: Game drives are in open vehicles
Bottom: Up close and personal from one of Makalolo's hides

Wildlife commonly seen include elephant (huge herds), rhino, giraffe, zebra, greater kudu, impala, buffalo, sable antelope, wildebeest, tsessebe, black-backed jackal, lion and hyena. On a recent visit in May, we saw sable antelope, lion, giraffe, hyena, buffalo, elephant, wildebeest, zebra and about a dozen bat-eared fox. On another visit we saw a very large, full-maned lion guarding a buffalo kill while a jackal darted in and out, snatching morsels as dozens of vultures waited their turn.

Another time we sat in a tree hide by a water hole and watched over 30 giraffe come to drink. From a ground-level hide, we watched as a herd of

An armed guide leads guests on a new adventure

over 70 eland passed within 65 feet (30 m) and 10 buffalo came within 30 feet (9 m) of us.

The area around Sinamatella Camp in the northern part of the park is good for spotting kudu, elephant, giraffe, impala, hippo, klipspringer, warthog, lion, hyena and leopard. The **Bumbusi Ruins** of ancient stone buildings are located behind Bumbusi Camp, 15 miles (24 km) northwest of Sinamatella Camp.

The **Sinamatella area** of the park differs from the Main Camp area as you are no longer on the Kalahari sands but in a very hilly area with lots of rocky outcrops. The predominant woodland is mopane with scattered open grassland. This area has become quite well known as it is an Intensive Protection Zone (IPZ) for the protection of the endangered black rhino, of which there is now a good population. The elephant population in this area is very large and visitors may see huge herds at the water holes. The region has three main year-round water sources (Masuma Dam, Manduvu Dam and Shumba), each with a thatched picnic area, allowing for some wonderful game sighting. The area also has many perennial springs that attract pockets of game that make this a wonderful walking area, especially in the dry season.

The **Robins area** of Hwange borders Sinamatella and offers similar terrain and has natural hot springs that can be accessed by road. They are all very saline but this doesn't stop the animals from drinking from them. There are more open grasslands supporting a lot more grazers and some large herds of roan and sable antelope. Although not part of the IPZ, there are a few rhinos that are residents of this area. Other wildlife includes a large lion population, impala (which attract the lion), buffalo, greater kudu, sable antelope, roan antelope, waterbuck, elephant, giraffe, reedbuck, tsessebe, side-striped jackal, cheetah and spotted hyena.

Hwange has approximately 300 miles (480 km) of roads, some of which are closed during the rainy season. All-weather roads run through most of the park. Some roads near the main camp are tarmac, which detracts a bit from the feeling of being in the bush.

Vehicles must keep to the roads (except in the private concession areas where limited off-road driving is allowed), and visitors arc not allowed to leave their vehicles unless escorted by a licensed Professional Guide, or in designated areas, such as hides, game-viewing platforms or at fenced-in picnic sites. Open vehicles are allowed only for licensed tour operators.

Airstrips for small aircraft are available at Makalolo, and at Main Camp; large and small aircraft may land at Hwange Airport. The closest rail station is Dete Station, 15 miles (24 km) from Main Camp.

Luxury mobile tented camp safaris to the Sinamatella and Robins areas (the best locations in the park for mobile tented camping) are available.

ACCOMMODATIONS: Makalolo Plains, Little Makalolo, Linkwasha, Little Linkwasha and Somalisa are located in exclusive areas deep within the park. Only guests of those camps are allowed in their respective regions. The Hide is located on a private reserve; guests enter the park through the Kennedy Pan entrance. Sable Valley Lodge, Sikumi Tree Lodge and Hwange Safari Lodge are all located in 60,000-acre (24,000-hectare) Dete Vlei (private reserve) bordering Hwange National Park, a 30 to 60-minute drive from Hwange National Park; guests of these camps enter the park through the Main Gate. CLASS A:

Makalolo Plains lounge

• **Little Makalolo**, totally rebuilt in 2008, has 6 luxury tents with en suite facilities, a plunge pool and "wood pile" hide overlooking the water hole in front of camp. • **Makalolo Plains** has 9 luxury en suite tents, including a family tent, set on raised wooden platforms. Raised walkways connect the sleeping tents with the lounge/dining room area and plunge pool. There is a raised viewing deck and underground hide overlooking the water hole. A recent 24-hour game count at the

waterholes in the Makalolo concession yielded 5,519 elephant and 1,271
buffalo!

Somalisa offers an authentic
bush experience

CLASS A/B: • **Somalisa Camp** is an
authentic bush camp, comprised of 6
tents with en suite bathrooms, flush
toilet and outdoor bush shower. The
main area and pool overlooks the pan
where the game congregate. Activities
include guided walks, day and night
game drives and game viewing from
hides. • **The Hide** has 10 luxury tents
under thatch with en suite facilities,
overlooking a water hole. Activities
include day and night game drives,
walks and bush dinners. Two guests may overnight in the romantic Dove's Nest
tree house. Walking safaris in Hwange National Park are available, using a fully
serviced mobile tented camp set up in an exclusive spot from which the walks
are conducted (minimum 3 nights).

CLASS B/C: • **Sable Valley Lodge** overlooks a water hole and accommodates up
to 30 guests in luxury thatched lodges with en suite facilities. Day game drives
and walks are offered. • **Sikumi Tree Lodge** has 13 thatched tree houses (maximum of 30 guests) set in acacia trees, all with private facilities, and a swimming pool. Activities include day game drives and walks. Children are welcome. • **Linkwasha Camp** consists of 7 tents with en suite bathrooms. • **Little
Linkwasha** consists of 3 tents with en suite bathrooms. Activities at these two
camps include day and night game drives (with up to 10 guests in a vehicle where
most other camps take a maximum of 7). • **Hwange Safari Lodge** has 100 double rooms with en suite facilities and a swimming pool, conference center and
elevated game-viewing platform with a bar overlooking a waterhole.

CLASS D, F & CAMPING: There are 7 National Park camps — **Main Camp,
Sinamatella Camp**, **Robins Camp**, **Bumbusi Camp**, **Lukosi Camp**, **Deka
Camp** and **Nantwich Camp** — all of which have basic lodge accommodation.
Some rooms have en suite facilities. Ablution blocks are available for campers
and for people in rooms without en suite facilities.

Matobo (Matopos) National Park

Hundreds of kopjes supporting thousands of precariously balanced rocks
give the 164-square-mile (424-km²) Matobo National Park one of the most

Top: Matobo Hills offers breath
taking views
Bottom: The giant boulders of
Matobo Hills

unusual landscapes in Africa. A jewel of a park, it is a well-kept secret and is a highlight for many that venture there. The park is divided into two sections — a general recreational area, with popular pony trails, and a game reserve.

Matobo National Park has the highest concentration of eagles in the world, with 58 pairs of black eagles, 45 pairs of African hawk eagles, 32 pairs of Wahlberg's eagles and 5 pairs of crowned eagles known to exist within the reserve.

Part of the park is an IPZ (Intensive Protection Zone) and contains one of the highest concentrations of black and white rhino in Africa. Leopard are plentiful but are seldom seen. Other wildlife includes a large population of sable antelope along with giraffe, zebra, civet, genet, black-backed and side-striped jackal, caracal and porcupine. Other birdlife includes purple-crested lourie, boulder chat, and both peregrine and lanner falcon.

In addition to viewing game, on our most recent visit we visited rock painting sites, a rural clinic, a primary school and an authentic African healer in her village. This is definitely one of the best areas to visit for a quality cultural experience.

The region has over 3,000 San Bushman rock paintings — more than any other place in Africa. **Nswatugi Cave** rock paintings include images of giraffe and antelope. For **Bambata Cave** rock paintings, allow 1.5 hours for the hike. **White Rhino Shelter** rock paintings are also worth a visit.

Cecil Rhodes was buried on a huge rock kopje called "**View of the World**," from which there are sensational panoramas of the rugged countryside, especially at sunrise. A colony of dazzling platysaurus flat lizards may be seen at Rhode's gravesite; the colorful reptiles provide great photographic opportunities.

ACCOMMODATION — CLASS A/B:
• **Amalinda Camp**, attractively built into enormous kopjes, has 9 chalets with en suite facilities, and a magnificent natural rock pool. Activities include game drives, walks, horseback riding on a nearby property, day visits to nearby villages and Bushman paintings in the park. The camp is located about a 10-minute drive from the park.

The Rhodes Suite at Amalinda Camp

CLASS B: • **Matobo Hills Lodge**, located in a beautiful "amphitheater" of rock kopjes about a 10-minute drive from the park, has 17 thatched chalets (doubles) and a swimming pool creatively built into the rocks. Game drives, walks and visits to Bushman paintings and local villages are offered.

CLASSES D & F: • National Park bungalows with and without en suite facilities are available.

CAMPING: Camping and caravan sites with ablution blocks are available at Maleme Dam and Toghwana Dam.

Bulawayo

Bulawayo is the second largest city in Zimbabwe and holds the **National Museum** and **Railway Museum** — both well worth a visit. Some visitors to Matobo National Park fly in to Bulawayo Airport.

ACCOMMODATION — TOURIST CLASS: • **Churchill Arms Hotel** is a modern Tudor-style hotel with 50 rooms with en suite facilities, located 4 miles (6 km) from the city center. • **Holiday Inn Bulawayo** is located in the center of town and has 150 air-conditioned rooms with en suite facilities. • **Nesbitt Castle**, built in 1906 by a Scottish architect, has 9 exclusive suites with en suite bathrooms and is located only a few miles/kilometers from the city.

THE NORTH

Kariba (Town)

Kariba is a gateway to both Matusadona and Mana Pools National Parks. Some people fly there from Harare, Victoria Falls, Hwange or Lusaka (Zambia) and are then transferred by aircraft, boat or vehicle to their respective camps. Most international travelers coming from within Zimbabwe, however, bypass Kariba and charter directly into Matusadona and Mana Pools. Kariba is a good place to meet Zimbabweans on vacation.

Kariba Dam, one of the largest in Africa, is a short distance from town. Water sports (beware of crocodile and hippo) and cruises on the lake are available.

ACCOMMODATION — TOURIST CLASS: • **Caribbea Bay Resort**, located on the shores of Lake Kariba, is a Sardinian-style resort with 83 rooms (some air-conditioned) with en suite facilities, 2 swimming pools, a popular poolside bar and a casino.

CAMPING: • M.O.T.H. Campsite.

Lake Kariba

Sunsets over the waters of island-dotted Lake Kariba are rated among the most spectacular in the world. One of the largest man-made lakes on earth, covering over 1,970-square-miles (5,100-km²), Kariba was formed in 1958 by damming the Zambezi River. The lake is 175 miles (280 km) long and up to 20 miles (32 km) in width and is surrounded, for the most part, by untouched wilderness.

When the dam was completed and the waters in the valley began to rise, animals were forced to higher ground, which temporarily became islands that were soon to be submerged under the new lake. To save these helpless animals, Operation Noah was organized by Rupert Fothergill. Over 5,000 animals, including 35 different mammal species, numerous elephant and 44 black rhino, were rescued and released in what are now Matusadona National Park and the Chete Safari Area.

The unique background of submerged trees in Lake Kariba

Lights from commercial kapenta fishing boats are often seen on the lake at night. Fishing is excellent for tigerfish, giant vundu, bream, chessa and nkupi. October is the optimum month for tigerfishing (although very hot), and November to April for bream. Bird life, especially waterfowl, is prolific and superb viewing of African fish eagles is guaranteed. Cormorants and kingfishers are in abundance.

The Lake Kariba Ferry usually takes 22 hours to cruise from Mlibizi (a few hours drive from Victoria Falls) to Kariba Town. If you are thinking of taking a vehicle through Zimbabwe from Victoria Falls to Kariba, this ferry will save you over 775 miles (1,250 km) of driving.

Matusadona National Park

Situated on the southern shore of Lake Kariba and bounded on the east by the dramatic Sanyati Gorge and the west by the Umi River, this scenic 543-square-mile (1,407-km^2) park has an abundance of elephant, lion, kudu, impala and buffalo — especially along the shoreline in the dry season (May to October). Other game includes sable antelope, roan antelope and waterbuck. Cheetah have been introduced into the area. This is one of the best parks in Africa to track black rhino on foot — a real adventure indeed! Part of Matusadona is, in fact, an IPZ for rhino. Leopard are occasionally spotted.

On my last visit, within 30 minutes of my first game drive, we spotted two sets of two black rhino from the vehicle — outstanding! Enroute to camp we stopped to see lion on a buffalo kill. On an afternoon game drive during another visit, we spotted elephant, impala, buffalo and a large male lion, and had an interesting excursion out tracking black rhino. During an afternoon

Matusadona National Park

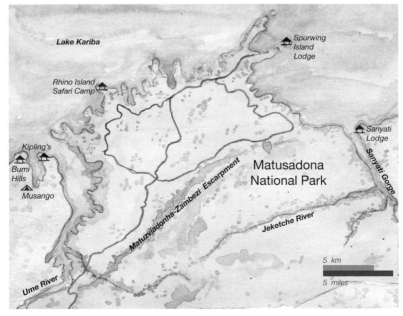

Top: A young wild black rhino looking for a scratch at Rhino Island Safari Camp
Middle: Lake Kariba is the backdrop for elephants and black rhinos
Bottom: A chalet at Rhino Island Safari Camp, Matusadona

boat ride we spent more than half an hour watching two bull elephants frolicking in the water — locking tusks and at times completely submerging, then popping up with water hyacinth on their heads.

Game viewing by boat is a real attraction, and walking safaris are popular. Fishing is excellent, but beware of crocodiles. Private mobile tented safaris with Professional Guides are another great way to experience the bush. Motor yachts complete with captain, staff and Professional Guide provide private parties with great freedom and comfort in exploring the region. Multi-day hiking and backpacking trips provide other options for adventure.

ACCOMMODATION — CLASS A/B:
• **Sanyati Lodge**, situated on the Sanyati Gorge, just outside the western border of the park, has 11 air-conditioned en suite luxury lodges, including a honeymoon suite and presidential suite, and a gym and plunge pool. Boat and vehicle game drives and fishing are offered. Escorted walks can be arranged.

ACCOMMODATION — CLASS B:
• **Rhino Island Safari Camp**, situated near Elephant Point, has 6 chalets with en suite bathrooms, and are set on wooden platforms with thatched roofs. Activities include game viewing drives, walks, and boat cruises on the lake along the Matusadona shoreline.
• **Musango** has 8 en suite tents including 2 honeymoon tents with private plunge pools and a swimming pool.

Walks, vehicle and boat game drives, canoeing, visits to dinosaur fossil sights, villages and the rhino orphanage are offered. • **Kiplings Lodge**, located at the mouth of the Ume River on the lake, has 10 rooms with en suite facilities and a plunge pool. Day game drives, walks, canoeing, boat game drives and fishing are offered. • **Bumi Hills Lodge**, located on the western outskirts of the park on a hill overlooking the lake, has 20 well-appointed luxury rooms with en suite facilities and a swimming pool. Walks, day and night game viewing by vehicle and by boat, fishing and village visits are offered. (Please note — Kiplings and Bumi Hills open for large groups on request.)

CLASS C: • **Spurwing Island** is a 40-bed camp with tents, cabins and thatched chalets with en suite facilities and a swimming pool. Walks, game drives by vehicle and by boat, and fishing are offered.

CLASS D: The National Park has 2 self-service camps — **Ume** and **Mbalabala**; each camp may be booked by only one party.

CAMPING: The 2 National Park Campsites, **Tashinga** and **Sanyati**, have ablution blocks.

A young black rhino cools off in the mud

Mana Pools National Park

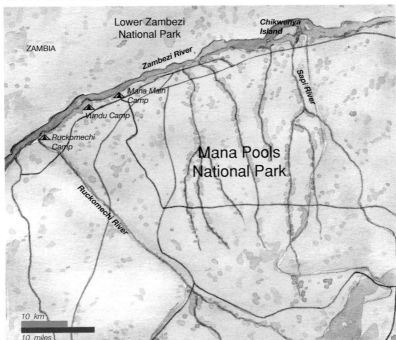

Mana Pools National Park

During the dry season, Mana Pools National Park has one of the highest concentrations of wildlife on the continent. This is in fact the best park in Africa for walking and canoe safaris. The park is situated on the southern side of the Lower Zambezi River downstream (northeast) of Lake Kariba and Victoria Falls.

This 845-square-mile (2,190-km²) park is uniquely characterized by fertile river terraces reaching inland for several miles from the slow-moving Zambezi River. Small ponds and pools, such as Chine Pools and Long Pool, were formed as the river's course slowly drifted northward. Reeds, sandbanks and huge mahogany and acacia trees near the river give way to dense mopane woodland to the park's southern boundary along the steep Zambezi Escarpment.

Mana Pools National Park covers part of the Middle Zambezi Valley, which is home for 12,000 elephant and 16,000 buffalo (with herds of over 500 each).

Mana Pools is one of the best parks on the continent for seeing African wild dog and greater kudu. Species commonly seen in the park include

An elephant stands to reach prized *acacia albida* pods

elephant, leopard, buffalo, waterbuck, zebra, eland, impala, bushbuck, lion and crocodile. Large pods of hippo are often seen lying on the sandbanks, soaking up the morning sun. Occasionally spotted are jackal, spotted hyena and the rare nyala. Large varieties of both woodland and water birds are present.

Walking Safaris

This is by far my favorite park in Africa for walking in the bush. On a recent visit we walked with our Professional Guide into a large herd of buffalo, and were, at one point, surrounded by them. Later in the walk we encountered lion, and an elephant that stood on its hind legs in an attempt to break off a large tree branch. In the afternoon we again tracked lion and approached the pride closely by a technique the Zimbabweans call "bum crawling" — sitting on your backside and using your arms to slowly push you forward. Great fun!

On foot early the next morning we approached a large bull elephant

A frequent sighting in Mana Pools — wild dog

Keeping a watchful eye on a herd of Cape buffalo

and a younger male elephant. The younger elephant gave us a mock charge but was "stopped" by the older bull, which seemed quite comfortable with our presence. A short time later we approached the older bull so closely that I could have leaned out and touched his tusks. This was certainly one of the most exciting experiences I have had in my 30 years of visiting Africa! This kind of adventure is only safe and only possible with a top Professional Guide. Mana Pools is by far the best reserve in Africa for this level of interaction with elephants.

On another visit we encountered a bull elephant that decided to mock charge us not once — but twice! On the first charge, it stopped about 30 feet (9 m) from us, and on the second charge — about 15 feet (4.5 m). Keep in mind that, as long as you do what your guide says, there is little danger — only a big rush of adrenaline!

Shortly after the charge, we reached camp. Later, under a full moon, the same elephant approached our camp, and we walked out to meet it. The elephant trumpeted, then gave us a mock charge in the moonlight!

Events like this are why walking safaris, and safaris in general, are so popular: You never know what is going to happen next!

Walking safaris like this one may sound a bit risky. They are, however, quite safe — as long as the safari is conducted by a fully licensed Professional Guide. Just use common sense and enjoy the adventure. To better understand the excitement of a walking safari, I suggest you obtain the video *As Close As You Dare* (2007) Crowe World Media. Please see page 672 for details.

Canoeing Safaris

For the adventurous traveler, canoeing safaris are one of the best ways to experience the African bush and is one of my favorite safaris on the entire continent. Traveling silently by canoe, you can paddle closely to wildlife that has come to drink along the shore. Most importantly, you actively participate in the adventure!

Canoe safaris are available, lasting from 3 to 9 days and covering different stretches of the river. They are operated from Kariba Dam downstream for up to 159 miles (255 km) past Mana Pools National Park to Kanyemba near the Mozambique border.

The river is divided into four canoeing segments: 1) from below Kariba Dam through the Kariba Gorge to Chirundu, 2) from Chirundu to the border of Mana Pools, 3) along Mana Pools National Park and 4) downstream (east) of the park through the rugged Mupata Gorge to Kanyemba. The section (3) along Mana Pools National Park is the best section for wildlife viewing. In addi-

An adventure unlike any other in Africa — canoeing in Mana Pools

tion, no motorized boats are allowed on the Zimbabwe side of this stretch of the river, making it all the more attractive.

Three different "levels" of canoe safaris are available:

(1) Budget (participation) canoe safaris do not have a support vehicle on land. Camping is often done on islands in the Zambezi where there are no facilities. Participants sleep in sleeping bags in small pup tents or under mosquito nets, and everyone pitches their own tents and helps with the chores. Walking inland is limited to 165 feet (50 m) from the riverbank.

(2) First class (full-service) canoe safaris are led by a Professional Guide licensed to escort you on walks. These safaris have a cook and camp attendants who take care of all the chores, which allows guests to spend all their time exploring the area and enjoying the bush. This option is far superior to the Budget option, because it allows you to canoe and go on vehicular game drives and walks. Guests are accommodated in comfortable tents (large enough to stand) with cots with mattresses, sheets and blankets. Bush shower tents and toilet tents are set up for the group. Bucket shower and bush toilet tents are usually separate from the sleeping tents, or in some cases, bush toilets may be en suite.

(3) Luxury (full-service) canoe safaris have all the benefits of the First Class option with the added attraction of larger sleeping tents that each have en suite bush showers and toilets.

On the second day of a recent canoe safari, we pulled onto the riverbank for lunch. As we started walking up the bank, we were greeted by a young bull elephant coming down for a drink. He trumpeted, kicked dirt and shook his head a number of times before he backed off enough to let us by.

Later, as we were having lunch, another bull elephant paid us a visit, approaching within 15 feet (4.5 m) of us. That's close when the elephant is almost 10 feet (3 m) in height at the shoulder! As we were about to return to the canoes, the bull elephant that had almost kept us from coming ashore earlier apparently decided he wanted a mud bath and completely covered our canoes with mud in the process. Our guide approached him from the riverbank above in an attempt to persuade him to leave, and the elephant responded by using the tip of his trunk to throw a large blob of mud, just missing our guide by inches!

On a previous canoe safari along Mana Pools, as we canoed past two large bull elephant walking along the river's edge, our guide instructed us to pull into shore about 50 yards (50 m) downstream of them. The larger of the elephants continued walking toward us, eating apple ring acacia *(Acacia albida)* pods that had fallen from trees along the river.

Our guide and I crouched silently behind our canoe, with the rest of the group doing the same behind us. The elephant came closer and closer and closer until he was not more than 6 feet (2 m) from us. One step more and he would have stepped into the canoe. What a thrill! Eventually, after having a drink, he turned around and walked back down the shoreline that he came from.

Several times we saw elephant swimming from the mainland to islands in the Zambezi in search of food. We also saw hundreds of hippo, buffalo, waterbuck and impala and countless elephant, crocodile, lion and many other species.

Although these canoe safaris are by no means marathons, participants must paddle their own canoes, which allows them to be more involved in the adventure. Your guide will instruct you on safety precautions. Previous canoe experience is not necessary. However, spending at least a few hours in a canoe before your African safari will allow you to feel more comfortable canoeing in a foreign environment. If you like the idea of canoeing but prefer to do little or no paddling, I suggest you book a private canoe safari and request paddlers.

The best time to visit the park, for one of the finest exhibitions of wild-life on the continent, is at the end of the dry season (July to October) when large numbers of elephant, buffalo, waterbuck and impala come to the river to drink and graze on the lush grasses along its banks. Game viewing is also good in May, June and November. During the rainy season (November to April), many large land mammals move away from the river toward the escarpment. However, game viewing in the area near Ruckomechi Camp is good year-round.

Because many roads within the park are closed during the rainy season, the camps (except for Ruckomechi) are also closed during that period. Charter flights operate into three airstrips in the park. Gasoline (petrol) is not available in the park, and powerboats are not allowed. Four-wheel-drive vehicles are recommended in the dry season and necessary in the rainy season.

ACCOMMODATION—CLASS A/B:
• **Vundu Tented Camp** is located right on the Zambezi River within the park and has 5 double tents and 3 singles with en suite, open-air bathrooms, bar and dining area. From your camp you may take leisurely canoeing safaris, game drives and walks to explore and appreciate the rich floodplains and river channels. • **Ruckomechi Camp**, completely rebuilt in early 2008, lies on the western boundary of the park. The camp has 9 luxury en suite tents and the main area offers a lounge, dining room, library and swimming pool. Game drives, walks, boat game drives, hides and canoeing are offered.

CLASS D & F: National Parks accommodations include **Musangu Lodge** and **Muchichiri Lodge**.

CAMPING: • **Nyamepi Camp** has 29 caravan/camping sites and ablution blocks with hot and cold water. The exclusive camps, which are limited to one group at a time, are **Mucheni Camp**, **Nkupe Camp**, **Ndungu Camp** and **Gwaya** (Old Tree Lodge) **Camp**.

Top: Vundu Tented Camp
Middle: Picnicking in style on the shores of the Zambezi River
Bottom: A newly remodeled tent at Ruckomechi Camp

Chizarira National Park

This remote, undeveloped park is situated on the Zambezi Escarpment overlooking the Zambezi Valley and the southern part of Lake Kariba. Chizarira covers 737-square-miles (1,910-km²) of wild, untouched bush with plateaus, deep gorges, thick woodlands and riverbeds.

Chizarira is a park for the adventurer more interested in experiencing the wilderness than in seeing huge herds of animals. Walking is allowed if accompanied by a Professional Guide, and that is the best way to explore the park.

The best view of Lake Kariba and the Zambezi Valley is from Mucheni View Point, which is also a great spot for birdwatching — especially for birds of prey.

Roads are rough and gas (petrol) not available; a 4wd vehicle is recommended year-round and is necessary in the rainy season. Chizarira National Park is a day's drive from Matusadona National Park. Easiest access is by charter aircraft. Some luxury, first class and budget group camping safaris include Chizarira in their itineraries.

ACCOMMODATION — CLASS B: • **Chizarira Lodge** has 8 thatched chalets (16 beds) with en suite facilities and a swimming pool. Activities include game drives, walks and overnight walking trails.

CLASS F & CAMPING: There are 4 exclusive national park campsites, **Kasiswi Bush Camp**, **Mobola Bush Camp**, **Mucheni Gorge Camp** and **Busi Bush Camp**. Each limited to 1 party (maximum 12 people).

THE EAST

Nyanga National Park

Most of this beautifully forested and mountainous park lies above 6,560 feet (2,000 m), rising to 8,504 feet (2,592 m). Mt. Inyangani is the highest mountain in Zimbabwe. Trout fishing, horseback riding, hiking and golf are just a few of the many sports enjoyed in the refreshing environment. The park covers 127-square-miles (330-km²) and is located near the Mozambique border north of Mutare.

This is the northern limit of the Eastern Highlands and is also the most accessible. The upland grasslands are a refuge for endangered birds, such as the blue swallow and wattled crane, while smaller mammal species, such as the oribi, are not uncommon. Numerous rare and endemic plants are found here, and blue duiker and Samango monkey may be found in the indigenous forests.

On our last visit we had a great time picnicking at World's View, horseback riding through the pine plantations, fishing for trout and playing a round of golf.

ACCOMMODATION — TOURIST CLASS: • **Inn on Ruparara** is a lovely country inn that accommodates a maximum of 36 guests in 17 lodges. Activities on the grounds and in the area include horseback riding, fishing, golf and gambling at a nearby casino. • **Pine Tree Inn** is a small country inn; rooms have facilities en suite. • **Troutbeck Inn**, a comfortable country resort with 70 rooms with en suite facilities, offers horseback riding, trout fishing, lawn bowling, squash, tennis and golf. • **Montclair Hotel** has rooms with en suite facilities, a golf course and casino.

CAMPING: Numerous camping and trailer (caravan) sites are available.

Bvumba Botanical Garden and Reserve

The Bvumba Highlands, situated about 15 miles (25 km) southeast of Mutare, is a cool and often misty area of major interest to naturalists. The beautiful **Bvumba** (formerly Vumba) **Botanical Garden** is a scenic and tranquil locality, not only for botanists but also for the general wildlife enthusiast. Excellent views of Samango monkeys can be enjoyed there, and it is a superb birdwatching locality for species such as silvery-cheeked hornbill and red-throated twinspot. Numerous small streams twist through the garden and there are breathtaking views out across Mozambique.

The nearby **Bunga Forest Reserve** supports populations of the tiny blue duiker and the secretive Swynnerton's robin, among many others. Small footpaths wind among the tall forest trees.

ACCOMMODATION — FIRST CLASS: • **Leopard Rock Hotel** has 58 rooms with en suite facilities, an 18-hole golf course (considered to be one of the most scenic in southern Africa), casino, swimming pool, tennis and squash courts. Horseback riding and fishing are available.

TOURIST CLASS: • **Inn on the Vumba** has 15 bedrooms with en suite facilities. • **White Horse Inn** is a small hotel (14 beds) with rooms that have en suite facilities. • **Eden Lodge** has 12 bedrooms, 2 luxury lodges and 2 family rooms, all with en suite facilities.

CAMPING: Camp and trailer (caravan) sites are available.

Chimanimani National Park

This rugged, mountainous 66-square-mile (171-km^2) park with deep gorges and numerous streams includes most of the Chimanimani Mountain Range, which rises to 7,995 feet (2,437 m). This is an excellent park for hiking and backpacking. Eland, sable antelope and bushbuck may be seen.

This is undoubtedly the most beautiful and undisturbed part of Zimbabwe's Eastern Highlands. The hiking trail winds among huge sandstone boulders, sculpted by wind and rain into bizarre shapes and forms. Crusty lichens in various colors adorn the rocks, and numerous isolated forms of stunted Afro-montane plants (including protea and erica) are present.

Birding is good in the forest areas of the gorges where orange thrush and Chirinda apalis are among the interesting species present. Nectar-feeding sunbirds thrive in the heathlands and forest fringes, where bokmakierie and stone chat may also be seen. A number of pairs of the endangered blue swallow breed in burrows on the upland grasslands.

ACCOMMODATION — CLASS F: A mountain hut is available for refuge.

CAMPING: Camping is allowed in the park.

Harare

Harare is the capital and largest city in Zimbabwe. Points of interest include the **National Art Gallery, Botanical Garden, Houses of Parliament** and the **Tobacco Auction Floors** (the largest in the world). **Mbare Msika Market** is good for shopping for curios from local vendors. Harare is a good place to shop for Shona carvings made of wood and soapstone, silverwork and paintings. A park adjacent to the Intercontinental Hotel features a large variety of brilliant flora. **Harare Botanical Gardens** has indigenous trees and herbs.

Harare's best restaurants include Tiffany's, L'Escargot, Amanzi, The Bagatelle, 22 Victoria Street, La Chandelle, Wombles and La Francais. Imba Matombo Lodge also has a restaurant that is open to the public and serves excellent food.

The **Larvon Bird Gardens** and **Lake Chivero (McIlwane) Game Park** are a short drive west of Harare. Larvon provides the opportunity to see (and photograph) a host of African bird species close-up, and this park has gained many accolades for its educational work and ability to raise endangered species. Lake Chivero is a popular fishing and boating destination, but there is also lion, white rhino, spotted hyena, cheetah, elephant, bushpig, giraffe, zebra and a variety of antelope present. The tall miombo woodland is home to a variety of birds, including miombo rock thrush, spotted creeper and white-breasted cuckooshrike.

West of the capital city are the **Ewanrigg Botanical Gardens**, famous for their collection of aloes, which are at their flowering peak between June and August. A huge variety of other African trees and other plants can be seen here.

ACCOMMODATION — DELUXE: • **Meikles Hotel**, one of the "Leading Hotels of the World," has 317 rooms and suites with en suite facilities, a swimming pool, sauna, gym and traditional Old World atmosphere.

FIRST CLASS: • **Imba Matombo**, located a 15-minute drive from Harare in the suburb of Glen Lorne, accommodates guests in rooms in a large home and chalets (20 beds total) with en suite facilities. The property has a tennis court, swimming pool and excellent restaurant. • **Rainbow Towers** (formerly the Sheraton Hotel) has 325 air-conditioned rooms and suites with en suite facilities, a swimming pool, tennis courts, and a sauna and gym. • **Crowne Plaza Monomatapa Hotel** has 240 air-conditioned rooms with en suite facilities, a swimming pool and convention facilities.

TOURIST CLASS: • **Wild Geese Lodge**, located 20 minutes by road from the city center and 30 minutes from the airport, is a private guesthouse set in beautiful gardens, with 9 chalets with en suite facilities. The lodge is adjacent to a private conservancy, with plains game including blesbok, eland, kudu, tsessebe and zebra. • **Holiday Inn** has 200 air-conditioned rooms with en suite facilities and a swimming pool. • **Best Western Jameson Hotel** has 128 air-conditioned rooms and suites with en suite facilities and a swimming pool.

THE SOUTH

Great Zimbabwe

These impressive stone ruins, a World Heritage Site, located 11 miles (18 km) from Masvingo, look distinctly out of place in sub-Saharan Africa, where almost all traditional structures have been built of mud, cow dung, straw and reeds. The origin of these ruins is rather confusing, but it is now widely believed that they represent an important ceremonial and residential center for former Zimbabwean rulers. Evidence of artifacts from the Far East indicates that the site was part of a trading center that involved the export of ivory and gold. Some historians believe it was an eleventh century Shona settlement. In addition to the astonishing archaeological interest, the area's antelope and birdlife are also attractions to naturalists.

In 1890, Fort Victoria (now Masvingo) became the first settlement of whites in what is now Zimbabwe. The settlers first discovered the Great Zimbabwe Ruins in 1888.

The city was at its prime from the twelfth to fourteenth centuries. The Acropolis or Hill Complex, traditionally the King's residence, is situated high on a granite hill overlooking the Temple (a walled enclosure) and the less-complete restoration of the Valley Complex.

ACCOMMODATION — TOURIST CLASS: • **Lodge of the Ancient City** has been attractively built in the style of the ruins. The lodge's comfortable rooms have en suite facilities and there is a swimming pool. • **Great Zimbabwe Hotel** is a country hotel, located a few minutes walk from the ruins, with a swimming pool and 56 rooms with private facilities. • **The Inn on Great Zimbabwe**, located on a hillside minutes from Great Zimbabwe, has 8 rooms with en suite facilities, 7 self-catering cottages and a campsite.

Mutirikwe (Kyle) Recreational Park

Located 20 miles (32 km) southwest of Masvingo, this 65-square-mile (169-km^2) park is a great place to go horseback riding among white rhino and a variety of other game. Rides on the pony trails are led by a park ranger into a fenced wildlife section of the park.

ACCOMMODATION — TOURIST CLASS: See "Great Zimbabwe".

CLASSES D & F: • National Park lodges, some with private facilities and others without, are available.

CAMPING: Camping and trailer (caravan) sites with ablution blocks are located near the National Park office and at Sikato Bay Camp on the west bank of Lake Mutirikwe.

Gonarezhou National Park

The second largest park in Zimbabwe, Gonarezhou borders the country of Mozambique in southeastern Zimbabwe and covers over 1,950-square-miles (5,053-km²) of bush.

Gonarezhou means "the place of many elephants" and is definitely elephant country. Other species commonly seen are lion, buffalo, zebra, giraffe and a variety of antelope species. Nyala are regularly seen in riverine areas. Rarely seen are roan antelope and Liechtenstein's hartebeest.

The park is divided into two regions, the Chipinda Pools section, which includes the Runde and Save subregions, and the Mabalauta section. Game viewing is best in the Runde subregion.

Perhaps the most beautiful part of the reserve is the Chilojo Cliffs on the broad Runde River. These impressive cliffs are composed of oxide-rich sandstone, which is spectacularly colorful at sunset.

The spectacular view from Pamushana

Much of the park is comprised of Mopane woodland and scrub, some of which has been drastically altered by the browsing activities of elephants. Gonarezhou was once home to some of the most magnificent baobab trees in Africa, but many of these were lost during a crippling drought from 1991 to 1993.

Visited mostly by the more adventurous, this park provides a true wilderness experience. Among the birds to be seen here are giant eagle owl, lappet-faced vulture, woolly-necked stork, Bohm's spinetail, red-billed helmetshrike and golden-breasted bunting.

Gonarezhou has been earmarked for incorporation into the proposed Great Limpopo Transfrontier Conservation Area.

The park is usually only open in the dry season, May 1 to October 31. Winter temperatures are mild; however, summer temperatures can exceed 104°F (40°C).

From Masvingo, drive southwest to Chiredzi, then continue either 36 miles (58 km) to Chipinda Pools or 105 miles (170 km) to Mabalauta Camp. Four-wheel-drive vehicles are highly recommended. The nearest airstrip is Buffalo Range.

ACCOMMODATION — CLASS A+:
• **Pamushana** is a luxury lodge consisting of 4 large double and 2 spacious family air-conditioned villas with en suite facilities, swimming pool and sauna. Activities include day and night game drives, walks, canoeing, bass and bream fishing and visits to San Bushman paintings. Access is by scheduled charter flights from Johannesburg on Mondays or Thursdays or private charter.

One of the luxurious suites at Pamushana

CLASS A/B:• **Nduna Lodge**, set on the 378-square-mile (980-km²) Lone Star Reserve bordering Gonarezhou National Park, has 6 air-conditioned luxury stone-and-thatch chalets (doubles) with en suite facilities and a swimming pool. The lodge is nestled in a rock amphitheater on the edge of a lake. Elephant, buffalo, lion, black rhino, leopard and a variety of antelope may be seen. Activities include day and night game drives, canoeing, walks and viewing San Bushman paintings. Easiest access is by private air charter.

CLASS B: • **Chilo Gorge Safari Lodge**, set on the cliffs of the gorge overlooking the Save River, has 14 thatched lodges (doubles) with en suite facilities.

• **Mahenye Safari Lodge** is situated on the Save River bordering the reserve and consists of 8 thatched lodges (doubles) with en suite facilities.

CAMPING: • **Chipinda Pools Camping and Caravan Site** and **Chinguli** have ablution blocks. Seven remote campsites with basic facilities are also available. • **Mabalauta** has 5 camping/trailer (caravan) sites.

Zambia

Zambia

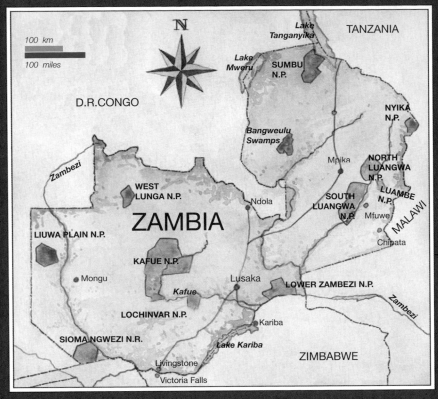

Zambia is one of Africa's least developed countries, with vast areas of wilderness and a comprehensive network of national parks protecting its wildlife. The landscape is an upland plateau ranging in altitude from 3,000 to 5,000 feet above sea level (915 to 1,525 m) with dry savannah and miombo woodland predominating. Zambia's economy is based on copper mining, agriculture and tourism. At 290,586-square-miles (752,614-km^2), Zambia is larger than Texas (or France), but has a population of some 11 million. Lusaka is the capital city with 1.3 million inhabitants. English is the official language, with Bemba, Tonga, Ngoni and Lozi widely spoken. Currency is the Zambian Kwacha.

Zambia
Country Highlights

- There is nothing like a walking safari for the ultimate adrenaline rush and Zambia is a top destination for them! The country combines outstanding guides, beautiful scenery and excellent game viewing.
- Zambia's bush camps are one of the last secret gems in southern Africa. For those who want to experience remote Africa, these are the ultimate destination. Reed chalets or huts in the most remote corners of Zambia offer the personal attention lacking in many larger lodges and camps.
- A microlight over the Zambezi River (South Luangwa National Park), giving you truly a bird's eye view of the animals and crocs in the river.
- Most safaris to Zambia include time in South Luangwa Valley and the Lower Zambezi region but Kafue National Park should not be missed. Two and half times the size of South Luangwa, it has more species of antelope than any park in Africa but almost no tourists!
- End your safari adventure with time in Livingstone in one of the luxury lodges along the Zambezi River. Sip a cold cocktail while listening to the world famous Victoria Falls, the "Smoke that Thunders".

Best Parks and Reserves to Visit   Best Times to Go

South and North Luangwa ....June to October
Lower Zambezi ....June to October
Kafue National Park ....July to October

Best Accommodations
Chiawa Camp, Sausage Tree, Tafika Camp, Shumba Bush Camp, Kapinga Camp, The River Club, Toka Leya, Tongabezi Camp, The Islands of Siankaba

ZAMBIA

A country rich in wildlife, Zambia has gained a well-deserved heightened popularity over the last few years as a top safari destination. Extraordinary game viewing, outstanding guides and a variety of accommodations, Zambia attracts those looking for a remote, authentic safari experience.

Zambia was named after the mighty Zambezi River, which flows through western and southern Zambia. The Zambezi River is fed by its Kafue and Luangwa tributaries, and forms the boundary between Zambia and Zimbabwe before flowing through Mozambique — eventually emptying into the Indian Ocean. The three great lakes of Bangweulu, Mweru and Tanganyika are in northern Zambia, and Lake Kariba is found along the southeastern border adjacent to Zimbabwe.

The country is predominantly a high plateau ranging in altitude from 3,000 to 5,000 feet (915 to 1,525 m), which is why it has a subtropical rather than a tropical climate. April to August is cool and dry, September to October is hot and dry, and November to March is warm and wet. Winter temperatures are as cool as 43°F (6°C) and summer temperatures can exceed 100°F (38°C). The dry season, with clear sunny skies, is May to October.

The Zambian people are predominantly composed of Bantu ethnic groups who practice a combination of traditional and Christian beliefs. English is the official language and is widely spoken, in addition to 73 other languages and dialects. In contrast to most African countries, over 40% of the population lives in urban areas, due mainly to the copper mining industry.

In 1888, emissaries of Cecil Rhodes signed "treaties" with African chiefs ceding mineral rights of what was proclaimed Northern Rhodesia, which came under British influence. In 1953, Northern Rhodesia, Southern

Rhodesia (now Zimbabwe) and Nyasaland (now Malawi) were consolidated into the Federation of Rhodesia and Nyasaland. The Federation was dissolved in 1963. Northern Rhodesia achieved its independence on October 24, 1964, as the Republic of Zambia. Since the elections in 1991, Zambia has a multi-party political system.

Zambia's economy is based primarily on copper mined in the "Copper Belt" near the Congo border. Other major foreign exchange earners are agriculture (exporting fruit, coffee, sugar) and the tourism industry.

🐾 WILDLIFE AND WILDLIFE AREAS

Zambia provides fabulous options for the wildlife adventurer, including both night and day game drives by open vehicle, walking safaris using remote bush camps or mobile tented camps, canoe safaris and white-water rafting.

Zambia boasts 19 gazetted national parks covering over 24,000-square-miles (60,000-km^2), and with the 34 game management areas adjacent to the parks, the country has set aside 32% of its land for the preservation of wildlife. However, some of the national parks and reserves are not open to the general public.

The country's four major parks are South Luangwa National Park, North Luangwa National Park, Lower Zambezi National Park and Kafue National Park. South Luangwa and the Lower Zambezi are the most popular of the four, largely due to their large concentrations of game. Kafue National Park offers great game viewing with few tourists, and North Luangwa is the ultimate park for walking.

Zambia is excellent for walking safaris, which are operated primarily in South Luangwa, North Luangwa, Lower Zambezi and Kafue National Parks. Virtually all of the camps offer morning walks and day and night game drives.

Fishing is very good for tigerfish in Lake Kariba and the Zambezi River, and for tigerfish, goliath tigerfish, Nile perch and lake salmon in Lake Tanganyika.

Visitors who have their own vehicles must return to the camps by nightfall, and, therefore, cannot conduct

The Busanga Plains are home to large herds of red lechwe (Kafue National Park)

night safaris on their own; neither may they leave the roads in search of game or walk in the park without the company of an armed wildlife guard.

More wildlife may be viewed June through October when the grass level is low and game is easier to see. Many of the rivers will have dried up and the game is concentrated around the lagoons and oxbow lakes — making game viewing all the more spectacular. Game viewing is good in November, April and May, and the bush is certainly more lush and beautiful and that time! December to March is the hot and humid rainy season when foliage becomes thicker, making wildlife more difficult to spot.

THE NORTH AND NORTHEAST

South Luangwa National Park

The natural beauty, variety and concentration of wildlife make this huge, 3,494-square-mile (9,050-km^2) park one of the finest in Africa. Game can be so prolific that Luangwa is called "The Crowded Valley."

Top: The magic of the South Luangwa at sunset
Bottom: A herd of buffalo drink from the Luangwa River

South Luangwa is home to savannah, wetland and forest animals. The southern regions are predominantly woodland savannah with scattered grassy areas. Leopard, kudu and giraffe are numerous. To the north, the woodlands give way to scattered trees and open plains, where wildebeest and other savannah animals dominate the scene.

Thornicroft's giraffe are indigenous to the park. Lion, hyena, buffalo, waterbuck, impala, kudu, puku, bushbuck and zebra are plentiful. There are also small herds of Cookson's wildebeest, unique to Luangwa, while African wild dog are present in small numbers and rarely seen. Leopard are most commonly sighted on night game drives from July to October.

November, with the onset of the rains, is a time of rebirth with the calving of impala, wildebeest and other species. Most of the Palearctic migrants have arrived, along with large flocks of Abdim's and white storks.

South Luangwa

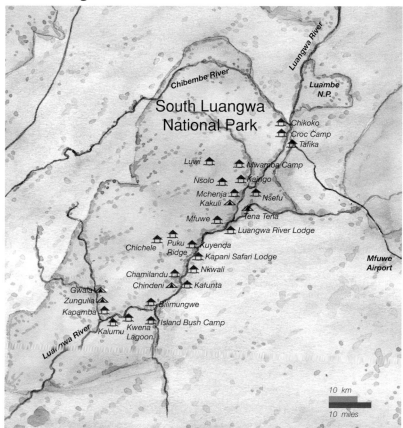

Hippo and crocs abound in the muddy Luangwa River, a tributary of the Zambezi which runs along much of the park's eastern boundary and then traverses the southern part of the park.

Over 400 species of birds have been recorded, including sacred ibis, saddle-billed storks, yellow-billed storks, Egyptian geese, spur-winged geese, fish eagles (Zambia's national bird), crowned cranes, carmine bee-eaters (spectacular breeding colonies September through November), woodland kingfishers, lilac-breasted rollers, bateleur eagles, Pel's fishing owl and long-tailed starlings. The best time for bird watching is November to April.

A real advantage of this great park is that visitors can experience day and night game drives in open vehicles, as well as participate in walking safaris ranging in length from a few hours to three or more days.

On a recent adventure with my wife and two sons, we saw lots of elephant and Cape buffalo, spotted hyena, greater kudu, civet, large spotted genet, Thornicroft's giraffe, Sharpe's grysbok, slender and white-tailed mongoose, porcupine, puku, common waterbuck, Cookson's wildebeest, warthog and Crawshay's zebra, among other game. The Luangwa River was full of hippo and crocs. In addition to game viewing, the boys played soccer almost daily with "newly found friends" within the camp grounds.

On another visit we saw very good game, including a huge herd of more than 500 buffalo, elephant (including a huge tusker), many hippo, including a large pod with several humorous juveniles, Thornicroft's giraffe, bushbuck, greater kudu, lion, serval and genet.

Top: A microlight is the ultimate way to experience South Luangwa
Bottom: When disturbed, crocodiles head for deep water

Over the years I have taken a number of **ultralight (microlight) flights** from Tafika Lodge over a wilderness region of the park, and must say that this is one of the most exciting adventures I have taken in Africa! I have seen huge herds of elephant and buffalo, large pods of hippo, a variety of antelope species and even lion. None of the wildlife even took note of us, except for crocs, which quickly fled to deep water. John, my pilot, surmised that they must have thought we were a pterodactyl.

South Luangwa is one of the best parks in Africa for **night drives**. On one of our visits, we followed what turned out to be a pride of seven lion while they hunted. We then followed a leopard at close range (20 ft./6 m), and had quite a thrill when the leopard jumped high into a bush after two sleeping doves. Other sightings included spotted hyena, Pel's fishing owl, several more leopard and lion, and a number of genet and civet.

Walking safaris were first pioneered in this park by Norman Carr, and are conducted by a licensed walking guide accompanied by an armed national parks game scout. Most lodges and camps offer morning and afternoon walks. Multi-day walks are also offered, during which guests hike from bush camp to bush camp or stay in mobile tents. Walking safaris are only conducted from June to October during the dry season when the foliage has thinned out enough for safe walking. Children under the age of 12 are not allowed on walks.

Walking safaris are the highlight of many visitors' trips to Africa and are certainly one of my favorite ways of experiencing the bush. Those who would enjoy walking 3 to 7 miles (5 to 11 km) per day at a reasonable pace and wish to experience nature up close, walking safaris are highly recommended. Many lodges have their own smaller bush camps, catering to a maximum of six or seven guests, set in remote regions of the park where walking is the main activity. However, bush camps are also excellent for those who do not want to do a lot of walking, but wish simply to relax and experience isolation in the bush.

Facilities in bush camps vary from comfortable chalets or tents with en suite facilities to simple chalets or tents with separate shower and toilet facilities (see "Accommodations" below for details). In addition to walking, some bush camps also offer day and night game drives.

Some camps offer programs whereby guests may walk from one bush camp to another. Your luggage is carried ahead to the next bush camp by vehicle or by porters who walk separately from the group. Guests usually carry only their cameras and a little water. The terrain is fairly flat but often rugged.

If you take a multi-day walking safari, I suggest you stay at least 2 additional nights in the park for day and night game drives by open vehicle; it will

A walking safari in South Luangwa

give you the opportunity to see many species that you might not have seen on your walking safari.

There are few all-weather roads in the park north of Mfuwe, so most of the northern camps are closed November to May, and the camps that stay open during that period are usually reachable only by motorboat.

Mfuwe International Airport is about an hour flight from Lusaka. South Luangwa's main gate is 433 miles (700 km) from Lusaka; driving takes about 10 hours and is not recommended. Some international visitors fly into Mfuwe from Lilongwe (Malawi) and Kariba (Zimbabwe).

ACCOMMODATION IN CENTRAL AND SOUTHERN SOUTH LUANGWA (this region of the park has many all-weather roads and is usually open year-round).

Puku Ridge's pool area

CLASS A: • **Puku Ridge**, set on a secluded ridge near Chichele Presidential Lodge, accommodates up to 12 guests in tented camp with en suite facilities. • **Chichele Presidential Lodge**, the former Presidential hideaway recently transformed into an "early-Victorian yet contemporary lodge", is set on a hill overlooking the surrounding plains. The lodge has a swimming pool and caters to 20 guests in cottages with en suite facilities, air-conditioning, ceiling fans and inclusive mini-bar, a spa treatment room is available to guests. Activities include day and night game drives and walks with a professional guide. • **Luangwa River Lodge**, located on the banks of the Luangwa River overlooking the Wafwa Oxbow Lagoon, has 5 chalets with en suite facilities. Day and night game drives and walks are offered.

CLASS A/B: • **Kalamu Tented Camp** is located in the Luamfwa Concession in the southern area of the South Luangwa National Park. The camp consists of 4 Meru-style tents with en suite facilities and an indoor shower. The dining and bar area sit under a canopy of trees and overlook the Luangwa River and there is a plunge pool. Activities include game drives and game walks. The camp is accessed by private airstrip. • **Kwena Lagoon**, also located in the Luamfwa Concession, is set on a beautiful permanent lagoon near the Luangwa River and consists of 8 en suite tents with both indoor and outdoor showers. Escorted walks as well as day and night game drives are offered. • **Kapamba Bushcamp** overlooks the Kapamba River and consists of 4 open-fronted stone chalets with en suite facilities, including large sunken bath and double shower. Daily walks and day and night game drives are offered. • **Chamilandu Bush Camp** overlooks the Luangwa River and consists of 3 grass-and-thatch chalets, built on raised wooden decks, with en suite facilities. Walks and limited day and night game drives are offered. • **Chindeni Bushcamp** overlooks a permanent oxbow lagoon and has 4 luxury tents (maximum of 8 guests), on raised wooden decks, with en suite facilities. Bush walks, as well as limited day and night game drives, are offered. • **Bilimungwe Bushcamp** is set on a permanent waterhole, and has 4 large reed-and-thatch chalets (maximum of 8 guests) with en suite facilities. Walking safaris are the primary activity, but limited day and night game drives are offered. • **Nkwali Camp**, situated just outside the park on the eastern banks of the Luangwa River, is open year-round and has 6 chalets with en suite facilities, and a swimming pool. Day and night game drives and walks are offered. • **Luangwa House**, situated next to Nkwali, is a private luxury residence for up to 8 guests (in 4 bedrooms). The house offers private guides and

Nkwali Camp's main lounge overlooks the Luangwa River

vehicles for game drives and walks as well as a swimming pool, private chef and staff. • **Robin's House,** also on the same property as Nkwali, has 2 bedrooms with facilities en suite and is great for families.• **Kapani Safari Lodge** has 8 standard chalets and 2 suites, with small refrigerators and en suite facilities, and a large swimming pool. Kapani was operated by the late Norman Carr, who introduced walking safaris to Zambia. The camp offers day and night game drives and walks. • **Mfuwe Lodge**, set on two picturesque lagoons, has 18 chalets (including 2 suites) with private decks and en suite facilities, a huge bar/dining/deck area and a large swimming pool. Day and night game drives are offered.

CLASS B: • **Kuyenda Bush Camp** has 4 grass chalets (preferred maximum of 6 guests), set on the banks of the Manzi River, with en suite bucket showers and flush toilets. Daily walks as well as day and night game drives are offered. • **Zungulila** offers walks only and is available for private parties with a minimum of 4 people. All tents have en suite facilities and sweeping views of the Kapamba River. • **Gwala** is located further up the Kapamba River from Zungulila set in the heart of an ebony grove. Only walks are offered.

CLASS D AND F: • **Flatdogs**, located near Mfuwe Bridge outside the park, has catered and self-catered bungalows and campsites.

ACCOMMODATION IN NORTHERN SOUTH LUANGWA — Because this region has few all-weather roads, the camps usually open in May and close at the end of October before the onset of the rains. This area is generally less crowded than Central Luangwa near Mfuwe, and many of the camps offer multi-day walking safaris. Tafika, Tena Tena, and Nsefu are located in the Nsefu Sector of the park.

Top: Tafika's lounge area
Bottom: A thatched reed chalet at Tafika

CLASS A/B: • **Tafika Camp** has 4 large thatched chalets and 1 2-bedroom family chalet plus a honeymoon suite — all with en suite facilities. Day and night game drives, walks, village visits, mountain biking, specialist painting safaris and exciting ultra-light (microlight) flights are offered. Because this is the only northern camp open in November, guests of that period have the entire region virtually to themselves. • **Kaingo Camp** overlooks the Luangwa River and has 5 thatched chalets with en suite facilities. Walks, day and night game drives, and photography from a hide are offered. • **Mchenja Camp**, set beneath a grove of ebony trees on the banks of the Luangwa River, has 5 stylish tents under its own thatched roof, each with en suite facilities. There is a small pool and bar next to the dining area. Day and night game drives and walks are offered. • **Tena Tena**, set on the banks of the Luangwa River inside the park, accommodates up to 10 guests in 5 tents under thatch overlooking a waterhole, with en suite facilities. Day and night game drives, morning walks, and community visits are offered as well as 6-day mobile tented walking safaris. • **Nsefu Camp**, located near the Luangwa River a 60- to 90-minute drive from Mfuwe Airport, has 6 tastefully decorated brick and thatch rondavels (12 beds) with open-roofed en suite facilities. Day and night game drives and morning walks are offered. The bar overlooks a water hole. Nsolo Camp, Luwi Camp and Kakuli Camp are in association with Kapani Camp and Chikoko and Crocodile Bushcamps are associated with Tafika Camp. Walking safaris from camp to camp are available and are usually limited to 6 guests.

CLASS B: • **Chikoko Bush Camp** is located on the western bank of the Luangwa River in an area with no roads, so it is highly unlikely that you will see other tourists. The area is specifically for walking. There are 3 tree chalets on raised platforms 10 feet (3 m) above the ground with en suite flush toilets, hand basins, and private showers. • **Crocodile Bush Camp** consists of 3 grass-and-pole chalets with en suite open-air bathrooms. The camp is located within the park, 2.5 miles (4 km) upstream from Tafika, and caters to a maximum of 6 guests. Walking safaris are conducted between Tafika, Crocodile Camp and Chikoko Bush Camp. • **Mwamba Bush Camp**, located on the banks of the Mwamba River a 3-hour walk from Kaingo Camp, has 3 reed-and-thatch chalets with en suite facilities. The chalets are uniquely designed with large skylights (protected by mosquito netting) to give you the feeling that you are sleeping "under

Top: River front dining at Tena Tena
Bottom: Guests from Crocodile Bush Camp gain a better view of nearby elephants

the stars." Walks, as well as day and night game drives, are offered. • **Nsolo Camp**, situated near a permanent waterhole, caters to a maximum of 8 guests in 4 chalets, with en suite facilities, set on decks overlooking an open vlei. The fronts of the chalets are completely open and are closed using tent material at night. There are some roads for game drives; however, walks are the most prominent activity. • **Luwi Camp** is located further inland than Nsolo and has 4 bamboo huts with en suite facilities, accommodating a maximum of 8 guests. Walking safaris from camp are offered, and some guests walk from this camp to Nsolo Camp. • **Kakuli Camp**, set on a riverbank overlooking the confluence of the Luangwa and Luwi Rivers, accommodates a maximum of 10 guests in tents with en suite facilities. Day and night game drives as well as walks are offered.

CAMPING: Camping is not allowed in the park except with a licensed tour operator.

North Luangwa National Park

As the name implies, this largely undeveloped 1,780-square-mile (4,636-km²) park lies north of South Luangwa National Park in the upper Luangwa Valley.

Mark and Delia Owens, coauthors of *Eye of the Elephant and Cry of the Kalahari* (Houghton Mifflan), conducted wildlife research here and were successful in reducing poaching and creating an infrastructure to attract tourists.

The park lies between the 4,600-foot-high (1,400-m) Muchinga Escarpment on the west and the Luangwa River on the east, with altitudes ranging from 1,640 to 3,610 feet (500 to 1,100 m). Vegetation includes miombo woodland, scrubland and riverine forest.

Wildlife includes lion, leopard, elephant, buffalo, zebra, eland, kudu, Cookson's wildebeest (much larger populations than in South Luangwa), impala, bushbuck, hippo, crocodile and a large population of spotted hyena. Black-maned lion are seen here more often than in South Luangwa. Nearly 400 species of birds have been recorded, including species not usually seen in South

Lions mating

Luangwa, such as the half-collared kingfisher, long-tailed wagtail, white-winged starling, yellow-throated long-claw and black-backed barbet.

Walking is by far the primary activity, however, there are now enough roads (about 60 mi./100 km) in the park for productive game drive/walk combinations and limited night drives.

This park is visited by very few tourists. It is in fact unlikely that you will encounter any other groups.

On one visit we walked from the airstrip for an hour and then crossed the crystal-clear, shallow Mwaleshi River (great for cooling off in hot weather) before coming to our camp.

In the afternoon we began driving toward the confluence of the Mwaleshi and Luangwa Rivers, when we spotted some vultures in the trees. We got out of the vehicle to investigate and found two lions on a buffalo kill, and after walking a bit more, found two more lion.

Other game seen enroute included a large herd of eland, wildebeest, impala, Crawshay's zebra, and double-banded sandgrouse. When we arrived at the confluence, we walked down to the river to a pod of over 100 hippos. As we approached, more than 50 ran out of the shallow water across the dry river-bed to deep water a few hundred yards (meters) away. The sight of 50 one-ton "bums" of bouncing fat running together was too funny for words! After sun-downers, we drove back to the buffalo kill and checked out the lions on spot-light. After watching the lions devouring their meal, we returned to our camp and fell upon our own finely prepared meals with equal gusto!

The next morning we left camp at 6:00 a.m., after a small breakfast, and went for a 5-hour walk along the Mwaleshi River. On the walk we saw impala, puku, wildebeest, zebra and brown snake eagle. We stopped for tea, and our porter reported hearing a roar that turned out to have come from a 9-foot croc hidden under some bushes high on the riverbank. In the afternoon we drove west on the road that goes toward the Mwaleshi Falls and saw more lion, white-tailed mongoose and wood owl, among other species.

Guests staying several days in the park may have time to visit the waterfalls located near the foot of the Muchinga Escarpment. The excursion involves a long drive and a two hour-walk. The water at the falls is so clear that you may see hippo and crocs swimming underwater. You can also swim (at your own risk) in some shallow pools nearby. Game seen enroute to the falls may include elephant, Lichtenstein's hartebeest, bushpig, roan antelope and Moloneys monkey.

The rainy season is November to March, and the best time to visit is June to October. Access to the park is best by a 45-minute or so charter flight from Mfuwe Airport; alternatively it is about a 6-hour drive. I suggest spending 6 or more nights divided between North and South Luangwa.

ACCOMMODATION — CLASS B:
• **Mwaleshi Camp** is a bush camp set on the banks of the Mwaleshi River with 4 reed-and-thatch chalets with en suite facilities with showers and flush toilets. Escorted walks, day and night game drives are offered. An early morning walk from camp is often followed by a bush breakfast and a game drive back to camp. • **Kutandala Bush Camp** is set on the banks of the Mwaleshi River and has 3 reed-and-thatch chalets with en suite facilities. Escorted walks and limited day and night game drives are offered.

Mwaleshi Camp is set on the banks of the Mwaleshi River

CLASS C: • **Buffalo Camp** is a rustic, 6-bed camp with separate facilities.

CAMPING: Campsites are available at Buffalo Camp, Mano Scott Camp (on northwestern boundary) and Luelo (east bank of the Luangwa).

Luambe National Park

This undeveloped, 99-square-mile (254-km²) savannah and woodlands park is located just northeast of South Luangwa National Park. Luambe has many of the same species and features of South Luangwa National Park, but has limited facilities to accommodate visitors.

ACCOMMODATION — CLASS B/C: • **Luangwa Wilderness Lodge**, the only lodge located within the park, has 5 safari-style tents built on wooden platforms overlooking the river, each with en suite facilities. Meals are served under the thatched dining area with open fireplace.

CAMPING: Campsites are available at Luangwa Wilderness Lodge.

Nyika Plateau National Park

The rolling highlands of Nyika are located in northeast Zambia and western Malawi. This 31-square-mile (80-km²) park includes the small Zambian portion of the Nyika Plateau. This is a good park to visit for a keen naturalist or anyone wishing to escape the summer heat of the valleys below. Due to the high altitude, night temperatures sometimes drop below freezing May to September.

Montane grassland and relic montane forest dominate the scene. A great variety of orchid and butterfly species are present, along with Moloney's monkey, blue monkey, civet and a number of other small mammals. Roan antelope, reedbuck, bushbuck, eland and bushpig and even leopard are regularly seen, while serval are present but rarely seen. The spotted hyena populations have increased dramatically over the last several years, and due to the colder climate, have thicker coats than those found in the lowland areas. Interesting bird species in the area include the moustached green bulbul, olive thrush, white-tailed crested flycatcher and bar-tailed trogon. The best time for bird watching is November to June.

ACCOMMODATION — See "Nyika National Park" in the chapter on Malawi.

Nsumbu National Park

Nsumbu National Park borders the huge inland sea of Lake Tanganyika in the extreme north of Zambia. Visitors come to this 780-square-mile (2,020-km²) park mainly for fishing and water sports. This part of Lake Tanganyika is reputedly bilharzia-free, but be sure to check the current status.

Forest and wetland wildlife species are plentiful. In fact, visitors are often accompanied to the sandy beaches by wildlife guards. Elephant, lion, buffalo, eland, puku, roan antelope, blue duiker and Sharpe's grysbok may be seen. The shoreline is inhabited by hippo, crocodile and water birds. Savannah dominates the park inland.

Day and night game drives in open vehicles, guided walks, and day and night game viewing by boat for crocodile are available.

Fishing for goliath tigerfish, vundu (giant catfish), lake salmon and Nile perch in Lake Tanganyika is excellent, especially December through April. The Zambia National Fishing Competition at Kasaba Bay is held every March or April, depending on the water level. Boats are available for hire.

ACCOMMODATION — CLASS C/D: • **Ndole Bay Lodge**, located just outside the park, has chalets (18 beds) with facilities en suite; game viewing, fishing and boating are available. • **Nkamba Bay Lodge**, located 15 miles (24 km) from Kasaba Bay in the park on a hill overlooking the beach, has 10 chalets (doubles) with en suite facilities. Activities include fishing, boating and game viewing. • **Kasaba Bay Lodge** has 18 chalets (doubles) with en suite facilities, a swimming pool and is located a few hundred yards from the beach. The lodge offers fishing, game viewing and boating.

Bangwelu Swamps

Lake Bangwelu, and the seemingly endless plains found to the east, have some unique mammal and bird species that, for some travelers, may be worth the effort of getting to this remote area. From May to July thousands of the endemic black lechwe are found in the wetlands. The rare and prehistoric looking shoebill and the shy sitatunga may be seen by boat or on foot in the swamps. Other game in the area includes oribi, tsessebe and side-striped jackal.

During the rainy season the floodplains are visited by over 370 species of migrant birds. Sightings may include the blue-breasted bee-eater, coppery-tailed coucal, white and pink-backed pelicans, herons, white storks, saddle-billed storks, ibises, pratincoles, Montagu's harrier, crowned cranes, jacanas and flamingos.

ACCOMMODATION — CLASS C: • **Shoebill Camp** has tents under thatch with separate facilities.

THE SOUTH AND WEST

Lower Zambezi National Park

Located along the Zambezi River across from Mana Pools National Park (Zimbabwe), the Lower Zambezi National Park extends 75 miles (120 km) along the Zambezi River between the Chongwe River on the west and nearly to the Luangwa River to the east, and approximately 20 miles (35 km) inland.

Lower Zambezi National Park

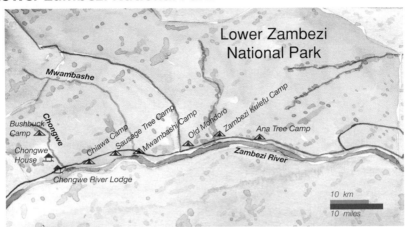

Walks, day and night game drives, and boat game drives are arranged to see elephant, buffalo, lion, leopard and a variety of antelope, and fishing is also offered. This is certainly one of the best parks in Africa!

When traveling with my wife and children not long ago we encountered hundreds of elephant and hippo, leopard, lion, Cape buffalo, large-spotted genet, civet, common waterbuck, greater kudu, dwarf mongoose, porcupine, and zebra along with many other species. For 3 days we enjoyed some fabulous game drives during the day and at night, and some great boating trips. A highlight was a day spent adventuring up river by boat. We had the most sumptuous lunch on a sandbar in the middle of the Zambezi River with some fond memories of a herd of buffalo crossing from one island to another, and the children partaking in a long jump hurdle competition on the sandbanks.

Guests from Old Mondoro enjoy game viewing by boat

On another visit, on an evening game drive we saw two civet, two genet, six lion killing an impala and mating porcupine — quite entertaining! On a 3-hour fishing excursion I caught over a dozen tigerfish weighing 6 to 10 pounds each. For a half an hour I fought what I thought was a giant vundu — but later turned out to be a 6-foot croc. You can see that catch recorded in Chiawa Camp's record book!

One afternoon we canoed for 2 hours along the narrow, beautiful Chifungulu Channel downstream from Sausage Tree Camp, and encountered an abundance of game.

Game viewing is best July to October and is good in May and June. The best fishing months are September, October, and the first two weeks of November.

ACCOMMODATION — CLASS A: • **Chiawa Camp**, located on the banks of the Zambezi River within the park, has 6 standard tents, 2 superior tents and 1 honeymoon tent (all 3 perfect for honeymooners) under thatch with facilities en suite, set on elevated wooden platforms. The charming thatched lounge/bar area has an upstairs observation deck and lounge, as well. Day and night vehicle game drives, morning and afternoon river cruises, visits to the hide, fishing (it's excellent here), canoeing and walking are offered. • **Sausage Tree Camp** has 6 Bedouin-style tents with en suite open-air bathrooms with hot/cold showers and flush toilets. Day and night game drives, boat game drives, fishing, walking and canoeing are offered. • **Zambezi Kulefu Camp** is located in the far eastern part of the Lower Zambezi Park overlooking one of the permanent channels of the Zambezi River. It consists of 7 spacious tented rooms (maximum of 12 guests) with private verandahs. Activities include day and night game drives in open 4 wd vehicles, walking safaris (June onward), boat and canoe excursions and fishing.

Top: One of Chiawa's superior tents, Lower Zambezi
Bottom: Elephants pay a visit to Sausage Tree Camp

CLASS A/B: • **Old Mondoro Bushcamp,** located on the banks of the Zambezi River within the park, has 4 reed-and-pole rooms with canvas roofs and en suite facilities. The focus is on walking trails; game drives, boat safaris and canoeing are also available. Many guests will spend a few nights here along with a few nights at either Chiawa or Sausage Tree camps, because they are located in different regions of the park and favor different activities. • **Chongwe River**

Top: The view from one of Chongwe River Camp's tents
Bottom: Fishing excursions are offered from most of the Lower Zambezi camps like Kulefu

House is a private house accommodating up to 8 guests in 4 bedrooms. The activities offered are exclusive to guests and include game drives, boat cruises walking and canoeing safaris and fishing. There is a swimming pool and private chef for guests' enjoyment. • **Chongwe River Camp** is a comfortable "bush camp" located just outside the western border of the Park consisting of 10 double chalets with 1 honeymoon suite, each with open air en suite bathrooms. Activities include game drives in open vehicles, guided walks, canoeing, boating and fishing.

CLASS B: • **Mwambashi Camp** has 11 tents with en suite bathrooms. Day and night game drives, walks in the bush and boat game drives are offered. • **Ana Tree Lodge** has 8 tents, each with en suite toilets, showers and hand basins. A vast plain stretches from the lodge to the banks of the Zambezi River. Game drives, walking safaris, boating and fishing are offered. • **Bushbuck Camp** is a seasonal rustic fly-camp overlooking the Chongwe River with tents with en suite flush toilets and hot bucket showers. Bushbuck is for guests who would like to include a night or two in the bush outside of Chongwe River Camp.

Lake Kariba

Lake Kariba is one of the largest man-made lakes in the world — 180 miles (290 km) long and up to 20 miles (32 km) wide (see "Lake Kariba" in the chapter on Zimbabwe for full details). Canoe safaris are offered downstream of Kariba Dam through the Kariba Gorge.

Siavonga

Siavonga is a small village situated on Lake Kariba just west of Lake Kariba Dam.

ACCOMMODATION — TOURIST CLASS: • **Lake Safari Lodge** has 26 rooms on Lake Kariba. The bar, restaurant and lounge have great views of the lake.

Lusaka

Attractions in Lusaka, the capital of Zambia, include the Luburma Market and Chieftainess Mungule's Village. Woodcarvings made by local craftsmen can be seen at Kabwata Cultural Center. There is also a museum near the city center. The international airport is 16 miles (26 km) from the city.

ACCOMMODATION — FIRST CLASS: • **Taj Pamodzi Hotel** is a 480-bed air-conditioned hotel with facilities en suite, a swimming pool and gym. • **Lusaka Inter-Continental Hotel** is an air-conditioned hotel with 402 rooms with facilities en suite, 24-hour room service, 3 restaurants, a casino, gym and a swimming pool. • **Holiday Inn** is an air-conditioned 215-bed hotel with facilities en suite and a swimming pool.

ACCOMMODATION NEAR LUSAKA — CLASS A/B: • **Protea Hotel Lusaka Safari Lodge**, located about an hour's drive from the airport and overlooking Lechwe Lake, has 20 thatched rooms with facilities en suite, private verandah and swimming pool. Kudu, sable, sitatunga, waterbuck and lechwe may be seen on the property.

CLASS B: • **Chaminuka** is a lodge situated on a game farm near the airport, convenient for travelers needing to overnight before catching charter flights into the parks the following day.

Lochinvar National Park

Lochinvar is a birdwatcher's paradise, with over 400 recorded species. In addition, the park is host to about 30,000 Kafue lechwe (their stronghold), 2,000 blue wildebeest and 700 zebra. Greater kudu, buffalo, bushbuck, oribi, hippo, side-striped jackal, reedbuck and common waterbuck are also present.

Kafue lechwe are unique to the Kafue Flats and are related to the red lechwe of the Busanga Swamps of Kafue National Park.

Birdwatching in this 153-square-mile (410-km^2) park is best February and March and also very good November to December and April to May. Water birds, such as the wattled crane, are especially abundant, and fish eagles are prolific. The park also encompasses part of Chunga Lagoon, which is fished by villagers living outside the park boundaries.

Although the park is open year-round, the roads are inaccessible during the rainy season. Lochinvar is located 145 miles (235 km) southwest of Lusaka, 30 miles (50 km) northwest of Monze off the Lusaka-Livingstone Road.

ACCOMMODATION — None as of this writing.

Kafue National Park

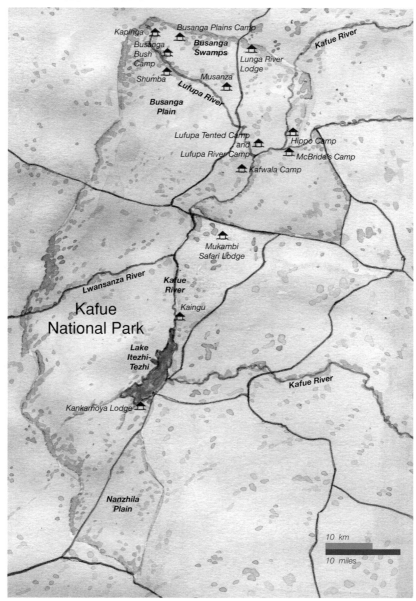

Kafue National Park

Kafue National Park, one of the largest in Africa, covers 8,687-square-miles (22,400-km^2), making it 2.5 times the size of South Luangwa National Park and half the size of Switzerland.

Kafue has the largest number of different antelope species of any park in Africa. Many of the species, such as greater kudu and sable antelope, are said to be substantially larger than elsewhere in the country. Visitors usually see a greater variety of species in Kafue, although not the quantity of wildlife that they might see in South Luangwa.

Game is especially difficult to spot in the rainy season. Game viewing in this park is sometimes a combination of riding in a vehicle, walking and boating on the rivers and swamp boats (great fun — operated by a few select camps) through the swamps, according to the wishes of the group.

Lake Itezhi-Tezhi, formed as the result of a hydroelectric dam constructed at the southern end of the Kafue Flats, provides fishing, birdwatching and boating opportunities for visitors.

The Busanga Plains and marshes in the north have a greater number and variety of wildlife species. Animals are easier to spot here than in the dense woodland savannah in the south. This region is predominantly miombo forest,

Zebras running across the Busanga Plains

Top: Untamed Zambia — lions versus hippos in Kafue
Middle: An aerial view of the vast Busanga Plains
Bottom: A surprise finding for guests — tree climbing lions of Busanga

which gives way to savannah grasslands, along with rock hills, marshes and riverine forests. The Kafue River runs through the northern part of the park and along its east central border.

Large herds of red lechwe may be seen on the Busanga Plains. Sitatunga may be found in the Busanga Swamps on the northern border of the park. Lion are often seen on day and night game drives. This is the best park in Zambia to see cheetah which are being seen quite frequently. Leopard are occasionally seen. Also present on the plains are buffalo, elephant, puku, wildebeest, impala, roan antelope, sable antelope, greater kudu, Lichtenstein's hartebeest, waterbuck, wild dog and hyena. More than 400 species of birds have been recorded.

The fact that Kafue has the largest number of antelope species of any park in Africa became immediately evident the following day on a 3-hour morning drive from the Lunga River to the Busanga Plains, during which we spotted 9 species: impala, puku, common duiker, sable antelope (herd of 34), Lichtenstein's hartebeest, roan antelope, reedbuck, blue wildebeest and oribi.

To leave the forest and watch the expansive plains of Busanga open before our eyes was truly an amazing sight. The 350-square-miles (900-km^2) of plains are broken by numerous small palm "islands," and have a feel of the openness of the short grass plains of the southeastern Serengeti coupled with the presence of water and landscape similar to Botswana's Okavango

Delta. Some of the camps are accessed by helicopter — a truly amazing way to see the plains!

We witnessed lion chasing a puku across the plains, and saw yellow baboon, buffalo, hippo, side-striped jackal, large grey mongoose, warthog, Defassa waterbuck, Burchell's zebra and zorilla. Bird life was prolific. We only encountered a few other vehicles — most of which were from our own camp. This is definitely a park for anyone wanting to get off the beaten track!

There is little to be seen on the 4-hour, 170-mile (275-km) drive from Lusaka; scheduled group charter flights from Livingstone, Lusaka and Lower Zambezi National Park are available and are a better alternative. Most safari camps are open from May to December.

ACCOMMODATION — CLASS A:
• **Shumba Bush Camp** has 6 luxury safari tents on raised platforms with views of the surrounding plains (accommodating a maximum of 12 guests). The camp's dining and bar area look out on the plains. Day and night game drives, swamp boat rides, walking safaris and services of a masseuse are offered. • **Kapinga Camp** blends into its surroundings and with only 3 luxury safari tents (accommodating a maximum of 8 guests), it offers very personalized service. Day and night game drives, swamp boat rides, walking safaris and spa treatments are offered. This camp, as well as Shumba Bush Camp are reached by helicopter transfer from an airstrip within the park.

Top: Shumba Camp's beautiful deck area
Middle: Sleeping in style at Kapinga Camp
Bottom: Lunga River Lodge offers waterfront dining

Top: A helicopter transfers guests to Shumba and Kapinga
Bottom: Kafue is home to a variety of antelope as well as predators

CLASS A/B: • **Lunga River Lodge** has 6 thatched cabins with en suite facilities, and a swimming pool. Activities include walks, day and night game drives, and boating. • **Busanga Bush Camp** has 4 thatched huts with en suite facilities. Day and night game drives and walks are offered. Access to the camp is via helicopter from the Busanga Airstrip. Vehicles can drive in from Lufupa after August when water levels drop. • **Mukambi Safari Lodge,** located at the entrance to Kafue National Park has 8 chalets, 1 luxury family unit and 7 traditional safari-style tents, each with en suite facilities, and 2 swimming pools. Morning and night game drives, boat trips and walking safaris are offered. • **Busanga Plains Camp**, sister camp to Mukambi Safari Lodge, has 4 en suite safari tents and offers game drives and walking safaris.

CLASS B: • **Lufupa Tented Camp**, situated in the center of the northern region near the confluence of the Kafue and Lufupa Rivers, has 9 canvas Meru tents with en suite bathrooms (including 1 family tent accommodating 4 people), and offers day and night game drives, walks, fishing and game viewing by boat. • **Lufupa River Camp** has 7 twin Meru tents with en suite bathrooms and 2 family tents. • **Konkamoya Lodge**, located on the southern edge of Lake Itezhi-Tezhi, consists of 3 chalets and offers game drives, walks, game viewing by boat and canoe and fishing. • **Musanza Bush Camp** has 4 simple walk-in tents featuring en suite toilets and hot bucket showers. • **Hippo Lodge**, located in the northern sector of Kafue, has 4 rustic chalets and 2 tents with open-air bathrooms. • **Kaingu Safari Lodge** offers 4 safari tents under thatch and 1 family house. Each has en suite facilities and outdoor shower. • **McBrides' Camp**, located in the northeast section of the park, consists of 5 thatched chalets with en suite bathrooms and private verandahs. The camp specializes in walking safaris.

CLASS D: • **Kafwala Camp** overlooks the Kafwala Rapids and is a self-catering camp. Game viewing activities can be booked through Lufupa Tented Camp.

CAMPSITES: Camping facilities are available at Lufupa River Café, located adjacent to Lufupa River Camp.

Victoria Falls

Called Mosi-oa-Tunya, "the smoke that thunders", Victoria Falls is one of the seven natural wonders of the world. Visitors may walk along the **Knife Edge Bridge** for a good view of the Eastern Cataract and Boiling Pot.

A **sunset cruise** is a very pleasant experience; hippo and crocodile are often seen. Fixed-wing aircraft and helicopter **flights over the falls** are a great way to get a bird's eye view of Victoria Falls.

A boat excursion to **Livingstone's Island** is highly recommended for great views of the falls. This only operates when the water flowing over the Falls is its lowest, from August to November. Half-day **elephant back riding** excursions are offered and highly recommended as a way to spend up close and personal time with these intelligent creatures. **Canoe safaris** are conducted upstream of the falls. **Fishing** for tigerfish on the Zambezi River is best from June to October (September is best), before the rains muddy the water.

One of the world's highest commercially run **bungee jumps** is operated on the bridge crossing the Zambezi River. After falling over 300 feet (100 m), a member of the bungee staff is lowered to the jumper and connects a cable to his harness. The jumper is winched into the upright position and then winched back up onto the bridge.

The Zambezi River below Victoria Falls is one of the most exciting **white-water rafting** experiences in the world.

Top: A spectacular aerial view of Victoria Falls
Bottom: Guests from Islands of Siankaba enjoy a sunset cruise

Victoria Falls

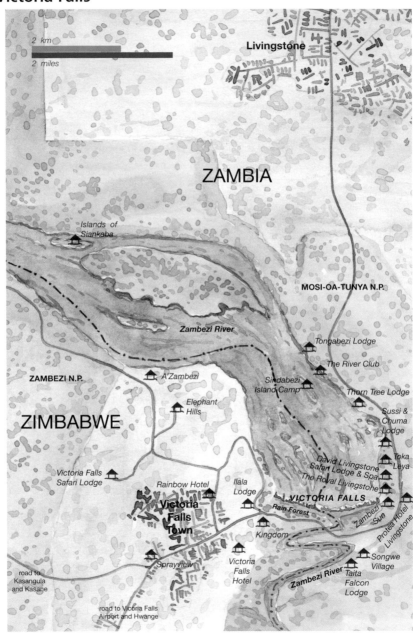

Numerous fifth-class rapids (the highest class runable) make this one of the most challenging rivers on earth. Trips are operated on the Zambezi River below Victoria Falls from the Zambia and Zimbabwe side of the Zambezi River. See the description of whitewater rafting in the "Victoria Falls" section of the chapter on Zimbabwe for further details.

The falls are located about 3 miles (5 km) from Livingstone. See the chapter on Zimbabwe for a detailed description of the falls.

The ultimate adrenaline rush — class five rapids on the Zambezi River

Mosi-oa-Tunya (Smoke That Thunders) National Park

Much of the area around the Victoria Falls on the Zambian side is positioned within the 4-square-mile (10-km^2) Mosi-oa-Tunya National Park. Only a small section is fenced off into a game park that has a small population of sable, eland, warthog, giraffe, zebra, buffalo and elephant. There are two monuments within the park — one where the pioneers used to cross the river, and the other at the old cemetery. There are no large predators in the park.

ACCOMMODATION WITHIN THE PARK — CLASS A: • **Toka Leya Camp** is situated on the banks of the Zambezi River in the eastern sector of the Mosi-oa-Tunya National Park. Accommodations consist of 12 safari-style tents (including 2 family tents), each en suite with a view of the Zambezi River and surrounding islands. There is a swimming pool and spa for guests to enjoy on hot African days. Activities include a tour of the falls on the Zambian side, game drives, river cruises and guided walks. • **Sussi Lodge** is located on the Zambezi River, just a 10-minute drive above Victoria Falls. The camp consists of 12 luxury rooms with en suite facilities, air-conditioning, and private decks. The main lodge consists of an upstairs sitting area and a nice downstairs dining area plus a beauty

The lounge at Toka Leya Camp overlooks the Zambezi River

Guests at Toka Leya Camp enjoy great views of the river

treatment room. There is a separate swimming pool, spa and sundowner deck. The camps offer tours to the falls, Livingstone Museum visits, and a cultural village tour as well as game drives within Mosi-oa-Tunya National Park. • **Chuma Houses** are 2 exclusive properties featuring 2 bedrooms en suite (1 double and 1 twin room). There is a spacious lounge and dining room area, kitchen, outdoor verandah, barbeque area and private swimming pool. Guests have their own private chef, butler and a private guide, vehicles and boat.

CLASS B: • **Thorn Tree River Lodge**, located in Mosi-oa-Tunya, has 7 stone rooms under thatch and 2 wood suites under thatch with en suite facilities, private verandahs with views of the river and bush. Activities include river cruises, tours of the Victoria Falls area, game drives and elephant back safaris are conducted from camp.

Livingstone

Livingstone is a city of over 100,000 inhabitants, 5 miles (8 km) from the town of Victoria Falls. Driving from Lusaka takes 5 to 6 hours (295 miles/ 470 km) and flying takes a little over an hour.

The **Livingstone Museum** is the National Museum of Zambia and is renowned for its collection of Dr. Livingstone's memoirs. Other exhibits cover the art and culture of Zambia. The **Maramba Cultural Center** exhibits bandas from various districts in Zambia and presents colorful costumed performances by Zambian dancers. The **Railway Museum** has steam engines and trains from the late 1800s and 1900s.

Livingstone Zoological Park is a small, fenced park near Livingstone covering 25-square-miles (65-km^2). It is stocked with giraffe, buffalo, impala and other wildlife. The best time to visit is from June to October.

ACCOMMODATION — DELUXE: • **The David Livingstone Safari Lodge and Spa**, recently constructed on the banks of the Zambezi River, is a colonial-style property with 72 luxury rooms and 5 loft suites accommodating a total of 154 guests. There is also a spa, tropical infinity swimming pool, restaurant and bar. • **The Royal Livingstone Hotel** has a total of 173 rooms including

3 standard suites, 1 presidential suite and 2 paraplegic (handicapped) rooms, restaurant and bar. All rooms have air-conditioning, satellite television, mini-bar and mini safe, and private balconies and terraces that offer views of the Zambezi River.

FIRST CLASS: • **Protea Hotel Livingstone**, recently built, consists of 80 deluxe rooms with en suite facilities and satellite TV. The hotel is situated next to the new shopping and entertainment center enroute from the falls to Livingstone town.

TOURIST CLASS: • **Zambezi Sun** has a total of 212 rooms with private balconies and satellite TV including 4 suites and 2 paraplegic rooms, and a restaurant and bar focused around the central swimming pool.

ACCOMMODATION NEAR LIVINGSTONE — CLASS A: • **The River Club** is located 12 miles (20 km) upstream from Victoria Falls and has a distinct Edwardian flavor with 10 luxury en suite chalets overlooking the Zambezi River. Visits to the falls and other local attractions, river cruises and village visits are offered. • **Tongabezi Lodge**, situated on the Zambezi River 12 miles (20 km) upstream from Victoria Falls, sleeps 22 guests in 5 thatched river cottages, 4 spacious stone-and-thatched houses, 1 enclosed house with private plunge pool and 1 Garden Cottage with 2 bedrooms set away from the river, all with en suite facilities. Guests enjoy the swimming pool and activities such as canoeing, boat excursions, fishing, croquet, and flights over the falls are offered. • **The Islands of Siankaba**, consisting of two islands in the Zambezi River, 24 miles (38 km) upstream from the Victoria Falls, has 7 teak-and-canvas chalets on raised platforms with facilities en suite and a swimming pool. The two islands are linked by a series of suspension bridges and overhead walkways. Activities include guided walks on the main island, village/school tour, mokoro trips, and sunset river cruises, as well as trips to Victoria Falls.

Top: A chalet at the River Club
Bottom: Dining riverside at Tongabezi

CLASS A/B: • **Sindabezi Island Camp**, located on an exclusive island in the Zambezi River 2 miles (3 km) downstream from Tongabezi Camp, has 5 romantic thatched cottages lit only by candles and lanterns with en suite bush (bucket) showers and flush toilets.

CLASS B: • **Songwe Village** is perched nearly 400 feet (120 m) above the Zambezi Gorge, just a short drive from the falls. There are 8 comfortable thatched huts built in the traditional style with en suite facilities.

CLASS B/C: • **Taita Falcon Lodge**, located 5 miles (7 km) downstream from the falls, overlooking the spectacular Batoka Gorge and the Zambezi River, has 6 chalets with verandahs and en suite facilities.

Sioma Falls

Sioma Falls, located a 6-hour drive and 185 miles (300 km) upstream (northwest) of Victoria Falls, is a magnificent series of 6 horseshoe-shaped falls stretching across the 1.5 mile-wide Zambezi River. The best time to visit is July through January.

Liuwa Plain National Park

Located in southwestern Zambia, this remote 1,413-square-mile (3,660-km^2) park of open plains contains large numbers of wildebeest along with lion, hyena and spectacular numbers of migrating birds.

Wildlife, however, should be considered a plus and not the main reason for traveling to this seldom-visited park. It is a remote wilderness that is more suited for birdwatchers and for those interested in meeting African villagers who are uninfluenced by modern culture.

ACCOMMODATION: None. Mobile tented safaris are available.

Namibia

Namibia

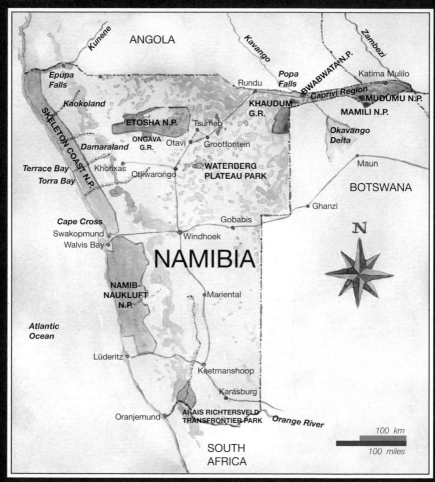

Namibia is one of Africa's driest countries, with the Namib and Kalahari Deserts dominating the landscape. Elevation ranges from sea level on the Atlantic seaboard to some 5,410 feet (1,650 m) at Windhoek on the central plateau. In the far north, the permanent water of the Kunene and Okavango Rivers allows for productive agriculture and it is here that most of the population live. Just over two million people inhabit the 318,250-square-miles (824,268-km²) of Namibia which is about the size of Texas and Oklahoma combined. Windhoek is the capital city. English is the official language. Currency is the Namibian Dollar.

Namibia
Country Highlights

- Seeing sun rise over the sand dunes at Sossusvlei
- Flying in a small charter plane or hot-air balloon over the unmistakable and epic scenery of Namibia
- Visiting UNESCO World Heritage Site at Twyfelfontein to see the ancient rock engravings
- Tracking desert elephant and black rhino in Damaraland
- Seal colonies, whale bones and shipwrecks on the Skeleton Coast
- Watching the pecking order of game around Etosha and Ongava's water holes
- Accompanying San bushmen on a traditional hunt
- Visiting the Himba, taking a boat cruise on the Kunene River and quad biking in Kaokoland

Best Parks and Reserves to Visit   **Best Times to Go**
Namib-Naukluft.................................Year round
Skeleton Coast..................................Year round
Damaraland.......................................Year round
Kaokoland..Year round
Etosha..May to November

Best Accommodations
Little Ongava, Serra Cafema, Little Kulala, Wolwedans Boulders Camp, Heinitzburg Hotel

NAMIBIA

In addition to wildlife, Namibia has some of the most spectacular desert ecosystems in the world. It is famous for its stark beauty and the diversity of its tribes, while it is a geologist's and naturalist's paradise.

Essentially a desert land, Namibia is one of the most interesting and unusual of African countries. The Namib, in fact, is considered to be the oldest desert in the world. It may seem inhospitable in its dryness, but an astonishing variety of wildlife exists there, including unique, desert-adapted species, together with the big game of the savannah. Namibia has a sparse population of about 1.8 million, the majority of which live in Windhoek (the capital city) or in the far northern regions of Ovamboland.

Namibia is situated in the sub-tropics, and flanked by the cold Atlantic Ocean. The cold Benguela current, which drifts northward from Antarctica, has a massive influence on the climate. Cool, dry air is pushed inland, creating a temperate coastline, and the extreme desert conditions of the Namib. Most of the country receives less than 10 inches (250 mm) of rain (the entire coastal region has less than 1 inch/25 mm); 80% of this rain falls between October and April.

Namibia has a subtropical climate. Inland summer (October to April) days are warm to hot with cool nights. From May to September (winter), days are warm with clear skies but the nights can become quite cold. Summer (December to March) is the "rainy" season, and most rainfall occurs in the north and northeast.

There are five perennial (permanent) rivers in Namibia, all forming a border with neighboring countries. The Gariep (Orange) River is in the south and divides Namibia from South Africa while the Kunene, in the far north, forms a natural border with Angola. The Kavango, Kwando, Linyanti and Chobe Rivers separate the country from Botswana, while the mighty Zambezi separates it from Zambia and Zimbabwe. All other rivers in the country are ephemeral, running only when good rains are received in their catchment areas.

Namibia is one of the world's most sparsely populated countries. Its population is 86% black, 7% white and 7% colored (of mixed descent). The Owambo tribe represents at least half of all the black Namibians, while other tribes include Damara, Herero, Kavango, Nama, Caprivian, San (Bushmen), Rehoboth Baster, Himba, Topnaar and Tswana. Herero women, colorfully dressed in red and black, continue to wear conservative, impractical and extremely hot attire that was fashioned for them by puritanical, nineteenth century missionaries. Most people live in the northern part of the country where there is more water.

In 1884 much of the coast became German South West Africa until 1915, when South Africa took control during World War I. In 1920 the Union of South Africa received a mandate by the League of Nations to govern the region as if it were part of South Africa. The United Nations retracted the mandate in 1966 and renamed the country Namibia. The country became independent on March 21, 1990.

Namibia is one of the world's largest producers of diamonds and has the world's second largest uranium mine. Tsumeb is the only known mine to have produced over 200 different minerals. Other major industries include fishing, agriculture and the burgeoning tourism industry.

🐾 WILDLIFE AND WILDLIFE AREAS

Namibia has set aside about 14% of its surface area as proclaimed national parks. Etosha is the most famous, and it offers game viewing on par with other top reserves in southern Africa.

The Namib-Naukluft and Skeleton Coast parks protect unique desert ecosystems, and are an attraction for smaller life forms and landscapes, as well as low concentrations of desert-adapted big game. Lion have returned to the Skeleton Coast, and elephant may be seen there as well. Other key areas to consider visiting are Kaokoland for spectacular scenery and to visit the Himba, and Bushmanland to visit the San.

Game viewing in Etosha and the Caprivi reserves is best during the

A desert elephant traverses Namibia's harsh landscape

A full mane lion stands out against the brush

dry season May to November. Due to Namibia's unique desert, game viewing in the desert areas is great all year round.

A few selected tour operators may use open-sided vehicles in Etosha National Park, however, self-drive travelers are only allowed in Etosha in closed vehicles. Open-sided vehicles are allowed in all other parks. Walking is allowed in all parks and reserves, except Etosha. However, walking is not recommended unless you are accompanied by an experienced guide. The parks are well organized and the facilities are clean.

THE NORTH AND WEST

Windhoek

Windhoek is the capital and administrative, commercial and educational center of Namibia, situated in the center of the country at 5,410 feet (1650 m) above sea level. Windhoek is also the starting point for most Namibian safaris. Eros Airport serves as the gateway for most charter flights departing for the safari camps.

The capital has been influenced greatly by German architecture from the early colonial days. Three castles were built between 1913 and 1918, and are located close together in what is now the fashionable suburb of Klein Windhoek. The **Heinitzburg** is now one of Windhoek's finest hotels, while Italy's ambassador to Namibia resides in the **Schwerinsburg**, and the **Sanderburg** has become a private dwelling. The **State Museum**, dating from the end of the nineteenth century, is housed in the **Alte Feste** (Old Fort), and is closer to the city center.

Other places of interest include Windhoek's **Botanical Gardens**, the **National Art Gallery**, **Post Street Mall** with its impressive collection of meteorite rocks, the **Supreme Court** building and **Heroes Acre** — a burial place reserved for Namibia's most revered freedom fighters — a few kilometers out of town on the B1 road, toward Rehoboth.

The NICE restaurant (Namibian Institute of Culinary Excellence) and bar are one of the city's hippest and most sophisticated new spots. It offers international cuisine infusing Namibian classics such as exquisite game dishes with Asian or Italian, along with traditional dishes. Am Weinberg serves wholesome and healthy Namibian haute cuisine, and offers a great outdoor venue.

Leo's at the Heinitzburg Hotel has varied cuisine ranging from international to French a la carte; the atmosphere is extremely formal. Joe's is a popular bar and restaurant known for its informal atmosphere and is loved by young and old, Namibians and travelers. The restaurant serves great steaks but is not a good choice for vegetarians. Luigi & The Fish is known for good seafood, has a pool table and is popular (especially among the young). Joe's Beerhouse is the iconic "watering hole", a legend in its own time; it's a popular bar and restaurant known for its informal atmosphere and is loved by young and old, Namibians and travelers. Restaurants offering a great African vibe include La Marmite, offering some fabulous West African cooking. African Roots is always full of locals and offers fresh and varied local fare. Iitumba is out in the bush, a few miles/kilometers from town, and specializes in braaiing (barbequing) local meats.

On a day trip from Windhoek you can visit the **Ombo Ostrich Farm** to see ostriches in all stages of development, from the egg to the grown bird, and the historic **Otjisazu Guest Farm** at Ovitoto where you can meet the colorful Herero people at Ovitoto.

ACCOMMODATION — FIRST CLASS: • **Heinitzburg Hotel**, the only member of the Relais and Chateaux group of excellence in Namibia, is an old castle with 16 air-conditioned rooms and en suite facilities. • **Hotel Thule**, situated on a hilltop location in upscale Eros, boasts 23 rooms with en suite facilities and air-conditioning. The restaurant and pool area have spectacular views! • **The Olive Grove** offers 10 en suite air-conditioned rooms and 1 executive suite in a location close to the city center. The veranda offers al fresco dining and there is a tranquil garden and pool. • **Windhoek Country Club Resort and Casino**, located several kilometers from the city, has 152 air-conditioned rooms with en suite facilities, tennis courts, an 18-hole golf course and a swimming pool. A complimentary shuttle takes guests to and from the city center. • **The Safari**

Top: The Heinitzburg's main façade
Bottom: One of the elegant bedrooms at the Heinitzburg

Court (4-star) and **Hotel Safari** (3-star) are located 2 miles (3 km) from the city center; The Safari Court has 257 rooms and Hotel Safari has 192. All are air conditioned with en suite facilities, a swimming pool and free transport to and from Windhoek. • **Kalahari Sands Hotel and Casino**, located in the center of town, has 173 air-conditioned rooms and suites with private facilities, a rooftop swimming pool, a fitness center and recently renovated reception area.

TOURIST CLASS: • **Hilltop House** is a luxurious bed and breakfast with commanding views over Windhoek, only a few minutes' walk from town. There is a swimming pool, and the seven rooms have facilities en suite. • **Villa Verdi**, a small guest lodge located a few minutes walk from downtown, has 13 standard rooms, 3 apartments and 1 luxury suite, all with private facilities and a swimming pool. • **Klein Windhoek Guest House** is a busy establishment with 9 air-conditioned rooms with en suite facilities, 6 self-catering flats and there are plans to expand with several luxury rooms. There is a small pool and 2 restaurants, 1 of which overlooks the Klein Windhoek River. • **Hotel Thüringerhof** recently underwent an extensive renovation and has 40 air-conditioned rooms with en suite facilities and a beer garden.

CAMPING: • **Monteiro Self-Catering and Camping** lays 7 miles (11 km) south of the city and offers camping in a natural setting but still close to Windhoek. There are 2 large chalets and 6 campsites and a swimming pool. • **Arebush**, located about 2.5 miles (4 km) from the city center, has a number of campsites and budget, self-catering chalets plus a restaurant. • **Daan Viljoen Game Park**, 17 miles (27 km) from Windhoek, has campsites and self-catering is available.

Namib-Naukluft Park

The consolidation of the Namib Desert Park and the Naukluft Mountain Zebra Park along with the incorporation of other adjacent lands, including most of what was called "Diamond Area #2", created the largest park in Namibia and one of the largest in the world. Namib-Naukluft Park covers 19,215-square-miles (49,768-km²) of desert savannah grasslands, gypsum and quartz plains, granite mountains, an estuarine lagoon and wetlands, a canyon and huge, drifting apricot-colored dunes.

The Kuiseb River runs through the center of the park from east to west and acts as a natural boundary separating the northern grayish-white gravel plains from the southern deserts.

Herds of mountain zebra, gemsbok, springbok and flocks of ostrich roam the region.

Many small, fascinating creatures have uniquely adapted to this environment and help make this one of the most interesting deserts in the world. The dunes are home to numerous unique creatures, such as the translucent Palmato gecko, shovel-nosed lizard and Namib golden mole.

The 5 main regions of the park are the Namib, Sandvis, Naukluft, Sesriem and Sossusvlei areas.

It is generally acknowledged that the **Namib** is the world's oldest desert. The Namib is known as the "living desert" because of the diversity of life existing in seemingly inhospitable conditions. In this dry place, an intriguing array of desert-adapted animals and plants are nourished by condensation from the sea mists off the distant Atlantic Ocean.

The Welwitschia Flats is located on a dirt road about 22 miles (35 km) north of the Swakopmund-Windhoek Road and is one of the best areas to see the prehistoric *Welwitschia mirabilis* plants. Actually classified as trees, many welwitschia are thousands of

A 4-wheel drive vehicle is a necessity in the desert

years old and are perfect examples of adaptation to an extremely hostile environment. The water holes at Hotsas and Ganab are good locations to spot game; Ganab and Aruvlei are known for mountain zebra.

If you plan to deviate from the two main roads through the park, a permit is required and is obtainable weekdays only at the Environment and Tourism Office in Swakopmund, Windhoek or Sesriem.

The **Sandvis** area includes **Sandwich Harbor**, 26 miles (42 km) south of Walvis Bay, and is accessible only by 4wd vehicles. Fresh water seeps from under the dunes into the saltwater lagoon, resulting in a unique environment. Bird watching is excellent September through March. Only day trips are allowed to the harbor. Permits are required and may be obtained from the Ministry of Environment and Tourism or from service stations in Walvis Bay.

The **Naukluft** region is an important watershed that is characterized by dolomitic mountains over 6,445 feet (1,965 m) in height with massive picturesque rock formations and thickly foliated riverbeds. Large numbers of mountain zebra, along with springbok, kudu, klipspringer, rock hyrax, baboon and black eagles are frequently sighted. Also present are cheetah and leopard.

Namib-Naukluft Park

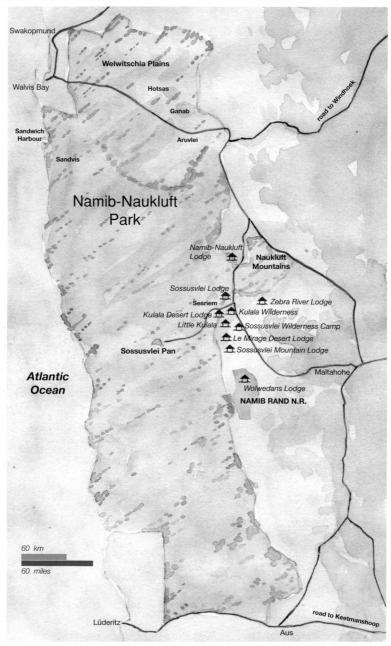

There are several hiking trails from which to choose. One of the more interesting trails is the Naukluft Trail, 10.5 miles (17 km) in length, requiring 6 to 7 hours of hiking. A 75-mile (120-km) trail, which takes 8 days, may also be hiked April to October, with prior permission.

Sesriem Canyon is about 0.6 mile (1 km) long and is as narrow as 6 feet (2 m), with walls about 100 feet (30 m) high. In some places the canyon takes on a cave or tunnel-like appearance.

Sossusvlei has the highest sand dunes in the world, exceeding 1,000 feet (300 m). The base of the second highest sand dune in the world can be closely approached by vehicle.

The hike along the knife-edge rim to the top is strenuous, requiring 60 to 90 minutes of taking 2 steps up and sliding 1 step down. The view from the top into other valleys and of the mountains beyond is marvelous. Even up there, colorful beetles, ants and other desert critters roam about.

Sunrise on these magnificent and colorful dunes is spectacular. Please note that to witness the dunes at sunrise, you must stay at lodges that are located close to the park gate.

Ballooning safaris are offered and can be reached from most lodges. At Sossusvlei, camping is not allowed and there are no accommodations.

Sossusvlei's epic scenery is best viewed from a balloon

Top: A stunning view from any corner of Little Kulala's bedroom
Bottom: One of the private bungalows at Sossusvlei Wilderness Camp

ACCOMMODATION: • Kulala Desert Lodge, Little Kulala, Kulala Wilderness Camp and Sossusvlei Wilderness Camp are located on the scenic, 52,000-acre (21,000-hectare) Kulala Wilderness Reserve, which is on the boundary of the park. A private entrance gate to the park provides quick access into the park. Activities include day visits to the Sossusvlei dunes, desert breakfasts under the camel-thorn acacia trees, visit to Sesriem Canyon, drives into the desert, ballooning, walking trails, horseback riding, and visits to Bushman paintings on the private reserve

CLASS A+: • **Little Kulala** has 11 thatch-and-canvas chalets or "Kulalas" (Oshiwambo word "to sleep") with en suite bathrooms set on wooden platforms, and private plunge pools. Guests may also sleep under the stars on the roof of their chalet — a private stargazing platform!

CLASS A: • **Sossusvlei Wilderness Camp** is built near the top of a mountain overlooking vast open plains. There are 9 bungalows with en suite bathrooms. The main living area is under thatch • **Sossusvlei Mountain Lodge** has 10 spacious air-conditioned stone-and-glass suites with en suite facilities. Activities include walks, ballooning, and scenic drives to Sossusvlei and the Sesriem Canyon.

CLASS A/B: • **Kulala Desert Lodge**, situated on the edge of Sossusvlei, has 15 stylish thatched and canvas "kulalas" with en suite facilities. A rooftop sleeping area allows guests to enjoy a night under the spectacular desert sky.

CLASS B: • **Kulala Wilderness Camp**, located on the Kulala Wilderness Reserve, has 10 tents with en suite facilities. • **Le Mirage Desert Lodge and Spa** boasts 26 rooms with full facilities just 12 miles (20 km) from Sesriem. • **The Desert Homestead** offers 20 en suite chalets just 20 miles (32 km) from ̄esriem, and has horse riding facilities including overnight trails. • **Zebra ̄ver Lodge** is located in the Tsaris Mountains and has 7 rooms with en suite ̄ities. Swimming, nature drives and hikes to 5 natural springs are offered on the farm. • **Sossusvlei Lodge**, located at the gate to the Sesriem area and about 37 miles (60 km) from Sossusvlei, has 45 rooms with en suite facilities, and an adventure center. • **Rostock Ritz Desert Lodge** is located 75 miles (120 km) from Sesriem (a suitable stopover for those traveling from Swakopmund and the coast), has 20 rock chalets, pool and restaurant.

CLASS D, F AND CAMPING: • **Sossusvlei Desert Camp**, a new camp with 20 chalets located only 3 miles (5 km) from Sesriem. • **Tsauchab River Camp**, located 44 miles (70 km) from Sesriem deep in the Naukluft and Tsaris mountains, has 8 campsites, 4 chalets and a tented camp. • **MET Campsites** in the Namib have no firewood or water. You must be self-sufficient. • **Naukluft Campsites** have water, charcoal and ablution facilities. • **The NWR Sesriem Campsite** has two ablution blocks with hot and cold water and a swimming pool. Firewood and fuel are available. This is a busy campsite frequented by large overland bus groups.

Namib Rand Nature Reserve

The 463-square-mile (1,200-km^2) Namib Rand Nature Reserve, situated in the pristine Namib Desert just east of the southern border of Namib Naukluft Park, is the largest private nature reserve in southern Africa. It is a world of wind-sculpted orange dunes and jagged mountains. There is plenty of opportunity here to experience true solitude in the desert, as the reserve is so huge compared to the number of guests hosted at any one time.

While this is not a game-rich area, you will find springbok, gemsbok, zebra, baboon, ostrich and more, which eke out their existence under the arid desert conditions. Across this diverse canvas of contrasting landscapes traverse an exciting variety of large and small desert creatures — as wild and ancient as their habitat.

CLASS A: • **Wolwedans Dune Lodge** has 9 chalets with private

Top: The epic beauty of the Namib Rand Nature Reserve
Bottom: Wolwedans Boulders Camp offers amazing views

A tent at Wolwedans Dune Camp

balconies built on wooden platforms with en suite facilities. • **Wolwedans Boulders Camp**, located 28 miles (45 km) from Wolwedans Dune Lodge, is an intimate camp with just 4 en suite tents. There is a dining and lounge tent, deck and open fireplace. • **Private Camp** (an extension of Boulders Camp) is an idyllic retreat for honeymooners and those looking to relax. The renovated farmhouse has 2 en suite bedrooms.

CLASS B: • **Wolwedans Dune Camp**, set on the 463-square-mile (1200-km²) Namib Rand Nature Reserve, has 6 tents with en suite facilities. Activities include desert drives, game viewing and walking trails

Swakopmund and Walvis Bay

The resort town of Swakopmund, located on the coast and surrounded by the Namib Desert, has many fine examples of German colonial architecture.

The coastal strip south of Swakopmund to Walvis Bay (a distance of about 20 mi./30 km) has the highest density of shorebirds in southern Africa and perhaps on the whole continent. In excess of 13,000 birds of more than 30 species feed on the nutrient-rich beaches. The majority are palearctic waders, including knot, Curlew sandpiper, turnstone and grey plover (present only between September and April). The threatened Damara tern and black oystercatcher may also be seen.

Walvis Bay plays an important role in Namibia's economy, with its international seaport and an airport that is the entry point for many visitors who embark on one of the many desert adventures the country has to offer. Another fun adventure is **quad biking** into the dunes just outside of Swakopmund.

Some travelers base themselves at Swakopmund and take day trips to the many attractions in the area. Some of the more interesting excursions include a visit to **Walvis Bay Lagoon**, home to the greater and lesser flamingos, a visit to the **Moon Valley** and the **Swakop River Canyon**, home to the world's oldest living fossil plant — the *Welwitschia mirabilis* — and the largest, man-made, offshore Guano Island, home to flocks of cormorants and Cape gulls, as well as pelicans. On the **Dolphin Cruise** you can enjoy champagne and oysters while having a very good chance of observing heavyside and bottlenose dolphins, as they swim along side the boat, turtles, and the huge seal colony at Pelican Point.

On a visit with my wife and two boys (5 and 8 years old at the time) we were hardly through our introductions to our boat captain when Flipper, a sub-adult seal, hauled himself aboard our 22-foot boat. The captain invited the kids to come closer, and he explained all about the seals. Finally, the kids built up the courage to offer a fish to their new-found friend. Their eyes sparkled with the wonder that only small children can show as they proudly looked back at us while 500 pounds of lumbering Cape fur seal flopped over the side of the boat to be transformed to weightless grace.

The best time to visit the coast for sunbathing, fishing and surfing is from December to February; June to July is cold with some rain.

Top: A dolphin cruise in Walvis Bay
Bottom: A seal hitches a ride in Walvis Bay

ACCOMMODATION — FIRST CLASS: • **Swakopmund Hotel & Entertainment Centre**, has 90 rooms with en suite facilities, a swimming pool, tennis courts and a gym. Guests have use of the Rossmund Golf Course, 1 of only 4 desert golf courses in the world. • **The Hansa Hotel** is an attractive hotel with 58 rooms with en suite facilities. • **The Sams Giardino House**, situated with a view of the dunes of the Namib Desert and within walking distance of the city center, has 9 rooms with en suite facilities and a wine cellar. • **The Stiltz** is set on the Swakop riverbed overlooking the sand dunes and bird rich lagoon at the river mouth. There are 10 very comfortable wooden bungalows, all of which are built on stilts and interlinked by wooden walkways to the main dining bungalow. A luxury villa, sleeping 6, is available for families.

TOURIST CLASS: • **The Strand Hotel** is located on the beachfront and has 45 rooms with private facilities. • **Hotel Schweizerhaus** has 24 rooms (some with sea views) with en suite facilities. Café Anton, part of the same premises, is famed for its pastries, cakes and refreshments.

Cape Cross Seal Reserve

Cape Cross Seal Reserve, home to the largest breeding seal colony in the southern hemisphere (approximately 200,000 seals), is open daily from 10:00 a.m. to 5:00 p.m.

ACCOMMODATION — CLASS B: • **Cape Cross Lodge**, located 75 miles (120 km) north of Swakopmund, has 30 en suite rooms with superb views of the ocean, and a restaurant and wine cellar.

Skeleton Coast Park

Skeletons of shipwrecks and whales may be seen on the treacherous coast of this park, which stretches along the seashore and covers over 2,000-square-miles (5,000-km²) of wind-sculpted dunes, canyons and jagged peaks of the Namib.

Skeleton Coast by Amy Schoeman (Struik Publishers) is a superb pictorial and factual representation of this fascinating region. This coastal stretch is without doubt inhospitable in the extreme. The San (Bushmen) who once lived in the area dubbed it "The land God made in anger!"

The freezing Benguela Current of the Atlantic flows from Antarctica northward along the Namibian coastline and meets the hot, dry air of the Namib Desert, forming a thick fog bank which often penetrates inland for more than 20 miles (32 km) almost every day and often lingers until the desert sun burns it off between 9:00 and 10:00 a.m. It is this very fog which brings life and sustenance to every living thing in the Namib. Yet when there is the occasional easterly wind instead of fog, there is sunshine.

The park is divided into southern and northern sections. The **southern section** is more accessible and lies between the Ugab and Hoanib Rivers. Permits and reservations (paid in advance) must be made with Namibia Wildlife Resorts (NWR) for stays at either Torra Bay or Terrace Bay.

Top: The majestic dunes of the Skeleton Coast
Bottom: Hidden surprises exist in this barren wasteland

The **northern part** of the park has been designated as wilderness area and can be visited only with fly-in safaris.

The northern region has many unusual and fascinating attractions. One such attraction is the **Cape Frio Seal Colony**, which has grown to about 40,000 individuals.

A walk down the **roaring dunes** will give you the surprise of your life. Suddenly, everyone is looking up to spot the B-52 bomber that must be overhead. Apparently, the sand is just the right diameter and consistency to create a loud noise when millions of its granules slide down the steep dune. Incredible!

Driving through **Hoarusib Canyon**, you will witness striking contrasts of dark-green grasses against verdite canyon walls and near-vertical white dunes.

Big game is present in surprisingly large numbers for a desert environment and includes desert elephant, cheetah, leopard and baboon. Brown hyena are plentiful but rarely seen. Black-backed jackal, springbok and gemsbok are often sighted. The big news is that lion, after decades of absence, have returned to the Skeleton Coast! They have been seen on the beaches, and will, like the hyena and jackal, hunt seals.

Birds may be sparse, but are interesting. Small flocks of Gray's lark forage off the gravel plains, while Ludwig's bustard, tractrac chat and bokmakierie are among the species likely to be seen near camps and on walks.

The east wind brings detritus (small bits of plant matter) providing much-needed compost for plants and food for lizards and beetles. The west wind brings the moisture on which most life depends in this desert — one that is almost completely devoid of water. The ancient "fossil" plant, *Welwitschia mirabilis*, is also found in the region.

On a recent visit we encountered many small and fascinating desert creatures as well as desert elephant, black-backed jackal (over 30, in fact, near the seal colony), herds of majestic gemsbok, springbok, and even a brown hyena!

On our last visit, my wife and I and the kids had the time of our lives. The activities included fascinating nature walks in the park. It supports some of the most harsh yet tranquil, inhospitable yet fragile environments in the world. Every participant in this unique ecosystem was carefully and cleverly designed for its role, be it the fog-gathering lichens or the water-independent gemsbok.

Our day trips included a visit to the nomadic and very tribal Himba people, bedecked in ritualistic jewelry and ochre skins, a fishing trip that did, in fact, provide supper, a visit to Cape Frio Seal Colony, where 40,000 lumps of fur and fat lie basking on the beach, a visit to the "Clay Castles" and an amethyst mine. Add to that a healthy dose of the most fantastic and variable scenery you can imagine, and that's about 10% of what the area offers!

The Skeleton Coast is at its finest from January through March, however, this is an excellent reserve to visit any time of the year.

A massive seal colony lines the coast

ACCOMMODATION—NORTHERN SKELETON COAST — CLASS A: • **Skeleton Coast Camp** has 6 stylishly appointed tents with en suite facilities. Each tent is set on decking off the ground and has a veranda area with private view. Only guests staying at this camp may visit the exclusive 600,000-acre (240,000-hectare) northern region of the park. In addition to exploring the park, guests may also visit local Himba tribes. The camp is open year-round and only accessible by air.

ACCOMMODATION — SOUTHERN SKELETON COAST — CLASS D: • **Terrace Bay** is open year-round and offers full board and lodging in basic bungalows with private facilities. There is a landing strip for light aircraft. This is a favorite haunt among beach fisherman.

CAMPING: • **Torra Bay** has campsites and caravan sites and is open only over the holidays (December 1 to January 31). You must be self-sufficient because supplies are not readily available.

ACCOMMODATION NEAR THE SKELETON COAST — CLASS A: • **Okahirongo Elephant Lodge** has 7 luxury chalets (including a 2-bedroom Presidential suite) with large en suite bathrooms complete with tub, indoor and outdoor showers and private gazebo.

CLASS C: • **Kuidas Camp**, **Purros Camp** and **Kunene Camp** accommodate guests in basic igloo huts with en suite chemical toilets and separate bucket showers. Guests normally fly from camp to camp and go on walks and nature drives from the camps.

CAMPING: **The Purros Community Campsite**, supported by the Namibia Community Based Tourism Assistance Trust (NACOBTA), provides a number of shady campsites close to the Hoarusib River. Elephants frequently wander through camp.

Damaraland

Damaraland is a large region with many attractions and is located east of Skeleton Coast National Park and southwest of Etosha National Park. This is an arid, mountainous region of spectacularly rugged scenery. Damara herders can be seen throughout this region.

The **Brandberg** is a massive mountain covering an area of 19-by-14 miles (23-by-30 km) and rises 6,500 feet (1,980 m) above the surrounding plains to 8,440 feet (2,573 m) above sea level. Its special attraction is that it harbors thousands of rock paintings, including one of the most famous in the region — "**The White Lady.**"

Twyfelfontein was declared a UNESCO World Heritage Site in June 2007. The geology of the area consists of great Etjo sandstone formations rising from the

A rock engraving at Twyfelfontein

Huab River valley, providing the "canvases" for the age-old art found there. Twyfelfontein or /Ui-//aes ("place among packed stones") boasts one of the largest concentrations of rock petroglyphs (engravings) on the African continent. Most of these well-preserved engravings represent rhinoceros, elephant, ostrich and giraffe, as well as drawings of human and animal footprints. The site also includes 6 painted rock shelters with motifs of human figures in red ochre. Twyfelfontein forms an extensive and high-quality record of ritual practices relating to hunter-gatherer communities (the San Bushmen) in this part of southern Africa over the last 2,000 or more years. The Petrified Forest has many broken, petrified tree trunks up to about 100 feet (30 m) in length. Welwitschia plants may also be seen here.

Burnt Mountain, a colorful mountain composed of many shades of purple and red, glows as if on fire when it is struck by the rays of the setting sun.

The **Spitzkoppe**, known also as "The Matterhorn of Namibia", peaks at 5,853 feet (1784 m) above sea level. These huge granite peaks stand out starkly against the surrounding gravel plains and provide some serious, high-quality rock climbing.

Vingerklip (Finger Rock), a massive limestone monolith, spearing 115 feet (35 m) into the sky, is the last remnant of a plateau formed 15 million years ago.

Wildlife is sparse and should be considered a bonus. However, many consider the search for wildlife, which has adapted to a near-waterless environment, well worth the effort. Wildlife includes desert elephant, desert black rhino, lion, desert-dwelling giraffe and Hartmann's mountain zebra. Wildlife migrates east and west along the dry riverbeds in search of food and water.

Among the interesting birds of the region are Ludwig's bustard, Ruppell's korhaan and rosy-faced lovebird.

Top: The endangered black rhino
Bottom: Tracking black rhino in
Damaraland

On a recent visit, some of our sightings included herds of desert elephant and giraffe. We searched for the elusive desert rhino and took nature walks that revealed much about this delicate and fascinating environment.

Damaraland is interesting to visit year-round, and the best time to see big game is April through December.

ACCOMMODATION — CLASS A: • **Damaraland Camp** is a recently renovated 20-bed tented camp with en suite facilities, pool and airstrip, situated in the Huab River valley where desert-adapted elephants are often seen and desert rhino may also be seen. Activities consist of guided walks and nature drives in open vehicles. Visits to Twyfelfontein are offered to guests staying three or more nights. • **Mowani Mountain Camp** has 12 luxury tented suites each with private facilities and wooden decks, and 1 suite with private butler, dining and lounge area. Activities include guided nature drives and visits to Twyfelfontein.

CLASS A/B: • **Hoanib River Camp** offers comfortable hexagonal walk-in Meru tents each with en suite facilities. Activities include game drives and walks in search of desert-adapted elephant and spectacular stark scenery. • **Doro Nawas Camp** is a 16-room lodge built on a rugged, rocky knoll in the middle of a plain adjacent to the Aba-Huab River. Activities revolve around game and bird viewing and visits to Twyfelfontein (offered daily). The camp is well placed to search for desert elephant.

CLASS B: • **Desert Rhino Camp** is a luxury mobile tented camp accommodating a maximum of 16 guests. The camp has large "Meru" tents with en suite facilities including bucket showers with hot water on call. Activities offered are rhino tracking on foot or by vehicle, night drives and full day outings (with a picnic lunch) on the concession. The rhino tracking runs in conjunction with the "Save the Rhino Trust" which gives guests an opportunity to see conservation in action and to raise funds for the endangered black rhino. • **Palmwag Lodge** offers 3 types of accommodations. The lodge has 2- and 4-bed thatched bungalows and the camp has 8 large Meru-style tents with en suite bathrooms, flushing toilets and hot/cold bucket showers. A campsite is also available. Activities include hiking and guided tours into their massive 1,737-square-mile (4,500-km²) private reserve that has one of the largest populations of black rhino in Africa. • **Vingerklip**

Doro Nawas Camp is surrounded by dramatic scenery

Lodge has 22 comfortable bungalows with en suite facilities, each with a view across the valley, and a swimming pool. • **Grootberg Lodge** was completely funded by the European Union (EU) and donated to the local community of the #Khoadi //Hoas Conservancy. Grootberg has 12 rooms and is located on the very edge of the Grootberg Plateau with stunning views overlooking the Klip River valley. Activities here include guided scenic walks and drives, elephant and rhino tracking and horse trails.

CLASS C: • **Etendeka Mountain Camp** is a tented camp (16 beds) with communal showers and flush toilets. Exploring the region by open 4wd vehicle and walks is offered. • **Khorixas Rest Camp** has rondavels with en suite facilities. • **Twyfelfontein Country Lodge**, which is the nearest accommodation to the World Heritage Site, has 56 rooms, restaurant and bar area plus a swimming pool.

CAMPING: • **Hoada Campsite**, located between Kamanjab and Palmwag, offers 3 campsites nestled among huge granite boulders with hot and cold water plus flush toilets, and is operated by the #Khoadi //Hoas Community. • **Khorixas Rest Camp** and **Palmwag Rest Camp** have campsites with an ablution block. Other NACOBTA supported campsites near Twyfelfontein include the **Aba Huab Campsite**, with shower and toilet facilities, and the more basic **Granietkop site**.

Kaokoland

This region of rugged mountain ranges interspersed with wide valleys is north of Damaraland and bordered on the west by Skeleton Coast National Park. Wildlife is sparse but includes elephant, giraffe, gemsbok, ostrich, some black rhino and lion. Himba tribes may be seen in the region. Kaokoland, or the

Top: Himba women standing in front of their dwelling
Bottom: Serra Cafema's deck offers a cool respite from the harsh surroundings

Kaokoveld as it is sometimes known, is generally acknowledged as being one of the last true wilderness areas remaining on the planet Earth.

If you wish to visit a Himba village, it is customary to wait a distance from the village until someone comes and invites you in. If you come across a village that is deserted, please do not take anything that you may find lying around. Due to their nomadic lifestyle, the Himba often leave possessions behind because they know they will return.

The best time to visit is May to December. A minimum of 2 fully self-contained 4wd vehicles per party is required, and a professional guide is highly recommended. There is no fuel in the western region. You will in most instances need to be totally self-sufficient; please respect this extremely fragile area, carry out all that you take in, leaving just footprints behind!

ACCOMMODATION — CLASS A+: • **Serra Cafema**, one of the most remote camps in all of southern Africa, is located on the Kunene River in an area of incredible beauty. Following months of research and participation from the semi-nomadic Himba, the design of Serra Cafema reflects the locale, striking geology and cultural uniqueness of the territory, and pays homage to the Himba and their traditional way of life. The camp offers 8 spacious canvas and thatch chalets with en suite bathrooms. Activities include walks, nature drives, boat game drives and visits to local Himba tribes. Access is by air charter.

CLASS B: • **Sesfontein Lodge**, located between Skeleton Coast Park and Etosha National Park, is an old fort with rooms and suites with en suite facilities. It is arranged around a swimming pool and central oasis-garden.

CLASS C: • **Epupa Camp** is located on the Kunene River near Epupa Falls and opposite the Angolan border. There are 9 safari-style tents with en suite facilities.

CAMPING: There are community-owned sites deep in Kaokoland abutting the Kunene River, one at **Okorohombo**, another at **Enyandi**, and one at **Epupa Falls**.

Etosha National Park

Etosha — the "great white place" or "place of emptiness" — is one of Africa's greatest parks in both size and variety of wildlife species. The park covers 8,569-square-miles (22,200-km^2) in the northern part of the country and lies 3,280 to 4,920 feet (1,000 to 1,500 m) above sea level.

Although still ranking as one of the biggest game reserves in Africa, it originally was several times larger and, in fact, the largest reserve in the world.

The park's vegetation is mainly mixed scrub, mopane savannah and dry woodland that surround the huge Etosha (Salt) Pan. The pan is a silvery white, shallow depression, dry except during the rainy season. Mirages and dust devils play across what was once a lake fed by a river that long ago changed course. Apart from evaporation, water present in the pan from time to time will also seep through to the impermeable clay floor of the area, thus producing plentiful springs, particularly in the southern parts of the pan. The water here might have twice the salinity of seawater. Along the edge of the pan are springs that attract wildlife during the dry winter season.

The eastern areas of the park experience the most rainfall and have denser bush than the northwestern region, which is mainly open grasslands. About 40 water holes spread out along 500 miles (800 km) of roads provide many vantage points from which to watch game. The rainy season here coincides with

Etosha National Park

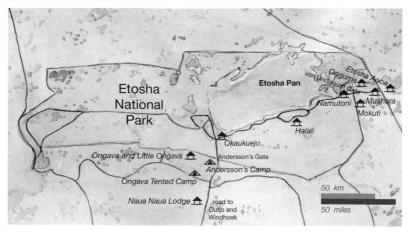

the summer months and visitors should bear in mind that, after any good rainfall that might occur in the period between November and April, animals will no longer have the need to visit the waterholes along the tourist road network, so game viewing in these months might prove to be less rewarding.

Etosha is famous for its huge elephant population, which is most visible July to September in the center of the park. Large numbers of elephant may also be seen in May, June and October. When the rains begin in January, some elephant herds migrate north to Angola and west to Kaokoland and begin returning in March. Large populations of zebra, blue wildebeest, springbok and gemsbok migrate westward from the Namutoni area in October and November to the west and northwest of Okaukuejo Camp, where they stay until around March to May. From June to August they migrate eastward again, past Okaukuejo and Halali Camps, to the Namutoni plains where there is water year-round. The calving season (which attracts predators) for a number of antelope species is November through April. The park is totally fenced, although this does not always stop the elephant from going where they please.

Lion are commonly seen, and zebra are often sighted way out on the barren pan where lions have no cover from which to launch an attack. Black-faced impala and Damara dikdik, one of Africa's smallest antelopes, are two distinctive species of this area. Black rhino occur throughout the park, with the best viewing opportunities at Okaukuejo. Leopard are seen fairly often.

A variety of antelope visit a water hole at Etosha

During one visit, we spotted black rhino, elephant, lion, red hartebeest, greater kudu, giraffe, gemsbok, zebra, blue wildebeest, springbok, black-faced impala, black-backed jackal, honey badger, warthog and mongoose. Other wildlife in the park includes brown hyena, spotted hyena, caracal, African wildcat, leopard, cheetah, aardwolf, Cape fox, bat-eared fox, eland, roan antelope and grey duiker.

A real attraction to photographers is that it is, in fact, common to see from five to eight or more mammal species at a waterhole at the same time.

Bird life is prolific, and 340 species have been recorded. The main pan is of importance as a regional breeding site for lesser and greater flamingos, as well as white pelicans. Over one million flamingos may gather to breed in the saline shallows of the salt pan, when conditions are suitable, but tourists are not given access to the breeding colonies of these sensitive birds. Birds of prey are particularly well-represented, with martial eagle, black-breasted snake eagle, bateleur, pale chanting goshawk, pygmy falcon and red-necked falcon among the most arresting. Other frequently seen species are red-billed teal, Namaqua sandgrouse, Burchell's sandgrouse, kori bustard, purple roller and crimson-breasted shrike.

Roads run along the eastern, southern and western borders of the Etosha Pan. The area around Namutoni Camp, in the eastern part of the park, receives more rain than the other regions of the park. Eland, kudu and Damara dikdik are often seen in the area. A good spot to see elephant is at Olifantsbad, a water hole between Halali and Okaukuejo Camps.

At the floodlit water hole at Okaukuejo Camp, we witnessed an hour-long standoff between a black rhino and two elephants over control of the water hole.

From Okaukuejo you can drive along the southwestern edge of the pan to Okondeka and west to the Haunted Forest, a dense concentration of eerie-looking African moringa trees. Etosha is a 5-hour drive on good, paved roads or a 1-hour charter flight from Windhoek.

Travel on all roads inside the National Park is restricted to the hours between sunrise and sunset, all resort gates being closed and locked outside these times. During the year sunrise occurs between 6:00 and 7:00, and sunset between 5:30 and 7:30 in the evening, depending on the season.

ACCOMMODATION — CLASS A+: see "Ongava Game Reserve" below.

CLASS A: • **Onguma Plains** is situated on the 50,000-acre (20,000-hectare) Onguma Private Nature Reserve near von Lindequist Gate (eastern side of the park). The lodge has 11 air-conditioned mini-suites and 1 maxi-suite each with a music system, mini-bar, telephone and computer/internet facilities, en suite bathroom as well as an outside shower and wooden verandas. The main area

Andersson's Camp — One of the newest camps in Namibia

is a fort with a classical African feel combined with Moroccan and Indian elements, with upstairs viewing decks and conference facilities for up to 40 guests. • **Onguma Tented Camp** overlooks a floodlit waterhole and has 7 en suite tents with both an indoor and outdoor shower. Unfortunately no children under the age of 12 are permitted.

CLASS A/B: • The brand new **Andersson's Camp** is situated only 2.8 miles (4.5 km) from Andersson's Gate at the southern entrance into Etosha. The resurrected former farmstead has 20 tented en suite units on raised decks for enhanced views of the waterhole. Care has been taken at this camp to make it as environmentally friendly as possible. • **Mushara Lodge**, located on the eastern boundary of Etosha, has 10 chalets, 1 family unit and 2 single rooms, all with air-conditioning, mini-bar, telephones and en suite facilities. • **Mokuti Lodge**, located 500 yards (500 m) from the von Lindequist Gate, has 106 air-conditioned thatched bungalows with en suite facilities, a swimming pool and an airstrip. • **Naua Naua Lodge**, a 45 minute drive from Andersson Gate, has 10 rooms with en suite facilities, restaurant, pool and a bar facing a floodlit waterhole.

CLASS B: • **Onguma Bush Camp** is a rustic camp with 6 en suite air-conditioned luxury bungalows, and 1 family room. The camp is most used by self-drive tourists and families. • **Epacha Game Lodge & Spa**, situated approximately 43 miles (70 km) southwest of Etosha on its own 52,500-acre (21,000-hectare) reserve, has 18 luxury Hillside Chalets plus 1 presidential suite, as well as a spa and swimming pool. Its companion establishment, sitting elsewhere on the same reserve, is **Eagle Tented Lodge & Spa**, offering 8 luxury tents and also 8 standard tents, with a spa and swimming pool.

CLASS C: • **Etosha Aoba** accommodates up to 18 guests in thatched cottages with en suite facilities and is located 7 miles (12 km) from the von Lindequist Gate.

CLASS B, B/C, C & D: There are 3 **National Park camps**, all operated by Namibia Wildlife Resorts (NWR), a parastatal and the only company allowed to build and operate tourist establishments in Etosha. These are situated at Namutoni, Halali and Okaukuejo respectively. The 3 camps have all recently undergone massive refurbishment, and have lodge accommodations, trailer (caravan) and camping sites, swimming pool, floodlit water hole, restaurant, store, petrol station and landing strip. The camps are fenced for the visitors' protection. • **Namutoni Camp**, situated 7 miles (11 km) from the eastern von Lindequist Gate, features an attractive fortress built in 1904 and converted into a restaurant, with a viewing platform on the upper ramparts. • **Halali Camp**, the newest of the camps, lies halfway between Namutoni and Okaukuejo Camps at the foot of a dolomite hill. Most rooms now have private facilities. • **Okaukuejo Camp**, situated 11 miles (18 km) from the Andersson Gate entrance, has some delightful chalets with private facilities, especially those closest to the waterhole.

CAMPING: There is a huge choice for those wishing to camp. The 3 NWR resorts inside the Park (at Namutoni, Halali and Okaukuejo) all have plentiful facilities, but so do many of the lodges around the perimeter of Etosha.

Ongava Game Reserve

Ongava Game Reserve is a 115-square-mile (300-km²) private reserve along the southern boundary of Etosha near Andersson Gate. The reserve is the top privately-owned rhino breeding area in the country, currently with 10 black and 19 white rhino, along with high concentrations of a variety of game.

Night game drives and walks, which are not allowed in Etosha, are allowed on the reserve. Guests staying on the reserve usua lly take morning game drives in Etosha and take afternoon game drives or walks and night game drives in the reserve. Birdwatching is good. Some of the key Namibian "specials" to be seen here include Hartlaub's francolin, white-tailed shrike, Monteiro's hornbill and bare-cheeked babbler.

ACCOMMODATION — CLASS A+: • **Little Ongava** is situated within the Ongava Game Reserve, a private

Top: Zebras drinking at an Ongava waterhole
Bottom: A game drive at Ongava

Little Ongava's refreshing pool

75,000-acre (30,000-hectare) game reserve that is located adjacent to the southern boundary of Etosha National Park. The camp offers 3 spacious luxury suites each with its own plunge pool, en suite bathroom, a "sala", an additional outdoor shower and a view of the waterhole in front of the lodge. Guests at Little Ongava share a dedicated guide and 4wd vehicle ensuring the optimum nature experience.

CLASS A: • **Ongava Lodge**, situated on Ongava Game Reserve near Etosha's Andersson Gate, has 14 luxury air-conditioned rock-and-thatch chalets with en suite facilities, overlooks a flood-lit waterhole, and has a swimming pool and a hide. • **Ongava Tented Camp**, also located on the reserve, has 9 large tents with en suite facilities and a private water hole. Both Ongava Lodge and Ongava Tented Camp offer day and night game drives and walks on the reserve and day game drives in open-sided vehicles into Etosha.

Bushmanland

Tsumkwe, the unofficial capital of Bushmanland and home to the Bushmen (San) people, borders Botswana and is situated south of Khaudom and east of Grootfontein.

One of the village elders

The Ju/'hoansi people were the last independent hunters and gatherers in southern Africa, planting no crops and domesticating no animals until 1920. The 2000 or so Ju/'hoansi are now permanently settled in approximately 30 villages where they continue to hunt and gather within n!oresi — areas of 115 to 230 square miles (300 to 600 km) where different bands have rights to the natural resources. They also keep cattle and earn income through tourism and by selling traditional crafts. They speak the central of three dialects of !Kung — the language spoken by the northern Bushmen.

The Nyae Nyae Conservancy was formed in 1998 and gives the Ju/'hoansi the right to benefit from wildlife and tourism activities in the area. A 4wd vehicle is required to explore the area.

ACCOMMODATION — CLASS B/C: • **Tsumkwe Lodge** can accommodate up to 12 people in 6 thatched rooms with en suite facilities. From here, the Nyae Nyae (Bushman) area and the Khaudum Game Reserve 30 miles (50 km) to the north can be explored. • Guests at **Nhoma Camp**, located 50 miles (80 km) west of Tsumkwe, are introduced to the cultures and traditions of the Ju/'hoansi San. The Ju/'hoansi show guests how they gather food and introduce them to many of their customs and beliefs. You see the San just as they really exist in their traditional villages. Access to the camp is by road and air charter.

Khaudum Game Reserve

Situated in the extreme northeast section of the country on the Botswana border, Khaudum National Park covers 1,483-square-miles (3,841-km²), primarily of Kalahari sand dunes and dry woodland savannah. This is one of the most remote and least visited reserves in Namibia.

Mammal species include elephant, lion, leopard, side-striped jackal, African wild dog, giraffe, wildebeest, eland, kudu, roan antelope and sable antelope.

During the dry season (June to October), game viewing can be good, especially at springs and water holes lying along dry riverbeds, which serve as "roads." However, wildlife is not nearly as concentrated as in Etosha National Park. Khaudum should be visited by primarily those seeking a wilderness experience in a reserve that they will most likely have to themselves.

The birdlife in the Park is thrilling, with some 320 species listed, such as martial and tawny eagles, white-backed vultures, southern yellow-billed hornbills, black kites, sharp-tailed starlings, and fork-tailed drongos. Birdlife is most interesting between January and April, when aquatic species are attracted to the rain-filled pan systems. Large numbers

Top: A Bushman heads out to hunt springhare
Middle: Tracking the game
Bottom: A successful hunt!

of knob-billed duck, open-billed stork, black-winged stilt and glossy ibis, to name just a few, crowd the productive waterholes. Palearctic migrants can be numerous in some years, as can be sandpipers, pratincoles and harriers.

Access to the park is from Tsumkwe in the south or Katere in the north. A minimum of two 4wd vehicles are required for each party visiting the reserve.

ACCOMMODATION — CLASS F and CAMPING: • **Sikareti**, located in the south of the reserve, has campsites and remnants of some thatched huts. • **Khaudum**, situated in the north of the park 43 miles (70 km) from Sikareti, has two rustic huts. Tourists must be totally self-sufficient

Waterberg Plateau Park

Situated south of Etosha National Park and east of the town of Otijiwarongo, this 156-square-mile (400-km²) park is the home of several scarce and endangered species, including black rhino, white rhino, roan antelope and sable antelope. Other species include brown hyena, eland, tsessebe, kudu, gemsbok, giraffe, impala, klipspringer and dikdik. Leopard are sometimes seen on the top of the plateau.

This is a prime area for seeing many of Namibia's near-endemic bird species, and a Mecca for birdwatchers from across the world. Hartlaub's francolin, Ruppell's parrot, white-tailed shrike, Monteiro's hornbill, rockrunner, bare-cheeked babbler and Bradfield's swift are all resident.

Waterberg Plateau Park also contains unique flora, along with rock paintings and engravings. Three trails lead up to the top of the sandstone plateau, which rises over 820 feet (300 m) above the surrounding plains, and one runs across the top. Walking on the plateau is restricted to organized, guided walking trails.

ACCOMMODATION — CLASS B: • **The Waterberg Camp**, operated by NWR, (formerly named the *Bernabe de la Bat Rest Camp*), accommodates guests in comfortable premier bush chalets, and 2- and 4-bed bush chalets and double rooms, all nestled along the base of the Waterberg Plateau cliffs. There is a swimming pool, and a restaurant and bar in the restored Rasthaus, built in 1908. • **Mount Etjo Safari Lodge** has comfortably furnished en suite rooms. The main lodge area overlooks a water hole.

ACCOMMODATION NEAR WATERBERG — CLASS B: • **Okonjima Lodge** is family-run and located on a private game reserve and has 10 comfortable, en suite rooms. The farm is the home of the AfriCat Foundation, which is committed to the long-term conservation of large carnivores, particularly cheetah and leopard. Their **Bush Camp** has 8 luxury, thatched African-style chalets, while the **Bush Suite** privately caters for 4. All 3 lodges have their own pools. Activities include walks and watching orphaned wild animals, adopted by the family, roam freely about the farm. • **African Wilderness Trails** is a farmstead with 5 en suite rooms, swimming pool and sauna. Game drives, hikes, and trips to the Waterberg Plateau Park and The Cheetah Conservation Fund project are offered. • **Waterberg Guest Farm** is a 103,784-acre (42,000 hectare) estate with 4 double guest rooms and 2 luxury bush bungalows, a pool and a floodlit waterhole.

CAMPING: Campsites with an ablution block are available at Waterberg Camp.

THE EAST

The Caprivi Region

The Caprivi Region of northeastern Namibia has long been very different from the rest of the mostly semiarid Namibian countryside, not only in terms of its river systems and wetlands, its vegetation, woodlands, weather patterns, game and birdlife, but even in its geographic make-up and the character of the traditional peoples who live in this unique area.

The Caprivi Region was known until the end of the nineteenth century as Itenga, meaning "separate" in the Zalamo dialect of Tanganyika, now Tanzania. And it's an accurate description for this finger of land measuring only 298 miles (480 kms) in length and from 20 miles (32 kms) to 62 miles (100 kms) in width. The Caprivi has always been set apart from the rest of the country. To its north lies Angola and Zambia, while Botswana borders it to the south and east and Zimbabwe just touches the eastern extremity.

The Caprivi Region measures some 7,720-square-miles (20,000-km²) in size and benefits from several perennial rivers running through its territories, making it a diverse wetlands paradise.

Much of the wildlife in this region has been poached, especially during the conflict with Angola. However, wildlife populations are increasing, and the Caprivi is well worth a visit for anyone looking for a wilderness experience first, with wildlife as a bonus.

Mudumu National Park and Mamili National Park are similar to Botswana's Okavango Delta. Over 400 species of birds have been recorded in the region.

Bwabwata National Park

Newly proclaimed in 2007, Bwabwata National Park covers 2,432-square-miles (6,300-km²) and incorporates the former West Caprivi Game Reserve plus Mahango and the Core Conservation Area at Buffalo — all the land up to the Kwando River. Settlements of indigenous peoples are allowed to remain within the new park at Omega and Chetto. Nearby **Popa Falls** features rapids (more so than "falls") of the Kavango River, which has numerous hippo and crocs.

Wildlife includes elephant, hippo, crocs, buffalo, waterbuck, lechwe, reedbuck, bushbuck, kudu, tsessebe, impala and the rare sitatunga. Bird life includes fish eagle, wattled crane, crowned crane and African skimmer. Four-wheel-drive vehicles are required to explore the most remote regions of the park, but 2wd vehicles may be used on the main route.

ACCOMMODATION IN CAPRIVI — CLASS A/B: • **Divava Okavango Lodge & Spa** offers 20 luxurious chalets, bush bar, restaurant, swimming pool and a viewing deck overlooking the Okavango River. Boat cruises to the Popa Falls and excursions to the Mahango section of Bwabwata National Park are offered. • **Ndhovu Safari Lodge**, situated close to the Popa Falls on the Okavango River, is just 1.5 miles (2 km) from Mahango, has 6 tents with en suite bathrooms, 2 wooden chalets, restaurant and bar. There is a "river tent" on the water for the adventurous! Boats are available for hire.

CLASS B & C: • **Ngepi Camp** has some tree-house chalets and some bush huts, all close to the river itself. There is a central bar and an intriguing caged swimming pool.

CLASS D: • **The Popa Falls Resort**, another of the parastatal NWR's establishments, offers some rustic thatched chalets with separate toilets and showers, located about 10 miles (16 km) north of Mahango.

CAMPING: • **Ngepi Camp** offers great riverside campsites. • The rustic **N//goabaca Community Campsite** is run by the local Khwe San of West Caprivi under the auspices of the Kyaramacan Trust. There are 4 large sites, some with wooden decks overlooking the Falls. From here is by far the best access to and views of the Popa Falls. There are full ablution facilities available. • **NWR Popa Falls** and **Ndhovu Safari Lodge** offer full camping facilities as well.

Kwando Region

The waters of the Kwando River, its banks with plentiful reed and papyrus beds and surrounding savannah are home to a wonderful array of wild and aquatic life and especially bird life. Small, scattered communities of the indigenous Mafwe people do their best to eke out a rudimentary but crucial living from the harsh splendor all around them.

The Kwando River is a real enigma. As it nears the Linyanti Swamps further to the east, the river becomes known as the Linyanti. Further toward its confluence with the Zambezi, it is re-titled the Chobe River. If the Zambezi is full and running fast, its waters will actually force the Chobe to back up and even flow back toward the Linyanti, thus linking with the Kwando itself. Should levels be so high as to fill Lake Liambezi, dry now since 1997, that route would also link the Kwando and Zambezi as well.

Permits available at the Susuwe Ranger Station close to Kongola or from the MET offices in Katima Mulilo will allow you to enter and enjoy the stunning scenery, wildlife and bird life of the eastern extremities of Bwabwata National Park, all close to the Kwando. A 4wd vehicle here is a necessity. A particularly awesome experience is to visit the "Horseshoe Bend" on the Kwando River; allow a half day (preferably afternoon, toward sunset) to reach this natural curve on the river. You may see elephant, sometimes in big numbers, buffalo and a number of antelope species along with myriad warblers, weavers and coucals.

ACCOMMODATION IN CAPRIVI (KWANDO AREA) CLASS A: • **Susuwe Island Lodge** is set on an island in the Kwando and provides 6 spacious brick and thatch suites equipped with double bathroom, bedroom, lounge and wooden viewing deck each with private plunge pool. Activities include boat trips, nature walks and game drives into Bwabwata National Park.

CLASS A/B: • **Camp Kwando** has 12 thatched tents alongside the river and 3 luxurious tree bungalows on higher ground. All accommodation is en suite. There is a swimming pool. Campsites are also available.

CLASS B: • **Namushasha Country Lodge** has 27 en suite bungalows, a small pool, bar, sundowner deck, curio shop and buffet restaurant.

CAMPING: • **Nambwa Campsite**, located in the park itself, has ablutions and is located on the Mashi River. • **Bum Hill Campsite** has some wonderful elevated camping decks allowing great views of the Kwando River and surrounding flood plains.

Mudumu National Park

This small 31-square-mile (80-km^2) park of forests, floodplains, islands and bush is similar to the Okavango Delta (Botswana), but with less game. The Kwando River runs along the park's western border.

While on walks on a recent visit we encountered elephant, impala and a number of other species. Other wildlife includes lion, hippo, crocs, roan antelope and sitatunga. Giraffe have been recently reintroduced.

Birdwatching is tremendous. Coppery-tailed coucal, slaty egret, greater swamp warbler, swamp boubou and brown firefinch are all resident, and flocks of migratory carmine

Lianshulu Lodge

Game viewing by boat from Lianshulu

and blue-cheeked bee-eaters may be seen between December and April.

Traditional villages operated by the local communities lie to either side of the park boundaries. Game viewing by open vehicle and walks are allowed. Four-wheel-drive vehicles are recommended.

ACCOMMODATION — *Lianshulu Lodge* and its sister lodge, *Lianshulu Bush Lodge*, are located on the banks of the Kwando River. Lianshulu has its own Namibian Border Post which allows guests to check out of Namibia, take a 45 minute boat ride down the Kwando/Linyanti River and embark into Botswana on the other bank at Kwando Lagoon Camp — making these great camps to add to a Botswana safari itinerary.

CLASS A: • **Lianshulu Lodge** has 10 thatched chalets (doubles) and 1 honeymoon suite, all with en suite facilities, and a swimming pool.

CLASS A/B • **Lianshulu Bush Lodge** has 8 rooms with en suite bathrooms. Activities include game drives, walks, game viewing by boat, sunset cruises on a double-decker barge and excursions to Mamili National Park. Access is by scheduled flights to Mpacha, air charter and by road.

CAMPING: Basic campsites with no facilities are available in the reserve.

Mamili National Park

This newly proclaimed park is predominantly floodplain and has similar wildlife as Mudumu National Park. The Linyanti River flows along its southeastern border, which it shares with Botswana. For those in search of a real wilderness experience, Mamili is the Caprivi's best kept secret.

Mamili National Park is predominantly wetlands where you may see hippo, and crocs, red lechwe, waterbuck, reedbuck and if you're really fortunate, the elusive sitatunga.

The bird life in the region includes Pels fishing owl on Impalila Island, wattled cranes in the Linyanti Swamps, iridescent carmine bee-eaters prevalent near the Zambezi, various sunbirds of the forests, the possibility of sighting a rosy-throated longclaw on the flood plains and the hauntingly striking cry of the African fish eagle above the Chobe and elsewhere.

ACCOMMODATION — CLASS B: • **Caprivi River Lodge** has 8 air-conditioned, en suite chalets and 3 more basic wooden cabins, and offers boating activities and excursions to the nearby Mamili National Park.

CLASS B/C: • **Island View Lodge**, overlooking Kalimbeza Island on a backwater of the Zambezi, offers accommodation in rustic thatch-roofed bungalows. • **Caprivi Houseboat Safaris**, based in Katima Mulilo, offer scenic, guided boating all the way to the Chobe. They have 3 waterside chalets for use before or after your trip.

CAMPING: Basic campsites with no facilities are available in the reserve. Camping is offered at **Caprivi River Lodge** and **Island View Lodge**, both with full facilities.

ACCOMMODATION IN CAPRIVI (ZAMBEZI AREA) — These properties are most easily accessed from the Kasane area of Botswana as they are near Chobe National Park.

CLASS A: • **Ntwala Island Lodge** offers 4 ultra-luxurious suites with en suite facilities, private plunge pools fringed by white sand and a viewing deck, outdoor bath and private sala. Game viewing is by private boat.

CLASS B: • **Impalila Island Lodge**, situated on an island with huge baobab trees, has 8 luxury en suite chalets. Activities include a guided walk to reputedly the only spot in the world where 4 different countries meet, river trips, fishing or simply relaxing poolside.

THE SOUTH

Intu Afrika

Situated near the town of Mariental, about a 3-hour drive south of Windhoek, Intu Afrika offers an insight into Bushman culture. A Bushman tracker takes guests into the Kalahari and shares secrets on survival in the bush. The walk usually covers less than a mile (1 km), and afterward guests may be taken to visit the tracker's family. Guests are also shown how the Bushmen make curios and weapons. Please note that this is not a pure bushman experience by any means — more of a commercial enterprise.

ACCOMMODATION — Class A/B: • **Dune Lodge** consists of 5 luxury chalets with en suite bathrooms and lounge area. A private game ranger is included.

CLASS B: • **Zebra/Main Lodge** consists of 8 air-conditioned colonial-type rooms with bathrooms en suite.

CLASS B/C: • **Camelthorn Lodge** has 10 bungalows situated about a 10-minute walk away from the Zebra/Main Lodge. Each bungalow has an en suite bathroom with shower and flush toilets, and electricity.

CLASS C: • **Surricate Camp** has bungalows with en suite open-air bathrooms with bath and shower and flush toilets. Each tent has electricity. Game drives and Bushman excursions are offered.

Ai-Ais/Richtersveld Transfrontier Park

In the south, August 2003 saw Namibia's Ai-Ais Hot Springs Resort and Fish River Canyon areas combine with South Africa's Richtersveld area to become the Ai-Ais / Richtersveld Transfrontier Park.

Second in size only to the Grand Canyon, **Fish River Canyon** is 100 miles (161 km) in length, up to 17 miles (27 km) in width and up to 1,800 feet (550 m) deep. The Fish River cuts its way through the canyon to the Orange River, which empties into the Atlantic Ocean.

The vegetation and wildlife are very interesting. Many red aloes make the area appear like you might imagine the planet Mars. Baboons, mountain zebra, rock hyrax, ground squirrel and klipspringer are often seen, while kudu and leopard remain elusive. The river water is cold and deep enough to swim in some areas.

There is a well-marked path into the canyon in the north of the park where the 4-day hike begins. For those hiking into the canyon for the day, allow 45 to 60 minutes down and 90 minutes back up. Permission to walk down to the canyon floor must first be obtained from the ranger at Hobas.

The main hiking trail is 53 miles (86 km) in length; due to possibly extreme summer temperatures and the risk of flash flooding, the hike is only open from the beginning of May until mid-September. It is also only recommended for those who are extremely fit, and you must have a doctor's certificate of fitness in order to obtain your permit. Advance bookings are necessary, and there must be a minimum of 3 per group. The going is tough because much of the walking is on the sandy, rock-strewn floor of the canyon. No facilities whatsoever exist en route, so this hike is not for the tenderfoot. Water is readily available (but do take purification tablets) from the many pools that join up to become a river during the rainy summers, but you must carry your own food supplies. Hot sulphur springs are located at Palm Springs, about halfway along the trail. The hike does represent a challenge to participants, but also a wonderful experience in the most remote nature imaginable.

ACCOMMODATION — CLASS A/B: • **Gondwana Canon Lodge**, located just 12 miles (20 km) from the main Canyon viewpoint at Hobas, has 28 thatched bungalows with en suite facilities, blending beautifully into their surroundings of massive granite boulders.

CLASS B: • **Vogelstrausskluft Lodge** is situated on the western rim of the Canyon, and offers 4 luxury suites as well as 20 twin rooms.

CLASS C: • **Canon Roadhouse** offers 9 en suite rooms, swimming pool and filling station. • **The Ai-Ais Hot Springs Resort**, operated by NWR, is located at the southern end of the canyon at the end of the hiking trail and boasts a large thermally-heated swimming pool and mineral baths.

CAMPING: • **Ai-Ais** campsites have hot showers. • **Hobas** campsite, located at the trailhead in the north of the park, has hot showers and a swimming pool. • The campsite at the **Canon Roadhouse** has just been extended and offers full camping facilities.

The "Green" Kalahari

The ancestral home of mankind's earliest forebears, the San (Bushmen), the Kalahari is a pristine, wildlife paradise, certainly one of Africa's most special wilderness frontiers.

This unique semi-desert area covers a vast 965,250-square-miles (2.5 million-km^2), spreading across nine countries in all. With its long hot summers, unpredictable rainfall, sandy, porous soils and resultant scarcity of surface water, little wonder that it has over the millennia earned its stirring pseudonym — "The Thirstland".

This huge sand mass is exemplified by primordial red dune lands stretching in parallel from southeast to northwest. Strips of grass studded with magnificent camelthorn trees (*Acacia erioloba*) and wrapped in vegetation unique to the Kalahari are commonly referred to as "The Streets". These separate the dunes and provide vital refuge and sustenance to a remarkable diversity of both wildlife and bird life.

Cheetah – one of the big cats of the "Green" Kalahari

Travel between Namibia, South Africa and Botswana in this Kalahari region has been hugely encouraged and eased as of October 2007 by the opening of the Mata Mata Gate to the **Kgalagadi Transfrontier Park**. It is for the use of bona-fide tourists only and visitors must book a minimum of a two night stay in the Kgalagadi Park on the South African side. The lodges listed below are located about a half day drive from the Mata Mata Gate.

Game species that may well be seen in the area include oryx, kudu, blue wildebeest, red hartebeest, springbok, steenbok, ostrich, eland, Burchell's Plains Zebra and giraffe. Felines will include lion, cheetah and perhaps

Top: Guests at Bagatelle enjoy dinners in the boma
Middle: Bagatelle Dune Chalet
Bottom: One of the chalets at Bagatelle

leopard. Raptors abound here in the Kalahari, especially martial, brown snake, black-breasted snake and bateleur eagles; you may also spot a number of pale chanting goshawks, and lappet faced vultures, perhaps even a pygmy falcon.

ACCOMMODATION — CLASS A/B:
• **Bagatelle Kalahari Game Ranch** is an exquisite boutique-style lodge with 4 chalets raised on stilts atop a Kalahari dune. Six intriguing Strohbale (Straw Bale) chalets complete the accommodation. These latter chalets have straw compressed between the structural walls, rendering them cool in summer and warm in winter. All rooms are en suite and air-conditioned; there is also a restaurant, pool, library and a well-stocked wine cellar! • **Guest Farm Kiripotib** sits on the extreme edge of the Kalahari, a 2-hour drive from Windhoek. There are 2 beautifully furnished chalets and 3 guest rooms and pool. Activities include the Kiripotib Farm Workshop, touring the farm, guided mountain hikes, savannah trails and stargazing on a visit to a private Observatory nearby.

South Africa

South Africa

At the southern end of the continent, South Africa is an extremely diverse country with temperate highlands, subtropical savannah, alpine-like mountains, semi-desert and unique Mediterranean-like shrub lands known as "fynbos". Much of the country is a high plateau averaging some 4,800 feet (1,500 m) above sea level, with the Drakensberg rising to 11,400 feet (3,450 m). The country is flanked by the cool Atlantic and warm Indian Oceans, each of which has a strong bearing on the climate. South Africa is the most industrialized nation on the continent but still has large protected areas including the famous Kruger National Park and surrounding areas which occupy most of the lowveld. Covering some 471,445-square-miles (1.2 million-km²), South Africa is twice the size of Texas. English is the official language, with Zulu, Tswana, Xhosa, Sotho and Afrikaans all widely spoken. The population is estimated at around 45 million. Pretoria and Cape Town are the capital cities but Johannesburg is the business hub. Currency is the Rand (ZAR).

South Africa
Country Highlights

- Visit one or more of the Private Game Reserves in Sabi Sand and Thornybush (near Kruger) that South Africa is so famous for. You'll have the opportunity to possibly see the "Big Five" on your first game drive! Bring a good camera and get ready for epic leopard shots!
- Take a five-star trip back in history and travel in style aboard the Blue Train or Rovos Rail.
- Spend time in Cape Town, one of the world's most beautiful cities.
- Travel up the Garden Route, stopping in charming towns like Hermanus, as well as up South Africa's diverse coast for whale watching and perhaps for a glimpse at a great white shark.
- Experience the finest wines and cuisine available on the continent.

Best Parks and Reserves to Visit	Best Times to Go
Private Game Reserves near Kruger	Excellent year round (best June to November)
Phinda	May to October; good year-round
Kwandwe, Shamwari	September to April; good year-round

Best Accommodations (Safari camps or lodges):
Singita Lebombo, Singita Sweni Lodge, Singita Boulders Lodge, Singita Ebony Lodge, Londolozi Private Granite Suites, Londolozi Tree Camp, Rattray's on MalaMala, Lion Sands Ivory Lodge, Earth Lodge, Ulusaba Rock Lodge, Royal Malewane, Mateya Safari Lodge, Royal Madikwe, Getty House, Phinda Rock Lodge, Phinda Vlei Lodge

SOUTH AFRICA

South Africa is commonly promoted as "The Rainbow Nation" and "A World In One Country", and with two oceans, subtropical savannah, arid scrubland, deserts, and the impressive Drakensberg Mountains, this is hard to deny. This large country is rich in natural beauty and wildlife diversity and covers about 4% of the continent's land surface. The southwestern corner (Cape Town and surroundings) is climatically and botanically unique. The country consists of a high-altitude central plateau surrounded by a rim of mountains, which are particularly impressive in the KwaZulu-Natal Drakensberg. Think of an inverted soup bowl, and you will have a rough idea of the country's landscape.

The plateau is temperate in climate, and it is there that most people live and where agriculture is most developed. In the south, the coastal plain is very narrow or non-existent, with cliffs often plunging directly into the sea. In the east, the lowlands are more extensive, most notably in the warm lowveld with the Kruger National Park and its rich wildlife. The country's largest river is the Orange, which rises in Lesotho and meanders some 1,400 miles (2,200 km) west to spill out into the Atlantic Ocean. A number of large rivers drain to the east into the Indian Ocean, predominantly the Limpopo, Olifants, Sabie, Komati, Umfolozi, Tugela and Kei.

There are three distinct climatic zones within South Africa. The entire central plateau and eastern parts, (including the lowveld) experience summer rainfall (October to March). It is warm to hot (depending upon altitude) in summer and cool to warm during winter (May to August). Nights can be cold, even at lower altitudes, in mid-winter. The southwestern corner, including Cape Town, experiences dry, warm summers and cool, wet winters — a Mediterranean climate not unlike California or southern France. The region east of the southwestern Cape, extending along the coast to East London, experiences rainfall throughout the year, but is prone to drought conditions.

Seventy percent of the population belongs to four ethnic groups: Zulu (the largest), Xhosa, Tswana and Bapedi. Fifteen percent of the population is white, of which 60% is Afrikaner. English and Afrikaans are spoken throughout the country.

In 1488 Portuguese navigator Bartholomew Dias discovered the Cape of Good Hope. The first Dutch settlers arrived in 1652 and the first British settlers in 1820. To escape British rule, Boer (which means farmer) Voortrekkers (forward marchers) moved from Cape Town to the north and east, establishing the independent Republic of the Transvaal and Orange Free State.

Two very big economic breakthroughs were the discovery of diamonds in 1869 and, even more importantly, the discovery of gold in Transvaal shortly thereafter. Conflict between the British and Boers resulted in two separate Anglo-Boer Wars beginning in 1899 and the ultimate British victory in 1902.

In 1910 the Union of South Africa was formed and remained a member of the British Commonwealth until May 31, 1961, when the Republic of South Africa was formed outside the British Commonwealth. On April 27, 1994, a national election open to all races was held and was won by the African National Congress (ANC) under the charismatic leadership of Nelson Mandela. Since that time, South Africa has been welcomed back into the international fold, and tourism has increased dramatically.

🐾 WILDLIFE AND WILDLIFE AREAS

In line with its numerous distinct geographic, altitudinal and climatic zones, South Africa supports a great diversity of wildlife and plants. In fact, well over 10% of all the world's plants and flowers occur in South Africa. Virtually all of Africa's great land mammals are to be found (mostly in the eastern lowlands), as well as whales, dolphins and other marine species in the surrounding oceans. In many places, large mammals have been reintroduced to locations where they were once hunted to extinction, with the white rhinoceros being perhaps the biggest success story.

Birdlife is outstanding throughout the country, with some 600 breeding species and close to 800 overall, including Eurasian migrants and seabirds. A good number of bird species are endemic (restricted) to South Africa, particularly in the Karoo, highveld grasslands and Cape fynbos regions, making this a highly popular destination among international birdwatchers.

Reptiles, frogs and other life forms are equally well represented. The Cape fynbos region is home to an astonishing 8,500 plant species and is considered to be one of the world's eight Floristic Regions. The plants in this winter

A safarier's favorite — the lilac breasted roller

rainfall area are characterized by relatively small leaves and include many varieties of erica and protea. The Karoo is a semi-arid scrubland, but it is a botanist's dream because of its astonishing number of hardy and succulent plants. The much-celebrated Namaqualand region is renowned for its springtime (late August to early September) displays of colorful flowers. True forests are sparse in South Africa, with only small patches on the southern coast near Knysna and Transkei, and along the Northern KwaZulu-Natal coast and in the eastern escarpment. Acacia, combretum and mopane dominate the sub-tropical lowlands, with taller, evergreen trees along rivers and watercourses.

South Africa has a good network of protected areas, with over 700 publicly owned reserves (including 19 national parks), which cover about 6% of the land surface. In addition to that, there are about 200 private game and wildlife reserves. The Kruger National Park is the largest park, and together with the second largest (Kgalagadi Transfrontier Park), accounts for about 40% of the total protected

A full mane lion pauses for a drink

area. The great majority of the other parks and sanctuaries are quite small.

In recent years, South Africa has been the primary catalyst for a number of proposed Transfrontier Conservation Areas (TFCAs), which link protected areas across national boundaries and form "corridors" to link separated parks. The idea is to have multi-use areas, which incorporate the needs of local people while safeguarding the natural resources over a larger area. The first of these areas to be formally promulgated was the Kgalagadi National Park, which is shared with Botswana, to embrace the Kalahari Gemsbok National Park. Other TFCAs are in various stages of negotiation and development in Mozambique, Swaziland, Namibia and Zimbabwe.

In many private reserves, seeing a white rhino is almost a guarantee

The Kruger and other national parks are frankly not well suited to international visitors with limited vacation time. They are ideally suited to self-drive visitors on tight budgets with lots of time, and are most popular with South African holiday-makers and larger coach-tour (40+ tourists) groups. Open vehicles are generally not allowed, although a few local companies are now allowed open sided and canvas-roofed vehicles. Visitors are required to stick to a designated road and track network.

Accommodation is mostly at large rest camps, although there are some smaller bush camps. Most campsites have ablution blocks (communal bathrooms) with hot and cold water, and many sites even have laundry facilities. Generally speaking, the major roads in the parks are tarred and the minor roads are constructed of good quality gravel, allowing for comfortable riding — and mass tourism.

In contrast, a number of **private reserves** offer premier accommodation, superb food, day and night game drives in open vehicles and escorted walks. Leopard, lion and other animals have become accustomed to game viewing vehicles at several of these comparatively small reserves, and local guides often know the territories or whereabouts of particular animals, which ensures more predictable and intimate encounters. Trained guides and trackers interpret the wildlife and ecosystem for guests. In a move toward partial privatization, the

Kruger has recently allocated sites within the park for experienced operators to set up and manage more exclusive camps and lodges.

GAUTENG

Johannesburg

Johannesburg began as a mining town when the largest deposits of gold in the world were discovered in the Witwatersrand in 1886. Since the Middle Ages, one-third of the gold mined in the world has come from the Witwatersrand field.

This "City of Gold," locally known as "Egoli," is now the country's largest commercial center and city and the country's main gateway for overseas visitors. The city itself has a population of approximately 2 million, while the total urban area including **Soweto** (**SO**uth **WE**stern **TO**wnships) has a population of approximately 4 million. Attractions include the **Museum Africa**, the **Gold Mine Museum** and **Gold Reef City**, a reconstruction of Johannesburg at the turn of the century, "**Cradle of Mankind**" anthropological excursions, and the **De Wildt Cheetah Centre**.

ACCOMMODATION — DELUXE: • **The Saxon Hotel**, located in the Sandhurst suburb of Sandton, makes a world-class statement of ethnic African elegance. Set in 6 acres (2.5 hectares) of lush landscaped gardens, there are 24 suites overlooking the gardens. • **The Grace in Rosebank**, located in Rosebank adjacent to The Mall, is surrounded by a variety of restaurants, boutiques and craft markets. The hotel has 73 rooms with en suite facilities, restaurant, sitting

One of the Egoli Suites at the Saxon

room with library and complimentary café and informal evening wine tasting, heated swimming pool and business center. A walkway connects the hotel directly to The Mall shopping center. • **The Michelangelo**, located on Nelson Mandela Square has 242 rooms with en suite facilities, restaurants, a heated swimming pool, steam bath, fitness center, business center and direct access to one of South Africa's best malls. • **The Westcliff Hotel**, set on a hilltop overlooking the city and zoo, has 115 rooms and suites with private facilities, a business center, spa facility and a swimming pool. Some of the

suites have private swimming pools.
• **InterContinental Johannesburg Airport Sun** is located right across from arrivals and departures at the airport, and it features a restaurant, bar, fitness center and indoor pool.
• **InterContinental Sandton Sun & Towers** is located adjacent to one of the country's finest shopping malls. The hotel has 564 air-conditioned rooms with en suite facilities and refrigerators; there is also a health club, swimming pool and five restaurants. • **Park Hyatt Johannesburg**, located in the suburb of Rosebank, has 224 rooms and suites with en suite facilities, a heated swimming pool, sauna, steam rooms and a gymnasium • **InterContinental Palazzo-Johannesburg Montecasino**, located in the heart of the Montecasino entertainment complex in the northern suburb of Fourways, has 246 rooms with en suite facilities.

Top: The Westcliff Hotel, framed by the beautiful jacaranda trees
Bottom: A dip in the Westcliff's pool is the perfect cure for jet lag

FIRST CLASS: • **D'Oreale Grand Hotel**, located a 5-minute drive from Johannesburg International Airport, has 196 air-conditioned rooms with en suite bathrooms in palatial-style buildings, with a health spa, tennis courts, swimming pool, bars and restaurants. • **Protea Hotel Balalaika**, located in Sandton, has 330 rooms with en suite facilities. • **Sandton Holiday Inn** has 249 rooms with en suite facilities. • **Southern Sun O.R. Tambo International Airport** has 366 air-conditioned rooms with en suite facilities and a swimming pool.

TOURIST CLASS: • **Metcourt Laurel** has 80 air-conditioned en suite rooms. Guests may use the facilities at The Emperor Hotel. • **Garden Court O.R. Tambo International Airport**, located less than a mile from Johannesburg International Airport, has 253 air-conditioned rooms with facilities en suite, a swimming pool and a sauna. • **City Lodges** have simple rooms with en suite facilities. • **The Airport Grand**, just three miles from the international airport has 149 air-conditioned en suite rooms, dining room, bar and guest swimming pool.

ACCOMMODATION NEAR JOHANNESBURG — DELUXE: • **Mount Grace Country House Hotel**, located in Magaliesburg less than an hour's drive from Johannesburg, has 80 luxuriously appointed rooms with en suite facilities, swimming pools, a tennis court, lawn bowling, a croquet lawn, walking trail, and a world-class spa. Other activities include horseback riding, mountain biking and fly-fishing. • **De Hoek Country House** lies in a serene country setting and is located an hour from Johannesburg and Pretoria. The hotel is built of sandstone and offers 20 luxurious rooms with 16 of the Superior suites overlooking the Magalies River.

FIRST CLASS: • **Kloofzicht Lodge** in Muldersdrift offers 42 suites with en suite facilities, each with great views over the Zwartkops Mountains. Activities offered include fly fishing, archery, hot-air ballooning, guided nature walks, hiking trails, game viewing and bird watching.

Pretoria

Pretoria is an attractive city and the administrative capital of South Africa. Points of interest include **Paul Kruger's house**, **Voortrekker Monument**, **Natural History (Transvaal) Museum**, **Union Buildings**, the **State Opera House** and **Church Square**.

ACCOMMODATION — DELUXE: • **Kievits Kroon Country Estate**, located 10 minutes north of Pretoria, is a Cape-Dutch themed hotel with 99 en suite rooms, 3 restaurants, swimming pool and conference facilities. The Wellness Centre has a heated pool, jacuzzis, sauna, steam bath, gym and health bar. • **Sheraton Pretoria Hotel & Towers**, set opposite the Union Buildings in Pretoria, has 175 en suite rooms in the Hotel section and 7 suites in the Towers section. • **Illyria House** is a privately owned residence in an exclusive suburb of Pretoria with 6 rooms with en suite facilities. • **Kloof House**, located in the suburb of Waterkloof, has 7 rooms with en suite or private facilities.

FIRST CLASS: • **Court Classique**, located in Arcadia (Pretoria), has rooms ranging from studios to 2-bedroom suites with kitchenettes and en suite bathrooms. • **Centurion Lake Hotel**, located outside Pretoria on a lake, has 160 rooms with en suite facilities.

TOURIST CLASS: • **Southern Sun Pretoria** (Formerly the *Holiday Inn Pretoria*) has 242 rooms and suites with en suite facilities and a swimming pool.

The Blue Train

The world-renowned luxurious Blue Train offers an experience that has all but disappeared in modern times. The train is promoted as "A Five-Star Hotel on Wheels," and that it is.

Two Blue Trains were built in South Africa and put into service in 1972. The suites have individual air-conditioning controls, television, radio and en suite bathrooms with shower or bathtub. The luxury compartments are only about 3 feet (1 m) wider than the deluxe cabins and also contain CD and video players. A staff of thirty-four is onboard to take care of guests.

The Blue Train rolls past Table Mountain

Five-star meals (two sittings for lunch and dinner) are served in the beautifully appointed dining car, which features exquisite table settings. Dress for lunch is "smart casual," and for dinner a jacket and tie are required for men and elegant dress for ladies.

The train runs overnight from Cape Town to Pretoria on average 3 times a week, and vice versa, year-round, and periodically there are special routings (such as Pretoria to Durban). Book well in advance because reservations are often difficult to obtain.

Rovos Rail

Rovos Rail has 5 restored luxury steam trains, each with 20 coaches accommodating up to 72 passengers, 2 dining cars and an observation car. Please note that the journeys are not all "steam-hauled". Every effort is made to use steam for at least a portion of the trip, usually arriving or departing Pretoria. The Deluxe Suites have en suite showers, while the Royal Suites have en suite showers and Victorian baths. Royal Suites are about 50% larger than Deluxe Suites. Rovos Rail recently introduced Pullman Suites to its range of accommodations. These are significantly smaller than the Deluxe Suites, however, they are a lot more affordable. Jacket and tie are required for men and elegant dress for ladies at dinner.

On our journey we enjoyed the magical atmosphere of this restored vintage steam train and the scenery enroute, along with quality wines and 5-star dining.

You have the choice of a two-night trip from Pretoria to Cape Town

The elegant Observation car of Rovos Rail

with a sightseeing stop in the old mining town of Kimberley and in the quaint village of Matjiesfontein; a two-night trip from Pretoria to see Victoria Falls; a two-night trip from Pretoria to Komatipoort (game drive in Kruger National Park), continuing to Swaziland (game drive in Mkhaya Game Reserve) and Zululand (game drive in Hluhluwe Umfolozi) ending in Durban; overnight trip along the Garden Route from Cape Town to Knysna via George; an annual six-night safari from Pretoria to Kimberley, Upington, Windhoek and Swakopmund (Namibia); and a once-a-year, 13-night safari from Cape Town to Dar es Salaam (Tanzania), and vice versa. Another annual favorite is the 8-night African Collage linking some of South Africa's scenic highlights between Pretoria and Cape Town including Kruger National Park, Swaziland, Durban, the Drakensberg Mountains and the lovely Garden Route.

MPUMALANGA AND LIMPOPO PROVINCES

Kruger and The Private Reserves

The most popular area in the country for wildlife safaris for international visitors is the private reserves that lie along Kruger National Park's western border.

There is a tremendous difference in the variety and quality of experience between visiting Kruger National Park and staying in the National Park rest camps versus visiting the adjacent private reserves. In Kruger, which has over 900,000 tourists each year, only closed vehicles are allowed, and off-road driving is not allowed. Park rangers in open park vehicles conduct night game drives, but driving after dark in private vehicles is not allowed. Facilities are fair but too basic for most international travelers.

In the adjacent private reserves, day and night game viewing is conducted in open vehicles, walking is allowed and facilities are excellent. In other words, visitors have a greater opportunity to experience the bush in the private reserves than in Kruger. A safari to Kruger National Park using national park camps is considerably less expensive than a safari of the same length in the private reserves, however, you generally see much less game — and the game you encounter could be hundreds of yards (meters) from the road.

The best game viewing in Kruger National Park is May to October, during the sunny, dry winter season, when the grass has been grazed down and the deciduous plants have lost their leaves. Game viewing in the private reserves is actually good year-round, because the guides are in radio contact with other vehicles (they can direct each other to the best sightings) and can drive off-road in search of game. Calving season is in early summer (November and December) for most game species.

Kruger National Park and Adjacent Private Reserves

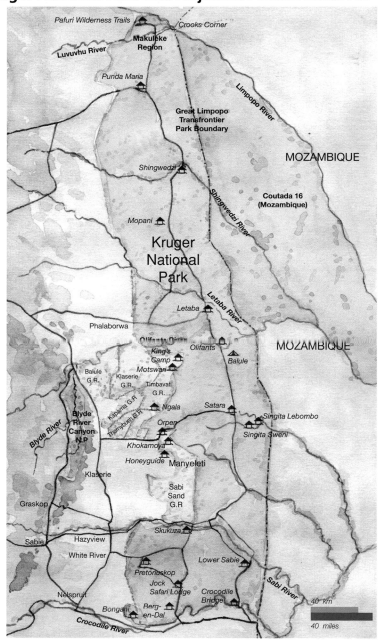

Winter days (June to August) are usually warm, with an average maximum temperature of 73°F (23°C) and clear skies. Late afternoons are cool, while temperatures at night and in the early morning sometimes drop below freezing. From October to February there are light rains, with December, January and February receiving the heaviest downpours. Temperatures from October to February sometimes rise to over 100°F (38°C). March and April are cooler as the rains begin to diminish.

The best time to look for over 450 bird species in this region is October to March — just the opposite of the best game viewing periods. However, bird watching is good year-round because less than half the bird population is composed of seasonal migrants.

To get to the area from Johannesburg, many people take about an hour's flight to Mpumalanga, Hoedspruit, or an air charter directly to their camp. Alternatively, the drive from Johannesburg to Kruger (Skukuza) is about 310 miles (500 km) northeast on good, tarred roads and takes 5 to 6 hours.

Kruger National Park

Kruger is the largest South African park and has more species of wildlife than any other game sanctuary in Africa — 130 species of mammals, 114

Leopard – one of the most stunning African animals

species of reptiles, 48 species of fish, 33 species of amphibians and 468 species of birds.

The park is home to large populations of elephant (over 8,000), buffalo (over 25,000), Burchell's zebra (over 25,000), greater kudu, giraffe, impala, white rhino, black rhino, hippopotamus, lion, leopard, cheetah, wild dog and spotted hyena, among others.

Kruger's 7,523-square-miles (19,485-km²) make it nearly the size of the state of Massachusetts. The park is 55 miles (88 km) wide at its widest point and 220 miles (355 km) long. The fences separating the park and the Timbavati and Sabi Sand Reserves were taken down years ago, effectively increasing the size of the reserve by 15% and allowing the wildlife greater freedom of movement. However, the annual winter migration routes of antelope, zebra and various other species in search of water and better grazing are still cut off by fences.

Several hundred windmills and artificial water holes have been constructed to provide the water that is so desperately needed in the dry season.

The park can be divided into three major regions: northern, central/southeastern and southwestern. Altitude varies from 650 feet (200 m) in the east to 2,950 feet (900 m) at Pretoriuskop in the southwest.

The northern region from the Letaba River to the Limpopo River is the driest. Mopane trees dominate the landscape, with the unique baobab (upside-down) trees becoming increas-

Cooling off with a mud bath

ingly numerous toward Pafuri and the Limpopo River. From Letaba to Punda Maria is the best region for spotting elephant, tsessebe and sable and roan antelope. Elephant prefer this area since it is less developed than the other regions, making it easier to congregate away from roads and traffic, and mopane trees (their preferred source of food) are prevalent.

The central/southeastern region is situated south of Letaba to Orpen Gate and also includes the eastern part of the park from Satara southward, covering Nwanedzi, Lower Sabie and Crocodile Bridge. Grassy plains and scattered knobthorn, leadwood, and marula trees dominate the landscape. Lion inhabit most areas of the park but are most prevalent in this region, where there is also an abundance of zebra and wildebeest — their favorite prey. Cheetah and black-backed jackal are best spotted on the plains. Wild dogs are mainly scattered through flatter areas, with possibly a better chance of finding them in

The impressive horns of a greater kudu

the Letaba-Malopene River area, Skukuza, and northwest of Malelane.

The southwestern part of the park, including a wide strip along the western boundary from Skukuza to Orpen Gate, is more densely forested with thorny thickets, knobthorn, marula and red bush-willow. This is the most difficult region in which to spot game — especially during the rainy season. Many of the park's 600 white rhino prefer this area.

Black rhino are scattered throughout the southern and central areas, often feeding on low-lying acacia trees. Although common, mostly nocturnal leopard are rarely seen. Buffalo roam throughout the park, while hippos prefer to inhabit the deeper parts of Kruger's many rivers by day.

Among the most conspicuous of Kruger's birds are the raptors. Commonly encountered throughout the year are the tawny eagle, bateleur, brown snake eagle and martial eagle, while the migratory Wahlberg's eagle is present in large numbers between September and March. A hundred or more white-backed vultures commonly show up at carcasses of large mammals, with lappet-faced, white-headed and hooded vultures in smaller numbers. Even without a prior interest in birds, you'll soon become captivated by the abundant lilac-breasted

Game drives are taken in open vehicles in the private concession areas and reserves

rollers, yellow-billed hornbills, greater blue-eared starlings, long-tailed shrikes and fork-tailed drongos. Several species of francolin can be seen crossing roads, particularly in the late afternoon, and red-billed oxpecker are always found pecking ticks from the coats of antelope, rhino and giraffe. In the wet season, carmine bee-eater, woodland kingfisher and European roller are conspicuous roadside birds. Some of the best bird watching is in the rest camps and picnic spots where you have a chance to walk around and listen. When out on the roads, it is advisable to switch off the vehicle motor on a regular basis to just listen and wait — you'll soon be rewarded with sightings of a variety of birds.

During the South African school holidays and long weekends, the number of day visitors to the park is limited and accommodations are almost impossible to obtain. Be sure to reserve in advance.

ACCOMMODATION IN PRIVATE CONCESSION AREAS WITHIN KRUGER NATIONAL PARK — CLASS A+: Singita Lebombo Lodge and Singita Sweni Lodge are located on a 37,500-acre (15,000-hectare) private concession area within Kruger National Park. Both camps offer day and night game drives and escorted walks. • **Singita Lebombo**, overlooking the confluence of the Nwanetsi and Sweni Rivers, has 15 luxurious air-conditioned suites with en suite facilities and private plunge pools, heath spa, gym and swimming pool. • **Singita Sweni Lodge**, the smallest of the Singita lodges, has 6 luxurious suites built on stilts and tucked away among the trees.

CLASS A: • **Ngala Lodge** has 20 air-conditioned cottages with separate lounge and en suite bathrooms and a swimming pool. Day and night game drives, walks, and three-day walking safaris are offered in a luxury mobile tented camp. • **Ngala Tented Safari Camp** has 6 spacious tents set on wooden platforms with en suite facilities and a swimming pool. • **Pafuri Wilderness Camp** lies within the 61,776-acre (24,000-hectare) Makuleke Concession in northern Kruger National Park where the borders of South Africa, Zimbabwe and Mozambique meet. The camp is located on the northern bank of the Luvuvhu River shaded by large ebony trees and consists of 20 East African style Meru tents — 6 of which can be used as family units. • **Pafuri Wilderness Trails** accommodates a maximum of 8 guests in en suite thatch-and-canvas tents raised on low platforms. The focus is on walking trails led by an armed guide and tracker. • **Jock Safari Lodge**, located on a private concession area within the southern part of Kruger, has 12 luxury suites with private salas (outdoor lounges) and a swimming pool. Day and night game drives are

Top: Singita Sweni Lodge offers gorgeous views of the river
Bottom: Luxurious Singita Lebombo

conducted. • **Hamilton's Tented Camp** offers 6 "Out of Africa" styled canvas tents complete with teak floors and private decks. The main lodge is connected by raised walkways. Game drives, guided walks and Nomadic African spa treatments are offered. • **Hoyo Hoyo Tsonga Lodge** is a unique lodge featuring 6 luxury air-conditioned "bee-hive" suites with private facilities, and game viewing decks. There is a swimming pool and game drives and guided walks are offered.

CLASS B/C, C, D & CAMPING: There are 16 National Park Rest Camps that offer a wide range of accommodations, including cottages with en suite facilities, thatched huts, with or without private facilities, and campsites. The larger rest camps have licensed restaurants. Many of the cottages and huts have cooking facilities and refrigerators.

ACCOMMODATION NEAR KRUGER NATIONAL PARK — CLASS A/B: • **InterContinental Malelane Sun Resort**, located near Kruger's southernmost gate, has 102 chalets and suites with en suite facilities overlooking several water holes.

The Private Reserves

A number of privately owned wildlife reserves are found along the western border of Kruger. Associations of ranchers have fenced the western boundary of their reserves but have not placed fences between their individual properties, allowing game to roam throughout the reserves and Kruger National Park. The private reserves, in general, have exceptionally high standards of accommodation, food and service.

A very important advantage private reserves have over national parks is that private reserves use open vehicles, which give not only a better view but also a much better feel of the bush. At most reserves, a game tracker sits on the hood or the back of each vehicle. Drivers are in radio contact with each other, greatly increasing the chances of finding those species that guests want to see most.

Vehicles may leave the road to pursue game through the bush. Night drives, which are only allowed in national park vehicles in Kruger, provide an opportunity to spot nocturnal animals rarely seen during the day. Walking safaris with an armed tracker are available.

During our family's most current visit to the Sabi Sands, we saw several leopard, lion, rhino, cheetah, white rhino, elephant, Cape buffalo, southern giraffe, bushbuck, duiker, hippo, spotted hyena, greater kudu, white-tailed mongoose, common waterbuck, steenbok, Burchell's zebra and black wildebeest, among other game. During the midday a guide took our two boys out for some target practicing and taught them how to drive a land rover — one of the highlights of their trip!

Sabi Sand Game Reserve

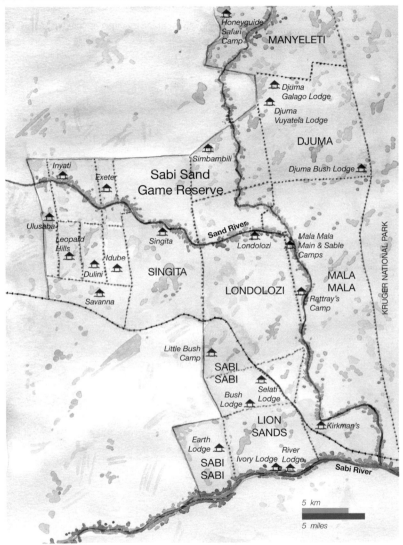

Over the years I have had the privilege of staying at virtually all of the lodges in this region, and I am happy to report that the great majority of them consistently offer good food, service and accommodations that range from comfortable to opulent.

Top: The ultimate in luxury —
Londolozi Private Granite Suites
Bottom: Londolozi Tree Camp's deck
is the perfect place for a cocktail

ACCOMMODATION — SABI SAND PRIVATE GAME RESERVE: Sabi Sand Private Game Reserve is situated about a 5-hour drive or 1 hour by scheduled air service from Johannesburg. There is also scheduled air service from nearby Kruger Mpumalanga International Airport located about 87 miles (140 km) from the reserve. All the lodges have airstrips for private air charters. Lodges in the reserve include Singita (Boulders and Ebony camps), MalaMala (MalaMala Main Camp, Rattray's and Sable camps), Londolozi (Granite, Tree, Pioneer, Founders and Varty), Ulusaba (Rock and Safari Lodge) and Djuma (Vuyatela and Bush Lodge), Sabi Sabi (Earth, Bush, Selati and Little Bush Camp), Simbambili, Exeter, Inyati and Idube reserves. All of the camps offer day and night game drives, and most offer walks.

CLASS A+: Singita has been rated by *Condé Nast Traveler Magazine* and *Travel & Leisure* as one of the top lodges in the world for many years. • **Singita Boulders Lodge** has 12 air-conditioned suites with en suite facilities, deck, fireplace and private plunge pool. • **Singita Ebony Lodge** has 12 air-conditioned rooms (including 2 family suites) with fireplace, deck, private plunge pool and en suite facilities. Boulders and Ebony share a gym and spa center. • **Londolozi Private Granite Suites** offers an unforgettable experience for no more than 6 guests in 3 well-appointed suites which are suspended over the Sand River. The suites share a private swimming pool, ranger, game viewing vehicle and masseuse. Londolozi is once again being run by the Varty family, who has recently upgraded all of their camps and is adding their personal touch to their guest's experiences. • **Londolozi Tree Camp** has 6 luxury

air-conditioned suites with en suite facilities. Each suite has its own plunge pool and a private sala. The camp has a boma, swimming pool and lounge deck.
• **Rattray's on MalaMala** represents a classical "into Africa" safari experience for the discerning traveler. This exclusive camp offers 8 comfortable suites, each overlooking the Sand River, with private heated plunge pools and secluded verandahs. The camp offers a maximum of 4 guests per safari vehicle.• **Lion**

Sands Ivory Lodge has 6 luxurious air-conditioned, thatched suites with en suite facilities, private plunge pools and decks, gym and health spa, and 2 hides. • **Earth Lodge** (Sabi Sabi Reserve) has 13 air-conditioned suites, including a presidential suite, each with their own plunge pools and patios. The lodge has a wine cellar, health spa, library and swimming pool. • **Ulusaba Rock Lodge** has 10 air-conditioned suites situated on top of an 800-foot (244 m) hilly outcrop, each with a private deck overlooking the savannah below. The lodge has a swimming pool surrounded by a natural waterfall, two tennis courts and a masseuse.

CLASS A: • **MalaMala Sable Camp**, adjacent to MalaMala Main Camp, caters to up to 14 guests in 7 luxurious suites. The camp has a swimming pool, boma, cozy bar, and lounge/dining room. The viewing deck provides a magnificent view over the Sand River. This camp may be reserved exclusively for a private party or individual guests. • **MalaMala Main Camp** is a luxurious camp with 18 air-conditioned, spacious thatched rondavels (each with two en suite "his" and "hers" bathrooms) and a swimming pool. Families with children are welcome.

Top: One of Rattray's decadent bedrooms
Bottom: Tucked among the trees, Rattray's offers the ultimate in privacy

Privacy and solitude at Djuma Vuyatela

• **Londolozi Pioneer Camp** has 6 large and luxurious air-conditioned suites with en suite facilities and a swimming pool. The cottages are themed with historic memorabilia and the history of Londolozi. • **Varty Camp** (Londolozi) is comprised of 8 chalets and 2 suites that are air conditioned with private plunge pools and elevated timber decks. En suite bathrooms have views of the lush green riverine vegetation. Children and families are welcome. The camp has a large swimming pool and wine cellar. There is also a boutique, gym and massage treatment room. • **Founders Camp** (Londolozi) offers 5 chalets, all with en suite facilities. The classic safari camp has a boma, swimming pool, and lounge deck. • **Vuyatela** (Djuma Game Reserve) has 8 unique chalet suites, each with a private lounge separated from the bedroom by a beautiful teak deck, ending with a private plunge pool. The main lodge overlooks a water hole and has a suspended bird watching tower. There is also a gym and relaxation room. • **Simbambili Lodge**, located in the northern part of the reserve, has 8 air-conditioned, thatched chalets with private facilities, plunge pools and salas. • **Sabi Sabi Bush Lodge** overlooks a water hole and has 25 air-conditioned thatched suites, including a spacious presidential suite, with private facilities and a swimming pool. • **Selati Lodge** (Sabi Sabi) has 8 air-conditioned chalets (including a presidential suite with private vehicle/guide) with en suite facilities and a swimming pool. • **Little Bush Camp** (Sabi Sabi) offers 6 air-conditioned suites with private facilities and intimate views of the bushveld. • **Leopard Hills**, located in the western part of Sabi Sands, is built on a hill overlooking a waterhole and has 8 air-conditioned suites with private plunge pools and swimming pool. • **Ulusaba Safari Lodge**, situated on the banks of the Mabrak River, has 10 luxurious "tree" chalets. A spa treatment center and tennis courts are shared with guests from Ulusaba Rock Lodge. • **Savanna** overlooks a series of 4 water holes and offers seven fully air-conditioned tented suites with private decks. Several of the suites have private plunge pools. • **Exeter** features 3 lodges, (Leadwood Lodge, River Lodge and Dulini Lodge), each offering elegant air-conditioned suites set on the banks of the Sand River with en suite bathrooms, private plunge pools and decks.

• **Kirkman's Kamp** overlooks the Sand River and has 18 air-conditioned rooms with en suite facilities and a swimming pool.

CLASS A/B: • **Djuma Bush Lodge** offers 7 comfortable air-conditioned thatched-roof rondavels with en suite facilities, a pool, bar and viewing deck. • **Lion Sands River Lodge** is located in the southern part of the reserve with 6 miles (10 km) of river frontage on the Sabi River. The lodge has 18 air-conditioned, thatched rooms with en suite facilities, gym and heath spa, swimming pool, sala and 4 hides. • **Idube Game Lodge** has 10 air-conditioned chalets with en suite facilities and a swimming pool. • **Inyati Game Lodge** has 10 thatched chalets (doubles) with en suite facilities and a swimming pool.

ACCOMMODATION — MANYELETI GAME RESERVE: Guests fly to Hoedspruit or by charter aircraft directly to their respective camps. CLASS A/B: • **Honeyguide Safari Camp** consists of 2 camps, Mantobeni and Khoya Moya, each consisting of 12 tents with en suite facilities and catering to a maximum of 48 guests. Daily walking trails and night game drives are offered.

ACCOMMODATION — TIMBAVATI GAME RESERVE: Guests of the camps listed below fly to Hoedspruit or by charter aircraft directly to their respective camps. Day and night game drives and walks are offered. CLASS A/B: • **Kings Camp** has 11 thatched colonial suites each with private facilities, romantic Victorian bathtubs, indoor/outdoor showers, air-conditioning, mini-bars, and a swimming pool. • **Motswari** has 15 rondavels with en suite facilities and a swimming pool. • **Tanda Tula Bush Camp** has 12 tents with en suite facilities.

ACCOMMODATION — THORNYBUSH GAME RESERVE — CLASS A+: • **Royal Malewane**, situated near Hoedspruit and adjacent to the Kruger National Park, has 8 regal suites plus 2 2-bedroom suites (the Royal and the Malewane, each accommodating 4 guests) with private vehicle and guide, providing a feel of original colonial elegance.
CLASS A: • **Thornybush Main Lodge**, located in the Thornybush Game Reserve adjacent to Kruger, has 20 glass-fronted air-conditioned suites including two family units with en suite facilities and decks overlooking a waterhole, and a swimming pool.
CLASS A/B: • **Serondella Lodge** is an 8-bed camp offering delightful thatched suites overlooking a waterhole. The lodge is flanked by two waterholes, where guests can enjoy an abundance of big game and birdlife from spectacular viewing decks. • **Jackalberry Lodge** is a rustic 10-bedded camp, with en suite facilities and offers views of the Drakensberg Mountains. Morning and night game drives as well as walking safaris are offered.

ACCOMMODATION — KAPAMA GAME RESERVE — CLASS A: • **Camp Jabulani** is located near Hoedspruit in the Limpopo Province, and is only 25 miles (40 km) from the Kruger National Park. The camp has just 6 secluded

rondavel suites, each with a private splash pool, fireplace, air conditioning, en suite bathroom and outside shower. Activities include day and night elephant-back safaris, morning and evening game drives, bush walks, bird watching and a visit to the Hoedspruit Endangered Species Center where they have a facility for cheetah conservation.

ACCOMMODATION — GARONGA SAFARI CAMP — CLASS A: • **Garonga Safari Camp** is an exclusive 14-bed camp in the greater Makalali Conservancy situated west of the Kruger National Park. The tents offer en suite facilities, private decks with views and an outdoor shower.

Top: A unique way to game view at Camp Jabulani
Bottom: Camp Jabulani's main lodge

Blyde River Canyon, Pilgrim's Rest and Bourke's Luck Potholes

West of the Kruger National Park, the landscape rises abruptly in altitude. This dramatic escarpment, which separates lowveld from highveld, is formed by the imposing Drakensberg range. The best way to appreciate this area is by driving from Hoedspruit, up and through the Strydom Tunnel, to Graskop and then south to the town of Sabie. The Blyde River Canyon is an area of great scenic beauty, with the impressive red sandstone gorge rising half a mile (1.5 km) above the river below. Three isolated rock pinnacles, each capped with vegetation, have the appearance of traditional African huts and are known as the **Three Rondavels**. This is a good lookout point for birds such as Alpine swift, jackal buzzard and red-winged starling.

South of the Three Rondavels lookout are the astonishing **Bourke's Luck Potholes**. There, the sandstone bedrock has been carved out at the confluence of the Treur and Blyde Rivers, to form a series of whirlpool-eroded potholes. Nearby, a number of beautiful waterfalls occur during the summer rainy season, and there are numerous lookout points and short walking trails. For the fit and enthusiastic, there are back-packing trails into the **Blyde River Canyon** itself.

The little village of **Graskop**, frequently covered in mist, is famous for its crafts and coffee shops. The grasslands fringing the village are home to a few surviving pairs of South Africa's rarest bird — the blue swallow. To the west of Graskop is the picturesque village of **Pilgrim's Rest**, a living museum. This was the site of major alluvial gold panning and dig-

Top: A special dinner set for guests at Cybele Forest Lodge
Bottom: The lush area surrounding Cybele Forest Lodge

ging between 1873 and 1876. Some of the original buildings remain standing, while many others have been meticulously restored. There is certainly great Old World charm about the tin-and-wood buildings — now shops, bars or guesthouses. Explore the unusual and quaint shops, take a drive in a horse-drawn carriage through the village, play golf, fish for trout or go horseback riding. The small village nature reserve supports a number of oribi and birds, such as bush blackcap and chorister robin.

South of Pilgrim's Rest is the town of **Sabie**, the center of the region's timber industry. This is the gateway to the winding **Long Tom Pass** — a smooth tarmac road meandering through highland meadows to the trout fishing havens of **Lydenburg** and **Dullstroom**. The modern road is set upon a wagon route that was charted in 1871, which allowed access to the lowveld and Indian Ocean for the isolated Boer Republic. The name of the pass is derived from a large field gun used by the Boers in a skirmish with the British in 1900.

ACCOMMODATION IN THE REGION — DELUXE: • **Cybele Forest Lodge** (White River) is a lovely lodge with luxuriously appointed rooms and cottages with facilities en suite and a swimming pool. This forested area is great for walks, horseback riding, and trout fishing. The Spa in the Forest offers a range of health and beauty treatments. • **Blue Mountain Lodge** (White River), located on a 500-acre (200-hectare) estate, offers a choice of 8 luxury Victorian Suites, or 1 of 4 "Quadrant Suites" with en suite facilities and a swimming pool. Activities include walking, bass fishing and bird watching. • **Highgrove House** is a renovated colonial farmstead featuring 8 decorated garden suites. Each includes full private bathroom with bath and shower, overhead fans, open fireplaces and secluded verandas with views of the forest or valley and avocado orchards. To maintain an atmosphere of fine dining, dress code for dinner is smart. • **The Coach House** (Tzaneen/Letaba) is situated on 1,384-acres (560-hectares) of the Letaba district in Limpopo Province, the hotel offers dramatic views of the Drakensberg Mountains. The hotel has 41 rooms with en suite facilities and a swimming pool.

FIRST CLASS: • **Hulala Lakeside Lodge** (White River) is set among great granite boulders and surrounded on three sides by a lake. The lodge has rooms and suites with en suite facilities, log fireplaces and private terraces, and a swimming pool. • **Royal Hotel** (Pilgrims Rest) has rooms and suites with en suite facilities.

TOURIST CLASS: • **Rissington Inn** is an affordable, award-winning country lodge in the heart of the Lowveld. • **Mount Sheba** (Pilgrim's Rest) has 25 rooms with en suite facilities and a swimming pool.

ACCOMMODATION BETWEEN THE REGION AND JOHANNESBURG — DELUXE: • **Mount Anderson Ranch** is an exclusive 20,000-acre (8,000-hectare) property with 3 rooms in a large ranch house with en suite facilities. Trout fishing, horseback riding, nature drives and walks are offered. The lodge is booked out to one private party at a time. • **Walkersons Country Manor** resembles a Scottish highland estate because it is surrounded by lakes and rivers. The suites have log fireplaces and en suite facilities. Mountain walks and trout fishing are the main attraction. • **Critchley Hackle** is a rustic stone-built complex with en suite facilities.

Welgevonden Game Reserve and Marakele National Park

Located about 2.5 hours northwest of Johannesburg, these reserves are destined to become one of South Africa's new wildlife hotspots. Welgevonden is an 85,000-acre (34,000-hectare) private game reserve that borders Marakele National Park's eastern boundary. When combined, these two parks are close to 250,000-acres (100,000-hectares) in size, with all the "Big 5" in this malaria-free region. The area is known as the "Valley of the Tuskers," because many of the elephant bulls have massive tusks with over 70 pounds (32 kg) of ivory on each side.

ACCOMMODATION — CLASS A: • **Shidzidzi** has 5 brick-and-thatch lodges with en suite bathrooms and indoor and outdoor showers. The main lodge has the dining room, a lounge, a bar and a pool. Day and night game drives are conducted in open vehicles. • **Makweti Safari Lodge** offers 5 romantic suites with views across the African plains. Activities include daily walks and open-vehicle game drives.

Top: Makweti Safari Lodge
Bottom: One of the palatial
suites at Makweti Safari Lodge

NORTH WEST PROVINCE

Pilanesberg Nature Reserve

An extinct volcanic crater was the site for one of the most ambitious wildlife restoration projects on the African continent. Officially opened in 1979, Pilanesberg Game Reserve was a joint project between the local community and the provincial administration to transform an area of marginal agricultural value into a productive wildlife estate. This was a highly controversial program at the time, but it proved to be a groundbreaking success. Livestock was removed, villages willingly relocated, and thousands of animals (only species known to occur historically) were reintroduced. The popularity of the neighboring Sun City Resort ensured that visitors came from afar, and in good numbers, to fulfill the promise of an improved livelihood for the local community.

This beautiful reserve covers 212-square-miles (550-km^2) and is located within a 17-mile- (27-km) wide volcanic bowl that rises over the surrounding plains, and it offers good game viewing in a beautiful, hilly setting. Both white and black rhino are fairly common; elephant, eland, red hartebeest and sable antelope are frequently seen. Lion, cheetah and leopard occur in reasonable numbers, and the elusive brown hyena occurs alongside its more gregarious relative, the spotted hyena. Close to 400 species of birds have been recorded, with crimson-breasted shrike, grey hornbill, pearl-spotted owl and golden-breasted bunting among the characteristic residents. Day and night game drives and hot-air balloon safaris are conducted in the reserve.

ACCOMMODATION — CLASS A: • **Kwa Maritane** has 90 comfortable rooms with en suite facilities and a swimming pool. • **Tshukudu** offers 6 luxury air-conditioned cottages each with elevated views of the surrounding reserve.

CLASS B: • **Bakubung** overlooks a hippo pool and has 76 air-conditioned en suite rooms and 66 self-catering cabanas with en suite bathrooms, conference center, restaurant, swimming pool and children's playground. Guests may take a 10-minute shuttle to Sun City.

CLASS C & D: • **Kololo**, • **Mankwe**, • **Manyane** and • **Metswedi** camps provide basic tented accommodation.

CAMPING: • **Manyane Caravan and Camping Site** have campsites and ablution facilities.

Sun City

Sun City is a premier entertainment vacation complex with numerous restaurants, Las Vegas-style floor shows, casinos, tennis and a variety of water sports. The Lost City Golf Course is an 18-hole Gary Player-designed course with desert style on the front 9 holes and African bushveld on the back 9 holes. The Gary Player Golf Course is an 18-hole bushveld course and is home of the annual Nedbank Golf Challenge. Sun City is a 2-hour drive (116 mi./187 km) or a short flight from Johannesburg. Excursions to Pilanesberg Nature Reserve are offered by some of the hotels.

ACCOMMODATION — DELUXE: • **The Palace Hotel of the Lost City** has been constructed as a royal residence from an ancient civilization and is set in 62-acres (25-hectares) of lush gardens. This lavish property has 338 rooms and four suites, a pool with 6-foot (2-m) surfing waves and water chutes, several restaurants and bars and 2 world-class Gary Player golf courses.

FIRST CLASS: • **The Cascades**, landscaped with lush gardens, waterfalls and a swimming pool, has 281 rooms with facilities en suite. • **Sun City Hotel** has 340 rooms with en suite facilities and a swimming pool.

TOURIST CLASS: • **Sun City Cabanas** has 380 cabanas with facilities en suite.

Madikwe Game Reserve

Following on the success of Pilanesberg, the North west provincial authorities embarked upon a similar transformation of a vast semi-arid area close to the Botswana border, known as Madikwe. A vast area of plains, interrupted in places by inselberg rock outcrops, Madikwe is dominated by acacias and sweet grasses. The absence of surface water limited agricultural development, but indigenous wildlife has thrived since "Operation Phoenix" translocated some 8,000 animals from other parks in South Africa, Namibia and Zimbabwe. Madikwe was the site for the first relocation of adult African elephants, moved from Gonarezhou in Zimbabwe in 1993. They have thrived to the point to which some have recently been translocated to Angola.

Two packs of the endangered wild dog occur in the 465-square-mile (750-km²) reserve, and this is one of the best places to see them in South Africa. In addition there are healthy populations of lion, cheetah and leopard. Black and white rhino and a wide range of antelope are numerous. After traveling on the African continent for over 30 years, I recently had the thrill of seeing my first aardvark here. This was really exciting!

Birdlife is outstanding, with numerous species characteristic of the Kalahari, such as violet-eared waxbill, swallow-tailed bee-eater and pied babbler.

A real plus for some travelers is that the area is malaria free.

Top: Madikwe River Lodge's main lounge
Bottom: The crisp comfort of Madikwe River Lodge

ACCOMMODATION — CLASS A+: • **Mateya Safari Lodge** consists of 5 individually designed luxury air-conditioned thatched suites — each offering uninterrupted views of the waterhole and plains and including a sala, plunge pool and outdoor shower. There is a restaurant, lounge and an 8,000 bottle wine cellar. Game viewing activities include day and night game drives in open vehicles (with a maximum of four people per vehicle) as well as bush walks. • **Royal Madikwe** is a luxury residence accommodating up to 10 people on an exclusive basis. All bedrooms are en suite and offer the finest furnishing and yet are family friendly. The main lodge houses the fireplace, dining room with open designer kitchen, lounge and viewing deck with hot tub. A private safari guide and vehicle are available throughout your stay.

CLASS A: • **Jaci's Safari Lodge** has 9 thatched chalets overlooking a small stream where the animals come to drink, with en suite bathrooms (including a 2-bedroom suite with private pool). • **Jaci's Tree Lodge** has 8 "tree houses" built on stilts with en suite facilities and large private decks. The main building includes an open-air dining room, lounge, swimming pool and 4-sided fireplace. Both of Jaci's lodges are very family friendly. • **Madikwe River Lodge** offers 16 split-level thatched chalets with en suite bathrooms, and a private deck set in a riverine forest. There is a main dining area, lounge, boma and swimming pool. Day and night game drives and walks are offered.

THE CAPE PROVINCES

Kgalagadi Transfrontier Park

In May 2000 Kalahari Gemsbok National Park was officially merged with Botswana's Gemsbok National Park to form the Kgalagadi Transfrontier Park. The park is located in the northwest corner of South Africa and the southwest corner of Botswana, bordering Namibia to the west. This huge 13,900-square-mile (36,000-km^2) park is predominantly semi-desert and open savannah. Scattered thorn trees and grasses lie between red Kalahari sand dunes. San Bushmen inhabited the area as far back as 25,000 years ago.

The most interesting (and productive from an animal-viewing perspective) habitat in the park is the fossil riverbeds. Tens of thousands of years ago, in a wetter era, the Auob and Nossob Rivers flowed into the Orange River, but today they are no more than furrowed drainage lines. They do, however, hold underground water, and once in a decade or so, they flow briefly after particularly heavy downpours. It is in the Auob and Nossob drainage lines that the largest camel thorn acacias grow, providing shade, nutrition and nesting sites for a host of creatures. Grasses grow taller and sweeter here, too. The two main roads in the park follow the Nossob and Auob (they are linked by the so-called "Dune Road") where a much higher concentration of animals are seen than in the surrounding dunes.

The park is famous for the majestic gemsbok (oryx), which occur in abundance. This is also one of the best places to see and photograph the gazelle-like springbok, the national sporting emblem of South Africa. Blue wildebeest occur in small numbers — a mere remnant of a migratory population that may have once rivaled the famed Serengeti herds. Predator viewing is often quite good, with lion, leopard and particularly cheetah, seen with frequency. The Kalahari lions are among the most handsome in Africa, for there is little dense bush to scratch or damage their coats and manes. The elusive, mostly nocturnal, brown hyena may be encountered in the early mornings or late afternoon. This park also offers

Gemsbok (Oryx) are frequently seen in Kgalagadi Transfrontier Park

Kgalagadi Transfrontier Park

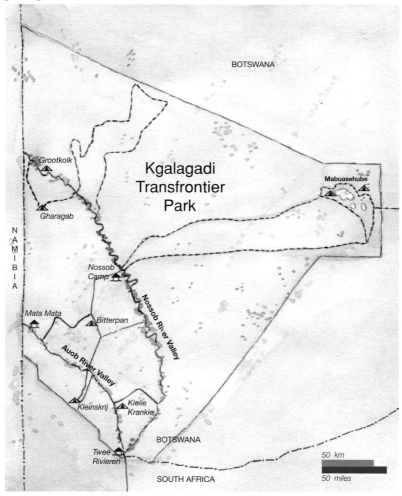

wonderful opportunities to see less common creatures such as honey badger, aardwolf, bat-eared fox and African wild cat, which, though primarily nocturnal, are often active during the day, especially in the cooler winter months.

Birdwatchers will not be disappointed, for the Kalahari supports a wide variety of species not commonly seen elsewhere. The gigantic thatched nests of sociable weavers are unmistakable wonders of avian architecture. Built by the small, sparrow-sized weavers, the huge structures commonly grow to a size that breaks the branches of the tree in which they are built. Birds of prey thrive in the

Kalahari, with pale chanting goshawk, gabar goshawk, bateleur, secretarybird, lanner falcon and the tiny pygmy falcon all very common. Giant eagle owls are regularly seen at their daytime roosts, while white-faced and pearl-spotted owls hunt about the rest camps after dark. Three species of sandgrouse can be seen quenching their thirst at waterholes, while the world's heaviest flying bird, the kori bustard, is extremely common.

Summer temperatures can exceed 104°F (40°C). Winter days are pleasant, but temperatures can drop below freezing at night. The animals have adapted to desert conditions by eating plants with high water content, such as wild cucumber and tsamma melon.

The southern entrance to the park is about 255 miles (411 km) north of Upington, which has scheduled air service from other major cities in the country. The park can be accessed from Namibia at the Mata Mata Gate by bonafide tourists only who are required to book a minimum of two nights stay.

ACCOMMODATION — CLASS B: • **Kgalagadi Kalahari Tented Camp**, set on a red sand dune overlooking a waterhole, has 15 tents, including 4 family units with en suite facilities, and swimming pool. • **Bitterpan**, located a 3-hour drive (4wd only) from Nossob, has 4 chalets on stilts with shared cooking facilities.

CLASS C&D: There are three rest camps with self-contained cottages with kitchens, huts with and without bathrooms, camping sites, stores, gas (petrol) and diesel. • **Twee Rivieren** is located at the southern entrance to the park. The camp has a restaurant, swimming pool and a landing strip for small aircraft. • **Nossob**, located in the northeastern part of the park near the Botswana border, has bungalows with en suite facilities and kitchens, as well as huts with separate facilities and communal kitchens. The camp has an information center for the plant and animal life in the park and has a landing strip for small aircraft. • **Mata Mata**, located on the western border of the park, has simple cottages with kitchens and en suite facilities, and huts with separate facilities and a communal kitchen.

ACCOMMODATION NEAR THE PARK — CLASS B&C: • **Molopo Kalahari Lodge**, located 37 miles (60 km) from the park, has 36 air-conditioned rondavels with en suite facilities and 5 chalets with separate facilities.

Tswalu Kalahari Reserve

Tswalu Kalahari Reserve

Tswalu Kalahari Reserve is the largest privately owned game reserve in South Africa, covering 290-square-miles (900-km²). Black rhino, roan and sable antelope may be seen, as well as up to 30 species of plains game.

This reserve has been made famous by the filming of "Meerkat Manor". Spending time with these habituated meerkats, possibly the cutest animals on earth, is not to be missed.

Other activities include morning and night game drives, guided walks, horseback riding, archery, star gazing, sun downers, and special activities for children. Ballooning and massage treatments are available but must be pre-booked.

The reserve is located west of Kuruman. Transfers are available from Kimberley or Upington; quickest access is by air charter from Johannesburg or Cape Town.

ACCOMMODATION: CLASS A+ —
• **The Motse** consists of 8 *legae* (a Tswana word for small house/suite), 2 of which are family units accommodating 4 people. Each legae includes a bedroom, en suite bathroom with both indoor and outdoor walk-in shower, open fireplace and private sun deck overlooking a waterhole. The main lodge has an outdoor heated swimming pool, terrace, boma, wine cellar, a gift shop and children's play room.
• **Tarkuni** is available for exclusive use for families and small groups of 8 to 12 guests. Accommodation includes 4 luxury bedrooms with en suite bathrooms, lounge and dining room, library, covered patio and heated swimming pool. For children, 2 sets of bunk beds and separate nanny quarters with 2 single beds and a bathroom en suite are available. Private guide and game viewing vehicles as well as a dedicated chef are included.

Top: The refreshing pool at Motse
Middle: Tswalu's Tarkuni offers an exclusive experience
Bottom: The popular show "Meerkat Manor" is filmed at Tswalu

Kimberley

Kimberley is the "diamond city," where one of the world's biggest diamond strikes occurred in 1868. Visit the open-air museum and the "Big Hole," where over 3 tons of diamonds were removed from the largest hole dug by man on earth.

ACCOMMODATION — FIRST CLASS: • **Kimberley Club** offers 21 en suite bedrooms with an ambience of a bygone era.

TOURIST CLASS: • **Garden Court Kimberley** has 135 rooms with facilities en suite and a swimming pool.

Cape Town

Sir Francis Drake once said of the Cape Town area, "The fairest cape we saw in the whole circumference of the globe." Today, Cape Town is still thought

Cape Point Lighthouse

by many well-traveled people to be one of the most beautiful settings in the world. The Cape reminds me of the California coast — stark, natural beauty and a laid-back atmosphere.

An afternoon **Champagne Cruise** past islands with hundreds of seals, and featuring rocky cliffs and sandy beaches, allows a delightful perspective of the area.

The **Victoria & Alfred Waterfront (V & A)** has a variety of shops, historical buildings, museums, waterfront walks, restaurants, nightclubs, luxury and first class hotels, three micro breweries, theater, boat trips, helicopter rides and the **Two Oceans Aquarium**, which exhibits species from both the Atlantic and the Indian Oceans.

Tours to **Robben Island**, where Nelson Mandela was held as a political prisoner for so many years, depart from the Nelson Mandela Gateway situated at the Clock Tower at the Victoria & Alfred Harbor. The boat transfer to the island takes about 30 minutes. An hour tour of the island includes a visit to Mandela's cell, a stone quarry, an old village and a drive around the island, where you may see African (jackass) penguins and have great views of the city.

The one-day excursion down the Cape Peninsula to the **Cape of Good Hope Nature Reserve** and **Cape Point** is one of the finest drives on the continent. The reserve has lovely picnic sites, a population of bontebok and a variety of beautiful wildflowers. Some people say this is where the Atlantic meets the Indian Ocean, but that actually happens at Cape Agulhas, the southernmost point of Africa.

Cape Town and Environs

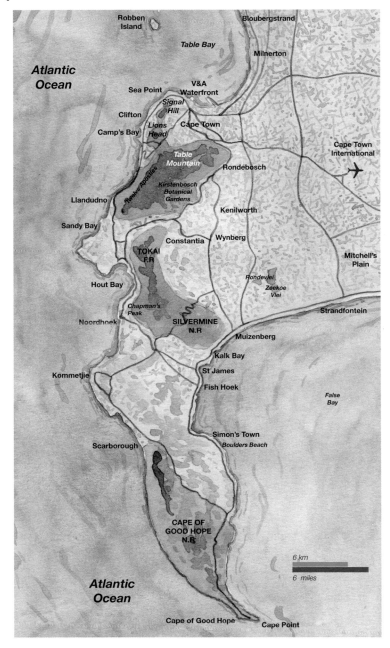

An adorable member of the African penguin colony

On our recent visit, we saw bontebok and ostrich, while baboons at the ocean's edge were eating mussels they had picked off the rocks. Be sure to stop in **Simon's Town** en route to visit the wonderful **African penguin colony** (formally called jackass penguins).

Whale watching in the Atlantic seaboard, Hout Bay and False Bay is good July and August and best September and October. **Kirstenbosch National Botanical Gardens**, one of the finest gardens in the world, has 9,000 of the 21,000 flowering plants of southern Africa. A recent addition to the gardens is a magnificent glasshouse conservatory containing succulent plants from all over southern Africa, including an exquisite baobab tree.

The **Cableway** (or 3-hour hike) up **Table Mountain**, with breathtaking views, is a must. The cable car can take 65 passengers at a time and does a full rotation on the way up. There is a good restaurant on the top of the mountain. Bring warm clothing because it is usually much cooler and windier on top. Table Mountain also offers the highest commercial abseiling or rappelling in the world.

The spectacular view of Cape Town from Table Mountain

A more active way to discover the area is by **kayaking** in single or double kayaks. Trips are available around Cape Point, from Table Bay to Clifton, in Hout Bay, in the Langebaan Lagoon and at Rictvlei (for bird watching), and from Simons Town to **Boulders Beach** to see the penguin colony. **Horseback riding** on beaches at Hout Bay, on the beaches, dunes and lagoons at Noordhoek Valley, or in the winelands is another great option. **Mountain biking** off Table Mountain to the Cape of Good Hope Nature Reserve and in the winelands is popular. From the Victoria & Alfred Waterfront, you may go **Ocean rafting** in rubberducks (Zodiacs), which reach speeds in excess of 80 mph (120km/hr). Wet bikes and jet skis may be rented in Blouberg and Muizenberg. **Quad bikes** may be rented in Melkbos, 30 minutes from central Cape Town. **Sand boarding** is offered on some of the biggest sand dunes in the Cape, about an hour's drive out of Cape Town, either in Atlantis or Betty's Bay. **Thunder City** offers 1-hour flights in fighter jets — with just you and the pilot!

The Atlantic Ocean and False Bay offer good angling and **deep-sea fishing**. Maasbanker and mackerel are numerous in the warmer waters in Table Bay in summer, while False Bay is one of the top angling areas with Gordon's Bay harbor as an entry point to the ocean. The fishing harbors of Kalk Bay and Hout Bay are excellent, particularly at the peak of the season around June and July. Simon's Town is the principle harbor for tuna boats, and there is a club for tuna fishermen which offers boats for charter. At the Cape of Good Hope Nature Reserve, fishing is particularly good from the rocky vantage points on both sides of the peninsula. The west coast offers good fishing at many points along the coast. At Bloubergstrand, fishing off the rocks is good. Fishing charters depart from the V&A Waterfront, Hout Bay, Simon's Town and Gordon's Bay and range from four hours to a full day.

Some of the finer **restaurant**s include the Atlantic Grill, Baia and Emily's (Victoria & Alfred Waterfront), Buitenverwachting, Constantia Uitsig, La Colombe and Cape Malay Kitchen (Constantia); Blue Danube (Tamboerskloof); Leinster Hall (Gardens) and Vilamoura (Camps Bay); the Africa Café, Aubergine, Caveau Wine Bar and Deli, Fork, Jardine, Five Flies, One.Waterfront at the Cape Grace and Theshowroom (Cape Town city), Brass Bell (Kalk Bay); and La Perla (Sea Point), and Salt and Jinga. Maestros Restaurant (located on Woodbridge Island)

Cape Town's vibrant Victoria & Alfred waterfront

situated across Table Bay, is exceptionally nice in summer; guests may watch the sun set behind Table Mountain.

Cape Town has many fabulous **shopping** areas, including The Victoria & Alfred Waterfront (small shops offering excellent quality and variety), Greenmarket Square (local stalls featuring African crafts, textiles and hand-made goods, Monday to Saturday only), Cape of Good Hope Fine Wine Exporters (will arrange to ship cases of wine home — you will probably have to pay duty), The Collector (Church Street — a small downtown gallery), Jewel Africa (City Centre — manufactures jewelery, enormous variety of precious and semi-precious stones, also curios and craftwork), Uwe Koetter (manufacturing jewelery), Cape Gallery and Pan African Market (Church Street), Waterkant Street area (home furnishings and accessories) Long Street Arcade (variety of antique and collectable dealers in one arcade) and La Cotte Wineshop (Franschhoek — noted for its extensive selection of older wines, shipping arranged).

February through April is the best time to visit the Cape because there is very little wind; October to January is warm and windy and is also a good time to visit. May to August can be rainy and cool. However, this is one of the most beautiful cities in the world to visit any time of the year.

Top: Ellerman House's serene pool area
Bottom: Prime location on the waterfront — The Cape Grace

ACCOMMODATION — DELUXE:
• **Ellerman House** is a grand old home with 11 suites with en suite facilities and a swimming pool, gym and steam bath. It is a historical landmark situated in the suburb of Bantry Bay within walking distance of the famous Clifton Beach. • **Cape Grace** is an elegant hotel located in the Victoria & Alfred Waterfront on its own quay, with 104 rooms and suites with en suite facilities, restaurant, lounge, spa, "Bascule" whiskey bar and a swimming pool. • **Table Bay** is a 329-room hotel located in the Victoria & Alfred Waterfront with en suite facilities, satellite television, a restaurant, conference facilities and a swimming pool, spa and health club. • **Mount Nelson Hotel** is set on nine landscaped acres near the base of

With Table Mountain in the background, The Mount Nelson is a Cape Town icon

Table Mountain and has luxurious rooms with en suite facilities, two swimming pools, tennis courts and a spa.

FIRST CLASS: • **Radisson Waterfront Hotel**, located a few minutes walk or complimentary hotel shuttle to the Victoria & Alfred Waterfront, has 181 rooms with en suite facilities, two restaurants and a pool. Rooms either overlook the ocean in front or Table Mountain behind. • **Le Vendome**, situated in Sea Point, is an elegant hotel with 143 rooms and luxury suites, 2 restaurants and a swimming pool. • **Peninsula Hotel**, located in Sea Point facing the Atlantic Ocean, has 110 suites with 1 to 3 bedrooms and 2 swimming pools. • **Victoria & Alfred Hotel**, located in the Victoria & Alfred Waterfront, has 68 air-conditioned rooms with en suite facilities. • **The Townhouse Hotel** is a 12-story hotel close to the historic Parliament Buildings, with 106 air-conditioned rooms with en suite facilities, small refrigerators, mini-bars, and free high speed Internet.

TOURIST CLASS: • **The Commodore Hotel** is located a few minutes walk from the Victoria & Alfred Waterfront and has 236 air-conditioned rooms. • **Portswood Hotel**, located a five-minute walk to the Victoria & Alfred Waterfront, has 103 air-conditioned rooms with en suite facilities. • **The Cullinan Inn**, located near the entrance to the Victoria & Alfred Waterfront, has 416 rooms all with bath and separate shower, a bar, swimming pool, gym and restaurant.

GUESTHOUSES: • **Kensington Place** is located within walking distance to Cape Town's trendy Kloof Street, with its diverse eating and shopping establishments. It has 8 suites with private balconies overlooking the bay and Table Mountain, and a swimming pool. • **Clarendon House** is an elegant guesthouse situated in Fresnaye, one of Cape Town's prime residential seafront suburbs. Each of the 7 bedrooms has en suite bathrooms. • **Welgelegen**, a beautiful double-story Victorian home in the popular suburb of Gardens within walking distance of Kloof Street, has en suite bedrooms and a swimming pool. • **Four Rosmead** consists of 8 en suite bedrooms (including the Bellegables Suite) in an exclusive guesthouse situated on the slopes of Table Mountain

Suites at Kensington Place overlook the bay and Table Mountain

in the residential suburb of Oranjezicht. Lunch and dinner are now offered to guests. • **Cape Cadogan** has 12 en suite bedrooms and the Owner's Villa that are decorated with an eclectic mix of contemporary and antique furniture using dramatic fabrics to maximum effect. • **Hemingway Lodge** offers 3 suites in an ideal location in the city. There is a swimming pool for guests.

ACCOMMODATION IN THE CAPE AREA — DELUXE: • **The Cellars-Hohenhort Hotel** is comprised of 2 luxury country houses with a swimming pool and is situated in the beautiful Constantia Valley, a 15-minute drive from Cape Town. All 38 rooms and 15 suites have en suite facilities. • **The Bay Hotel**, located opposite the beach at Camps Bay, a 10-minute drive out of Cape Town, has 72 rooms and 6 suites with en suite facilities and a swimming pool. • **Twelve Apostles Hotel** has 70 en suite rooms, some with sea and some with mountain views, swimming pool and restaurant. • **Colona Castle** is a spectacular villa with 3 standard suites and 5 full suites, each decorated with sumptuous furnishings and antiques. The hotel is located on the False Bay coastline and offers views of Table Mountain, the peninsula, winelands and South African Ocean. Guests can enjoy a gourmet restaurant, and swimming pool and spa treatments are available upon request. • **The Vineyard Hotel & Spa** is a 175-room hotel situated in the suburb of Newlands on six acres, a 15-minute drive from the City Center and the Victoria & Alfred Waterfront, and within easy walking distance of the up-market Cavendish Shopping Centre. It has three restaurants, a health and fitness center, spa and swimming pool.

FIRST CLASS: • **Constantia Uitsig**, located on a 200-acre (80-hectare) private wine farm in the Constantia Valley, offers simple elegance with 10 rooms and 7 suites with en suite bathrooms, Uitsig and La Colombe (2 of the top restaurants in South Africa) and a swimming pool. • **Greenways**, located near Kirstenbosch Botanical Gardens, is a magnificent mansion with eight rooms and 6 suites with en suite facilities, a swimming pool and a croquet lawn. • **The Palm House** is an elegant guesthouse with 10 rooms with en suite facilities.

The Winelands

From humble beginnings as an experimental vineyard below Table Mountain by the Dutch East India Company during the seventeenth century, the wine industry in South Africa today has spread over a large and diverse area. Grapes are grown in nearly 60 officially declared appellations covering over 250,000-acres (100,000-hectares).

There are 6 important wine producing areas within a 2-hour drive of Cape Town, offering an amazing array of different wine styles from the many estates, private wine cellars and cooperatives. A superb marine- and mountain-influenced climate, coupled with stunning scenery, makes this an attractive area to visit. Hundreds of restaurants serve interesting regional cuisine matched to

The Grande Roche is the perfect example of classic Cape Dutch architecture

the local wines, which helps to drive the continuing Cape wine renaissance. The areas close to Cape Town are 1) Constantia, 2) Durbanville, 3) Paarl, Wellington and Franschhoek, 4) Stellenbosch, 5) Swartland, and 6) Walker Bay. **Constantia** is sometimes referred to as the cradle of wine making in the Cape; Simon vander Stel was granted land here in 1685. Constantia is a leafy zone on the southeast of the Cape Peninsula facing the Atlantic Ocean. It is cooled by sea breezes from two sides, southeasterly from False Bay, and northerly gusts over the Constantiaberg mountain spine. Red and white wines are produced, but the area is recognized for whites, especially sauvignon blanc.

Durbanville is an area in transition from rustic tradition to modern development. The area of rolling hills north of the city gets cooling nighttime mists and influences from both Table and False Bays. Wine farming dates from 1716, and the area was originally known for bulk wine production, but is now recognized for sauvignon blanc and merlot. **Paarl, Wellington and Franschhoek** have a variety of microclimates, soil types and grape varieties, with German and Huguenot heritage as well as the Dutch dating from the seventeenth century. Paarl is noted for shiraz, and more recently viognier, while **Franschhoek** has become a center for food and wine appreciation. The area is better known for white wine styles, especially chenin and semillon, but some wonderful shiraz and "bordeaux style" red blends are also being produced.

Stellenbosch is known to most as the red wine producing area in South Africa. However, the local estates produce great sparkling, white and fortified wines, as well. Cooler mountain slopes and cooling sea breezes from False Bay help moderate summer temperatures. The Simonsberg and Helderberg mountain areas fall within the Stellenbosch region. The area is recognized for cabernet, pinotage, shiraz and sparkling wines.

Swartland is the wheat and tobacco farming area north of Cape Town, and it is traditionally associated with big red wines. Swartland is now producing very good white wines — especially in the Groenekloof area that provides cooling Atlantic Ocean breezes. Swartland, along with the Malmesbury and Tulbagh areas, is recognized for pinotage, shiraz and sauvignon blanc.

The age-old adage that the best wine is grown within sight of the ocean is true for **Walker Bay**. Famous also for the winter whale watching, the area, which includes Elgin, is recognized for pinot noir, chardonnay and pinotage.

The main towns of the Cape Winelands are Stellenbosch, Paarl and Franschhoek. **Stellenbosch** is known for its unique Cape Dutch architectural heritage and the Stellenbosch (Maties) University. The town is also home to the Bergkelder wine complex, the Village Museum, and many galleries, specialty and antique shops. **Paarl** is the home of the Afrikaans Language Museum and the Taal Language Monument, and the KWV wine complex located in the Berg River Valley between the dramatic mountain scenery of the Paarlberg and the Klein Drakenstein Mountains. **Franschhoek**, nestled in the Valley of the Huguenots among spectacular mountains, is a charming village with many galleries, shops, cafés and fine restaurants and is also home to the Huguenot Monument and Museum.

There are four popular wine routes through the beautiful wine country northeast of Cape Town. The Stellenbosch Route covers 55 private cellars and cooperative wineries, including the Bergkelder, Blaauwklippen and Delheim, and the Van Ryn Brandy Cellar. The Paarl Route covers 26 cooperative wineries and estates, including Nederburg Estate and KWV Cooperative. The Franschhoek Route covers 24 cooperative wineries and private wine estates, including Bellingham and Boschendal. The Worcester Route has 20 cooperative wineries and estates.

There are a number of excellent restaurants in the region, including 96 Winery Road, 33 and Auberge Paysan (Stellenbosch), Bosman's (Paarl) and La Petite Ferme, Haute Cabriere and the Tasting Room at Le Quartier Francais (Franschhoek).

ACCOMMODATION — DELUXE:
• **Grand Roche**, a luxury estate hotel located in Paarl, has 34 rooms and suites with en suite facilities and a swimming pool, fitness center and tennis courts. Bosman's is one of the finest restaurants in the country. • **Le Quartier Francais**, a lovely country inn located in Franschhoek, has 15 deluxe rooms and 2 luxurious suites and the "Four Quarters" which consists of 4 exclusive suites with fireplaces, an excellent restaurant and swimming pool. • **Lanzerac Manor & Winery** has 48 luxurious en suite bedrooms and suites, authentic Cape Dutch architecture, restaurant, bar, Craven Lounge with a cigar bar, and three outdoor swimming pools. • **The Lord Charles Hotel**, located in Somerset West, has 198 rooms with en suite facilities.

Top: The main terrace at the Grand Roche overlooks the vineyard
Middle: Le Quartier Francais' main house and pool
Bottom: The "Four Quarters" at Le Quartier Francais

FIRST CLASS: • **D'Ouwe Werf**, located in Stellenbosch, is a beautiful old inn with 32 rooms and suites with private facilities, tennis courts, restaurant, vine-covered terrace, garden and swimming pool. • **Roggeland Country House** is a stately Cape Dutch farmhouse located near Paarl, with 10 bedrooms with en suite facilities, and a swimming pool. • **La Provence**, a quaint country inn situated in the middle of the FranschhoekValley, has rooms with facilities en suite, a restaurant and swimming pool. • **Auberge Rozendal Wine Farm Country House**, a 140-year-old homestead located near Stellenbosch, has Victorian-style cottages with en suite facilities and a swimming pool. Horseback riding is available. • **Mont Rochelle**, surrounded by the estates vineyards high on a mountain overlooking the Franschhoek Manor, has 22 rooms with en suite facilities, restaurant, swimming pool and sauna. • **River Manor**, a 2-minute stroll from the charming village center of Stellenbosch, has 16 en suite rooms, a swimming pool and spa. • **La Petit Ferme** has 3 private cottages set among the vineyards, each with private patio and plunge pool. Spacious bedrooms have fireplaces and bathrooms with large tubs and showers. • **Le Franschhoek Hotel and Spa** offers 79 en suite rooms with views of the gardens, a wellness spa, tennis and bicycling to wine farms in the surrounding vineyards, and a restaurant.

GUEST HOUSES: • **Rusthof Franschhoek** is an exclusive country house in Franschhoek with 8 air-conditioned rooms with en suite facilities, and swimming pool. • **Residence Klein Olifantshoek**, is located in Franschhoek and has 6 spacious en suite bedrooms and saltwater swimming pool.

North of Cape Town

This region has attractions that easily rival those on the more well-known Garden Route. Fabulous mountain scenery, whale and bird watching along the stark Atlantic Coastline and the magnificent proliferation of flowers in August and September make this a region well worth visiting. The **West Coast Ostrich Farm** is located 20 minutes north of Cape Town on the way to the West Coast National Park.

West Coast National Park

West Coast National Park covers 107-square-miles (276-km^2) along the Atlantic Ocean about an hour's drive north of Cape Town and includes the Langebaan Lagoon, several islands and coastal areas.

Whales can be seen from the park's shoreline between July and November.

Langebaan Lagoon, a wetland of internationally recognized importance, often has populations of over 50,000 birds comprised of 23 resident species and dozens of migrants from northern Europe and Asia. In total, over 250 different species have been recorded. Bird hides allow close viewing of the thousands of waders that migrate here in the summer months. Langebaan is also the site of a fossil footprint approximately 117,000 years old. Strandloper is an open-air restaurant on the beach serving a BBQ of the seafood caught in the area.

During spring, the land is in full flower. The **Postberg Nature Reserve** section of the park is open for visitors to enjoy from mid-August until the end of September. Bontebok, Cape mountain zebra, eland and Cape grysbok can be seen. A special bird is the black harrier. At Geelbek there is a historic farm and national monument with a country-style restaurant. It also serves as National Park Headquarters.

Another attraction in the area is the **West Coast Fossil Park**, located in Langebaanweg. The park has a visitor center with fossil displays, laboratory and lecture room, coffee shop and tea garden.

ACCOMMODATION IN THE REGION: FIRST CLASS: • **Bartholomeus Klip Farmhouse**, located in the Swartland region, is a restored Victorian farmhouse with 5 bedrooms with facilities en suite, set on an historic wheat and sheep farm combined with thousands of acres (hectares) of private nature reserve. Walks, mountain biking, and water sports at the dam are offered along with game drives to look for wildlife such as the Cape mountain zebra, and explore unique fynbos of the reserve. The lodge is located about a 75-minute drive from West Coast National Park and a 3-hour drive from Lambert's Bay.

ACCOMMODATION — GUESTHOUSES: • **Farmhouse Guest House**, located in Langebaan, has 18 rooms with en suite facilities. • **Kersefontein Guest House**, located on a working farm on the Berg River, has 6 en suite rooms and is a national monument.

Lambert's Bay

Lambert's Bay is famous for the crayfish and fish industry. Bird Island (now more a peninsula than an island) is found near the entrance of the harbor and is the breeding ground of thousands of Cape gannets, cormorants, penguins and other seabirds. There is a new information center, restaurant and truly sensational bird hide which offers outstanding photographic opportunities.

Muisbosskerm is an open-air seafood restaurant on the beach. Meals are prepared on open fires behind a hedge of thorny shrubs that are traditionally used for building sheep pens. The west coast crayfish is excellent.

The Cedarberg

This rugged, mountainous 502-square-mile (1,300-km^2) wilderness area dotted with interesting rock formations created by erosion, also features waterfalls, clear mountain pools, rock paintings and beautiful fynbos flora.

This is a fabulous area (along with Namaqualand to the north) in which to see millions of flowers blooming in the spring and is part of the "Wildflower Route". The best time to see wildflowers in the Cedarberg is August to early September.

There are over 250 marked hiking trails in the Cedarberg.

From the Cedarberg consider taking a day trip to Lamberts Bay to visit the gannet colony and see the whales in season.

The area is also known for the cultivation of unique products such as Rooibos Tea. There are a number of vineyards in the region, and tobacco is also cultivated, especially around the Rhenish Mission Station at Wupperthal. The nearby **Biedouw Valley** is famous for the profusion of wild flowers in spring (August and September) and the large variety of colorful vygies *(mesembryanthemums)* reaching right up to the mountains.

Clanwilliam, located 150 miles (240 km) from Cape Town, is the gateway to the Cederberg, via the Packhuis Pass, and much of the Karoo and the Maskam areas. It is famous for the Clanwilliam Dam (recreational water sports), the Ramskop Flower Reserve, Rooibos Tea factory and the many restored historic buildings.

ACCOMMODATION — CLASS A: • **Bushmans Kloof Lodge**, a Relais & Chateaux property and a South African Natural Heritage site, is located on

the 19,275-acre (7800-hectare) Bushmans Kloof Wilderness Reserve and provides a sanctuary for indigenous wildlife, birdlife and 755 species of plants. Wildlife on the reserve includes bontebok, red hartebeest, black wildebeest, Cape mountain zebra, Burchell's zebra, eland and springbok, however, the game is often difficult to approach closely. The lodge has 13 rooms and 3 suites. • **Koro Lodge**, situated 1.5 miles (2 kms) away from the main lodge, is a renovated farmhouse which has been transformed into a stunning private villa — consisting of 2 luxury en suite bedrooms and a loft large enough to accommodate 4 children. The villa comes equipped with its own chef, game ranger and vehicle. Besides the

Top: Bushmans Kloof's fire pit is the ideal spot to gather for a drink
Bottom: A unique element of Bushmans Kloof is the ancient rock art

guided game drives, guests can go on guided rock art walks (more than 125 rock art sites, some dating back 10,000 years), botanical tours, mountain biking, nature hikes, abseiling, canoeing, archery, croquet, fly fishing and swimming in crystal clear rock pools.

TOURIST CLASS: • **Saint Du Barry's Country Lodge**, located in Clanwilliam, has 4 rooms and 1 family unit with en suite facilities and a plunge pool.

GUESTHOUSES: • **Oudrif Guest House**, situated in the Cederberg on the banks of the Doring River, has 5 straw-baled, solar-powered cottages with en suite bathrooms and a restaurant. This is more an "eco-lodge" than a B&B.

Namaqualand

Namaqualand is located north of the mouth of the Olifants River and south of the Orange River, and it is a place of rare and exquisite beauty, with vivid contrasts between vast expanses of space and brilliant displays of flowers in spring (August to early September). The area is largely semi-desert with warm dry temperatures year-round, and it has about 4,000 species of plants.

The flora of this region is unique. After a good rainy season there are not only carpets of annual flowers, but also a wide variety of geophytes (plants with bulbs, corms and tubers), dwarf shrubs and succulents that vary from creepers to large-stem succulents like the chubby kokerboom *(Aloe dichtoma)*, a tree-succulent.

The reason for this unique flora is the region's low and sporadic winter rainfall, which gives rise to plant adaptations for survival during moist winters and to dry and very hot summers. In winter and spring the plant cover is high with perennials and many annuals, but in the summer Namaqualand becomes a barren scene. This winter-summer transformation is almost unimaginable and must be seen to be believed.

There are many towns in this region that are famous for their flowers. Nieuwoudtville is home to many of the geophytes; Van Rhynsdorp

Some of the beautiful flowers of Namaqualand

features many of the succulents in the area; and Garies, Kamieskroon and Springbok become carpeted with wildflowers such as daisies, herbs, succulents and lilies in the springtime.

ACCOMMODATION — TOURIST CLASS: • **O'Kiep Country Hotel**, located in O'Kiep, 5 miles (8 km) north of Springbok, is a comfortable country hotel with 18 air-conditioned rooms with en suite facilities, restaurant and bar. • **Kamieskroon Hotel**, located in the heart of Namaqualand, has 24 rooms with en suite facilities, lounge, restaurant and bar. • **Karoo Lodge Guest House** located in the center of Springbok, has 26 air-conditioned rooms with en suite facilities, restaurant and bar. • **Annie's Cottage**, a beautifully restored manor house situated in the heart of Springbok, has 11 en suite rooms (all individually decorated) and a very relaxing garden and pool area. • **Mountain View Guest House** in Springbok has 10 air-conditioned suites all with private facilities and mini-bars.

East of Cape Town
Hermanus, Gansbaai and De Kelders

This beautiful region is located less than a 2-hour drive from Cape Town or Franschhoek (The Winelands). Explore this charming seaside town, walk in the **Fernkloof Reserve** with magnificent views over scenic Walker Bay,

The spectacular coastline of South Africa

stroll along the cliff paths, and visit the Saturday Craft Market. The Hamilton Russell and Bouchard & Finlayson wineries have tasting facilities not far from Hermanus. There are also specialist wine shops in Hermanus that offer wine tasting to showcase the local wine estates in the Hermanus area.

Hermanus and the Walker Bay area, which encompasses Gansbaai, are some of the best land-based **whale-watching** sights in the world. The whales come into these waters from the Antarctic Convergence between July and November.

The southern right whale is eight times as big as a large bull elephant, and it reaches over 50 feet (15 m) in length and 50 tons in weight. It is so aware of its exact position that it is able to pass under, or next to your boat with its tail fluke curved around you. Breaching is an incredible sight and can only be likened to a missile being launched from a submarine.

Boat trips to Walker Bay and Gansbaai for whale watching, and to nearby Dyer Island to view Cape fur seals, African (jackass) penguins, thousands of cormorants and other seabirds, and to great white shark dive (see description under "Scuba Diving in the Southern Cape") are highly recommended. A visit to Grootbos Nature Reserve is also recommended (see the description that follows).

ACCOMMODATION HERMANUS — DELUXE: • **The Marine Hotel**, situated in Hermanus on a cliff overlooking Walker Bay, is a Relais & Chateaux hotel with 43 rooms and suites, 2 restaurants, a swimming pool and a helipad. Golf, tennis, bowls and squash are available at a nearby Country Club. • **The Western Cape Hotel and Spa** has 145 en suite rooms and suites, golf courses, swimming pool, and Acquabella Spa and Wellness Centre. • **Birkenhead House**, perched high on the cliffs of Hermanus overlooking the whale watchers paradise of Walker Bay, has 10 luxurious rooms with mountain or sea views.

GUEST HOUSES: • **Auberge Burgundy Guest House**, situated on Walker Bay, has 18 garden rooms, either sea or garden facing, 3 poolside rooms and 3 suites with sea views. The Burgundy Restaurant offers outstanding cuisine, featuring fresh local seafood. • **Sandbaai Country House**, located on the beachfront, has 11 rooms with en suite bathrooms. • **De Kelders Bed and Breakfast**, located near Gansbaai overlooking the cliffs of De Kelders and the sea, has 5 rooms with facilities en suite. • **Anlo Guest House**, situated 5 minutes from Gansbaai in De Kelders, has 8 en suite rooms set back from the ocean with sea views. • **Blue Gum Country Estate** is located outside of Stanford, 12 miles (20 kms) beyond Hermanus. The lodge features 10 suites, decorated in English country or African style, each with private facilities. Guests enjoy the swimming pool and exclusive access to a boat on the Stanford River. Morning and evening cruises are offered.

Top: Grootbos Lodge — a leader in responsible tourism
Bottom: Enjoy the incredible view over Grootbos Nature Reserve

Grootbos Nature Reserve

Grootbos is a private fynbos reserve located between Hermanus and Gansbaai about a 2-hour drive from Cape Town. This is an excellent place to stay if you plan to whale watch, take boat excursions to see seal colonies and dive with great white sharks.

Grootbos Nature Reserve has a diversity of fynbos vegetation with over 740 plant species and over 100 bird species. Activities available at Grootbos include nature drives, walks, horseback rides, and walks along the 20 miles (30 km) of beaches.

During our visit we were treated to the most interesting guided presentation of fynbos ecology that I have ever had. The next day we went whale watching on Walker Bay and came within a few yards (meters) of several southern right whales, which seemed to enjoy our presence. That same afternoon we boarded a 30-foot (9-m) rubber duck (Zodiac) and zoomed across the waves at speeds over 50 miles per hour (80 km/h) to Dyer Island, where we found a large seal colony and watched great white shark diving in action — and even had a great white at least 16 feet (5 m) in length swim right under our boat. That's enough to stop your heart for a few seconds!

ACCOMMODATION: CLASS A — • **Grootbos** has 2 lodges, the **Garden Lodge** and the **Forest Lodge**, with 23 private luxury cottages that include a separate lounge, en suite bathroom, fireplace and mini-bar. There is a restaurant with central fireplace, full bar and lounge area with wooden deck overlooking Walker Bay, library and gift shop, large swimming pool, ecological interpretation and research center and Leica spotting scopes for whale watching. From the deck, you may have a vista all the way to Cape Point. Children are very welcome.

Scuba Diving in the Southern Cape

The world's two great oceans, the cold south Atlantic and the warm Indio-Pacific, rub brawny shoulders along the southernmost curve of Africa. This contrast of temperatures produces two extremes in underwater habitats and at least three unique opportunities for the adventurous diver: the Southern Cape, Southern Natal Coast (Durban area) and Northern Natal Coast (near Sodwana Bay and Rocktail Bay).

For those seeking the ultimate underwater thrill, the Southern Cape offers the magnificent cold-water predator — the great white shark. South Africa is one of the few places in the world where divers can encounter this formidable creature from the safety of a shark cage. The great white shark is a protected species in South Africa and reaches heroic proportions in these rich waters.

Dyer Island is believed to be one of the best places in the world to view the great white shark. The island is 6 nautical miles from Gansbaai and is a bird sanctuary and a brooding site of the African penguin. Adjoining the island is a smaller rocky island called Geyser Rock, which supports a large seal population. Separating Geyser and Dyer Island is a channel named "Shark Alley" where the boats anchor hoping to sight these magnificent predators.

A thrill of the aquatic kind! Whale watching on Walker Bay

There have been a few licenses granted to commercial shark divers in the Southern Cape area, and all operations have experienced skippers and divers on board who supply all the necessary equipment required to enter the cages under the water. You do need a diving qualification to enter the cage. Non-divers can see the sharks from the boat because they come very close to the surface. The best time to see the great white sharks is between May and October. The probability of seeing a shark during January, February and March is about 50%.

The boats go out to sea between 7:00 and 9:00 a.m. and, depending on weather conditions, they reach the anchoring spot in about 20 to 25 minutes. The anchor is put down, the cage goes into the water and a scent trail is begun. Once final preparations for the dive are made, you settle down to spend the rest of the time watching, diving and enjoying the day. A light lunch and drinks are available on the boat, and there is a toilet on board.

Not for the faint of heart. A great white shark comes up for a closer look

The water temperature can be anywhere between 54° and 61°F (12° and 16°C). Visibility is usually 20 to 26 feet (6 to 8 m), but it can go up to 40 to 50 feet (12–15 m) on a good day and down to 7to 10 feet (2 to 3 m) on a bad day.

Diving facilities, equipment and training in South Africa are generally excellent.

The Garden Route

One of the most beautiful drives on the continent, the Garden Route is lined with Indian Ocean coastal scenery, beautiful beaches, lakes, forests and mountains, with small country hotel accommodations and large resort hotels. The Garden Route runs between Mossel Bay (east of Cape Town) and Storms River (west of Port Elizabeth).

A number of tours and self-drive options are available from Cape Town to Port Elizabeth (or vice versa) for a minimum of 2 nights/3 days. These programs visit a variety of areas and attractions. The **coastal route** from Cape Town passes through the winelands, Hermanus, Mossel Bay and the coastal areas of Wilderness, Knysna and Plettenberg Bay to Port Elizabeth.

The **mountainous route** from Cape Town passes through the winelands, Caledon, Swellendam, over magnificent Tradouw Pass to Barrydale and Calitzdorp, and then to Oudtshoorn. Continue over the Outeniqua Mountains to Wilderness and through the coastal areas to Port Elizabeth. The **northern route** from Cape Town passes through the winelands, Matjiesfontein, and Prince Albert to Oudtshoorn. From there you can join the coastal areas route to Port Elizabeth.

Departing Cape Town, the better way to begin the **coastal route** is to drive to Somerset West, turn toward the coast at The Strand, and continue along False Bay passing Gordon's Bay, Betty's Bay (where there is a mainland colony of African penguins) and onward to Hermanus. The road down to the coast yields fine views of the rugged coastline. The southernmost vineyards in Africa are located nearby.

One of the most scenic regions along the coast – the Garden Route

Southern right whales usually start arriving in **Walker Bay** (Hermanus) in June or July and usually depart by December, with the peak season being August and September. The best time for whale watching in general along the Garden Route is also August and September.

You may continue to **Cape Agulhas**, the southernmost tip of Africa, where the Atlantic and Indian Oceans meet, and to **Waenhuiskrans** (Arniston), a 200-year-old fishing village. An interesting day visit from Arniston is the **De Hoop Nature Reserve**, which is a pristine reserve with magnificent, unspoiled beaches. It is the breeding ground of the African black oystercatcher and has a colony of Cape vultures. Other species seen include bontebok, eland and Cape mountain zebra.

Continue to the town of **Mossel Bay** and then drive north to **Oudtshoorn** where you can ride an ostrich — or at least watch them race — and tour an ostrich farm. Located about 16 miles (26 km) north of Oudtshoorn are the

Cango Caves, the largest limestone caves in Africa, with colorful stalactites and stalagmites.

Return to the coast via **George**, an Old World town with oak-tree-lined streets set at the foot of the Outeniqua Mountains. A narrow-gauge steam train runs in the morning from George across the **Knysna Lagoon** to Knysna and back to George that same afternoon.

Continue east to the **Wilderness Area**, which encompasses a number of interlinking lakes, and onward to Knysna, a small coastal town with a beautiful lagoon excellent for boating. The Knysna Forest and the Tsitsikamma Forest together form South Africa's largest indigenous high forest.

The Pletternberg offers incredible views of the bay

Farther east lies **Plettenberg Bay**, the Garden Route's most sophisticated resort area. The new boardwalk complex has many shops, restaurants and a casino. Whale-watching boat trips depart from the beach.

My family and I have spent a day in Plettenberg, walking Robberg Nature Reserve and enjoying the dolphin cruise with one of the local boat operators. We saw three of the marine "Big 5," with humpback and southern right whales, Cape fur seals and bottlenose dolphins.

Nearby is **Tsitsikamma National Park** — a lushly vegetated 50-mile (80-km) strip along the coast. Wildlife includes the Cape clawless otter, grysbok, bushbuck and blue duiker. Over 275 species of birds have been recorded. The park has hiking trails, including the famous **Otter Trail**, and underwater trails for both snorkelers and scuba divers. At **Bloukran's Bridge**, about 25 miles (40 km) from Plettenberg Bay, is the highest **bungee jump** in the world — 708 feet (216 m)!

The northern route passes the Paarl winelands area through a portion of the Great Karoo (semi desert) to **Matjiesfontein**, a charming little town where the buildings and railway station have been preserved in their original Victorian style. From there the route runs southeast through Prince Albert to Oudtshoorn, where it meets the southern route.

One of the luxury rooms at The Plettenberg

From Plettenberg Bay you may continue to St. Francis Bay, Jeffrey's Bay (famous for surfing) and to Port Elizabeth.

ACCOMMODATION — SOUTHWEST TO NORTHEAST:

WAENHUISKRANS — FIRST CLASS: • **The Arniston** has 31 rooms with en suite facilities and a swimming pool. Whales are often seen May to October.

SWELLENDAM — FIRST CLASS: • **Klippe Rivier Homestead** is a Cape Dutch homestead in which the old wine house and stables have been converted into 6 luxury bedrooms and 1 honeymoon cottage with en suite facilities.

OUDTSHOORN — FIRST CLASS: • **Rosenhof Country Lodge** has 12 rooms and 2 executive suites with en suite facilities and a swimming pool.

GUEST HOUSE: • **Altes Landhaus**, cradled in the Schoemanshoek Valley, is a Cape Dutch-style homestead offering all suites with private facilities.

TOURIST CLASS: • **De Opstal Farm**, a working ostrich farm located between Oudtshoorn and the Cango Caves, has air-conditioned rooms with en suite facilities and a swimming pool. • **Queens Hotel** has 40 en suite rooms and is located in downtown Oudtshoorn.

PRINCE ALBERT — TOURIST CLASS: • **The Swartberg Hotel**, located north of Outdshoorn, is a charming hotel with 14 rooms in the main house and 5 cottages that are ideal for families, all rooms are en suite.

GEORGE — DELUXE: • **The Fancourt Hotel & Country Club Estate** is an elegant hotel (a National Monument) with 100 rooms and suites with en suite facilities, 4 championship golf courses, swimming pool, tennis and a spa.

FIRST CLASS: • **Hoogekraal Country House**, an eighteenth century coastal estate, has 10 rooms with facilities en suite.

WILDERNESS — TOURIST CLASS: • **Wilderness Hotel** is situated close to the ocean and the lagoon and has 155 rooms with en suite facilities.

GUEST HOUSE: • **Wilderness Manor** is situated on Wilderness Lagoon within walking distance of the beaches and village shops. The manor is known for its elegant rooms decorated in afro-colonial style. Each of the 4 bedrooms has an en suite bathroom.

BETWEEN WILDERNESS AND KNYSNA — DELUXE: • **Lake Pleasant Hotel**, a converted 1840 manor house situated within a bird sanctuary on a natural freshwater lake, has 20 air-conditioned self-contained suites and 6 villas with en suite bathrooms, a restaurant, beautifully restored bar, wine cellar, indoor swimming pool, spa (wellness center), steam room, sauna and tennis courts.

The golf course at Pezula Resort offers incredible views

KNYSNA — DELUXE: • **Pezula Resort** is a retreat overlooking Knysna Lagoon, with suites with private balconies, health spa and 18-hole champion golf course. • **St. James Club** is located on the shores of the Knysna Lagoon, with 15 suites with en suite facilities, a swimming pool and floodlit tennis courts. • **Phantom Forest Lodge**, located on the Phantom Forest Eco Reserve, is situated on the Knysna River and offers guests a unique bio-diversity of Afro-montane forest, estuarine wetland and Cape coastal fynbos. The lodge has 12 tree suites that are comprised of a sitting room, bedroom with private forest bathroom and an outside deck area. Activities include walking trails, canoeing and bird watching.

FIRST CLASS: • **Belvidere Manor** has guest cottages with en suite facilities. • **Ai Due Camini Guest House**, located on the eastern head of Knysna Lagoon, has 5 bedrooms with facilities en suite and a swimming pool.

TOURIST CLASS: • **Yellowwood Lodge**, a restored Victorian house, has 11 rooms with en suite facilities. • **Point Lodge**, set on the water's edge, has 9 rooms with facilities en suite and a swimming pool. • **Brenton-on-Sea**, located in the secluded Brenton Cliffs area, has rooms with en suite facilities.

PLETTENBERG BAY — DELUXE: • **Tsala Treetop Lodge** has 10 secluded suites built with natural stone, wood and glass set at the top of the canopy of the trees about 20 feet (6 m) above the forest floor. Each suite has an en suite bathroom, outdoor shower and a plunge pool. • **Kurland**, a luxury country hotel established in old Cape Dutch tradition surrounded by polo fields, has 8 large and beautifully furnished rooms with facilities en suite situated around the swimming pool, and a health spa with fully equipped gymnasium, sauna and steam bath. • **Hunter's Country House** has 21 elegantly decorated thatched cottages with en suite facilities. • **The Plettenberg** is a 5-star Relais & Chateaux Hotel built on a rocky headland with breathtaking vistas of the sea with 37 air-conditioned luxury rooms and suites, and 2 swimming pools. The adjoining Beach House has its own pool and is ideal for a family or small group of friends.

FIRST CLASS: • **Hog Hollow**, set on the edge of the forest with great views of the Tsitsikamma Mountains, has 12 suites (chalets) with en suite facilities, private decks and fireplaces. • **Lodge on the Bay** has 6 luxury suites with a contemporary flair and en suite bathrooms.

TOURIST CLASS: • **Formosa Inn**, an old established coach house, has 38 garden chalets with en suite facilities. • **Country Crescent Hotel**, located just outside of Plettenberg Bay, has 39 rooms with facilities en suite and a swimming pool.

STORMS RIVER — TOURIST CLASS: • **Protea Hotel Tsitsikamma Village Inn** has 49 Swiss-style chalets with facilities en suite.

ST. FRANCIS BAY — FIRST CLASS: • **Jyllinge Lodge**, located on the beach in a charming coastal resort town, has 8 rooms with facilities en suite.

PORT ELIZABETH — DELUXE: • **Courtyard Suites Hotel**, a new hotel located on the beachfront in front of the new Boardwalk Complex, has 64 suites and a swimming pool. • **Hacklewood Hill Country House**, built in 1898, is an elegant residence located in a suburb, with 8 rooms with en suite facilities, a swimming pool and tennis courts.

FIRST CLASS: • **Marine Hotel**, located near the beach, has 98 rooms with en suite facilities and a swimming pool.

TOURIST CLASS: • **Protea Hotel Edward**, a historical landmark, has 97 rooms with facilities en suite and a swimming pool. • **Garden Court Kings Beach Holiday Inn** has 285 rooms with en suite facilities and a swimming pool.

MATJIESFONTEIN (NORTHERN ROUTE) — TOURIST CLASS: • **The Lord Milner** is located just off the Cape Town-Johannesburg Road (N1).

Shamwari Private Game Reserve

Shamwari is a 35,000-acre (14,000-hectare), malaria-free private game reserve located 47 miles (75 km) northeast of Port Elizabeth.

Wildlife on the reserve includes white rhino, black rhino, elephant, buffalo, lion, hippo and 17 species of antelope. Day and night game drives and walks are offered.

ACCOMMODATION — CLASS A: • **Eagles Crag Lodge** features 9

One of the sumptuous bedrooms at Eagles Crag Lodge

superior suites each with private facilities, a private deck with pool, as well as, indoor and outdoor showers. The lodge has a spa, dining room, library, lounge and cocktail bar. • **Long Lee Manor** is an Edwardian mansion with 19 air-conditioned rooms with private balconies and en suite facilities. • **Lobengula Lodge** has 5 air-conditioned suites with en suite facilities. • **Riverdene** is a restored settler's home accommodating 18 guests with facilities en suite. • **Bushman River Lodge** is also a restored settler's home, with 4 suites with en suite facilities. • **Bayethe Tented Lodge** offers 9 tents nestled along the bed of the river, camouflaged under trees. Each tent is air-conditioned and has an en-suite bathroom, shower, private plunge pool and viewing deck.

Addo Elephant National Park

This 29,000-acre (11,718-hectare) park, located in a malaria-free area about 45 miles (72 km) north of Port Elizabeth, was formed to protect the last of the elephant and Cape buffalo in the Eastern Cape. Other wildlife in the park includes black rhino, greater kudu, eland, red hartebeest and bushbuck. By far the main attraction of the park is the opportunity for close encounters with elephants. We saw hundreds during out last visit!

ACCOMMODATION — CLASS A: • **Gorah Elephant Camp**, set on a private concession area in the park, has 11 luxurious tents with en suite bathrooms. Gorah House, the main lodge building, was built in 1856 and has been restored to its colonial style.

FIRST CLASS: • **Riverbend Country Lodge**, located on a private game farm adjacent to the park, has 8 rooms with bathrooms en suite and a swimming pool. Walks on the farm and horseback riding are offered. A spa facility has recently been added. • **Kuzuko Lodge**, which opened in October 2007, adjoins Addo Elephant National Park and has 24 en suite air-conditioned chalets. Day and night game drives are offered with access into the national park.

Kwandwe Great Fish River Lodge's main lounge

Kwandwe

Kwandwe is a 62,000-acre (25,000-hectare) private reserve of rolling hills and savannah located in the malaria-free Eastern Cape, about 20 minutes by road from Grahamstown and 2 hours from Port Elizabeth. The reserve includes 19 miles (30 km) of river frontage on the Great Fish River. Over 7,000 head of game was reintroduced into the reserve, including both black and white rhino, lion, elephant, cheetah, Cape buffalo and a variety of antelope.

ACCOMMODATION — CLASS A: • **Kwandwe Great Fish River Lodge** overlooks the Great Fish River and has 9 air-conditioned suites with bathrooms, indoor and outdoor showers, private plunge pools and salas, a swimming pool and wine cellar. Activities include day and night game drives, walks, fishing, rhino tracking, overnight fly-camping and visits to historical Grahamstown. • **Uplands Homestead** has 3 en suite bedrooms, private game ranger, chef and butler, and is ideal for families and private parties. • **Kwandwe Ecca Lodge** features 6 intimate suites, each with a luxurious en suite bathroom and sitting area. Main guest areas include a dining room and bar area, interactive kitchen, and lap pool. • The newest addition, **Melton Manor**, is a sole-use safari villa with 4 spacious en suite bedrooms, an interactive kitchen, private butler, ranger and chef.

Top: The refreshing pool at Kwandwe Ecca Lodge
Bottom: The topography surrounding Kwandwe Melton Manor

KWAZULU-NATAL

KwaZulu-Natal is located in eastern South Africa along the Indian Ocean. The Drakensberg Mountains rise to 11,420 feet (3,482 m) and run roughly north and south along its western border, which it shares with Lesotho.

KwaZulu-Natal is the home of the Zulu. A large variety of wildlife concentrated in several small yet interesting reserves. Hiking in the Drakensberg Mountains is popular.

Durban

The largest city in KwaZulu-Natal, Durban has a beachfront called The Golden Mile that features amusement parks, amphitheater, colorful markets

KwaZulu-Natal

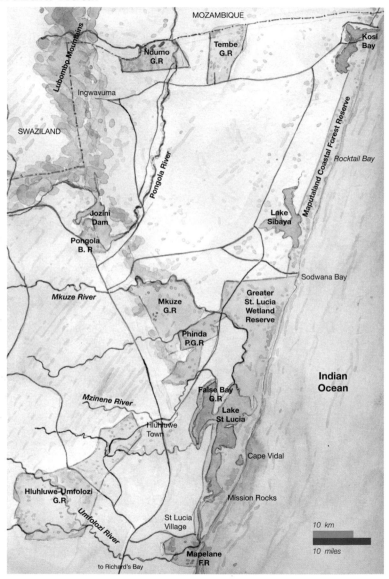

and aquarium (Sea World). Rickshaws, with drivers in traditional Zulu costume, are available along the beachfront. The Victoria Market and Grey Street Mosque are evidence of the strong Indian influence in this area.

ACCOMMODATION — FIRST CLASS: • **Quarters Hotel**, set in a trendy suburb of Durban, consists of 4 restored Victorian homes and features 24 en suite bedrooms. There is a restaurant on site. • **Hilton Durban**, a 327-room business hotel located next to the International Convention Centre, has a restaurant, bar and swimming pool. • **Holiday Inn Crown Plaza** has 450 rooms and suites with en suite facilities and two swimming pools.

TOURIST CLASS: • **Protea Edward Hotel**, a hotel with Old World charm and located on the beachfront, has 101 rooms with en suite facilities and a swimming pool. • **The Royal Hotel**, located in the city center, has 230 rooms and 21 suites with en suite facilities and swimming pool. • **Garden Court Marine Parade** has 346 sea-facing rooms and suites with en suite facilities and a swimming pool. • **Southern Sun North Beach** has 285 rooms and suites with facilities en suite and a swimming pool.

ACCOMMODATION NEAR DURBAN — DELUXE: • **Zimbali Lodge**, located 26 miles (42 km) north of Durban, has been built in a forest and is surrounded by a championship 18-hole Tom Weiskopf golf course. The lodge has 76 rooms, colonial-style restaurant with views over the Indian Ocean, tennis courts, a private beach, outdoor pool, a health spa, conference facilities, golf club and pro shop. Nearby attractions include the traditional Zulu village of Shakaland, Crocodile Creek, Zulu Battlefields, Chaka's Rock and Hluhluwe Game Reserve. • **Beverly Hills**, located north of Durban on the beach at Umhlanga Rocks, has 88 rooms and suites with en suite facilities and a swimming pool. • **Shorten's Country House**, an old colonial homestead built in 1905, is located a 20-minute drive from Durban and has chalets with en suite facilities, an 18-hole golf course, squash and tennis courts and bowling greens. • **Selbourne Lodge and Golf Resort** is an English manor-style resort set close to the Indian Ocean, with 72 rooms and suites with en suite bathrooms. Facilities include an 18-hole golf course, restaurant, private beach club, tennis courts and swimming pool.

Zimbali Lodge's spectacular pool area

Zululand

This is the most tropical part of South Africa, with many plant and animal species typical of East Africa, extending south along what is a broad coastal

An example of a traditional "beehive" Zulu hut made of thatched grass

plain. It is not surprising that Zululand also has the greatest concentration of wildlife areas and game ranches in the country. This is also the land of scenic hills and valleys, dotted with Zulu homesteads, many still in the traditional "beehive" style.

ACCOMMODATION — CLASS A/B: • **Shakaland**, a resort built on the movie set for the films *Shaka Zulu* and *John Ross,* offers a look into the Zulu culture. Take a walk through a typical Zulu village where you may be shown the art of bead making, spear throwing and beer brewing, visit the Sangoma (witch doctor) and enjoy a display of Zulu dancing. Guests are accommodated in 55 traditional beehive huts with en suite bathrooms.

CLASS B: • **Simunye Pioneer Settlement**, located between Durban and Hluhluwe Umfolozi Park, allows guests to experience contemporary Zulu culture. Accommodations are rock chalets built into the side of a cliff, with facilities en suite and a rock pool. There is no electricity; lighting is supplied by lamps and candles. Guests may learn to drive a single-horse ox cart or horseback ride in the valley.

Drakensberg Mountains

Referred to as uKhahlamba — "Barrier of Spears", this 120 mile (200 km) long mountain range rises on the eastern escarpment of South Africa and borders the mountain Kingdom of Lesotho. This region was witness to much of the early history of South Africa such as the Stone Age occupation, the San hunter-gatherers referred to as "Bushmen", migrating chiefdoms from the Great Lakes of Central Africa in the 1300s, and the ox wagons of Boer settlers negotiated the pass in the 1830s and 1840s. Now a World Heritage Site, the mountain flora and fauna are complimented by the 35,000 San rock art images.

ACCOMMODATION — CLASS A/B: • **Cleopatra Mountain Farmhouse** is located at the foot of the Drakensberg Mountains. The owners of the property, Richard and Mouse Poynton were also the originators of the Country House movement in South Africa in the 1980s. Accommodations include 11 standard rooms, suites and private cottages. Activities include hiking on mountain trails, horseback riding, fishing, birding and swimming in mountain pools. • **Cathedral Peak's** accommodation range from inter-leading family rooms, to private rondavels tucked away between the trees. The exclusive honeymoon suites with private gardens offer breathtaking mountain views. Guests can enjoy daily horseback riding, squash, tennis, swimming pool, boule, badminton, volleyball, croquet, lawn chess, mini golf, gym, sauna, mountain bike trails, trout fishing and a challenging 9-hole golf course.

Midlands — Rorke's Drift

There are numerous Zulu War and Anglo-Boer War battle sites in the region, including Isandlwana and Rorke's Drift. Tour guides who are superb storytellers make the history of that day come alive, and long, family associations with the area and its people allow you some unique Zulu perspectives on the battles fought with the British soldiers.

Overlooking the Battlefield of Isandlwana, the 6,250-acre (2,500-hectare) **Fugitive's Drift Game Reserve** is 5 miles (8 km) from Rorke's Drift on the Buffalo River in KwaZulu Natal. Diverse and abundant wildlife includes giraffe, zebra, kudu, hartebeest and a host of smaller antelope, as well as 275 recorded bird species. The **Buffalo George** is a Natural Heritage Site where spectacular walks can be enjoyed.

ACCOMMODATION — CLASS A: • **Isandlwana Lodge** is carved into the iNyoni rock overlooking Mt. Isandlwana and offers 12 luxury rooms with en suite facilities, and a swimming pool.

CLASS B: • **Fugitives' Drift Lodge** consists of 8 colonial-style cottages with en suite facilities. Most people who stay here are interested in tours of the Anglo/Zulu battlefields. • **Zulu Wings Game Lodge** is located close to Isandlwana, Rorke's Drift and Blood River Battlefield sites and offers 6 cozy rooms with en suite facilities. Home-style meals are served in the dining room and there is a lounge, pool table and swimming pool. • **Three Tree Hill Lodge** specializes in the second Anglo-Boer War (1899–1902) and overlooks The Battle of Spioenkop. There are 6 cottages with facilities en suite, swimming pool and library. Tours of the battlefield are given.

Hluhluwe Umfolozi Park

The Hluhluwe and Umfolozi Reserves, the oldest reserves in Africa (proclaimed in 1895), were combined to form Hluhluwe Umfolozi Park — now the third largest reserve in South Africa. As there are no roads directly connecting Hluhluwe and Umfolozi, each section of the park must be visited separately. The best time to visit is during the dry winter months (May to September). Game drives by open vehicle and walks with national park guides are available.

The Umfolozi section of the park is located about 165 miles (265 km) north of Durban. This 185-square-mile (478-km²) reserve of open grassland

and savannah woodland is best known for having the world's largest concentration of white rhino — approximately 1,900. Other species include black rhino, elephant, nyala, greater kudu, waterbuck, zebra, wildebeest, buffalo, giraffe, black-backed jackal, lion and cheetah. Over 400 species of birds have been recorded.

The 90-square-miles (231-km^2) of grassland, forest and woodland of the Hluhluwe section of the park is host to a variety of wildlife, including large numbers of white rhino, along with black rhino, elephant, buffalo, southern giraffe, wildebeest, Burchell's zebra, kudu, lion, cheetah, Samango monkeys, hippo and crocs. This is one of the best parks in Africa to see the splendid nyala antelope. Over 425 bird species have been recorded, with narina trogon, cinnamon dove and Natal robin among the more interesting species.

On one visit we spotted over 20 white rhino, 12 nyala and southern giraffe, along with buffalo and grey duiker, among other species.

The Hluhluwe section of the park is located about 18 miles (29 km) from St. Lucia and 175 miles (282 km) from Durban. The park contains walking trails.

ACCOMMODATION IN THE UMFOLOZI SECTION — CLASS C & D:
• The park has self-service chalets, huts and bush camps with ablution blocks.

ACCOMMODATION IN THE HLUHLUWE SECTION — CLASS B:
• **Hilltop Camp**, an attractive camp run by the park, has chalets with en suite facilities and a restaurant.

CLASS C & D: The park has cottages with en suite facilities and self-service huts with ablution blocks. A small self-service bush camp with an ablution block is also available.

CAMPING: None.

ACCOMMODATION NEAR THE PARK — CLASS A/B: • **Zululand Tree Lodge**, located on the Ubizane Game Reserve near the Hluhluwe entrance, has 24 fan-cooled tree-house-style chalets with en suite facilities and a swimming pool. Game drives to Hluhluwe Umfolozi and Mkuzi Game Reserves, walks, horseback riding, local community visits and cruises on Lake St. Lucia are offered.

Itala Game Reserve

This scenic 116-square-mile (300-km^2) reserve consists of open savannah, deep valleys, granite outcrops and rivers.

The reserve has a high concentration of wildlife, including black rhino, white rhino, giraffe, eland, kudu, tsessebe and waterbuck. Over 300 bird species have been recorded, including birds of prey such as martial eagle, black eagle, Wahlberg's eagle and brown snake eagle.

Game drives by park rangers are in open vehicles; wilderness trails and guided day walks are also available. The park is located in northern Natal just south of the Pongola River.

ACCOMMODATION — CLASS B: • **Ntshondwe Camp** has 67 thatched chalets with en suite facilities, overlooking a water hole.

CLASS D: A small, self-service bush camp with separate facilities is available.

CAMPING: Campsites with ablution blocks are available.

Phinda Private Game Reserve

Phinda covers 85-square-miles (220-km^2) of landscape, much of it reclaimed from former livestock and pineapple farms. The habitats are extremely diverse, with acacia and broad-leafed savannah, riverine woodland, marshes and rocky hillsides. Groves of unique sand-forest exist on ancient dunes, and this remarkable dry forest is home to rare plants and mammals such as suni, bushpig and nyala, and unusual birds, including African broadbill, Neergaard's sunbird and pink-throated twinspot.

Wildlife at Phinda includes white rhino, giraffe, elephant, hippo, zebra and buffalo, as well as the big carnivores — all reintroduced since 1991 and thriving in this reborn wilderness. This is one of the best reserves in southern Africa for seeing cheetah. Bird watching is outstanding; among the more interesting species are crested guineafowl, gorgeous bushshrike, pygmy kingfisher, lemon-breasted canary and Eastern Nicator.

Phinda operates along the lines of private reserves bordering Kruger, with day and night drives in open 4wd vehicles, bush walks and boma

Top: A luxurious bedroom at Phinda's Getty House
Middle: Giraffes were reintroduced to Phinda Game Reserve in 1991
Bottom: The dining room at Phinda Vlei Lodge

Top: A boat cruise at Phinda
Middle: Dining al fresco in the boma at Phinda Zuka Lodge
Bottom: Phinda is one of the best places in southern Africa to see cheetah

dinners. Additional experiences offered include boat cruises and canoeing on the Mzinene River, excursions to the nearby Indian Ocean, and flights to enjoy an aerial perspective of the region. Loggerhead turtles, bottlenose dolphins, whale sharks and rays are among the marine animals often seen from the air. Three-day walking safaris with overnights in a luxury mobile tented camp, and a Bush Skills Academy are also offered.

Phinda is very important from a regional perspective because it forms an ecological link between the St. Lucia reserves and Mkuze Game Reserve — a vast area that is soon to have all fences removed. Phinda has also pioneered successful community development projects in the region, providing employment, skills development and infrastructures, such as clinics and schools, to a previously impoverished area. Guests are invited to visit nearby communities to see how the lives of many people have been transformed, thanks to the revenue earned from tourism. The rights to the land itself were recently returned to the community.

ACCOMMODATION — A+: • **Getty House** is a luxurious private villa on Phinda Private Game Reserve situated in the west of the Reserve. The villa includes 4 spacious suites and a private butler, chef, guide and 4wd safari vehicle for exclusive use of the guests. • **Phinda Rock Lodge** has 6 air-conditioned suites nestled on the edge of a rocky cliff, each with en suite bathroom, indoor and outdoor showers and plunge pool. • **Phinda Vlei Lodge** has 6 air-conditioned suites on stilts, each with their own bathroom and plunge pool.

CLASS A: • **Phinda Forest Lodge** has 16 air-conditioned chalets, surrounded on three sides by glass and built on stilts between the forest floor and the towering torchwood trees, and a swimming pool. The windows open up to the canopy beyond. • **Phinda Mountain Lodge** has 25 spacious air-conditioned chalets with en suite facilities and a swimming pool. • **Phinda Zuka Lodge** offers 4 thatched Zululand bush cottages with en suite facilities and private verandahs overlooking the waterhole. Private guide/host, butler and chef are exclusive to the camp.

Mkuze Falls Private Nature Reserve

This private game reserve in northern KwaZulu-Natal is located close to the southern boundary of Swaziland. The reserve boasts two significant biomes: the montane grassland and lowveld bushveld, which offers a great diversity of species from leopard and lion to buffalo and a healthy population of elephant. The rich grasslands support large numbers of grazing herbivores such as wildebeest and zebra, which attract the attention of the reintroduced cheetah population.

ACCOMMODATION — CLASS A: • **Mkuze Falls Lodge** has 8 en suite air-conditioned suites with private plunge pools and views across the Mkuze River gorge. • **Mkuze Falls Tented Camp** is more intimate in size and has only 5 luxury safari tents, each with en suite facilities. Both properties include morning, afternoon and night safaris as well as guided bush walks.

Mkhuze Game Reserve

This 131-square-mile (340-km^2) park has a diversity of vegetation including riverine forest, savannah woodland and forests of large sycamore fig trees. Wildlife includes leopard, side-striped jackal, white rhino, black rhino, eland, kudu, nyala, bushbuck, reedbuck, klipspringer, hippo, crocs and a variety of aquatic birds.

Mkhuze is one of South Africa's top bird watching localities, and most serious birders should visit both Mkhuze Game Reserve and Mkuze Falls Private Nature Reserve, which is only a few hours drive away. A particular highlight at Mkhuze is the various observation hides (blinds), which overlook key points and provide unrivalled viewing and photographic opportunities, not only of birds such as purple-crested turaco and yellow weaver, but also of rhino, nyala and warthog quenching their thirst. The fig forest walk offers an outstanding chance to see Narina trogon, white-eared barbet and trumpeter hornbill, to name just a few.

ACCOMMODATION — CLASS C & D: • **National Park bungalows**, an 8-bed bush camp with facilities en suite, and huts with ablution blocks.

St. Lucia and Maputaland Marine Reserves

These two reserves combined to form Africa's largest marine conservation area, covering 342-square-miles (885-km^2). The reserve runs along the coastline from 0.6 mile (1 km) south of Cape Vidal to the Mozambique border and 3.5 miles (5.6 km) out into the Indian Ocean.

Several species of turtles, including loggerhead and the endangered leatherback, lay their eggs on the northern beaches. St. Lucia includes the southernmost coral reefs in the world and is the only breeding spot for pink-backed pelicans in South Africa. Flamingos migrate to the reserve, depending upon the salinity levels in the lakes and lagoons. Boat tours are available from the village of St. Lucia.

ACCOMMODATION — CLASS B: • **Makakatana Bay Lodge**, located within the Greater St. Lucia Wetland Park Reserve, has 5 air-conditioned suites and 1 honeymoon suite with en suite bathrooms, swimming pool, restaurant and bar.

CAMPING: Campsites are available.

Maputaland Coastal Forest Reserve

Top: The pristine coastline at Rocktail Bay
Bottom: A scuba diver's thrill — a whale shark

The Maputaland Coastal Forest Reserve is a remote reserve containing very possibly the highest forested sand dunes in the world. No construction is allowed on the ocean side of these huge dunes. The beach is, in fact, rated as one of the most beautiful and pristine beaches in the world!

Maputaland is one of the best areas for scuba diving in southern Africa. The Indian Ocean "Big Five" — humpback whales, whale sharks, huge leather back turtles, bottlenosed dolphins and ragged-tooth sharks — can be seen on dives.

Wildlife includes large spotted genet, water mongoose, hippos and turtles (in season). During our visit we saw a variety of birdlife, including scarlet-chested sunbirds and dusky flycatchers. KwaZulu locals are often seen collecting mussels and catching reef fish in the reserve.

Beach walking, snorkeling, surf casting and fly-fishing, and exploring the unique flora and bird life of this region provide visitors with plenty to do. Black Rock, a large sandstone protrusion into the Indian Ocean about 4 miles (6.7 km) from Rocktail Bay, is one of the few places in the world where pelagics may be fished from shore. Lala Neck, located south of Rocktail Bay, is very good for snorkeling. Lake Sibaya, the largest freshwater lake in South Africa, is separated from the Indian Ocean by only the coastal dunes.

ACCOMMODATION — CLASS A/B:
• **Rocktail Beach Camp** lies within the coastal forest, 765 yards (700 m) inland from the warm Indian Ocean. Its 12 en suite chalets (including 3 family rooms) with private verandahs are tucked away in the indigenous forest, some with ocean views. A fully

Top: A loggerhead turtle comes ashore to nest at Rocktail Bay
Bottom: Rocktail Bay Lodge

accredited dive center provides scuba diving and snorkeling activities offshore. Other activities include surf fishing, quad biking, birding, horseback riding guided drives to various sites and the local village. • **Rocktail Bay Lodge** has 10 attractive wooden chalets and 1 family suite, with en suite facilities and a swimming pool. Fishing, snorkeling, scuba diving, nature drives and excursions to Black Rock, Lala Neck and Lake Sabaya are offered.

Ndumo Game Reserve

Located in northeastern KwaZulu-Natal, on the border with Mozambique, Ndumo comprises a mosaic of woodland and wetland, and is known by some as the "Little Okavango" (in reference to the Okavango Delta in Botswana).

Although only 39-square-miles (100-km²) in extent, this is undoubtedly one of the finest reserves for birding in South Africa. The vegetation is dense and there are no large herds of game — and neither elephant nor lion — but the tropical setting and semi-aquatic wildlife is spectacular. Both black and white rhino occur, but it is hippo, nyala, suni and red duiker that are most often seen.

The beautiful Nyamithi Pan is a small lake ringed by ghostly fever trees and home to some massive Nile crocodiles. Nyamithi (and other pans) is also a haven for waterfowl, including white pelican, goliath heron, yellow-billed stork and black egret. Pied and malachite kingfishers feed in the shallows, alongside black-winged stilt and African jacana. In the woodlands and forests, birds such as tambourine dove, Natal robin, crowned hornbill and green coucal are fairly common. Known as the "birding Mecca" of South Africa, Ndumo has recorded over 60% of the 700 species found in the country.

ACCOMMODATION — CLASS D: • **National Parks cottages** with ablution facilities.

CAMPING: None.

Sodwana Bay National Park

Fishing (especially for marlin) and scuba diving are the main attractions of this 1.6-square-mile (4.1-km²) reserve.

ACCOMMODATION — CLASS B/C: • **Sodwana Bay Lodge** has chalets with en suite facilities and offers scuba diving and big-game fishing.

CAMPING: Campsites are available.

Scuba Diving — Natal Coast

In the transition zone between Sodwana and Rocktail Bay's coral reefs and the Cape's kelp forests is the city of Durban and the southern Natal Coast. Aliwal Shoal, Lander's Reef and the Produce wreck are the diving focal points of the region.

Escorted boat dives to these rocky reefs are opportunities to view a wide variety of southern Africa's marine animals, including potato bass (a large grouper), eels, rays, turtles and myriad reef fish.

The best time to see Aliwal's famed "ragged tooth sharks" is June and July. A group of huge resident bridle bass (jewfish) and schools of dagger salmon make the nearby wreck of the Produce their home.

Zululand's semitropical coast has South Africa's warmest and clearest waters — ideal for scuba diving and snorkeling. Because the coral reefs are home to both warm- and cold-water fishes, there are more fish families to be found on the reefs off shore of Rocktail Bay and Sodwana Bay than in the whole of the Great Barrier Reef. Escorted boat dives are offered from Sodwana Bay and Rocktail Bay (see above).

Africa's most southern coral reefs are composed of hard and soft reefs. Named according to their distance from the Sodwana launch site, these reefs are called Quarter-, Two-, Three-, Four-, Seven- and Nine-Mile reefs. The reefs are home to many species of colorful Indian Ocean tropical fish, rock cods (groupers), kingfish (a large jack), barracudas and moray eels. Dolphins are sometimes sighted on the way to dive sites, and humpback whales migrate through the area in February and September. "Ragged tooth" sharks and enormous whale sharks (the world's biggest fish) are sometimes seen by divers in January and February. Manta rays and pelagics are also part of the fish mix. Loggerhead, green and leatherback sea turtles use the undeveloped coastline for nesting from December to March. Night drives and walks to see turtles nesting can be arranged.

Diving is possible year-round, with the best conditions between February and June. Visibility ranges from 20 to 100+ feet (6 to 30+ m), depending on sea conditions, with an average of 65 feet (20 m). Water temperature ranges from 70 to 80°F (21 to 27°C). Most diving is conducted from 25 to 125 feet (8 to 38 m) below the surface.

East Africa

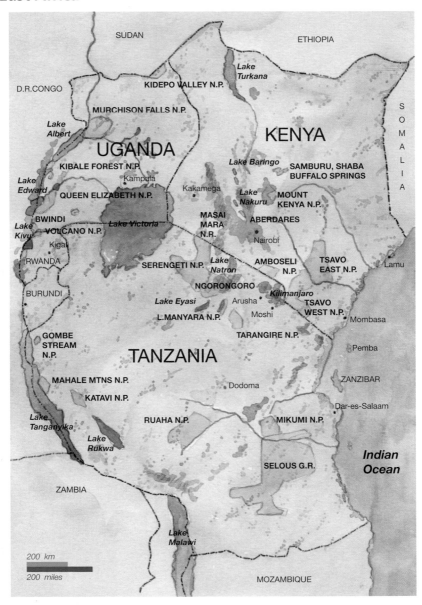

Tanzania

Tanzania

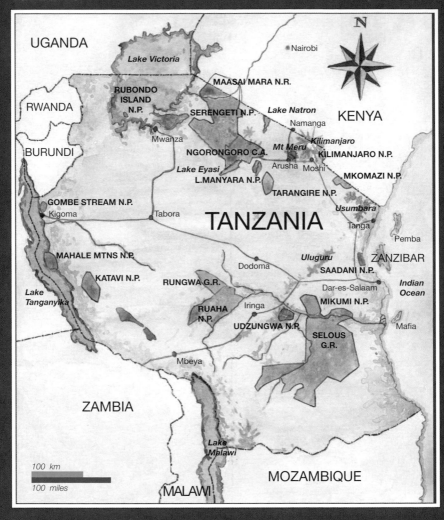

Set between the tropical Indian Ocean and the two arms of the Rift Valley, Tanzania is one of Africa's most scenically beautiful countries. It also has some of the most extensive protected areas including the fabled Serengeti. The landscape rises from sea level to 19,000 feet (5,894 m) at the summit of Mt. Kilimanjaro. Covering 365,000-square-miles (945,000-km²), Tanzania is about the same size as Texas and Oklahoma combined. The population numbers some 36 million, with Dodoma as the administrative capital. The famous port city of Dar es Salaam has been a key trading center for centuries. KiSwahili is the most widely spoken language, but English is also commonly used. Currency is the Tanzanian Shilling.

Tanzania
Country Highlights

- Tanzania is considered by many experts as one of the two top wildlife countries on the continent (along with Botswana)
- Have front row seats to the spectacle known as the Migration of the Wildebeest across the majestic Serengeti plains
- Experience world-class luxury private mobile camping with your own staff and luxury tent in Tarangire or the Serengeti
- Descend into the Ngorongoro Crater for a day of game viewing and opportunity to see the "Big Five"
- Climb Mt. Kilimanjaro – the highest peak in Africa
- Spend time with the Hadzape Bushmen, the Datoga and the Maasai
- Fly to the Selous and experience guided walking safaris and game viewing by boat
- Trek chimpanzees at Mahale or Gombe and visit remote Katavi to see big game with very few tourists
- Finish your safari adventure with a stay on Zanzibar or one of the charming outer islands offering barefoot luxury

Best Parks and Reserves to Visit　　**Best Times to Go**

Serengeti, Grumeti Reserves and....................Year round (rainy period
　Ngorongoro　　　　　　　　　　　　April through mid May)
Tarangire, Selous, Ruaha and Katavi.............June to November
Mahale ....mid-May through mid-
　　　　　　　　　　　　　　　　　　October/December to
　　　　　　　　　　　　　　　　　　February

Best Accommodations

Sasakwa Lodge, Sabora Plains and Faru Faru, Migration Camp, Tarangire Treetops, Lake Manyara Tree Lodge, Ngorongoro Crater Lodge, Sand Rivers, Beho Beho, Lupita Island Lodge

TANZANIA

Between Africa's highest mountain (Kilimanjaro) and Africa's largest lake (Victoria) lies one of the best game viewing areas on the continent. This region also includes the world's largest unflooded intact volcanic caldera (Ngorongoro) and the most famous wildlife park (the Serengeti). To the southeast lies one of the world's largest game reserves — the Selous.

Volcanic highlands dominate the north, giving way southward to a plateau, then semidesert in the center of the country and highlands in the south. The coastal lowlands are hot and humid with lush vegetation. One branch of the Great Rift Valley passes through Lakes Manyara and Natron in northern Tanzania to Lake Malawi (Lake Nyasa) in the south, while the other branch passes through Lakes Rukwa and Tanganyika in the west.

The "long rains" usually occur in April and May, however, this does not mean it rains all the time, as the thundershowers will come and go. Lighter rains often occur in late October and November. Altitude has a great effect on temperature. At Arusha (4,600 ft/1,390 m), the Southern Highlands (6,700 ft/2,030 m) and the top of Ngorongoro Crater (7,500 ft/2,285 m), nights and early mornings are especially cool. Tanzania's highest temperatures occur December to March and are lowest in July.

Some scientists debate that East Africa was the cradle of mankind. Some of the earliest known humanoid footprints, estimated to be 3.5 million years old, were discovered at Laetoli by Dr. Mary Leakey in 1979. Dr. Leakey also found the estimated 1.7-million-year-old skull Zinjanthropus boisei at Oldupai (formerly Olduvai) Gorge in 1957.

From as far back as the tenth century, Arabs, Persians, Egyptians, Indians and Chinese were involved in heavy trading on the coast. The slave trade began in the mid-1600s and was abolished in 1873.

British explorers Richard Burton and John Speke crossed Tanzania in 1857 to Lake Tanganyika. Speke later discovered Lake Victoria, which he mistakenly thought was the source of the Nile.

The German East Africa Company gained control of the mainland (then called German East Africa) in 1885, and the German government held it from 1891 until World War I, when it was mandated to Britain by the League of Nations. Tanganyika gained its independence from Britain in 1961, and Zanzibar gained its independence in December 1963. Zanzibar, once the center of the East African slave trade, was ruled by sultans until they were overthrown in January 1964. Three months later, Zanzibar formed a union with Tanganyika — the United Republic of Tanzania.

There are 120 tribes in Tanzania. Bantu languages and dialects are spoken by 95% of the population, with KiSwahili the official and national language. Over 75% of the people are peasant farmers. Export of coffee, cotton, sisal, tea, cloves and cashews bring 70% of the country's foreign exchange. Tourism is now one of the country's top foreign exchange earners.

🐾 WILDLIFE AND WILDLIFE AREAS

Reserves cover over 95,000-square-miles (250,000-km²); only a few countries on earth can boast having a greater amount of land devoted to parks and reserves. The 15 national parks, 17 game reserves and 1 conservation area comprise over 15% of the country's land area. In total, over 25% of the country has been set aside for wildlife conservation. Tanzania's great variety of wildlife can be at least partially attributed to its great diversity of landscapes, with altitudes ranging from sea level to 19,340 feet (5,895 m).

Tanzania is one of the best wildlife countries in Africa for mobile tented camp safaris. Vehicles with roof hatches or pop-tops are used on driving safaris. Safari camps and lodges that have guides and vehicles based at them may in many cases use open-sided vehicles.

No two zebras have the same stripe pattern

Top: A lioness decides to take it easy in
the morning sun
Bottom: The excitement of a game drive

If accompanied by a national park guide, walking is allowed in Arusha, Mt. Kilimanjaro, Gombe Stream, Ruaha, Mahale Mountains, Katavi National Park, Rubondo Island National Park, Selous Game Reserve and Loliondo Game Reserve (bordering the eastern side of the Serengeti National Park). Areas for walking have recently been designated in Tarangire National Park and more areas are expected to be opened. Walking is also allowed in the Ngorongoro Conservation area (but not within the Ngorongoro Crater itself) if accompanied by a conservation ranger.

The best weather for viewing game in northern Tanzania is June through March. Christmas to February and July and August are the busiest periods. April and May is traditionally the rainy season and travel in 4wd vehicles is highly recommended, however, as the seasons are not as pronounced as they were a few decades ago, travelers during that period may in fact encounter little rain. Advantages of traveling in April and May include lower rates, fewer tourists, and great game viewing in some parks, such as the Serengeti and Ngorongoro Crater. This is a great time to drive through the Great Serengeti Migration, with possibly no other vehicles in sight!

Light rains usually fall late October to early December, but, in fact, have little negative effect on game viewing. A little rain is nice because it helps drop the dust out of the air, and the bush turns from brown to green. In southern Tanzania the best months for game viewing are June to November due to the longer 6 month dry season compared to the north.

The country contains 35 species of antelope and over 1.5 million wildebeest — over 80% of the population of this species in Africa. The calving season for wildebeest is from mid-January to mid-March.

Northern Tanzania

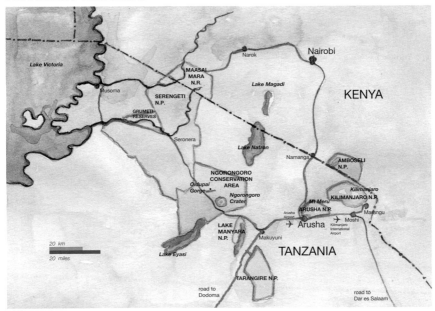

THE NORTH

This region, from Mt. Kilimanjaro in the east to Serengeti National Park in the west, is the area most visited by tourists and boasts many of the country's most famous parks.

Some visitors reach Arusha, gateway to the area, by flying directly into Kilimanjaro International Airport. Others fly into Nairobi (Kenya) and then take a one-hour flight to Kilimanjaro or a 4- to 5-hour drive via Namanga to Arusha, or they fly into Dar es Salaam and then take an hour's flight to Kilimanjaro or Arusha airports. Kilimanjaro International Airport is located 34 miles (54 km) east of Arusha and 22 miles (35 km) west of Moshi, and has a bank, bar, shops and a restaurant.

The "Northern Circuit" includes Arusha National Park, Tarangire National Park, Lake Manyara National Park, Ngorongoro Conservation Area, Oldupai Gorge and the Serengeti National Park.

From Arusha the Northern Circuit runs 45 miles (73 km) west on a good tarmac road, across the gently rolling Maasai plains with scattered acacia trees, to Makuyuni. You can then either continue on the main road toward Dodoma for another 20 miles (32 km) to Tarangire National Park or turn right (northwest) to Mto wa Mbu (Mosquito Creek) on a recently paved road.

Enroute you pass many Maasai bomas (villages) and Maasai in their colorful traditional dress walking on the roadside, riding bicycles, herding their cattle and driving overloaded donkey carts.

Maasai Morani completing the circumcision ritual are sometimes seen clad in black with white paint on their faces. They leave the village as children for a period of training and instruction by elders and return as men.

Mto wa Mbu is a village with a market filled with wood carvings and other local crafts for sale. Be sure to bargain. If you take a few minutes to walk into the village behind the stands, you will get a more realistic (and less touristy) view of village life.

Continuing west, you soon pass the entrance to Lake Manyara National Park. The road then climbs up the Rift Valley escarpment past huge baobab trees and numerous baboons looking for handouts (please do not feed any wild animals). Fabulous views of the valley and Lake Manyara Park below can be seen. Next you pass through beautiful cultivated uplands, the village of Karatu and other small villages, past the turnoff to Lake Eyasi, and on up the slopes of the Crater Highlands to Ngorongoro Crater. The road then follows the rim of the crater and finally descends the western side of the crater to Oldupai Gorge and Serengeti National Park, the Loliondo Game Conservation Area and the Grumeti Reserves.

Arusha

This town is the center of tourism for northern Tanzania and is situated in the foothills of rugged Mt. Meru. Named after a sub-tribe of the Maasai, the Wa-Arusha, it is located on the Great North Road midway between Cairo and Cape Town. Makonde carvings and other souvenirs are available in the numerous craft shops at the center of town. Walking around the Arusha Market, located behind the bus station, is an interesting way to spend a few hours. Consider visiting a school or clinic to better experience the local culture.

ACCOMMODATION: Also see "Accommodation" under "Arusha National Park."

DELUXE: • **Arusha Coffee Lodge**, located near the Arusha Airport on a coffee plantation, has 18 rooms with large en suite bathrooms with separate shower and bath, telephones, mini bar, ceiling fans and fireplaces. There is a swimming pool and 24-hour room service. • **Serena Mountain Village, Arusha** has recently been renovated and has 42 rondavels with en suite facilities, swimming pool and conference center. The lodge is set in lovely gardens and is located 6 miles (10 km) east of Arusha overlooking Lake Duluti. • **Kigongoni Lodge** is located on 70-acres (28-hectares) with 18 stand alone cottages and 1 family room, each with a private verandah and views of Mt. Kilimanjaro and/or Mt. Meru. • **Safari Spa**, situated in a valley between Mt. Kilimanjaro and Mt. Meru, has cottages with en suite facilities, fitness center, sauna, steam room, jacuzzi, and swimming pool. Polo matches are often played on the grounds.

FIRST CLASS: • **Karama Lodge**, located about 3 miles (5 km) from Arusha, consists of 22 bungalows with en suite bathrooms, and it is built on stilts. On a clear day there are spectacular views of Mt. Meru and Mt. Kilimanjaro. • **Moivaro Lodge**, situated outside of Arusha on a coffee plantation, has 40 double (or triple) cottages with en suite facilities and a swimming pool. • **Dik Dik Hotel** has

Serena Mountain Village, Arusha

9 bungalows with 2 double rooms in each bungalow, with en suite facilities, and a swimming pool. Horseback riding and fishing are available. • **Rivertrees Country Inn** is a country-style hotel with 8 rooms with en suite facilities, set in tranquil gardens and farmland, situated midway between Arusha and Kilimanjaro airport. • **Ngare Sero Mountain Lodge** is a farmhouse situated on the slopes of Mt. Meru, with rooms that have private facilities. • **Mt. Meru Hotel** is a 200-room hotel with en suite facilities and a swimming pool. • **Mount Meru Game Lodge** is located in 33 acres of gardens bordered by the Usa River and the animal sanctuary. The lodge consists of 15 rooms and 2 newly constructed suites. • **The Arusha Hotel**, located in the heart of Arusha, offers 86 stylish rooms with en suite facilities, air-conditioning, satellite television, WiFi, electronic safes and a swimming pool. • **Kibo Palace Hotel**, in Arusha's Town Center, has 65 well-appointed rooms with en suite facilities, mini-bar, in-room safe, satellite television and WiFi. Amenities include a fitness center, massage room, and swimming pool.

TOURIST CLASS: • **The Impala Hotel** has 160 rooms, including several suites, with en suite facilities and a swimming pool.

Arusha National Park

This highly underrated park is predominantly inhabited by forest animals, while in the other northern parks, savannah animals are more prevalent. Arusha National Park is the best place in northern Tanzania to spot black-and-white colobus monkeys and bushbuck and to photograph larger species with Mt. Kilimanjaro or Mt. Meru in the background. Early mornings are best for this because Mt. Kilimanjaro is less likely to be covered with clouds. Travelers should consider spending at least half a day here as this park is so different from the other parks and reserves on the "Northern Circuit".

Arusha National Park

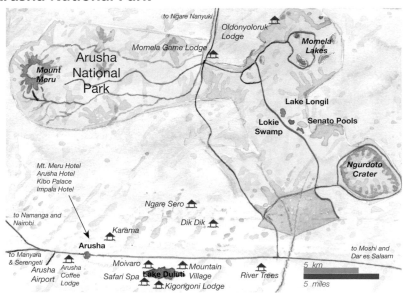

This 53-square-mile (137-km²) park is actually the merger of three regions: Meru Crater National Park, Momella Lakes and Ngurdoto Crater National Park. The wide range of habitats, from highland rain forest to acacia woodlands and crater lakes, hosts a variety of wildlife. Armed park guides are required to accompany you for walks in the western part of the park or for climbing Mt. Meru; guides are available at Park Headquarters at Momella Gate.

On the open grassland near the entrance to the park, Burchell's zebra are often seen. High in the forest canopy of the Ngurdoto Forest is a good place to find blue monkeys and black-and-white colobus monkeys. Olive baboons are common and red duiker are sometimes seen.

Canoeing on the Momella Lakes

Walking is not allowed in the 2 mile (3 km) wide Ngurdoto Crater, which is, in essence, a reserve within a reserve. However, there can be good views (especially in the early morning) of the crater, Momella Lakes and Mt. Kilimanjaro.

Driving north from Ngurdoto, you pass Ngongongare Spring, the Senato Pools (sometimes dry) and Lokie Swamp and are likely to see

Arusha National Park is one of the best places to view black-and-white colobus monkeys

common waterbuck and maybe Bohor reedbuck. Buffalo are often seen around Lake Longil.

As you continue past Kambi Ya Fisi (hyena's camp), the landscape becomes more open, and elephant and giraffe can be seen. Hippo and a variety of water fowl can be seen at the shallow, alkaline Momella Lakes, where canoe safaris are offered.

From Kitoto, a 4wd vehicle is needed to reach Meru Crater. The sheer cliff rises about 4,920 feet (1,500 m) and is one of the highest in the world.

At the base of Mt. Meru, you may encounter elephant and buffalo. Kirk's dikdik, banded mongoose and klipspringer can also be seen in the park. On one visit we saw giraffe lying down — very unusual indeed! The best time to visit for game viewing is June through March.

Over 400 species of birds have been recorded, with Hartlaub's turaco, red-fronted parrot and brown-breasted barbet among the species not easily found elsewhere in northern Tanzania.

Mt. Meru (14,977 feet/4,566 m) is an impressive mountain that is classified as a dormant volcano; its last eruption was just over 100 years ago. The mountain can be climbed in 2 days, but it is more enjoyable to take 3 days, which allows more time for exploration.

On the morning of the first day of a 3-day climb, walk for about three hours from Momella Gate (about 5,000 feet/1,500 m) to Miriakamba Hut.

In the afternoon, hike to Meru Crater. On the second day, hike 3 hours to the Saddle Hut, and in the afternoon walk for about 1 and 1.5 hours to Little Meru (12,530 feet/3,820 m). On day 3, reach the summit and return to Momella Gate.

The best months to climb are June to October and late December to February. Bring all your own gear and make your reservations in advance.

The turnoff to the park entrance is 13 miles (21 km) east of Arusha and 36 miles (58 km) west of Moshi. Continue another 7 miles (11 km) to Ngurdoto Gate. Walking is allowed in the western part of this park where there are a number of hikes and picnic sites to enjoy when accompanied by a park ranger.

ACCOMMODATION IN THE RESERVE — CLASS F: One self-service rest house (5 beds) is located near Momella Gate.

ACCOMMODATION NEAR THE RESERVE — CLASS A/B: • **Hatari Lodge** has 9 bungalows (doubles) with open fireplace and en suite facilities, designed in a classic retro style. The central living and dining room welcome guests for meals and there is a lounge area and deck with views of Mt. Kilimanjaro.

CLASS C/D: • **Momella Game Lodge**, located just outside Arusha National Park, has 57 rooms with en suite facilities.

CAMPING: One campsite is located near Ngurdoto Gate, in the forest, and 3 are at the foot of Tululusia Hill. All have water, long-drop toilets and firewood.

The colorful dress of the Maasai

Ndarakwai Ranch

Ndarakwai is a 10,000-acre (4,000-hectare) private wildlife reserve located on the northwest slopes of Mt. Kilimanjaro about a 1.5 hour drive from Arusha. The area is dominated by acacia woodlands. There is permanent water on the ranch — a key element in making it a haven for wildlife — especially in the dry season.

Activities include day and night game drives in open vehicles, escorted walks with armed guides, and visits to Maasai villages that are far off the tourist track.

During a morning and afternoon game drive we saw a large herd of lesser kudu (this is one of the best places for lesser kudu in East Africa), eland, bushbuck, gerenuk, Defassa waterbuck, Burchell's zebra, Thomson's gazelle, impala, baboon and vervet monkey, eland, ostrich and other game. On a night drive we spotted marsh mongoose, bushpig, springhare and bush duiker. Elephant are prevalent in the dry seasons.

ACCOMMODATION — CLASS B: • **Ndarakwai Ranch** has 10 permanent tents on platforms under thatch, with bush (bucket) showers and en suite flush toilets.

Ndarakwai Ranch

Sinya

The Sinya region is Maasailand bordering the southwestern corner of Amboseli National Park in Kenya. Mt. Meru lies to the southwest and Mt. Kilimanjaro to the southeast. This area of hills and acacia woodland has seldom been visited by tourists until recently.

Unlike at Amboseli, one seldom if ever encounters other tourists on the Tanzania side of the border. From the time we left Namanga until the time we left the region, we encountered no other vehicles.

There is no permanent water in the area except for a few boreholes used by the Maasai for their livestock. In addition to seeing resident game, wildlife can be seen traversing the area, moving to and from permanent water in Amboseli National Park to permanent water on the slopes of Mt. Kilimanjaro.

Two Maasai morani joined us on 2 game drives during which we spotted lesser kudu, African wild cat, eland, cheetah, elephant, Maasai giraffe, dikdik, impala, dwarf mongoose and Burchell's zebra.

Game viewing in Sinya is good; however, its major attraction may be that it offers very good opportunities for a non-touristy, cultural experience with the Maasai.

Sinya is about an hour and a half drive from Namanga and about a two-hour drive from Arusha.

ACCOMMODATION — CLASS B/C: • **Kambi ya Tembo** has 8 tents with en suite bucket showers and flush toilets.

Tarangire National Park

Large numbers of baobab trees dotting the landscape give the park a prehistoric look, the likes of which I have never seen. This 1,003-square-mile (2,600-km²) park has a different feel to it than any other northern park — and an eerie feeling at that, making it one of my favorites.

Tarangire National Park

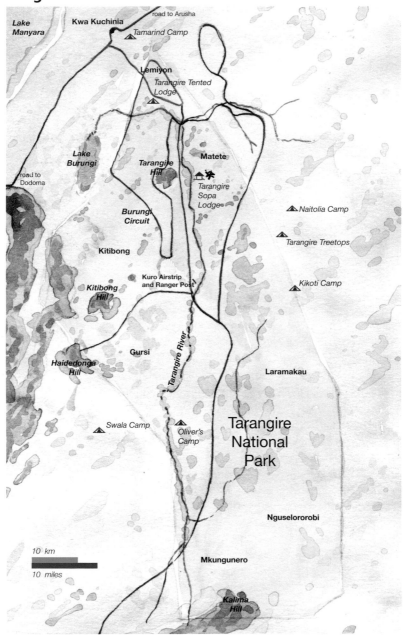

Lake
Manyara

Kwa Kuchinia

road to Arusha

Tamarind Camp

Lemiyon

*Tarangire Tented
Lodge*

Lake
Burungi

road to
Dodoma

*Tarangire
Hill*

Matete

*Tarangire
Sopa
Lodge*

Naitolia Camp

*Burungi
Circuit*

Kitibong

Tarangire Treetops

*Kitibong
Hill*

Kuro Airstrip
and Ranger Post

Kikoti Camp

Gursi

*Haidedonga
Hill*

Tarangire River

Laramakau

Tarangire
National
Park

Swala Camp

*Oliver's
Camp*

Nguselororobi

10 km

10 miles

Mkungunero

Kalima
Hill

Tarangire is the best park on the northern circuit to see lions in trees and elephant. Many years ago while in the park I met Cynthia Moss, author of *Elephant Memories and Portraits in the Wild* (Chicago University Press), who told me that she had identified over 500 individual elephants within the park during one week!

Fewer tourists visit this park than Manyara, Ngorongoro and Serengeti, allowing a better opportunity to experience it as the early explorers did — alone. This park should not be missed; wildlife viewing is excellent, especially from July to November, when many animals concentrate near the only permanent water source in the area — the Tarangire River and its tributaries.

At the beginning of the short rainy season (November), migratory species including wildebeest and zebra, soon followed by elephant, buffalo, Grant's gazelle, Thomson's gazelle and oryx, begin migrating out of the park. However, as most migration routes have been cut off from the expansion of man's presence, many of these animals are, in fact, remaining in the park and few are migrating out of the park or far beyond the park's borders, also making December to February a good time to visit. Giraffe, waterbuck, lesser kudu and other resident species remain in the park. The migratory animals that do manage to leave the park usually return at the end of the long rains in June.

On a recent two-day visit during November we saw more than 600 elephant, several prides of lion, leopard in a tree with an impala kill, eland, oryx, along with a variety of other antelope. The game viewing was excellent!

Tarangire wildlife populations include approximately 30,000 zebra, 25,000 wildebeest, 5,000 elephant, 5,000 buffalo, 5,000 eland, 2,500 Maasai giraffe and 1,000 oryx. Other prominent species include Grant's and Thomson's gazelle, hartebeest, impala, lesser and greater kudu, reedbuck and gerenuk. Lion and leopard are frequently seen. Cheetah and spotted hyena are also present, as are the banded, slender, dwarf and marsh mongoose. African wild dog may also be seen.

Lions are often seen in trees in Tarangire

The **Lemiyon region**, the northernmost region of the park, is characterized by a high concentration of baobab trees that is unmatched by any park I've seen. This unique landscape is also dotted by umbrella acacia trees, as well as some open grasslands and wooded areas. Elephant, wildebeest and zebra are often seen. Visitors with little time for game viewing may want to concentrate on the Matete and the Lemiyon areas, including the Tarangire River.

The majestic baobabs of Tarangire

The **Matete region** covers the northeastern part of the park and is characterized by open grasslands with scattered umbrella acacia and baobab trees and the Tarangire River. Lion, fringe-eared oryx and klipspringer are seen quite often. Bat-eared fox are also present.

On the 50-mile (80-km) **Burungi Circuit**, you pass through acacia parklands and woodlands. You are likely to see a number of species, including elephant, eland and bushbuck.

The eastern side of the **Kitibong area** is a good place to find large herds of buffalo. The eastern side is mainly acacia parklands, and the western side is thicker woodlands.

The **Gursi section** is similar to the Kitibong area with the addition of rainy season wetlands, which are home to large populations of water birds.

The **Larmakau region**, located in the central eastern part of the park, has extensive swamps. **Nguselororobi**, in the south of the park, is predominantly swamp with some woodlands and plains. The **Mkungunero section** has a few freshwater pools and a variety of bird life.

On one visit, we spotted eland, giraffe, buffalo, a few lion, oryx, elephant, impala, Grant's gazelle, zebra, hartebeest, warthog, baboon and ostrich.

Game viewing is excellent during the dry season from July to October, and is, in fact, very good in June, November and December. Well over 300 species of birds have been recorded at Tarangire, with lappet-faced vulture, yellow-necked spurfowl, Fischer's lovebird, white-bellied go-away bird, rosy-patched bushshrike and ashy starling among the characteristic species. Bird watching is best December through May. During the rainy seasons, some roads become impassable.

Oliver's Camp is located in the southern region of the park

ACCOMMODATION IN THE RESERVE — CLASS A/B: • **Oliver's Camp**, located inside the southern region of the reserve and sits on an elevated ridge overlooking a flood plain, has 8 tents with private bush showers and flush toilets. Day game drives and walking safaris are offered within the park. • **Swala Camp** is a permanent tented camp, located on the western side of the park, with 9 tents with en suite facilities, and a swimming pool. The camp sponsors a local school which can be visited when in session.

CLASS B:✳**Tarangire Sopa Lodge** has 75 rooms with en suite facilities and a swimming pool.

CLASS B/C: • **Tarangire Tented Lodge** is set on a high ridge overlooking the Tarangire River, and has 35 tents (doubles) and 6 bungalows (triples) with private facilities and a large swimming pool.

ACCOMMODATION ON THE PERIPHERY OF THE PARK — CLASS A: • **Tarangire Treetops Camp** is set in a private reserve just outside the border of the park, about a 45-minute drive from the park entrance. Each of the 21 luxurious tents has bathroom facilities en suite,

Top: Built around trees, Tarangire Treetops is a unique and luxurious camp
Bottom: The interior of a tent at Tarangire Treetops

and it features a deck built around one of the trees. Activities offered outside the park include walking, night game drives and mountain biking.

CLASS B: • **Kikoti Camp** is a 20 bed permanent tented camp, with en suite facilities, perched high on a ridge on the eastern periphery of the park only 4 miles (7 km) from the park gate. Activities include day game drives into the park, nature walks with a Maasai guide, escorted mountain biking, night game drives outside the park and visits to local villages. • **Naitolia Camp**, located in a private concession area northeast of the park, has 4 stone and grass cottages with en suite toilets and bucket showers, and 1 tree camp (used only in the dry season). Walking safaris and night game drives can be arranged from this camp.

CAMPING: There are campsites for private and public use throughout the park. All facilities have to be brought into the park.

Lake Manyara National Park

Once one of the most popular hunting areas of Tanzania, this 125-square-mile (325-km^2) park has the Great Rift Valley Escarpment for a dramatic backdrop. Two-thirds of the park is covered by alkaline Lake Manyara, which is situated at an altitude of 3,150 feet (960 m).

Lake Manyara National Park

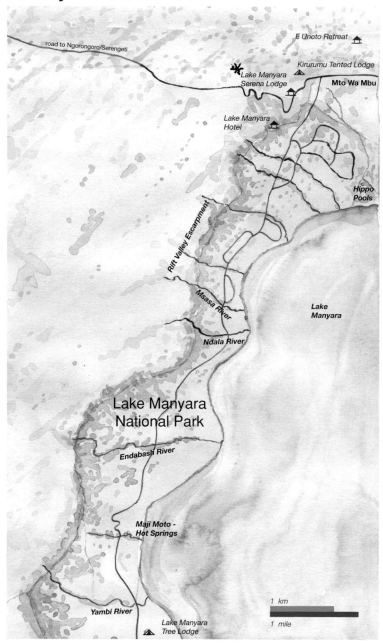

road to Ngorongoro/Serengeti

E Unoto Retreat

Kirurumu Tented Lodge

Lake Manyara
Serena Lodge

Mto Wa Mbu

Lake Manyara
Hotel

Hippo
Pools

Rift Valley Escarpment

Msasa River

Lake
Manyara

Ndala River

Lake Manyara
National Park

Endabash River

Maji Moto -
Hot Springs

Yambi River

Lake Manyara
Tree Lodge

1 km

1 mile

The turnoff to Lake Manyara is past Mto wa Mbu on the road from Makuyuni to Ngorongoro Crater, about 75 miles (120 km) west of Arusha.

Despite its comparatively small size, the park has five distinct vegetation zones and a remarkable diversity of wildlife. From the crest of the Rift Valley to the shores of the lake, the varied topography and soils support characteristic plants and animals. The first zone reached from the park entrance is ground-water forest that is fed by water seeping from the Great Rift Wall, with wild fig, sausage, tamarind and mahog-

A glimpse into village life at Mto wa Mbu

any trees. Elephant prefer these dense forests, as well as marshy glades. The other zones include the marshlands along the edge of the lake, scrub on the Rift Valley Wall, open areas with scattered acacia, and open grasslands.

Manyara, like Tarangire National Park (Tanzania) and Ishasha in Queen Elizabeth National Park (Uganda), is well known for its tree-climbing lions, which may be found lazing on branches of acacia trees. Some people believe that lions climb trees in Manyara and Tarangire to avoid tsetse flies and the dense undergrowth while they remain in the cool shade. They also believe that lions of the Ruwenzori National Park in Uganda climb trees to gain a hunting advantage. Finding lion in the trees in Lake Manyara is rare, so don't set your heart on it — look at it as an unexpected bonus.

Manyara features large concentrations of elephant and buffalo. Other wildlife includes common waterbuck, Maasai giraffe, zebra, impala, baboons and blue monkeys.

Some 450 species of birds — including an astonishing total of over 40 varieties of birds of prey — have been recorded, which makes Manyara one of Tanzania's best birdwatching localities and one of the world's most impressive raptor havens. Among the exciting birds regularly seen are saddle-billed stork, crowned eagle, southern ground hornbill, silvery-cheeked hornbill, grey-hooded kingfisher, long-tailed fiscal, spotted morning thrush and black-winged red bishop.

The fantastic views of the Rift Valley from the Lake Manyara Serena

The level of the lake fluctuates with rainfall, and it rose to its highest level in over 30 years in 1998, when El Niño rains caused flooding in northern Tanzania. When the lake is high, the fish population increases and pelicans and storks flourish. At lower levels, the salinity of the water increases, and vast flocks of lesser and greater flamingo feed on brine shrimp and algae in the shallows.

The northern part of the park can be crowded, but as the southern part has very few visitors, consider packing a breakfast and/or a picnic lunch and spend most of a day exploring the south.

The traditional migration route from Lake Manyara to Tarangire National Park has been all but cut off by villages. Nevertheless, much of the wildlife is resident year-round, making this a good park to visit any time. The best time to visit is December to March and June to October. A 4wd vehicle is recommended for travel in April and May.

On our most recent family visit we saw elephant, hippo, wildebeest, zebra, olive baboon, Kirk's dikdik and a variety of birds in a few hours. On a previous visit we encountered a pride of lion lying only a few yards (meters) from the road. Later, as we were rounding a bend, we almost ran right into two huge bull elephants that were sparring with tusks locked, pushing each other from one side of the road to the other, trumpeting and kicking up mounds of dust in their fight for dominance. Birds spotted included white-breasted cormorant, red-billed oxpecker, African spoonbill, lesser flamingo, white pelican, grey-headed gull, wood sandpiper, black-winged stilt, white-faced duck, white-crowned plover, blacksmith plover, long-toed plover, avocet, water dikkop, cattle egret, common sandpiper, painted snipe and sacred ibis.

Other activities offered in and near the park include night game drives (with bush dinner), walking on the edge of the escarpment and mountain biking (E Unoto Retreat Lodge only).

Roads in the northern part of the park are good year-round and 4wd is not

Lake Manyara Tree Lodge offers luxurious treehouses

needed, although in the rainy season some side tracks may be temporarily closed. Four-wheel-drive vehicles are sometimes necessary and highly recommended for travel in the more remote southern part of Lake Manyara.

ACCOMMODATION — CLASS A+:
• **Lake Manyara Tree Lodge**, located in the southwestern area of the park in a mahogany forest, has 10 luxury treehouses with facilities en suite and a swimming pool. Usually guests have this area of the park all to themselves. As it

takes at least 2 hours to drive from the park gate to the lodge, a 2-night stay is recommended.

CLASS A/B✳ **Lake Manyara Serena Safari Lodge**, magnificently set on the Rift Valley Escarpment overlooking the park and the Rift Valley 1,000 feet (300 m) below, has 67 rooms with en suite facilities and a swimming pool. The hotel offers walks along the Rift Valley escarpment and to Mto wa Mbu Village.

CLASS B: • **E Unoto Retreat Lodge** is a totally Maasai inspired and owned lodge with 25 en suite bungalows. It is located on a hill overlooking a natural spring outside the park. Mountain biking, nature walks and exclusive visits to their nearby village are offered. • **Kirurumu Camp** is set on the escarpment overlooking the Rift Valley, outside the reserve, and has 20 tents covered by thatched roofs, with en suite facilities. Short nature walks around the area as well as hikes down the escarpment to Mtu wa Mbu village are offered. • **Lake Manyara Hotel**, set on the escarpment overlooking the park, has 100 rooms with en suite facilities and a swimming pool.

CLASSES D & F: • **National Park Self-Service Bandas** (10 doubles) are located near the park entrance. Some bandas have private facilities and everyone shares a communal kitchen.

CAMPING: Two campsites are located near the park entrance, both with toilet and shower facilities. One campsite is situated within the park with no facilities; this site requires a special permit.

The Karatu Area

This is a highland area of rich farmland near the town of Karatu, located between the Rift Valley Escarpment overlooking Lake Manyara National Park and the Ngorongoro Conservation Area. Many visitors stay in comfortable accommodations here and take day trips into the Ngorongoro Crater and to Lake Manyara.

The **Iraqw Cultural Center** allows visitors the opportunity to learn more about the local Iraqw tribe, who have inhabited the immediate Ngorongoro highlands near Gibb's Farm for over 200 years. Guests will have the chance to tour a traditional Iraqw home that has been built entirely using traditional materials and methods of construction, just as it would have been 200 years ago. While here, there

Nicholas Nolting at the Iraqw Cultural Center

is also the opportunity to observe a biogas plant used for producing cooking and lighting gas from animal dung for a home — eliminating the need for firewood or charcoal and thereby helping to minimize the effects of deforestation. Our kids particularly enjoyed trying their hand at throwing the traditional spears.

ACCOMMODATION — CLASS A and B: • **Gibb's Farm** has 14 Farm Cottages (Class A) and 8 Standard Cottages (Class B), all with en suite facilities. Wireless internet is available near the lobby area. Walks to nearby waterfalls, hikes to the Ngorongoro Crater rim, mountain biking and village visits can be arranged. Special Masaai massage and therapy treatments are available.

CLASS B: • **Plantation Lodge**, set in lovely gardens on a coffee farm near Karatu, has 14 rooms with facilities en suite and a swimming pool. • **Tloma Lodge** offers 20 rooms with en suite facilities. The lodge is located close to the Tloma Primary School where guests can visit and meet the children. • **Ngorongoro Farmhouse** is located 2.5 miles (4 km) from the Ngorongoro park gate and has 56 rooms with en suite facilities. Walks are available in the surrounding area.

Lake Eyasi

Lake Eyasi lies on the southern border of the Ngorongoro Conservation area and is Tanzania's largest soda lake. The remote region is seldom visited by travelers and is home for the Hadzape Bushmen and the Datoga (also called the Barabaig or Mang'ati) tribe. Here you can have a much truer picture of tribal life than in the more touristy areas.

Hadzape Bushmen are traditional hunter-gatherers who speak a "click" language similar to the Bushmen of southern Africa. The men hunt in the early mornings and afternoons with bows and arrows. Poison arrows are used for large game and non-poison arrows for birds and small game. The women gather wild fruits, roots and tubers. The Mang'ati (also called the **Datoga**) is a tribe similar to the Maasai, that herd cattle and goats. Their diet primarily consists of meat, milk, and blood.

Top: Miles and Nicholas Nolting with the Datoga tribe
Bottom: Miles and Nicholas Nolting learning the fine art of shooting arrows from the Hadzape Bushmen

Hunting with the Bushmen is one of the most exciting cultural experiences you can have in Africa. Recently my wife and I and our two children (age 11 and 14 at the time) spent two days at Lake Eyasi and enjoyed every minute of it. We left the lodge before sunrise and with the assistance of a local guide found a bushman encampment that had apparently been deserted just a few days earlier.

After about 45 minutes of searching, we located their new camp, and shortly thereafter set off with five hunt-

Members of the Datoga tribe

ers armed with traditional bows and arrows (they gave our boys bows and arrows as well). Their first mission was to find a dikdik that they had shot the night before which had escaped. My son Nicolas became the "hero" of the day by finding the lost metal arrowhead on the pathway, as arrowheads require a relatively high price in the form of trade with the local blacksmith. We never found the dikdik, but they did shoot a bushbaby, and quickly made a fire the traditional way, cooked and ate it. We returned to their camp, where we were invited to dance with them and to take target practice. Shooting those bows is harder than you might think!

Later that day we visited the local blacksmith, and spent a few hours with the Datoga (Mang'ati) tribe. The women invited our children to dance (jump) with them, and we spent some time in huts, seeing how they lived. What made the experience with the bushmen and the Datoga even more special is that we had them to ourselves — just our family and our guide.

During another visit the Bushmen shot a baboon out of the top of a tree, cooked it and then returned to their village where the meat was shared among their families. That afternoon we visited a family of the Mang'ati, which slaughtered a goat and cooked it while our guide showed us around their boma.

Only travelers with a keen interest in culture should venture here. If you visit the area, please do your part in helping them maintain their culture by not giving the Bushmen or the Mang'ati any clothing or other western articles. Your guide will know what is appropriate. Lake Eyasi is a perfect family destination as children are welcome to get involved in all the activities.

Lake Eyasi is about a 3-hour drive from the Karatu — Ngorongoro Crater road.

ACCOMMODATION: CLASS A/B: • **Kisima Ngeda Camp** is located on the eastern shore of Lake Eyasi and has 6 permanent tents with en suite facilities.

CAMPING: Campsites are available.

Ngorongoro Crater Conservation Area

Ngorongoro Crater is the largest unflooded, intact caldera (collapsed cone of a volcano) in the world. Known as the eighth Wonder of the World, its vastness and beauty are truly overwhelming, and it is believed by some to have been the proverbial Garden of Eden. Many scientists suggest that before its eruption, this volcano was larger than Mt. Kilimanjaro.

Ngorongoro contains possibly the largest permanent concentration of wildlife in Africa, with an estimated average of 30,000 large mammals. In addition, this is one of the best reserves in Africa in which to see black rhino.

Large concentrations of wildlife make Ngorongoro Crater their permanent home. Game viewing is good year-round. Because there is a permanent source of fresh water, there's no reason for much of the wildlife to migrate as it must do in the Serengeti.

Ngorongoro Crater itself is but a small portion of the 3,200-square-mile (8,288-km²) Ngorongoro Conservation Area, a World Heritage Site that is characterized by a highland plateau with volcanic mountains as well as several craters,

Ngorongoro Crater

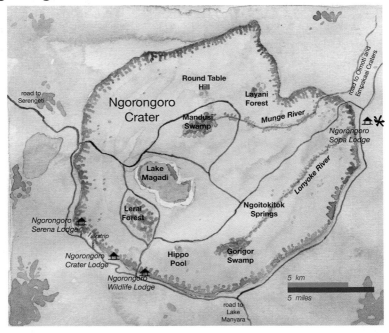

extensive savannah and forests. Altitudes range from 4,430 to 11,800 feet (1,350 to 3,600 m).

Ngorongoro Crater is about 12 miles (19 km) wide and its rim rises 1,200 to 1,600 feet (365 to 490 m) off of its expansive 102-square-mile (265-km^2) floor. From the crater rim, elephant appear as small dark specks on the grasslands.

The steep descent into the crater along winding roads takes 25 to 35 minutes from the crater rim. The crater floor is predominantly grasslands (making game easy to spot) with two swamps fed by streams, and the Lerai Forest. The walls of the crater are lightly forested. You may descend on a road beginning on the western rim or on the eastern rim. Once on the floor, your guide may turn left on a dirt road and travel clockwise around the crater floor.

Lake Magadi, also called Crater Lake and Lake Makat, is a shallow soda lake near the western rim entry point of the crater that attracts thousands of flamingos and other water birds.

The dirt road continues past Mandusi Swamp. Game viewing is especially good in this area during the dry season (July to October) because some wildlife migrates to the fresh water. Hippo, elephant and reedbuck, among many other species, can usually be found here.

You then come to Round Table Hill, which provides a good view and excellent vantage point to get your bearings. The circular route continues over the Munge River,

Top: Elephants make their way across the crater floor
Middle: A zebra enjoying a dust bath
Bottom: The crater is one of the few places in Tanzania to see black rhino

The awe-inspiring view from the Ngorongoro Crater Lodge

the source of which is in the Olmoti Crater north of Ngorongoro Crater, to Ngoitokitok Springs. From there, you journey past Gorigor Swamp, fed by the Lonyokie River, to the Hippo Pool, which is probably the best place to see hippo.

The Lerai Forest, primarily composed of fever trees (a type of acacia), is a good place to spot elephant and waterbuck and, if you are very lucky, leopard. There are 2 picnic areas here with long-drop toilets and running water. The "exit only" road climbs the wall of the crater behind the forest. The road from the eastern rim can be used as both a down and up road into the crater.

On our family's most recent visit we spent a morning and afternoon on the crater floor spending time looking for the elusive rhino! Even though we ran into more vehicle traffic than on the rest of our trip we still have to appreciate that 5 or more vehicles at a sighting is not huge when you consider how many travelers around the world have their heart set on seeing one of the Natural Wonders of the World! We in fact never had more than 2 other vehicles on our sightings as our naturalist guide knew that we wished to avoid other vehicles when possible.

I feel many tour companies that tell prospective clients that Ngorongoro Crater is not worth a visit are just trying to avoid the expensive entry fees in order to make their tours less expensive. That's like saying that if you go to Delhi it's not worth going to see the Taj Mahal!

On another visit we saw three lion, hippo and black rhino within one hour on the crater floor. On another game drive we saw a variety of wildlife including two black rhino and one of the large tusker elephant that we found near the Lerai Forest. On a full-day's game drive during another visit, we saw several black rhino (including one mother with her baby), 27 lion, several golden jackal, a spotted hyena, numerous elephant, buffalo, zebra, wildebeest, flamingo, kori bustard, bat-eared fox at their den and an ostrich guarding the eggs in her nest. Later we spotted a leopard crossing the rim road around the crater. Bull elephant are also found in the wooded areas and on the slopes of the crater. Cheetah are present, but there are no giraffe, topi or impala.

Close to 400 bird species have been recorded in and around the Ngorongoro Crater. Birds commonly encountered on the crater floor are kori bustard, northern anteater chat, rufous-naped lark, rosy-breasted longclaw,

Buffalo keep a watchful eye on a pride of lions on the floor of the crater

superb starling and rufous-tailed weaver, as well as a host of waterfowl and waders. Different bird life thrives on the forested crater rim and misty highlands, with augur buzzard, golden-winged sunbird, malachite sunbird, tacazze sunbird, Schalow's turaco, white-eyed slaty flycatcher and streaky seedeater all being common.

At the picnic sites, vervet monkeys are very aggressive in getting at your food. Black and yellow-billed kites (predatory birds) habitually make swooping dives at lunch plates out in the open, and it is advisable to eat inside your vehicle! Once you've enjoyed your food, you'll be able to stretch your legs by walking around without being harassed by the kites. Camping has not been allowed on the crater floor since 1992.

One important thing to remember: game is not confined to the crater; wildlife is present throughout the conservation area, including near hotels and lodges.

Since this is classified as a conservation area and not a national park, wildlife, human beings and livestock exist together. Ground cultivation is not allowed. The Maasai are allowed to bring in their cattle for the salts and permanent water available on the crater floor, but they must leave the crater at night.

Ngorongoro Crater is about 112 miles (180 km) west of Arusha. An airstrip is located farther along the crater rim, but fog often keeps it closed in the mornings. Four-wheel-drive vehicles are required for game drives into the crater, and guests must be accompanied by a licensed guide or ranger.

Olmoti Crater, located about an hours drive from where the Eastern ascent/decent road intersects with the Ngorongoro Crater rim, is the perfect excursion for travelers who would like to explore more of the Crater Highlands and to possibly encounter Maasai going about their daily lives. From the Maasai village of Nainokanoka at the base of the crater, you hike with a ranger from Ngorongoro Conservation Area Authority for about an hour to the top of the 10,165 ft. (3,099 m) crater rim.

Another interesting excursion — for the adventurous and hardy only — is to take the beautifully scenic drive past Olmoti Crater through Maasailand to the 10,700 foot- (3,260 m) high **Empakaai Crater**, situated 20 miles (32 km) northwest of Ngorongoro Crater on a road that is difficult (and sometimes impossible) to negotiate, even with a 4wd vehicle. The crater is 5 miles (8 km) in diameter and is absolutely beautiful. The 1,000 foot (300 m) decent to the crater floor takes less than an hour. Flamingos and a variety of other bird life are often found lining the shores of Lake Empakaai.

Ol Doinyo Lengai (10,600 feet/3,231 m) — an active volcano and holy mountain of the Maasai, **Lake Natron** and possibly even Mt. Kilimanjaro may be seen from the crater's rim. The hike into Empakaai Crater is amazing. Maasai are often encountered on the drive as well as on the hike in and out of the crater. Allow a very long day for this excursion, or camp on the rim of the crater if you can stand the cold!

Oldupai Gorge

About 30 miles (50 km) west of Ngorongoro Crater and a few miles off the road to the Serengeti is **Oldupai Gorge**, site of many archaeological discoveries, including the estimated 1.7-million-year-old Zinjanthropus boisei fossil. The fossil is housed in the National Museum in Dar es Salaam. A small museum overlooks the gorge itself, and a guide there will tell you the story of the Leakeys' research and findings. Due to efforts in conserving the area, trips into the gorge where the *Zinjanthropus boisei* fossil was found are only allowed by special permit.

On our family's recent safari, the drive to Oldupai Gorge brought us into contact with "the old" with a visit to Richard Leakey's Museum & Archaeological Site, and "the present" with further interaction with the Maasai people living near the Gorge. My older son especially enjoyed listening to the museum guide talk about man's predecessors, and having his picture taken next to the marker where the famous fossil was discovered.

Miles and Nicholas Nolting on the "Shifting Sands"

We then drove to the **Shifting Sands**, located 4 miles (6 km) northwest of Oldupai Gorge. These crescent-shaped sand dunes, called "barchans", are about 100 yards (100 m) long and about 30 feet (9 m) high, and were formed by volcanic ash spewed from the active volcano Ol Donyo Lengai. The strong prevailing winds move the dunes an average of 55 feet (17 m) per year. Enroute to the Shifting Sands you can see signs that have been posted over the years showing the dune's "progress". This is one of the few places in the world where these dunes exist. While climbing a dune we were joined by three Maasai boys who spent some time playing with our children.

The vast flat plains around Oldupai Gorge and west toward Ndutu and the Naabi Hills are underlain with volcanic ash, which promotes the growth of highly nutritious annual grasses. These plains are the principle breeding grounds of the one and a half million Serengeti wildebeest, which drop their calves in January or February and feed on the lush but short-lived grasses. When the rains come to an end, the wildebeest move north and the plains bake under the relentless sun.

To the north of Oldupai are the **Gol Mountains**, a range of jagged hills and deep valleys. A great number of vultures nest in the **Ilkarian Gorge**, and the elusive striped hyena may sometimes be seen. At the western end of the Gols, the huge monolith of **Nasera Rock** is a striking landmark and — if you have the energy to climb to the top — allows for breathtaking views across the endless wilderness.

The western part of the conservation area is covered by the Serengeti Plains. Game viewing in this region bordering the Serengeti National Park is best between December and May, when the Serengeti migration is usually in the area.

The Serengeti is so large, I recommend spending at least 2 days in each of 2 regions. Many travelers spend 5 to 7 days in this great park. On our last visit, our family spent 10 days and did not want to leave!

The Ngorongoro Serena Safari Lodge is perched on the rim of the crater

ACCOMMODATION — CLASS A+: • **Ngorongoro Crater Lodge**, set on the southwestern rim of the crater, has 3 separate camps: North and South Camp, each with 12 suites and Tree Camp with 6 suites. Each stilted suite is elegantly furnished with full en suite facilities and butler service.

CLASS A/B: • **Ngorongoro Serena Safari Lodge**, situated on the western rim of the crater, has 75 rooms with en suite facilities. Escorted walks are offered. **✱Ngorongoro Sopa Lodge**, located on the eastern rim of the crater, has 97 suites with en suite facilities and a swimming pool. There is a down-and-up access road into the crater nearby.

CLASS B: • **Ngorongoro Wildlife Lodge**, a 75-room hotel with en suite facilities, has a wonderful view of the crater.

SEASONAL CAMP: • **Lemala Ngorongoro**, located just below the crater rim 2 miles (3km) from the Ngorongoro Sopa Lodge, has 8 heated tents with hot showers and flush toilets en suite, and a tented dining room.

CAMPING: Campsites are located on the crater rim.

Serengeti National Park

The Serengeti is Tanzania's largest and most famous park, and it has the largest concentration of migratory game animals in the world. It is also famous for its huge lion population and is one of the best places on the continent to see them. The park has received additional notoriety through Professor Bernard Grzimek's book, *Serengeti Shall Not Die* (Hamish Hamilton) and the feature film *Serengeti* (IMAX).

Serengeti is derived from the Maasai language and appropriately means "endless plain." The park's 5,700-square-miles (14,763-km²) makes it larger than the state of Connecticut. Altitude varies from 3,120 to 6,070 feet (950 to 1,850 m).

The park, a World Heritage Site, comprises most of the Serengeti ecosystem, which is the primary migration route of the wildebeest. The Serengeti ecosystem also includes Kenya's Maasai Mara National Reserve, bordering on the north; the Loliondo Controlled Area, bordering on the northeast; the Ngorongoro Conservation Area, bordering on the southeast; the Maswa

Serengeti National Park

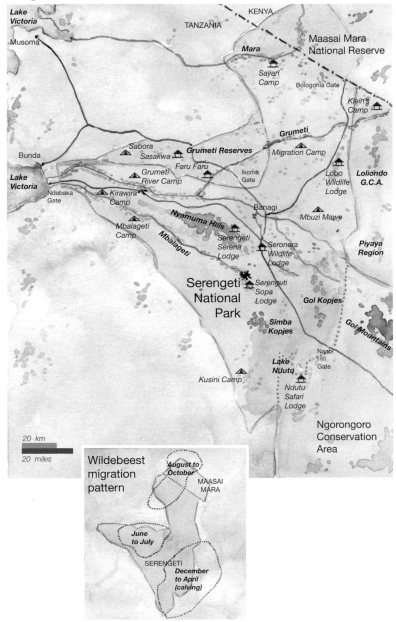

Lake Victoria
Musoma
TANZANIA
KENYA
Maasai Mara National Reserve
Mara
Sayari Camp
Bologonia Gate
Klein's Camp
Grumeti
Sabora
Sasakwa
Grumeti Reserves
Migration Camp
Bunda
Faru Faru
Grumeti River Camp
Ikoma Gate
Lobo Wildlife Lodge
Loliondo G.C.A.
Lake Victoria
Ndabaka Gate
Kirawira Camp
Banagi
Mbuzi Mawe
Mbalageti Camp
Nyamuma Hills
Mbalageti
Serengeti Serena Lodge
Seronera Wildlife Lodge
Piyaya Region
Serengeti National Park
Serengeti Sopa Lodge
Gol Kopjes
Gol Mountains
Simba Kopjes
Lake Ndutu
Naabi Hill Gate
Kusini Camp
Ndutu Safari Lodge
Ngorongoro Conservation Area

20 km
20 miles

Wildebeest migration pattern

August to October
MAASAI MARA
June to July
SERENGETI
December to April (calving)

The Serengeti migration is one of the greatest spectacles in the natural world

Game Reserve, bordering on the southwest; and the Grumeti Reserves and the Ikorongo Controlled Areas, bordering on the northwest. The "western corridor" of the park comes within 5 miles (8 km) of Lake Victoria.

Nearly 500 species of birds and 35 species of large plains animals can be found in the Serengeti. The park may contain as many as 1.5 million wildebeest, 500,000 zebra, 300,000 Grant's gazelle, 250,000 Thomson's gazelle, 120,000 impala, 70,000 topi, 20,000 buffalo, 9,000 eland, 8,000 giraffe, 1,000 lion and 800 elephant.

Most of the Serengeti is a vast, open plain broken by rocky outcrops (kopjes). There is also acacia savannah, savannah woodland, riverine forests, some swamps and small lakes.

The north is more hilly, with thick scrub and forests lining the Mara River, where leopards are sometimes spotted sleeping in the trees. Acacia savannah dominates the central region, with short- and long-grass open plains in the southeast and woodland plains and hills in the western corridor.

It is impossible to predict the exact time of the famous Serengeti migration of approximately 1.3 million wildebeest, 200,000 zebra and 250,000 Thomson's gazelle, which covers a circuit of about 500 miles (800 km).

The key element in understanding of "The Greatest Wildlife Show on Earth" is that it follows the general "rainfall gradient" across the ecosystem, with lower rainfall in the southeast (short-grass plains) and higher rainfall in the northwest. The migration moves from Kenya back to the short-grass plains of the Serengeti and Ngorongoro Conservation Area once the short rains have begun (usually in late October into November), and after the short-grass plains have dried out (usually in May), the migration moves northwest to higher rainfall areas and areas of permanent water — and fresh grass.

From December to May wildebeest, zebra, eland and Thomson's gazelle usually concentrate on the treeless short-grass plains in the extreme southeastern Serengeti and western Ngorongoro Conservation Area near Lake Ndutu in search of short grass, which they prefer over the longer dry-stemmed variety. In April and May, the height of the rainy season, a 4wd vehicle is highly recommended.

Other species common to the area during this period are Grant's gazelle, eland, hartebeest, topi and a host of predators including lion, cheetah, spotted hyena, honey badger and black-backed jackal. Kori bustard, secretarybird, yellow-throated sandgrouse and rufous-naped lark are resident birds of the open plains, which attract large numbers of migratory Montagu's and pallid harriers (from Europe) between September and March.

During the long rainy season (April and May), nomadic lions and hyena move to the eastern part of the Serengeti. The migration, mainly of wildebeest and zebra, begins in May or June. Once the dry season begins, wildebeest and zebra must migrate from the area.

There is no permanent water, and both of these species must drink on a regular basis.

The rut for wildebeest is concentrated over a three-week period and generally occurs at the end of April, May or early June. After a gestation period of eight and one-half months, approximately 90% of the pregnant cows will give birth on the short-grass plains within a six-week period between the mid/end of January and February. Zebra calving season is spread out over most of the year, with a slightly higher birth rate December through March. The best time to see wildebeest and zebra crossing the Grumeti River is in June/ early July and November, and the best time to see them crossing the Mara River is from July to November.

Wildebeest move about 6 to 10 abreast in columns several miles long toward the western corridor. Zebra do not move in columns but in family units.

A family of cheetah resting on the plains

As a solitary hunter, a leopard cannot afford to become injured and avoids confrontation

As a general rule, by June the migration has progressed west of Seronera. The migration then splits into three separate migrations: one west through the corridor toward permanent water and Lake Victoria and then northeast; the second due north, reaching the Maasai Mara of Kenya around mid-July; and the third northward between the other two to a region west of Lobo Lodge, where the group disperses.

During July through September, the Serengeti's highest concentration of wildlife is in the extreme north. The first and second groups meet and usually begin returning to the Serengeti National Park in late October; the migration then reaches the central or southern Serengeti by December.

Short-grass plains dominate the part of the Ngorongoro Conservation Area bordering the Serengeti. As you move northwest into the park, the plains change to medium-grass plains and then into long-grass plains around **Simba Kopjes** north of Naabi Hill Gate. Topi, elephant, Thomson's and Grant's gazelle, bat-eared fox and warthog are often seen here.

There are two saline lakes in the south of the park, **Lake Masek** and **Lake Lagaja,** known mainly for their populations of lesser and greater flamingos.

During our last family visit we saw a leopard climb up a tree to its kill, a cheetah on its kill, and several other cheetah, a pride of six lion stalk and attempt to pull down a buffalo, and two lion cubs on a high rock kopje watching as three female lions hunted on the plains below them. Other wild-life we saw included herds of elephant, eland, more lion, bushbuck, dikdik, Grants and Thompson's gazelle, Maasai giraffe, hartebeest, spotted hyena, impala, golden jackal, banded mongoose, black tailed mongoose, common reedbuck, topi, Defassa waterbuck, warthog, western black-and-white colobus monkey, and thousands and thousands of wildebeest and zebra.

While game viewing in the Seronera Valley, one December morning, we found leopard and watched a large running herd of zebra splash through a marsh swamp in the soft morning light. Under some nearby bushes, a pride of five lion looked on in total disinterest as they continued their morning snooze. Later we drove around the Moru Kopjes and found a lone lion sunning himself on a rock, surrounded by the magnificent spectacle of the larger herds of wildebeest and zebra on the grassy plains.

On another visit, only an hour after stepping off the charter flight at the Seronera airstrip, we saw leopards mating in clear sight on a kopje. Other game spotted in a 24-hour period included Maasai giraffe, elephant, lion, spotted hyena, black-backed jackal, klipspringer, dikdik, bushbuck, buffalo, topi, Bohor reedbuck and steenbok.

On yet another visit, we watched a pride of lion with five cubs play for hours. Later we came upon a fire in the northern Serengeti, where hundreds of storks were feeding on the insects that were fleeing the flames.

Seronera

The **Seronera Valley** is located in the center of the park and is characterized by large umbrella thorn trees — the archetypal image of the African savannah. Game is plentiful, and the area is famous for lion and leopard. Other wildlife includes hyena, jackal, topi, Maasai giraffe and Thomson's gazelle. This is the best area of the park to find cheetah, especially in the dry season. In the wet season, many cheetah are found in the short-grass plains. They are, however, found throughout the park.

Banagi Hill, 11 miles (17 km) north of Seronera on the road to Lobo, is a good area for Maasai giraffe, buffalo and impala. Four miles (6 km) from Banagi on the Orangi River is a hippo pool.

In the northern Serengeti we saw lion, cheetah, lots of elephant, and hippo in the Mara River. In the Loliondo Game Conservation Area we went on escorted walks and night drives.

A unique way to experience the Serengeti is by **hot air balloon.** Guests from the Serengeti Sopa, Serengeti Serena and Seronera lodges are transferred to the balloon launch site near Maasai Kopjes in the central Serengeti in time for a dawn takeoff. A new site has also been designated in the west-

Top: Balloon safari over the
Serengeti
Bottom: Following the exciting
balloon safari, a champagne
breakfast is served on the plains

ern part of the Serengeti and guests can experience this activity from Grumeti River Camp, Kirawira and Mbalageti Lodges. Your pilot may fly you, at times, over 1,000 feet off the ground for panoramic views, and at other times at a very low altitudes (a few yards/meters off the ground) for great game viewing and photographic opportunities. The flight lasts about an hour, depending on wind conditions. After landing, guests enjoy a champagne breakfast.

Our last balloon safari took us over vulture nests, hippos and crocs, eland, a hyena den, large herds of Thomson's gazelles and part of the zebra migration as it moved northwards across the plains. Following our "crash" landing we celebrated with a glass of champagne and a sumptuous breakfast.

Lobo

From Banagi northward to Lobo and the Bologonja Gate are rolling uplands with open plains, bush, woodlands and magnificent kopjes. This is the best area of the park to see elephant. Forests of large mahogany and fig trees are found along the rivers where kingfishers, fish eagles and turacos can be seen. Other wildlife found in the Lobo area includes grey bush duikers and mountain reedbuck. Large numbers of Maasai giraffe are permanent residents.

Large herds of wildebeest are often in the region from July until the rains begin, usually in November. During this period, many wildebeest drown while attempting to cross the Mara River.

Western Corridor

Beginning 3 miles (5 km) north of Seronera, the western corridor road passes over the Grumeti River and beyond to a central range of hills. Eighteen miles (29 km) before Ndabaka Gate is an extensive area of black cotton soil, which makes rainy season travel difficult. This area is best visited June to March for its fabulous resident game. For the migration, it is best visited June, July and late October to early December. Colobus monkeys may be found in the riverine areas. Other wildlife includes eland, topi, impala, dikdik, hippo and crocodile.

The area is known for its huge crocodiles, which reach 20 feet in length. I saw one specimen that was 17 feet long and about 1,500 pounds! There is a swinging bridge across the Grumeti River that provides a great viewpoint down the river. In this remote region of the Serengeti, we also saw a mother cheetah with six cubs, along with a variety of other game.

The granite kopjes or rocky out-crops that dot the plains are home to rock hyrax, Kirk's dikdik and klip-springer. Banded, dwarf and slender mongoose are occasionally seen nearby. Verreaux's eagle are sometimes sighted near the Moru Kopjes.

Three species of jackal live in the Serengeti: black-backed, side-striped and golden. Side-striped jackal are rare, golden jackal are usually found in the short grass plains and black-backed jackal are quite common. The 6 species of vultures found in the park are white-backed, white-headed, hooded, lappet-faced, Ruppell's and Egyptian.

Clients are met on the airstrip by their guide

At the time of this writing, the border with Kenya between Serengeti National Park and the Maasai Mara is officially closed, and is expected to remain closed. There is a dry-weather road (often impassable in the rainy season) from Mwanza and Musoma (Lake Victoria) to the west through Ndabaka Gate. The main road from the Ngorongoro Conservation Area via Naabi Hill Gate is open year-round.

Vehicles must stay on the roads within a 10 mile (16 km) radius of Seronera, Lobo, Kirawira and Grumeti (Western Corridor), as well as around Simba Kipjes, Moru, Naabi and Gol Kopjes. Off-road driving is allowed in some other areas of the park, making a safari with a 4wd vehicle all the more attractive. Travel in the park is allowed only from 6:00 a.m. until 7:00 p.m. Visitors may get out of the vehicle in open areas if no animals are present. Do stay close to the vehicle, and keep a careful lookout.

From late July to September, when one arm of the migration is usually in the Maasai Mara in Kenya, consider focusing your time in the northern Serengeti. You will have a very good chance of seeing the migration, with only a fraction of the tourists that you would probably encounter game viewing in the Maasai Mara. Having those expansive Serengeti Plains almost to yourself is a priceless experience for travelers who are looking for more out of a safari than just seeing animals.

Park Headquarters are located at Seronera, while the park staff housing is located at Ft. Ikoma, outside of the park.

Top: The verandah of Sayari Camp offers endless vistas
Middle: Kirawira Luxury Tented Camp
Bottom: The lounge at Migration Camp beckons guests with its comfortable furnishings

ACCOMMODATION — CLASS A: • **Sayari Camp** has been completely rebuilt and is located in the northern region of the park, with loads of resident game year-round, peaking during the Migration crossings from July through November. The permanent tented camp is divided into 2 wings of 6 and 9 luxury en suite tents, each with private bath, shower, flush toilet and a verandah. Each wing enjoys its own bar, dining room and lounge with a shared swimming pool. Activities include open vehicle game drives and fly camping expeditions. • **Migration Camp**, located 14 miles (22 km) west of Lobo Lodge, has 20 tents with en suite facilities and a swimming pool. • **Kirawira Luxury Tented Camp**, located in the western corridor approximately 55 miles (90 km) west of Seronera and 6 miles (10 km) east of the Kirawira Ranger Post, has a classic Victorian atmosphere, with 25 luxury tents with en suite facilities and a swimming pool. • **Grumeti River Camp**, located in the Western Corridor 53 miles (85 km) west of Seronera Lodge and 31 miles (50 km) east of Lake Victoria, has 10 tents with en suite facilities and a plunge pool.

CLASS A/B: • **Mbuzi Mawe Camp** is located on a kopje between Seronera and

Lobo in a wilderness zone where walking is allowed. The camp consists of 16 luxurious tents with en suite facilities. • **Mbalageti Camp** is a permanent tented camp located in Western Serengeti overlooking the Mbalageti River Valley, consisting of 24 luxury tented en suite chalets, each with a private verandah. • **Serengeti Serena Safari Lodge**, set on a hill overlooking the Serengeti Plains about 18 miles (29 km) northwest of Seronera Lodge, has 66 rooms with en suite facilities and a swimming pool. • **Kusini Camp**, located in the southern Serengeti, has 12 tents with en suite facilities scattered around a rock formation. The camp is ideally located for the calving season of the wildebeest which takes place in this area in February of each year. Game viewing is at its best from December through March. ✷**Serengeti Sopa Lodge**, located 25 miles (40 km) southwest of Seronera Lodge and 60 miles (96 km) from Naabi Hill Gate, has 69 suites with en suite facilities and a swimming pool.

CLASS B: • **Seronera Wildlife Lodge**, situated in the center of the park 90 miles (145 km) from Ngorongoro Crater, has 57 double rooms with en suite facilities. **Lobo Wildlife Lodge**, located in the north of the park 43 miles north of Seronera, is uniquely designed around huge boulders. All 75 double rooms have en suite facilities.

ACCOMMODATION ON THE PERIPHERY OF THE PARK — CLASS A: • **Kleins Camp** is situated in a 25,000-acre (10,000-hectare) private reserve bordered on the west by Serengeti National Park and the north by the Maasai Mara in Kenya. Each of the 10 thatched cottages are made from local rock and have en suite facilities. Day and night game drives, guided bush walks and visits to local Maasai are offered.

CLASS B: • **Ndutu Safari Lodge** is a rustic lodge with 34 rooms (doubles) with en suite facilities, located on the edge of the park in Ngorongoro Conservation Area. • **Speke Bay Lodge**, located on the southeastern shore of Lake Victoria, 10 miles (15 km) from the Serengeti National Park and 78 miles (125 km) north of Mwanza has 8 thatched bungalows on the lakeshore, with en suite facilities. Fishing, boat excursions and mountain biking are offered.

CAMPING: Campsites are available at Seronera, Ndutu, Naabi Hill Gate, Moru Kopjes, Kirawira and Lobo. Camping in other areas requires permission from the warden and higher fees. It is best to book well in advance.

SEASONAL CAMPS: • **Sayari South Camp** is based in the Piaya region just outside the southeastern border of the Serengeti from December to March. The camp has only 5 luxury en suite tents, each with a private verandah, • **Suyan Camp** has 6 en suite tents located in a private conservation area in Loliondo, immediately bordering the northeastern Serengeti. Activities may

Top: The dining tent at Suyan Camp
Bottom: The ultimate experience —
luxury mobile camping

include game drives during the day and at night, walking, and cultural interaction with the local Maasai. • **Olakira Camp** is a 5 tented traditional mobile safari camp with en suite facilities that moves through the Serengeti following the movements of the migration. • **Nduara Camp** (formerly *Loliondo Safari Camp*) is situated in a private conservation area in Loliondo immediately bordering the northeastern Serengeti. Day and night game drives, walking, and Maasai visits are offered. • **Serengeti Safari Camp** makes use of a Traditional Mobile Tented Camp with en suite facilities on a shared-use basis for up to 8 guests, periodically moving location within the Serengeti according to migration game movements and weather conditions.

Grumeti Reserves

Grumeti Reserves is located adjacent to the Western Corridor of the Serengeti, bordering the national park, and encompasses over 350,000-acres (40,000-hectares) of unrivaled wilderness. The area forms part of the famous migratory route, which is traveled by hundreds of thousands of animals every year.

The real advantage of this reserve is that guests can enjoy the splendor of the Serengeti Plains and it's spectacular wildlife with only a few other vehicles ever in sight.

Sasakwa Lodge, Sabora Plains and Faru Faru are three of the best properties in Africa — with Sasakwa providing true elegance in the wilderness. Our family had a fabulous time here on a recent visit. We saw the migration in all its glory with endless wildebeest columns moving through the area.

As the reserve is so large, we hardly encountered another vehicle on our game drives. While staying at Sasakwa, my wife Alison went horseback riding while our boys Miles, Nicholas and I tried our hand at archery, played some tennis and went for a swim to get some much appreciated exercise.

Other wildlife spotted included Cape buffalo, bushbuck, cheetah, eland, elephant, Maasai giraffe, spotted hyena, black-backed jackal, lion, dwarf

The breath taking vistas of the Grumeti Reserves

mongoose, slender mongoose, white-tailed mongoose, black-and-white colobus monkey, porcupine topi, warthog, Defassa waterbuck and Patas monkeys in the riverine forest.

Game drives and walks are enjoyed with resident professional guides. Other activities include archery, lawn croquet, mountain biking, equestrian pursuits, and hot air ballooning.

ACCOMMODATION — CLASS A+: • **Sasakwa Lodge** offers 7 individually air-conditioned cottages (ranging in size from 1 to 4 bedrooms) that have been positioned in the garden for complete privacy, each with its own heated plunge pool, a comfortable lounge area, elegantly appointed bathrooms and generous sized bedroom. More experienced riders can enjoy rides onto the Serengeti plains. • **Sabora Plains Tented Camp** accommodates 12 guests in 6 luxurious tents reminiscent of Hemingway, Blixen and Roosevelt. The spacious air-conditioned tents are decorated in rich fabrics, antiques and Persian rugs. • **Faru Faru River Lodge** accommodates 12 guests in luxurious comfort. Offering fantastic views across the Grumeti River, the lodge is built in a rustic style with huge windows where guests can watch the constant stream of game to the river's edge.

Top: Faru Faru's fire pit and surrounding wilderness
Bottom: Saskawa's elegant accommodation

Lake Natron Region

Located between the Ngorongoro Conservation Area and the Kenya border, **Lake Natron** is a shallow, alkaline lake approximately 38 miles long and 15 miles wide (60-by-25 km). This remote lake is one of East Africa's largest breeding areas for both lesser and greater flamingos.

This is a remote wilderness with limited wildlife, a few scattered Maasai settlements, rugged sand tracks and only a few choices for tourists to stay. You may encounter Maasai tribesmen as they tend their herds of cattle, visit the waterfalls and see the inland cliffs that are home to thousands of Ruppell's vultures.

South of Lake Natron is **Ol Doinyo Lengai**, the only active carbonatite volcano in the world and holy mountain of the Maasai. This steep mountain takes about 10 hours to climb and return to its base. The climb starts at midnight, due to the extremely high mid-day temperatures and to allow the opportunity to enjoy the beauty of the volcano at night.

ACCOMMODATION — CLASS B: • **The Ngare Sero Lake Natron Camp** offers 8 self-contained tents with an open yet private feeling. Activities vary and include bird and nature walks and climbs on Ol Doinyo Lengai.

CLASS C: • **Moivaro Lodge's Lake Natron Tented Camp** is more rustic than Ngare Sero but offers comfortable en suite accommodations, and can arrange climbs on the mountain.

Rubondo Island National Park

Located in the southwestern part of Lake Victoria, the main attractions of this 93-square-mile (240-km^2) island are sitatunga (indigenous) and small groups of chimpanzees. Walking is allowed and the wildlife that may be seen includes black-and-white colobus monkey, giraffe, bushbuck and otters. There are no large predators. Nearly 400 species of birds have been recorded, including storks, herons, ibises, kingfishers, bee-eaters, flycatchers and an abundance of fish eagles.

In addition to the main island, there are about a dozen small islands that make up the park. Habitats include papyrus swamps, savannah, open woodlands and dense evergreen forests. Visitors, accompanied by a guide who is usually armed, may walk along forested trails in search of wildlife or wait patiently at a number of hides. The best time to visit is November to February. A few boats are available for hire.

Flying by air charter is the only easy way to get to the park. An airstrip is located at Park Headquarters. From Mwanza, it is a 7-hour drive by vehicle and a 2-hour boat ride by one route and a 10-hour drive and half-hour boat ride by another route. Visitors are not allowed to bring their vehicles to the island.

ACCOMMODATION — CLASS A/B:• **Rubondo Island Camp** has 10 tents under thatch with en suite facilities and a swimming pool. Activities include fishing, walks in search of chimpanzees and other wildlife, and birdwatching.

Mt. Kilimanjaro National Park

Known to many through Ernest Hemingway's book *The Snows of Kilimanjaro* (Arrow), Mt. Kilimanjaro is the highest mountain in the world that is not part of a mountain range, and it is definitely one of the world's most impressive mountains. Kilimanjaro means "shining mountain"; it rises from an average altitude of about 3,300 feet (1,000 m) on the dry plains to 19,340 feet (5,895 m), truly a world-class mountain. On clear days, the mountain can be seen from over 200 miles (320 km) away.

The mountain consists of three major volcanic centers: Kibo (19,340 feet/5,895 m), Shira (13,650 feet/4,162 m) to the west and Mawenzi (16,893 feet/5,150 m) to the east. The base of the mountain is 37 miles (60 km) long and 25 miles (40 km) wide. The park is a World Heritage Site and covers 292-square-miles (756-km^2) of the mountain above 8,856 feet (2,700 m). The park also has six corridors that climbers may use to trek through the Forest Reserve.

Hikers pass through zones of forest, alpine and semidesert to its snow-capped peak, situated only three degrees south of the equator. It was once thought to be an extinct volcano, but due to recent rumblings, it is now classified as dormant.

One of the mobile camps providing shelter to climbers

Climbing Mt. Kilimanjaro was definitely a highlight of my travels. For the struggle to reach its highest peak I was handsomely rewarded with a feeling of accomplishment, fabulous views of the African plains, and many exciting memories of the climb. In fact, with over 30,000 climbers a year, Kilimanjaro is second only to the Everest and Annapurnas areas in Nepal in popularity as a trekking destination outside of Europe.

Kilimanjaro may, in fact, be the easiest mountain in the world for a climber to ascend to such heights. But it is still a struggle for even fit adventurers. On the other hand, it can be climbed by people from all walks of life who are in good condition and have a strong will. Mind you, reaching the top is by no means necessary; the flora, fauna and magnificent views seen enroute are fabulous.

A Christian missionary, Johann Rebmann, reported his discovery of this snow-capped mountain, but the Europeans didn't believe him. Hans Meyer was the first European to climb Kilimanjaro, doing so in 1889.

The most unique animal in this park is the Abbot's duiker, which is found in only a few mountain forests in northern Tanzania. Other wildlife includes elephant, buffalo, eland, leopard, hyrax, and black-and-white colobus monkeys. However, very little large game is seen.

Bird life is sparse but interesting, with bronze sunbird, red-tufted malachite sunbird, alpine chat and streaky seedeater not uncommon. You might see augur buzzard and white-necked raven soaring above you, and you may even be lucky enough to see the rare bearded vulture.

The best time to climb is mid-December to mid-March and June to October during the drier seasons when the skies are fairly clear. The temperatures in July and August can be quite cool. April and May should be avoided because of heavy rains and overcast skies.

From April to May, during the long rainy season, the summit is often covered in clouds, with snow falling

Taking a moment to enjoy the view

Preparing to make the summit

at higher altitudes and rain at lower altitudes. The short rains (November) bring afternoon thunderstorms, but evenings and mornings are often clear.

Many routes to the summit require no mountaineering skills.

Mountaineers wishing to ascend by technical routes may wish to get a copy of *Guide to Mt. Kenya and Kilimanjaro* (Mountain Club of Kenya), edited by Iain Allan.

The Park Headquarters is located in Marangu, about a 7-hour drive from Nairobi, or 2 hours from Arusha. Children under 10 years of age are not allowed over 9,843 feet (3,000 m).

Travelers wishing to see Mt. Kilimanjaro, but who do not wish to climb it, may do so (provided the weather is clear) from Arusha National Park or Amboseli National Park (Kenya).

Zones

Mt. Kilimanjaro can be divided into five zones by altitude: 1) cultivated lower slopes, 2) forest, 3) heath and moorland/lower alpine, 4) highland desert/alpine and 5) summit. Each zone spans approximately 3,300 feet (1,000 m) in altitude. As the altitude increases, rainfall and temperature decrease; this has a direct effect on the vegetation each zone supports.

The rich volcanic soils of the **lower slopes** of the mountain around Moshi and Marangu up to the park gate (6,000 ft./1,830 m) are intensely cultivated, mostly with coffee and bananas.

The **forest** zone (5,900–9,185 ft./1,800–2,800 m) receives the highest rainfall of the zones, with about 80 inches (2,000 mm) on the southern slopes and about half that amount on the northern and western slopes. The upper half of this zone is often covered with clouds, and humidity is high, with day temperatures ranging from 60 to 70°F (15 to 21°C). Don't be surprised if it rains while walking through this zone; in fact, expect it.

In the lower forest, there are palms, sycamore figs, bearded lichen and mosses hanging from tree limbs, tree ferns growing to 20 feet (6 m) in height, and giant lobelia which grow to over 30 feet (9 m). In the upper forest zone, giant groundsels appear. Unlike many East African volcanic mountains, no bamboo belt surrounds Kilimanjaro.

Black-and-white colobus and blue monkey, olive baboon and bushbuck may be seen. Elephant, eland, giraffe, buffalo and suni may be seen on the northern and western slopes. Also present but seldom seen are bushpig, civet, genet, bush duiker, Abbot's duiker and red duiker.

Zone three, a lower alpine zone ranging from 9,185 to 13,120 feet (2,800 to 4,000 m), is predominantly **heath** followed by moorlands. Rainfall decreases with altitude from about 50 inches to 20 inches (1,250 to 500 mm) per year. Giant heather (10 to 30 feet/3 to 9 m high), grasslands with scattered bushes and beautiful flowers, including "everlasting" flowers, protea and colorful red-hot pokers, characterize the lower part of this zone.

You then enter the **moorlands** with tussock grasses and groups of giant senecios and lobelias — weird, prehistoric-looking Afro-alpine vegetation that would provide a great setting for a science fiction movie. With a lot of luck, you may spot eland, elephant, buffalo or klipspringer.

The **highland desert/alpine zone** is from around 13,120 to 16,400 feet (4,000 to 5,000 m) and receives only about 10 inches (250 mm) of rain per year. Vegetation is very thin and includes tussock grasses, "everlasting" flowers, moss balls and lichens. The thin air makes flying too difficult for most birds, and the very few larger mammals that may be seen do not make this region their home. What this zone lacks in wildlife is compensated for by the fabulous views. Temperatures can range from below freezing to very hot, so be prepared.

The **summit** experiences arctic conditions and receives less than 4 inches (100 mm) of rain per year, usually in the form of snow. It is almost completely devoid of vegetation.

Kibo's northern summit is covered by the Great Northern Glacier. On Kibo there is an outer caldera about 1.5 miles (2.5 km) in diameter. Uhuru peak is the highest point on the outer caldera and also the highest point on the mountain. Kilimanjaro's glaciers are shrinking and trends in global warming suggest that the mountain may lose most of its ice peak in the foreseeable future.

Within the outer caldera is an inner cone that contains the Inner or Reusch Crater, which is about .5 mile (1 km) in diameter. Vents (fumaroles) spewing steam and sulfurous gasses are located at the Terrace and the base of the crater. Within the Inner Crater is an ash cone with an ash pit about 1,100 feet (335 m) across and about 400 feet (120 m) deep.

Routes

In regard to routes, Kilimanjaro is divided into two halves by a line running north/south between Barafu Camp and Kibo Hut. All climbers who ascend on the Machame, Shira, Lemosho, and Umbwe routes must descend on the Mweka route. All climbers who ascend on the Rongai and Marangu routes must descend on the Marangu Route. The Marangu Route is the only two-way route; all other routes are one way only. Climbers from the Rongai and Marangu routes only meet climbers from the other routes on the Kibo Crater rim. This system is effective in reducing the impact of large numbers of climbers on all routes, except for the Marangu Route.

Success after the long trek!

Climbers on the Machame, Shira, Lemosho, and Umbwe routes may approach the summit via the Western Breach or may skirt around to Barafu and climb up to Stella Point.

Climbing Kibo Peak via the routes described below requires no mountaineering skills. A guide for each climbing party is required. Porters are highly recommended. The Marangu and the Machame routes are the most popular, carrying 85% of all climbers, while the Shira, Lemosho, Rongai and Umbwe routes are much less used. Climbers stay in basic mountain huts on the Marangu Route and camps on all other routes.

Your porters will bring fuel (kerosene or gas) for cooking and heating because cooking with firewood has been banned. The national park guides are not qualified to lead glacier- or ice-climbing routes. The services of a professional guide must be arranged in advance.

The park has rescue teams based at the Park Headquarters, on the eastern edge of the Shira Plateau, and rangers at various points spread over the mountain.

For the quality of your experience to be the best possible on this busy mountain I recommend a 6 day-Rongai route or an 8 day-Shira route climb.

Kilimanjaro routes

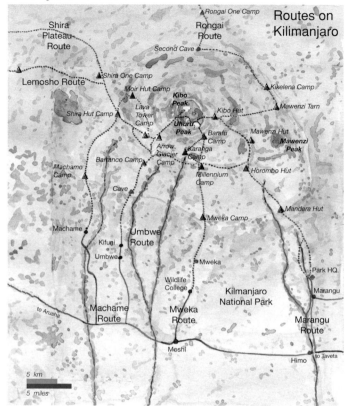

Routes on Kilimanjaro

Shira Plateau Route

Rongai Route

Rongai One Camp

Second Cave

Shira One Camp

Lemosho Route

Moir Hut Camp

Kikelena Camp

Kibo Peak

Mawenzi Tarn

Lava Tower Camp

Kibo Hut

Shira Hut Camp

Uhuru Peak

Barafu Camp

Mawenzi Hut

Mawenzi Peak

Arrow Glacier Camp

Karanga Camp

Barranco Camp

Machame Camp

Millennium Camp

Horombo Hut

Cave

Mweka Camp

Mandera Hut

Machame

Kifuni

Umbwe Route

Umbwe

Mweka

Park HQ

Wildlife College

Kilimanjaro National Park

Marangu

to Arusha

Machame Route

Mweka Route

Marangu Route

Moshi

Himo

to Taveta

5 km

5 miles

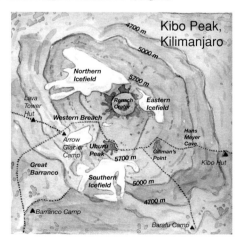

Kibo Peak, Kilimanjaro

4700 m

5000 m

5700 m

Northern Icefield

Rensch Crater

Eastern Icefield

Lava Tower Hut

Western Breach

Hans Meyer Cave

Arrow Glacier Camp

Uhuru Peak

Gillman's Point

Kibo Hut

5700 m

Great Barranco

Southern Icefield

5000 m

4700 m

Barranco Camp

Barafu Camp

These two routes allow you to visit some of the quieter areas of Kilimanjaro, are scenically interesting and the itineraries are structured to give the best chance to reach the summit.

Rongai Route

The Rongai route starts just south of the Kenya-Tanzania border. It is as easy as the main Marangu trail and more attractive as it travels from the northern side of the mountain right across it to the southern slopes. The route has extensive views and spends one night at Mawenzi Tarn, the mountain's most beautiful campsite.

DAY ONE: MARANGU (6,398 ft./1,950 m) to RONGAI ONE CAMP (8,530 ft./2,600 m) — THREE to FOUR HOURS. ALTITUDE GAIN 2,133 ft.(650 m).

Drive for 2.5 hours from Marangu to Rongai Gate and start the climb through the forest where there is a good chance of seeing colobus monkeys. As the forest starts to thin, you cross a small stream and reach Rongai One Camp.

DAY TWO: RONGAI ONE CAMP to KIKELEWA CAMP (11,811 ft./3,600 m) — SIX to SEVEN HOURS. ALTITUDE GAIN 3,281 ft.(1,000 m).

A steady climb all morning brings you to Second Cave, where there is a break for lunch. After lunch, depart toward Mawenzi Peak. The Kikelewa Camp will be reached in late afternoon.

DAY THREE: KIKELEWA CAMP to MAWENZI TARN (14,104 ft./4,300 m) — THREE to FIVE HOURS. ALTITUDE GAIN 2,293 ft. (700 m).

A short, steep climb, leaving all vegetation behind, brings you closer to Mawenzi Peak and after topping a small rise you enter the striking Tarn valley. After lunch in camp, take an acclimation walk.

DAY FOUR: MAWENZI TARN to KIBO CAMP (15,420 ft./4,700 m) — THREE to FOUR HOURS. ALTITUDE GAIN 1,316 ft. (400 m).

Cross the saddle between the Mawenzi and the main summit, Kibo. This are is very desert-like. Arrive at the Kibo Camp for a late lunch. The afternoon is spent preparing for the summit push.

DAY FIVE: KIBO CAMP to UHURU PEAK (19,344 ft./5,896 m) AND DOWN TO HOROMBO CAMP (12,139 ft./3,700 m) — TEN to FIFTEEN HOURS.

Wake up around midnight and start the climb by flashlight (headlamps are better), plodding slowly up the switchbacks to pass Hans Meyer Cave and Jamaica Rocks and reach Gilmans Point. On the crater rim there is a real sense of achievement to get here. After a short rest those strong enough can continue for another 1.5 hours to the very top, Uhuru Peak (19,344 ft./5,896 m). The descent to Kibo Camp is surprisingly fast and after a small rest and some food the descent continues down to Horombo Camp.

DAY SIX: HOROMBO CAMP to MARANGU MAIN GATE — FIVE to SIX HOURS.

A steady descent takes you down into the forest and on through rich forest to the main park gate at Marangu (6,070 ft./1,850 m).

Shira Route

This route is from the west and is planned to give the best acclimation, while views are not as extensive as on Rongai, they are constantly changing as you traverse the mountain which is quite interesting.

DAY ONE: LONDOROSSI GATE (9,842 ft./3,000m) to SHIRA ONE CAMP (11,483 ft./3,500 m) — FOUR to SIX HOURS. ALTITUDE GAIN 1,650 ft (500 m).

Drive 2.5 hours from Arusha to Londorossi Gate, register and drive up to 9,842 ft/3,000 m within the park to start the walk. The trail climbs up to the Shira Plateau and then heads along a small path into the middle of the Shira Plateau and reaches Shira One Camp.

DAY TWO: SHIRA ONE CAMP to SHIRA HUT CAMP (12,598 ft./3,840 m) — FIVE HOURS. ALTITUDE GAIN 1,115 ft (340 m).

Walk south across the plateau to its rim, there is a chance to get to the top of the Shira Cathedral (12,303 ft./3,750 m) before following the old crater rim around and up to the Shira Hut Camp.

DAY THREE: SHIRA HUT CAMP to MOIR HUT CAMP (13,120 ft./4,000 m) — FOUR to SEVEN HOURS WALKING (INCLUDING AFTERNOON WALK FROM CAMP). ALTITUDE GAIN 522 ft. (16 m).

A short morning walk through the moorlands brings you to Moir Hut Camp (13,451 ft./4,100 m). After having lunch at the camp, there is time to acclimatize with an ascent of the nearby Lent Hills.

The Arrow Glacier

DAY FOUR: MOIR HUT CAMP to LAVA TOWER CAMP (13,780 ft./4,200 m) — FOUR to FIVE HOURS.

Another morning walk which traverses the side of Kibo to reach Lava Tower Camp (13,780 ft./4,200 m). In the afternoon there is a chance to acclimatize by following a trail up toward Arrow Glacier, reaching a height of 15,420 ft. (4700 m) before returning to camp.

DAY FIVE: LAVA TOWER CAMP to KARANGA CAMP (13,123 ft./ 4,000 m) — FIVE to SEVEN HOURS.

From Lava Tower you drop down to the Barranco Valley and then climb up steeply on the Barranco Wall. An undulating trail that continues and eventually drops into the Karanga Valley, the last water source on the way to the summit. After crossing the stream, a steep climb up the other side of the U-shaped valley leads to Karanga Camp.

DAY SIX: KARANGA CAMP to BARAFU CAMP (15,092 ft./4,600 m) — FOUR to FIVE HOURS. ALTITUDE GAIN 1,969 ft (600 m).

Today you will walk across the compacted scree and rocks onto the Barafu Ridge and on to the Barafu Camp for lunch. There is a short acclimation walk in the afternoon.

DAY SEVEN: BARAFU CAMP to UHURU PEAK (19,344 ft./5,896 m) AND DOWN TO MILLENNIUM CAMP (13,123 ft./4,000m) — TEN to FIFTEEN HOURS.

Midnight you will wake up and head off to the summit over the rocky ridge behind camp and then switchback up the main slopes to reach Stella Point on the crater rim. It is another 45 minutes to the very top, Uhuru Peak. The descent back to Barafu Camp is rapid and after a rest and some food, continue your descent to Millennium Camp.

DAY EIGHT: MILLENNIUM CAMP to MWEKA GATE (5,413 ft./1,650 m) — FOUR to SIX HOURS.

The route heads straight off Kilimanjaro through the lush rainforest to reach Mweka Gate.

Marangu Route

The Marangu Route is the least expensive route to climb and is second in popularity only to the Machame Route. Marangu has hut accommodations with separate long-drop toilets, and is the second easiest (most gradual) route to the summit (Rongai is the easiest).

This route may be completed in 5 days, but it's best to take 6 days, spending an extra day at Horombo Hut to allow more time to acclimatize to the altitude. The huts are dormitory-style with common areas for cooking and eating.

Most climbing tours originate in Nairobi, Arusha or Kilimanjaro Airport and last 7 or 8 days. The night before the climb is often spent in the village of Marangu or in Arusha.

DAY ONE: MARANGU (6,004 ft./1,830 m) to MANDARA HUT (8,856 ft./2,700 m) — FOUR to FIVE HOURS. ALTITUDE GAIN: 2,854 feet (870 m).

An hour or so is spent at Park Headquarters at Marangu Gate handling registration and arranging the loads for the porters. Try to leave in the morning to allow a leisurely pace and to avoid afternoon showers. The trail leads through the forest and is often muddy.

Mandara has a number of small wooden A-frame huts that sleep 8 persons each, 4 to a room, and a main cabin with a dormitory upstairs and dining room downstairs, for a total of 60 beds. Kerosene lamps, stoves and mattresses are provided.

DAY TWO: MANDARA to HOROMBO HUT (12,205 ft./3,720 m) — FIVE to SEVEN HOURS. ALTITUDE GAIN: 3,346 feet (1,020 m).

On day two, you pass through the upper part of the rain forest to tussock grassland and fascinating Afro-alpine vegetation of giant groundsels and giant lobelias to the moorlands. Once out of the forest, you begin to get great views of the town of Moshi and Mawenzi Peak (16,893 feet/5,149 m). If you can spare an extra day for acclimatizing, Horombo is the best hut for this. There are some nice day hikes that will help you further acclimatize. Kibo is too high to allow a good night's sleep. Horombo has 120 beds and is similar to but more crowded than Mandara.

DAY THREE: HOROMBO HUT to KIBO HUT (15,430 ft./4,703 m) — FIVE to SIX HOURS. ALTITUDE GAIN: 3,225 feet (983 m).

On the morning of day three, the vegetation begins to thin out to open grasslands. You pass "Last Water" (be sure to fill your water bottles because this is the last source of water). The landscape becomes more barren as you reach "The Saddle," a wide desert between Kibo and Mawenzi Peak. Kibo Hut does not come in to view until just before you reach it. Kibo Hut has 58 beds and is located on the east side of Kibo Peak.

With the wind-chill factor, it can be very cold, so dress warmly. This is the day many hikers feel the effects of the altitude and may begin to experience some altitude sickness. Most people find it impossible to sleep at this height because of the lack of oxygen and the bitter cold, not to mention the possibility of altitude sickness. Get as much rest as you can.

DAY FOUR: KIBO HUT to GILLMAN'S POINT (18,635 ft./5,680 m) and UHURU PEAK (19,340 ft./5,895 m) AND DOWN TO HOROMBO HUT — TEN to TWELVE HOURS.

Your guide will wake you shortly after midnight for your ascent, which should begin around 1:00 a.m. Be sure not to delay the start; it is vital that you reach the summit by sunrise. The sun quickly melts the frozen scree, making the ascent all the more difficult.

The steep ascent to Gillman's Point on the edge of the caldera is a grueling 4- to 5-hour slog up scree. Hans Meyer Cave is a good place to rest before climbing seemingly unending switchbacks past Johannes Notch to Gillman's Point.

From Gillman's Point, Uhuru Peak is a fairly gradual climb of 705 feet (215 m). It will take another hour to hour and a half. Uhuru Peak is well marked, and there is a book in which you may sign your name.

If you are still feeling strong, ask your guide to take you down into the caldera to the inner crater, which has some steam vents. You return to Gillman's Point by a different route.

The feeling of accomplishment upon reaching the summit, as I said, is one of the highlights of my life. I was amazed at the tremendous size of the glaciers so close to the equator.

Standing over 16,000 feet (4,900 m) above the surrounding plains, the view was breathtaking in every direction. Sunrise over Mawenzi is a beautiful sight. You truly feel that you're on the top of the world!

Shortly after sunrise, you begin the long walk down the mountain to Kibo Hut for a short rest, then continue onward to Horombo Hut. Provided you are not completely exhausted, the walk down is long but pretty easy going. From Gillman's Point to Horombo takes about 4 hours and from Uhuru Peak, about 5.

DAY FIVE: HOROMBO HUT to MARANGU

Another long day of hiking as you descend past Mandara Hut to Park Headquarters, where you receive a diploma certifying your accomplishment. Many climbers then spend the night in a hotel in Marangu or Arusha and have the pleasure of sharing their experiences with unwary visitors planning to begin their Kilimanjaro adventure the following day.

Machame Route

This is the most popular and one of the most beautiful routes up the mountain. It is also one of the steepest routes. The park gate is located a few miles above Machame village. Hike 4 to 6 hours through rain forest to Machame Huts (9,843 ft./3,000 m).

The following day you hike 5 to 7 hours to the defunct Shira Hut (12,467 ft./3,800 m) on the Shira Plateau (see Shira Plateau Route for description of the area). Continue hiking about 4 hours to Lava Tower Hut. From Lava Tower Hut there had been two choices to reach Uhuru Peak. The route via the Western Breach with an overnight at Arrow Glacier (15,744 ft./4,800 m) before reaching the Inner Crater has been closed due to concerns about the possibility of falling ice chunks from the glacier. The route now used continues along the Southern Summit Circuit path to Barranco and Barafu before climbing to Uhuru via Stella Point (18,811 ft./5,735 m).

Lemosho Route

Next to the Umbwe Route, this is the least-used route and requires a minimum of 7 days. As with the Shira Plateau Route above, drive to the Londorossi Gate. Then drive to Lemosho Glades and hike through the rainforest to Forest Camp (8,000 ft./2,440 m). On the second day, take a full day's hike into the Shira Caldera, a high grassy plateau, to Shira One Campsite (11,500 ft./3,500 m). On day 3, trek for 3 to 4 hours across the Shira Plateau to Shira 2 Campsite (12,200 ft./3,700 m). Those who feel strong can take an acclimatizing trek to Shira Cathedral. On Day 4, hike 7 hours down the Barranco Valley over 15,000 feet (4,570 m). This is great for acclimatization. Next go to the camp at Barranco Wall (12,900 ft./3,940 m). On day 5, climb up Barranco Wall (14,000 ft./4,270 m). On Day 6 trek to Barafu Camp (16,000 ft./4,600 m). On Day 7, begin trekking up the scree slopes just after midnight to Stella Point on the rim and onward to Uhuru Peak. Return to Barafu Camp and continue your descent to Mweka Hut (10,170 ft./3,100 m). On Day 8, hike to Mweka Gate.

Umbwe Route

The Umbwe Route is very steep and strenuous. The route begins at Umbwe (about 4,600 ft./1,400 m), a village 10 miles (16 km) from Moshi. Walk 2 miles to Kifuni village and into the forest. Follow the path for another 3.5 miles (5km) and then branch left into a mist-covered forest until you reach the forest cave (Bivouac #1) at 9,515 feet (2,900 m), 6 to 7 hours from Umbwe. Overhanging ledges extending about 5 feet (1.5 m) from the cliff provide reasonable protection for about 6 people; however, it is recommended you use your own tents. Water is available, but not close by.

Continue through moorlands and along a narrow ridge with deep valleys on either side. The thick mist and vegetation covered with "Old Man's Beard" moss creates an eerie atmosphere. The second caves at 11,483 feet (3,500 m) are still another 2- to 3-hour hike from Bivouac #1. The vegetation thins out, and you branch right shortly before arriving at Barranco Hut (12,795 ft./3,900 m) about 2 hours later.

From Barranco you can backtrack to the fork and turn right (north) and hike for 3 hours to where Lava Tower Hut (15,092 ft./4,600 m) used to stand. From there, the climb is up steep scree and blocks of rock to the floor of the crater and Uhuru Peak via the Great Western Breach. The climb from Lava Tower Hut to the caldera takes about 9 hours. An alternative from Barranco Hut is to traverse the mountain eastward and follow the Summit Circuit path to Barafu Camp. Descend via the Mweka Route, regardless of the summit routes used.

Summit Circuit

There is a circuit between 12,139 and 15,092 feet (3,700 and 4,600 m) completely around the base of Kibo Peak. Horombo, Barranco and Moir Huts are on the circuit, while Lava Tower, Shira, Kibo and Mawenzi Huts are on side trails, not far from the circuit. A tent is needed since there is no hut on the northern side of Kibo. Be sure to bring a well-insulated pad for your sleeping bag.

As of this writing, Lava Tower and Arrow Glacier are closed due to safety reasons. Therefore the routes trekking through these two areas are being rerouted.

Equipment Checklist

The better equipped you are for climbing Mt. Kilimanjaro, the higher your chances of making the summit. When it comes to clothing, the "layered effect" works best. Bring a duffel bag to pack your gear in for the climb. Wrap your clothes in heavy garbage bags to keep them dry. Keep the weight under the porter's maximum load of 33 pounds (15 kg). Here's a suggested checklist of items to consider bringing:

CLOTHING

- ☐ Gortex jacket (with hood) and pants, and a light raincoat
- ☐ polypropylene long underwear — tops and bottoms, medium and heavy weight
- ☐ wool sweater (one or two)
- ☐ Gortex gaiters (to keep the scree/rocks out of your boots at higher altitudes)
- ☐ tennis shoes or ultralight hiking boots (for lower altitudes)
- ☐ medium-weight insulated hiking boots for warmth and to help dig into the scree during the final ascent
- ☐ heavy wool or down mittens with Gortex outer shell and glove liners
- ☐ several pairs of wool socks and polypropylene liner socks

- ☐ several pairs of underwear
- ☐ track or warm-up suit (to relax and sleep in)
- ☐ long trousers or knickers (wool or synthetic)
- ☐ light, loose-fitting cotton trousers
- ☐ shorts (with pockets)
- ☐ wool long-sleeve and cotton long sleeve shirts
- ☐ T-shirts or short-sleeve shirts
- ☐ turtleneck shirt
- ☐ down vest
- ☐ balaclava (wool or synthetic)
- ☐ wide-brimmed hat or cap for protection from the sun
- ☐ bandana
- ☐ wool hat
- ☐ sleeping pad (for all routes except the Marangu Route)

MISCELLANEOUS

- ☐ day pack large enough to carry extra clothing, rain gear, two plastic water bottles (1 liter/quart each), camera and lunch
- ☐ sleeping bag (rated at least 0° F [–18° C])
- ☐ pocket flask for summit climb
- ☐ flashlight with extra bulb and batteries and a head lamp
- ☐ light towel
- ☐ sunglasses and mountaineering glasses
- ☐ camera and film
- ☐ strong sunblock
- ☐ protective lip balm, such as Chapstick brand
- ☐ body lotion (otherwise skin may get dry and itchy)
- ☐ water purifiers
- ☐ duffle bag
- ☐ half-dozen heavy garbage bags in which to wrap clothes
- ☐ toilet paper
- ☐ moist towelettes
- ☐ pocket knife with scissors
- ☐ granola bars, trail mix and sweets that travel well
- ☐ powered drink mix

BASIC FIRST AID KIT

- ☐ malaria pills
- ☐ moleskin and second skin
- ☐ plastic bandage strips, such as Band-Aid brand
- ☐ elastic bandages
- ☐ gauze pads (4" × 4")
- ☐ diuretics (diamox) — by prescription from your doctor
- ☐ broad-spectrum antibiotics (pills) — as above
- ☐ laxative
- ☐ antihistamine tablets
- ☐ antibiotic cream
- ☐ antidiarrheal preparation — Imodium or Lomotil
- ☐ iodine
- ☐ aspirin or acetaminophen for headache/muscle pain
- ☐ throat and cough lozenges
- ☐ decongestant (can be found in combination with antihistamine tablets)

Please note that it requires more time to boil water at higher altitudes to successfully kill the parasites that cause illness.

Huts

Mandara, Horombo and Kibo Huts are described under the Marangu Route above. The other huts are prefab metal huts, either 10 or 15 feet (3 or 4.5 m) in diameter in varying states of disrepair; most are basically uninhabitable. Many of the wooden floors have been ripped up and used for firewood. Tourists are not allowed to sleep in any of the huts on the mountain (other than Mandara,

Horombo and Kibo) so you must plan on sleeping in your own tent and let the guides and porters use the huts. Drinking water should be filtered and treated because some sources on the mountain are polluted.

• MAWENZI HUT (15,092 ft./4,600 m): From "The Saddle" on the Marangu Route, just after passing East Lava Hill, hike 1.25 miles (2 km) east-northeast on a marked path to the hut at the base of the West Corrie. Mawenzi Hut sleeps 5 and is about a 3-hour hike from Horombo or Kibo Huts. There are no toilets. Mawenzi Peak should be attempted only by well-equipped, experienced mountaineers.

• MAWENZI TARN HUT (14,206 ft./4,330 m): This hut is situated northeast of Mawenzi Hut; it is an easy hike around the foot of the peak. There are toilets there, and water is also available.

• MWEKA HUTS (10,170 ft./3,100 m): There are two large huts. There is a stream nearby.

• BARAFU HUT (15,092 ft./4,600 m): There is no water.

• BARRANCO HUT (12,795 ft./3,900 m): There is a bivouac site about a 600-foot (180 m) walk above the hut under a rock overhang. A stream is located nearby.

• MOIR HUT (13,780 ft./4,200 m): This hut is located on the northwest side of Kibo north of the Shira. There is water nearby.

Climbing Tips

There are a number of ways to increase your chances of making it to the top. One of the most important things to remember is to take your time. Polepole is Swahili for "slowly," which is definitely the way to go. There is no prize for being the first to the hut or first to the top.

Pace yourself so that you are never completely out of breath. Exaggerate your breathing, taking deeper and more frequent breaths than you feel you actually need. This will help you acclimatize and help keep you from exhausting yourself prematurely, and it will help lower the chances of developing pulmonary or cerebral edema.

Ski poles make good walking sticks; they can be rented at Park Headquarters and are highly recommended. Bring a small backpack to carry the items to which you wish to have quick access along the trail, such as a water bottle, snacks and a camera. Most importantly, listen to what your body is telling you. Don't overdo it! Many people die each year on the mountain because they don't listen or pay attention to the signs and keep pushing themselves. Stop and enjoy the view from time to time and watch your footing while you climb.

On steep portions of the hike, use the "lock step" method to conserve energy. Take a step and lock the knee of your uphill leg. This puts your weight on the leg bone, using less muscle strength. Pause for a few seconds, letting your other leg rest without any weight on it, and breath deeply. Then repeat. This technique will save vital energy that you may very well need in your quest for the top.

Some climbers take the prescription drug Diamox, a diuretic which usually reduces the symptoms of altitude sickness; but, there are side effects from taking the drug, including increased urination. You should discuss the use of Diamox with your doctor prior to leaving home.

Drink a lot more water than you feel you need. High-altitude hiking is very dehydrating, and a dehydrated body weakens quickly. Climbers should obtain 4 to 6 quarts (4 to 6 liters) of fluid daily from their food and drinks. Consume foods such as soups, oatmeal porridge, and fresh fruits to supplement water and other liquids. Climbers should drink until the color of their urine is clear.

Most hikers find it difficult to sleep at high altitude. Once you reach the hut each afternoon, rest a bit, then hike to a spot a few hundred feet in altitude above the hut and relax for a while. Acclimatizing even for a short time at a higher altitude will help you get a more restful night's sleep. Remember, "Climb high, sleep low!"

Consume at least 4,000 calories per day on the climb. This can be a problem. Most climbers lose their appetite at high altitude. Bring along trail mix (mixed nuts and dried fruit), chocolate, and other goodies that you enjoy, to supplement the meals prepared for you.

Forget about drinking alcoholic beverages on the climb. Altitude greatly enhances the effects of alcohol. Plus, alcohol causes dehydration. A headache caused by altitude sickness can be bad enough without having a hangover on top of it.

As the entire descent is made in two days, your knees take a hard pounding; you may want to wrap your knees with elastic bandages or use elastic knee supports.

Park Headquarters is located in Marangu, 29 miles (47 km) from Moshi, 63 miles (101 km) from Kilimanjaro Airport and 75 miles (120 km) from Arusha.

Equipment is available for rent from Park Headquarters and Kibo and Marangu Hotels, but it may not be of top quality. If possible, I recommend that you bring your own gear.

ACCOMMODATION NEAR MARANGU — TOURIST CLASS: • **Kibo Hotel**, situated less than a mile (1.6 km) from Marangu village, has rooms with en suite facilities (150 beds). • **Marangu Hotel**, located 1.5 miles (2.4 km) from Marangu village, is a rustic lodge with 29 double rooms with en suite facilities.

ACCOMMODATION NEAR MACHAME — TOURIST CLASS: • **Protea Machame Aishi Hotel** is located about a mile (1.6 km) from the Machame Gate. It offers 30 rooms and a heated swimming pool.

THE SOUTH

The "Southern Circuit" of wildlife reserves includes the Selous Game Reserve, Ruaha National Park and Mikumi National Park. The Selous and Ruaha are less visited than the northern Tanzania parks and offer a great opportunity to explore wild and unspoiled bush. Daily scheduled charter flights link the Selous and Ruaha with Dar es Salaam and Zanzibar.

Selous Game Reserve

This little-known reserve happens to be the second largest game reserve in Africa, and it is a World Heritage Site. Over 21,000-square-miles (55,000-km²) in area, the Selous is more than half the size of the state of Ohio, twice the area of Denmark and 3.75 times larger than Serengeti National Park. Unexploited and largely unexplored, no human habitation is allowed in this virgin bush, except at limited tourist facilities.

The Selous is a stronghold for over 50,000 elephant, 150,000 buffalo (herds often exceed 1,000), and large populations of lion, leopard, Lichtenstein's hartebeest, greater kudu, hippo, crocodiles, and numerous other species, including giraffe, zebra, wildebeest, waterbuck, African wild dog, impala and a small number of black rhino. Colobus monkey can be found in the forests along the Rufiji River. Over one million large animals live within its borders. Over 350 species of birds and 2,000 plant species have been recorded.

Almost 75% of this low-lying reserve (360 to 4,100 ft./110 to 1,250 m) is composed of miombo woodlands, with a balance of grasslands, floodplains, marshes and dense forests.

Morning walks accompanied by an armed ranger and guide are popular and are conducted by all the camps. Fly camping for a few nights is available.

This reserve can give you the feeling of exploring the bush for the first time, because you will encounter few other visitors during your safari.

The Rufiji River, the largest river in East Africa, roughly bisects the park as it flows from the southwest to the northeast. The Rufiji and its tributaries,

Wild dogs — Africa's voracious hunters

Selous Game Reserve

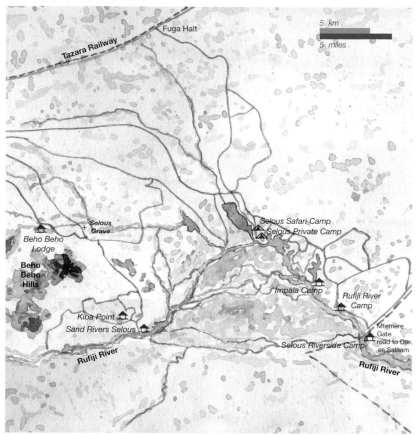

A walking safari in the Selous is a
highlight for many guests

including Great Ruaha and Luwego, have high concentrations of hippo and crocs. Fish eagles are numerous.

Exploring the Rufiji River, its channels, swamps and lakes by boat is another great way to view game and experience the reserve. You should consider adding the Selous onto a northern Tanzania itinerary, because game viewing by boat is not possible in the Serengeti, Ngorongoro, Lake Manyara or Tarangire. Fishing is also popular.

On a recent visit, we encountered numerous lion, including two females and four cubs on a Defassa waterbuck kill, a pack of wild dogs, large herds of elephant, eland, buffalo and giraffe, banded mongoose, Defassa waterbuck and blue wildebeest. Bird life was prolific; our sightings on a boat game drive included African spoonbill, black-winged stilt, fish eagle, gray heron, great white egret, little egret, open-billed stork, and Pel's Fishing Owl found in Stigler's Gorge.

A boating activity from Sand Rivers Selous

All photographic safari activities are restricted to the northern 20% of the reserve. The best time to visit the reserve is during the dry season, June to November. Game viewing from December to February is good, although it is quite hot during that period. During the rainy season, many of the roads are impassable and wildlife is scattered. The reserve is usually closed from mid- to end of March to the end of May.

Most visitors fly to the Selous by scheduled or private air charter from Dar es Salaam, while others take advantage of scheduled and charter flights from Arusha, Zanzibar or other parks. Access by road is difficult and only possible in the dry season. A novel way to experience the vastness of Selous is to arrive from Dar via the Selous Safari Train which is due to be re-launched late in 2009. The train journey will take about 5 hours and will allow travelers to enjoy the scenery enroute.

ACCOMMODATION: The camps are located about 160 to 235 miles (260 to 380 km) from Dar es Salaam, requiring a 6- to 12-hour drive in a 4wd vehicle. All camps have private airstrips and flying is highly recommended.

CLASS A: • **Lukula Selous** is a luxury seasonal camp located on a remote private 300,000-acre (120,000-hectare) reserve in the southern region of the Selous. The camp consists of 4 large sleeping tents set along the riverbank with en suite flush toilets and hot water safari showers. The camp is open late-June to mid-November and is booked on an exclusive basis for a

An aerial view of Lukula Selous' private game reserve

The open airy tents at Selous Safari Camp

minimum of 3 nights. Activities include game drives, guided walking safaris, fly camping and canoeing, all personalized to a guest's preference. • **Beho Beho** has 10 luxury en suite stone cottages offering panoramic views over the Rufiji River flood plain, and a swimming pool. Game drives, boating on a nearby lake and superb walking is offered. • **Sand Rivers Selous** is situated on the banks of the Rufiji River and has 8 luxury open-fronted chalets (5 standard rooms, 2 suites and 1 Honeymoon cottage) looking out over the river, each with en suite facilities. The 2 suites have plunge pools and a lounge area and the Honeymoon Cottage (known as The Rhino House) has its own plunge pool, lounge/dining area and private guide and vehicle. Game drives, walks, boat safaris, fishing, multi-day walking safaris with fly camping are offered. • **Kiba Point**, downstream from Sand Rivers Selous, is a new private camp featuring 4 large open-fronted rooms with en suite facilities and private plunge pool. This 8-bedded camp is booked on a totally exclusive basis only and includes game drives, walks, fly-camping, boating and fishing. • **Selous Safari Camp**, a luxury tented camp set on the shores of Lake Nzerakera, has 9 tents with en suite facilities and a swimming pool. The camp also has a "dungo," a large elevated platform overlooking Lake Nzerakera for relaxing and watching game and bird life during the midday. Game drives, escorted walks, boat safaris, fishing and fly camping and multi-day walking safaris are offered. • **Selous Private Camp**, located next to Selous Safari Camp, has 4 luxury tents with en suite facilities and a swimming pool, and can only be booked on an exclusive basis. • **Retreat Selous** is one of the newest camps in the reserve. It is located in the west past Stieglers Gorge. The camp has a selection of hillside, riverside and private riverside tents. The main facility is built like an Arabian Fort with a sunset bar and infinity pool, and will soon launch a wellness center with spa treatments offered. Boat excursions are carried out on the Ruaha River.

CLASS A/B: • **Rufiji River Camp**, a comfortable tented camp with 20 tents (doubles) with en suite facilities, offers game drives, fishing, walking and boat safaris.

CLASS B: • **Selous Impala Camp** is located on the banks of the Rufiji River. There are 6 tents with spectacular views of the river with en suite facilities, private verandahs and swimming pool. The camp offers game drives, walking safaris and boat rides on the Rufiji River. • **Selous Riverside Camp** is a new camp with 10 tents with views of the river. The camp is located just outside the park but offers game drives, boat safaris and walking safaris inside the park.

MOBILE CAMPING: • **Selous Walking Safaris** (based from Sand Rivers Selous) offer exciting and exclusive walks based out of mobile fly camps, through some of the most diverse and game-rich habitats in the Selous. Walks are offered from June to October and are concentrated around early morning and late afternoon, with opportunities for fishing in the middle of the day. The walks are based out of a fully staffed fly camp with simple tents, bedrolls with sheets, a dome tent at the rear for changing and storing luggage, and a shared long drop toilet and bucket shower.

Top: Retreat Selous' pool offers fantastic views of the surrounding area
Bottom: Game drives in the Selous take place in open vehicles

CAMPING: Sites are available.

Ruaha National Park

Ruaha, known for its great populations of elephant, buffalo, greater and lesser kudu, hippo, crocs and magnificent scenery, is one of the country's newest and best national parks, and because of its location, it is one of the least visited.

Ruaha's scenery is spectacular, and its current 5,000-square-mile (12,950-km^2) area makes it almost as large as Serengeti National Park. The landscape is characterized by miombo woodland with rocky hills on a plateau over 3,300 feet (1,000 m) in altitude. Park elevation ranges from 2,460 feet (750 m) in the Ruaha Valley to the 6,230 foot (1,900 m) Ikingu Mountain in the west of the park.

Jongomero Camp

Ruaha National Park

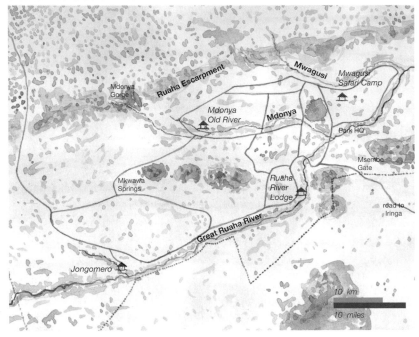

A walking safari from Jongomero Camp

Once referred to by the early explorers as the Garden of Eden, Ruaha was originally part of the Saba Game Reserve formed in 1910 before becoming part of the Rungwe Game Reserve that was established in 1946. The Ruaha National Park was gazetted as a park in 1964 when all hunting was prohibited. In 2006, the Tanzanian Government announced that the bordering game reserves including Rungwe and the Usangu wetlands were to be upgraded to expand the Ruaha National Park to approximately double its size. It is set to become one of the largest parks in Africa with an area roughly the size of Belgium and twice as big as the Serengeti National Park. One of the most important aspects of this is the overlapping of East African and southern African species of plants, trees, birds and mammals.

The Great Ruaha River, with its impressive gorges, deep pools and rapids, runs for 100 miles (160 km), close to the park's southern boundary, and it is home to many hippo and crocodiles. The black rocks of the riverbed contrasted against the golden grass on the riverbank dotted with baobab trees is a beautiful sight indeed. This is an excellent area for walking.

The dry season, June to November, is the best time to visit the park, when game is concentrated along the Ruaha River. Large numbers of greater and lesser kudu, elephant, wildebeest and impala can be seen, along with eland, sable antelope, roan antelope, buffalo, Defassa waterbuck, ostrich and giraffe. Lion, leopard, spotted and striped hyena, black-backed jackal, bat-eared fox and African wild dog are also present in significant numbers. Black rhino are present but seldom seen. Over 523 species of birds have been recorded.

On our most recent visit, we saw 25 greater kudu, two eland and herds of buffalo and zebra on the drive from the airstrip to the camp alone. Other game spotted included leopard, lion, elephant, lesser kudu and a pack of wild dog that ran right through our camp!

In addition to morning and afternoon excursions, midday game viewing in this park can also be very productive because wildlife can be seen walking to and from the river.

During the wet months of December to March, wildlife is scattered, but viewing is still good. Game viewing from February to June is difficult due to high grass.

The park is about a 2.5-hour charter flight from Dar es Salaam, or a 2-hour drive from Iringa, through the villages of Mloa and Idodi and across the Ruaha River. Park Headquarters and an airstrip are located at Msembe, 70 miles (112 km) from Iringa and 385 miles (615 km) from Dar es Salaam.

ACCOMMODATION — CLASS A/B:
• **Jongomero Camp**, located on the banks of the Jongomero Sand River in the southwestern section of Ruaha, has 8 tents with flush toilets and bucket showers. The camp specializes in day long game drives to the remote areas of Ruaha. • **Mwagusi Safari Camp** has 11 tents under thatch with en suite bathrooms, bucket showers and flush toilets. Game drives in open vehicles and walks are offered. • **Ruaha River Lodge** is located on the banks of the

Ruaha River Lodge is set on the banks of the Ruaha River

Ruaha River and offers stunning views. The spacious 20 stone and thatch bandas with en suite facilities are located in prime positions on the river bank, each with a private patio.

CLASS F: • **National Park Rondavels** (self-service) are situated at Msembe.

CAMPING: Campsites are available.

Mikumi National Park

Mikumi is the closest park to Dar es Salaam (180 miles/288 km), and it takes about 4 hours to drive on tarmac from Dar es Salaam via Morogoro. The park covers 1,247-square-miles (3,230-km²) and borders the Selous Game Reserve to the south along the Tazara Railroad line, which runs down to Zambia and divides the park.

The park is dominated by the Mkata River floodplain, with swamps and grasslands dotted with baobab trees and miombo woodlands at an average altitude of 1,800 feet (550 m) above sea level. Elephant, buffalo, lion, hippo, zebra, wildebeest and Maasai giraffe are prevalent. Sable antelope, common waterbuck, Lichtenstein's hartebeest, eland, Bohor reedbuck and impala may also be seen. Black-and-white colobus monkey are frequently seen in the south of the park.

During a 2-day stay, we saw elephant, zebra, six lion, giraffe, buffalo, impala, ground hornbill and guinea fowl, among other species. There is a variety of bird life, because Mikumi is in the transition zone between north and south.

The long rains are from March to May and the short rains from November to December. Rainfall within the park ranges from 20 to 40 inches (510 to 1,070 mm) yearly.

It is difficult to say when the best time is to visit Mikumi. Unlike most parks, wildlife concentrates in this park during the wet season, when the vegetation is the thickest, making game viewing more difficult. Fewer animals are present in the dry season, but the ones present are easier to spot. Lion and elephant are two mammals that are more likely to be seen in the dry season. Considering this, the best time to visit is June through February.

This park is open all year, although some roads are closed during the rainy season. There is an airstrip, gas (petrol) station and garage at Park Headquarters.

ACCOMMODATION — CLASS A/B: • **Vuma Hill Tented Camp** has luxury tents under thatch and set on platforms with en suite facilities and a swimming pool. Day trips to the Udzungwa Mountains are available. • **Foxes Safari Camp** offers 8 custom designed tents with en suite bathrooms and raised on wooden platforms and located around the rock kopje overlooking the Mkata floodplain and Mwangambogo water hole. Day trips to the Udzungwa Mountains are available.

CLASS D: • **Mikumi Wildlife Camp** has self-contained bandas and a restaurant and bar.

CAMPING: Campsites are available.

Enjoying a cocktail by the fire pit at Vuma Hill Tented Camp

Udzungwa Mountains National Park

Udzungwa is one of Tanzania's most recent national parks and many of the park's secrets are yet to be revealed due to the relative inaccessibility of its rainforests and mountain ranges that vary from 655 feet (200 m) to 9,840 feet (3,000 m) in altitude with an area about 385-square-miles (1,000-km²).

Often referred to as a "Mountain Archipelago of Rainforest" or the "Galapagos of Africa", the Udzungwa Mountains National Park is a remnant of the ancient forest that stretched along the eastern arc rift of Tanzania. Today all that remains are a few island patches of rainforest that evolved in isolation over the millennia and are widely considered to be one of the planet's richest in biodiversity. A quarter of the plant species are unique to Udzungwa and found no where else!

Having recently discovered within these remote forests numerous endemic birds (including the Udzungwa Partridge, Rufus Winged Sunbird, and Iringa Akalat), 4 of the 11 primates were unique (such as Hehe Red Colobus, Sanje Mangabey, a couple of Galagoes), and other mammals such as Phillips' Congo shrew, along with endemic amphibians and reptiles, all unique species found no where else. Scientists are still getting excited with new species being discovered often.

You can reach Udzungwa from Mikumi National Park where there are several permanent tented camps to choose from (see "Accommodations" above).

THE WEST

The Western Circuit includes Gombe Stream National Park, Mahale National Park, Katavi National Park and Lake Tanganyika, and is the most remote and least visited of the "Circuits" covered in this book. For those wishing to get off the beaten path — read on!

Lake Tanganyika

Lake Tanganyika forms much of the western border of Tanzania and is indeed an "inland sea." This is the world's longest lake (446 mi./714 km) and the world's second deepest lake (over 4,700 ft./1,433 m). Only Lake Baikal in Russia is deeper, at over 5,700 feet (1,738 m). More than 400 species of fish inhabit Lake Tanganyika's clear waters. Easiest access to the lake in Tanzania is by flying to Kigoma.

Lupita Island

Lupita is a 110-acre (44-hectare) island nestled among the only group of islands in the lake. The topography offers a little of everything from indigenous forest, open grassland and rocky outcrops. This has to be one of the most remote and exclusive island lodges in the world!

Access is by scheduled charter flights from Arusha and private charter flights from other parks and reserves in Tanzania.

ACCOMMODATION — CLASS A+: • **Lupita Island Lodge** is an all-inclusive luxurious resort with 12 luxury suites and 2 executive suites, each with private plunge pools and lake views. Each suite offers total privacy and has been designed to blend into the environment. There is a swimming pool and fully equipped spa and gym. Activities include lake cruises, picnics on secluded islands, snorkeling, biking, hiking, bird watching, fishing and sundowner cruises.

One of the luxury suites on Lupita Island

Kigoma

Kigoma is the country's major port on huge Lake Tanganyika. From there you can catch a steamer to Burundi or Zambia. Kigoma is the closest town to Gombe Stream National Park and many travelers stay there while in transit to and from the park. Kigoma can be reached by air, by road or by a 2.5-day train ride (the train schedules are not dependable) from Dar es Salaam.

Ujiji, a small town 6 miles (10 km) south of Kigoma, is where the line, "Dr. Livingstone, I presume?" was spoken by Stanley in 1872. Buses run there regularly from the Kigoma Rail Station.

ACCOMMODATION — FIRST CLASS: • **Kigoma Hilltop Hotel**, located just outside Kigoma on the edge of Lake Victoria, has 30 air-conditioned cottages with en suite bathrooms.

TOURIST CLASS: • **Aqua Lodge**, located 50 yards (50 m) from the lake, has 9 rooms with private facilities.

Gombe Stream National Park

Gombe Stream is the setting for Jane Goodall's chimpanzee studies and her films and books, including *In the Shadow of Man* (Houghton Mifflin). The

Chimpanzees are the main attraction at Gombe

remote 20-square-mile (52-km^2) park is situated along the eastern shores of Lake Tanganyika 10 miles (16 km) north of Kigoma in remote northwestern Tanzania. This tiny park covers a thin strip of land 3 miles (5 km) wide and stretches for 10 miles (16 km) along Lake Tanganyika. A mountain range ascends steeply from the lake at an altitude of 2,235 feet (681 m) to form part of the eastern wall of the western branch of the Great Rift Valley, rising to 5,000 feet (4,524 m).

Thick gallery forests are found along Gombe Stream and many other permanent streams in the valley and lower slopes of the mountains. Higher up the slopes are woodlands with some grasslands near the upper ridges.

The experience of seeing chimpanzees in the wild is by far the major attraction of this park. Other primates include red colobus monkey, blue monkey and baboon. Other wildlife of note includes buffalo, Defassa waterbuck and leopard.

Chimpanzees can usually be found around the research station and are quite habituated to humans. Two-hour morning and afternoon hikes into the forest searching for chimps can be arranged. The Kakombe Waterfall is worth a visit. There is also a nice walk along the lake shore northward from the guest house.

You can reach the park by water taxi (about 3 hours) from Ujiji or Kigoma.

ACCOMMODATION — CLASS B: • **Gombe Forest Lodge** is the only tented camp in the park and has 6 comfortable tents with en suite facilities. Meals are served in the dining tent and are a 3-course affair. Transfers from Kigoma to Gombe are by way of boat and take you past fishing villages and scenic hills.

CLASS F: There is a basic, self-service guest house and one hostel with separate facilities. Book well in advance or bring a tent, because the guest house may be full. Only basic supplies are available in Kigoma.

CAMPING: Allowed on special request.

Mahale Mountains National Park

Like Gombe Stream, the main attraction of this remote park, which was only gazetted in 1985, is to be able to walk among large populations of chimpanzees. The chimps have been studied by Japanese researchers for more than 35 years, and now many chimps have been habituated to humans.

Located about 95 miles (150 km) south of Kigoma, this 609-square-mile (1,577-km^2) park is situated on the eastern shores of Lake Tanganyika. The Mahale Mountains, featuring deep ravines, permanent streams and waterfalls, run through the center of the park, forming the eastern wall of the Great Rift

Valley — with altitudes up to 8,075 feet (2,462 m) above sea level. The western side of the mountains, where the chimp trekking occurs, is primarily composed of semitropical rain forest with *brachystygia* (semideciduous) woodland on the ridges and montane forest at higher altitudes.

Trekking in the park occurs in the range of the M Group, which as of this writing consists of 57 individuals that have been habituated to human presence. Once found, trekkers can watch them naturally go about their normal daily activities from often just a few yards (meters) away.

In addition to over 1,000 chimpanzees, the park is also home to 8 other species of primates, including red colobus monkey

A habituated chimp in Mahale

and Angolan black-and-white colobus monkey. Other wildlife includes bushbuck, otters, banded mongoose, Sharpe's grysbok and blue duiker.

Seasons are fairly predictable. The main dry season usually runs from mid-May to mid-October, with mid-December to mid-February also being quite dry. Rainy seasons are usually mid-October to mid-December and mid-February to mid-May. Nights are often cool and rainfall ranges from 60 to 100 inches (1,500 to 2,500 mm) per year. The best time to visit is during the two dry seasons mentioned above.

There are scheduled charter flights operating a few times a week from Arusha to Mahale and scheduled flights most days of the week from Dar es Salaam to Kigoma. Otherwise, a private charter from Nairobi, Dar es Salaam, Arusha or any Tanzanian park is required.

To reach Mahale by boat from Kigoma (not recommended), take the weekly steamer MV Liemba for 8 to 10 hours to the village of Lagosa (Mugambo). You usually arrive in the middle of the night and must be transferred ashore. From there you may be able to charter a boat for a 3-hour ride to Kasoge (Kasiha village) in the park. Small boats from Kigoma make this journey in about 16 hours. The park cannot be reached by vehicle.

ACCOMMODATION — CLASS A: • **Greystoke Mahale** is located on the eastern shores of the lake and features 6 open-fronted bandas with dressing rooms, bathrooms are accessible via a short boardwalk and include showers and flush toilets and upstairs relaxation decks. Hikes to see chimpanzees, sailing by dhow, dugout canoeing, snorkeling and fishing are offered. The camp

Greystoke Mahale as viewed from the lake

is open June to mid-October and mid-December to mid-February.

CLASS B: • **Kungwe Beach Lodge** (formerly *Nkungwe Camp*) is set on the shores of Lake Tanganyika and has 6 comfortable tents with en suite facilities. Chimpanzee tracking, fishing and bird watching are offered.

CLASS F: There are 2 small resthouses, but you will need to bring your own food, crockery and cutlery, bed linens and stove. No supplies are available in the park.

CAMPING: Camping sites are available.

Katavi National Park

Katavi offers incredible game viewing and remains virtually unvisited by travelers due to its remoteness. This undeveloped 1,545-square-mile (4,000-km^2) park is located between the towns of Mpanda and Sumbawanga on the main road running through western Tanzania from north to south.

Chimp trekking is the highlight of a stay at Greystoke Mahale

Lake Katavi and its extensive floodplains are in the north of this park, which is about 2,950 feet (900 m) above sea level. To the southeast is Lake Chada, which is connected with Lake Katavi by the Katuma River and its extensive swampland. Miombo woodlands dominate most of the dry areas, except for acacia woodlands near Lake Chada.

Wildlife includes hippo, crocs, elephant, zebra, lion, leopard, eland, puku, roan antelope and sable antelope. Herds of several thousand buffalo are sometimes seen. Over 400 species of birds have been recorded.

The long rains are March to May. The best time to visit is July to October. Scheduled charter flights to the park are available several times a week from Arusha.

Top: One of Chada Katavi's tents
Bottom: Past the palms, the open plains of Chada Katavi

ACCOMMODATIONS — CLASS A/B: • **Chada Katavi** is located in the heart of Katavi National Park with views over the wide Chada Plain. Accommodations include 6 spacious safari tents with bush showers (hot water) and bush (long-drop) toilets. Activities include game drives, walks and optional fly-camping. • **Katavi Wildlife Camp** offers 6 spacious tents all with en suite bathrooms with solar heated showers and flush toilets. The tents are set on wooden platforms with verandas overlooking the herds of game on the Katisunga plain. Activities include game drives, walks, and fly-camping.

CLASS B: • **Katuma Bush Lodge** has 10 tents with en suite facilities. It offers game drives in open sided vehicles and walking safaris.

CLASS F: There are only a few huts for shelter. Very basic hotel accommodation is available in Mpanda and Sumbawanga.

CAMPING: Sites are available in the park. Campers must be self-sufficient, as there are no facilities.

THE COAST

Dar Es Salaam

Dar es Salaam, which means "haven of peace" in Arabic, is the functional capital, largest city and commercial center of Tanzania. Many safaris to the southern parks begin here. Among the more interesting sights are the harbor, **National Museum**, **Village Museum** and the **Kariakoo Market**. Ask at your hotel about traditional dancing troops that may be performing during your stay.

Once the German capital, hub of the slave trade and end point of the slave route from the interior, **Bagamoyo** is an old seaport 46 miles (75 km) north of Dar es Salaam. Fourteenth century ruins, stone pens and shackles that held the slaves can be seen.

ACCOMMODATION — FIRST CLASS: • **The Kilimanjaro Kempinski Hotel** is a large, 191 room air-conditioned hotel with en suite facilities, a swimming pool and a fabulous view of the harbor. • **The Movenpick Royal Palm** (formerly the *Sheraton Hotel*) has 250 air-conditioned rooms with en suite facilities, two restaurants, and a bar, swimming pool and health club. • **Holiday Inn**, located in the city center, has 154 rooms with en suite bathrooms, 2 restaurants and cocktail lounge • **Golden Tulip Inn** has 84 air-conditioned rooms and 7 suites — all with private balconies and sea views. • **Oyster Bay Hotel** is 4 miles (6 km) from town on the coast and has been recently renovated. All rooms have en suite facilities. • **Hotel Sea Cliff** (the hotel was gutted by a fire in 2007 and is currently closed. No date to open has been set).

TOURIST CLASS: • **The New Africa Hotel**, situated in the heart of Dar es Salaam's shopping and banking district, has 126 air-conditioned rooms and 7 suites with en suite facilities, 2 restaurants, 2 bars, a casino and business center.

ACCOMMODATION NEAR DAR-ES-SALAAM — LUXURY: • **Amani Beach Club**, situated on the coast south of Dar es Salaam, has 12 luxury air-conditioned cottages, each with garden terrace and hammock overlooking the Indian Ocean, and swimming pool.

FIRST CLASS: • **Ras Kutani Beach Resort**, located on a beautiful, remote beach 17 miles (28 km) south of Dar es Salaam, has 9 spacious cottages and 4 suites with en suite facilities. Wind surfing, sailing, snorkeling, deep sea fishing and horseback riding are offered. Humpback whales can sometimes be seen from shore. Access is by a 10-minute charter flight or 1 hour road transfer from Dar es Salaam.

Lazy Lagoon Island

Lazy Lagoon Island is a private island retreat 44 miles (70 km) north of Dar es Salaam in the Zanzibar channel. It is approximately 4 miles (6 km) off shore from the historic slave town of Bagamoyo. The island is protected by coral and the delicate ecosystem still attracts suni antelope, duiker, and Galago bushbabies.

TOURIST CLASS: • **Lazy Lagoon Island Lodge** is the only lodge on the island and offers 12 individual beach cottages with en suite facilities each opening out on the white sand beach. Activities include sailing, windsurfing, kayaking and snorkeling as well as a guided tour around the Kaole ruins and Bagamoyo Slave Town.

Lazy Lagoon's main lodge with its refreshing pool

Zanzibar

Zanzibar (known to the locals as Unguja) and its sister island, Pemba, grow 75% of the world's cloves. A beautiful island, Zanzibar is only 22 miles (35 km) from the mainland — a 25-minute, scheduled or charter flight from Dar es Salaam or a 90-minute hydrofoil ride. There are also several scheduled flights from Arusha taking about 75 minutes.

The narrow streets and Arabic architecture of historical Zanzibar City are exceptionally mystical and beautiful on a moonlit night. Main attractions include the **Zanzibar Museum**, former British Consulate, **Arab Old Fort**, the **Anglican Cathedral** built on the site of the former slave market, **Sultan's Palace**, clove market and Indian bazaar. Livingstone's and Burton's houses are near the picturesque Dhow Harbour, where 20 to 30 large Arab dhows can often be seen having their cargos loaded or unloaded. Antique shops stocked with Arab clocks, kettles, brass trays, Zanzibar beds, carved doors and frames have special atmospheres all their own.

The **Spice Tour** travels north of Stone Town and includes a visit to one or more spice gardens and farms. Various spices and plants, including cinnamon, cloves, nutmeg, vanilla, ginger and black pepper, along with fruits such as tamarind, guava, rose-apple and several types of mango and bananas, may be seen, touched, smelled and purchased.

Good restaurants include Mecury's, the Zanzibar Serena Inn, and The Fisherman, located across

A dhow cruising off the coast of Zanzibar

Zanzibar

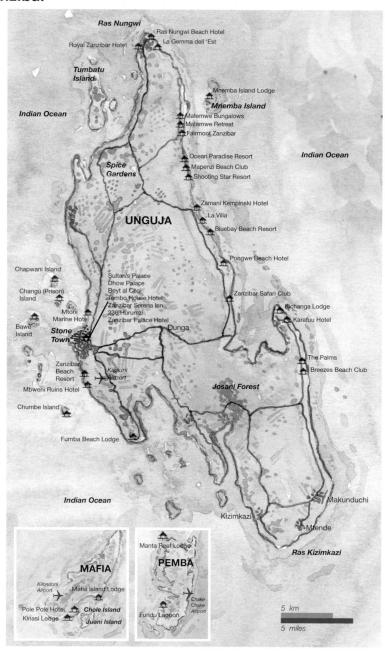

Ras Nungwi

Ras Nungwi Beach Hotel
La Gemma dell 'Est
Royal Zanzibar Hotel

Tumbatu
Island

Mnemba Island Lodge

Indian Ocean

Mnemba Island
Matemwe Bungalows
Matemwe Retreat
Fairmont Zanzibar

Ocean Paradise Resort   Indian Ocean
Spice   Mapenzi Beach Club
Gardens   Shooting Star Resort

Zamani Kempinski Hotel
UNGUJA   La Villa
Bluebay Beach Resort

Pongwe Beach Hotel

Chapwani Island
Sultan's Palace
Changu (Prison)   Dhow Palace
Island   Beyt al Chai   Zanzibar Safari Club
Tembo House Hotel
Mtoni   Zanzibar Serena Inn   Kichanga Lodge
Marine Hotel   236 Hurumzi   Karafuu Hotel
Bawe   Zanzibar Palace Hotel
Island   Stone   Dunga
Town

The Palms
Zanzibar   Breezes Beach Club
Beach   Kisauni
Resort   Airport
Mbweni Ruins Hotel   Josani Forest

Chumbe Island

Fumba Beach Lodge

Indian Ocean   Makunduchi

Kizimkazi
Mtende

Manta Reef Lodge   Ras Kizimkazi

MAFIA   PEMBA

Kilondoni
Airport   Mafia Island Lodge   Chake
Chake
Pole Pole Hotel   Chole Island   Airport   5 km
Kinasi Lodge   Juani Island   Fundu Lagoon
5 miles

from the Tembo Hotel in Stone Town. Just outside of town, Mtoni Marine also has a good restaurant. At 236 Hurumzi (formerly *Emerson & Green*) the Tower Top Restaurant serves a limited seating for dinner each night and is quite popular.

The more pristine coral reefs off Zanzibar offer a superb diving or snorkeling experience. In addition to a mind-boggling diversity of brightly colored reef fish, dolphins, green turtles and the largest of all fishes — the harmless whale shark — are fairly numerous in the waters around Zanzibar.

For a taste of what Zanzibar was like prior to the arrival of the traders, sultans and farmers, a visit to **Jozani Forest** is highly recommended. This small patch of remaining forest — mostly palm, pandanus and mahogany trees — is home to the unique Zanzibar red colobus, one of Africa's rarest and most endangered primates. Among birds, the equally rare Fischer's turaco may also be seen at Jozani, along with paradise flycatcher, banded wattle-eye and numerous other species.

Top: The narrow alleyways of Stone Town
Bottom: The old Dispensary in Zanzibar exhibits colonial architecture

ACCOMMODATION IN ZANZIBAR TOWN — FIRST CLASS: • **The Beyt Al Chai** — Stone House Inn, located on the famous Kelele Square, has 6 air-conditioned suites with en suite facilities. • **Zanzibar Serena Inn**, located on the waterfront in Stone Town, has 51 rooms (most with private balconies) with en suite facilities, seafront restaurant, bar and swimming pool. Guests have access to a beautiful private beach at the Mangapwani Caves.

TOURIST CLASS: • **Dhow Palace**, located in the heart of Stone Town about 300 yards (300m) from the waterfront and has 17 tastefully decorated rooms with en suite facilities and rooftop restaurant (no alcoholic beverages served), with panoramic views of Stone Town. • **Tembo Hotel** has 29 air-conditioned rooms with en suite facilities, restaurant (no alcoholic beverages served), and a swimming pool. From its waterfront location, ships are constantly seen, passing enroute to and from the harbor. • **236 Hurumzi** (formerly *Emerson's & Green*)

The Palms

offers elegant rooms decorate in period antiques and is located in the heart of Stone Town on a narrow alleyway. Dinner is served nightly with limited seating. • **Zanzibar Palace Hotel** has 9 rooms (2 of which are suites), all with en suite facilities. The hotel is located in the heart of Stone Town.

ACCOMMODATION ON THE BEACH — DELUXE: • **The Palms** is situated along a pristine white beach on the east coast of the island and consists of 6 luxurious villas featuring a bedroom, living room, en suite bathroom, Jacuzzi and private terrace overlooking the Indian Ocean. There is a swimming pool, dining room, evening bar and pool bar and massage facilities. • **Gemma Del Est**, the largest resort in Zanzibar, is located on the Northwest coast of Zanzibar on a magnificent stretch of beach where you are able to swim during low and high tide. The resort has 138 rooms including 41 suites, and a massive swimming pool with a sunken bar, restaurant, full water sports centre, big game fishing facility, full PADI certified dive school, diving, snorkeling, water-skiing, windsurfing, kayaking, and dhow cruises. • **The Fairmont Zanzibar** is located on the northeastern coast of the island and has over 380 yards (350 m) of pristine beach. This resort offers 109 air-conditioned guest rooms and cottages each with private facilities and satellite television, 2 swimming pools, a main restaurant, several lounges and 2 poolside bars. Guests enjoy a 24-hour fitness center, a PADI certified dive center, Burahi Spa, and free-of-charge non-motorized water sports such as sea kayaking, sailing, windsurfing and snorkeling. • **Royal Zanzibar Hotel** is a new property located on the northern tip of the island with a spectacular beach, and will have 100 rooms and suites with private facilities • **Matemwe Retreat** is a private section to Matemwe (see below in First Class) which features 3 exclusive 2-story suites with air-conditioned en suite bedrooms on the first floor and a private sun terrace with plunge pool on the second.

A luxurious bedroom at Matemwe Retreat

FIRST CLASS: • **Blue Bay Beach Resort** is situated on a fine, white-sand beach on the east coast of Zanzibar, a 45-minute drive from Stone Town. This 25-acre (10 hectare) property has 112 air-conditioned rooms and suites in 2-story bungalows with en suite bathrooms, 2 restaurants, 2 bars and a large swimming pool. Scuba diving and water sports are offered. • **Karafuu Hotel Village**, located on the east coast of Zanzibar about a 90-minute drive

The pristine white beach at Matemwe

from the airport or Stone Town, has 89 air-conditioned rooms in bungalows with en suite facilities, 5 restaurants, 2 bars, sports and entertainment facilities, and swimming pool. • **Breezes Beach Club**, located on the east coast near the village of Bwejuu, about an hour's drive from Zanzibar airport, has 70 en suite bedrooms in 2-story bungalows set on an unspoiled beach, 2 restaurants, 2 bars, conference facility, fitness center, flood-lit tennis court, disco and scuba diving center. • **Ras Nungwi Beach Hotel**, located about 36 miles (60 km) north of Zanzibar airport on the northern tip of the island, has 32 rooms with facilities en suite, 2 restaurants, bar, swimming pool, PADI dive center, deep-sea fishing, water skiing and windsurfing. • **PlanHotel Mapenzi Beach Resort**, located on a beautiful beach on the east coast 28 miles (45 km) from the airport, has 87 spacious rooms (all with air-conditioning) with en suite facilities, 2 restaurants, 3 bars, tennis courts and a swimming pool. Activities include mountain biking, archery, snorkeling, beach volleyball, table tennis, wind surfing, canoeing and deep-sea fishing. • **Mbweni Ruins Hotel**, located on the west coast of the island and a 15-minute drive from

Stone Town, has 12 sea-facing, air-conditioned rooms with en suite facilities, restaurant, bar and swimming pool. • **Matemwe**, located on cliffs overlooking the northeast coast, has 12 rooms, all with en suite facilities, 2 swimming pools and a restaurant.

Chumbe Island Coral Park

Located 6 miles (10 km) by boat from Stone Town, this nature reserve offers forest and marine nature trails,

Aerial view of Chumbe Island

The unique design of
Chumbe's bungalows

over half a mile (1 km) of protected reef, great bird watching and snorkeling. Over 40 species of birds, including the endangered roseate tern, have been recorded on the island, and 370 families of fish have been identified on the colorful reefs that drop off to about 50 feet (16 m).

ACCOMMODATION — TOURIST CLASS: • **Chumbe Island Lodge** offers 6 palm-thatched bungalows with en suite facilities set in the forest and facing the ocean. Each bungalow has solar-powered lights and is equipped to catch, filter and solar-heat its own water for warm showers. This lodge has recently won prestigious environmental awards for its sensitive ecotourism.

Mnemba Island

Mnemba is an exclusive island located 2 miles (3 km) northeast of the Zanzibar mainland. The island is only 1 mile (1.5 km) in circumference and is idyllic for anyone who wants to truly get away from it all.

Top: Mnemba's thatched bandas are an idyllic retreat
Bottom: The pristine beach of Mnemba

Mnemba's reefs are among the best around Zanzibar, and, along with a bewildering variety of spectacular reef fish, encounters with green turtles and whale sharks are fairly common. Humpback whales pass through the straits between Mnemba and the mainland, and pods of common dolphins are seen almost daily. The huge coconut crab is an occasional visitor and the charming little ghost crabs are abundant on the pearly white beach. A variety of birds roost on Mnemba's secure sandbanks, including crab plovers, dimorphic egret, lesser crested tern and a host of Eurasian migratory waders.

ACCOMMODATION — DELUXE: • **Mnemba Island Lodge** is an exclusive island getaway with 10 thatched beach cottages with en suite facilities. This is "barefoot luxury" at its finest. Wind surfing, big-game fishing, skiing, snorkeling and scuba diving are available. The lodge is an hour by road, followed by 20 minutes by boat from Stone Town.

Pemba Island

Pemba is located 16 miles (25 km) north of Zanzibar Island near the Kenyan border and offers some of the best scuba diving and deep-sea fishing in all of sub-Saharan Africa. The Pemba Channel runs between Pemba and the mainland with depths

Crisp, cool comfort at Mnemba

up to 2,625 feet (800 m). Sheer underwater walls drop 150 to 600 feet (45 to 183 m) just off the coastline. Divers often see eagle ray, grouper, tuna and a variety of tropical fish.

Access to the island is by boat transfer to Pemba Harbor (Mkoani) or by a 20-minute scheduled or private charter flight.

ACCOMMODATION — FIRST CLASS: • **Fundu Lagoon**, set on 3 miles (4.5 km) of private beach, has 16 bungalows (some on the beach and some on the ridge), a restaurant, 2 bars and a PADI dive center. Activities include snorkeling, scuba diving, sailing, fishing, water skiing and kayaking.

TOURIST CLASS: • **Manta Reef Camp** has 15 comfortable rustic cabins, completely open in the front and built on raised platforms with en suite facilities, and a dive shop. Scuba diving and snorkeling are offered.

Mafia Island

A 40-minute flight south from Dar es Salaam or Zanzibar, this island offers some of the best big-game fishing in the world. Species caught include marlin, sailfish, tuna and shark. The diving is also very good.

ACCOMMODATION — FIRST CLASS: • **Kinasi Lodge** has 20 private chalets with en suite facilities, and is set on a hillside overlooking Chole Bay. Scuba diving, snorkeling, sport fishing, sailing and wind surfing are offered. Other activities include excursions to historic sites, villages, forests, secluded beaches and bays. • **Pole Pole Resort** offers 7 luxury bungalows with facilities en suite. Built into its natural surroundings with traditional makuti roofin, the resort offers a variety of different activities including scuba diving, snorkeling and fishing.

TOURIST CLASS: • **Mafia Island Lodge**, located on Chole Bay, has 40 rooms with en suite facilities. Scuba diving, snorkeling, deep-sea fishing, water skiing, sailing and motor boating are offered.

Kenya

Kenya

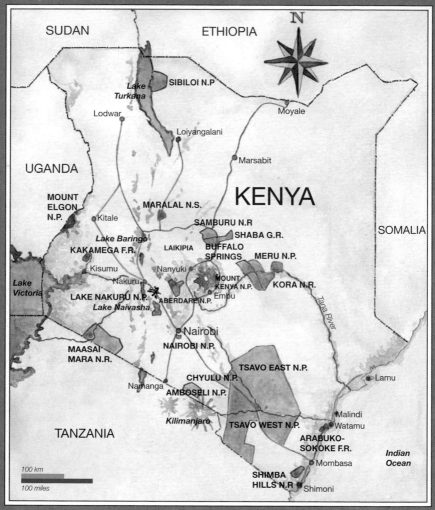

SUDAN

ETHIOPIA

N

Lake Turkana

SIBILOI N.P

Lodwar

Moyale

Loiyangalani

Marsabit

UGANDA

KENYA

MOUNT ELGON N.P.

Kitale

MARALAL N.S.

SAMBURU N.R

SHABA G.R.

SOMALIA

Lake Baringo

KAKAMEGA F.R.

LAIKIPIA

BUFFALO SPRINGS

MERU N.P.

Kisumu

Nanyuki

Nakuru

MOUNT KENYA N.P.

KORA N.R.

Lake Victoria

LAKE NAKURU N.P.

ABERDARE N.P.

Embu

Tana River

Lake Naivasha

Nairobi

MAASAI MARA N.R.

NAIROBI N.P.

TSAVO EAST N.P.

Lamu

CHYULU N.P.

Namanga

AMBOSELI N.P.

Kilimanjaro

TSAVO WEST N.P.

Malindi

Watamu

TANZANIA

ARABUKO-SOKOKE F.R.

Indian Ocean

Mombasa

100 km

100 miles

SHIMBA HILLS N.R

Shimoni

From the warm tropical waters of the Indian Ocean, to the icy heights of Mount Kenya at 17,058 feet (5,199 m), this is truly "a world in one country". Desert and arid savannah prevails in the northern frontier and southeast, while remnant forests extend over the high country and wetter west. Covering 225,000-square-miles (582,750-km^2), Kenya is about the same size as Texas or France. The population numbers some 33 million, with over 2.5 million in the capital city of Nairobi. KiSwahili and English are the official languages. Currency is the Kenyan shilling.

Kenya
Country Highlights

- See the Great Serengeti Migration and game view off-road at Kenya's finest reserve — the Maasai Mara
- Get up close and personal with a baby elephant at Daphne Sheldrick Elephant Orphanage in Nairobi
- Sunrise balloon safari across the Maasai Mara
- Checking off the "Big Five" game viewing
- Sundowners at Ol Donyo Wuas or Campi ya Kanzi with Mt. Kilimanjaro in the background
- Nature walk with a Maasai or Samburu guide

Best Parks and Reserves to Visit	Best Times to Go
Maasai Mara National Reserve	December to March / July to October
Amboseli National Park	January to March / July to October
Ol Donyo Wuas and Campi ya Kanzi Private Game Reserves	June to March
Samburu National Reserve	January to March / July to September

Best Accommodations
Ol Donyo Wuas, Mara Explorer, Governor's Ilmoran Camp, Bateleur Camp, Shompole, Borana, The Sanctuary at Ol Lentille, Lewa House, Samburu Sasaab, Finch Hattons, Elsa's Kopje, Joy's Camp

KENYA

The word "safari" is Swahili for "a journey," and Kenya is where it all began. Hemingway immortalized the safari experience, although he was a sport and trophy hunter rather than a naturalist or photographer.

Joy Adamson was among the group of expatriates, in the 1960s and 1970s, whose endeavors to conserve African wildlife captured the world's attention. The writings of Karen Blixen, and the adaptation of her classic book *Out of Africa* into a motion picture starring Robert Redford and Meryl Streep, helped establish Kenya as a great safari destination in the modern era.

Visitors to Kenya can enjoy fabulous game viewing, birdwatching, hot-air ballooning, mountaineering, scuba diving, freshwater and deep-sea fishing, and numerous other activities.

Kenya is well known for the magnificent Serengeti Migration (shared with Tanzania) of more than one million wildebeest and zebra in the Maasai Mara and for the colorful Maasai, Samburu and other tribes that contribute so much to making this a top safari destination.

Kenya has one of the most diversely majestic landscapes on the continent. The Great Rift Valley, with the steep-walled valley floor dropping as much as 2,000 to 3,000 feet (610 to 915 m) from the surrounding countryside, is more breathtakingly dramatic here than anywhere else in Africa.

The eastern and northern regions of the country are arid. Most of the population and economic production are in the south, which is characterized by a plateau that ranges in altitude from 3,000 to 10,000 feet (915 to 3,050 m), sloping down to Lake Victoria in the west and to a coastal strip to the east.

Over half the country is Christian, although many people still retain their indigenous beliefs. There is a Muslim population concentrated along the coast.

The Maasai are found mainly to the south of Nairobi, the Kikuyu in the highlands around Nairobi, the Samburu in the arid north, and the Luo around Lake Victoria.

Bantu and Nilotic peoples moved into the area before Arab traders, who arrived on the Kenyan coast by the first century A.D. The Swahili language was created out of a mixture of Bantu and Arabic and became the universal trading language.

The Portuguese arrived in 1498 and took command of the coast, followed by the Omani in the 1600s and the British in the late nineteenth century. Kenya gained its independence within the British Commonwealth on December 12, 1963. Key foreign exchange-earners are tourism, coffee, tea and horticulture (flowers and vegetables exported to Europe, especially in the European winter).

🐾 WILDLIFE AND WILDLIFE AREAS

Kenya is one of the best countries on the continent for seeing large amounts of wildlife. In addition, lodge safaris, where guests are driven from park to park, are generally less expensive here than in Tanzania, Botswana or Zambia. Prices are even more attractive in Kenya's low season (April, May and November). Game viewing is still good in the low season due to the excellent visibility of the open plains of the Maasai Mara and other reserves.

Kenya's well-known parks have the reputation of being crowded in high season, and compared to less popular reserves, they are. However, I feel this should be put into perspective. There are very few reserves in Africa that have such great sightings of the game many safariers want to see most (leopard, lion, cheetah) than in reserves like the Maasai Mara and Samburu, so having several other vehicles on some sightings is perhaps not a bad tradeoff.

Booking a safari with a private vehicle and guide is a great way to maximize the quality of your game

Cheetah using a termite mound to look for prey on the Maasai Mara viewing experience. If a few vehicles show up on your sighting, if you wish, you can simply search for another game viewing opportunity perhaps further off the beaten path. In other words, you have much more control of your experience in the bush.

It is possible to get totally away from the crowds in some of the splendid private reserves or the less popular national parks. Many private reserves cater to a maximum of 12 to 24 guests in luxury accommodations and offer activities not allowed within the parks, such as night game drives and escorted walks. Ol Donyo Wuas and Campi ya Kanzi, for instance, each cover 250,000-acres (100,000-hectares) and cater to no more than 16 guests. You can also visit the major reserves at times other than during peak seasons.

The Kenya Wildlife Services, formed to monitor the national parks and reserves, has instituted changes that have reduced poaching and limited the building of new lodges and camps in parks and reserves.

The Maasai Mara is the best reserve in Kenya for wildlife viewing and should, if at all possible, be included in your itinerary, unless you will be touring the Serengeti National Park in Tanzania at the times of the year when the Serengeti Migration is more concentrated there.

In general, game viewing is best during the dry seasons, mid-December to March and July to October. Wildlife is easiest to spot in the Maasai Mara, Amboseli and Nairobi National Parks, which have vast wide-open plains.

Cuddly at birth, lions will grow to be an average of 260–400 pounds for females and 330–550 pounds for males

The awe inspiring beauty of a leopard

Samburu/Buffalo Springs National Reserves and Lewa Downs are the country's best northern reserves and are also excellent for game viewing

The country is an ornithologist's paradise, with over 1,000 species of birds recorded within its borders. Greater and lesser flamingos migrate along the Rift Valley and prefer the alkaline lakes of Magadi, Elmenteita, Nakuru, Bogoria or Turkana. Lakes Naivasha and Baringo are freshwater lakes. Birdwatching is good year-round, but is perhaps best between September and March when many species of Eurasian migratory birds are present alongside the breeding residents.

Flying safaris are available as Kenya has an excellent network of scheduled flights to all the reserves. Unique, camel-back safaris are operated in the north, where guests spend time riding these "ships of the desert" and walking down dry riverbeds.

To give you the greatest variety of experiences on a safari in Kenya, I highly recommend combining visits to some of Kenya's top parks with stays in some private reserves.

THE SOUTH

Nairobi

Nairobi, situated at an altitude of about 6,000 feet (1,830 m), means "place of cool waters" in the Maasai language.

The **National Museum** of Nairobi has been recently refurbished and features the Leakey family's paleo-anthropological discoveries, botanical drawings and the original tribal paintings of Joy Adamson. Studying the taxidermy displays of birds and wild animals will help you identify the live game while on safari. Across from the museum is the **Snake Park**, exhibiting over 200 species of the "well-loved" reptilian family. At the **Municipal Market** in the center of town on Muindi Mbingu Street, vendors sell and produce unusual and beautiful curios (be sure to bargain). The **Railroad Museum** will be of interest to railroad enthusiasts. The **Nairobi Race Course** has horse racing on Sunday afternoons (in season); the track is an excellent place for people to watch and meet a diverse cross section of Nairobians.

Top: Feeding time at Daphne Sheldrick Elephant Orphanage
Bottom: An up close and personal moment at the Giraffe Centre

One of the more popular dining and disco spots is the Carnivore, famous for its tasty selection of meats cooked on giant open grills. The Tamarind is known for excellent seafood. The Minar and Haandi are possibly the finest of Kenya's great Indian restaurants. The Thorn Tree Cafe is a renowned meeting place for travelers on long safaris who leave messages on a bulletin board; it is one of the best spots in town for people-watching. The Talisam in Karen, the Osteria del Chinati on Lennon Road and the Mediteraneo at the Junction are the best restaurants in Nairobi and its suburbs. Other excellent restaurants include Alan Bobbies' Bistro and 'Thai Chi' at The Stanley Hotel. The most happening disco in Nairobi these days is The Pavement in Westlands.

Other attractions include the **Bomas of Kenya**, which features regular performances of ethnic dances and 16 varying styles of Kenyan homesteads. At the **Giraffe Centre**, guests can learn more about the Rothschild's giraffes and even feed them from an elevated platform. The **Karen Blixen**

Museum is also an interesting attraction, featuring many of this famous author's personal possessions on display in her restored home. The trained team at the **Daphne Sheldrick Elephant Orphanage** have brought sick and abandoned elephants back to health and released them into the wild at Tsavo East National Park. Using a milk formula she created, Daphne was the first person to success-fully bottle-raise an orphaned milk-dependent elephant.

ACCOMMODATION — DELUXE:
• **Fairmont Norfolk Hotel**, a land-mark in Nairobi, has a traditional safari atmosphere, a swimming pool, the fabulous Ibis Grill, and an open-air bar that is especially popular on Friday nights. The hotel was recently renovated, and all rooms are air-conditioned with en suite facilities.
• **Nairobi Serena**, located a few min-utes drive from town, is a member of the "Leading Hotels of the World," and has been completely remodeled with 184 air-conditioned rooms and suites with en suite facilities, business center, conference facilities, Maisha Spa and a large swimming pool. • **The Palacina**, located about 10 minutes from the city center, has 14 suites each with its own living room, en suite bathroom and a private furnished bal-cony, and the award winning Moonflower Restaurant.

Top: The Fairmont Norfolk Hotel in downtown Nairobi
Bottom: The Nairobi Serena

FIRST CLASS: • **The Panari Hotel** is conveniently located a few minutes away from the International Airport, just 3 miles (5 km) from the city cen-ter, with 135 rooms and two suites, a restaurant, coffee shop and bar. • **Hilton International** is centrally located and has 329 air-conditioned rooms with facilities en suite and a swimming pool. • **Inter-Continental Hotel**, near the center of town, has a swimming pool, 440 air-conditioned rooms with en suite facilities and a casino. • **The Stanley Hotel**, located in the center of town, has 240 air-conditioned rooms with en suite facilities. • **Grand Regency Hotel** is a 300-room high-rise hotel with en suite facilities and a swimming pool, restau-rant, rooftop lounge, conference center and casino. • **Nairobi Safari Club** is an air-conditioned, all-suite hotel (146 rooms) with en suite facilities, a health club and swimming pool.

TOURIST CLASS: • **Fairview Hotel**, set on 5 acres of gardens just over a mile (2 km) from the city center, has 103 rooms and 11 apartments with en suite facilities. • **Landmark Hotel**, located in the suburb of Westlands outside the city center, has 124 rooms with en suite facilities. • **Mayfair Court Holiday Inn** located in the suburb of Westlands, has 108 rooms with en suite facilities, two swimming pools, a restaurant and a casino.

Top: The lounge area at Ngong House
Bottom: The House of Waine

ACCOMMODATION OUTSIDE OF NAIROBI — DELUXE: • **House of Waine**, situated in the suburb of Karen, is set on 2.5 acres and offers 11 bedrooms, each with a large marble bathroom. Meals are served in various locations on the property and there are two bars exclusively for hotel guests. • **Ngong House**, located in the suburb of Karen/Langata, has 4 elevated log cabins set in beautiful natural gardens, with en suite facilities and excellent food. • **The Windsor Golf and Country Club**, located 11 miles (17 km) outside Nairobi, is a colonial-style hotel with 130 rooms with en suite facilities, an 18-hole golf course, tennis courts, and a health club and gymnasium.

FIRST CLASS: **Safari Park Hotel**, located 7 miles (11 km) from the city center in a quiet, country setting, has 228 rooms with en suite facilities, a huge swimming pool, tennis and squash courts and several restaurants — all in a lush garden setting. • **Giraffe Manor**, located in the suburb of Karen/Langata, is famous for having Rothschild's giraffes roaming about the property, often sticking their heads through open windows looking for handouts. This unique lodge has 3 bedrooms with en suite facilities and 2 without. • **Karen Blixen Cottages**, situated 20 miles (32 km) from Nairobi and a half mile (1 km) from the Karen Blixen Museum, has 16 suites with en suite bathrooms, restaurant, bar and swimming pool. • **Macushla House**, a private guesthouse located near Giraffe Manor, which is just a 20-minute drive from downtown Nairobi, caters to a maximum of 10 guests in rooms with en suite facilities and swimming pool.

The "Lunatic Express"

The service and standard of accommodations on this overnight train between Nairobi and Mombasa has, unfortunately, deteriorated over the last two decades, and at this point should be considered only by hardy travelers. Dinner and breakfast are served on this journey that passes Mt. Kilimanjaro in the night. There are departures three times a week from both Nairobi and Mombasa.

Nairobi National Park

Nairobi National Park is only 8 miles (13 km) south of Nairobi, and has a variety of game including several types of antelope, hippo, black rhino, and even the occasional lion and cheetah — a bit of everything except elephant. The park has one of the highest concentrations of black rhino in Africa, with a current population of over 60.

Most of the park is open plains with areas of scattered acacia bush.

The permanent Athi River is fringed by yellow-barked fever trees, and there is a small patch of highland forest dominated by crotons. An impressive list of birds has been recorded, but occurrence is seasonal for many species. Among the characteristic varieties are ostrich, secretary bird, black-headed heron, augur buzzard, little bee-eater and Jackson's widowbird.

There is something very strange about being in the midst of wild game while still within sight of a city skyline. Altitude ranges from 4,950 to 5,850 feet (1,500 to 1,785 m) above sea level.

The Animal Orphanage, a small zoo near the main park entrance, cares for hurt, sick or stray animals. The side of the park facing Nairobi is fenced. A 4wd vehicle is recommended in the rainy season.

Amboseli National Reserve

Set on the Tanzanian border, Amboseli is one of the most scenic of Kenya's wildlife reserves. Every vista is dominated by the majestic, snow-capped peak of Kilimanjaro in neighboring Tanzania. The grandeur of this imposing feature provides a superb backdrop for photographing and viewing big game.

Amboseli is perhaps best-known for its abundant (over 1,000) and approachable elephants — the subject of several documentary films

A game drive from Tortilis Camp

Amboseli National Reserve

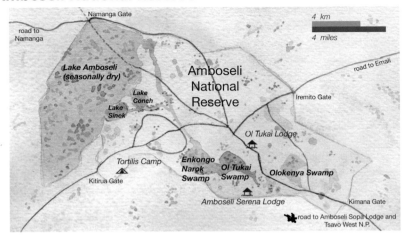

and researcher Cynthia Moss' classic book *Elephant Memories* (University of Chicago Press).

Amboseli National Reserve covers 150-square-miles (390-km^2) and averages about 3,900 feet (1,190 m) in altitude. Elephant and giraffe are easily found, and many visitors enjoy photographing them as they pass in front of majestic Mt. Kilimanjaro. The mountain seems so close, but it is actually located in Tanzania, more than 30 miles (48 km) from the park.

The reserve lies in the rain shadow of Kilimanjaro and receives, on average, just 12 inches (300 mm) of rain per year. Interestingly, however, subterranean water draining off the northern slopes of Mt. Kilimanjaro surfaces in Amboseli in the form of freshwater springs. These springs are a major draw for wildlife, and the surrounding papyrus beds are an attractive habitat for wetland species. The dominant habitat is acacia-commiphora scrub or woodland, much of it on rocky, lava-strewn plains.

A dry and ancient lakebed occupies the western part of the reserve, but when it fills after heavy rains it can be a huge attraction for birds. Over 400 bird species have been recorded here, including three varieties of sandgrouse, rosy-patched bushshrike, Taveta golden weaver and purple grenadier. In addition to the plain's game typical of East Africa, the arid-adapted gerenuk, lesser kudu and fringe-eared oryx may been seen.

From Nairobi, travel south across the Athi Plains inhabited by the Maasai pastoralists. Visitors enter the reserve on a badly corrugated road from Namanga and pass Lake Amboseli (a salt pan), which is bone dry except in the rainy seasons, eastward across sparsely vegetated chalk flats to Ol Tukai. Mirages are common under the midday sun. ··

Approaching the center of the reserve, the barren landscape turns refreshingly green from springs and swamps fed by underground runoff from the overshadowing Mt. Kilimanjaro. These swamps give life to an otherwise parched land, providing water for nearby grasslands and acacia woodlands and attracting a profusion of game and waterfowl. Superb starling, red-and-yellow barbet and silverbird are among the bush birds in residence.

Large herds of elephant and buffalo are often seen around the swamps, especially at **Enkongo Narok Swamp**, where it is easy to obtain photos of animals (especially elephant) in the foreground and Mt. Kilimanjaro in the background. Early morning is best, before Mt. Kilimanjaro is covered in clouds; the clouds may partially clear in late afternoon.

Observation Hill is a good location from which to get an overview of the reserve. There is a pretty good chance of spotting cheetah, giraffe and impala, but oryx and gerenuk are less likely to be seen. Game viewing is best from mid-December to March (also the best views of Mt. Kilimanjaro) and from July to October, and due to the open terrain, is actually good year-round except for possibly April and May when it can be quite wet.

To limit destruction to the environment, driving off the roads is forbidden, and heavy fines are being levied against those who break the rules. Please do not ask your driver to leave the road for a closer look at wildlife. The park is about 140 miles (225 km) from Nairobi.

ACCOMMODATION — CLASS A:
• **Tortilis Camp** is located just outside the reserve and has 17 luxury tents and one family unit with two rooms, each with en suite facilities. Day game drives within the park, bush breakfasts, guided walks, cultural visits, massage and beauty treatments are available as well as a swimming pool.

A luxury tent at Tortilis Camp

CLASS A/B: • **Amboseli Serena Safari Lodge** has 92 rooms including five family rooms and one suite, with en suite facilities and a swimming pool. The lodge has recently been completely remodeled and refurbished.

CLASS B: • **Ol Tukai Lodge** has 80 rooms with facilities en suite and a swimming pool. • **Amboseli Porini Camp**, located in the Selenkay Conservation Area just north of Amboseli, has six tents with en suite bathrooms including shower, wash basin and flush toilet. Activities include day and night game drives and walks led by Maasai warriors. ✱**Amboseli Sopa Lodge** offers

Top: Mt. Kilimajaro provides a spectacular background for a picnic at Ol Donyo Wuas
Middle: Aerial view of Ol Donyo Wuas
Bottom: Some of the giant tuskers of Ol Donyo Wuas

47 rooms with private veranda and en suite facilities. There are also several bars, a pool and dining room.

CAMPING: Campsites are located outside the park on Maasai land, 4 miles (6 km) past Observation Hill. No facilities exist except long-drop (pit) toilets. Bring your own water.

Ol Donyo Wuas

Ol Donyo Wuas is set on a 270,000-acre (125,000-hectare) Maasai Group Ranch (part of the Amboseli ecosystem) in the foothills of the Chyulu Range, halfway between Tsavo West, Amboseli National Park and Chyulu National Park. Guests of the lodge have panoramic views of Mt. Kilimanjaro and exclusive access to the ranch.

On game drives during my last visit we saw Maasai giraffe, oryx, Grant's gazelle, eland, bush duiker, dikdik, Coke's hartebeest, black-backed jackal and serval, among other game. Lion, cheetah and elephant may also be seen. Massive elephant bulls with close to 100 pound tusks are a feature and are resident at the waterhole below the lodge. On a recent game drive 16 different cheetah were sighted. It is one of the few areas in Kenya outside of a National park where lion concentrations are increasing, due mainly to Richard Bonham's innovative predator compensation scheme that is now reaping rewards.

On horseback we cantered among herds of zebra and wildebeest and came fairly close to giraffe, oryx and eland. This is certainly one of the best places for horseback riding in East Africa.

Easiest access is by air on the daily 50-minute shuttle flight from Nairobi.

ACCOMMODATION — CLASS A+: • **Ol Donyo Wuas** has been completely rebuilt with improved facilities and accommodates guests in six thatched luxury cottages (including two single rooms and four doubles) with open fireplaces, verandas, private pools, and en suite facilities. Day and night game drives in open vehicles and escorted walks with excellent resident guides, Maasai visits, horseback rides ranging from an hour's ride to multi-day safaris, and fly camping are offered. This is an ideal venue for families with children who enjoy private game drives. Sleep outs under the stars are also possible on "Seduction Rock" and in a tented camp — but these should be booked in advance. The camp has been a leader in preserving wildlife and simultaneously providing benefit to the local communities.

Ride Kenya is a sister organization to Ol Donyo Wuas that offers superb 3- and 6-night horseback safaris with guaranteed departures nine months out of every year. Each night is spent in luxury tented camps (arguably some of the finest in all of Kenya) that are permanently erected.

Campi ya Kanzi

Campi ya Kanzi is located on a 280,000-acre (115,000-hectare) Maasai Group Ranch surrounded by Chyulu, Tsavo and Amboseli National Parks, and stretching to the foothills of Mt. Kilimanjaro. The landscape is quite varied from lush forests to riverine forest and savannah grasslands, as the altitude ranges from 3,000 to 6,900 feet (900 to 2,100 m). Wildlife includes elephant, lion, cheetah, lesser kudu, giraffe, fringe-eared oryx, gerenuk and mountain reedbuck. Over 400 species of birds have been recorded. Easiest access is by a 55-minute charter flight from Nairobi.

ACCOMMODATION — CLASS A: • **Campi ya Kanzi** has six luxury tents and two suites under thatch, set

Top: Horseback riding at Ol Donyo Wuas
Bottom: Guests enjoy the view from Campi ya Kanzi

on raised wooden decks with verandahs and en suite bathrooms. Activities at this family-run lodge include day and night game drives, escorted walks with the Maasai trackers, Maasai cultural visits, and excursions to Tsavo West, Chyulu and Amboseli national parks. There are lovely views of Mt. Kilimanjaro from the camp. The camp is a great contributor to the welfare of the local Maasi community.

Tsavo West National Park

Halfway between Nairobi and Mombasa lie **West** and **East Tsavo National Parks**, which together with **Chyulu Hills National Park** total 8,217-square-miles (21,283-km^2). Large herds of over 100 elephant are part of the massive population of over 15,000 in Tsavo West and East combined. The park has a number of large prides of lion and a good leopard population. Also present are caracal, giraffe, zebra and a variety of antelope.

Tsavo National Park

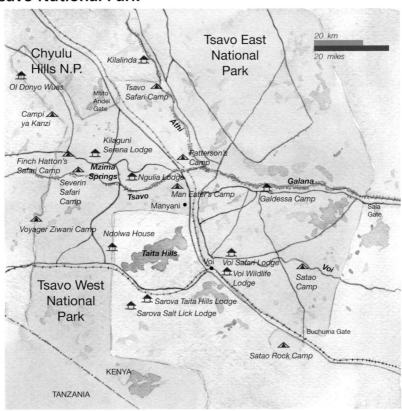

Acacia and Commiphora woodland dominates the landscape, with ribbons of taller trees along the Galana, Tsavo and other rivers. The graceful doum palm, with its forked trunk, is a common sight. The many enormous baobab trees provide plenty of breeding cavities for barbets, starlings, parrots, rollers, kestrels and owls.

Big game is less concentrated here than in Amboseli National Park; however, the park's rugged terrain is quite impressive in itself.

Tsavo has a healthy population of elephant

Tsavo West National Park is predominantly semi-arid plains broken by occasional granite outcrops. Lava fields are located near Kilaguni Lodge. Altitudes range from 1,000 feet (305 m) to nearly 6,000 feet (1,830 m) in the Ngulia Mountains located in the northern region of the park.

From the **Mzima Springs** underwater viewing platform, located just south of Kilaguni Serena Safari Lodge, visitors may be lucky enough to watch hippo swim in the clear waters among the crocs and fish. Otters also inhabit these waters. The best viewing is early in the morning. Kilaguni Serena Safari Lodge is about 180 miles (290 km) from Nairobi.

ACCOMMODATION — CLASS A: • **Finch Hattons Safari Camp** overlooks a hippo pool, and has 35 tents with en suite facilities and a swimming pool. The camp is well regarded for its excellent cuisine and service. • **Ndolwa House** is a small, luxury lodge on a 10,000 acre private ranch of the Ndolwa Wildlife Sanctuary. The lodge consists of five stone cottages with en suite

Tented accommodations at Finch Hattons Camp

facilities. The main lounge consists of a dining room and bar area. Day and night game drives and bush walks are offered.

CLASS A/B: • **Severin Safari Camp** has 20 unique octagonal en suite tents overlooking a waterhole and Mt. Kilimanjaro beyond. • **Kilaguni Serena Safari Lodge** has 52 rooms with facilities en suite and a swimming pool. • **Ngulia Lodge** has 56 rooms with en suite facilities and a swimming pool.

CAMPING: Campsites are available at Kitani, Kamboyo and Kangechwa and at the following park gates: Mtito Andei, Chyulu (Kilaguni), Kasigau and Tsavo. Chyulu has showers and toilets; the other campsites have basic (if any) facilities.

ACCOMMODATION NEAR TSAVO WEST NATIONAL PARK — CLASS B/C: • **Voyager Ziwani,** situated just outside the southwestern boundary of the park, overlooks a freshwater dam and has 16 tents with en suite showers and long-drop toilets. Day and night game drives, walks and excursions to the volcanic Lake Chala and walks among the World War I battlefields along the Tanzanian border are offered.

Tsavo East National Park

Tsavo East is mostly arid bush dotted with rocky outcrops that are traversed by seasonal riverbeds lined with riverine forest. Tsavo East is generally hotter and drier, as it lies at a lower altitude (about 1,000 ft./305 m) than its western

Tsavo's endless vistas

counterpart. The 3,000-square-miles (7,770-km²) south of the Galana River is the main region open to the public.

Substantial numbers of elephant, lion, cheetah, Maasai giraffe, lesser kudu and other large mammals occur, as well as a small number of highly endangered hirola (Hunter's hartebeest), which were relocated here in 1996 and seem to be holding their own. Among the interesting dryland birds are vulturine guineafowl, orange-bellied parrot, white-bellied go-away bird and golden-breasted starlings.

East Tsavo's only permanent water hole is at Aruba Dam, and the drive from Voi makes for a good game drive. Just north of Voi is an isolated hill, Mudanda Rock, another good spot for game. The scenic drive along the Galana River often produces sightings of hippo and crocs.

Voi is about 210 miles (340 km) from Nairobi.

ACCOMMODATION — CLASS B/C: • **Galdessa Camp**, situated on the banks of the Galana River, has 11 rustic tented bandas in Main Camp and 3 in Private Camp, all under thatch with en suite bucket showers and flush toilets. Activities include day and night game drives. Black rhino have been reintroduced locally. • **Satao Camp** has 32 tents with en suite flush toilets and bush (bucket) showers. • **Voi Safari Lodge**, in the hills above the town of Voi, has

52 rooms with facilities en suite, a swimming pool and photographic hide. • **Voi Wildlife Lodge**, situated just outside the main gate, offers 72 rooms with en suite facilities, several bars, a restaurant, health club and swimming pool.

CLASS C: • **Patterson's Camp,** set along the banks of the Athi River in this historical "man-eaters" area of the park, has 20 basic tents with en suite facilities.

CAMPING: Campsites are available at Voi, Sala and Buchuma Gates. There are few or no facilities.

ACCOMMODATION NEAR THE PARK — CLASS A: • **Kilalinda,** set on the banks of the Athi River at the edge of the park, has six cottages (one of which has a private jacuzzi), with verandahs, en suite facilities and a swimming pool. Activities include day and night game drives, walks, escorted game walks and fishing.

CLASS B: • **Man Eaters Camp,** located on the banks of the Tsavo River, less than a mile (1.2 km) from the main highway and is within easy reach of both Tsavo East and West national parks, and has 30 en suite tents, restaurant, bar and swimming pool.

Within The Tsavo Ecosystem

The Tsavo Kasigau Wildlife Corridor is a wildlife conservancy in the making, encompassing an enormous 380,000-acre (152,000-hectare) stretch of unspoiled private wilderness that is nestled between Tsavo East and West. This area forms a vital corridor route for a population of almost 1,000 elephants as they disperse between the Galana River in Tsavo East and south to Lake Jipe in Tsavo West.

Located within this ecosystem is the **Taita Discovery Centre,** dedicated to the environmental education of foreigners and Kenyans alike through their participation in a variety of community service programs. It is also the motivating epicenter for the testing and establishment of a variety of environmentally based

Participants in the community service program at Taita Discovery Centre

micro-enterprises including aquaculture, apiculture, sericulture and many more. Volunteers from around the world are accommodated at nearby Satao Rock Camp. This is a great program to consider if you are looking to do some short or long-term volunteer work in Africa!

ACCOMMODATION — CLASS A: • **Sarova Salt Lick Game Lodge** and **Sarova Taita Hills Game Lodge** (Class B) are situated on the 28,000 acre privately managed Taita Hills Wildlife Sanctuary between the southern extensions of Tsavo East and West parks, about 240 miles (390 km) from Nairobi and 125 miles (200 km) from Mombasa. • **Sarova Salt Lick Game Lodge**, built on stilts to enhance viewing of wildlife visiting the salt lick, has 96 rooms with en suite facilities and a photographic hide.

CLASS B: • **Sarova Taita Hills Game Lodge** has 60 rooms with en suite facilities and a swimming pool. Night game drives and trips to nearby Lake Jipe can be arranged.

CLASS C: • **Satao Rock Camp** has 12 tents with en suite bathrooms, and it sits on a rock kopje overlooking a waterhole. Guides and resident researchers assist guests in "service learning" activities from the **Taita Discovery Centre** that assist the local communities.

Maasai Mara National Reserve

This is undoubtedly the finest wildlife area in Kenya. Unlike many reserves in Africa that are seasonal, game viewing here is in fact fabulous year-round. Off-road game viewing is allowed, making it all the more attractive.

All of the big game is here: elephant, lion (prides of up to 40 or more), leopard, cheetah and buffalo are prevalent, along with a small population of

The Maasai Mara at sunset

black rhino. Other commonly sighted species include zebra, wildebeest, Thomson's gazelle, Defassa waterbuck, eland and Maasai giraffe. This is the only place in Kenya where topi are common.

Maasai Mara National Reserve, a northern extension of the Serengeti Plains (Tanzania), is located southwest of Nairobi and covers 590-square-miles (1,530-km^2) of open plains, acacia woodlands and riverine forest along the banks on the Mara and Talek Rivers, which are home for many hippo, crocs and waterfowl.

One of the better places to look for wildlife is in the **Mara Triangle** in the western part of the reserve, which is bounded by the Siria (Esoit Oloololo) Escarpment rising about 1,000 feet (305 m) above the plains on the west, by the Tanzanian border to the south and by the Mara River to the east. A multitude of

Maasai Mara National Reserve

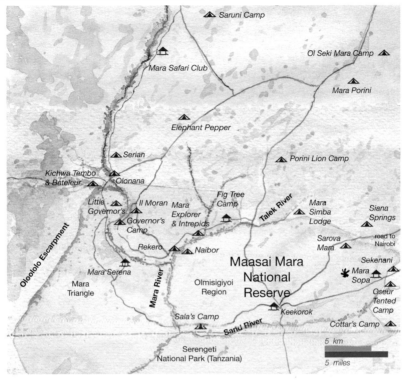

savannah animals can be found on these open grasslands and other areas to the northwest of the reserve.

The western part of the Mara is less crowded than the eastern part of the reserve. Most adventurers visiting the camps in the western part of the reserve fly into the Mara, while most people visiting the lodges and camps in the eastern Mara are driven into the reserve.

Lion are distributed throughout the park. Cheetah are most often seen on the short-grass plains. Black rhino are most concentrated in the Olmisigiyoi Region in the center of the park, in the northwest and in the extreme eastern parts of the park; and are now starting to forage in the Mara Triangle.

The best time to see the migration is from approximately mid-July to mid-November when great herds of wildebeest (1.4 million) and zebra (250,000) reside in the Mara region and northern Tanzania before returning to Serengeti National Park. From the southern Serengeti of Tanzania, a major portion of the migration moves northwest toward Lake Victoria, then north

4-wheel drive game viewing vehicle on the Mara

across the Mara River into Kenya in search of grass, usually returning to Tanzania in late October or early November. The best time to witness large numbers of wildebeest and zebra crossing the Mara River is from mid/late July to late October.

As the park teems with resident wildlife, game viewing is good year-round. There is a real advantage in visiting the reserve November to June as there are fewer travelers at that time. On a recent visit in February we spotted several different leopard and cheetah in just a few days, along with many lion.

On another visit we saw lion, cheetah, thousands of wildebeest and zebra, and the unforgettable experience of witnessing part of the migration crossing the Mara River! We patiently sat at the river's edge for four hours and were handsomely rewarded for our patience. On another visit we saw a mother leopard and two cubs with their kill in a tree, several cheetah, numerous prides of lion, thousands of wildebeest and zebra, a large breeding herd of elephant and a variety of other game.

The Mara is a paradise for birds and birdwatchers. Over 400 species have been recorded, with grassland and wetland birds especially well represented. Martial eagle, long-crested eagle and bateleur are common, while large numbers of vultures follow the great migration of wildebeest and zebra, feeding on the remains of those that die of exhaustion, old age or predator attacks. The Mara River and some of its tributaries are forested along their banks, providing ideal habitat for exciting birds such as Ross's turaco, black-and-white-casqued hornbill, blue flycatcher and the narina trogon.

Balloon safaris are very popular and certainly a unique way of experiencing Africa. On my last balloon safari we flew over part of the great migration

The thrill of watching a wildebeest "crossing"

and saw a variety of wildlife. The pilot was extremely entertaining as well as knowledgeable of the flora and fauna enroute. The champagne breakfast that followed was great fun for the entire group.

Fishing safaris by private air charter to **Mfangano Island, Rusinga Island** and **Takawiri Island** on Lake Victoria are available from all the camps (book in advance).

In the Mara Triangle and the northwestern part of the park, 4wd vehicles are recommended. There are at least two flights a day from Nairobi that serve the park. Keekorok Lodge is located about 170 miles (275 km) and the Mara Serena Safari Lodge about 210 miles (340 km) from Nairobi.

ACCOMMODATION — All lodges and camps listed below either conduct hot-air balloon safaris or will take you to where one is being offered; be sure to book well in advance. Many guests fly into the Mara (highly recommended) and are taken game viewing in 4wd vehicles (preferably) or minivans. Most camps and lodges are a five- to six-hour drive from Nairobi.

Ready! Set! Go!

Top: Mara Explorer tents offer comfort and privacy
Middle: Luxury accommodations at Governor's Ilmoran Camp
Bottom: Mara Intrepids' inviting pool

ACCOMMODATION IN THE RESERVE — CLASS A+: • **Mara Explorer**, situated on the Talek River in the middle of the Mara, has 10 luxurious tents with facilities en suite (five include private outdoor Victorian bathtubs). Activities include game drives, walking safaris outside the reserve, balloon safaris, private bush meals and visits to Maasai communities. • **Governor's Ilmoran Camp** is located within the reserve, and has 10 huge tents lining the winding banks of the Mara River — all with en suite bathrooms. Group morning and afternoon game drives and walks on the periphery of the reserve are offered.

CLASS A: • **Mara Intrepids Club** is situated on the Talek River and has 30 tents with four-poster beds, en suite facilities and a swimming pool. The camp has two unique family tents. Game drives are offered three times a day as well as walks in the adjacent Maasai land. There is an "Adventurers Club" for guests ages 4 to 12. • **Little Governor's Camp**, located in the northwest part of the park on the Mara River, has 17 tents with facilities en suite. Guests reach the camp by crossing the Mara River. Walks are offered outside the reserve.

• **Governor's Camp**, located a few miles from Little Governor's Camp on the Mara River, has 38 tents with en suite facilities and excellent food and service. Walks outside the reserve are offered. • **Sala's Camp** is located on the banks of the Sand River in a private and secluded corner of the Mara, offering views across the plains toward Tanzania (and the Serengeti). The camp has six double tents and one honeymoon tent with en suite facilities and hot showers and flushing toilets. Activities include morning and afternoon game drives, bush breakfasts and optional balloon safari or visit to a Maasai village.

CLASS A/B: • **Mara Serena Safari Lodge**, set on a hill in the central western part of the park, has 76 rooms with private facilities and a swimming pool. Because it is set far from any other camps or lodges, guests encounter very few other vehicles. The view from the lodge of the expansive plains below is spectacular.

CLASS B: • **Mara Simba Lodge** has 36 rooms with facilities en suite and private verandas overlooking the Talek River and a swimming pool. • **Governor's Private Camp** caters to private parties of up to 16 guests in tents with en suite flush toilets and bush (bucket) showers. • **Keekorok Lodge** is an old-style lodge with 72 rooms and 12 cottages with en suite facilities and a swimming pool. • **Sarova Mara Camp** has 75 tents with en suite facilities and a swimming pool.

ACCOMMODATION ON THE PERIPHERY OF THE RESERVE — CLASS A+: • **Bateleur Camp** at Kichwa Tembo, situated on the western border of the Mara, is actually two camps, each with nine luxuriously furnished tents with facilities en suite. Morning and afternoon game drives, night game drives on a private concession, guided walks and Maasai visits are offered. • **Cottar's 1920s Mara Safari Camp**, set outside the eastern border of the reserve on a 250,000-acre (100,000-hectare) private concession, accommodates up to 12 clients in authentic, spacious white canvas tents, and incorporates original safari antiques from the '20s. Four adjoining tents share their own dining tent and are perfect for families. Each tent has a dressing room and bathroom (old-fashioned tub), a main bedroom and private verandah. Day game drives are conducted in the reserve while both day and night game drives are provided on the concession along with walking and fishing.

CLASS A: • **Kichwa Tembo** has 28 standard (Class A/B) and 12 luxury tents (Class A) and two thatched rondavels with en suite facilities and swimming pool. Escorted walks, Maasai village visits, day and night game drives in a private concession area are offered.
• **Olonana**, set on the banks of the Mara River, has 12 luxury tents built on wooden platforms, each overlooking the river with en suite facilities. The camp has a swimming pool and activities include game drives, walking safaris and tour of a local village.
• **Saruni Lodge**, located north of the reserve, has 12 deluxe en suite tents and offers game drives, walking and spa services.

Kichwa Tembo is located on the edge of the Maasai Mara Reserve

CLASS B: • **Siana Springs Intrepids** has 38 tents with facilities en suite, and a swimming pool. Walks and day and night game drives are offered. • **Mara Bushtops** (formerly Bush Tops) offers 12 en suite tents and a swimming pool. ✱ • **Mara Sopa Lodge** located on the eastern border of the park high on a ridge overlooking the Mara near Ololaimutiek Gate, has 72 rooms with facilities en suite and a swimming pool.

CLASS B/C: • **Mara Porini Camp** is situated in the northeast area of the Mara, adjacent to the park, on the Ol Kinyei game conservancy. The 6 guest tents have an en suite bathroom with flush toilet and safari shower. Guests may enjoy day and night game drives, sundowners and escorted walks with Maasai guides. • **Fig Tree Camp**, located on the Talek River, has 30 basic chalets and 30 tents with facilities en suite and a swimming pool.

SEASONAL CAMPS: The following camps are open seasonally and offer many of the comforts of a permanent tented camp. • **Naibor Luxury Camp** is located within the Mara Reserve and has 9 spacious, classic safari tents with en suite bathrooms, pull shower and verandas. Morning and afternoon game drives, walks in nearby game concession, and visits to the Maasai village are offered. • **Rekero Tented Camp** is located very close to the confluence of the Mara and Talek Rivers. The 6 tents are equipped with toilets and hot showers, and has a large dining tent. Game drives, walks and bush picnics are offered. • **Elephant Pepper Camp** is a seasonal permanent tented eco-friendly camp situated on the northern edge of the Maasai Mara reserve. The 8 tents (including one honeymoon/family tent) have en suite bathrooms, solar lighting and verandahs. Activities include extended game drives in 4wd vehicles, guided bush walks with Maasai, cultural visits, night game drives, picnics and sundowners. • **Olseki Mara Camp** is a seasonal camp located on the

Top: A tent at seasonal camp —
Elephant Pepper
Bottom: The unique tents at Olseki
Mara Camp

Innisikera River. The camp offers 6 spacious tents featuring solar lighting and flush toilets. • **Serian** is an exclusive wilderness camp set close to the Siria Escarpment, with 8 en suite marquee tents, each with a private butler. The camp operates from June until the end of March and offers game drives as well as escorted walks and fly camping. • **Richard's Camp** is an eco-friendly camp and offers 8 en suite tents.

CAMPING: Sites are located outside the park along the Talek River.

THE WEST

Kakamega Forest

Kakamega is the eastern-most remnant of the great West African rain forests that once stretched the width of Africa. There are 4 miles (7 km) of walking trails through a forest that includes some of Africa's greatest hard and soft woods, including Elgon Teak, red and white stink woods, and several varieties of Croton.

Kakamega is an ornithologist's dream, alive with different species of birds — some are found only in this part of Kenya. Avifauna specialties include great blue turaco, African gray parrot, blue-headed bee-eater, black-and-white casqued hornbill, emerald cuckoo, black-billed and Vieillot's black weavers, Chubb's cisticola, Turner's eremomella, joyfull greenbul, Luhder's bushshrike, honeyguide greenbul, Uganda woodland warbler, yellow-bellied wattle-eye and chestnut wattle-eye. Black-and-white colobus monkey, blue monkey and red-tailed monkeys may also be seen.

ACCOMMODATION — CLASS B: • **Rondo Retreat** has 4 rooms in the main house (originally built in the 1920s) and 4 cottages with 2 to 4 rooms each, some with en suite facilities.

Mt. Elgon National Park

Seldom visited, this 65-square-mile (169-km²) park is a huge, extinct volcano shared with Uganda, and at 14,178 feet (4,321 m) it is the second highest mountain in Kenya. Mt. Elgon also has the giant Afro-alpine flora found on Mt. Kenya and Mt. Kilimanjaro.

The forests are often so thick that a full-grown elephant could be standing 20 feet (6 m) from the road and not be seen. Buffalo, waterbuck and bushbuck are more likely to be spotted.

Mt. Elgon is of great botanical interest and offers a wealth of Afro-alpine plants on the high-altitude moorlands. Giant podocarpus, olive and juniper trees form a dense forest on the mid-slopes, where epiphytic orchids and lichens abound. The spectacular black-and-white colobus and blue monkey are the most common primates, while small numbers of giant forest hog feed on the forest floor. The cliffs and caves are home to lanner falcon, scarce swift and hill chat, while keen birdwatchers can look for the elusive bar-tailed trogon and Doherty's bushshrike in the dense forest.

Kitum and Makingeny Caves are unique; they were partially formed by the resident herds of elephant. Small herds often enter the caves near dusk to spend several hours in the company of thousands of bats, mining salts with their tusks. Makingeny is the largest, but Kitum is more frequently visited by elephants. During our visit, elephant droppings were everywhere, foreshadowing the real possibility of their sources being inside.

Access to the park is difficult in the rainy season, when 4wd vehicles are recommended. There are no huts on the mountain, and campers must bring their own tents. The park is 255 miles (360 km) from Nairobi.

ACCOMMODATION — CLASS D: • **Mt. Elgon Lodge**, situated less than a mile (1.5 km) before the park entrance, has 17 rooms with private facilities.

CAMPING: Several campsites and self-service bandas are available in the park.

ACCOMMODATION NEAR THE RESERVE — CLASS B/C: • **Lokitela Farm** is located on the foothills of Mt. Elgon, 11 miles (19 km) from the town of Kitale. Up to 24 guests are accommodated in the main house and in lodge cottages.

Lake Victoria

Lake Victoria is the largest lake in Africa and the second largest freshwater lake in the world (Lake Superior is the largest). The lake is approximately 26,650-square-miles (69,000-km^2) in size and is bordered by Kenya, Tanzania and Uganda.

Fishing for the giant Nile perch is excellent; the largest one taken from the lake was reported to weigh 520 pounds (236 kg)! Nile perch weighing in excess of 100 pounds (45 kg) are sometimes caught.

Unfortunately, the Nile perch is not native to Lake Victoria. It was introduced in the 1950s and is a major predator of indigenous fish, some of which have become extinct. In recent years, the gigantic lake has also been plagued by the rapidly spreading water hyacinth, an aquatic plant from tropical America that has blanketed much of the water surface and starved it of oxygen. This has had grave consequences for aquatic wildlife as well as for local fishing communities.

Over 100 species of birds have been recorded on the islands. Spotted necked otters may also be seen.

Easiest access to the island camps in the lake is by air charter from the Maasai Mara or from Nairobi.

ACCOMMODATION — CLASS A: **• Rusinga Island Lodge** has 7 cottages (8 bedrooms) with en suite facilities, including a two-bedroom family unit. Fishing, boating, birdwatching, water skiing, wind surfing, pre-historic fossil digs, visits to nearby Ruma National Park, health spa, and mountain biking are offered.

CLASS A/B: **• Mfangano Island Camp**, just a 40-minute charter flight and 15-minute boat ride from the Maasai Mara, has 7 cottages with en suite facilities. Fishing, boating, birdwatching and visits to Luo fishing villages are offered.

CLASS B/C: **• Takawiri Island Resort** has 4 cottages, each with 2 rooms and en suite facilities. Fishing, sailing, wind surfing, birdwatching and visits to local villages are offered.

Top: The thatched cottages at Rusinga Island Lodge
Bottom: A game drive at nearby Ruma National Park

Kisumu

Kisumu, located on the shores of Lake Victoria about 215 miles (345 km) from Nairobi, is the third largest city in Kenya, with a population over 125,000.

ACCOMMODATION — TOURIST CLASS: **• Imperial Hotel** has 87 rooms (most of them air-conditioned) with en suite facilities.

THE MT. KENYA CIRCUIT

Aberdare National Park

This 296-square-mile (767-km^2) park of luxuriant forest includes much of the Aberdare (renamed Nyandarua) Range of mountains.

The park can be divided by altitude into two sections. A high plateau of undulating moorlands with tussock grasses and giant heather lies between Ol Doinyo Lasatima (13,120 ft./3,999 m) and Kinangop (12,816 ft./3,906 m). This region affords excellent views of Mt. Kenya and the Rift Valley. Black rhino, lion, hyena, buffalo, elephant, eland, reedbuck, suni, bushpig and, very rarely, the nocturnal bongo can be seen.

On the eastern slopes below lie the forested hills and valleys of the Salient, home to black rhino, leopard, elephant, buffalo, waterbuck, bushbuck, giant forest hog, and black-and-white colobus monkey.

The park is also rich in bird life, including many species not easily seen elsewhere. The moorlands and montane forest are home to Jackson's and Moorland francolins, Aberdare cisticola and Cape eagle owl, as well as various eagles and buzzards. Several species of dazzling sunbirds, the ecological equivalents of the American hummingbirds, occur on the mountains and are frequently seen in the gardens of the various camps and lodges.

Night temperatures range from cool to freezing, as most of the park lies above 9,800 feet (2,988 m). A 4wd vehicle is required for travel within the park. The Ark and Treetops are about 110 miles (175 km) from Nairobi.

ACCOMMODATION: Guests of two tree hotels, Treetops and the Ark, are entertained by a variety of wildlife visiting their water holes and salt licks.

CLASS B/C: • **The Ark**, a "tree hotel" overlooking a water hole, has small rooms with en suite facilities (104 beds total), a glass-enclosed main viewing lounge, outside verandas on each level (floodlit for all-night game viewing) and ground-level photo hide. The area near the Ark is a rhino reserve. Game drives in the Salient are offered. Guests usually have lunch at the Aberdare Country Club before transferring to the Ark and are transferred back to the Aberdare Country Club by 9:00 the following morning to depart to their next safari destination. Children under seven are not allowed.

CLASS C: • **Treetops**, the first of the "tree hotels" (on stilts), is older and more rustic than the Ark. Only the suites have en suite facilities. Guests usually have a buffet lunch at the Outspan Hotel before transferring to Treetops and are returned to the Outspan by 9:00 the following morning to continue their safari. Children under seven are not allowed.

CAMPING: There are several public campsites.

ACCOMMODATION NEAR THE PARK: CLASS B/C: • **Sangare Tented Camp** is located on a 6,500-acre (2,630-hectare) private ranch and has 12 spacious tents with en suite facilities. Game drives, birdwatching and horseback riding are offered.

Solio Ranch and Wildlife Sanctuary

This private 18,000-acre (7,200-hectare) rhino sanctuary has approximately 140 black rhino and white rhino. On my last visit I watched a black rhino with the largest horns I think I have ever seen!

Other wildlife includes lion, leopard, cheetah, hippo, reticulated giraffe, oryx, and a variety of plain's wildlife and bird life. The reserve is situated near Aberdare National Park, a three-hour drive from Nairobi or a 20-minute private air charter from Nanyuki. A visit to the Solio can be easily combined with a visit to Aberdare National Park.

ACCOMMODATION: None. See "Aberdare National Park" above.

Mt. Kenya National Park

Kenya's highest mountain and the second highest on the continent, Mt. Kenya lies just below the equator, yet it has several permanent glaciers.

Mt. Kenya's two highest peaks, **Batian** (17,058 ft./5,199 m) and **Nelion** (17,023 ft./5,188 m), are accessible by about 25 routes and should be attempted only by experienced rock climbers. **Point Lenana** (16,355 ft./ 4,985 m) is a non-technical climb that is accessible to hikers in good condition and is best climbed in the dry seasons. January to February is the best time to go, when views are the clearest and temperatures are warmer on top; July to October is also dry but colder. Vegetation changes are similar to those described for the Ruwenzori Mountains (see The Congo) and Mt. Kilimanjaro (see Tanzania).

Rock-climbing routes on the south side of the mountain are in best condition from late December to mid-March, while routes on the north side are best climbed from late June to mid-October. Ice routes are best attempted during the same periods but on opposite sides of the mountain. Howell Hut (17,023 ft./ 5,188 m), located on the summit of Nelion, sleeps two.

Although rarely seen, climbers should be on the lookout for buffalo and elephant. Other wildlife that may be encountered includes leopard, duiker, bushbuck, giant forest hog, Syke's monkey and colobus monkey.

Because climbers can ascend to high altitudes very quickly, Mt. Kenya claims more than half of the world's deaths from

The eastern wall of the Great Rift Valley

pulmonary edema. My climbing partner had symptoms of pulmonary edema after reaching Austrian Hut (15,715 ft./4,790 m), and we had to abandon our attempt of Batian Peak and return to lower altitudes. Therefore, a slow, sensible approach is recommended.

The world's highest altitude scuba diving record was shattered at Two Tarn Lake (14,720 ft./4,488 m), one of more than 30 lakes on the mountain. The previous record of 12,500 feet (3,811 m) was set at Lake Titicaca in Bolivia. In addition, climbers are occasionally seen ice skating on the Curling Pond below the Lewis Glacier.

Naro Moru Route

The Naro Moru Route is a steep, quick route up the mountain. The climb to Point Lenana normally takes two or three days up and one or two down. The first night is often spent at Naro Moru Lodge or, better yet, at the Met — Meteorological Station — (10,000 ft./3,050 m) to assist altitude acclimatization.

From Nairobi, drive 105 miles (168 km) to Naro Moru, then 10 miles (16 km) on a dirt road to the park gate (7,874 ft./2,400 m). You may be able to drive to the Met Station, unless the rains have washed out the road.

From the park gate, it is a three and one-half hour (6 mi./10 km) hike through conifer, hardwood and bamboo forests to the Met Station. Beware of buffalo enroute. The Met Station has self-service bandas with mattresses, cooking facilities, long-drop toilets and water. To help you acclimatize, consider hiking for about an hour up to the tree line (10,500 ft./3,200 m) in the afternoon, returning well before dark.

From the Met Station, hike through the **Vertical Bog**, a series of muddy hills with patches of tussock grass. To keep your boots dry, you may want to wear tennis shoes through the bog. Cross the Naro Moru River and continue to **Teleki Valley**, where Mt. Kenya's peaks finally come into clear view (if it's not cloudy). After leaving the tree line, vegetation will change to tussock grass and heather moorlands with everlasting flowers, giant groundsel and giant lobelia that sometimes exceed 30 feet (9 m) in height.

From the Met Station, it takes about six hours to reach Mackinder's Camp (13,778 ft./4,200 m), which has a brick lodge and campsites. American Camp (14,173 ft./4,320 m), a camping spot one hour from Mackinder's Camp, is used by some campers who bring their own tents. Water is available from a nearby stream.

Austrian Hut (15,715 ft./4,790 m) is a three- to four-hour hike from Mackinder's Camp. Another hour is usually required to gain the additional 640 feet (195 m) in altitude needed to reach Point Lenana, only a half-mile away.

Austrian Hut is bitterly cold at night and is most often used by technical rock climbers attempting Nelion or Batian Peaks. Many climbers wishing to conquer Point Lenana begin from their camps in the Teleki Valley (Mackinder's) long before sunrise, reaching Point Lenana shortly after sunrise and return to Teleki Valley for the night. The view from Point Lenana is the clearest and one of the most magnificent panoramas I've seen from any mountain — and well worth the effort!

Around the Peaks

From Mackinder's Camp, it is a two- to three-hour hike to Two Tarn Hut (14,731 ft./4,490 m). You may stop for the night or continue for another three or four hours over two passes exceeding 15,000 feet to Kami Hut (14,564 ft./ 4,439 m), located on the north side of the peaks. From Kami Hut, it is a five- to six-hour hike up the north ridge of Point Lenana or directly to Austrian Hut. Return via the Naro Moru Route described above. Due to the path's continuous gain and loss of altitude, this is a very strenuous hike — the equivalent of climbing to Point Lenana two or three times!

Chogoria Route

This is the most scenic route on the mountain. From the Chogoria Forest Station on the eastern side of Mt. Kenya, hike or drive 10 miles (16 km) to Bairunyi Clearing (8,858 ft./2,700 m) and camp. You may choose to continue for another 4 miles (6 km) (4wd vehicle required) to Meru Mt. Kenya Lodge (9,898 ft./3,017 m) and stay in its self-catering bandas.

Hike through hagenia forest to Urumandi Hut (10,050 ft./3,063 m), owned by the Mountain Club of Kenya. Room for camping is available nearby. Minto's Hut (14,075 ft./4,290 m) is about a six-hour hike from Meru Mt. Kenya Lodge. Space for tents is available nearby. Two Campsites, situated a mile beyond Minto's Hut, is another good place to camp.

Austrian Hut is a four-hour hike from Minto's Hut. Some climbers descend using the Naro Moru Route.

The access road to the Chogoria Forest Station is very bad, so allow plenty of time for the drive.

Sirimon Route

The Sirimon Route is a long, slow route up the mountain. Ten miles (16 km) past Nanyuki on the Nanyuki-Timau Road, turn right on a dirt road and drive 6 miles (10 km) to the park gate. Sirimon is the least used and most strenuous of the three major routes on Mt. Kenya.

The northern side of the mountain, much drier than the western side (Naro Moru Route), has no bamboo or hagenia zone. Acacia grasslands cover much of the northern slopes, and zebra and a variety of antelope are likely to be seen.

Although the track continues up to the moorlands to about 13,000 feet (3,960 m), it is better to make your first camp around 8,000 to 9,000 feet (2,440 to 2,745 m) so you can acclimatize. There is another campsite at 10,990 feet (3,350 m), 5 miles (8 km) from the park gate. About a mile (1.5 km) farther is Judmeier Camp (operated by the Mountain Rock Hotel). Liki North Hut (13,090 ft./ 3,990 m) is about a four hour hike from Judmeier. Another four-hour hike brings you to Shipton's Cave Campsite (13,450 ft./4,100 m). Shipton's Camp (operated by Bantu Lodge) is a little farther up the mountain. Austrian Hut is a five-hour hike from Shipton's Cave.

Lone climbers are not usually allowed to enter the park. Little equipment is available in Kenya, so bring whatever you need. For climbing tips and equipment checklist, see "Mt. Kilimanjaro" in the chapter on Tanzania.

ACCOMMODATION NEAR THE PARK — CLASS A: • **The Fairmont Safari Club** (formerly the *Mt. Kenya Safari Club*) is located on the slopes of Mt. Kenya, outside the national park near Nanyuki, about 140 miles (224 km) from Nairobi. It was partially owned by actor William Holden and became one of the most famous "country clubs" in Africa. The property underwent extensive renovations in 2008. The spacious gardens are frequented by many species of exotic birds. Facilities include swimming pool, Irish Pub, 9-hole golf course, and very comfortable rooms, suites and luxury cottages with fireplaces (264 beds total). The Animal Orphanage contains a number of rare species, such as zebra duiker and

bongo. High-altitude flights around the peaks of Mt. Kenya in a Beaver aircraft are available. Game drives are not conducted on the property.

CLASS B: • **Mountain Serena Lodge**, about 110 miles (177 km) north of Nairobi, is a "tree hotel" set in a forest reserve near the park overlooking a water hole and salt lick, similar to Treetops and the Ark (see "Aberdare National Park"). All 42 double rooms have en suite facilities and face the water hole. • **Lake Rutundu Cottages** is a rustic yet comfortable fishing lodge set on a small tarn (mountain lake) at 10,200 feet (3,100 m) altitude. Guests are accommodated in two cedar cabins with en suite facilities and hot tub. The lodge is self-catering, but most tour companies will provide full-service catering. The trout fishing is some of the finest in the world! Best access is by charter flight to Africa's highest airstrip, at 11,000 feet (3,355 m).

Top: All rooms at Mountain Serena Lodge overlook the water hole
Bottom: Elephants visit the water hole at Mountain Serena Lodge

CLASS B/C, D & E: • **Naro Moru River Lodge**, located below the entrance to the park, has chalets (Class B/C) with en suite facilities and rustic, self-service cabins (Class D & E). Climbers often stay here before and after their attempts at Mt. Kenya's peaks. Trout fishing is good.

CLASS C/D: • **Mountain Rock Hotel** has a few simple chalets in a patch of forest near Naro Moru.

CAMPING: Camping is allowed at the **Naro Moru Lodge** and at sites in the park.

Ol Pejeta Ranch

This 110,000-acre (44,000-hectare) private game reserve of savannah and riverine forest has a variety of wildlife, including black rhino, reticulated giraffe, buffalo, Grevy's zebra, oryx, Coke's hartebeest and Thomson's gazelle. Walks, day and night game drives, boat rides and camel rides are offered. There is also a chimpanzee sanctuary/rehabilitation center. A 4wd vehicle may be necessary to reach the camp from the main road during the rains.

ACCOMMODATION — CLASS A/B: • **Serena Sweetwaters Tented Camp** has 39 recently refurbished large tents with en suite facilities facing a water hole, and a swimming pool. The camp is located 150 miles (240 km) north of Nairobi.

CLASS B: • **Ol Pejeta Ranch House** has six luxury en suite bedrooms and was restored to the former farmhouse glory of its previous owner, Lord Delamere, by tycoon Adnan Kashoggi. The house is available for private parties.

CLASS B/C: • **Porini Rhino Camp** is an eco-friendly camp with solar powered lighting and no generator. The camp offers six tents with en suite facilities.

Meru National Park

Meru is best known for Elsa, the lioness of Joy Adamson's *Born Free,* which was rehabituated to the wild. This 300 square-mile (870-km^2) park is located 220 miles (355 km) east of Mt. Kenya, from Nairobi (via Nanayuki or Embu).

The swamps are host to most of Meru's 5,000 buffalo, sometimes seen in herds of more than 200, and a number of elephant. Oryx, eland, reticulated giraffe and Grevy's zebra are plentiful on the plains, where lion and leopard are also most likely to be seen. Lesser kudu, gerenuk and cheetah can be found along with hippo and crocs within the Tana River area.

Over 400 species of birds have been recorded, including palm nut vulture, African finfoot, Pel's fishing owl, violet woodhoopoe, and the spectacular golden-breasted starling, which move about in small flocks.

Top: The cottages at Elsa's Kopje are open to the plains
Bottom: Elsa's Kopje has a spectacular infinity pool

ACCOMMODATION — CLASS A: • **Elsa's Kopje** is built on Mughwango Hill, the site of George Adamson's first camp in Meru. There are eight open-faced stone cottages and one three-tiered Honeymoon Suite, each with en suite bathrooms and open verandahs overlooking the plains, and a swimming pool. There is also a family unit called the "Private House" with a separate living room, private garden and pool. Game drives are taken in open 4wd vehicles, walks, a masseuse, and bush meals are offered.

CLASS A/B: • **Leopard Rock** is a 60-bed lodge with en suite facilities, and swimming pool. Guests are offered game drives, walks and fishing.

CLASS F: Self-service bandas are located at Park Headquarters and at Leopard Rock.

CAMPING: Sites are available at Murera Gate and Park Headquarters.

The Rift Valley

Stretching some 4,000 miles (6,500 km) from the Red Sea to the Zambezi River, the Rift Valley is one of the most distinctive ruptures on the Earth's surface, and one of the few geological features that can be seen from the moon. The Rift Valley is thought to have begun to form some 40 million years ago, at a time when mankind's ancestors emerged onto the African savannahs. The slow rending apart of the Earth's crust also led to the formation and eruption of many volcanic mountains along or adjacent to the Rift Valley.

The Rift Valley is split into two arms: the Eastern Arm, which cuts through the center of Kenya, and the Western Arm, which forms the border between Uganda and the Democratic Republic of the Congo. A chain of beautiful lakes have formed along the length of the Rift Valley, and when combined with sheer cliffs and acacia flats, they make for breathtaking scenery.

Lake Magadi Region

Lake Magadi is a soda lake near the Tanzanian border. Nearby is Shompole — a 35,000-acre (14,000-hectare) conservancy surrounded by a 140,000-acre (56,000-hectare) group ranch on the Tanzanian border near Lakes Magadi and Natron, about 75 miles (120 km) south of Nairobi.

ACCOMMODATION — CLASS A+:
• **Shompole**, set on the edge of the Nguruman Escarpment, has six impressively designed open-sided bedrooms with en suite bathrooms and private plunge pools. An exclusive 4-guest villa is the latest edition to the property and includes a split floor plan, two en suite bedrooms, swimming pool, dining area and outside shower and bath. Activities at Shompole include day and night game drives, escorted walks, visits to Lake Natron and fly camping.

Each room at Shompole has its own private plunge pool

Lake Naivasha

Lake Naivasha, located just 55 miles (89 km) northwest of Nairobi, is one of the most beautiful of Kenya's Rift Valley lakes, and features fringing papyrus beds, secluded lagoons and the picturesque Crescent Island. It is a favorite spot for picnics and water sports for Nairobi residents, and it is a birdwatcher's paradise. African fish eagles are abundant. Waterfowl, plovers, sandpipers, avocet, terns, kingfishers, storks and ibis are plentiful. This is a freshwater lake with a suspected underground outlet, so it is less attractive to flamingos, which prefer soda lakes.

Take a boat ride to **Crescent Island** and walk around this game-and-bird sanctuary, which is host to zebra, giraffe, waterbuck, several antelope species and a few camels.

ACCOMMODATION — CLASS A: • **Loldia House**, a cattle ranch located on the northern side of Lake Naivasha, accommodates up to 10 guests in rooms at the main house and a cottage with en suite facilities. • **Chui Lodge** is located on the Oserian Wildlife Sanctuary and has eight individual cottages built in the same fashion as the main building. Each room has en suite bathrooms and a veranda with its own view of the sanctuary and Rift Escarpment. The property has a heated swimming pool and a highlight of a stay is the multicultural cuisine. Activities include game drives and bush walks. • **Kiangzai**

House, also located on Oserian Wildlife Sanctuary, has five luxury bedrooms based in the renovated homestead house. Amenities include a sitting room, dining room, bar, library and pool.

CLASS A/B: • **Longonot Game Ranch** has three double rooms with en suite facilities. Horseback riding is the main attraction. ✱**Lake Naivasha Sopa Lodge** has 21 cottages, consisting of four rooms each, totaling 84 en suite rooms all with panoramic views of the southern shores of the lake. • **The Great Rift Valley Lodge and Golf Resort** is perched on the Eburu Escarpment overlooking Lake Naivasha. The resort offers 30 en suite rooms with private balconies. Activities include walking and horseback riding safaris as well as golf on the championship course (additional fee).

CLASS C: • **Lake Naivasha Country Club** is a beautifully landscaped hotel on the lake shore, built during the colonial era with 51 rooms with somewhat dated en suite facilities and a swimming pool. Sunset cruises are offered and a special Sunday afternoon tea is served.

CAMPING: • **Fisherman's Camp** has a restaurant, bar and a wide-screen TV, and is popular with Nairobi residents.

Hell's Gate National Park

Located to the south of Lake Naivasha, this ruggedly scenic park covers 26-square-miles (68-km²) of high cliffs and scattered grassy areas. The deep gorge is great for hiking and for spotting raptors. Klipspringer, mountain reedbuck, eland, giraffe, and Grant's and Thomson's gazelles may also be seen. Cliff-dwelling birds such as Verreaux's eagle and Ruppell's griffon vultures breed here, and the rare lammergeyer or bearded vulture was reintroduced during the year 2000.

ACCOMMODATION: See "Lake Naivasha" above.

Lake Elmenteita

Lake Elmenteita is a shallow, alkaline lake located between Lakes Naivasha and Nakuru. The lake only holds surface water for a brief period after heavy rain, and it rapidly evaporates. A white soda crust covers much of the lake. A number of hot springs feed permanent lagoons on the fringes of the lake — very attractive to a host of birds.

Up to 50,000 lesser flamingos may feed here, and the uncommon great white pelican, avocet and chestnut-banded plover are breeding residents. The sparse, open bushland surrounding the lake is home to Grant's and Thomson's gazelle, as well as Rothchild's giraffe.

ACCOMMODATION — CLASS C/D: • **Lake Elmenteita Lodge** has 33 rondavels with en suite facilities. Nature walks and ox-wagon rides to the lakeshore are offered.

Lake Nakuru National Park

Lake Nakuru National Park encompasses the alkaline lake of the same name and is frequently visited by hundreds of thousands (sometimes more than a million) of greater and lesser flamingos — and more than 400 bird species in all. Located 100 miles (160 km) northwest of Nairobi on a fair road, the park covers 73-square-miles (188-km^2) — most of which is the lake itself.

Nakuru has been declared a black rhino sanctuary and has a fair number of these endangered animals. A small

Flamingos congregate along the shores of Lake Nakuru

population of white rhino has been reintroduced from South Africa. Other wildlife includes lion, leopard, Rothschild's giraffe (introduced), waterbuck, reedbuck, hippo, baboon, pelican, and cormorant. The lake is an important stopover for thousands of migratory wading birds that head to and from Europe each year.

ACCOMMODATION — CLASS B: • **Sarova Lion Hill Lodge** is located in the park and has air-conditioned cottages (150 beds total) with en suite facilities and a swimming pool.

CLASS C: • **Flamingo Hill Camp** offers 25 tents with canopy beds and en suite facilities. Game drives, sundowners and massages (additional fee) are available for guests. • **Lake Nakuru Lodge** has rooms and cottages (120 beds) with en suite facilities and a swimming pool. Horseback riding just outside the park and nature walks within the park are offered.

CAMPING: Campsites with running water are available in the park.

ACCOMMODATION NEAR LAKE NAKURU — CLASS A: • **Deloraine** is an old, colonial home set on a 5,000-acre (2,000-hectare) farm, and offers 6 rooms with en suite facilities, tennis court and swimming pool. Horseback riding is available.

CLASS B: • **Gogar Farm House**, a picturesque colonial farm owned by the same family for almost 100 years, has 6 rooms with en suite bathrooms, tennis court and large swimming pool. Walks on the farm, birdwatching and horseback riding are offered.

Nyahururu (Thompson's) Falls

Thompson's Falls is located at 7,745 feet (2,360 m) altitude about 115 miles (185 km) from Nairobi, above the Rift Valley between Nanyuki and Nakuru.

ACCOMMODATION — CLASS C/D: • **Thompson's Falls Lodge** is a rustic country hotel; rooms have private facilities.

Lake Bogoria National Reserve

Lake Bogoria National Reserve, located north of Nakuru, has numerous hot springs and geysers along the lakeshore. Thousands of flamingos frequent this alkaline lake, as do greater kudu on the steep slopes of the lake's eastern and southern shores.

ACCOMMODATION — CLASS C/D: • **Lake Bogoria Lodge** has 45 rooms with en suite facilities.

CAMPING: Campsites are available with no facilities.

Lake Baringo

Lake Baringo, a freshwater lake located 20 miles (32 km) north of Lake Bogoria, is a haven for a colorful and mixed variety of bird life (over 400 species recorded). There is a sporting center for waterskiing, fishing and boating. The early morning boat ride along the lakeshore and a walk below the cliffs were two of the finest birdwatching excursions I've experienced. I was also entranced by hippo, crocodile, fishermen and villages along the shore.

ACCOMMODATION — CLASS A/B: • **Samatian Camp** is located on an island in the middle of Lake Baringo and offers 5 thatched chalets with lake views and en suite facilities. The camp has a large pool and provides a variety of water-based activities like fishing, boating and bird watching.

CLASS B: • **Island Camp** is located in the center of Lake Baringo on Ol Kokwa Island. All tents have en suite facilities. Take a walk and you may see a few waterbuck and meet the Njemps tribes people who also inhabit the island. Boat safaris and water sports (beware of hippo and crocs) are available. • **Lake Baringo Club** has 52 rooms with en suite facilities and a swimming pool. Boat and fishing trips are offered.

CLASS D: • **Betty Robert's Campsite**, situated on the lakeshore, has bandas.

CAMPING: • **Betty Robert's Campsite**.

THE NORTH

Laikipia

Laikipia, located north of the Aberdares and northwest of Mt. Kenya, is a wild and sparsely populated region considered to be the gateway to Kenya's Northern frontier.

Much of Laikipia is composed of large, privately owned ranches that cover a wide range of landscapes from high plains to low forested valleys. On most ranches, cattle share the land with free-ranging wildlife. Some sanctuaries were created by local communities, which have combined small farms and grazing land into large group ranches — some of which are active in significant conservation programs. These community ranches are great places to learn about traditional cultures. A visit to one of these private ranches is highly recommended as a way to get off the beaten path.

Ol Lentille, Borana Ranch, Ol Malo Ranch, Loisaba Ranch, Ol Ari Nyiro Ranch and Mugie Ranch are located in Laikipia. Although Lewa Downs, Il'Ngwesi and Tassia are technically outside Laikipia, I have included them in this section because they offer similar experiences.

Laikipia

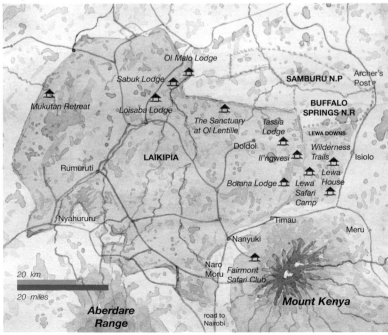

Top: The colorful Maasai
Middle: Colonel's House at
Ol Lentille
Bottom: Chief's Lodge at Ol Lentille

Ol Lentille

Ol Lentille is located on 14,500-acres (6,000-hectare) in the extreme northern escarpment of the Laikipia plateau.

I had the pleasure of spending three days here on a recent safari with my wife and two children (10 and 13 years old at the time) and thoroughly enjoyed it. This fabulous property is an example of cutting edge conservation tourism and joint-partnership with the Maasai community and owners, John and Gill Elias. The concept is that you have your own villa and stay for several days to a week or more. We enjoyed the camel rides, riding out on the quad bikes, climbing Ol Lentille Hill, riding the horses along the animal trails and hanging out (plus playing soccer) at the local Maasai school.

We spent an afternoon in a Maasai Community Village that was set up for tourists and run by a woman's group from the four neighboring villages. We enjoyed watching them dance (and joining in), seeing the differences between the old manyattas and new manyattas (higher ceilings), how they packed their donkeys when they moved their belongings from one grazing area to the other, and taking blood from a cow. As we were the only foreign guests, the experience did not particularly have a touristy feel to it.

ACCOMMODATION-CLASS A+: • **The Sanctuary at Ol Lentille** has 4 luxury houses each with their own living and dining rooms, kitchens and bedrooms with en suite bathrooms. Guests enjoy the service of their own butler, valet, Maasai guide and 4wd vehicle. Activities include day and night game drives, escorted walks, Maasai village visits, horseback riding and quad biking.

Sabuk

This wilderness area, located in Northern Laikipia, has plains, valleys, acacia forest and wild olive forest. Kudu, zebra, eland, elephant, giraffe, gazelle, and, of course, the predators, leopard, lion and cheetah are found here.

ACCOMMODATION — CLASS A: • **Sabuk Lodge** has six beautiful open-fronted stone-and-thatch cottages with en suite bathrooms and private verandahs overlooking the Ewaso Nyiro River Gorge below. There is also a family unit with two rooms. The lodge has a swimming pool for guests' enjoyment. Day and night game drives, escorted walks, and walking/camel safaris as well as fly camping with Lailipiak Maasai warriors as your guides are available.

Loisaba Ranch

Loisaba is a 65,000-acre (26,000-hectare) ranch located on the northern edge of the Laikipia Plateau. Day and night game drives, escorted walks, fly camping, horseback riding, helicopter rides and hot air balloon safaris are offered. I highly recommend spending a night in one of the star-bed camps.

Top: Sabuk Lodge's lounge
Bottom: Sabuk Maasai with a camel

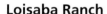

Set on an elevated platform, your bed is rolled out from under the roof and you spend the night looking up at thousands of stars.

ACCOMMODATION — CLASS A: • **Loisaba Lodge,** perched on the edge of a cliff overlooking Mt. Kenya in the distance, has 7 chalets with private verandas, star-beds, and en suite facilities, a swimming pool and tennis court. There is also a separate two-bedroom Loisaba House and Cottage that provide private staff and guide for those guests.

CLASS B: **Loisaba Star Beds** offer an opportunity for a unique cultural experience and to sleep "under the stars". Two Star Bed camps, Kiboko and Koija, each have two raised platforms with en suite facilities and

A unique adventure is to sleep out under the stars on one of Loisaba's Star Beds

4-poster double beds that are rolled out from under a thatched roof at night for a magnificent star-gazing experience. This is a joint project run by the Maasai from the local community. I felt the cultural experience was one of the best I have ever had with Maasai, and highly recommend it!

A view from Borana Lodge over Hyena Valley Dam

Borana Ranch

Borana is a 32,000-acre (12,950-hectare) ranch located in the Laikipia area about 6,500 feet (2,000 m) above sea level. Dedicated to sharing its wealth with the surrounding communities, projects such as a mobile health clinic, ancillary program, scholarship program and job training have been set up. Elephant, lion, buffalo, greater kudu and klipspringer and a variety of antelope may be seen. The activities are day and night game drives, escorted walks, horseback riding and camel riding.

ACCOMMODATION — CLASS A: • **Borana Lodge** is set on the edge of the escarpment and has eight luxury chalets with en suite facilities and a swimming pool. • **Laragai House** is a private residence that can be rented to accommodate 12 guests with a staff to take care of any needs. There is a heated swimming pool and clay tennis courts.

Ol Malo Ranch

Ol Malo Ranch, located along the Uaso Nyiro River on the edge of Kenya's North Eastern Province, covers 5,000-acres (2,000-hectares). Day and night game drives, escorted walks, overnight fly camping, horseback riding and camel treks are offered.

During my last visit we saw lion, giraffe, greater kudu, elephant and a variety of other game while on game drives and on walks.

ACCOMMODATION — CLASS A: • **Ol Malo Lodge**, located on an escarpment with dramatic views of the bush below, has four beautiful chalets with en suite bathrooms with large tubs, and a swimming pool. • **Ol Malo House** is a private house that can be rented for up to 12 guests.

Ol Ari Nyiro Ranch

The ranch is a rhino sanctuary, and Mukutan Retreat is owned by Kuki Gallmann, author of *I Dreamed of Africa* (Penguin Books). The lodge is built on the edge of a gorge on the top of the Rift Valley wall, and overlooks Lakes Baringo and Bogoria.

The bush is quite thick, which makes game viewing a bit difficult. The real attraction is spending time with Kuki herself; however, she does not guarantee that she will be at the lodge. Only one group of guests is accommodated at a time.

ACCOMMODATION — CLASS A: • **Mukutan Retreat** has three stone-and-thatch cottages with en suite facilities.

Lewa Downs

Located between Mt. Kenya and Samburu National Reserve, the privately owned, scenic 45,000-acre (18,000-hectare) Lewa Wildlife Conservancy has a variety of wildlife, adapted to the semi-arid environment, including a large black and white rhino population (Lewa is a rhino sanctuary), elephant, lion, leopard, cheetah, reticulated giraffe, Grevy's zebra, buffalo, hartebeest, bushbuck, gerenuk, Gunther's dikdik and Somali ostrich. Lewa is one of the few places in Kenya where the rare, semi-aquatic sitatunga antelope and African wild dog are sometimes seen, and we were fortunate to have seen sitatunga on our last visit!

During a previous visit we spotted Beisa oryx, Grant's gazelle, a large herd of elephant and a few smaller herds, Mt. Kenya hartebeest and Somali ostrich, among other species.

Horseback riding, hiking, camel riding, day and night game drives in open 4wd vehicles and a cultural visit to the nearby Il N'gwesi Maasai tribal community are offered. The Lewa Wildlife Conservancy is a unique experiment in wildlife conservation and community development and is a not-for-profit organization.

Top: A Park Ranger keeps a watchful eye over two black rhino
Bottom: A walking safari at Wilderness Trails

The spectacular view from Wilderness Trails

ACCOMMODATION — CLASS A+: • **Lewa House** has 3 large cottages which accommodate up to 12 guests. There is a dining room, bar and swimming pool.

CLASS A: • **Wilderness Trails** accommodates up to 16 guests in cottages with en suite facilities and a swimming pool. • **Ngarie Niti** is a large two-bedroom stone house with two separate cottages with en suite facilities. Horseback riding is available to guests. • **Kifaru House** accommodates 12 guests in 6 thatched bandas with en suite bathrooms and an infinity swimming pool. In addition to game drives, horseback riding and visits to the rhino sanctuary are available.

CLASS A/B: • **Lewa Safari Camp** has 12 tents, set on elevated platforms with en suite facilities, and a swimming pool. In addition to game drives, horseback riding and visits to the rhino sanctuary are available.

Il'Ngwesi

The Il'Ngwesi Conservation Area is adjacent to Lewa Downs. Wildlife includes a variety of species that have adapted to dry conditions, including oryx, reticulated giraffe, Grevy's zebra, gerenuk and dikdik.

ACCOMMODATION — CLASS B: • **Il'Ngwesi** has 6 bandas with en suite bathrooms and a swimming pool. The lodge has a covered viewing platform and offers cultural visits and camel safaris.

Tassia

Tassia is owned and managed by the Lekurruki Community Conservation Group Ranch. Walks, Maasai cultural visits and game drives are the main activities.

ACCOMMODATION — CLASS B: • **Tassia Lodge** has 6 rooms with en suite bathrooms, and a plunge pool. The lodge is booked on an exclusive-use basis.

Samburu National Reserve

This relatively small (64-sq.-mi./165-km²) but excellent reserve of scrub desert, thornbush, riverine forest, and swamps along the Ewaso Nyiro River is situated north of Mt. Kenya and the Laikipia region.

Elephant and lion are plentiful, as are Beisa oryx, reticulated giraffe, gerenuk, Grevy's zebra and other species adapted to an arid environment. Leopard are often seen.

Bird life is strikingly colorful and abundant, with golden-breasted starling, white-headed mousebird, sulphur-breasted bushshrike and a variety of weaver birds. Larger birds include the blue-necked Somali ostrich, martial eagle, Egyptian vulture and vulturine guineafowl.

Grevy's zebra

Samburu, probably the best-known reserve in northern Kenya, is located about 220 miles (355 km) north of Nairobi. Under special arrangement, walking may be offered just outside the reserve.

ACCOMMODATION — CLASS A: • **Sasaab** is located on Samburu community land and was constructed using local materials with a Moroccan

Samburu and Buffalo Springs

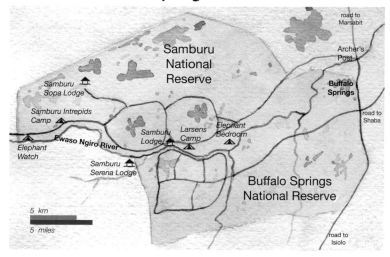

Top: The area surrounding Sasaab Camp
Middle: The rooms at Sasaab overlook the Ewaso Nyiro River
Bottom: Sasaab's open-air lounge

flair. The camp accommodates 18 guests in 9 individual rooms each with en suite facilities and private plunge pools. Activities include game drives, camel walks, cultural visits and bush walks. • **Larsen's Tented Camp**, situated on the banks of the Ewaso Nyiro River, has 20 recently refurbished spacious tents, all with facilities en suite and a swimming pool. • **Samburu Intrepids Camp** has a swimming pool and 27 luxury tents, each with a private terrace and facilities en suite. Game drives, escorted walks, camelback safaris and visits to neighboring Samburu communities are offered. • **Elephant Watch Camp**, set on the northern bank of the Ewaso Nyiro River, has 5 spacious desert-style tents with en suite bathrooms. The camp is run by Oria Douglas-Hamilton who has been working alongside her husband Iain in elephant conservation for 30 years. Activities include trailblazing elephant walks, tracking of elephant from the research camp, and visits to local Samburu projects.

CLASS B: • **Samburu Lodge**, located on the banks of the Ewaso Nyiro River, has rooms, cottages and tents (75 units) with private facilities and a swimming pool. This lodge also baits for crocs and leopard. • **Elephant Bedroom** is a small camp located on the banks of the Ewaso Nyiro River in Samburu National Reserve. The 12 tents are furnished in rustic African style and feature en suite facilities. Activities include guided nature walks, game drives and cultural visits.

CLASS C: • **Samburu Sopa Lodge** has 30 cottages featuring 2 bedrooms in each (total of 60 beds) with en suite facilities, a water hole and swimming pool. Game drives, nature walks and visits to local Samburu tribe are offered.

CAMPING: Campsites are located along the north bank of the Ewaso Nyiro River between the West Gate and Samburu Lodge. Public sites have long-drop toilets.

Top: Larsen's Tented Camp
Bottom: A game drive from Larsen's Tented Camp

Buffalo Springs National Reserve

Buffalo Springs is a 50-square-mile (131-km²) reserve located south of the Ewaso Nyiro River, which serves as its northern border with Samburu National Reserve. The unusual doum palm, the only palm tree species whose trunk divides into branches, grows to over 60 feet (19 m) in height in this arid park. Wildlife is similar to what is seen in Samburu National Reserve.

On a two-hour game drive, we encountered oryx, gerenuk, Grant's gazelle, waterbuck, Somali ostrich and two large herds of elephant. Baboons are often found drinking at the springs.

ACCOMMODATION — CLASS A/B: • **Samburu Serena Safari Lodge**, situated on the banks of the Ewaso Nyiro River, has 62 rooms with facilities en suite and a swimming pool. The lodge baits for crocs and leopard. The camp conducts game drives in Samburu as well as in Buffalo Springs.

CAMPING: Campsites have no facilities.

Shaba National Reserve

The turnoff to the entrance to Shaba National Reserve is located east of Samburu National Reserve, 2 miles (3 km) south of Archer's Post. The Ewaso Nyiro River forms the reserve's northwestern border and flows through the western part of the reserve.

This 92-square-mile (239-km²) reserve is characterized by rocky hills and scattered thornbush. Volcanic rock is present in many areas. Mt. Shaba, a

5,320-foot- (1,622-m) high volcanic cone, which the park was named after, lies to the south of the reserve.

Shaba became famous for hosting the 2001 "Survivor" television series as well as the location of George Adamson's film *Walking with Lions*. A marsh in the center of the reserve is a good spot to look for wildlife.

The lounge area at Joy's Camp

Wildlife is less abundant and cannot be approached as closely as in the Samburu and Buffalo Springs National Reserves. However, there is much less traffic in this reserve.

ACCOMMODATION — CLASS A: • **Joy's Camp** offers 10 large Bedouin style tents with en suite facilities and swimming pool. Situated at Joy Adamson's (of *Born Free* fame) original campsite, these luxury tents are set on raised platforms with great views of the surrounding hills. The camp overlooks a large natural spring and offers game drives, bush meals, massages, cultural visits and walks.

CLASS B: • **Shaba Sarova Lodge**, situated on the Ewaso Nyiro River, is a resort-style lodge with 85 rooms with facilities en suite, and a huge swimming pool.

CAMPING: Ask at the gate.

Maralal National Sanctuary

Maralal National Sanctuary, located northwest of Samburu and 95 miles (153 km) north of Nyahururu (205 mi./330 km from Nairobi) near the town of Maralal, has zebra, buffalo, eland, impala and hyena.

ACCOMMODATION — CLASS C: • **Maralal Safari Lodge** has 12 cottages with fireplaces and en suite facilities, a swimming pool and a waterhole.

CLASS D, F & CAMPING: • **Yare Safaris Hostel and Campsite**, located 2 miles (3 km) south of Maralal, has bandas, dormitories and campsites.

Mathews Range

Located northwest of Samburu National Reserve, this remote wilderness area with lush green vegetation rises above the surrounding semi-desert lowlands. Elephant, lion, buffalo, greater kudu, waterbuck and other game may be seen, and over 100 bird species have been recorded. The real attraction of this area is its stark beauty, remoteness and opportunity for a cultural interaction with the Samburu. Camel safaris are operated in the area. Access to the region is by air charter or 4wd vehicles, which are necessary in this region.

ACCOMMODATION — CLASS A/B: • **Desert Rose**, perched on a cliff high up on the remote Mt. Nyiru, has 5 houses with open-air bathrooms. The camp offers remote cultural interactions, forest walks up Mt. Nyiru and exciting camel treks. Easiest access to the camp is by an approximately 100-minute charter flight from Nairobi.

CLASS B • **Kitich Camp** is situated on a private concession of more than 150,000-acres (60,000-hectares) in the southern part of the Mathews Range at an altitude of 4,300 feet (1,300 m). It has 6 tents with en suite long-drop toilets and bucket showers. Walks in the forests with local Samburu tribesmen, game tracking, swimming in nearby natural rock pools and visits to Samburu villages are offered. • **Sarara Camp**, located on the Namunyak Conservancy, has 5 tents each with flushing toilets and open-air showers. There is a rock swimming pool near the watering hole for guests' enjoyment. This is one of the best bird-watching areas in Kenya.

Lake Turkana

Sometimes referred to as the Jade Sea because of its deep green color, Lake Turkana is a huge inland lake surrounded by semi-desert near the Ethiopian border. It can be reached in three days of hard driving over rough terrain or a few hours by air charter from Nairobi.

Formerly named Lake Rudolf, this huge lake, which is over 175 miles (280 km) long and 10 to 30 miles (16 to 48 km) wide, is set in a lunar-like landscape of lava rocks, dried-up river beds and scattered oases.

The brown Omo River flows from the Ethiopian Highlands into the northern part of the lake, where the water is fairly fresh but becomes increasingly saline further south due to intense evaporation. The presence of puffer fish implies that the lake was at one time connected to the Mediterranean Sea by the River Nile.

One of the continent's largest populations of crocodile is found here. Because the bitter alkaline waters render their skins useless for commercial trade, crocodile are not hunted and grow to abnormally large sizes. Although the water is very tempting in such a hot, dry climate, swim only at your own risk!

Forty-seven species of fish live in the brackish waters, seven of which are found nowhere else. This is a very worthwhile location for keen birders, as aquatic birds abound. Expect to see pink-backed pelican, greater flamingo,

Top: An aerial view of Lake Turkana
Bottom: The lunar-like landscape of
Lake Turkana

spur-winged plover and African skimmer. Up to 100,000 little stint winter here on their annual migration from northern Europe. In the dry scrublands, birds that are absent or seldom seen elsewhere in Kenya include the swallow-tailed kite, fox kestrel, Abyssinian roller, star-spotted nightjar and Jackson's hornbill.

Fishing is a major attraction at Lake Turkana. Nile perch, the world's largest freshwater fish, can exceed 400 pounds (180 kg). Tigerfish, however, put up a more exciting fight. The El Molo tribe, the smallest tribe in Kenya (about 500 members), can be found near Loiyangalani.

Central Island National Park, a 2-square-mile (5-km²) island containing three volcanic cones, is the most highly concentrated breeding ground of crocodile in Africa. Excursions to **South Island National Park**, also volcanic and full of crocodile, are available from the Oasis Lodge.

Easiest access to the park is by small aircraft. Four-wheel-drive vehicles are necessary. Loiyangalani is about 415 miles (665 km) and Ferguson's Gulf is about 500 miles (805 km) north of Nairobi.

ACCOMMODATION-CLASS C: • **Oasis Lodge**, located on the southeastern shore of the lake at Loiyangalani, has 24 basic cottages with facilities en suite, 2 swimming pools, fishing boats and equipment for hire. Excursions to South Island National Park are available.

CLASS D: • **El Molo Lodge** has bandas. There are also self-catering bandas at Koobi Fora.

CAMPING: At **El Molo Lodge**, **Sunset Strip Campsite** and **El Molo Bay**.

Chalbi Desert

The Chalbi Desert is home to 30,000 nomadic Gabra tribesmen, who are still living an unaffected lifestyle in an untouched, harsh wilderness, east of the southern part of Lake Turkana. The Gabra water their goats, oblivious of the visitors, at oases and deep wells set on the edge of the Dida Galgalu plains.

The Kalacha Oasis is a natural spring attracting jackals, ostrich, sandgrouse and other wildlife.

ACCOMMODATION — CLASS B: • **Kalacha Community Bandas**, a unique community project with the Gabra people, consists of 4 bungalows set among the palm trees of the Oasis with en suite facilities and swimming pool.

THE COAST

Mombasa

Mombasa is the second largest city in Kenya, with a population of over 600,000. Situated on an island, 307 miles (495 km) from Nairobi on a paved road, it is a cultural blend of the Middle East, Asia and Africa.

The **Old Harbour** is haven for dhows carrying goods for trade between Arabia and the Indian subcontinent and Africa, especially from December to April. **Kilindini**, "place of deep water," is the modern harbor and largest port on the eastern coast of Africa.

Built by the Portuguese in 1593, **Fort Jesus** now serves as a museum. The **Old Town** is Muslim and Indian in flavor, with winding, narrow streets and alleys too narrow for cars. The tall, nineteenth century buildings with handcarved doors and overhanging balconies, and small shops of Old Town and Fort Jesus are best seen on foot.

Mombasa is the best place in Kenya for excellent Swahili food. The Tamarind Restaurant, located on the water's edge overlooking Mombasa Island and Aquamarine Restaurant at Mtwapa Creek serve excellent seafood.

The city of Mombasa has no beaches, so most international visitors stay on the beautiful white sand beaches to the south or north of the island. Nyali Beach, Mombasa Beach, Kenyatta Beach and Shanzu Beach are just to the north of Mombasa, while Diani Beach is about 20 miles (32 km) to the south.

Most beach hotels on the coast offer a variety of water sports for their guests, including sailing, wind surfing, water skiing, deep-sea fishing, scuba diving and snorkeling on beautiful coral reefs.

ACCOMMODATION IN MOMBASA — TOURIST CLASS: • **Castle Hotel**, located on the main shopping street in central Mombasa, has 60 simple rooms with facilities en suite and a busy café/bar on the ground floor terrace — an ideal place for people-watching across the bustling streets.

Top: One of Alfajiri's amazing villas
Bottom: The main house at Alfajiri

ACCOMMODATION JUST NORTH OF MOMBASA — DELUXE: • **Mombasa Serena Beach Hotel** has 166 remodeled air-conditioned rooms with en suite facilities, a new Maisha Spa, a swimming pool and tennis, scuba diving and other water sports.

FIRST CLASS: • **Nyali Beach Hotel** has 235 air-conditioned rooms with en suite facilities, minibars, a small night-club, 2 swimming pools, 2 tennis courts, shops and a very popular kite surfing center. • **Voyager Beach Resort**, located on Nyali Beach, has 233 spacious rooms (decorated as a ship's cabin) with en suite facilities, restaurant, 3 swimming pools, tennis courts, dive center, water-sports and children's adventure club. • **Sarova Whitesands Beach Resort** has 346 air-conditioned rooms with en suite facilities, 3 swimming pools, tennis and water sports.

TOURIST CLASS: • **Mombasa Beach Hotel** has 150 air-conditioned rooms with en suite facilities, a swimming pool, and tennis courts.

ACCOMMODATION JUST SOUTH OF MOMBASA — DELUXE: • **Leopard Beach Resort & Spa**, located on 30 acres along Diani Beach, has 160 rooms and suites with en suite bathrooms, 4 restaurants, bar, swimming pool, business center, floodlit tennis courts, scuba diving and water sports center and the delightful new "Uzuri Spa Fitness Forest" with gym, steam and sauna. • **Alfajiri** consists of 3 of the finest villas on the Kenya coast. Cliff Villa accommodates 8 guests in 4 bedrooms with en suite facilities, dining room, kitchen, lounge, large veranda and private pool overlooking the Indian Ocean. The Beach Villa and Garden Villas share a pool and can accommodate 4 and 8 people respectively • **Diani Reef Hotel** has 304 air-conditioned rooms with facilities en suite, a swimming pool, dive school and tennis courts.

FIRST CLASS: • **Pinewood Village** has 20 private villas with en suite facilities and private chefs. • **Indian Ocean Beach Club**, set on a beautiful beach, has 100 air-conditioned rooms with en suite facilities, a swimming pool, tennis, scuba diving and water sports. • **Diani House**, set on 12-acres (5-hectares) of forested garden along 820 feet (250 m) of beachfront, has 4 rooms with private verandahs and en suite facilities, and a single room with shared facilities. Snorkeling, fishing, windsurfing, visits to the local market and walks in the Kaya Kinondon and the Jadini Forest are available.

CAMPING: Campsites available at **Twiga Lodge** (Tiwi Beach).

South Of Mombasa
Shimba Hills National Park

This 74-square-mile (192-km^2) reserve of rolling hills and forests is located an hour's drive south of Mombasa and 10 miles (16 km) inland. At 1,500 feet (460 m) above sea level, this is a good place to cool off from the heat of the coast. From the park there are magnificent views of the Indian Ocean, and Mt. Kilimanjaro can even be seen on exceptionally clear days.

Wildlife includes elephant and buffalo and occasional sightings of genet, civet, serval, leopard and roan antelope. This is the only park in Kenya with sable antelope.

ACCOMMODATION — CLASS B: • **Shimba Hills Lodge** is a three-story "tree hotel" with 80 beds, overlooking a floodlit water hole.

ACCOMMODATION NEAR THE RESERVE — CLASS B: • **Mukurumuji Tented Camp**, set in the privately owned Sable Valley Sanctuary overlooking Shimba Hills Reserve, has 4 basic but comfortable tents under thatch with en suite facilities. Activities include day trips into Shimba Hills and to the Mwaluganje Elephant Sanctuary.

Kisite Mpunguti Marine Reserve

Kisite Mpunguti Marine Reserve is situated near the small fishing village of Shimoni ("place of the caves"), where slaves were held before shipment, near the Tanzanian border far from the mainstream of tourism. Delightful boat excursions to Wasini Island, an ancient Arab settlement across a channel from Shimoni, and snorkeling excursions are available.

The **Pemba Channel**, just off of Shimoni, is one of the world's finest marlin fishing grounds.

ACCOMMODATION — CLASS C: • **Pemba Channel Lodge** accommodates up to 14 guests in bungalows with en suite facilities. Boats are available for hire for deep-sea fishing. The lodge is closed from April 1 to July 31st. • **Shimoni Reef Lodge** has 10 basic thatched cottages with en suite facilities, a swimming pool and a PADI Dive Center.

North Of Mombasa
Malindi-Watamu Marine National Reserve

Malindi-Watamu Marine National Reserve encompasses the area south of Malindi to south of Watamu, from 100 feet to 3 nautical miles (30 m to 5 km) offshore, and it has very good diving and snorkeling. During a recent visit we snorkeled in the park and were very impressed by the clarity of the water and the great variety of tropical reef fish.

ACCOMMODATION IN WATAMU — FIRST CLASS: • **Hemingway's** is a 175-bed hotel with en suite facilities, swimming pool and charter boats for deep-sea fishing and diving. • **Turtle Bay Beach Club** has 154 air-conditioned rooms with en suite facilities.

Malindi

Malindi, located 75 miles (120 km) north of Mombasa (2 hours by car), has numerous beach hotels, nightclubs and shops. The International Bill Fishing Competition is held here every January. On our last visit we went out for a fun day of fishing and caught 10 wahoo weighing over 40 pounds each!

The **Sokoke Arabuko Forest** is Africa's northernmost brachystegia forest and Kenya's last remaining area of extensive lowland forest. The forest contains a variety of interesting wildlife, including Adder's duiker, bushy-tailed mongoose, golden-rumped elephant shrew, the Sokoke scops owl, the Sokoke pipit and Clarke's weaver.

The **Gedi Ruins**, last inhabited in the thirteenth century by about 2,500 people, is a mystery in that there are no Arabic or Swahili records of its existence.

TOURIST CLASS: • **Driftwood Beach Club** has 27 cottages (some air-conditioned) with en suite facilities and a swimming pool.

CAMPING: • Silversands Campsite is 1 mile (2 km) north of town.

Lamu

Swahili culture has changed little in the past few hundred years on the island of Lamu. There are only a few motorized vehicles on the island that are owned by government officials, but plenty of donkey carts provide substitutes. Narrow, winding streets and a maze of alleyways add to the timeless atmosphere. Many travelers have compared Lamu to a mini-Katmandu.

The **Lamu Museum** has exhibits of Swahili craftwork. Of the more than 30 mosques on Lamu, only a few are open to visitors. The best beaches are at **Shela**, a 45-minute walk or short boat ride from the town of Lamu to the Peponi Beach Hotel. **Matondoni** is a fishing village where dhows, fishing nets and traps are made. Numerous attractions are also found on nearby islands.

Sailing off the Kenya coast

The best way to reach the island is to fly. Driving is not recommended because the road from Malindi is very rough and may be impassable in the rainy season.

ACCOMMODATION — DELUXE: • **Kipungani Explorer Lamu**, set on the southern end of Lamu Island, is a perfect "Robinson Crusoe hideaway" and has 13 beach bandas with en suite facilities, hanging moon-beds, butler service and a swimming pool. Water-skiing, sailing, deep-sea fishing and snorkeling are offered.

FIRST CLASS: • **Peponi Beach Hotel**, a pleasant beach resort, is located about 1 mile (2 km) from the town of Lamu. All 25 rooms are fan-cooled and have facilities en suite. • **The Island Hotel**, located in the center of Shela Village, has 14 fan-cooled rooms with en suite facilities.

TOURIST CLASS: • **Lamu Palace Hotel** has air-conditioned rooms (50 beds) with en suite facilities and is located 200 yards (200 m) from the jetty. • **Petley's Inn** has been a landmark since the nineteenth century. The hotel has a rustic atmosphere and rooms with private facilities. • **Kizingo Hotel** has 6 beachfront bandas with en suite facilities and offers shaded balconies and ocean views. Beyond the spectacular beach, guests can fish, snorkel and even swim with wild dolphins.

Top: The lounge at Manda Bay
Middle: Aerial view of Manda Bay
Bottom: Barefoot luxury at Kiwayu

ACCOMMODATION IN THE REGION OF LAMU — DELUXE:
• **Manda Bay** is located on the north-western tip of **Manda Island** and has 16 cottages, 11 are set right on the seafront and 5 are slightly behind on higher ground. All the cottages have en suite bathrooms, and private veranda overlooking the Indian Ocean. Deep-sea fishing, windsurfing, sailing, snorkeling, water skiing and several other options are available. The property also features dhow excursions, spa and massage, cultural visits and a swimming pool.
• **Kiwayu** is situated on a peninsula 30 miles (50 km) northeast of Lamu in the **Dodori National Reserve** on a beautiful beach. There are 18 large, fan-cooled but simple cottages with private verandahs (with hammocks) and en suite facilities set right on the beach. Activities include snorkeling, wind surfing, sailing, water-skiing, deep-sea fishing, game drives in the Dodori National Reserve and visits to local Bajuni villages.

Uganda

Uganda

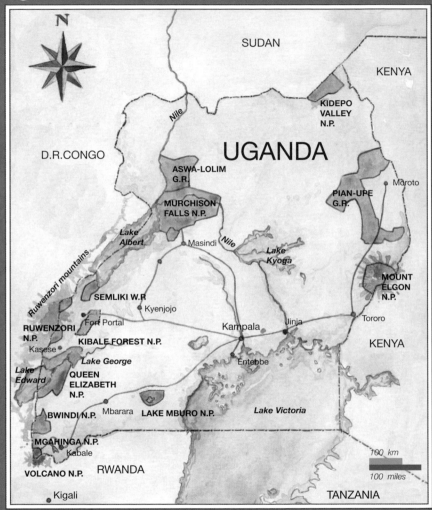

Straddling the equator, Uganda is a verdant country once referred to as the "Pearl of the British Empire in East Africa." Most of Uganda is an upland plateau averaging 3,000 feet (1,000 m) above sea level. With the enormous Lake Victoria occupying the southeastern part of the country, and numerous other Rift Valley lakes as well as the mighty Nile River, one-sixth of Uganda is fresh water. Approximately the size of Oregon (or Great Britain) Uganda covers 93,000-square-miles (240,000-km²). Almost all of the 27 million population are either subsistence farmers or employed in agriculture. Kampala is the capital city with over 1.2 million inhabitants. KiSwahili and English are the main languages. Currency is the Ugandan Shilling.

Uganda Country Highlights

- A safari to Uganda is like visiting your own Garden of Eden. Parks are not congested with vehicles and hotels and lodges give you the personal attention rarely found in this day of international travel.
- Bwindi Impenetrable Forest is known the world over for gorilla trekking. A visit to this park will reveal a unique African adventure and one of the most fascinating primates.
- Visit Murchison Falls and view the dramatic waterfall, lush foliage and the largest concentration of crocodiles on the continent.
- Trek into Kibale Forest National Park for the ultimate chimpanzee experience as well as the opportunity to see black-and-white colobus monkey, red colobus, gray-cheeked mangabey and red-tailed monkey.
- Experience Queen Elizabeth National Park and view an astonishing 547 bird species — one of the highest figures for any single protected area in the world.

Best Parks and Reserves to Visit	Best Times to Go
Bwindi Impenetrable Forest	December to March / June to September
Kibale Forest National Park	December to March / June to September
Queen Elizabeth National Park	December to March / June to September
Murchison Falls National Park	December to March / June to September

Best Accommodations

Apoka Lodge, Gorilla Forest Camp, Emin Pasha, Kampala Serena Hotel, Kampala Sheraton Hotel

UGANDA

Uganda, once the "Pearl of the British Empire in East Africa," is one of the most beautiful countries on the continent. One-sixth of its area is covered by water. Along its western boundary lie the Ruwenzori Mountains, Africa's highest mountain range, and Ptolemy's fabled "Mountains of the Moon." The Ugandans claim the source of the Nile is at Jinja, where it leaves Lake Victoria.

The climate in Uganda is similar to Kenya except that Uganda is wetter. The driest times of the year are December to February and June to July, and the wettest is from mid-March to mid-May, with lighter rains October to November.

English is spoken as widely here as in Kenya or Tanzania. The main religions are Christianity and Islam.

In the eighteenth century, the Kingdom of Buganda became the most powerful in the region. Together with three other kingdoms, and several native communities, it was made a British Protectorate in 1893 and achieved independence in 1962.

Over 90% of the population is employed in agriculture, with coffee as the major export.

🐾 WILDLIFE AND WILDLIFE AREAS

Uganda's tremendous diversity of wildlife is due to its situation at the junction of the East African savannahs, the West African rainforests and the semiarid Sahelian zone of North Africa. There are 10 national parks and 15 wildlife reserves, but most are much smaller than those in Tanzania or

Kenya. Clever planning of the parks and reserves has, however, resulted in most of the different habitats being conserved, enabling visitors to enjoy a wide variety of wildlife and nature experiences.

Primates, including gorillas, large numbers of chimpanzees and an array of smaller monkeys are a major attraction. The endemic Uganda kob (a beautiful antelope), as well as lion, leopard, elephant and giraffe inhabit the savannahs while the great wetlands are home to large numbers of hippo and crocodile.

Gorillas remain the greatest international attraction, and there is nothing comparable to the thrill of a close encounter with these magnificent, peaceful apes. Travelers from all over the world venture to Bwindi to experience these magnificent animals in their native environment. Gorilla trekking is so popular that I suggest you book your safari a year or so in advance if possible, as permits are limited.

Relative to its size, Uganda is the richest country for birds in Africa, with over 1,000 species in an area the size of Great Britain. A wealth of hornbills, turacos, barbets, sunbirds, kingfishers, weavers and storks are present, as well as the bizarre and much sought-after shoebill.

A real advantage of parks in Uganda is that they are not anywhere near as crowed as those in Kenya or Tanzania. You meet very few other vehicles on game drives — in some cases, you even have the parks almost to yourself!

The view across Bwindi Impenetrable Forest toward the Virunga Mountains in neighboring Rwanda

NORTHERN AND WESTERN

Kidepo Valley National Park

Isolated from the Ugandan mainstream by the harsh plains to the north of Mount Elgon, Kidepo Valley National Park is Uganda's second largest national park. Kidepo is one of Africa's last great wilderness areas, a tract of rugged savannah dominated by Mt. Morungole and transected by the Kidepo and Narus Rivers. Perennial running water in the Narus River makes Kidepo an oasis in this semidesert.

While the game viewing is excellent, it is the sense of supreme isolation that distinguishes this rare slice of wild Africa — as yet undiscovered by the mass safari market. Wildlife includes elephant, giraffe, buffalo, lion, cheetah, ostrich, Jackson's hartebeest, waterbuck, zebra, Guenther's dikdik, kudu, lesser kudu, eland, aardwolf, bat-eared fox and Patas monkeys. Occasionally African wild dogs are spotted near Kanantarok Hot Springs close to the border of Sudan.

Bird watchers will relish their time spent in Kidepo as it boasts 475 species, some not found anywhere else in Uganda. Bird such as the black-breasted barbet, Karamoja apalis and the rose-ringed parakeet are just some of the rarer birds to see (and hear).

Top: The surrounding vistas of the Apoka Lodge
Bottom: One of Apoka's roomy cottages

The park can be explored by traditional vehicle game drives as well as tracking game on foot. You may also take a cultural excursion to nearby villages. Ask your lodge to pack a picnic lunch as there are some spectacular spots to enjoy the scenery and solitude.

Getting to Kidepo can take up to 2 days driving from Entebbe on extremely rough roads. The recommended mode of transportation is private charter flight from Entebbe. Currently there are scheduled flights to Kidepo but they are limited to just one day a week.

ACCOMMODATION — CLASS A:
• **Apoka Lodge** has 10 roomy cottages, built of wood, canvas and thatch with en suite facilities, a swimming pool

carved out of rock, and private balconies. The lodge has a waterhole and has fantastic views down the Narus Valley. Game drives in 4wd vehicles and escorted walks are offered.

CLASS C/D: • **Apoka Rest Camp** is located about a 100 yards (100 m) from Apoka Lodge and offers bandas with solar lighting and hot showers. Bottled water, soda and beer are usually available but no food.

A visiting elephant in front of one of the chalets at Apoka Lodge

CAMPING: A few miles/kilometers from Apoka there is a campsite but no services.

Murchison (Kabalega) Falls National Park

This park is named after the famous falls where the Victoria Nile rushes with tremendous force through a narrow, 20-foot-wide (6-m) rock gorge to crash onto the rocks 150 feet (45 m) below. Fish dazed by this fall are easy prey to one of the largest concentrations of crocodile on the continent.

Located in northwestern Uganda, this park covers approximately 1,500-square-miles (3,885-km^2) of predominantly grassy plains and savannah woodlands, with altitudes ranging from 1,650 to 4,240 feet (500 to 1,292 m). Riverine forest with giant tamarind trees lines some parts of the Victoria Nile, which traverses the park from east to west.

In addition to Murchison Falls, a highlight of the park is the three-hour, 7-mile (11 km) boat trip from Paraa Lodge to the foot of the falls. Numerous crocodile and hippo inhabit the river and along its banks, as well as buffalo, elephant, and prolific bird life (over 400 species) including red-throated bee-eater, piapiac, silverbird and black-headed gonolek.

Mist rising from Murchison Falls

At the base of the falls, an intrepid fisherman tries his luck

Another great excursion is a 6-hour launch trip from Paraa Lodge to the delta where the Victoria Nile flows into Lake Albert. Shoebills (whale-headed storks) are a popular feature of this trip.

The park is also home to Rothchild's giraffe, Defassa waterbuck, oribi, hartebeest and Uganda kob. Record Nile perch over 200 pounds (90 kg) have been caught in the Nile. Some of the best fishing is just below Karuma Falls and Murchison Falls.

The easiest time to spot animals is January to February and the short dry season from June to July. Game viewing August to December is also good. From March to May, the landscape is more attractive, but the wildlife is less concentrated.

Park headquarters and the most extensive road system for game viewing are near the Paraa Lodge. The Buligi Circuit arrives at the confluence of the Albert Nile and Victoria Nile. Waterfowl are especially abundant, along with a variety of game. Fuel is usually available at the Paraa Lodge.

Top: Nile Safari Camp's open-air lounge
Bottom: A view of Nile Safari Camp from the Nile River

ACCOMMODATION — CLASS A/B: • **Nile Safari Camp** is nestled on the southern bank of the Nile River and offers exclusive accommodation in 5 wooden chalets and 5 luxury tents, each with en suite facilities, private verandas and views of the Nile River. The lodge has a swimming pool, lounge and restaurant. Boat trips to the base of Murchison Falls, game drives and nature walks are offered. • **Paraa Lodge** is located on the north side of the river with views of the River Nile. The 53 en suite rooms are equipped with ceiling fans and private verandahs. Lodge amenities include a swimming pool with a swim-up bar, souvenir shop, conference room, Captain's Table Restaurant and Explorer's Bar.

CLASS B/C: • **Sambiya River Lodge** is located in the southern section of the park on the Sambiya River and 23 miles (20 km) from the falls (a 25-minute drive). The lodge offers 25 en suite cottages with private verandahs, a restaurant, swimming pool and a telescope.

CLASS D/F: • **Red Chilli Rest Camp** is set on the southern bank with easy access to Park Headquarters. There are 13 simple bandas (some en suite), camping facilities, a restaurant and bar.

Paraa Lodge's pool area

CAMPING: Sites available at Red Chilli Rest Camp or Nile Safari Lodge.

Semliki Game Reserve

Formerly called the *Toro Game Reserve,* this 85-square-mile (220-km²) reserve of grassland, savannah, forest and wetland habitats is bordered by Lake Albert to the north and the Ruwenzori Mountains to the southwest.

The tropical lowland forest conserved in this park is ecologically linked to the Congo basin and provides a very different Ugandan wildlife experience. The giant hardwood trees and tangled undergrowth of the forest are home to many fascinating mammals such as Africa's smallest ungulate—the tiny pygmy antelope, which is hardly bigger than a hare. Chimpanzees in the area are becoming habituated and sightings are now quite good. Other primates including the gray-cheeked mangaby, red-tailed monkey and De Brazza's monkey may also be seen.

Other wildlife includes elephant, the Uganda Kob (the most common large mammal) and warthog as well as infrequently seen buffalo, leopard, lion, hyena, bushbuck, waterbuck, reedbuck, duiker and forest hog.

The reserve is an absolute paradise for birdwatchers, with 35 of the 385 species occurring nowhere else in East Africa. Specials such as the chestnut owlet, white-crested hornbill, African piculet and fiery-breasted bushshrike attract enthusiastic observers from far and wide.

The park has an airstrip and is about a 6-hour drive from Kampala, a 3-hour drive from Queen Elizabeth National Park and a 2-hour drive from Kibale Forest National Park.

A tent at Semliki Safari Lodge

ACCOMMODATION — CLASS A/B: • **Semliki Safari Lodge** has 8 tents with en suite facilities and a swimming pool. A newly constructed waterhole is attracting animals and is quite popular during the dry season. Activities include night game drives, chimpanzee tracking, boat trips on Lake Albert, fishing for Nile perch, tilapia and tiger fish, and visits to Nkusi Waterfalls.

Ruwenzori Mountains National Park

This is the highest mountain range in Africa and home of the legendary "Mountains of the Moon." They rise 13,000 feet (3,963 m) above the western arm of the Rift Valley to 16,762 feet (5,109 m) above sea level, just north of the equator, and are usually covered in mist. See "Ruwenzori Mountains" in the chapter on the Congo for a general description. The only mountains that are higher are Mt. Kilmanjaro and Mt. Kenya.

Hikers in good condition can enjoy walking a strenuous circuit for 6 or 7 days that rises to over 13,000 feet (3,963 m) in altitude through some of the most amazing vegetation in the world. Walking routes trace the lower slopes and it is a region of great biological beauty. Successive zones of distinct vegetation ring the six major massifs of the Ruwenzori with woodland, evergreen forest, bamboo, boggy heathland and Afro-alpine moorland in a sequence up the slopes. Large mammals are few, but the Ruwenzori colobus, giant forest hog and yellow-backed duiker may be encountered. The exquisite Ruwenzori turaco is fairly common, while the Ruwenzori batis and

Ruwenzori Mountains

bamboo warbler are found nowhere else in Uganda.

The main trailhead begins near Ibanda. Drive 6 miles (10 km) north from Kasese on the Fort Portal road, then turn left (west) for 8 miles (13 km). The mountain huts take up to 15 people. It is best to bring all your own gear, although equipment may be available for hire.

The Central Circuit

Hikers begin the Central Circuit trek

On day one, a dirt road from Ibanda runs 3 miles (5 km) to the Park Headquarters at Nyakalengija (5,400 ft./1,646 m). There is a 5-hour hike past village huts, into the park and onward to Nyabitaba Hut (8,700 ft./2,652 m). You may be lucky enough to see black-and-white colobus monkeys or the Rwenzori turaco. Many climbers prefer staying in a nearby rock shelter instead of the hut. Water and firewood are not available near the hut. Tent spaces are located nearby.

Day two is the most grueling of the circuit. Climbers hike 5 or 6 hours past a bamboo forest to Nyamileju Hut (10,900 ft./3,322 m) and a nearby rock shelter. Time and energy permitting, you may continue hiking through a bog in the giant heather, lobelia and groundsel zone for about an hour to John Mate Hut (11,200 ft./3,414 m).

On day three, hikers must traverse a muddy bog to Bigo Hut (11,300 ft./ 3,444 m). A rest is recommended before continuing through Upper Bigo Bog to Bujuku Lake, where there are views of Mt. Baker, Mt. Stanley and Mt. Speke, to Bujuku Hut (13,000 ft./ 3,962 m). From John Mate Hut to Bujuku Hut should take about 5 to 6 hours. Technical climbers attempting Mt. Speke often use this hut as a base.

On day four, the hike crosses Groundsel Gully toward Scott Elliot Pass to Elena Hut (14,700 ft./ 4,372 m). Elena is the base camp for

An example of the lobelia plant that grows in the Ruwenzori Mountains

climbing Margarita Peak, which requires 2 more days, previous permission from National Parks and the proper equipment (crampons, ice axe, ropes, etc.). As you hike over Scott Elliot Pass you enter the alpine zone of limited vegetation, but with fabulous views of Margarita Peak, Mt. Baker, Elena and Savoia Glaciers. From there, the trail continues to Lake Kitandara and Kitandara Hut (13,200 ft./4,023 m) and then goes on to Kabamba Rock Shelter (12,400 ft./3,779 m). The hike from Bujuku Hut takes about 5 hours.

On day five, hike to Freshfield Pass and then descend past the rock shelters at Bujongolo and Kabamba (an optional overnight stop) onward to Guy Yeoman Hut (10,700 ft./3,261 m). The hike to Guy Yeoman Hut takes 6 to 7 hours.

On day six, there is a 5-hour hike down to Nyabitaba Hut, with an optional overnight stop, or you may choose to finish the journey with a 3-hour hike to the park gate.

The Rwenzori Mountains have two rainy seasons, from March to May and September to mid-December. The best time to climb is mid-December through February and June through August during the dry season. However, no matter when you climb, you will still get wet. Wood fires are prohibited, so be prepared to use paraffin or gas stoves.

For information on climbing the summits and glaciers, I recommend the books *East Africa International Mountain Guide,* by Andrew Wielochowski (1986), and *Guide to the Ruwenzori,* by Osmaston and Pasteur (1972), both published by West Col Productions in England. Maps of the area include "The Central Ruwenzoris" with a scale of 1:250,000 and "Margherita" with a scale of 1:50,000.

ACCOMMODATION — CLASS C/D: See "Kasese" below.

Kibale is one of the best places in Uganda to see chimpanzees

CLASS F: A few dormitory huts are available from RMS at Ibanda. Many of the huts on the hiking trails are in poor condition but are in the process of being renovated. Bring a ground sheet and insulated pad for your sleeping bag. Because not all of the huts are in good repair, it is best to bring your own tent.

Kibale Forest National Park

This 296-square-mile (766-km^2) park consists of lowland tropical rain forest, tropical deciduous forest, marshes, grasslands and crater lakes, and is the best place in Uganda for chimpanzee trekking.

In addition to escorted walks, the park offers a Chimpanzee Experience. The program starts at 6:00 a.m., from the time the chimpanzees leave their nests until slightly before dark, which allows guests to observe the chimps de-nesting and nesting as well as their other daily activities. The Chimpanzee Experience needs to be booked well in advance.

Kibale is home to 12 other species of primates including black-and-white colobus monkey, red colobus, gray-cheeked mangabey and red-tailed monkey. Some of the other wildlife species include blue duiker, Harvey's red duiker, bushbuck, bushpig and over 100 species of butterflies.

Over 300 species of birds have been recorded, and experienced local guides — with their knowledge of calls and behavior — are invaluable in this challenging bird watching environment. Green-breasted pitta, black bee-eater, white-headed woodhoopoe and the tiny chestnut wattle-eye are among the possible delights for keen observers.

The park is located northeast of Queen Elizabeth National Park, 22 miles (35 km) south of Fort Portal.

ACCOMMODATION — CLASS A/B: • **Ndali Lodge** is perched on a hillside above Nyinambunga Crater Lake, in the heart of Uganda's crater lake region (a 45-minute drive from the park). The lodge has 8 en suite cottages with private verandahs, lounge, dining room, and swimming pool. Boating, nature walks and cultural farm walks are offered.

CLASS B: • **Primate Lodge**, located adjacent to Park Headquarters, has 8 large en suite tents which are privately located long a pathway in the forest. The main building houses the reception, bar and dining room. • **Mantana Safari Camp** is a permanently based mobile camp with 7 tents with en suite bush shower (hot water) and long-drop toilet, located

Top: A porch at Ndali Lodge
Bottom. An interior bedroom at Ndali Lodge

2 miles (3 km) from the park. • **Mountains of the Moon Hotel**, located about an hour's drive from the park in Fort Portal, is a newly renovated colonial-style hotel with 33 en suite rooms, lounge, dining room, 2 bars, conference center, swimming pool and gym. The hotel is set in a tropical garden with views of the Ruwenzori Mountains.

Primate Lodge's tents are raised up to give views of the forest

Southwestern Uganda, Rwanda and Eastern Congo

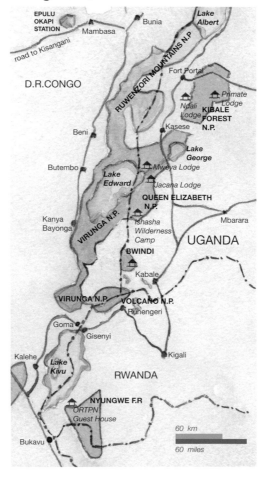

Queen Elizabeth National Park

The park contains about 770-square-miles (1,995-km^2) of tremendous scenic variety, including volcanic craters and crater lakes, grassy plains, swamps, rivers, lakes and tropical forest. The snowcapped Ruwenzori Mountains lie to the north and are not part of the park itself. The park has been extended to give migratory species more protection as they move to and from Kibale Forest.

A 2-hour launch trip on the **Kazinga Channel**, which joins Lakes Edward (Lake Rwitanzige) and George, affords excellent opportunities for viewing hippo and a great variety of waterfowl at close range. Truly marvelous photographic opportunities present themselves from the boat. The launch trip departs from just below Mweya Lodge and should not be missed.

The Katwe-Kikorongo area in the north of the park has several saline lakes. The **Chambura Gorge**, located on the northeast boundary of the park, has a population of chimpanzees. Trekkers descend from the savannah into a tropical rain forest within the gorge where turacos, hornbills and flycatchers abound.

South of the Kazinga Channel, the **Maramagambo Forest** is home for chimpanzees, black-and-white colobus monkeys, red colobus monkeys, blue monkeys, red tailed monkeys and baboons. The **Ishasha** region in the south of the park is famous for its tree-climbing lions.

Elephant are present, as well as buffalo, leopard, sitatunga, giant forest hog, Uganda kob, topi and Defassa waterbuck.

Interestingly enough, there are no giraffe, zebra, impala or rhino, and only a few crocodile have been sighted in the Kazinga Channel, while none have been seen in Lakes Edward or George. The crocodiles are believed to have been killed long ago by volcanic activity.

Guests enjoying a game drive in Queen Elizabeth National Park

An astonishing total of 547 bird species have been recorded here, one of the highest figures for any single protected area in the world. Twelve species of kingfisher, including the giant (the world's largest) and the dwarf (the world's smallest) are to be seen on waterways, in forest, and in the open savannah. There are 17 varieties of nectar-feeding sunbirds, flocks of red-throated bee-eaters, gangs of crow-like piapiacs, families of spectacular Ross's turacos in fruiting trees, and the rare, prehistoric-looking shoebill, which may be sighted along the shores of Lake George and in the Ishasha region.

Queen Elizabeth National Park

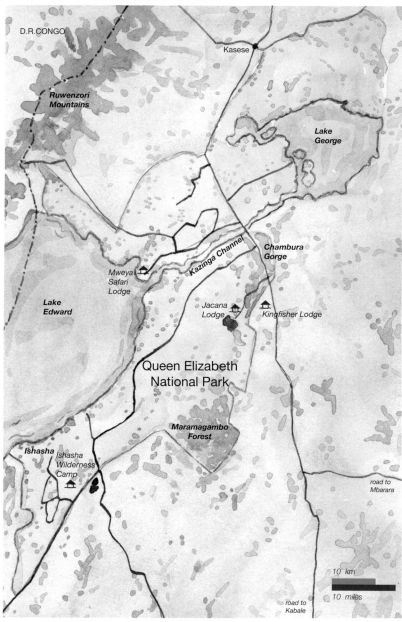

From Kampala, the park is 260 miles (420 km) via Mbarara and 285 miles (460 km) via Fort Portal. A landing strip is located at Mweya for light aircraft; larger planes can land at Kasese.

ACCOMMODATION — CLASS A/B: • **Mweya Safari Lodge**, scenically situated on a high bluff overlooking the Kazinga Channel and Lake Edward, has 49 fan-cooled rooms with en facilities and private verandahs, swimming pool, Kazinga Restaurant and Tembo Safari Bar, and a souvenir shop. • **Jacana Safari Lodge**, located on the edge of the Maramagambo Forest on the banks of Lake Nyamusingire, has 7 luxury en suite wooden chalets and 1 family cottage, swimming pool, restaurant, 2 bars and the Captain's Table (a pon

Mweya Safari Lodge overlooks Lake Edward

toon boat serving as a floating restaurant). Game drives, boating and nature walks are offered. The lodge is located on the butterfly migration route.

CLASS B/C· • **Ishasha Wilderness Camp**, a permanent tented camp located on the banks of the Ntungwe River in the southern sector of the park, features 10 tents with en suite facilities.

CAMPING: Sites are available near Mweya Lodge and along the Kazinga Channel.

Kasese

Kasese is the largest town situated near Queen Elizabeth National Park and Ruwenzori National Park, and it is a good place to purchase supplies.

ACCOMMODATION — CLASS C/D: • **Margherita Hotel** has rooms with private facilities and is located 2 miles (3 km) out of town.

SOUTHERN

Bwindi Impenetrable Forest National Park

The major attraction of the 127-square-mile (330-km^2) Bwindi Impenetrable Forest is the population of over 300 gorillas known to inhabit the park, that are in fact a different sub-species (yet to be named) from the mountain gorillas of Rwanda.

Bwindi is a forest of enormous hardwood trees, giant ferns, tangled undergrowth and hanging vines — the quintessential equatorial jungle. The size and altitudinal range of montane and lowland forests at Bwindi support more species of trees, ferns, birds and butterflies than any other forest in East Africa. It is also the only one inhabited by both chimpanzees and gorillas.

As of this writing, four groups may be visited by up to eight tourists per day — the Mubare, Habinyanja and Rushegura groups from Buhoma Park Headquarters, and the Nkuringo group from Nkuringo Park Headquarters.

Also as of this writing, the Mbare Group (M-Group) consists of 9 gorillas, including one silverback. The Habinyanja Group (H-Group) consists of 23 gorillas, including two silverbacks, the Rushegura Group (R-Group) consists of 15 gorillas including one silverback, and the Nkuringo Group consists of 18 gorillas including two silverbacks. Once found, visitors spend one hour with the gorillas.

Gorillas form themselves into fairly stable groups of 3 to 40. They are active by day and sleep in nests at night.

Gorillas eat leaves, buds and tubers (like wild celery), and are continuously on the move, foraging for their favorite foods. They eat morning and afternoon, interspacing their dining habits with a midday nap.

Searching for gorillas can be likened to an adventurous game of "hide and seek" in which the guides know where they were yesterday but must find their

Trekking through Bwindi Impenetrable Forest

trail again today and follow it. Finding gorillas can almost be guaranteed for those willing to hike 1 to 4 hours or more in search of them.

Each group of visitors is led by a park guide, an armed guard and one tracker. Porters may be hired to carry lunch, drinks, etc., and to assist anyone who may wish to return early.

The search often involves climbing down into gullies, then pulling yourself up steep hills by holding onto vines and bamboo. Even though the pace is slow, you must be in good condition to keep up; the search may take you to altitudes of 3,800 to over 6,500 feet (1,160 to 1,982 m) or more. While this sounds difficult, almost anyone in good physical condition can do it.

The guide looks for nests used the night before, and then tracks them from that spot. Once the gorilla group has been located, he then calms them by making low grunting sounds and imitates them by picking and chewing bits of foliage. Juvenile gorillas are often found playing and tend to approach their human guests. The guide will do his best to keep you the required distance (primarily to help insure the gorillas do not catch any communicable human diseases) of 22 feet (7 m). For the Ugandan Wildlife Authority's "Gorilla rules" brochure, visit *www. igcp.org/pdf/gorillarulesbrochure.pdf.*

Top: Tourists are briefed on the adventure they are about to experience
Bottom: Visitors begin their trek through Bwindi

Adult females are a little more cautious than the juveniles. The dominant male, called a silverback because of the silvery-grey hair on his back, usually keeps a bit further from his human visitors.

In terms of sensitivity toward the great primates and to afford you the best chances of a close and relaxed encounter, simple gorilla-viewing "etiquette" is critical. Never make eye contact with a silverback. If a silverback begins to act aggressively, look down immediately and take a submissive posture by squatting or sitting, or he may take your staring as aggression and charge. The key is

Top: Striking a thoughtful pose
Bottom: A gorilla on the floor of
the forest

to follow the directions of your well-trained guide. Gorillas are herbivores (vegetarians) and will not attack a human unless provoked. Your guides will instruct you not to touch the gorillas because they are susceptible to catching human colds and diseases.

For photography, bring a camera that either does not have a flash or one that can be turned off, as flash photography is not allowed. Videos and digital cameras are excellent for photography as gorillas are often found in the shadow of the forest in low-light conditions. If you are using film, use 400 ASA film or higher; you will probably want to "push" 400 ASA to 800 ASA to get enough light, or even use 1000 and 1600 ASA films. Bring extra data cards or several rolls of film on the trek — you very well may need them! Be sure you do not spend all your time looking through your camera lens as you will miss most of the experience. After spending up to 60 minutes visiting with these magnificent animals, visitors descend to a more open area for a picnic lunch.

Mornings are almost always cool and misty; even if it doesn't rain, you will undoubtedly get wet from hiking and crawling around wet vegetation. Wear a waterproof jacket or poncho (preferably Gortex), leather gloves to protect your hands from stinging nettles, waterproof light- or medium-weight hiking boots, to give you traction on muddy slopes and to keep your feet dry, and a hat. Bring a waterproof pouch for your camera, a water bottle and snacks. Do not wear bright clothes, perfumes, colognes or jewelry, because these distractions may excite the gorillas.

Visiting the gorillas is one of the most rewarding safaris in Africa. The park fees, which are among the highest in Africa, go toward the preservation of these magnificent, endangered creatures.

Other primates resident in the Bwindi forest include chimpanzee, black-and-white colobus monkey, red colobus monkey, grey-cheeked mangabey,

A baby gorilla clings to its mother

Top: Gorilla Forest Camp's open-air lounge
Middle: A tented bedroom at Gorilla Forest Camp
Bottom: Volcanoes Bwindi Lodge

L'Hoest's monkey and blue monkey. Other wildlife includes elephant, giant forest hog and duiker. Among the 345 species of birds recorded are the great blue turaco, yellow-eyed black flycatcher, Lühder's bushshrike, vanga flycatcher, black-faced rufous-warbler, black-throated apalis, and elusive green broadbill.

Park Headquarters is based at Buhoma, a 3-hour drive (67 mi./108 km) from Kabale. Because trekkers must be at the park by 8:30 a.m., it is necessary to overnight at a nearby guesthouse or permanent tented camp. Neither children under 15 years of age nor contagiously ill adults are allowed near the gorillas.

ACCOMMODATION AT BUHOMA–CLASS A: • **Gorilla Forest Camp** is a luxury permanent tented camp situated 5 minutes from the base station at Buhoma with 8 large tents set on raised wooden platforms, with en suite facilities including flushing toilets and a bathtub — great for soaking sore muscles after a long trek. There is also a restaurant and lounge.

CLASS A/B: • **Buhoma Homestead**, located near Park Headquarters, has recently been refurbished and offers 8 raised wooden cottages with en suite facilities.

CLASS B: • **Gorilla Resort** is a new property located walking distance from Park Headquarters with 2 cottages and 4 tents raised on platforms with en suite facilities (including bathtubs), bar, lounge, dining room and elevated campfire deck overlooking the forest.

CLASS B/C: • **Volcanoes Bwindi Lodge**, located about half a mile (1 km) from Park Headquarters, has 8 en suite tents, each with bush showers and short-drop toilets.

CLASS C: • **Mantana Safari Camp** is a permanently based mobile camp with en suite bush shower (hot water) and long-drop toilet.

CLASS D: • **National Park bandas** have rooms with separate facilities.

CAMPING: Campsites are available near the park entrance.

ACCOMMODATION AT NKURINGO: None. As of this writing, a lodge is under construction. Basic hotel accommodation is available at Kisoro, over an hour's drive from the park.

CAMPING: Campsites are available near the park entrance.

Mgahinga Gorilla National Park

Mgahinga Gorilla National Park is situated on the slopes of Mt. Muhabura and Mt. Gahinga in the southwestern corner of Uganda, bordering Rwanda and the Congo.

A joint commission has been set up by Uganda, Rwanda and the Congo to protect the mountain gorilla in the Virunga Mountains where the borders of the three countries meet, and despite human conflict over the past decade, the population of gorillas has actually undergone a slight increase.

One gorilla group has been habituated for tourism, however, as its natural range lies across political borders, gorilla viewing at Mgahinga cannot be guaranteed.

While gorilla tracking is the main activity in this 12-square-mile (34-km²) reserve, other mammals such as the rare golden monkey (a sub-species of the blue monkey), buffalo, black-fronted duiker, leopard, golden cat and serval may be encountered.

A gorilla relaxes in the thick vegetation of Bwindi

Bird life is not prolific, however, gems such as the red-tufted malachite sunbird, white-starred robin and Ruwenzori turaco may be observed in this highland region.

ACCOMMODATION — CLASS B/C: • **Mount Gahinga Rest Camp** has 4 rondavels and 3 tents with private facilities.

CAMPING: By permission of the landowner. There are no facilities.

Kabale

Kabale is Uganda's highest town, situated in a beautiful area called "The Little Switzerland of Africa" in southwestern Uganda.

ACCOMMODATION — TOURIST CLASS: • **White Horse Inn** has rooms with private facilities. • **Victoria Inn** has basic rooms, some with en suite facilities.

Lake Mburo National Park

Lake Mburo National Park is located in southwestern Uganda between Masaka and Mbarara. This approximately 200-square-mile (520-km²) park is named after the largest of the park's 14 lakes.

Located in the rain shadow between Lake Victoria and the Ruwenzori Mountains, the park is characterized by open plains in the north, acacia grassland in the center and lakes and marshes in the south. It is bounded by the Kampala-Mbarara road on the north, Lake Kachera on the east and the Ruizi River on the west.

Herds of zebra, impala (found nowhere else in Uganda) and buffalo enjoy this habitat, and the wetland system around the lake is home to the aquatic sitatunga antelope and hippo. Other game includes leopard, eland, reedbuck, topi, bushbuck and klipspringer.

Birds more typical of dryer Tanzanian savannah such as emerald-spotted dove and bare-faced go-away bird occur alongside lilac-breasted roller and pennant-winged nightjar. The lake's edge is busy with the feeding activities of herons, storks, cormorants, ducks and pelicans.

The park offers bush walks and boating on the lake, and is a good place to overnight when driving between Bwindi and Kampala.

Travelers experience a bushwalk in Lake Mburo National Park

ACCOMMODATION — CLASS A/B: • **Mihingo Lodge** offers 10 spacious tents with thatched roofs, en suite facilities and private verandahs, each individually placed to ensure spectacular views (of either the lake or forest) and privacy. There is an infinity pool and thatched dining room. Massages and game walks are offered.

CLASS B: • **Mantana Tented Camp** has 8 tents with en suite bush showers and toilets. Game drives and escorted bush walks are offered.

CLASS F: • Park bandas with shared facilities are available.

CAMPING: Campsites are available in the park.

ACCOMMODATION NEAR THE RESERVE — CLASS D: • **Lake View Hotel** and the • **Katatumba Resort** are located in Mbarara.

Top: Mihingo Lodge's thatched lounge area
Bottom: Mihingo's thatched tents offer great views

Kampala and Entebbe

Kampala, the capital of Uganda, is built on seven hills. Points of interest include the **Uganda Museum** and the **Kasubi Tombs of the Kabakas** — a shrine to the former Baganda kings and a fine example of Baganda craftsmanship.

For thrill seekers wanting a close encounter with the mighty River Nile, enthralling **white-water rafting** adventures operate from near the town of Jinja, east of Kampala.

The international airport is at Entebbe, about an hour's drive from Kampala.

ACCOMMODATION — DELUXE: • **Emin Pasha** is Uganda's only "boutique" hotel, offering 20 rooms in the colonial country house, a restaurant, bar and swimming pool set in a tropical garden. • **Kampala Serena Hotel** (formerly the *Nile Hotel*) has been completely remodeled and offers 152 air-conditioned rooms and suites with en suite facilities, 24-hour room service, 3 restaurants, a lounge, a large swimming pool and gym. • **Kampala Sheraton Hotel**, situated in an attractive park setting, has 251 newly renovated rooms and suites (most with air-conditioning) with private

The pool area of the Kampala Serena Hotel

facilities and balconies, a health club, several restaurants, 2 bars and a swimming pool.

FIRST CLASS: • **The Lake Victoria Hotel** is located near Entebbe airport overlooking Lake Victoria. The hotel's 99 rooms and suites have been completely renovated and offer en suite facilities, swimming pool, health club and restaurant. • **Imperial Resort Beach Hotel** with its 181 rooms is located in Entebbe, only a short drive from the airport. The hotel offers a 24-hour restaurant, swimming pool and a half mile (1 km) private stretch of beach on Lake Victoria. • **Golf Course Hotel** has 115 air-conditioned en suite rooms, 2 bars, 2 restaurants (1 revolves with views of the city), Olympic-size swimming pool and complementary golf and health club membership. • **Grand Imperial Hotel** is located in the center of town and has 80 air-conditioned rooms with en suite facilities, a swimming pool, health club, shops and restaurants. • **Mamba Point Guesthouse**, located in the suburb of Nakisero, has 6 en suite rooms with mini-bars, gym, sauna, bar and restaurant.

TOURIST CLASS: • **Protea Hotel,** located in the suburb of Kololo, has 70 en suite rooms, bar and restaurant. • **Fairway Hotel** has en suite facilities and overlooks the Kampala Golf Course. • **Hotel Equatoria** has rooms (most of them are air-conditioned) with en suite facilities. • **Hotel Africana** is a standard 3-star hotel only 3 minutes from Kampala's city center and 40 minutes from Entebbe. • **Fang Fang Hotel** is located in the hub of Kampala's business district and offers air-conditioned rooms and a restaurant on site. • **Speke Hotel** had 50 en suite rooms and several restaurants to choose from. The hotel is located close to Kampala's city center. • **Imperial Botanical Hotel** overlooks Lake Victoria in Entebbe and has a restaurant and swimming pool for guests' enjoyment.

Ngamba Island Camp

Ngamba Island (Chimp Island)

Ngamba Island Chimpanzee Sanctuary is situated in Lake Victoria, 90 minutes by boat from Entebbe Pier. The tropical 100-acre (40-hectare) island is home to approximately 42 orphaned chimpanzees, which are free to roam the forest during the day and return to the holding facility at night.

Chimpanzee viewing is the main activity. There are 2 daily viewing times during which you can watch the chimps being fed. A raised viewing platform allows you to view the chimps very closely and provides great photographic opportunities. Day visits and overnight stays are allowed but must be booked in advance. Swimming, kayaking, bird watching, sunset cruises and fishing are other optional activities.

ACCOMMODATION: CLASS C:
• **Ngamba Island Camp** has 4 tents set on raised wooden platforms with en suite facilities.

Top: Visitors at Ngamba Island Chimpanzee Sanctuary
Bottom: One of the adorable orphaned chimps at Ngamba

Rwanda

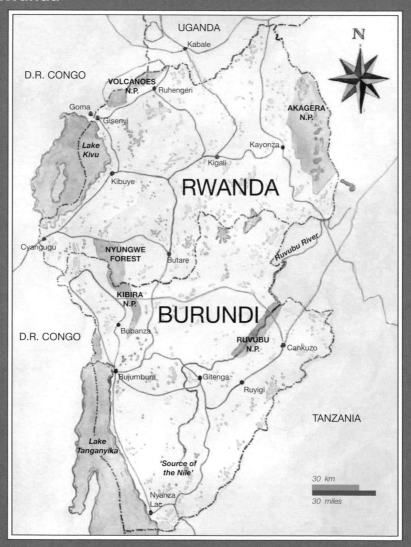

Rwanda is characterized by rolling hills and volcanic peaks with altitudes varying from 3,960 feet (1,207m) to 14,786 feet (4,507m) above sea level. Mt. Karisimbi in the Virunga range is the highest peak. Both Rwanda and Burundi are former Belgian colonies, previously united as Ruanda-Urundi. Although the country covers only 10,160 square miles (26,638-km²) it has a population of close to 10 million, making these fertile landscapes among the most densely populated in the world. Kinyarwanda is the predominant language, while French and English are widely spoken. The currency used is the Franc.

Rwanda
Country Highlights

- Gorilla Trekking!!!! A once-in-a-lifetime experience that will take your breath away! As there are only a few hundred of these endangered mountain gorillas remaining, the time to visit them is NOW!
- Travel to Nyungwe Forest to see 13 species of primates including habituated chimpanzees.
- Enjoying a sundowner cruise on Lake Kivu, one of the most beautiful lakes on the continent.
- Kigali's Genocide Museum and Women for Women Organization.
- The Rwandan government has created a very safe and inviting environment for international tourists, who are warmly welcomed by its people.

Best Parks and Reserves to Visit   **Best Times to Go**
Volcanoes National Park...............................December to March /
June to September
Nyungwe Forest ....December to March /
June to September

Best Accommodations
Sabyinyo Silverback Lodge, Lake Kivu Serena Hotel

RWANDA

Appropriately called "The Land of a Thousand Hills," Rwanda is predominantly grassy highlands and hills, with altitudes above sea level varying from a low of 3,960 feet (1,207 m) to Mt. Karisimbi, the highest of a range of extinct volcanoes in the northwest, which reaches 14,786 feet (4,507 m). Lake Kivu forms part of the border with the Congo and is one of the most beautiful lakes in Africa. In fact, most visitors are impressed by the beauty of the country as a whole.

Also called "The Country of Perpetual Spring," Rwanda's comfortable climate is temperate and mild with an average daytime temperature of 77°F (25°C). The main rainy season is from mid-February to mid-May, and the shorter one is from mid-October to mid-December.

Almost all (97%) of the people live in self-contained compounds and work the adjacent land. Over half of the population is Christian (most of which are Catholic), though many people follow traditional African beliefs. Hutu (Bahutu) and Tutsi (Batusi) tribes make up the majority of the population. The Tutsi long dominated the Hutu farmers in a feudal system analogous to that of medieval England. Their feudal system was second in size only to Ethiopia's, and was based on cattle.

Because of its physical isolation and the fearsome reputation of its people, Rwanda was not affected by the slave and ivory trade from Zanzibar during the 1800s. The area became a German protectorate in 1899 and in 1916 was occupied by the Belgians.

Following World War I, Rwanda and Burundi were mandated by the League of Nations to Belgium as the territory of Ruanda-Urundi. Full independence for Rwanda and Burundi was achieved on July 1, 1962.

Rwanda — "The Land of a Thousand Hills"

In 1994, a civil war (actually begun in 1990) between the Hutus and the Tutsis resulted in over a million deaths and even more refugees fleeing to neighboring Congo and Tanzania. The Tutsi forces were victorious, and many refugees have returned.

Rwanda is a remarkable country that has stabilized and become a role model in good governance in a little over a decade, under the leadership of President Kagame. The country aims to become the "Singapore of Africa". Crime and litter are almost non-existent. Even plastic bags are banned, and on the last Saturday of the month (Umunganda Day) the entire country does communal work for public good — from street cleaning to building homes for genocide survivors.

International tourists have returned to gorilla trek in Volcanoes National Park (Parc National des Volcans) and to visit other areas of the country.

High population density is at the root of Rwanda's economic problems. Almost all arable land is under cultivation. Tourism is now the country's major foreign exchange earner after tea and coffee.

French, English, and Kinyarwanda are widely spoken, and Kiswahili is spoken in the major towns and regions close to the borders of Uganda and Tanzania.

🐾 WILDLIFE AND WILDLIFE AREAS

Mountain gorilla trekking in Volcanoes National Park is by far Rwanda's major international attraction. After the release of the feature film, *Gorillas in the Mist*, about the late Dian Fossey's pioneering work habituating the gorillas, interest in gorilla trekking reached new heights and continues to grow yearly.

THE NORTH

Volcanoes National Park
(Parc National des Volcans)

Volcanoes National Park is home to the mountain gorilla, first documented by Europeans in the early 1900s. The peaks of the Virunga Mountains, heavily forested extinct volcanoes, serve as a border with the Congo and Uganda and are part of the watershed between the Congo and Nile river systems.

The 62-square-mile (160-km²) park supports several vegetation zones, from lush bamboo stands to luxuriant mountain forest to Afro-alpine. From 9,020 to

Top: Beginning the search for gorillas
Bottom: Climbers take a break to enjoy the view

10,825 feet (2,750 to 3,300 m), primary forest is dominated by hagenia trees growing 30 to 60 feet (9 to 18 m) in height. Hagenia have twisted trunks and low branches covered with lichen, out of which epiphytic orchids, moss and ferns often grow.

Volcanoes National Park borders both Virunga National Park in the Congo and the Mgahinga Gorilla National Park in Uganda. The park receives a high amount of rainfall, over 70 inches (1,800 mm) per year. Daytime temperatures at Park Headquarters range from 70 to 90°F (21 to 32°C).

Other wildlife in the park includes the blue monkey, golden monkey (a rare subspecies of blue monkey), black-fronted duiker (very common), bushbuck, giant forest hog, African civet, genet, and buffalo. One hundred nineteen species of birds have been recorded, including

Volcanoes National Park

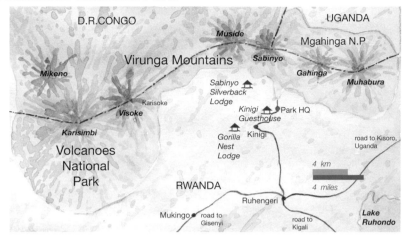

spectacular mountain turacos (the Rwenzori turaco is the most common) and forest francolin.

The mountain gorilla grows to 6 feet (1.8 m) in height and weighs up to 450 pounds (205 kg). For a description of gorilla trekking, see the "Dwindi Impenetrable Forest" section of the chapter on Uganda.

There have been some changes to the dynamics of the gorilla groups that are acclimated for tourist visits and several new ones have been added. As of this writing, travelers can visit Group Sabyinyo, Group Susa, the Amahoro Group, Group 13, Group Umubano, Group Hirwa and Group Kwitonda. The makeup of the gorilla groups were as follows: the Susa Group — 38 members including four silverbacks; The Sabyinyo Group — 8 individuals including the largest of the silverbacks (named Guhonda); The Amahoro Group — 17 members including one silverback; Group 13 — 23 members including one silverback (it had 13 members

Top: Thick vegetation poses a new challenge for climbers
Bottom: A gorilla's soulful eyes

Top: Getting up close and personal with a mountain gorilla
Middle: A gorilla mom, sister and twin babies
Bottom: A gorilla family goes about its business undisturbed by the trekker

during the 1980s, when the group was habituated); The Umubano Group — 9 members including one silverback; The Hirwa Group — 12 members including one silverback; and The Kwitonda Group — 16 individuals with one silverback.

A maximum of eight tourists can visit each gorilla group daily.

For an in-depth treatise on gorillas and this region beautifully presented with color photographs, I suggest you pick up a copy *of Mountain Gorillas: Biology, Conservation and Coexistence* by Gene Eckhart (University Press).

Visitors check in at the Volcanoes National Park Headquarters, which is 20 minutes from Ruhengeri, at 7:00 a.m. where they will meet their guides. At that time, guides will direct travelers to the various departure points where the searches begin. Departure points can be a 30 to 40-minute drive from Headquarters and difficult to find if you are not with a knowledgeable driver. Before departing Park Headquarters, make sure that you have the necessary vouchers.

Please note that children under 15 years of age or anyone having the flu or other sickness that might be transmitted to the gorillas are not allowed to visit the gorillas. Permits must be purchased in advance through an international tour operator, or in Kigali where a copy of the first three pages of a visitor's passport must be presented at the time of purchase. As there are only 40 to 56 people allowed to gorilla trek each day, you need to purchase permits for specific days well in advance (several months is recommended).

The most popular time to visit the gorillas is during the dry seasons, which occur mid-June to September and December to March.

It is difficult to get to the park and departure points unless you have pre-booked a safari (the best option) or rent your own vehicle (expensive). There is no public transportation from Ruhengeri to the Park Headquarters or to the trek departure points.

Mountain Climbing

Hiking in the beautiful Virunga Mountains is an adventure in itself. Trails lead to the craters or peaks of the park's five volcanoes, upward through the unique high vegetation zones of bamboo, hagenia-hypericum forests, giant lobelia and senecio, and finally to alpine meadows. Views from the top, which overlook the lush Rwandan valleys and into the Congo and Uganda, are spectacular.

Some travelers spend a day or two of gorilla trekking interspersed with hikes to one or more of the volcanoes.

Karisimbi (14,786 ft./4,507 m), which is occasionally snowcapped, is Rwanda's highest mountain. It is the most arduous ascent, requiring two days from the Visoke departure point. The night may be spent in a metal hut at about 12,000 feet (3,660 m).

Visoke (12,175 ft./3,711 m) has a beautiful crater lake and requires four hours of hiking, up a steep trail from the Visoke departure point, to reach

Top: Cameras ready! Gorilla trekkers enjoy a maximum of one hour with the primates
Middle: Two gorillas survey the scene
Bottom: A baby gorilla is never far from mom

the summit. The walk around the crater rim is highly recommended. Allow seven hours for the entire trip.

Lake Ngezi (9,843 ft./3,000 m), a small, shallow crater lake, is the easiest hike in the park; it takes only three to four hours round-trip from the Visoke departure point.

Sabyinyo (11,922 ft./3,634 m) can be climbed in five to six hours, starting at Park Headquarters near Kinigi. A metal hut is located just before you reach the lava beds. The final section is along a narrow, rocky ridge with steep drops on both sides.

Gahinga (11,398 ft./3,474 m) and **Muhabura** (13,540 ft./4127 m) are both reached from the departure point at Gasiza. The trail rises to a hut in poor condition on the saddle between the two mountains. Gahinga's summit can be reached in four hours, while two days are recommended to reach the summit of Muhabura.

A park guide must accompany each group, but porters are optional. Should you encounter gorillas on your hike, you may not leave the path to follow them. You may only track gorillas if you have previously purchased the proper permits.

Top: Sabyinyo Silverback Lodge offers great views of the mountains
Bottom: Sabyinyo Silverback Lodge's luxury accommodations

ACCOMMODATION — CLASS A+:
• A new small luxury lodge with 6 standard suites and 2 2-bedroom suites is being designed at the time of this writing and is scheduled to open in mid-2009.

CLASS A: • **Sabyinyo Silverback Lodge** is adjacent to the Parc National des Volcans and is comprised of a central building, with reception, bar, dining room, library/games room, community awareness center and shop. There are 5 rooms, 1 family cottage and 2 suite cottages, each with a private veranda, a sitting room with fireplace, bedroom, dressing room and a large modern bathroom. The family suite has an extra bedroom and bathroom incorporated. The lodge is an innovative conservation project conceived and constructed by the African Wildlife Foundation in which the local community is to receive economic benefits as a result of visiting tourists. • **Jack Hanna's Guesthouse** is a ranch-style home with 2 en suite bedrooms, located adjacent to Gorilla Nest Lodge.

CLASS B: • **Gorilla Nest Lodge** is about 1.5 miles (2 kms) from the Park. It currently has 45 standard rooms (with shower) and 2 suites with bath and shower. Renovations are scheduled, and the property may be upgraded in the near future.
• **Virunga Lodge** is an eco-lodge, set on a hillside with views of the Virunga volcanoes and Lakes Ruhondo and Bulera. The lodge consists of 8 bandas with en suite bathrooms, a bar with fireplace and dining room, and is located an hour drive from Park Headquarters.

The view from the patio of Sabyinyo Silverback Lodge

CLASS C: • **ASOFERWA Guest House** has 15 simple rooms with en suite facilities. • **Hotel Muhabura** is a very rustic hotel with 10 simple rooms and 2 pavilions with bathrooms en suite, and a bar and dining room. The hotel is located about 10 miles (16 km) from Park Headquarters which takes about 20 minutes to drive. • **La Palme Hotel**, located in Ruhengeri about a 20 minute drive from Park Headquarters, has 12 rooms with en suite facilities.

CAMPING: Campsites at Park Headquarters are near Kinigi, and cold shower and toilet facilities may be available. Beware of thieves.

Gisenyi — Lake Kivu

Gisenyi is a picturesque resort on the northern shores of beautiful Lake Kivu. Lake Kivu has some nice, white beaches and is believed to have little or no bilharzias (a disease). Crocodiles are absent from the lake due to volcanic action, eons ago, that wiped them out. Beware, however, of rising sulpher gas, which can be fatal. Gisenyi is a 75-minute drive from Volcanoes National Park, and is well worth the visit if time permits.

Catch of the day on the shores of Lake Kivu

ACCOMMODATION — DELUXE: • **Lake Kivu Serena Hotel** is located on the shores of Lake Kivu, the sixth largest lake in Africa. Accommodation comprises of 66 air-conditioned rooms, including 6 luxury suites, 23 family rooms. The restaurant offers a stunning view of the lake as you have breakfast, lunch or dinner. The hotel also has a gym, outdoor swimming pool and two tennis courts.

FIRST CLASS: • **Hotel Palm Beach** has 20 rooms, some with en suite facilities, and is located on the lakeshore drive. • **Stipp Hotel** is popular for its charming courtyard garden and pool area. The hotel offers 25 en suite rooms, restaurant and massage facilities.

TOURIST CLASS: • **Ubumwe Hotel** is a basic hotel featuring 15 rooms with en suite facilities.

Kibuye

Kibuye, located on Lake Kivu midway between Gisenyi and Cyangugu, is a small town with an attractive beach. Be sure not to miss the over 330 foot (100 m) high **Ndaba Waterfall** (Les Chutes des Ndaba), not far from Kibuye.

ACCOMMODATION — TOURIST CLASS: • **Centre Bethanie Mission** has 24 rooms, half of which have facilities en suite. • **Moriah Hill Resort** has 15 en suite rooms facing Lake Kivu, and a restaurant.

Nyungwe Forest National Park
(La Foret de Nyungwe)

The Nyungwe Forest is one of the most biologically diverse, high-altitude rain forests in Africa. Located in southwestern Rwanda and bordering the country of Burundi, this 375-square-mile (970-km²) reserve is home for 13 species of primates including a rare subspecies of black-and-white colobus monkey (documented in groups of several hundred), L'Hoest's monkey, blue monkey, grey-cheeked mangabey and habituated chimpanzees.

In addition to a variety of butterflies and more than 100 different species of orchids, more than 275 species of birds have been recorded. Some of the over 250 species of trees and shrubs grow to over 165 feet (50 m) in height. This mountainous national park has a variety of habitats, including wetlands, forested valleys and bamboo zones. Elevation ranges from 5,250 to 9,680 feet (1,600 to 2,950 m).

Although Nyungwe Forest National Park is situated at a lower altitude and receives less rain than Volcanoes National Park, hiking is more difficult in Nyungwe. The vegetation at Nyungwe is much thicker, and many slopes are steeper, if not impossible, to ascend. Colobus and the other primates may be difficult to approach closely. Chimpanzee trekking is gaining popularity.

ACCOMMODATION — CLASS C/D: • **ORTPN Guesthouse** (also referred to as *Gisakura Guesthouse*), located on the southwest edge of the forest, has 9 basic rooms most of them with en suite facilities. • **Peace Guesthouse** has 30 basic en suite rooms.

CAMPING: Campsites are available at the Park Headquarters in the middle of the forest.

Please note: A new property, Nyungwe Eco-Lodge is scheduled to be completed in 2009.

Butare

Located in southern Rwanda, not far from the border with Burundi, Butare is the intellectual capital of Rwanda. There you will find the **National Museum** (good archaeology and ethnology exhibits) and the **National University** and **National Institute of Scientific Research** (ask about folklore dances). Several craft centers are located in villages within 10 miles (16 km) of Butare. **The Ballet National du Rwanda** is located in Nyanza, 22 miles (35 km) from Butare.

ACCOMMODATION — CLASS C: • **Hotel Credo** has 25 rooms with en suite facilities, tennis court and swimming pool. • **Hotel Faucon** has 13 rooms with en suite facilities. • **Hotel Ibis** has 15 rooms with en suite facilities. • **Le Petit Prince Hotel** has 23 rooms with en suite facilities.

CENTRAL AND EAST

Kigali

The capital of Rwanda, Kigali is the commercial center of the country. A number of very good restaurants are located in the first class hotels. The Genocide Museum and Women for Women Organization are well worth visiting.

ACCOMMODATION — DELUXE: • **Kigali Serena Hotel** (previously the *Kigali Intercontinental*) is located a few miles outside the city center. It has 104 rooms and suites with en suite facilities, health/fitness center, restaurant, patio bar and a swimming pool.

The Women for Women Organization in Kigali

Top: Kigali Serena Hotel
Bottom: A standard bedroom at the
Kigali Serena Hotel

FIRST CLASS: • **Kigali Novotel Umubano**, located a few miles outside the city center, has 96 rooms with en suite facilities, swimming pool and tennis courts. • **Hotel des Mille Collines** has 112 rooms and suites with en suite facilities and a swimming pool. • **Hotel Gorillas** has 31 en suite rooms, a restaurant and bar for guests. • **Garni du Centre** offers 11 rooms with en suite facilities, breakfast is included in room rate. • **Stip Hotel** has 50 rooms with en suite facilities, restaurant, swimming pool and gym.

TOURIST CLASS: • **Hotel Chez Lando**, located 2 miles (3 km) from the airport, has 42 rooms with en suite facilities. • **Hotel Isimbi**, located in the center of Kigali, has 26 rooms with en suite facilities. • **Hotel Okapi**, located in the center of Kigali, has 24 rooms with en suite facilities. • **Ninzi Hill** is 10 minutes from the airport and offers 15 rooms with en suite facilities, restaurant and business center with internet connection.

Akagera National Park

Akagera National Park is located about a 2-hour drive from Kigali in northeastern Rwanda along the Akagera River (a Nile affluent) bordering Tanzania. This 348-square-mile (900-km²) park is a scenic combination of savannah, woodland and wetlands comprised of a dozen lakes linked by small channels and papyrus swamps.

Wildlife includes the world's largest antelope, the Cape Eland, and some of the largest buffalo in Africa. Other wildlife includes zebra, giraffe, hippo, crocodile, lion, leopard, impala, Defassa waterbuck, eland, sable antelope, bushbuck, oribi, roan antelope and black-backed jackal. Unfortunately much of the wildlife was killed during the civil war in the '90s, but it is slowly coming back. Birdlife is excellent with over 525 different species of birds recorded — including the papyrus gonolek and the rare shoebill.

The best time to visit the park is during the dry season July to September, while February, June and October are also good.

ACCOMMODATION — CLASS B: • **Akagera Game Lodge**, located inside the park overlooking beautiful Lake Ihema, has 60 standard rooms and 2 suites with private facilities, restaurant, bar and swimming pool.

Seychelles

Seychelles

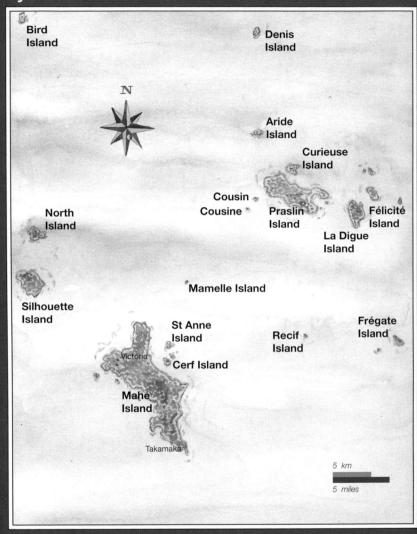

The Seychelles comprise 115 islands which cover a collective land area of just 171 square miles (433 km²) in the western Indian Ocean. Mahé, the largest of the islands is located 4 degrees south of the equator. The islands are made of either granite or coral, with the former having peaks rising up to 2,970 feet (905 m). Most of the coraline or "outer" islands are just a few feet above sea level. Due to its geographic isolation, most of the flora and fauna is unique, but plants and animals introduced by man have greatly altered the landscape and endangered many species. The resident population is less than 100,000 with Creole, French and English widely spoken.

SEYCHELLES

The Seychelles are unspoiled islands that have a charm all their own, complimented by the genuine friendliness of the people. To help maintain the unspoiled nature of the islands, construction of new hotels (additional beds) is strictly limited. The beauty and variety of the islands make the Seychelles a vacation in itself or an excellent add-on to any safari. With numerous scheduled flights it's easy to hop from island to island. The Seychelles is certainly a fabulous place for a honeymoon!

The Seychelles are comprised of 115 islands spread over an Exclusive Economic Zone (EEZ) of no less than 500,000-square-miles (1.3 million-km^2) in the Western Indian Ocean, situated northeast of Madagascar and approximately 1,100 miles (1,800 km) east of Kenya. Mahé, the largest of the islands, is located 4 degrees south of the equator.

Forty granitic and 75 coraline islands make up the Seychelles. The granitic group are mountainous islands with peaks rising up to 2,970 feet (905 m) and surrounded by narrow coastal strips. These include the three main and most visited islands of Mahé, Praslin and La Digue. Félicité, Frégate, Silhouette and North Island are smaller granite islands with only one resort on each island. Many of the islands in the coraline group, or "outer islands," are only about 3 feet (1 m) above sea level. Visitors should consider including at least one granite and one coral island in their stay.

The crystal blue water of the Seychelles is a snorkeler's paradise

The people of the Seychelles are a mixture of African, Asian and European cultures. About 85% of the population resides on Mahé, the largest and the most economically important island in the Seychelles archipelago. About 89% of the population is Roman Catholic, 7% belongs to the Church of England, and the balance divided among Pentecostal, Seventh-Day Adventists, Jehovah's Witnesses, Hindus and Muslims.

Creole cuisine, like the origins of the racially mixed backgrounds, brings together a concoction of interesting recipes from the far corners of the world. Delicate local touches, such as varieties of curries with wonderful spices from India, stir fries and rice from Asia, and garlic-flavored dishes from France, are all enjoyed on the Seychelles. Locally brewed beers are Seybrew and Eku.

The tranquil beaches and swaying palms are just two of the reasons people visit the Seychelles

The Seychelles is very diverse, with something to suit a great variety of travelers. Accommodations vary from luxurious five-star hotels and island resorts the less expensive family-owned guest houses, most with fewer than 15 rooms.

The islands have a tropical climate, which is generally warm and humid year-round. There are two tradewinds: The Southeast Tradewinds blow from May to September, during which it is relatively dry (although possibility of rain is year round), and the Northwest Tradewinds blow from November to March. The rainy season starts at the end of November and continues until the beginning of February. The temperature throughout the year varies between 75 to 90° F (24° to 32° C). The average monthly rainfall in January is 15.2 inches (386 mm) and in July is 3.3 inches (84 mm). Fortunately, the Seychelles lies outside the cyclone belt.

There is much speculation about the early discovery of the Seychelles by Arab traders but no documentary evidence exists. Vasco de Gama visited part of the archipelago, the islands known as the Amirantes, in 1502. In 1756, the French were the first to colonize the islands, on which they established spice plantations. The English conquered the islands in 1794 and abolished slavery in 1835. In 1903 it became a British Crown Colony and claimed it's independence in 1976. Tourism is the major foreign exchange earner.

🐾 WILDLIFE AND WILDLIFE AREAS

Seychelles exhibits unique flora and fauna, due to its geographic isolation. Nearly 50% of the land area has been set aside for national parks, nature reserves and World Heritage sites. The Aldabra Atoll is a World Heritage site, boasting a population of 150,000 giant land tortoises—more than can be found on the Galapagos. Though the giant Aldabran tortoise (*Geochelone gigantea*) originated in the Aldabran Islands, a small breeding colony was set up in the Seychelles islands to ensure its chance of survival.

Giant Aldabran tortoises can grow a carapace as long as 56 inches (140 cm). They can live to be 150 years of age. The tortoises found on mainland Africa are smaller than these island giants and are found mostly in tropical areas. They are primarily herbivores.

The raised shell of terrestrial tortoises, such as the Aldabran, probably evolved from the flatter shell of their aquatic ancestry for two reasons: 1) as a defense against predators, who otherwise might have been able to crush the reptile in their jaws, and 2) to provide for increased lung capacity, since they have proportionately larger lungs than do turtles.

The Seychelles has five species of frogs (four are endemic), including the smallest frog in the world, which rarely reaches 1 inch (2 cm,) at maturity. Marine life is prolific, and places like Alphonse and Desroches provide some of the best diving in the world.

The flora is as exotic and unique as the islands themselves. The most exotic and strangest palm in the world is the famous "coco-de-mer," which has the largest and heaviest seed in the world.

There are seven established walking trails in the Seychelles — six on Mahé Island and one on La Digue Island. These walks offer great opportunities to enjoy the flora and fauna unique to these beautiful islands.

Bird Life

The Seychelles are the "Galapagos" of the Indian Ocean. Many tropical species of birds are not afraid of man and can be approached within a few feet (less than a meter). Colonies of over 200,000 sooty terns can be found nesting on some of the islands.

For twitchers (keen birders), these islands offer an opportunity to add several species to their lists.

The Seychelles offers more than just beautiful beaches

Birdwatchers will be well entertained by 10 endemic species and 17 endemic sub-species, which are found on the granitic islands, plus 3 endemic ones found on the coraline islands. The rare black parrot is found only on Praslin and the Seychelles black paradise flycatcher is found only on La Digue. Other rarities include magpie robins and the Seychelles fody.

Fly Fishing

The Seychelles Islands are a superb saltwater fly-fishing destination for both "flats" and blue water species. The coral islands to the south of Mahé is the region where most of the flats are to be found. St. Josephs, Poivre, Farquhar and Cosmeledo groups all offer excellent fishing for bonefish and giant trevally. St. Francois is rated by experts as one of the best bonefish destinations in the world. The area's potential has only recently been recognized, and a reasonable fisherman can expect to catch in excess of 20 of these elusive fish per day. Deeper water fishing on the drop-off, using heavier, faster-sinking lines, is productive. Several species of trevally are to be found in one spot off of Alphonse. Other species to be found are bonito, rainbow runner, dogtooth tuna, dorado, wahoo, sailfish, milkfish and triggerfish.

Access to the best areas is not easy. Places like Alphonse have a lodge where fishermen can be based and from which all the different types of fishing are available. To reach the rest of the areas, live-aboard sailing or motor yachts are the answer. The distances are formidable but the rewards are great.

Mahé Island

Mahé is the largest and most developed island, and it is the economic and political center of the Seychelles. The island covers 59-square-miles (152-km^2)

Aerial view of Mahé, Seychelles

and is 17 miles (27 km) long and 8 miles (12 km) wide. It offers a variety of hotels and guesthouses and many lovely beaches. Both the international airport and major harbor (Victoria) are found on Mahé.

The interior of the island is mountainous, rising to 2,668 feet (905 m) at Morne Seychellois. One of the most scenic drives on the island is from Victoria through the highlands, south of Morne Seychellois National Park, to Port Glaud on the west coast. Île Thérèse, located off the west coast of Mahé, is home to a colony of giant tortoises.

There are 75 white sandy beaches, the most popular of which is Beau Vallon Beach, a 2-mile (3-km), crescent-shaped beach on the northwest coast. Grand' Anse is a good beach for surfing. Anse Royale is a 2-mile (3-km) beach protected by a coral reef and located on the southeast coast of the island. There is a better opportunity to find deserted beaches on the south side of the island than on the more developed north side.

Mahé provides hikers several trails, including 1) Victoria to Beau Vallon Bay to Victoria, 2) The Trois Freres Trail, which runs through Morne Seychellois National Park to the summit, 3) La Réserve and Brulee, which lead through a palm forest, 4) Danzil, which takes you to the secluded beach Anse Major, 5) Val Riche to Copolia, which runs through Morne Seychellois National Park, and 6) the Tea Factory, which goes to Morne Blanc in Morne Seychellois National Park.

Victoria

Victoria is the capital city and the major port of the Seychelles. Places of interest include the market, the Capuchin House, built in colonial Portuguese style, the State House, a fine example of Seychelles architecture, the Cathedral of the Immaculate Conception, the National Museum and the Botanical Gardens. The "Pirates Arms" bar and restaurant is a popular meeting point.

Morne Seychellois National Park

This 11-square-mile (30-km²) park covers much of northwest Mahé, with altitudes ranging from sea level to 2,969 feet (905 m). There are hiking trails from Sans Souci Road to Copolia (1,630 ft./497 m), Morne Blanc (2,188 ft./ 667 m) and Trois Freres (2,293 ft./699 m).

Bird life includes the blue pigeon, Seychelles bulbul, Seychelles kestrel, cave swiftlet and Seychelles white-eye.

Flora in the park includes five different species of palm trees, the vanilla orchid (*Vanilla phalaenopsis*), the extremely rare jellyfish tree (*Medusagyne oppositifolia*) and the bwa-d-fer (*Vateria seychellarum*).

Top: One of Banyan Tree's ultra-exclusive villas
Middle: Spectacular views are found in every room of Maia Resort villas
Bottom: A bedroom at Maia Resort

ACCOMMODATION ON MAHÉ — DELUXE: • **Banyan Tree**, located on the southwest coast overlooking Anse Intendance, has 60 air-conditioned, luxury 1- and 2-bedroom villas with private swimming pools and sundecks, gym, spa, 3 restaurants and a communal swimming pool. The Beach Villas are more spacious, and have an outdoor jacuzzi, steam shower room and feature larger private swimming pools than the Hillside Villas. • **Maia Resort** offers 30 spacious en suite villas scattered throughout the lush hills and beach. The resort has a luxury spa, restaurant, and swimming pool. Water activities can be arranged on site. • **Hilton Seychelles Northolme Resort & Spa** offers forest and ocean view villa rooms and suites. There are 2 restaurants, 2 bars, and a spa. • **The Four Seasons** is building a brand new resort on Mahé. Opening date and details are unknown as of this writing.

FIRST CLASS: • **Le Meridien Fisherman's Cove**, located on Beau Vallon Bay in the northwest part of Mahé Island, has 44 air-conditioned rooms and cottages with their own private balcony or terrace, plus 26 new suites — all with en suite facilities. The hotel offers 2 restaurants, a bar overlooking the bay, swimming pool, tennis court and many other recreational activities. • **Sunset Beach Hotel**, situated on Mahé's northwest coast, offers a good standard of accommodation, particularly in the junior suites. The hotel is set on a rocky promontory with a pathway that leads down to a secluded sandy cove. It has 29 air-conditioned rooms with baths, and the junior suites have sitting areas. Facilities include a restaurant, bar, boutique and swimming pool. • **The Wharf Hotel and Marina** is conveniently located 5 minutes from the airport. It offers 15 en suite rooms and 1 suite, 40 berth marina, pool, restaurant and bar.

TOURIST CLASS: • **Sun Resort** is a short stroll from Beau Vallon Beach. It has 20 air-conditioned rooms with shower, sitting area, and a balcony or patio overlooking the swimming pool. The restaurant serves Creole cuisine, and there is a small bar and coffee shop. • **Lazare Picault** overlooks Baie Lazare on the southwest coast and has 14 rooms, with en suite facilities, perched on the hillside.

Top: Northolme Resort & Spa's infinity pool
Bottom: Surrounded by lush vegetation, an example of one of Northolme Resort's villas

Sainte Anne Marine National Park

Located east of Victoria, Sainte Anne Marine National Park includes 6 small islands and the waters that surround them. Île Ronde (Round Island), Île au Cerf and Île Moyenne islands have lovely coral beds and are excellent for snorkeling or exploring in glass-bottom boats. Among the granite islands, Sainte Anne Island is the most important nesting site for hawksbill turtles.

ACCOMMODATION ON SAINTE ANNE ISLAND — DELUXE: • **Sainte Anne Resort and Spa** is located on Sainte Anne Island, a 494-acre (200-hectare) private island and nature reserve in the Marine National Park. The resort is 10 minutes away by private launch from Mahé. The 87 luxurious sea-facing villas, some with private pools, are spread along the island's pristine beaches. Two gourmet restaurants, a Clarins Spa, and a full range of water sports are available.

ACCOMMODATION ON ÎLE AU CERF — DELUXE: • **Cerf Island Resort** offers 12 luxury villas with views of the tropical gardens or Indian Ocean. Each is fully equipped with en suite bathrooms, air-conditioning, satellite television, mini-bar and private terrace. The resort boasts a fine dining restaurant, infinity pool, pool bar, beach-side dining, a lounge and mini spa. The property is located at the entrance of the Marine Park.

Praslin Island

Praslin, a granite island located 25 miles (40 km) northeast of Mahé, is the second largest island in the archipelago. Praslin is 6.5 miles (10.5 km) long and 2.3 miles (3.7 km) wide. The island is less mountainous than Mahé but still has hills over 1,150 feet (350 m) high. Beaches are less crowded than on Mahé, and Anse Lazio is considered the best beach on the island. Praslin is home to the famous Vallée de Mai National Park, which was declared a World Heritage Site by UNESCO in 1984.

Vallée de Mai National Park

The Vallée de Mai National Park contains over 4,000 coco-de-mer palm trees that grow in excess of 100 feet (30 m) in height and have a unique double-lobed coconut in the provocative shape of the human female pelvic region. At 20 pounds (9 kg), this is considered to be the world's largest fruit and takes over 10 years to ripen! Many myths and legends have arisen from the presence of this fruit, thought by some to be the original "forbidden fruit," and the island is considered the proverbial "Garden of Eden."

Allow 2 or 3 hours for your walk in this lovely park. The sale of the coco-de-mer (a unique souvenir, indeed) is strictly controlled, and a specimen may be purchased at the park or from other shops on the island. We were also amazed at the gigantic size of some of the palm fronds and were lucky enough to spot the rare black parrot on our visit.

Curieuse Marine National Park

Curieuse Marine National Park includes the waters between Curieuse Island and the northwestern coast of Praslin. The park covers 5-square-miles (14-km^2) and reaches depths of 100 feet (30 m). A large colony of giant land tortoises is protected in Laraie Bay.

Lemuria Resort sits poised on two pristine beaches

ACCOMMODATION ON PRASLIN — DELUXE: • **Lemuria Resort** is situated in the northwest, straddling 2 beaches — Anse Kerlan and Petite Anse Kerlan. This luxury resort has 96 suites plus 8 2-bedroom villas with sea-facing balconies or patios.

Facilities include a choice of 3 restaurants, bars, lounge, health spa, boutique, children's club, swimming pool, tennis courts, 18-hole championship golf course and water sports. There is a third, more private beach located nearby.

FIRST CLASS: • **L'Archipel** has 30 air-conditioned rooms and suites with en suite facilities, 2 restaurants, lounge, bar, swimming pool, gym, boutique, and free water sports including windsurfing, canoeing and snorkeling. • **La Réserve**, located on Anse Petite Cour, has 40 elegant air-conditioned Superior and Deluxe rooms with en suite facilities. The hotel offers a weekly Sundown and Discovery Cruise. • **Hotel Coco de Mer**, located on Anse Takamaka, has 40 air-conditioned rooms with en suite facilities, sitting area and terrace. Facilities include a restaurant, 2 bars, swimming pool, tennis and water sports, including wind surfing and canoeing. The hotel's 2 catamarans are available for charter. • **Hotel Acajou**, named after the timber used in its log cabin-style accommodation, is located on the Cote d'Or beach. It has 32 air-conditioned rooms with balconies facing the sea. Facilities include a restaurant, bar, beach snack bar, cocktail lounge and a swimming pool. Diving and bicycle hire can be arranged.

Top: The pool and sundeck of L'Archipel
Middle: Tropical furnishings at La Réserve
Bottom: A thatched dining area of La Réserve overlooks the water

TOURIST CLASS: • **Le Duc de Praslin** is just a few minutes walk from Cote d'Or Beach. Each of the spacious 27 rooms and suites are air conditioned and has a bath, shower and veranda. Facilities include swimming pool, 2 restaurants and bar.

Cousine Island

Cousine, not to be confused with Cousin Island (listed below), is a privately owned, 175-acre (70-hectare) island situated between Praslin and Mahé islands. The island has large granitic outcrops, open plains and pristine sandy-white beaches with beautiful coral reefs just offshore.

Wildlife above and below the sea is superb; many rare and endangered species, such as brush warblers and giant tortoises, may be found on and around the island.

At certain times of the year, turtles come ashore during the day and night to lay their eggs. Over 200,000 noddy terns plus a host of other interesting seabirds, such as tropicbirds and frigatebirds, roost and breed on the island.

Access to the island is only by helicopter.

ACCOMMODATION — DELUXE: • **Cousine Island Lodge** caters to a maximum of 8 guests in luxurious villas with en suite facilities. Resident scientists conducting research on the island act as your guides. No day-trippers are allowed — which guarantees an intimate meeting with nature for guests. Activities include nature walks and lectures, beach walking, boating, fishing, snorkeling and scuba diving.

Cousin Island

Cousin Island is located 2 miles (3 km) from Praslin. It was bought by the International Council for Bird Preservation with assistance from the World Wildlife Fund to establish a bird sanctuary to protect endangered species, including the Seychelles fody and Seychelles brush warbler. Between May and October, thousands of seabirds can be seen nesting on the island.

The island can be visited only on Tuesdays, Thursdays and Fridays, with groups limited to 20 people.

Aride Island

Aride Island is located 6 miles (10 km) due north of Praslin. It was bought by the Cadbury Family (of chocolate fame) and donated to the Royal Society of Wildlife Trusts. Today it is managed by Seychelles Island Conservation Society. Aride Island is probably the most natural and least touched of all the islands of Seychelles. Its spectacular wildlife makes it one of the world's most important nature reserves. The island is uninhabited except for a handful of researchers and no overnight accommodation is available. However, day visits are encouraged and should, where possible, be included on any visit to Seychelles.

Aride Island offers white sand beaches and crystal blue water

La Digue Island

La Digue is a granite island that has spectacular rock formations and secluded beaches. The best way to travel around this, the fourth largest island in the archipelago, is by foot, bicycle or ox cart. There are only a few vehicles on the island.

The highest point on this small 2-by-3 mile (3-by-5 km) island is 1,092 feet (333 m). A lovely walking trail from La Passe to Grand' Anse can be completed on foot or by bicycle. We spent 3 days exploring the island by bicycle and on foot, and would have loved to have stayed longer.

The island is reached by a 30-minute boat ride from Praslin.

ACCOMMODATION — FIRST CLASS: • **La Digue Island Lodge**, located on the west coast, has 69 air-conditioned rooms, most of which are thatched roofed A-frame chalets, with en suite facilities. Amenities include a beachfront restaurant, bar, boutique, swimming pool, wind surfing, snorkeling and a dive center.

TOURIST CLASS: • **Fleur de Lys**, located about 150 yards (150 m) from the ferry jetty and about the same distance from Anse Reunion Beach, has 8 air-conditioned bungalows with kitchens and en suite facilities. • **Patatran Village**, located on the northwest coast, has 21 air-conditioned rooms and suites with private facilities. It has a restaurant, bar, swimming pool and a small beach close by.

An inquisitive bird takes a closer look

Bird Island (Ile Aux Vaches)

Bird Island is a small coral island (1.5-by-0.5 mi./2.5-by-1 km) that is located about 60 miles (100 km) north of Mahé — about a 30-minute flight. A leisurely walk around this pristine island, with stops for an occasional swim and snorkel, takes about 2 to 3 hours. Over 500,000 sooty terns nest on the island, an event that usually occurs May through October.

ACCOMMODATION — FIRST CLASS: • **Bird Island Lodge**, the only property on the island, has 24 fan-cooled, spacious and comfortable bungalows with en suite facilities. Facilities include a restaurant, bar, lounge, boutique and the use of snorkeling equipment.

Desroches Island

Desroches, a coral island 6 miles long and 1.5 miles wide (10-by-2 km), is the largest island in the Amirantes group. It is situated 30 minutes by air from Mahé with a scheduled flight every day. This is an excellent island for those who enjoy water sports. Scuba diving, big game fishing and fly-fishing are excellent.

Desroches Island Lodge is located on a sublime stretch of beach

ACCOMMODATION — DELUXE: • **Desroches Island Lodge**, the only lodge on the island, has 20 air-conditioned Junior Suites rooms with en suite facilities. Water sports include hobie cat sailing, snorkeling, scuba diving, wind surfing and deep-sea fishing.

Denis Island

This small (350-acre/140-hectare) coral island is only 25 minutes by air north of Mahé, and is often thought of as the "perfect desert island." Denis is located on the edge of the Seychelles Bank, where water depths quickly reach over 6,500 feet (2,000 m). Deep-sea fishing for barracuda, dog-tooth tuna, marlin and sailfish is excellent. There is only one exclusive lodge on the island.

ACCOMMODATION — FIRST CLASS: • **Denis Island Lodge** has 25 large, spacious individually air-conditioned cottages with en suite facilities, a restaurant and a small swimming pool.

Frégate Island

Frégate Island, historically a haven for pirates, is a granite island that is 1.5 miles long and a quarter-mile wide (2.5-by-0.4 km). It is situated about 20 minutes east of Mahé by air. The island has magnificent beaches and a variety of flora and bird life, including the Seychelles magpie robin and Seychelles blue pigeon.

ACCOMMODATION — DELUXE: • **Frégate Island Private**, the only accommodation on the island, has 16 air-conditioned villas with en suite facilities. Each Indonesian-style villa overlooks the sea and consists of a separate bedroom and lounge divided by a foyer. The sun deck includes a private pool and sunbeds. Activities include scuba diving, snorkeling and guided nature walks.

Silhouette Island

Located 15 minutes northwest of Mahé by helicopter, this unspoiled

Top: One of Frégate Island's luxury villas, perched on granite boulders
Bottom: Indonesian-inspired furnishings at Frégate Island Private

granite island is the third largest island in the Seychelles and can be seen from the north coast of Mahé. Mountains rise to 2,427 feet (740 m) on this thickly forested, round island, which is approximately 3 miles (5 km) in diameter.

ACCOMMODATION — FIRST CLASS: • **Labriz** is a resort featuring 110 air-conditioned villas and pavilions with en suite bathrooms, outdoor showers, terraces and courtyard gardens. Some beach villas and pavilions have a private plunge pool. Labriz features 3 restaurants, a spa and wellness center and numerous water activities such as diving, snorkeling and fishing.

Top: The calm waters off Alphonse Island are ideal for anglers
Bottom: One of the white sand beaches of North Island

Alphonse Island

Alphonse Island is located in the Amirantes Group some 300 miles (500 km) and an hour by plane from Mahé. It boasts 2 miles (3 km) of reef-protected coastline and a tranquil lagoon.

ACCOMMODATION — • **Alphonse Island Lodge**, at the time of this writing, is closed for a complete rebuild. From October to April the lodge is open for small groups of fly-fishing anglers.

North Island

North Island is a privately owned island consisting of over 497-acres (201-hectares) in size, with 4 wonderful white sand beaches, mountains and freshwater lakes. One of the world's most progressive island rehabilitation and conservation programs is underway; alien fauna and flora is being removed, and the Seychelles' endemic fauna and flora are being reintroduced. Great snorkeling and scuba diving is a specialty.

For the fisherman, blue water fishing is excellent. Due to environmental conservation, trawling on a short line is used. Working from a boat is the most productive method of fishing and the drop off is a 2-hour boat ride from the island. Trevally, dorado, bonito, tuna and sailfish are all found in the area.

ACCOMMODATION — DELUXE:
• **North Island Lodge**, the only property on the island, has 10 presidential villas (approximately 4,500 sq. ft./ 420 m²) and 1 larger villa, #11 (approximately 7,000 sq. ft/650 m²) — providing a "Robinson Crusoe," barefoot luxury experience for guests. Each luxurious villa has an en suite sunken bath, indoor and outdoor shower, bidet, private rock pool, study, sala and butler service. Dining is a sumptuous affair with custom designed meals based around a guest's desires and preferences. Exploring the island can be done on foot, mountain bike or by your private Island Buggie (electric powered golf cart). Activities include snorkeling, scuba diving, health spa treatments and interactions with the scientists on the island.

Top: A quiet corner to enjoy the turquoise water
Bottom: Barefoot luxury of North Island's private villas

Mauritius

Mauritius

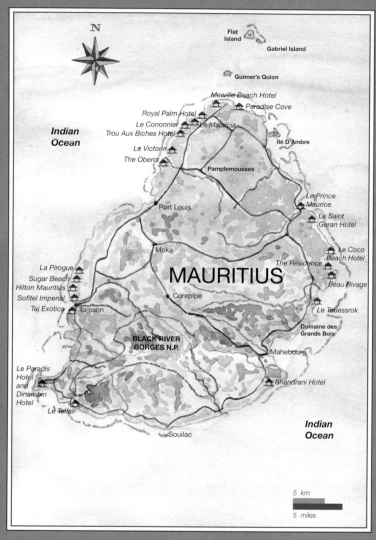

Mauritius is a volcanic island in the southwestern Indian Ocean, 520 miles (840 km) east of Madagascar. The island extends over 720-square-miles (1,865-km²), which is about the size of Rhode Island (or Luxembourg). The terrain of Mauritius is hilly with some small but spectacular mountains, the highest of which rise to some 2,700 feet (824 m). The 125 mile (200 km) coastline is fringed by coral reef, although much of this is not in a pristine state. The island was previously forested but — along with much of the native fauna — much of this has been lost to development. The dodo is the most famous victim of colonization by humans. The resident population is estimated at 1.2 million. Creole, French and English are predominate languages.

MAURITIUS

Mauritius lies east off the coast of southern Africa and is a favorite destination of international travelers looking for a fabulous beach holiday. The combination of a cosmopolitan atmosphere, virgin-white beaches, crystal-clear waters, chic hotels with service to match — along with exquisite Creole, Indian, Chinese and European cuisine — is difficult to beat.

The beaches, water sports, fabulous holiday hotels and exquisite dining are by far the major attractions of the island. Most visitors come for four days to a week or more and base themselves in one of the island's beach hotels for their entire stay.

This mountainous island paradise lies in the middle of the Indian Ocean in the tropics about 1,200 miles (1,935 km) east of Durban (South Africa), 1,100 miles (1,775 km) southeast of Mombasa (Kenya), 2,900 miles (4,675 km) southwest of Bombay (India) and 3,700 miles (5,970 km) west of Perth (Australia). Combining a visit to this remote island with a safari on the African mainland or an around-the world vacation should be considered.

The most appropriate and frequently heard phrase on this island is, "No problem in paradise." Unlike the populations of many other "paradises," most of the people in Mauritius have maintained their genuine and refreshing friendliness in the face of tourism.

Mauritius features world-class resorts

The 720-square-mile (1,865-km²) island features a central plateau, with the south more mountainous than the north. Much of the lush, native vegetation has been destroyed in favor of sugarcane and other crops.

The population of just over one million consists of Indians, Creoles, French and Chinese. Hindu, Muslim, and Christian festivals are frequent. English is the official language, and French is widely spoken, but most of the native people prefer to speak Creole. Creole cooking, which emphasizes the use of curries, fresh seafood and tropical fruits, is often served. Mauritian beer and rum are popular.

The island is known for the awkward dodo, which, living on an island free of large predators, never needed to evolve the ability to fly. This evolutionary trait ironically contributed to its demise; the dodo was easily hunted to extinction during Dutch rule in the 1800s.

One of the sublime beaches of Mauritius

Mauritius has a tropical, oceanic climate. The best time to visit for a beach holiday is from September through mid-December and from April through June, when the days are sunny and the temperatures are warm. From mid-December through March is the cyclone season, which brings occasional tropical rains. June to August (winter) nights are cool and the temperatures along the coastline are pleasant. The average daily maximum temperature in January is 86°F (30°C) and in July is 75°F (24°C). Surf temperatures around the reefs average 74°F (23°C) in winter and 81°F (27°C) in summer.

The first known discovery of Mauritius was by colonizers from Iran in 975 A.D., but they chose not to settle. They moved on to what is now Mombasa and Pemba Island. In the sixteenth century, the Portuguese used the island as a staging post along their trade route to India.

The Dutch came in 1598, led by Wybrandt van Warwyck, who named the island Mauritius after Prince Maurice of Nassau. However, the Dutch did not settle on the island until 1638. In 1710 they left the island to be replaced by the French in 1715, and the French renamed it Isle de France. The island then became a "legal" haven for pirates who preyed on British cargo ships during the war between Britain and France. In fact, this type of pirating was viewed by many at the time as a respectable business.

After 95 years of French control and influence, the British took over Mauritius in 1810. Slavery was abolished in 1835. As the emancipated slaves no longer wished to work on the sugar plantations, thousands of indentured Chinese and Indian workers were brought in to fill their places.

Mauritius became an independent member of the British Commonwealth in 1968. Mauritius has a parliamentary democracy, holding elections every five years. Republic Day was proclaimed on March 12, 1992.

Industrial products and sugar are the country's major exports.

Scuba Diving/Snorkeling

The 205 mile (330 km) coastline of Mauritius is almost completely surrounded by coral reefs, making it an excellent destination for snorkeling and scuba diving. You can dive on the colorful coral reefs and over 50 wrecks, which harbor a great variety of sea life.

The best conditions for scuba diving and sailing are during the period from October through March. Most of the larger beach hotels offer dive excursions and lessons, and they rent equipment. Spearfishing while snorkeling or diving with scuba equipment is prohibited.

Big-Game Fishing

Big-game fish, including blue marlin (plentiful), black marlin, yellowfin tuna, skipjack tuna, jackfish, wahoo, barracuda, sea bass and many species of shark can be caught. Fishing is excellent only a few miles offshore; the ocean drops to over 2,300 feet (700 m) in depth just one mile from shore! The best fishing is from December to March and is sometimes good as late as May. An international fishing tournament is held every year in December.

The largest fleets of deep-sea fishing boats are based at the Centre de Pêche at Rivière Noire (Black River) and at the Organization de Pêche du Nord at Trou-aux-Biches. Boats can be hired through your hotel or through travel agencies and should be booked well in advance during the prime fishing season. Fishing in the lagoons during this same period is also very good.

🐾 WILDLIFE AND WILDLIFE AREAS

Mauritius's major wildlife attractions are found both on land and below the surface of the Indian Ocean.

Bird Life

Mauritius has a number of endemic species of birds — many of which are found nowhere else in the world. Ornithologists or keen birders who wish to add unique species to their lists will find the long journey to this birder's paradise well worthwhile.

The pic-pic (Mauritian grey white-eye) is the only commonly seen bird of the island's 9 known remaining endemic species. The pink pigeon is thought to be the rarest pigeon in the world, and the echo parakeet is the world's rarest parrot, with approximately 40 birds alive. The Mauritius kestrel is also one of the rarest birds in the world; only 4 were known to exist in 1974. Fortunately, due to conservation efforts, populations of all the rare bird species are increasing. Other endemic species include the flycatcher, parakeet, Mauritius fody, olive white-eye, the merle and the cuckoo shrike. In total, about 45 species are found on the island. *Birds of Mauritius* by Claude Michel is available in many Mauritius shops.

Casela Bird Park

This peaceful, 25-acre (10-hectare) park harbors over 140 varieties of birds from 5 continents, including the Mauritian pink pigeon.

Black River Gorges National Park

Proclaimed as the country's first national park in 1994, this 25-square-mile (65-km^2) park covers 3.5% of the island and protects much of its remaining native forests. Nine endemic bird species, including the pink pigeon and Mauritius kestrel, are present.

The Black River Gorges are located in the highest mountain chain on the island and offer splendid views of the countryside. There are several scenic hiking trails, including a 4 mile (7 km) hike to the Macchabee Forest and a 9 mile (15 km) hike through the gorges to the Black River.

Domaine Des Grands Bois

Introduced stags, deer, wild boar and African monkeys roam this 2,000-acre (800-hectare), forested park, located north of Mahebourg on the east coast.

La Vanille Crocodile & Tortoise Park

Located in the south, this farm breeds Nile crocodiles from Madagascar. There is a small zoo featuring the wild animals found on Mauritius, as well as a nature walk.

Port Louis

Port Louis, the chief harbor and capital city, is partially surrounded by mountains and is multifaceted in character. The city has a large **market** where indigenous fruits and vegetables, spices, pareos (colorful cloth wraps) and other clothing and souvenirs are sold. Just off the main square along Place d'Armes are some eighteenth century buildings, including the **Government House** and **Municipal Theatre**. The **Caudan Waterfront** and the **Port Louis Waterfront** are good areas for shopping. There are also a few movie houses and numerous eateries.

Curepipe

Curepipe, a large town located on the central plateau, is a good place to shop and cool off from the warm coast. Garment manufacturing is one of the principal industries in Mauritius and there are several international designer outlet shops located in Curepipe. An extinct volcano, **Trou aux Cerfs**, may be visited nearby.

Pamplemousses

The world-renowned botanical gardens of Pamplemousses have dozens of bizarre plants and trees including the talipot palm — at age 60 it blooms only once, then it dies. Giant water lilies imported from Brazil are also found here.

Terres de Couleurs

On sunny days, the land takes on the colors of the rainbow at Terres de Couleurs (the colored earth), located in the southwestern mountains near Chamarel.

Grand Bassin

Grand Bassin is a lake in an extinct volcano's caldera; it is the holy lake of the Hindus, who celebrate the Maha Shivaratree, an exotic festival held yearly in February or March.

Accommodation – Beach Hotels

Hotels are spread out, so visitors spend most of their time enjoying the many activities and sports their particular hotel has to offer. In many of the top hotels, most water and land sports, with the exception of scuba diving, horseback riding and big-game fishing, are free, including wind surfing, water skiing, sailing, snorkeling, volleyball, golf and tennis. Small sailboats are available at most resorts. Casinos are operated at the Trou aux Biches, as well as at the Casino of Domaine Les Pailles in Pailles and the Casino de Maurice. If you wish to visit the island during the high season (December to February and July to August) and Easter, I suggest that you book your trip several months in advance. Demand for accommodation in the top hotels is high year-round.

ACCOMMODATION — DELUXE: • **The Taj Exotica,** located on the west coast of Mauritius, is spread over 27-acres (11-hectares) and overlooks tranquil Tamarin Bay. Sixty-five spacious villas, each with a private pool and garden, exude an intimate ambiance for guests combined with all the modern day luxuries. There

is a spa, lounge, 2 restaurants serving international dishes and local cuisine, and a variety of water sports are offered. • **Le Prince Maurice,** set in 60-acres (24-hectares) of private land, tropical gardens and sheltered beaches on the northeast coast of the island, has 89 air-conditioned junior and senior suites. The hotel has two à la carte restaurants — one of which is a "floating" restaurant — 2 bars, health and fitness centers, and water sports. • **The**

Oberoi, located at Baie of Tortues on the northwest coast, has 72 luxuriously furnished rooms with sunken baths. Facilities include 2 restaurants, bar, an ocean-front swimming pool, gym, health spa, tennis courts and water sports. • **Royal Palm Hotel** is an elegant, 84-all suite, deluxe hotel located on Grand Baie on the northwest tip of the island. • **One & Only Le Saint Géran,** located on Pointe de Flacq on the east coast of the island, has 3 restaurants, Givenchy Spa, 9-hole golf course, sailing and scuba diving. All 162 junior and ocean suites are air-conditioned with en suite facilities. • **Le Touessrok,** situated on the east coast at Trou d'Eau Douce, offers 200 air-conditioned rooms and villas with en suite facilities, spa, swimming pools, restaurants, shops, Ilot Mangenie (a private "Robinson Crusoe"-style island retreat), and Ile de Cerfs — an offshore water-sport playground which also offers secluded

Top: The expansive lobby at Le Prince Maurice
Middle: Le Prince Maurice's pool and dining area
Bottom: The powder white sand beach at One & Only Le Saint Géran

542

coves for sunbathing and an 18-hole golf course. • **Le Paradis Hotel and Golf Club** is located in the southwest of the island on a lagoon at the foot of the dramatic Le Morne Mountain. The hotel has 286 air-conditioned rooms and 13 villas, all with facilities en suite, 4 restaurants, swimming pools, 18-hole golf course, spa, casino, disco, nightly entertainment, scuba diving, water sports and a fleet of deep-sea fishing boats. • **Dinarobin Hotel Golf**

A junior suite at One & Only Le Saint Géran

comprises 172 suites, 3 restaurants, swimming pools and a spa. It is located adjacent to Le Paradis on a private peninsula, and the two hotels share all their facilities. • **Beau Rivage**, situated at Belle Mare on the east coast, has 162 air-conditioned junior suites plus 1- and 2-bedroom villas, 4 restaurants, bars, swimming pool, gym, sauna, floodlit tennis courts and water sports. • **Shandrani Hotel** is conveniently located 4 miles (6 km) from the international airport on Blue Bay on the southeastern coast. This 327-room hotel has 3 separate beaches, all the usual water sports and tennis. All rooms are air-conditioned with en suite facilities.

FIRST CLASS: • **The Residence**, set on a lovely stretch of beach on the east coast of the island, has 135 luxury air-conditioned rooms and 28 suites with balconies or terraces and butler service. Facilities include 2 restaurants, snack bar, health center, beauty salon and water sports. • **The Hilton Mauritius**, located on the island's western coast, has 193 richly decorated rooms. The hotel has 4 restaurants, fitness club, jacuzzi and sauna, hairdressing salon, water sports and an 18-hole golf course nearby. • **Le Mauricia** offers 198 rooms and is located close to Grand Baie. The property is ideal for families and there is evening entertainment and discos. • **Le Victoria**, located between Grand Baie and Port Louis, has 248 extra large rooms and suites (all sea facing) and is ideal for families. • **Paradise Cove Hotel**, located at Anse La Raie on the north coast, has 67 air-conditioned rooms with en suite facilities, 2 restaurants, bars, swimming pool and water sports. • **Sugar Beach Resort** is a plantation-style resort, set on the west coast of the island, with a total of 238 air-conditioned rooms with en suite facilities located in the Manor House and 16 Creole-style beach villas. Guests may enjoy a variety of water sports and the island's largest landscaped swimming pool, and they may also use the amenities of the nearby sister hotel, La Pirogue. • **La Pirogue** is located on a fine, white beach at Flic-en-Flac on the island's west coast. Thatched cottages spread out from the main building that features a distinctive, sail-like roof. All 248 rooms are air-conditioned with en suite facilities. • **Le Canonnier** has 248 rooms with en suite facilities. The property is ideal for families and there is evening entertainment and discos.

TOURIST CLASS: • **The Merville Beach Hotel** is a comfortable hotel situated on Grand Bay near the northern tip of the island, with 169 air-conditioned rooms with private facilities, a swimming pool and the usual water sports. • **Sofitel Imperial**, located at Flic-en-Flac on the island's west coast, has 191 air-conditioned rooms with en suite facilities, 3 restaurants, a piano bar and the usual water sports.

Ethiopia

Ethiopia is a mountainous country situated in the Horn of Africa, covering some 435,070-square-miles (1,127,127-km²) about twice the size of Texas. It has three distinct climate zones relative to topography. The highest peaks in the Simien mountains rise above 14,400 feet (4,400 m), while those in the Bale mountains are just slightly lower. These cool temperate uplands are in stark contrast to the low-lying Danakil and Ogaden deserts which are among the hottest places on Earth. A number of endemic mammals, birds and other species are confined to Ethiopia. There are 84 indigenous languages, but English is widely used. Currency is the Birr.

ETHIOPIA

The Federal Democratic Republic of Ethiopia stands out as the country with the richest history and culture in all of sub-Saharan Africa. It is one of the oldest nations in the world and has the third highest population of any country in Africa.

Located in southern Ethiopia, Omo River Valley is home to some of the most traditional tribes on earth. Isolated from the rest of the world for centuries, the distinct groups still follow their own customs. Lalibela features twelfth century rock-hewn churches that are used daily by the local people. Visiting these churches during services provides an opportunity to witness "living history" and is a very moving experience.

When many people think of Ethiopia, television images from the 1980s of starving people come to mind. During my visits I not only did not see any "starving" people; what I did see were large fields of crops from a land blessed with several years of good rain, resulting in lots of food for the country.

Geographically, Ethiopia is a land-locked country located in the Horn of Africa, dominated by highland plateaus with semi-deserts and deserts in the east and rain forest near the Sudanese border near Gambella on the west. Major rivers include the Blue Nile that flows from Lake Tana in the northwest of the country into Sudan; the Tekezze which flows into Sudan to join the main Nile flow; the Wabe Shabelle which flows east into Somalia; the Awash which empties into lakes straddling the border with Djibouti; the Baro which flows through Gambella into Sudan and the Omo River that flows south and eventually empties into Lake Turkana.

Ethiopia is bordered by Kenya to the south, Somalia, and Djibouti to the east, Eritrea to the north and Sudan to the west. Altitudes range from 380 feet

A young Karo family

(116 m) below sea level in the Danakil Depression in the east to 15,155 ft. (4,620 m) Ras Dashen in the beautiful Simien Mountains in the north.

The scenery in Ethiopia is spectacular. To the north on the "Historic Route" there is dramatic mountain scenery, particularly around the Simien Mountains. South of Addis Ababa there is a string of seven lakes along the floor of the Rift Valley — Lakes Zwai, Langano, Abiata, Shalla, Awassa, Abaya and Chamo — each in some way different from the other, and Bale Mountains National Park. South of Awassa the road passes through coffee plantations before reaching the more arid, acacia forested areas of Borana. In the west, on the road from Jimma to Gambella, there are vast stretches of tropical rain forest, while Gambella itself with its Nilotic ethnic groups provides a taste of the vast swamps and savannah of southern Sudan. In the east there is the Dalol Depression, the hottest place on earth, with its salt mines and a little to the south, Erta Ale, the only volcano in the world with a permanent lava lake.

The highlands and the lowlands have distinctly different rainy patterns. The highlands usually experience the main rains July to September and short, light rains April to June. The lowlands main rains usually occur April and May, with the short rains falling in November and December.

Ethiopia may have been the cradle of mankind. The world's oldest known nearly complete hominid skeleton, Lucy, is 3.3 million years old. According to legend, Menelik I, the son of King Solomon and the Queen of Sheba, brought the Ark of the Covenant to Axum from Jerusalem. From about 1000 B.C., the reign of Emperor Menelik I began what became one of the longest known uninterrupted monarchial dynasties in the world.

After the decline of the Axumite Empire, Ethiopia's rulers retreated with their Christian followers to the high escarpment of the central plateau. There, protected by mountains,

Karo women dancing before a bull jumping ceremony

they were able to repel Muslim invaders. From approximately the seventh to the sixteenth centuries A.D. the Ethiopians were surrounded by their enemies and in effect lived in isolation for 1,000 years. This cut them off from the evolving mainstream of Christian culture and helped preserve the values of their Christian Ethiopian culture. What resulted was an isolationist society suspicious of strangers and fearful of invasions.

Parts of the country were occupied by Italy from 1936 until 1941 when the country was liberated by the British and the Ethiopian patriotic forces.

Haile Selassie I became emperor in 1930 and ruled until 1974 when he was deposed by a group of soldiers, who later became known as the *Derg*. For seventeen years Ethiopia suffered from civil war and state sponsored famines, until the military regime was overthrown by a coalition of rebel groups which still dominate contemporary politics, after several elections, the most recent being in 2005.

Although still poor and underdeveloped with a very high population growth rate, over the last few years Ethiopia has achieved an economic growth rate of over 10% per annum, and the future looks considerably brighter than in the past.

The headquarters of the United Nations Economic Commission for Africa and the African Union are based in Addis Ababa. The country has some of the best middle and long-distance runners in the world, often placing well in the Olympics and other world meets.

A painted Hamar man

There are 70 languages from a variety of linguistic groups spoken in Ethiopia. The national language is Amharic which descended from Ge'ez, the language of Ancient Axum, and still used by the Ethiopian Orthodox Church today.

Ethiopia is one of the world's poorest countries. Per capita income is less than US$ 200.00 per annum. Average age expectancy is around 50 years and infant mortality is around 10%.

The economy is predominately agricultural. Approximately 25% of the population is occupied with the production of coffee, which accounts for 50% of all Ethiopia's exports. Ethiopia in fact is celebrated as the birthplace of coffee. Mining and horticultural projects are becoming more important contributors, as is the export of hydroelectric power to neighboring countries.

Ethiopia really is an amazing country to travel in, full of "real experiences" that I don't think can be found in many other places in the world. But

Hamar Koke tribal women prepare for a celebration dance

in regards to travel, it can be disorganized, chaotic, basic and unpredictable. Travelers to this country (unless you just plan on staying in Addis) need to be flexible and bring a sense of humor with them.

Currently, accommodations in some of the prime sites are still Government-owned and quite basic. However, the situation is rapidly improving as there are many new 3-, 4- and 5-star hotels and lodges under construction. In any case, I feel that for the adventurer, having to stay in meager facilities on parts of their trip will be far outweighed by the amazing history and cultural experiences available. For travelers that demand 5-star facilities, an option is to base themselves at a top hotel in Addis and take day trips by private air charter to the sights that are currently offering only basic accommodation.

Found only in the Ethiopian highlands, the gelada is an herbivore

🐾 WILDLIFE AND WILDLIFE AREAS

Wildlife enthusiasts looking for endemic species should consider visiting the Bale Mountains to see the Simien wolf and Menelik's bushbuck, and the Simien Mountains for the elusive Walia ibex and to enjoy the entertaining antics of the gelada. For big game it is necessary to go to the Omo and Mago parks in the south, or to Gambella, and even here sightings cannot be guaranteed.

More than 800 bird species are found in Ethiopia, of which 16 are endemic. A further 14 species are shared with Eritrea, which was part of Ethiopia until 1991. Ethiopia's diverse habitats, highlands, lowlands, forests, lakes, wetlands and riverine systems provide sites for migrants. For butterfly enthusiasts there are eight families, 93 genera and 324 species to be found in the country.

Addis Ababa

Addis Ababa is a bustling, seemingly chaotic city of nearly 5 million people of many ethnic backgrounds. Addis grew like an expanding village, with modern hotels, open markets,

Top: A troop of geladas with the Simien Mountains as a backdrop
Bottom: A member of the goat family, the Walia Ibex are a critically endangered species

slums, nineteenth century Armenian- and Indian-style buildings, churches, parks and malls are all mixed together. This was, in fact, still a city of tents just over 100 years ago. Founded in 1887 by Emperor Menelik I, Addis is the political, economic and social capital of Ethiopia. At between 7,545 to 8,200 feet (2,300 to 2,500 m) above sea level, it is the third highest capital in the world.

The **National Archaeological Museum** is located in the center of town and houses a replica of **Lucy**, the 3.3 million year old hominid skeleton along with a number of other hominid specimens over 1 million years old. Lucy was discovered in 1974 near the town of Hadar by Donald Johanson and Tom Gray, who recovered about 40% of the hominid skeleton. The museum also has artifacts and relics from the Axumite and Gondorene periods up to the rule of Menelik II. This is probably the museum of greatest interest to tourists.

We also visited the **Institute of Ethiopian Studies** and the **National Anthropological Museum**, founded by Professor Richard Pankhurst, OBE, a member of the family made famous by Sylvia Pankhurst the Suffragette who led the women's rights movement in Britain (she was buried in Addis). Professor Pankhurst is the leading expert on ethnology and this museum has a fascinating wealth of information and exhibits relating to Ethiopia's cultural and ethnographic heritage. The displays provide insight into the cultural crossroads that is modern day Ethiopia, with its elaborate festivals and immense spiritualism amongst many different faiths. This building was once the Genete Palace of Emperor Haile Selassie I, and visitors can see his bedroom.

A trip up **Mount Entoto** to see the expanse of Addis and to visit a church dedicated to the Holy Virgin (Maryam) and another dedicated to "Saint Raguel" is recommended if time allows.

The **Menelik Mausoleum** was constructed in 1911 in the old Baata church and it serves as a tomb for emperors, princes and martyrs of freedom. Built to house the tomb of Emperor Menelik II it also includes the graves of members of his family and the Emperor Haile Selassie I. **St. George's Cathedral** was built in 1896 in the traditional octagonal shape by the Emperor Menelik II to commemorate his victory at Adwa; it is dedicated to the national saint of Ethiopia. The museum houses a wide collection of important religious paintings, crosses of many designs, historic books and parchments, and beautiful handicrafts. There are also fine examples of modern paintings by the famous Ethiopian artist Afewerke Tekle. The **Trinity Cathedral** was built in 1941 in commemoration of Ethiopia's liberation from Italian occupation.

The **Jubilee Palace** is a modern palace completed to commemorate the Silver Jubilee of the coronation of Emperor Haile Selassie I. The park is home to a collection of rare indigenous wildlife.

A variety of cuisines are available in Addis, including Italian (try Castelli's, in Piassa), Greek, Armenian, Korean, Chinese, Arabic, Indian and Georgian. I highly recommend dining in one or more of the traditional Ethiopian restaurants, many of which have floor shows, such as Habesha Restaurant, Dashen Restaurant, Yod Abyssinia or the Crown Hotel.

There are some good **shopping opportunities** in Addis — whereas it's relatively poor outside the city. In general one is presented with traditional clothes and textiles, weavings, carvings, ethnic artifacts, spices/coffee, silver and gold jewelry and paintings with both modern and religious influences.

If you buy any souvenir that is worth more than US$ 500.00 you need to have a certificate confirming that the goods you have purchased are exportable and that they are not classified as irremovable heritage items. This is easy to obtain during normal office hours from the Ethiopian National Museum.

Churchill Road is the main souvenir shopping area of Addis. Close to the main post office are a number of souvenir shops selling silver jewelry, ethnic artifacts and carpets. Further up the road are several shops selling cotton weavings (tablecloths, embroidered shirts and dresses, scarves). Another good place for Ethiopian fabrics that are made into traditional dresses, scarves, shawls and purses is Mesfin Tesfa's on Bole Road. The lobby and pool level of the Hilton Hotel has some extensive and good shopping opportunities. Most of the best gold shops are at Teclu Desta in the piazza (the "downtown" from the Italian period).

Ethiopian art is another popular item, St. George Gallery behind the Sheraton has international quality handmade furniture, fabrics, paintings and jewelry, and the nearby Asni Gallery features modern art by young Ethiopian artists, as does the Makush Gallery on Bole Road which is inside a reasonably good restaurant if you get hungry.

Be sure to visit the **Mercato**, the largest market area on the continent, where you can bargain for Ethiopian crafts and virtually everything else under the sun.

Nightlife in Addis is exciting and gets moving around 10:30 p.m. In addition to modern discos, there are a large number of *azmari bait* (traditional music houses) where singers and musicians perform using traditional instruments such as the *kirar* (a kind of lyre) and the *masinqo* (a single stringed violin). Addis is actually quite safe at night — unlike most large cities.

ACCOMMODATION — DELUXE: • **Sheraton Luxury Collection Hotel** is the most luxurious accommodation in Ethiopia with spacious rooms and magnificent suites set in beautifully landscaped gardens. There are several restaurants, two bars, a large heated lap swimming pool, full spa, business center and conference facilities. The hotel is located about a 25 minute drive from the Bole International Airport.

FIRST CLASS: • **Hilton Hotel** has 356 en suite rooms with private balconies, four restaurants, swimming pool, tennis courts, health club, jogging track and shopping mall, set on 15 acres. This is one of the older style Hiltons as it was built in 1969.

The Sheraton Luxury Collection Hotel in Addis Ababa

TOURIST CLASS: • **Ghion Hotel** is centrally located and has 60 rooms and four suites with en suite facilities, restaurant and swimming pool. • **Imperial Hotel** has 57 en suite rooms and six suites, restaurant, bar and jazz club.

THE NORTH

The **Historic Route** and dramatic mountain scenery, particularly around the Simien Mountains is found in the north of the country.

Unlike most other African countries, Ethiopia was never colonized. This allowed them to develop relatively unaffected — resulting in unique cultures and an amazing wealth of historic sights. The best known historic sites on the Historic Route are Axum, Lalibela, Gondar and Bahir Dar.

The easiest and fastest way to get around is by scheduled flights or private air charter. In order not to miss some of the stunning scenery and other interesting, though less well-known sites, a combination of road and air travel is recommended.

If it is done by road, others sites and activities can easily be added, such as the rock hewn churches of Tigray, the markets of Senbete and Bati (where the highlanders and lowlanders meet for trade) and the beautiful Simien Mountains. Ideally, two days in each place should be allowed for Axum, Lalibela, Gondar and Bahir Dar. Two weeks plus should be allowed for doing the Historic Route by road.

Travelers can experience and even participate in ancient religious festivals (some with over 100,000 pilgrims) in this and other regions of the country. Some of the more prominent festivals include Timket (Ethiopian Epiphany), Fasika (Easter), Genna (Christmas) and Mesqal (the finding of the true cross), and the special feast days of individual churches.

Every day of the month is named after a patron saint, and subsequently there is a festival somewhere in the country every day celebrating that saint. Therefore travelers really do not need to get too preoccupied with timing their visits around "festivals". If fact, travelers can get overwhelmed by millions of Ethiopians during the major festivals. I'd encourage people to avoid these big festivals as there can be real chaos, and it is much nicer and more authentic to hit one of the "living museums" (local churches) on the day of a saint.

Timket (Ethiopian Epiphany) is one of the most colorful festivals and occurs on the 19th of January, when the church Tabots are paraded to a body of water in order to commemorate Christ's baptism.

Maskal is celebrated in memory of the Finding of the True Cross by Empress Eleni and coincides with the mass blooming of the golden Maskal daises. **Genna (Christmas)** is celebrated by church services on the 7th of January throughout the night, with worshipers moving from one church to another.

Ethiopia has a number of pilgrimage sites, Christian and Muslim, visited on certain days by thousands (in some places, tens of thousands) of pilgrims.

The most important sites include the **Mariamtsion Church** in Axum, **Debre Damo Monastery, Hamad al-Negash** (site of the first Muslim settlement in the world), **Gabriel Kolubi** near Dire Dawa and **Sheikh Hussain** near Bale.

Axum

Axum was the capital of an Empire which even included parts of Arabia across the Red Sea. It was rated as one of the four greatest powers of the ancient world (along with China, Persia and Rome) by fourth century Persian philosopher Mani. Axum had its own alphabet and notational system, constructed dams and traded with partners as far away as India and China.

Highlights in the area include stelae, the largest single pieces of stone erected anywhere in the world (one of which was returned from Italy in 2005 after being in Rome for 68 years), **Axum Museum**, the castles and tombs of the kings, and **Mariamtsion Church** that was built on the site of Ethiopia's first church. A chapel within the church compound is believed by Ethiopian Orthodox Christians to house the **Ark of the Covenant** (see Graham Hancock's *The Sign and the Seal*).

Other sites in the area include the **pre-Axumite temple** built in 800 B.C. at Yeha, 34 miles (55 km) east of Axum, and the seventh century monastery at **Debre Damo**, where the only access is by rope and women are not allowed).

ACCOMMODATION — CLASS D: • **Ramhai Hotel** has rooms with en suite facilities. • **Yeha Hotel** has 60 rooms and three suites all with en suite facilities, bar and restaurant. There is a great view from the property.

Gondar

Gondar was the capital of the Ethiopian Empire from the seventeenth to mid-nineteenth centuries and is distinguished by its castles and imperial compound and by its churches. **Debre Berhan Selassie** is one of the most spectacularly painted churches in the country with its walls completely covered in murals and its ceiling covered with murals of angels' faces — each slightly different that the others. The **Palace of Emperor Fasilidas** is the most impressive of the castles and well worth a visit.

The remains of the Palace of Emperor Fasilidas

Gondar is located 464 miles (748 km) by road from Addis Ababa, and is best accessed by scheduled flights.

ACCOMMODATION — CLASS C: • **Goha Hotel** has 60 rooms and four suites all with en suite facilities, two bars and a restaurant.

CLASS D: • **Hotel Lemmergeryer** is located closest to the airport and offers basic rooms. The restaurant is popular with locals.

Simien Mountains

The Simien Mountains present perhaps the most dramatic mountain scenery in Africa, and are certainly one of the most beautiful mountainous regions in the world. Huge volcanic plugs formed 40 million years ago have eroded into fabulous pinnacle peaks (many over 13,100 feet/4,000 m) and river valleys. Ras Dashen at 15,155 feet (4,620 m) is in fact the fourth highest peak in Africa; if you wish to climb it allow eight days.

Wildlife enthusiasts venture here to see endemic species including the Gelada (a type of baboon), the Walia ibex (a member of the goat family) and the Simien wolf. Simien wolves are in fact seldom seen here as there may be less than 20 individuals in the park, and are better viewed in Bale Mountains National Park.

During our visit we spent hours with different troops of Gelada — often sitting as close as 20 feet (6 m) from them. Observing how the members of the troop interact with each other at such close range is very entertaining! We were also fortunate enough to see several Walia ibex as we hiked on the higher mountain slopes.

Endemic birds in the region include wattled ibis, white-billed starling, thick-billed raven, back-headed siskin, white-collared pigeon, and white-backed black tit. Lammergeyers may also be seen.

The Simien Mountains can easily be combined with a tour on the Historic Route, as the park entrance at Debark is only about 60 miles (100 km) from Gondar.

The Simien Mountain range is a World Heritage site

ACCOMMODATION — CLASS B: • **Simiens Lodge** offers twenty rooms and one suite with en suite facilities and under-flo or solar heating to help keep guests warm on the cold nights. There is a main lodge that has a fireplace, restaurant and bar. The gelada often visit the grounds. There is also a 16-bed dormitory with shared bathrooms and showers.

CAMPING: Campsites are available in the park.

Lalibela

Lalibela means "the bees recognized his sovereignty" (in the Agnew language) and is one of the most amazing historical sites on earth. At the end of the twelfth and beginning of the thirteenth centuries King Lalibela of the Zaghwe dynasty built a series of rock hewn churches. The **New Jerusalem** is in fact rightly categorized as one of the wonders of the world. The excavations were dug deep in order to enable the churches to reach three stories below ground level. All of the churches were decorated with fine carvings, which have been well preserved.

The churches are naturally divided into the Eastern and Western groups by the dry riverbed of the Yordanus River (River Jordan). There are 11 churches within the town, all of which are still in use today. There are also a number of outlying churches that can be visited if you stay for a few days. This must have been a wealthy kingdom, as it is estimated that the churches in Lalibela took 25 years to construct, and there must have been economic surpluses to pay for the large work force required for the construction.

These are indeed "living museums" used daily by the local people. Approximately 5,000 monks and priests live here, working in the churches and

Top: Looking regal, a priest in Lalibela
Bottom: Praying between church columns

Top: The Church of St. George is one of the unique monolith churches in Lalibela
Bottom: The village of Lalibela

performing the annual Ethiopian Christian ceremonies year round.

During our visit we were able to visit one of the churches during a festival celebrating a patron saint, and I must say it was one of the most moving experiences of my life. The church was full of worshipers, the priests were burning incense, chanting and beating drums — and I was just a "fly on the wall" observing it all. I truly felt I had been taken 800 years back in time!

Lalibela is located 398 miles (642km) from Addis, and is most easily accessed by air.

ACCOMMODATION — CLASS C: • **Jerusalem Guesthouse** has 11 rooms with en suite facilities and a restaurant. • **Seven Olives Hotel** is a popular choice among independent travelers and is located close to the main entrances of the churches. The hotel offers en suite rooms and a restaurant on the premises. • **Roha Hotel** is a government run hotel and offers 60 rooms and four suites, each with private bathrooms. There is a restaurant, bar and laundry facilities.

One of the intricate murals found in Bahir Dar

Bahir Dar

Bahir Dar is situated on Lake Tana which has many island monasteries and churches — many of which are closed to women. However, the churches on the **Zeghie Peninsula** are open to all. Be sure to visit the recently restored medieval church of **Debre Sina Mariam**.

Visitors can cross the lake, which is the source of the Blue Nile, from Bahir Dar to Gorgora, and vice versa. The **Blue Nile Falls** are only worth seeing when the dam gates are open.

White water rafting is generally done on the Blue Nile near Bahir Dar (a few days), along the Omo River (the whole stretch can take up to a month) and on the Awash River (one or two days). Rafting can only be done at certain times of the year, after the rains, and needs to be set up well in advance.

ACCOMMODATION — There are currently 15 properties under construction along the lake shore. Two of the properties will be 5-star and scheduled to open in the future, the Bahir Dar Resort and another property owned and operated by Kuriftu Resorts. Additional details are not available at this time.

CLASS C: • **Tana Hotel**, set on the shores of Lake Tana, has 64 en suite rooms and suites, bar and restaurant.

The circular architecture of the Giorgis Monastery

CLASS D: • **Dib Anbessa Hotel** is decorated with wood carvings and traditional paintings of historical and artistic values. The rooms have en suite facilities and there is a restaurant on the property. • **Papyrus Hotel** is a new and modern hotel with indoor and outdoor restaurants, rooms and suites, multi-purpose conference hall, swimming pool and other facilities. • **Ghion Hotel** faces the southern shore of the lake and is surrounded by a lush garden, offers simple guest rooms.

CAMPING: Sites area available at the Ghion Hotel.

THE SOUTH

Rift Lakes

South of Addis Ababa there is a string of seven lakes along the floor of the Rift Valley — Lakes Zwai, Langano, Abiata, Shalla, Awassa, Abaya and Chamo — each with a character of its own. At Lake Ziway we spent time at the jetty and saw a variety of wildlife, including 20 hammerkops perched on a partially sunken boat near the jetty — an unusual site indeed!

ACCOMMODATION — CLASS B: • **Bishangari Lodge** is located on the eastern bank of Lake Langano and has eight chalets and one suite, all with private facilities, a bar and restaurant. Guests are taken with their luggage from reception to their chalets via donkey carts. Over 300 bird species have been recorded in the area. The lodge is located 155 miles (250 km) from Addis, and is a good overnight option if you are driving from Bale Mountains National Park to Addis.

Bale Mountains National Park

Bale Mountains National Park is situated on the southern plateau approximately 8,200 feet (2,500 m) above sea level, rising up to 14,360 ft. (4,377 m). This is the largest alpine area in Africa covering over 386-square-miles (1,000-km²). It also has the highest all-weather road in Africa running through it.

Bale encompasses a high altitude plateau with volcanic crags and lakes, forests, alpine moor land, trout filled streams and a great variety of fauna and flora. Several endemic mammals including the mountain nyala, Simien wolf

and Menelik's bushbuck may be found, and 16 endemic bird species have been recorded. Plant life includes giant lobelia, St. John's Wort and thistle flowers.

The park contains over half of the world's population of Semien wolves *(Canis simensis),* which is listed as critical endangered by the World Conservation Union (IUCN).

After arriving in Goba by charter, we drove to Park Headquarters at Dinsho. We hiked in a fenced area about 1 km square and had good sightings of two endemic mammals — the mountain nyala and Menelik's bushbuck *(Tragelaphus scriptus meneliki).* Although the fenced area offers protection, nyala are seen in other areas of the park, especially in the Gaysay area. Mountain nyalas have longer hair than common species of nyala due to the cold climate in its high altitude habitat. We also saw Menelik's

Top: The striking Bale Mountains is a unique eco-system
Bottom: A Simien wolf

bushbuck, an endemic sub-species in which the male is much darker than the common bushbuck.

The highlight of the visit was seeing over 20 Simien wolves and watching them from the vehicle and on foot while they hunted. We saw them stalk and kill several of their key prey — mole rats.

The park can be explored by vehicle, on foot and on horseback. The underwater river and caves of Sof Omar can be visited in a day trip from Goba.

The park is a two day's drive from Addis, and is best reached by taking a 1 hour 20 minute charter flight to the nearby town of Goba.

ACCOMMODATION — CLASS D: • **Goba Wabe Shabelle Hotel** has very basic rooms with facilities en suite, and a restaurant.

Omo River Valley

The Omo River Valley and Omo River Delta are one of the few great tribal lands of vanishing cultures left in the world today. As the world becomes more modernized, the opportunity to go "back in time" is becoming rarer by the day. I really do wonder how long these tribes will remain relatively untouched. One thing for sure is that we are the last generation to see "real cultural integrity". If this type of travel interests you, my advice is to go now!

Some of the different ethnic groups situated along the Omo River include the Karo, the Dus, the Nyangatom, the Hamar, the Kwegu (Mogudji) and the Mursi. Except for the past few decades, these tribes have lived in isolation from the modern world. Marvelous scenery, birdlife (over 300 species recorded) and wildlife provide an added bonus to visiting this region. My favorite sighting during my last visit was a Pel's fishing owl that landed on the Omo River bank opposite camp.

The Omo River flows for close to 620 miles (1,000 km) from the highlands southwest of Addis Ababa to Lake Turkana (Kenya), and offers white-water rafting opportunities.

The east side of the Omo is accessible by a three day drive from

Top: The best way to reach the most remote tribes is on the Omo River
Bottom: Karo men paint their bodies in preparation for a village ceremony

Top: The women and babies watch
Bottom: Karo men posing in front of
a hut

Addis. The west side of the river is currently accessible only for guests booked on boat-based safaris, or for those willing to take several days and drive from Addis Ababa to Jimma, Mizan Teferi, Tum, Tulgit and Kibish, where the Suri (Surma) people can be visited. A bridge is planned to be built across the Omo at Omo Rate, and will make access to the west bank and the Omo National Park easier.

Visitors should allow at least eight days to explore the Omo and the Omo River Delta. On my last visit I stayed 12 days — nine days based at Lamule Camp and three days camping in the Omo River Delta and had the time of my life. Over the last 10 years, the owner of Lamule Camp has developed relationships within each village that we visited — and that made all the difference.

We were shown the proper ways to act in the villages and paid the required "photographic fees" set by each community. When appropriate, we gave gifts including cowries shells and razor blades that the men used to shave their heads in preferred designs. At many times a flat fee (in Ethiopian Bir) was paid to the headmen of the village and we were able to take all the photos we wanted. At other times we paid on a per photo basis in Ethiopian Bir. Throughout the Omo the set rate for photos is 2 Birr — about 25 cents. While in Addis I loaded up with 500 one-Bir, 100 5-Birr and 100 10-Birr notes so I was well prepared. I figured the leftover would go for tips so there would be no waste.

The key is that the local people benefited economically from our presence, and we and they, in almost all cases, enjoyed and benefited from the experience as well. This is a way for the villages to make a living out of retaining their culture.

Most all of the men carry AK-47, Kalashnikov and other rifles. However, I never at any time felt unsafe. As long as you do not try to steal their cattle or their land, you are viewed as a neutral guest who is bringing economic benefit to their community.

The **Karo,** who number only about 3,000 people, mainly practice flood retreat cultivation on the banks of the Omo River, as do many of the tribes. When the level of the Omo drops (usually in September or October), they

Karo men with their rifles

cultivate the river banks — and continue to cultivate more of the river bank as the river level continues to drop. During my visit the river was the highest it had been since El Niño in the early '90s, and was only about 5 feet below the level of our camp when we arrived. The Omo was estimated to be about 80 feet (25 m) deep at that time. Their women make clay pots for trading with other tribes.

The Karo are exceptional in their face and body painting for their dances and ceremonies. Karo women scarify their chests to beautify themselves. The scars are cut with a knife and ash is rubbed in the wound to produce a raised welt. Their traditional evening dances are exceptional and a thrill — especially if you are asked to join in!

We went by boat to visit the Karo village of **Korcho,** set on a high sand bluff about 300 feet (90 m) above the level of the Omo a few minutes downstream by boat. Korcho children met us on arrival and walked with us on the 10 minute uphill hike to the village. We were offered "*buna geleba*" — or "coffee" by one of the guide's friends. The "coffee" was actually the husks or outside of the coffee beans as real coffee is much too expensive for these people. The taste was similar to weak coffee and it was quite good.

Top: A Karo family
Bottom: An example of a Karo hut

The following morning we walked into **Dus,** a village located only a few hundred meters from our camp,

I had the special pleasure of visiting a family that one of my clients had befriended the previous year. We had "coffee" with them and communicated through a translator. A few nights later we were invited back to the village in the late afternoon for a celebration which had much of the village dancing — and with its guests joining in!

The following day we went by boat up the Omo to visit the **Nyagatom** tribe who have settled primarily on the western side of the river. This tribe is quite warlike and was pushing across the Omo, taking over territory normally held by the Mursi tribe. We went in the morning to the village and witnessed the men shooting an arrow into the neck of a cow and capturing the blood — as do the Masai and other herders of cattle. We were invited back in the afternoon for some dancing put on by the three closest villages. The elders watched as the younger tribespeople danced. Our party was invited to join, and everyone seemed to have a great time.

Top: Nyagatom female bedecked in necklaces
Middle: An example of how the Nyagatom men paint their bodies
Bottom: A Nyagatom hut

There are about 30,000 members of the **Hamar** tribe, who are known for their practice of body adornment. The women are classically beautiful with long braided hair, and wear heavy polished iron jewelry around their necks.

One morning we drove about three hours to the Hamar Mountains near the town of Turmi to witness a *"Bullah"* (**Bull Jumping Ceremony**) — the right of passage for young Hamar warriors to pass into adulthood.

There were already over 200 Hamar when we arrived. The women were begging the men to whip them — picking out the whip to be used from the assortment each man had in his hand. The man would then crack the whip over her shoulder onto her back or directly on the back. Many women had wounds that were bleeding. The women are very proud of the welts and scars that mark their lower backs. These scars are a symbol of a woman's strength, love and devotion, received — at the woman's request — in ritualized whippings during and after the bull jumping ceremony. None of the women showed any sign of pain. The only time I saw a woman crying was when she asked a man to whip her and he refused. She then ran away crying. Except for two other visitors, we were the only *forengi* (foreigners).

We went back the following day for the feast which usually precedes the bull jumping. We were invited guests of the father of the bull jumper, (we were the only *forengi*). More than 150 Hamar were sitting under a low shade hut. There were two groups — the larger of which were friends of the bull jumping family and the other group were invited guests. Women would lead each group in traditional songs and everyone would clap. We were all accepted into the party and communicated as well as we could with sign language.

After the Hamar had drunk much sorgum beer, and after we tried their honey (take a lump, chew it up and spit out the wax) they began a traditional dance with the men on one side in a semi-circle, and with the women occasionally running in and out of the semi-circle. A few men would

Top: The Hamar Koke tribe gather for a ceremony
Middle: Young men with their weapons
Bottom: A young Hamar Koke man prepares for the bull jumping ceremony

A warrior comes of age by jumping the "bullah"

start jumping behind each other and then one at a time the women would run out and kick the man they wished to dance with above the ankle. After awhile a few men in our party joined in jumping with the Hamar men and following a few jumps we were each kicked and danced (jumped) for a few moments with the women that had chosen us.

Later they slaughtered a goat and a bull which were accepted by each of the two groups — the goat by the guests and the bull by the family. The family group was initially offered goat after goat and they refused to accept any of the goats. They told the father of the bull jumper that was holding the party that he was very rich and they were very many guests and he should slaughter a cow — and eventually he gave in. It was a fascinating night and one I was honored to be included in. On our drive back to camp we saw two bat eared fox and many dikdiks.

The **Hamar Market** in **Dimika** is held every Saturday. Hundreds of Hamar traders displayed their goods including honey, tobacco, sorghum, coffee substitute, gourds, jewelry, bananas, sorghum beer, rust colored dust used to dye their hair, and much more. I enjoyed bargaining with some of the vendors, which made it fun. As far as I could tell, everything for sale was goods that the Hamar themselves would purchase.

The **Kwegu** or **Mogudji** live on banks of the Omo River at its junction with the Mago River, and number only a few hundred people. They are good fishermen and also trap small game and collect honey and wild fruits. There

Members of the Kwegu

were about 75 people in the village, and very few of the adults and most certainly none of the children had seen Europeans (whites). These are the poorest of the poor on the Omo. They have no cattle and no land, and have some sort of a serfdom arrangement with the Nyagatom (previously it was with the Mursi). It was great fun showing the children their photos on our digital cameras, as they apparently find it hard to believe that you are showing them their own image.

I also took some video and played it back for them and they were truly amazed.

During my visit most of the **Mursi** tribe had moved away from the river, so we decided to drive to a Mursi Village about five hours away by road, to their dry-season range in the Mursi Hills. During the wet season they are mainly on the Tama Plains north of Mago Park, and within the park itself.

There are about 5,000 members of the Mursi tribe, who are best known by the large lip plates (up to 7 inches in diameter) worn by their women. The Mursi have a war-like culture, predominantly fighting to control large tracts of land for grazing. The men practice light scarification on their shoulders after killing an enemy, and paint most of their bodies with white chalk paint during dances and ceremonies.

Mago National Park

Mago National Park was established in 1978 and covers an area of 8,348-square-miles (21,620-km^2). The Mago Mountains form the northern border and the Mago River and Mursi Hill Range form the western border. There used to be thousands of lesser kudu in this reserve, however most of them along with elephant and other wildlife have been poached.

The Mursi are best known for their lip plates

The Mursi inhabit the park — just as many of Ethiopia's parks are inhabited by people. Physical features of the park include part of the Lake Turkana Basin to the south, the Great Rift Valley and the Ethiopian Highland massif. Visitors should be sure to note that according to the "Prohibited Activities within the Park" in the Mago National Park Visitor's Guide, that "carrying machine guns" is not allowed!

Mursi Hill range

On our drive through the park we saw gerenuk, Defassa waterbuck, black tailed mongoose and dikdik. Other wildlife includes lion, cheetah, tiang (a subspecies of topi), lesser kudu, oryx, Lelwel's hartebeest, Grant's gazelle, bushbuck, duiker, klipspringer, warthog, bushpig, bat eared fox, baboon and black-and-white colobus monkey. On a boat excursion along Mago National Park, which is situated on the eastern bank of the river, we saw lots of crocs and approached three on one sandbar so closely that the boat got stuck just a few yards (meters) from them.

The Mursi were quite commercial compared to the other tribes we visited as they are more easily visited by tourists in vehicles. The lip plates were huge and quite incredible — and made good souvenirs.

All visitors need to check in at the Mago National Park offices at Neri and pick up an armed national parks ranger to ride with them to see the Mursi. From wherever you enter the park you must first drive to Neri, pay park fees and take a park ranger with you.

ACCOMMODATION IN THE REGION– CLASS B: • **Lamule Camp** is a seasonal mobile camp set on the banks of the Omo River within the southern edge of Mago National Park. The camp consists of eight large standup sized tents (about 10 ft. × 13 ft./ 3m × 4m) with a private shower and toilet tent set back from each of the sleeping tents, and a large dining tent. There is generator to run the refrigerators and freezers that can be used by guests to charge batteries during the day. The food is superb. Over the last 10 years, the owner/operator of the camp has developed excellent relations with local chiefs and tribes in the area. At the time of this writing, the camp offers the only boat-based exploration of the Omo — giving access to more remote tribes not easily accessible (if at all) by vehicle. Lamule Camp and the Omo River are best accessed by a two-hour private charter flight from Addis Ababa to a nearby airstrip, or by a two-hour private charter flight from Nairobi to Illeret, the Kenyan town closest to the Ethiopian border with an airstrip, followed by a road transfer across the border to the camp. It takes two to three days to drive from Addis Ababa.

CLASS D: • **Murulle Omo Explorer's Lodge** has eight basic chalets with en suite cold showers and flush toilets. The camp is used for hunting as well as photographic guests.

CAMPING: Campsites are available at the Mago National Park offices.

Omo River Delta

The Omo River Delta is about 22 miles (35 km) across and covers about 230-square-miles (600-km²). The Omo empties into Lake Turkana in northern Kenya.

From Lamule Camp we went downstream by boat. Enroute we saw many naked men bathing and walking along the river, as well as good birdlife and crocs. After clearing immigration we boated to the seasonal Dassenech Camp, our home for the next three nights.

There are about 13,000 **Dassenech** living on islands throughout the delta, as well as in Kenya along the north-eastern side of Lake Turkana. They are primarily pastoralists who also practice flood retreat cultivation. Their cultural practices are similar to those of the Samburu and Rendille tribes in Kenya, with whom they share the custom of male and female circumcision.

We went to several remote Dassenech villages that are seldom visited by tourists as a boat is required to reach them — making them one of my favorite tribes to visit. The kids had great fun looking at their reflections in our sunglasses, and rubbed my arms as the Dassenech do not have body hair as is true with most of the Omo tribes.

We took an afternoon boat trip all the way to Lake Turkana through a myriad of channels — some as narrow as 33 feet (10 m) apart. We saw huge flocks of white pelicans, hammerkops, white faced whistling tree ducks, a

Top: Dassenech women
Bottom: White pelicans taking off in the Omo River Delta

European barn owl, African skimmers, fish eagles, yellow billed storks, maribu storks, white faced whistling ducks, pied kingfishers and malachite kingfishers along with many crocs. We also spotted a Egyptian plover, which hasn't been recorded in Kenya although this sighting took place only a mile from the Kenyan border. As the speedboat traveled at about the same speed as the birds flew, we had flocks of African skimmers and white pelicans flying alongside the boat for a few minutes at a time before flying off.

Omo National Park

Ethiopia's largest nature reserve, Omo National Park, covers 1,570-square-miles (4,068-km^2) and is located north of Mago National Park and is on the west side of the Omo River. Although wildlife is sparse compared to parks in Kenya and Tanzania, visitors may see buffalo, elephant, eland, Burchell's zebra, and perhaps lion and leopard.

Due to its relative inaccessibility, the park is seldom visited. Access is by ferry across the Omo River at Omarate (about a three day drive from Addis) or by air charter to an airstrip near Park Headquarters.

ACCOMMODATION: None.

CAMPING: Sites are available.

THE EAST

Danakil Depression

Located in the northeast of the country, the Danakil Depression is one of the hottest places on earth with summer temperatures exceeding 122°F (50°C). **Dalol**, at over 330 feet (100m) below sea level, is in fact the lowest point below sea level on earth. Travelers interested in geology will especially find **Mount Erta Ale** fascinating as it the only volcano in the world with a permanent lava lake. Mount Erta Ale can be accessed by road, with the ascent being made on foot with camels carrying the supplies, or by a helicopter flight from Mekele.

Harar

Harar is a walled, Muslim city considered to be the fourth most holy Islamic city after Mecca, Medina and the Dome of the Rock in Jerusalem. The city was extremely religious and in fact was closed to visitors until 1887. The most impressive of its 99 mosques is the sixteenth century **Grand Mosque** with its twin towers and minaret (women are not permitted to enter). Other attractions include the nineteenth century **Medhane Alem Church** housing examples of traditional regional art, the **Community Museum** depicting the earlier ways of life in the area and the markets — rated as some of the most colorful in the country. The **Hyena Men** Harar feed bones to wild hyenas from about 7:00 p.m. to 8:00 p.m. just outside the Fallana Gate of the old city.

Harar is located 325 miles (523km) east of Addis Ababa.

ACCOMMODATION — CLASS D: • **Ras Hotel** has very basic rooms.

THE WEST

Gambella National Park

Gambella shares its western border with Sudan and is one of Ethiopia's least developed parks, with limited wildlife. The plains are dominated by high Sudanese grass and the park has populations of Nile lechwe and white-eared kob, which are not found elsewhere in the country. Other wildlife includes crocs, hippos, topi, giraffe, buffalo and elephant.

During World War II, the British shipped coffee and other goods from Gambella on the Baro River to Kharthom (Sudan) and up the Nile to the Mediterranean Sea.

The Anuak, Nuer and Misingir peoples can be found along the Baro River.

Gambella is located about 370 miles (600km) by road (two days drive) from Addis Ababa. Gambella town is serviced by scheduled flights from Addis.

ACCOMMODATION — CLASS D: • **Ethiopian Hotel** is a government owned property on the banks of the Baro River. It is very basic.

There are other basic hotels in Gambella Town.

Mozambique

Mozambique

Mozambique is a huge country of about 308,640-square-miles (799,380-km²), which is larger than either Texas or France. Maputo is the capital city, and more than 80% of the population lives on or near the Indian Ocean. Much of the country is a low-lying coastal plain, drained by the Zambezi and Limpopo river systems. The climate is warm to hot, and frost free, with rainfall between October and March. Moist miombo woodland is the dominant habitat of the interior, with semiarid acacia and mopane woodland-savannah along the low-lying drainage systems. Much of the coastal vegetation has been replaced by sugarcane and other forms of agriculture, but the coast and offshore islands are spectacularly beautiful. A colony of Portugal until 1976, Portuguese is still widely spoken and forms a common language among the many ethnic groups. The currency is the meticais.

MOZAMBIQUE

Mozambique's greatest attraction to the international traveler is its pristine beaches, and especially the idyllic islands off its 1,550 mile (2,500 km) coastline with properties offering barefoot luxury at its finest.

In addition to beautiful white sandy beaches, adventure activities including diving, snorkeling and fishing are world class. A visit to this country can be the perfect beginning or ending to a safari in east or southern Africa. I encourage you to visit while this is still relatively "undiscovered" and certainly not a crowded destination.

For the true adventurer, the country holds large wildlife reserves of interest primarily to travelers looking for a remote bush experience, wishing to explore new territory or to see its amazing birdlife. Progressive conservation programs are underway to help to one day bring back the wildlife concentrations that were once here.

Mozambique is bordered on the southeast by South Africa and Swaziland, on the west by Zimbabwe, Zambia and Malawi, and on the north by Tanzania. The country encompasses nearly 309,000 square miles (800,000 km²) and is three times the size of the United Kingdom.

Most of the country is comprised of coastal lowlands which are wide in the south and narrow as one travels northward, where the plains rise to plateaus and mountains along the borders of Zimbabwe, Zambia and Malawi. The highest point in the country is Binga Peak (7,993 ft/ 2,436 m) on the Zimbabwean border. The Zambezi River's floodplains are the dominant feature in the center of the country, with the river flowing from the Cahora Bassa Dam near the Zimbabwe border to the 62-mile wide (100 km) Zambezi Delta and emptying into the Indian Ocean. The far north is characterized by striking inselbergs (tall granite outcrops). The other main rivers transecting the country are the Rio Limpopo in the south, the Rio Save in the center and the Rio Rovuma which serves as a border with Tanzania in the north.

As Mozambique lies primarily in the tropics, the climate is warm to hot and humid. Generally, the rainy season is from November to March. However, the weather patterns are not as consistent as they were a few decades ago. Cyclone season is February to March, with the "cyclone belt" covering just the south of the country.

Quilálea Island

Bantu-speaking tribes migrated to the area around the first century A.D. Small chiefdoms formed and many consolidated into larger kingdoms. Arab traders arrived by ship around the eighth century A.D. Vasco da Gamma "discovered" Mozambique by landing on Ilha de Mozambique in 1497. The Portuguese quickly gained control of a number of islands along the coast in a quest to control the gold trade and later the ivory and slave trades from the mainland. The Portuguese signed a treaty with Britain in 1891 which set the boundaries of Portuguese East Africa. The country became independent on June 25, 1975 with Samora Machel as president. A long civil war decimated much of the country and ended with a peace agreement in 1992. The country has been steadily recovering since that time.

One of Mozambique's quaint streets

Mozambique has an approximate population of 20 million — nearly half of which are under the age of 14. About 30% of people live in towns and cities, and almost 80% are subsistence farmers. Of the major tribal groups, the Makua-Lomwe is the largest representing nearly half of the population, followed by the Tsonga, Shona, Sena, Nyungwe, Chuabo, Sena and Yao.

There are over 60 languages and dialects spoken. About a quarter of the people speak Portuguese, with English being spoken in the major cities, as well as in most of the hotels, safari camps and beach resorts attracting international guests.

The country is a melting pot of African, Portuguese, Arabic and Indian cultures. About 35% are Christian (most are Roman Catholics), 25% Muslim and the majority of the rest follow traditional religions (ancestor worship and animism). Due to the multi-cultural influence the food is interesting and the seafood is in fact spectacular. Be sure to try the piri piri prawns!

Paradise found!

WILDLIFE AND WILDLIFE AREAS

Much of Mozambique's wildlife was decimated during the civil war that ended in the early 1990s. However, the wildlife populations are growing, and through innovative conservation efforts, some parks are being restocked with indigenous species. The major wildlife reserves to consider visiting on the mainland are Reserva do Niassa (Niassa Reserve), Parque Nacional da Gorongosa (Gorongosa National Park) and the Parque Nacional do Limpopo (Limpopo Transfrontier Reserve) bordering Kruger National Park (South Africa). The wildlife is relatively sparse compared to the better reserves in Zambia, Botswana and South Africa, and for the most part more difficult to approach as closely. A real plus is that you will virtually have the parks to yourself. The story with regard to birdlife is more encouraging, with over 600 species recorded.

These parks draw adventurers looking for pristine bush experiences and ones looking for new frontiers. A visit to one or more reserves can be combined with a wonderful beach holiday.

One of the exotic flowers of Mozambique

Marine Life

Mozambique's greatest wildlife attractions lie below sea level. The coast and the islands support an amazing variety of fish, coral, marine mammals and plants. Around two thousand species of fish representing over 80% of the families of the Indo-Pacific region occur here. Among the most interesting is

Scuba diving is a popular activity at Marlin Lodge

the whale shark, the largest fish in the world growing up to 50 feet in length. Whale sharks are often sited by divers and boaters especially from December to February.

Other sea life includes the dugong (similar to the manatee), several species of dolphin (bottlenose, striped, spinner and humpback), humpback whales, turtles (leatherback, loggerhead, hawksbill and green) and manta rays. Mozambique is certainly one of the best-kept secrets for divers.

The best sightings of humpback whales in the south is during the late winter (June to October) and may also be seen in the north in the Pemba area July to November. Water temperatures range from 82°F/28C in summer (and up to 86°F/30C December to February) to 72°F (22C) during the winter months (May to July).

Marine parks include Parque Nacional de Querimbas (Quirimbas National Park) and Parque Nacional de Bazaruto (Bazaruto National Park).

Fresh catch of the day

THE NORTH

Pemba

Pemba is the capital of the province of Cabo Delgado and the major city in the north of the country. The town is situated on the Bay of Pemba, a huge, natural deep-water bay.

Formerly known as Porto Amelia, this traditional Mozambique fishing port features interesting Portuguese-colonial architecture, and offers scuba diving and world-class blue water fishing close-by. The coral reefs lie close to the shore and within reach are the abundant fishing waters at St. Lazarus Banks.

The white sand beach at Londo Lodge

Pemba can be accessed by scheduled or private air service from Maputo, Johannesburg (South Africa), Nairobi (Kenya) and Dar-es-Salaam (Tanzania). Some visitors stay at this quaint coastal town and enjoy the beaches and diving, while others use it as a waypoint and connect to the more exclusive islands in the Quirimbas Archipelago.

ACCOMMODATION — FIRST CLASS: • **Pemba Beach Hotel** has Arabian-influenced architecture with 100 rooms comprising of standard and luxury room types, self-catering villas and 5 suites, 2 restaurants, 2 bars, 2 salt-water pools, a spa and beach club. • **Londo Lodge,** situated on a peninsula just south of the Quirimbas National Park, has only 6 private villas (5 Beach View and 1 Executive), infinity swimming pool and massage facilities.

The Arabian-influenced architecture of Pemba Beach Hotel

Quirimbas Archipelago

The Quirimbas Archipelago consists of 32 tropical coral islands and stretches for 62 miles (100 km) along the coast from Pemba to the Tanzanian border.

It contains one of the world's richest reefs and most bio-diverse marine areas in the world, with dugongs, fish eagles and turtles. Humpback whales pass through the islands on their annual migration and can be seen during the months of July to November. Humpback and spinner dolphins may be seen year round. The area has very little development, making it all the more attractive to international visitors.

The impressive marine area of **Quirimbas National Park** covers 580-square-miles (1,500-km²) and includes 11 coral islands. These islands feature phenomenal vertical drop-offs, some up to 1,300 feet (400 m). These walls are abundant with coral covered caves and tropical fish and game fish. The park is also home to a wide variety of bird species such as mangrove fish eagles, herons, flamingos, kingfishers, plovers and coucals.

Vamizi Island (Ilha Vamizi)

Vamizi Island is an 8-mile (12 km) crescent-shaped idyllic tropical island situated a short charter flight from Pemba.

The inviting waters and pristine beaches of Vamizi Island

Activities offered at the lodge include world-class scuba diving and snorkeling in the pristine coral reefs, deep sea, fly or shore fishing, kayaking, cruising by dhow and being pampered in the spa. Guided walks and a day trip to nearby Rongui Island are available.

ACCOMMODATION — DELUXE: • **Vamizi**, the only lodge on the island, offers 10 spacious sea-facing beach villas nestled under trees. Built and crafted by local islanders, the palm-thatched villas have expansive verandas and Swahili daybeds perfect for an afternoon siesta, and en suite Mozambiquean marble bathrooms. Access is via a short charter flight from Pemba.

Quilálea Island

Quilálea Island, situated in the southern region of the Quirimbas Archipelago, is a unique island marine sanctuary, fringed with pristine beaches and surrounded by the tropical Indian Ocean. The island is only 88-acres (35-hectares) in size and offers the ultimate in seclusion and privacy as the only residents are the hotel guests and staff.

ACCOMMODATION — DELUXE: • **Quilálea** accommodates up to 18 guests in 9 luxury air-conditioned villas, with en suite facilities and private verandas with panoramic sea views. Each villa was constructed entirely with indigenous materials. Scuba diving, snorkeling, fishing, and excursions on their 38 foot sailing yacht are available. Access is via a short charter flight from Pemba.

Matemo Island

Matemo Island is located approximately 20 minutes flying time north of Pemba. Palm groves, lush vegetation, white beaches and an azure sea provide an idyllic setting for this

Top: A luxury villa at Quilálea
Middle: One of the bedrooms at Quilálea
Bottom: The pool area at Quilálea

Top: The turquoise water off Matemo Island
Bottom: Matemo's chalets line the beach

exotic Quirimbas island destination. Ideal for honeymooners or families, Matemo offers a wide range of marine activities plus a fascinating insight into local culture.

ACCOMMODATION — DELUXE: • **Matemo Island** accommodates a maximum of 48 guests in 24 luxury air-conditioned chalets, each located just yards (meters) from the beach, with private patios with hammock, indoor and outdoor showers and panoramic ocean views. Private in-chalet spa treatments, diving, snorkeling, fishing and cultural island excursions to Ibo Island are offered.

Medjumbe Private Island

True hedonistic pleasure awaits at this romantic and exclusive island getaway. A perfect backdrop of endless white sand and translucent sea mesmerizes all who visit, while the untouched marine environment allows for constant new discoveries, whether your passion is diving, fishing, snorkeling, or simply exploring the spectaular beaches.

This small island of unspoiled beaches surrounded by translucent waters is just 875 × 380 yards (800 × 350 m) in size and offers total exclusivity and privacy, as the only human inhabitants being guests and staff. The diving off the island is world class, and the first of many exquisite sites can be found just 1.5 miles (2 km) from shore. Snorkeling and fishing, waterskiing, sailing, kayaking and sunset cruises are also offered.

ACCOMMODATION — DELUXE: • **Medjumbe Private Island** accommodates just 26 guests in 13 secluded luxury air-conditioned chalets each with panoramic sea views, their own plunge pool, deck, patio and sala.

Ibo Island (Ilha Do Ibo)

Ibo Island lies within Quirimbas National Park and is historically the most interesting island in the archipelago, and has been nominated for World Heritage status. For 500 years it was a prominent trading post on the East African coast, and had, in fact, become the most important town in Mozambique by the late eighteenth century. The island has three forts, an old catholic church and other historic buildings, and is virtually untouched by large commercial developments. Visiting here is like going back in time.

ACCOMMODATION — TOURIST CLASS: • **Ibo Island Lodge** is located on the waterfront and incorporates three mansions each over a century old with walls a yard (1 m) thick, with 12 en suite air-conditioned rooms.

Top: The veranda at Ibo Island Lodge
Bottom: One of the mansions at Ibo Island Lodge

Niassa Reserve (Reserva Do Niassa)

This 16,200-square-mile (42,000-km²) park is set on the southern border of Tanzania, and is about twice the size of Kruger National Park (South Africa). The scenery is incredible, with giant inselbergs, baobab trees and palms reaching out to the sky from what is one of the largest protected areas of miombo *(brachystegia)* woodland on the continent.

The park is the largest reserve in Mozambique and has highest concentration of game of any reserve as well. Due to its remoteness, the wildlife populations here were much less affected by the civil war than the country's other reserves.

Wildlife includes approximately 12,000 elephant, 9,000 sable antelope, 5,000 buffalo and 200 wild dog, along with good populations of lion, leopard, eland, Lichetenstien's hartebeest, kudu, bushbuck, impala, wildebeest, zebra, waterbuck and hippo. The elephant are famous for their large tusks. Three subspecies endemic to the park include Boehm's zebra, Niassa wildebeest and Johnstone's impala.

Top: The open-air bar at Lugenda Wilderness Camp
Bottom: Bright colors and tropical woods welcome guests

Over 370 bird species including Pel's fishing owl, Taita falcon, African skimmer, Stierling's woodpecker and the African pitta.

ACCOMMODATION — CLASS A/B: • **Lugenda Wilderness Camp**, located on the Lugenda River, has 8 fan-cooled luxury tents with large verandahs and en suite facilities, and a swimming pool. Game drives and escorted walks are offered. Access is by private air charter from Pemba and other cities to an airstrip near camp. The camp is open from June 1st until December 15th. Children under the age of 12 are not allowed.

CLASS D: • At Park Headquarters there are simple en suite chalets with en suite facilities.

CENTRAL

Gorongosa National Park (Parque Nacional da Gorongosa)

Gorongosa National Park covers approximately 1,455-square-miles (3,770-km²) of the floor of the Great East African Rift Valley and is considered to be the country's most biologically diverse reserve. Habitats include lowland miombo woodland, mopane woodland, rainforests, extensive grasslands and swamps.

The park was named after 6,107 foot (1,862 m) Gorongosa Mountain which dominates the landscape. Many rivers formed on its slopes flow into Lake Urema, which is centrally located in the park.

Much of the wildlife here was killed during the civil war, however, it is starting to rebound. The Carr Foundation is working to help restore the park by restocking buffalo, wildebeest and zebra. Other wildlife that may be seen includes elephant, hippo, crocodile, kudu and waterbuck, eland, sable, hartebeest, oribi, nyala, two species of bushbaby, and with luck, leopard, lion, and wild dog.

The diversity of soil types in the valley support an astonishing number of plant species that in turn support many different species of reptiles, frogs, and fish; more than 400 bird species.

Attractions within the park include the Lake Urema wetlands, the limestone gorges of the Cheringoma Plateau and Murombodzi Waterfall. There are approximately 93 miles (150km) of game viewing roads in the park. The best time to visit is during the dry season May to November. During the rainy season (January to April) the park is closed. The best access is by charter flight, or a long drive from Beira.

ACCOMMODATION — CLASS B: • **Chitengo Camp** has 9 new air-conditioned cabanas with en suite facilities, restaurant and pool.

CAMPING: Campsites with hot showers are available at Chitengo Camp.

SOUTH

Limpopo Transfrontier Reserve (Parque Nacional do Limpopo)
Located along the South African border, much of the wildlife in this reserve was killed off during the civil war that ended in 1992. Wildlife populations are fortunately slowly recovering.

The 75,000-acre (30,000-hectare) "Sanctuary" area, located within the reserve borders Kruger National Park, has the best game viewing, and is where most of the game is being trans-located in an effort to help restock the park.

Easiest access is by charter flight from Maputo or by 4wd vehicle from Kruger National Park.

ACCOMMODATIONS — CLASS C: **Machampane Wilderness Camp** is located in the Sanctuary Area and has 5 tents with en suite facilities, on raised decks overlooking the Machampane River.

CAMPING: **Campismo Agula Pesqueira** has campsites and a few tents for rent.

Vilanculos
Vilanculos is the gateway coastal city to the Bazaruto Archipelago, 435 miles (700 km) north of Maputo, directly opposite the islands of the Bazaruto Archipelago in the tropical Inhambane province.

Bazaruto Archipelago
Bazaruto and Benguerra Islands are the two largest islands off the Mozambican coast and feature beautiful white-sand beaches, world-class scuba diving and snorkeling, magnificent high sand dunes, coastal bush and green fresh-water lakes inhabited by crocodiles. Bird "specials" include the Blue-throated sunbird and Rudd's apalis.

For the avid angler, the Bazaruto Archipelago is ranked as the best marlin-angling destination in the eastern Indian Ocean. The best time for marlin fishing

Pansy Island, part of the Bazaruto Archipelago

is from mid-September until the end of December and for sailfish fishing is from April to August, with smaller game fish available year-round.

Bazaruto National Park includes Bazaruto, Benguerra, Magaruque, Santa Carolina and Bangue Islands, all of which are located 6 to 9 miles (10 to 15 km) off the coast just north of Vilanculos.

There are accommodations ranging from comfortable to deluxe from which to choose on Bazaruto Island (Indigo Bay Island Resort and Spa and Bazaruto Lodge) and on Benguerra Island (Azura, Marlin Lodge and Benguerra Lodge).

Benguerra Island

Benguerra Island is the second largest island in the chain, covering approximately 21-square-miles (55-km²) of magnificent beaches and surrounded by coral reefs. The island was declared a National Park in 1971, and includes forest, savannah, dunes and wetlands including freshwater lakes.

ACCOMMODATION — DELUXE: • **Azura**, Mozambique's first luxury eco-boutique retreat, was built entirely by hand in partnership with the local community. Azura has just 15 villas including 3 Luxury Beach Villas, 11 Infinity Beach Villas and the Presidential Villa. Each beachfront villa has a private bathroom with an indoor/outdoor shower, pool, air-conditioning, private sun deck, mini-bar, and butler service. Activities include snorkeling and scuba diving, big game fishing (marlin, sailfish, tuna), dhow trips, cruises to remote beaches and island walks. • **Marlin Lodge,** located on Benguerra Island, accommodates 34 guests in 14 luxury Beach Chalets and 3 Executive Beach Suites constructed from local hardwoods and elevated on stilts with deck platforms. Each air-conditioned en suite room has an indoor and an outdoor

A chalet at Marlin Lodge

shower, and a private, thatch-covered deck with sea facing views and direct beach access. There is a swimming pool with beach gazebo and serviced pool bar. The lodge welcomes children 14 years and older. Activities at the lodge include free wind-surfing, catamaran sailing, kite-flying and ocean ski paddling, water-skiing, snorkeling and scuba diving, sunset cruises on a dhow.

Picnicking in style at Benguerra Lodge

ACCOMMODATION — FIRST CLASS: • **Benguerra Lodge** is set within Benguerra Bay on the protected northwest side of the island. There are 4 types of accommodations: Bungalows, Cabanas, Casitas and the Villa — all with en suite facilities. Activities include wind surfing, snorkeling and scuba diving, hobie cat sailing, dhow rides and deep-sea and saltwater fishing.

Bazaruto Island (Ilha do Bazaruto)

Bazaruto is 23 miles (37 km) long and 4 miles (7 km) wide, making it by far the largest of the islands in the archipelago. Savannah grassland dominates the western part of the island while large sand dunes dominate the eastern part of the island.

ACCOMMODATION — DELUXE: • **Indigo Bay**, on the southwest shore of Bazaruto Island, offers guests a variety of accommodations including 29 Beach Chalets, 1 Honeymoon Chalet, 12 Luxury Bay View Villas, 1 Executive Suite and a Presidential Villa. Each chalet and villa offers a private bathroom, air-conditioning, mini-bar and private balcony. The Bay View Villas and Honeymoon Chalet also feature private plunge pools. Facilities include two swimming pools and a pool bar, beach snack bar, and the Sanctuary Spa. Activities available include scuba diving, snorkeling, hobie cat sailing,

Top: The decadent luxury of Indigo Bay
Bottom: The white sand beach at Bazaruto Lodge

Guests can enjoy the refreshing pool at Bazaruto Lodge

horseback riding, sundowner cruises, dune boarding, land rover safaris, catamaran island hopping and salt-water fly-fishing.

TOURIST CLASS: • **Bazaruto Lodge** has 25 A-frame thatch roofed bungalows (12 standard, 11 superior and 1 honeymoon) set in lush tropical gardens. All units are air-conditioned with private facilities and ceiling fans.

Maputo

Maputo, formerly known as Lorenzo Marques, is the capital of Mozambique. The city is a hodgepodge of new and old buildings with wide streets lined with jacaranda and palm trees, and is humming with activity.

The **Museu de Historia Natural** (Natural History Museum) is worth a visit, if only to see what may be the world's largest collection of elephant foe-

Sailing the calm waters off Mozambique's coast

tuses. The **Museu Nacional de Art** (National Art Museum) features the works of many of Mozambique's best contemporary artists. The nineteenth century **Fortaleza** (Fort) has a small museum. The **Mercado Municipal** will give you an insight into the life of the people and the variety of local produce available. One of the most unusual buildings in Africa is the **Iron House of Maputo**, located near the city center. This house was made entirely of iron and was designed by Gustav Eifel. Built in the late nineteenth century to be the governor's home, it proved to be far too hot for residence. **Inhaca Island** is a densely wooded island off Maputo, 10 minutes by small aircraft and two hours by ferry boat.

Be sure to try a few local restaurants and enjoy the local beers and a plate of piri piri prawns. **Piri Piri**, opposite the Polana Shopping Centre, serves sumptuous piri piri chicken, fantastic prawns and long glasses of cold local beer in "Giraffe" glasses. **Gianni's**, on the other side of the Polana Shopping Centre serves fresh ice cream made with local fruit and served with waffles and pancakes. **Costa do Sol**, located at the end of the Marginal coast road, is famous for its shellfish.

ACCOMMODATIONS—DELUXE:
• The **Polana Serena** Hotel is situated ten minutes away from the city center and the airport. This majestic colonial building offers 164 air-conditioned rooms and 23 suites each with en suite facilities and satellite television. The hotel overlooks the Bay of Maputo and offers landscaped gardens, a swimming pool and several restaurants and bars.

The pool area at the Polana Serena

ACCOMMODATION — TOURIST CLASS: • **Cardoso** has 114 air-conditioned standard rooms, 4 luxury suites and 12 executive rooms, gymnasium, swimming pool and wireless Internet throughout the hotel. • **Holiday Inn,** located just 5 miles (8 km) from the international airport, is the only beachfront hotel in the city of Maputo. Facilities include a swimming pool, sea view restaurant, bar and fitness center, and free Internet access in all guest rooms.

Malawi

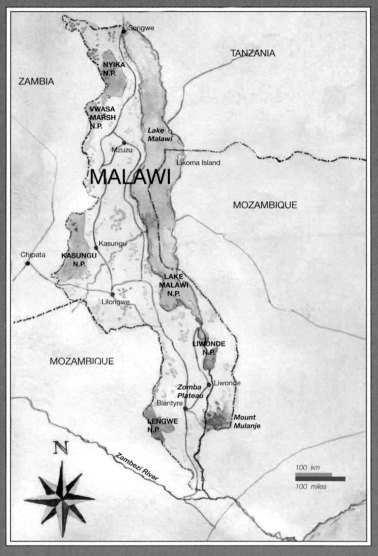

Known to many as the "Warm Heart of Africa" Malawi is a beautiful country dominated by the great lake of the same name. The altitude varies from 120 feet (37 m) in the Shire Valley to 9,847 feet (3,002 m) on the summit of Mount Mulanje. Brachystegia (miombo) woodland prevails over most of the country, with open grassland and moorland on higher ground. The population of Malawi is around 12 million, with about 500,000 In the capital of Lilongwe. The majority of the population are subsistence farmers. Chichewa and English are the official languages. Currency is the Malawian Kwacha.

MALAWI

Malawi, the warm heart of Africa, is a beautiful country with a variety of holiday attractions, interesting cultures and a few wildlife reserves of interest to the international traveler. Lake Malawi is a popular beach destination for travelers who have been on safari in Zambia or other southern African countries.

Geographically, the country is dominated by Lake Malawi, which stretches along the spine of the country. It is often referred to as the "calendar lake" because its surface dimensions are 365 miles (568 km) long and 52 miles (84 km) wide.

This freshwater lake, the southernmost in the Rift Valley chain, is the third largest in Africa. It is also one of the deepest of the Great Rift Valley lakes (2,296 feet/700 m deep), with its deepest point 755 feet (230 m) below sea level. Lake Malawi has over 400 species of freshwater fish and the largest number of cichlid fish species in the world.

Malawi is bordered by Zambia to the west, Tanzania to the north and Mozambique to the east, southwest and south. From north to south, Malawi is about 560 miles (900 km) long. The dominant geographical features in the south of the country are the Shire River and the high plateau of Dedza, Zomba and the Kirk Mountain Range, reaching an altitude from 5,050 feet (1,540 m) to 8,000 feet (2,440 m) above sea level.

As a whole, the country ranges in altitude from 120 feet (37 m) in the lower Shire Valley in the south to a height of 9,847 feet (3,002 m) at Mt. Mulanje, also in the south. The northern lakeshore and adjacent low country rise steeply to the west. Several areas, the Misuku Hills, the Nyika Plateau (Nganda Point is the highest peak on the plateau at 8,551 ft./2,607 m) and the Viphya Plateau, dominate the areas of higher ground.

The dominant vegetation of Malawi is *brachystegia* or miombo woodlands. Malawi has a tropical climate with a rainy season extending from November to March in the south and November to April in the north. Its climate is influenced locally by the lake and by altitude. A curious weather effect, known as *chiperoni* — low clouds, condensation and a light drizzle, precipitated by a high-pressure system in Mozambique, forces moist, cool air over higher ground — is a frequent occurrence during the dry season in the south of the country, particularly around Blantyre and Thyolo. Temperatures vary considerably, from a maximum of 104°F (40°C) in the low-lying Shire Valley (pronounced shirry) to below freezing on the plateaus, where frost may occur.

In the early fifteenth century, the area was inhabited by the Maravi people (a derivation of the word Malawi), who moved in from the west of the continent around the twelfth century. Arab slave traders were well established in the area by 1870 and were handling more than 20,000 slaves per year. David

Livingstone first visited the area in 1859, and on his subsequent visits brought many British missionaries.

Nyasaland became a protectorate of the British Empire in 1891 and in 1953 joined the Federation of Northern (now Zambia) and Southern (now Zimbabwe) Rhodesia. Malawi became independent in 1964.

Chichewa is the national language, but English is the official language and is widely spoken. The most popular beer is Carlsberg, brewed according to Danish traditions. You may want to try some Malawi Gin, and do not miss out on Malawian cashew nuts, peanut butter and Mulanje Gold, an admirable substitute for Kahlua.

The country's economy is based on agriculture; 90% of its population is rural, and agriculture accounts for 40% of the gross domestic product and 90% of its export revenues. Almost 70% of agricultural produce comes from small land holding farmers, whose principal crops are maize, tobacco, tea, sugarcane, groundnuts and coffee. With a population in excess of 11 million, almost every available piece of arable land is cultivated.

🐾 WILDLIFE AND WILDLIFE AREAS

Great importance has been attached to the protection of Malawi's natural heritage, which is reflected in the number of national parks and reserves within the country. Despite the burdens of overpopulation, almost 20% of Malawi's land area is set aside as either national park, game reserve or forest reserve.

Malawi's primary wildlife attractions are Liwonde National Park, Nyika National Park and Lake Malawi itself. Zambia is an excellent country to combine with Malawi, because South Luangwa National Park (Zambia) is easily accessible by air from Lilongwe.

Nyika National Park

The Nyika Plateau is a wild, remote and spectacular area of rolling montane grasslands interspersed with pockets of evergreen forest. The upland area of the Nyika (which means wilderness in the local Tumbuka language) Plateau was designated as Malawi's first national park in 1966. An important extension to the park, effectively doubling its size, was gazetted in 1976. Today it is the country's largest park, encompassing a total area of 1,210-square-miles (3,134-km^2).

Game on the plateau is plentiful; reedbuck, common duiker and roan antelope are the dominant animals, along with eland and Burchell's zebra. Leopard, hyena and bushpig may be seen on evening drives. An excellent way to explore the park is on horseback

The flower-filled, rolling grasslands of the Nyika are home to wattled crane, Denham's bustard, churring and black-lored cisticolas, common quail, rufous-naped lark, red-tufted malachite sunbird and mountain nightjar. The evergreen forest pockets, often beginning in valley heads and following drainage lines, are sanctuary to the large checkered elephant shrew, bushpig and forest duiker. They are also home for a number of forest-dwelling birds such as moustached green tinkerbird, Fulleborn's black boubou, Sharpe's akalat, olive-flanked alethe, scaly francolin, white-tailed flycatcher and bar-tailed trogon.

The best time to visit the park for botanists (for wildflowers and orchids) is September to January. For birders, September to March is best, although the heavy rains in January through April can restrict access and activities in the park. Wildlife viewing is good throughout the year.

A network of dirt roads meanders across the plateau. Access to the park is via Thazima Gate, 34 miles (55 km) from Rumphi and 81 miles (130 km) from Mzuzu. From Thazima Gate, it is about 37 miles (59 km) to the Malawian Parks Board Camp of Chelinda.

ACCOMMODATION — CLASS A/B: • **Chelinda Lodge** has 8 deluxe log cabins, each with private facilities, lounge with a fireplace, and balcony. Raised wooden walkways link the cabins to the central restaurant and lounge. As of this writing it is closed but may open soon under new ownership.

CLASS C: • **Chelinda Rest Camp** has 4 two-bedroom self-service cottages with private facilities and kitchen, and 6 twin-bedded rooms with private facilities. There is a restaurant and bar nearby.

CAMPING: A campsite with pre-erected tents and limited ablution facilities is available. You may also bring your own tent.

Lake Malawi

Magnificent Lake Malawi is the country's largest tourist attraction. The huge lake supplies a seemingly endless number of protein-rich fish to the local people. Chambo, a sought after tilapia (freshwater bream), is a good-eating fish.

On the lake you will see fishermen in their bwatus (dugout canoes) fishing either with nets or with lines. Sometimes at night you will see the twinkling of lights on the lake from bwatus and boats with small outboard motors.

The mostly clear waters of the lake make this an inviting environment for recreational activities. The southern lakeshore hotels are best equipped for watersports, and boardsailing, water skiing, sailing, snorkeling and scuba diving are all available.

Lake Malawi offers some of the best inland sailing in Africa. Although rough waters can suddenly develop with the onset of strong winds, there are no tides or currents in the lake. The prevailing wind is southeasterly, and the lake is generally at its calmest around March to June and is roughest in July and August, however, the lake can be rough at any time.

Likoma Island

Likoma Island is located in the far north of Lake Malawi on the east side of the lake very close to the Mozambique coastline. To visit the island is to step back in time. Just 7-square-miles (17-km²) in size with one small dirt road and a few vehicles, the local people survive largely by fishing, and rice and cassava farming. The island has hundreds of huge baobab trees and a number of glorious sandy beaches and rocky coves. The waters are crystal clear throughout the year and the diving and snorkeling is among the best in Lake Malawi.

ACCOMMODATION — FIRST CLASS: • **Kaya Mawa Lodge** is situated on the southwestern tip of the Island at the head of a crescent-shaped bay, surrounded by mango trees and ancient baobabs. It consists of 10 stone and teak-framed thatched cottages each with a shower, sunken bathtub, a "loo with a view", and private terrace with direct water access. The Honeymoon Room is tucked away on its own private island and offers incredible views. Activities include snorkeling, scuba diving (additional fee), swimming, sailing and visits to the local villages. Day trips to Mozambique can be arranged.

Top: Kaya Mawa Lodge's main area
Bottom: Kaya Mawa's jetty and view of the lake

TOURIST CLASS: • **Chintheche Inn**, situated on a sandy beach just south of Nkhata Bay on the western shore of the lake, has 10 fan-cooled rooms with en suite bathrooms, restaurant, and swimming pool.

Lake Malawi National Park

Lake Malawi National Park is the first national park to provide protection to the freshwater life of a deep-water Rift Valley lake. The 34-square-mile (88 km²) park is located in the southern part of the lake and includes 12 islands and most of the Nankhumba Peninsula. Its crystal clear waters and myriad of colorful cichlid fish darting among the rocky shoreline entice one to don a mask and snorkel and join the fish in their daily activities.

Wildlife that may be seen includes bushbuck, klipspringer, crocs and hippos. Bird life includes fish eagles, trumpeter hornbill, white-breasted cuckoo-shrike, crowned and black eagles, golden-backed pytilia and mocking chat.

ACCOMMODATION ON THE SOUTHERN LAKESHORE — CLASS A/B: • **Pumulani** is a brand new lodge located on the shores of Lake Malawi. The lodge features 10 individual villas with en suite facilities, a large bedroom, living area and private deck with lake views. Activities include snorkeling, fishing, sailing, dhow cruises, nature walks and kayaking. Optional activities for an additional charge are waterskiing, scuba diving, wake boarding and tube rides. • **Club Makakola**, set on a sandy beach on the shores of Lake Malawi, has cottages and 55 refurbished rooms with en suite facilities, 2 swimming pools, tennis courts, squash court, 9-hole Mlambe Golf Course and a conference center. Fishing, parasailing, diving and excursions to the Cape Maclear area are offered.

CLASS B: • **Livingstonia Beach Hotel**, once one of the finest hotels in Malawi (and still retains some of its former splendor), has 18 rooms and 8 rondavels, all fan-cooled, with en suite facilities, a restaurant and swimming pool. Sailboards, kayaks and boats are available for hire. • **Nkopola Lodge** is set on a hillside on the shore of Lake Malawi about 12 miles (20 km) north of the town of Mangochi. The lodge has 55 air-conditioned rooms with en suite facilities and a restaurant.

ACCOMMODATION ON MUMBO ISLAND — CLASS B: • **Mumbo Island Camp** has recently been upgraded to include en suite facilities, while on Domwe Island each 2 tents share a separate bathroom with a bucket shower and chemical toilet. Guests paddle their own kayaks out to the island, which is set off the Cape Maclear Peninsula. Activities include swimming, snorkeling, and exploring the local islands and lakeshore.

Lilongwe

Lilongwe became the capital in 1975 and features Old Town and New Town. **Old Town** hustles and bustles with markets and buildings close together, and the **New Town** (also known as the Garden City) offers modern architecture, open pedestrian precincts and parklands.

A visit to the market in the Old Town is a worthwhile experience. There, one can buy anything from live chickens to used motorcar parts. The air is ripe with the aroma of dried fish, spices and fresh vegetables.

For six months of each year (April to September) the **Tobacco Auction Floors** in Lilongwe and the nearby city of Limbe are hives of activity as buyers gather from around the world. Those thinking of visiting the floors should call in advance.

The **Lilongwe Nature Sanctuary**, located between the old and new towns, is a good place for seeing small mammals, such as porcupine, civet and vervet monkeys. It is also a good place for spotting birds, such as red-throated twinspot and perhaps African finfoot.

ACCOMMODATION — FIRST CLASS: • **Capital Hotel** is located in the New Town, adjacent to the commercial and diplomatic areas. The hotel has 185 air-conditioned rooms with en suite facilities, 2 restaurants and a swimming pool.

TOURIST CLASS: • **Heuglin's Lodge**, an exclusive guesthouse with a large swimming pool set in a quiet area of the Garden Suburbs of New Town, has 6 bedrooms with en suite facilities. The lodge has an excellent wildlife library and can arrange local sightseeing trips. • **Lilongwe Hotel**, situated on 3 acres of landscaped gardens in the heart of the Old Town, has 91 air-conditioned rooms with en suite facilities, 2 restaurants and a swimming pool.

Blantyre

Blantyre, named after the birthplace of the great explorer David Livingstone, began as a mission station in 1876. Its position in the agriculturally rich highlands, which has a more temperate climate, made it attractive to the first commercial traders.

Today, Blantyre is the largest city in the country and is also the commercial and industrial center of Malawi. Historical sites include the **Blantyre Mission**, the beautiful church of **St. Michael's and All Angels**, and the **Mandala House**, the oldest building in the country (erected in 1882).

Blantyre's market is more modern and does not have quite the same appeal as that of Lilongwe.

ACCOMMODATION — FIRST: • **Ryall's Hotel Blantyre** is the oldest established hotel situated in the middle of town and has been recently refurbished. The hotel offers 120 comfortably appointed rooms and a range of facilities including swimming pool, gym and wireless internet access throughout. • **Sunbird Mt. Soche Hotel**, located very close to the city center, has 132 air-conditioned rooms with en suite facilities, 2 restaurants and a swimming pool.

Liwonde National Park

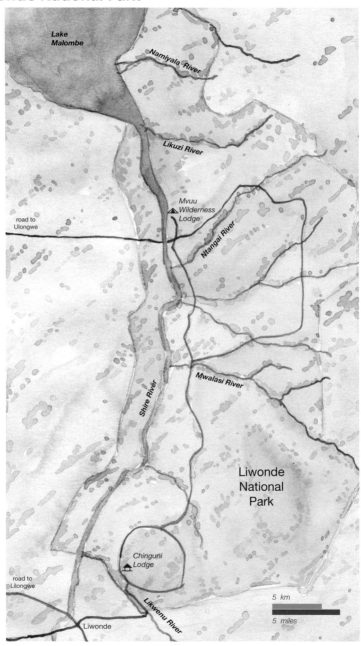

Liwonde National Park

Established in 1973, the 212-square-mile (548-km^2) Liwonde National Park was created to protect the important riverine vegetation and mopane woodland of the upper Shire Valley and is now Malawi's showpiece park.

A major feature of the park is the Shire River, which provides one of the last refuges in the country for hippo and Nile crocodile. The river flows out of Lake Malawi and forms the western boundary of the park. It forges its way southward over tumultuous rapids and falls to join the Zambezi River beyond Malawi's borders.

In Liwonde you have a good chance of seeing good numbers of impala, sable antelope, common water-buck, warthog, hippo, elephant and crocodile. Lion are also seen. This is a birder's paradise with over 400 species recorded, including Boehm's bee-eater, Lilian's lovebird, brown-breasted barbet, Pel's fishing owl, white-backed night heron and marsh tchagra.

Top: One of Mvuu Wilderness Lodge's luxury chalets
Bottom: A view of Mvuu Wilderness Lodge from the Shire River

The best time for game viewing is during the dry season, May to October. Birding is best November to April, but is very good year-round.

Liwonde National Park lies 75 miles (120 km) from Blantyre and 152 miles (245 km) from Lilongwe, via the town of Liwonde.

ACCOMMODATION — CLASS A: • **Mvuu Wilderness Lodge**, set on a quiet backwater area of the Shire River, offers splendid views of the mighty river from its bar/dining deck. The lodge has 8 luxury units with en suite facilities, and offers day and night game drives in open vehicles, boat game drives and escorted walks.

CLASS C AND D: • **Mvuu Camp** is a 36-bedded camp with attractive en suite stone chalets split into double chalets and specially designed 2-room family units.

CAMPING: Sites are available.

Mulanje

In the southeast of the country lies Mt. Mulanje, an impressive hunk of rock that juts out from the surrounding featureless plains. This is one of the finest scenic areas in the country. Sapitwa is the highest peak at 9,847 feet (3,002 m).

There are a number of forestry rest huts on the plateau, and there are trails leading from hut to hut. Several footpaths lead up to the massif from its base; the most popular is Likhabula, on the west side of the mountain. A Forestry Rest House at the foot serves as a base camp, and from there you can organize your climb. Porters may be hired to carry your gear because you must take all your supplies with you. The path is quite steep in places.

Mulanje is a flower-lover's paradise. A variety of soil types have resulted in a range of habitats from evergreen rain forests, with begonias on the sides of the plateau, to heath-like grasslands that are covered in ericas and giant lobelias at higher altitudes.

Helichrysum daisies dominate the landscape in the spring, as do a number of species of iris and brilliantly colored red-hot pokers. Two interesting birds seen here are the cholo alethe and the yellow-streaked bulbul.

Unfortunately, most game animals have been eliminated, but Mulanje can be very rewarding for botanists and birders.

The mountain is subject to extremes of climate, so if you are planning to walk on Mulanje, it is best to avoid the rainy season, January to April. Daytime temperatures May to August (the southern winter) are cool, with the likelihood of heavy mists in the mornings and frost at night. Between August and November, it can get quite hot. Thunderstorms occur November through April.

ACCOMMODATION — CLASS F: • **Forestry Rest House** at Likhabula provides bedding. Forestry huts on the plateau have wooden bunks; you must bring all necessary equipment.

ACCOMMODATION NEAR MULANJE — CLASS C: • **Chawani Bungalow**, located on the Satemwa Tea Estate below Thyolo Mountain, and about 20 miles east of Mulanje has four rooms with separate facilities. Bring your own food and drink. • **Lujeri Lodge** located on Lujeri Tea Estate on the eastern side of the mountain is an old tea plantation house with 4 large en suite rooms. Bring your own food.

Zomba Plateau

The Zomba Plateau, decreed a forest reserve in 1913, rises 3,300 feet (1,000 m) above the surrounding plains. Although much of the plateau is covered in commercially planted Mexican pine (for the timber and wood pulp industries), the forest reserve protects some patches of exquisite indigenous forest and some extensive grassland.

A series of walking trails meander through the plateau. Those who are less energetic can drive, although some roads may become impassable during the wet season. The highest point on Zomba is Chiradzulu at 6,835 feet (2,084 m), and the climatic extremes are very similar to those on Mt. Mulanje. A narrow, one-way road leads to the top of the plateau from the town of Zomba, and another takes you down.

Clear, cool mountain streams drain the plateau. Trout fishing in these streams and dams on the plateau is a popular pastime. Indeed, Malawi's only fish-fly-making factory is found in Zomba, home to the University of Malawi and one-time capital of the country. Fishing licenses are required and can be obtained from the Ku-Chawe Inn.

ACCOMMODATION — FIRST CLASS: • **Ku-Chawe Inn**, located on the top of the Zomba Plateau, has 40 rooms with en suite facilities and a restaurant.

CLASS C: • **Zomba Forest Lodge** located halfway up the mountain offers 4 en suite rooms and a full restaurant.

CLASS D: Self-service cottages are available.

CAMPING: Forestry campsites area available.

Swaziland

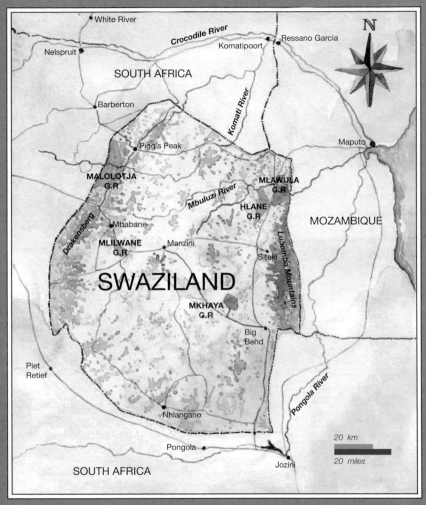

Swaziland is a small country divided into a temperate mountainous highveld in the west, and a subtropical lowveld in the east. The Lubombo hills form the eastern border with Mozambique. Elevation ranges from around 6,000 feet (1,829 m) at Malolotja to 2,100 feet (640 m) in the Komati River valley. With an area of 6,704-square-miles (17,364-km²) Swaziland is about the size of New Jersey, and has a population of about 1.5 million. SiSwati and English are the languages. Mbabane is the capital city. Currency is the Lilangeni.

SWAZILAND

The combination of friendly people, interesting culture, beautiful country-side and small game reserves makes Swaziland an attractive country to visit.

Swaziland, along with Lesotho and Morocco, is one of the last three remaining kingdoms in Africa. The country is deeply rooted in tradition — an important part of present-day life.

Although Swaziland is the second smallest country in Africa, within its boundaries is found a rich diversity of landscapes. Swaziland offers several wildlife reserves, fine examples of Stone Age San Bushmen rock paintings, international-class resorts and superb scenery.

Unlike most African countries, Swaziland has never been a totally subject nation. Although the British administered the country for 66 years, the people have always been governed by their own rulers according to their own traditions.

Swaziland has an excellent climate. The higher altitudes have a near-temperate climate, while the rest of the country is subtropical. Summers (November to January) are rainy, hot and humid. Winters (May to July) are crisp and clear, with occasional frosts in the highveld (higher altitudes). August is usually windy and dusty.

Geographically, the country is divided into four belts of about the same width that run roughly north to south: 1) the mountainous highveld in the west, 2) the hilly middleveld, 3) the lowveld bush, and 4) the Lubombo mountains, which are located along the eastern border with Mozambique.

Evidence suggests that Swaziland may have been inhabited by Bushmen between the early Stone Age and the fifteenth century. During the fifteenth century, descendants of the Nguni migrated to what is now Maputo, the capital of Mozambique, from the great lakes of Central Africa. Around 1700, the Nkosi Dlamini settled within the present-day borders of Swaziland.

Mswati II was proclaimed king of the people of the Mswati in 1840, forming the seed of a Swazi nation. By that time, the kingdom had grown to twice its present size, and whites (Europeans) began to secure valuable commercial and agricultural concessions. Dual administration of the country by British and Boer (Transvaal) governments failed. The Boers took over from 1895 until the Anglo-Boer War broke out in 1899. Swaziland became a High Commission Territory under the British after the war ended in 1903.

In 1921, Sobhuza II became king and remained on the throne until his death in 1982, making him the longest ruling monarch in history. The length of his reign gave Swaziland a higher level of political stability than experienced by most of the world. Only four rulers in modern times have reigned over 60 years: Sobhuza II, Queen Victoria of Great Britain, Louis XIV of France, and Karl Friedrich the Grand Duke of Badan.

Swaziland regained its independence on September 6, 1968. It was the last directly administered British colony in Africa. The Queen Regent, Indlovukazi ruled after the death of Sobhuza II and until Prince Makhosetive was crowned king in 1986.

The mining of the highlands' (Ngwenya's) iron ore began as early as 26,000 B.C. and continued until 1980, when deposits were exhausted. In the late 1800s, the Swazi gold rush centered around Pigg's Peak and Jeppe's Reef and lasted for 60 years.

The people are called Swazi(s), most of whom are subsistence farmers, and most follow a mixture of Christian and indigenous beliefs. About 95% of the population is of Swazi descent. The rest are Zulu, European, Mozambiquean and mulatto. Most prefer to live in scattered homesteads rather than concentrating themselves in villages and cities. Much of Swazi tradition revolves around the raising of cattle.

More than 15,000 Swazis work outside the country, primarily in South African gold and platinum mines. The country's main crops are maize, sugar, citrus, cotton, pineapples and tobacco. Seventy-five percent of the population works in agriculture.

🐾 WILDLIFE AND WILDLIFE AREAS

Less than 100 years ago, Swaziland was abundant in most forms of wildlife. In recent times, however, the introduction of large-scale commercial plantations (timber, sugar and citrus), combined with a growing population of subsistence farmers, have transformed most of the country and displaced most of its wildlife. Fortunately, some small natural ecosystems remain and are protected within a few beautiful nature reserves.

The two most important protected areas are Malolotja and Hlane-Mlawula. Malolotja protects a host of restricted-range or threatened species. Eliminated by hunters in the middle of the last century, elephant, white rhino, black rhino and lion have all been reintroduced. Because potentially dangerous large mammals are limited to only a few areas, many of the Swaziland reserves are ideal for horseback riding and hiking. Populations of waterbuck and oribi have declined, but typical savannah species are well represented in the lowveld.

Close to 500 species of birds have been recorded in this tiny, land-locked country — a diversity that can be attributed to the altitudinal range discussed earlier. Bald ibis, blue crane, blue swallow, Stanley's bustard and ground woodpecker all breed in the mist-belt grasslands of Malolotja. Saddle-billed stork, bateleur, ground hornbill and pink-throated twinspot are among the notable species of the lowveld. There is a great diversity of reptiles and amphibians, with many endemic forms of lizards and frogs identified in recent years.

Remarkably, 6,000 plant species have been identified in Swaziland, including 8 species of rare, primitive cycads. These living fossils date back to the age of dinosaurs and are the oldest known seed-bearing plants on the planet. Highly valued by illegal collectors, all species are protected by law.

THE NORTH

Malolotja Nature Reserve
Malolotja is a 70-square-mile (180-km²) highland wilderness of rolling, boulder-strewn grassland, rivers and streams, deep gorges and tall, montane forests. The vistas are quite breathtaking; the reserve varies in altitude from 6,000 feet (1829 m) to 2,100 feet (640 m) along the Nkomati River. Tumbling some 300 feet (90 m), the **Malolotja Falls** are Swaziland's highest waterfall, and the reserve is also home to the world's oldest known mine — **Ngwenya** — where hematite was extracted for rituals and cosmetics around 41,000 B.C. Game such as wildebeest, zebra and blesbok have been reintroduced, to add to the already-present oribi, Vaal rhebok and mountain reedbuck.

Malolotja is possibly the best place in Africa to see the elusive aardwolf — a nocturnal, termite-eating member of the hyena family. Black-backed jackal and serval are the major predators, although leopard may be found in remote areas.

A total of 290 bird species have been recorded, including numerous grassland-dependent species. A small colony of the highly endangered blue swallow exists close to the reserve's tourist camp. Blue crane are often seen. A small colony of bald ibis breed on the cliffs opposite the Malolotja Falls. Characteristic flora include proteas, erica and other Cape fynbos varieties. Rock-dwelling streptocarpus and 3 species of cycad are found on Ngwenya Mountain.

Because of a limited number of roads, the park is best suited for walkers and backpackers. Well-marked wilderness trails that require hikes of 1 to 7 days are available, and they require a permit to be hiked. Day trails may be used without first seeking a permit. Camping along the trail is allowed only at official sites; these sites have water but no facilities. Permits for backpacking and fishing must be obtained from the tourist office at the Forbes Reef Dam and Upper Malolotja River.

The best time to visit Malolotja is August to April; June to July is cold and windy. The main gate is located 22 miles (35 km) northwest of Mbabane on the road to Pigg's Peak.

ACCOMMODATION — CLASS C and D: • **National Park Cabins** features 6 cabins, each with 13 fully furnished rooms, private facilities, crockery and cutlery. Bring your own food, bedclothes and towels.

CAMPING: Campsites with ablution blocks are available.

Hlane-Mlawula Game Reserves

This 190-square-mile (484-km²) reserve complex is situated in northeastern Swaziland and includes both lowveld savannah and the Lubombo Mountains. Hlane was initially set aside by King Sobhuza II as a royal hunting ground, and it was proclaimed as a game reserve in 1967. Hlane is a fairly uniform, flat savannah dominated by knob thorn and marula trees.

The adjoining Mlawula Reserve, to the north, was established in 1980 and has more diverse topography, vegetation and wildlife. Impala, greater kudu and warthog are common larger mammals of open woodlands, while Sharpe's grysbok and mountain reedbuck are present in open grasslands on the Lubombo Heights, which provides wonderful views of the Mozambique coastal plain. The groves of Lubombo ironwood trees in the ravines of the Mbuluzi Gorge are fascinating in terms of their rare cycads and epiphytic orchids. Red duiker and samango monkey coexist with a variety of interesting birds, such as the African broadbill and narina trogon. Interestingly, some typically coastal birds from Mozambique, such as yellow weaver, yellow-spotted nicator and grey waxbill, may be seen along the Mbuluzi River.

The once-thriving population of white rhinos (originating from South Africa's Zululand reserves) crashed during the 1990s due to poaching, but it is slowly recovering. Reintroduced elephant are confined to select areas within Hlane. The complex is renowned for its abundance of birds of prey, including eagles, vultures and goshawks, and a lone family group of ground hornbills.

Game drives are best in Hlane, where waterholes provide excellent viewing in the dry winter months. The emphasis at Mlawula is on walking and backpacking on the network of trails.

ACCOMMODATION — CLASS C: • **Sara Bush Camp** has 3 tents set on wooden decks with en suite, open-air bathrooms.

CAMPING: • **Siphiso Camp** has campsites for caravans and tents, and an ablution block.

Mlilwane Wildlife Sanctuary

The first modern nature reserve to be established in Swaziland, it is owned and operated by the well-known Reilly family. It is located in the Ezulwini Valley. Mlilwane means "little fire" and is named for the lightning that often strikes a nearby hill. This 17-square-mile (45-km²) game sanctuary has a variety of wildlife, including giraffe, hippo, zebra, crocodile, jackal, caracal, serval, civet, nyala, blue wildebeest, eland, kudu, waterbuck, blesbok, reedbuck, bushbuck, oribi, duiker and klipspringer. Not all of these species are indigenous to the area, so the reserve is really more of an animal sanctuary than a natural ecosystem.

The sanctuary setting is middleveld and highveld, with altitudes ranging from 2,200 to 4,750 feet (670 to 1,450 m). It is located on an escarpment that was once a meeting point of westerly and easterly migrations of animals. The result is the congregation of a large number of wildlife species.

The northern limits of Mlilwane stretch to the outskirts of Mbabane and are visited only by guided, overnight trips on horse, mountain bike or on foot. Landmarks in the park include the twin peaks of "Sheba's Breasts," and "Execution Rock" — a legendary peak (the siSwati name is Nyonyane), where common criminals were supposedly pushed to their deaths.

Over 60 miles of gravel roads run throughout the sanctuary. Guided tours in open vehicles, on foot, mountain bike or on horseback can be arranged in advance. A network of self-guided walking trials covers approximately 12 miles (20 km). The best time to visit is during the dry season, May to September.

ACCOMMODATION — CLASS A/B: • **Reilly's Rock Hilltop Lodge**, situated on the Mlilwane Hill inside the sanctuary, is an old homestead that has been converted into a colonial-style lodge featuring only 6 rooms with en suite facilities. Game drives, horseback riding, escorted walks and mountain bike tours are offered.

CLASS C AND D: • **Mlilwane Rest Camp** has thatched wooden huts with en suite facilities and traditional "beehive" huts and an ablution block, a deck overlooking the hippo pool, and a restaurant. Traditional dancing is enjoyed by guests in the evening. • **Sondzela**, located inside the southern boundary of Mlilwane, caters primarily to backpackers, and it offers a variety of self-catering huts and dormitories, and a swimming pool.

CLASS D: • **Nyonyane Camp** has 4 self-catering log cabins with 4 to 8 beds each.

CAMPING: Campsites are available.

Ezulwini Valley

The Ezulwini Valley, or "Place of Heaven," is the entertainment center of the country and is the most convenient area in which to stay when visiting the Mlilwane Wildlife Sanctuary.

ACCOMMODATION — DELUXE: • **The Royal Swazi Sun Hotel, Casino and Country Club**, situated on 100-acres (40-hectares), has 149 rooms with en suite facilities, a swimming pool, a large al fresco spa, nearby mineral springs and sauna, casino, cinema, 18-hole championship golf course, horseback riding, tennis, squash, lawn bowling and a large convention center. Guests of the Ezulwini Sun and the Lugogo Sun may use the facilities of the more exclusive Royal Swazi Sun Hotel; a courtesy inter-hotel shuttle service is provided.

FIRST CLASS: • **Ezulwini Sun** has 60 air-conditioned rooms with private facilities, a swimming pool and tennis courts.

TOURIST CLASS: • **Lugogo Sun** has 202 air-conditioned rooms with en suite facilities and a swimming pool.

Lobamba

Lobamba is the spiritual and legislative capital of the country. The Queen Mother's village is situated there. The King Sobhuza II Memorial and National Museum, concentrating on Swazi culture and traditions, and the House of Parliament are prime attractions. The country's two premier ceremonies are the Ncwala and Umhlanga, both of which take place at the Ludzidzini Royal Residence. The more important of the two ceremonies is the **Ncwala**, or First Fruit Ceremony, usually held in December and January. Its exact date depends on the phases of the moon as analyzed by Swazi astrologers. The Ncwala symbolizes the religious spirit uniting the Swazi people with their king. The Ncwala is spread over about a three-week period and involves the entire Swazi nation.

The famous week-long **Umhlanga** (Reed Dance) is a colorful ceremony in which hundreds of Swazi maidens gather reeds and march to the royal residence at Ludzidzini, where the reeds are used to repair the windbreakers around the residence of the Queen Mother, Indlovukazi. Traditionally, at the final dance, the king chooses a wife from among these performing maidens. The Umhlanga occurs in late August/early September. Photographs of these two ceremonies may be taken only with permission from the Swaziland Information Services (P.O. Box 338, Mbabane, Swaziland, telephone: 011-268-4-2761).

Pigg's Peak

Pigg's Peak, located in one of the most scenic areas of the country, was named after William Pigg, who discovered gold there in January of 1884. Nearby is the country's most famous bushman painting, located at the **Nsangwini Shelter**. Ask the District Officer at Pigg's Peak to find a guide to take you there.

ACCOMMODATION — FIRST CLASS: • **Orion Pigg's Peak Hotel & Casino**, located 9 miles (15 km) north of Pigg's Peak, has 102 rooms with en suite facilities, a swimming pool, sauna, gym, tennis and squash courts, bowling green, clay pigeon shooting, cinema and casino.

Mbabane

Mbabane, the capital of Swaziland, is located in the mountainous highveld overlooking the Ezulwini Valley. Mbabane has a number of shops that sell local crafts. Most international visitors stay in Ezulwini Valley instead of Mbabane as the accommodations are superior. The international airport (Matsapha) is located about 15 miles (24 km) from Mbabane, between Mbabane and the industrial city of Manzini.

THE SOUTH

Nhlangano

Nhlangano means "The Meeting Place of the Kings" and commemorates the meeting between King Sobhuza II and King George VI in 1947. Nhlangano is located in the southwestern part of the country in an unspoiled mountainous area and is the burial place of many Swazi kings.

ACCOMMODATION — FIRST CLASS: • **The Nhlangano Sun** has a casino, disco bar, swimming pool, tennis, and 47 chalet-type rooms with en suite facilities.

Mkhaya Game Reserve

Swaziland's official refuge for endangered species, Mkhaya covers 25-square-miles (65-km^2) with sandveld savannah in the north and acacia-dominated savannah in the south. Altitude ranges from 6,170 to 1,150 feet (1,880 to 350 m). Winters are warm by day but cold at night; summers are hot, and temperatures exceed 100°F (38°C).

Mkhaya Game Reserve is a private enterprise of the Reilly family, who have set out to conserve and breed endangered species, such as black rhino and roan antelope. The Reillys have also devoted considerable attention to the breeding of pure Nguni cattle — a traditional, disease-free strain — which are considered to be in danger of becoming genetically polluted. The breed is considered a cornerstone of Swazi culture. Bird life at Mkaya is good and typical of the eastern lowveld.

Wildlife includes elephant, hippo, black and white rhino, zebra, roan antelope, sable antelope, buffalo, eland, wildebeest, red hartebeest, waterbuck, kudu, tsessebe, reedbuck, red duiker, grey duiker, steenbok, ostrich, spotted hyena, black-backed and side-striped jackal, and crocodile.

No self-driving is allowed in the reserve, and all visits must be booked in advance.

ACCOMMODATION — CLASS B: • **Stone Camp** has semi-open, stone-and-thatch chalets with en suite facilities. Game drives in open 4wd vehicles and walks are offered. White-water rafting is also available.

Lesotho

Lesotho is a small mountainous country, surrounded on all sides by South Africa. The landscape is spectacular with jagged peaks of the Maluti and Drakensberg mountains rising to over 11,200 feet (3,482 m) and deep river valleys. Nowhere is the elevation below 4,530 feet (1,380 m), ensuring that the climate is cool throughout the year, with snow being regular from May to August. With an area of some 11,720-square-miles (30,355-km²) Lesotho is about the size of Maryland (or Belgium). An estimated 2.2 million people inhabit the cool grasslands, with many living in and around the capital city of Maseru. Sesotho and English are the languages. Currency is the Loti.

LESOTHO

Lesotho is a rugged country with spectacular mountain scenery. Despite the cool climate and poor soils, the landscape has been intensively settled by subsistence farmers, and wildlife is restricted to hardy and adaptable species. This is certainly not a country to visit if you are looking for a big-game experience, but there are several rare and endemic birds and reptiles that will excite the genuine enthusiast. Infrastructure is limited. The countryside is best explored on pony treks and hiking trails, although a new, high-quality tar road allows access to the center of the country, and the legendary Sani Pass allows for 4wd vehicle access from South Africa's KwaZulu-Natal Province.

Called the "Kingdom in the Sky," Lesotho's lowest point (4,530 ft./1,380 m above sea level) is higher than the lowest point of any other country. Most of the country lies above 6,000 feet (1,830 m).

Lesotho is an "island" surrounded by the Republic of South Africa, which makes it one of only three countries in the world (including The Vatican and the Republic of San Marino) surrounded entirely by only one other country.

The country is called Lesotho (pronounced Lesutu), a citizen is called Mosotho and the people Basotho. Many men wear multicolored, traditional blankets to keep them warm in the often-freezing air, and they also wear the traditional conical basket hats. The Basotho are, in fact, known as the "Blanket People."

The Basotho are the only Africans to adapt to below-freezing temperatures, which can drop to –8°F (–22°C). Snow can fall in the mountains any time of the year, and it falls in the lowlands between May and August. Summer temperatures seldom rise over 90°F (32°C). The rainy season is during the summer with 85% of the annual rainfall (about 28 in./710 mm) occurring October to April, making many roads impassable.

The western part of the country is "lowland," with altitudes of 5,000 to 6,000 feet (1,525 to 1,830 m). The eastern three-quarters of the country is highland, rising to 11,420 feet (3,482 m) in the Drakensberg Mountain Range, bordering the KwaZulu-Natal Province of South Africa.

Bushmen (Qhuaique) inhabited Basutoland (now Lesotho) until the end of the sixteenth century. For the following 300 years the area was inhabited by refugees of numerous tribal wars in the region; these refugees formed the Basotho tribal group.

Moshoeshoe I reigned from 1823 to 1870, and his kingdom was powerful enough to keep even the warring Zulus at bay. Wars with South Africa, from 1823 to 1868, resulted in the loss of much land, now called "The Lost Territory." Lesotho asked to become a British protectorate to gain assistance in halting the encroachment of its lands by the Orange Free State (South

Africa). Lesotho was a British protectorate from 1868 until its independence on October 4, 1966.

Lesotho is one of Africa's poorest countries, but it benefits from its proximity to South Africa and derives income from labor export and, most recently, from fresh water diverted from the Lesotho Highlands Water Project (LHWP) to the industrial and economic center of Johannesburg. Light manufacturing and tourism are also important foreign exchange earners.

The headwaters of the Senqu (Orange) River rise in Lesotho, and they cut deep gorges through the Drakensberg and Maluti Mountains. The mighty river, critical for development and agriculture in neighboring South Africa and providing the water requirements for Johannesburg, eventually empties into the Atlantic Ocean, some 600 miles (1,000 km) from its source. The LHWP has brought revenuc and development to Lesotho. It harnesses water resources in a series of dams, produces hydro-electric power and provides employment to both rural and urban people.

🐾 WILDLIFE AND WILDLIFE AREAS

Lesotho is notable for its Afro-alpine plants and animals, many of which are found nowhere else (endemic) or found only in other highlands of the continent. Among larger mammals, the eland, black wildebeest, mountain reedbuck and chacma baboon occur only in small numbers. Large predators have been eliminated by stock farmers, though leopard and brown hyena may survive in remote areas. The endangered Cape vulture breeds at several localities in cliff-face colonies, while the spectacular but solitary bearded vulture occurs at a higher density in the Drakensberg than anywhere else in Africa. Among the interesting smaller birds are the orange-breasted rockjumper, sentinel rock thrush, Drakensberg siskin and mountain pipit. Good numbers of bald ibis are also found.

Sehlabathebe is the Lesotho's only national park, situated on the edge of the great escarpment on the eastern border and adjacent to South Africa's much larger Natal Drakensberg Park.

Pony Trekking

Lesotho is one of the best countries in the world for pony trekking. The Basotho pony is the chief means of transportation in the mountainous two-thirds of the country and the best way to explore this land of few roads. Bridle paths crisscross the landscape from one village or family settlement to the next.

The Basotho pony is perhaps the best pony in the world for mountain travel and was highly prized during wartime. It can easily climb and descend steep, rocky paths that other breeds of horses would not attempt. The riding style in Lesotho, as in most countries in Africa, is English.

Pony Trekking From Molimo Nthuse

Molimo Nthuse, located about an hour's drive (34 mi./54 km) on a good, tarred road from Maseru, is the center for pony trekking in this region. Escorted day trips to the refreshing rock pools of **Qiloane Falls**, and other rides of up to seven days in length, are offered. The ponies are well trained and a pleasure to ride.

Pony treks are conducted year-round — in summer "swimsuit" weather as well as in cold, snowy weather. Remember, the seasons are reversed from the northern hemisphere! Accommodation on overnight treks is in Basotho huts or you can camp (bring your own tent).

Pony Trekking From Malealea To Semonkong

One of the most interesting pony treks in Lesotho (offered from September to April) is a four- to six-day ride from Malealea, in southwestern Lesotho, to Semonkong and Maletsunyane Falls.

The pony trek often begins after examining some interesting Bushmen rock paintings and rock pools located near **Malealea**, about 50 miles (80 km) from Maseru. Riding east, the dark-blue skies are broken by high mountains in the distance. Basotho, wrapped in their traditional blankets and traveling on foot and by pony, offer friendly greetings and warm smiles. Riding in a cool breeze on a moonlit night in these remote mountains calms the soul and brings peace and harmony to one's spirit.

The nights are spent in traditional huts that are usually owned by the headman of the village. He provides firsthand knowledge of how the people live. Hikes to view **Ribaneng Falls** (328 ft./100 m) and **Ketane Falls** (401 ft./122 m) are made along the way.

The final destination is **Maletsunyane Falls**, a few miles and less than a half-hour ride (or a one and a half-hour walk) from Semonkong. Maletsunyane is one of the highest waterfalls in southern Africa, falling 635 feet (196 m) in a single drop. The impressive falls are best viewed from the bottom of the gorge, where camping is allowed overnight.

Semonkong, meaning "Place of Smoke" (probably from the mist from Maletsunyane Falls), is a dusty little town resembling America's "Wild, Wild West," with a general store, hitching posts and stables with horses providing the main means of transportation. Activities in the area, other than horse treks, include 4wd excursions, mountain bike and motorbike trails, hiking, bird watching and trout fishing.

ACCOMMODATION — CLASS D&F: MALEALEA: • **Malealea Lodge** is a small, self-service lodge featuring 22 new rondavels with en suite facilities, 18 en suite bedrooms in the farmhouse, 5 Basotho huts with communal bathrooms and kitchens, 9 budget rooms, and campsites. Day pony treks are available. The lodge specializes in horse treks from one hour to six days in length. CAMPING: Campsites are available at Malealea Lodge and Fraser Lodge (Semonkong).

ACCOMMODATION — CLASS D&F — SEMONKONG: • **Semonkong Lodge** has stone-and-thatch cottages with separate facilities, communal kitchen, bar and restaurant. • **Mountain Delight Lodge** is a small, self-service lodge with 10 beds.

The Mountain Road

This route cuts through the center of Lesotho, from west to east, and through spectacular mountain scenery to "the roof of Africa." From Maseru, the road ascends over **Bushmen Pass** (Lekhalong la Baroa) to **Molimo Nthuse** ("God Help Me Pass"). Between December and March, colorful scarlet-and-yellow red-hot pokers (flowers) may be seen in this area.

Continue to **Thaba Tseka**, where the good road ends and 4wd is necessary to negotiate the tracks that pass small villages and isolated herd boys. After **Sehonghong**, the route descends into the **Senqu (Orange) River Canyon**, which is dotted with unusual rock formations, then it climbs over **Matebeng Pass** (9,670 ft./2,948 m), which had snow, sleet and icicles during my visit one April, and onward to Sehlabathebe National Park.

Katse Dam

An incredible structure on the Malibamatso River, Katse Dam was completed in 1997 and is central to the Lesotho Highlands Water Project. The project funnels water through a series of tunnels through numerous ranges of the great Maluti Mountains, and it leads all the way to Gauteng (Johannesburg) and South Africa's industrial hub. The LHWP is one of the most ambitious, multipurpose water schemes in the world and the dam (over 600 ft./185 m high) is second in size only to Ghana's Lake Volta Akosombo Dam. An interpretive center offers visitors a view of the impressive features of the dam, and one can go on tours through the dam wall. It is also a great area for water sports.

ACCOMMODATION — CLASS C and D: • **Katse Lodge**, situated at the banks of Katse Lake close to the Katse Dam wall, has 10 single and 10 double rooms with en suite bathrooms, plus 2 self-catering units of 6 bedrooms, each unit with its own kitchen, lounge with fireplace and communal ablutions.

AfriSki

AfriSki, an Austrian-themed ski resort located 8 miles (12 km) from Oxbow, a village set in the Mahlasela Valley set at 10,570 feet (3,222 m) above sea level. AfriSki is the largest ski resort in Southern Africa, with the longest ski lift on the continent. AfriSki can accommodate 250 guests in the various accommodation types on site ranging from comfortable lodges to a hostel for backpackers. Summer activities include golf, trout fishing, hiking, horseback riding and a variety of other outdoor activities

Sehlabathebe National Park

Sehlabathebe has the highest sandstone formations (including arches) in southern Africa. This park, situated on a high plateau with small lakes, offers tremendous views of the Drakensberg Mountains and Natal. Sehlabathebe means "Plateau of the Shield" and has an average altitude of over 8,000 feet (2,440 m). Three peaks, called "The Three Bushmen" (Baroa-ba-Bararo), dominate the skyline.

This small, 25-square-mile (65-km²) fenced park is dominated by open grasslands, with evergreen shrubs forming thickets at the bases of cliffs. High-altitude shrubs form a heath landscape dominated by showy ericas. The meandering Tsoelikana River, marshlands and rock pools provide habitats for aquatic creatures. There is a small population of black wildebeest, as well as oribi, eland and mountain reedbuck.

Bearded vulture (lammergeyer) may be seen soaring overhead, along with Cape vultures, lanner falcon and jackal buzzard. The strange, crab-eating aquatic river frog is fairly common in the cold waters of the Tsoelikana.

The best time to visit Sehlabathebe for game viewing, hiking and some of the best freshwater fishing in southern Africa is November to March. Quickest access is by charter flight. Land access is by a 185 mile (300 km) drive across Lesotho from Maseru or from South Africa via Qacha's Nek, Sani Pass, or a five- to six-hour hike (or three- to four-hour pony trek) of 15 miles (24 km) from Bushman's Nek Lodge.

ACCOMMODATION — CLASS D: • **Sehlabathebe Park Lodge** is a self-service lodge with 4 double rooms.

CLASS F: Dormitory accommodation is available.

CAMPING: Campsites are available near the lodge.

Sani Pass

The Sani Pass is in the Drakensberg Mountains on the border between the Republic of South Africa and Lesotho. It is the most famous of three road crossings through the Drakensbergs — the other two are Bushman's Nek and Qacha's Nek. The nearest town of any note in Lesotho is Mokhotlong (31 mi./50 km), and the nearest city in the Republic of South Africa is Pietermaritzburg.

Sani Pass is a very steep and twisting road pass that can be driven only in a 4wd vehicle, or walked. The pass drops (or climbs, if you are heading into Lesotho) over 2,600 feet (800 m) in just under 5 miles (8 km) — an average grade of 1:10.

ACCOMMODATION — CLASS D: • **Sani Top Chalet**, set right on top of the pass at 9,425 feet (2,874 m), is home to the highest pub in Africa, and has rondavels with en suite facilities. The main chalet has three basic rooms which is perfect for a family. There are rustic self-catering accommodations for backpackers at the nearby village.

Maseru

Maseru is the capital and largest city and is located in the western lowlands. Sights include the Cathedral and the Royal Lesotho Carpet Factory, where some of the world's finest, hand-woven, woolen carpets may be bought. Some interesting day excursions from Maseru include **Thaba-Bosiu** (The Mountain at Night), the table mountain fortress that is 19 miles (30 km) from Maseru, where the Basotho fought off the Boers, and the **Ha Khotso** rock paintings, considered to be some of the finest in southern Africa, located 28 miles (45 km) from Maseru off the mountain road.

ACCOMMODATION — FIRST CLASS. • **The Lesotho Sun** is situated on a hill overlooking Maseru, with 194 rooms and suites with en suite facilities, a swimming pool, tennis courts, health club, casino, tenpin bowling, several restaurants and conference facilities.

TOURIST CLASS: • **Maseru Sun** has 112 rooms with en suite facilities, tennis courts, a swimming pool, conference rooms and a casino.

Burundi

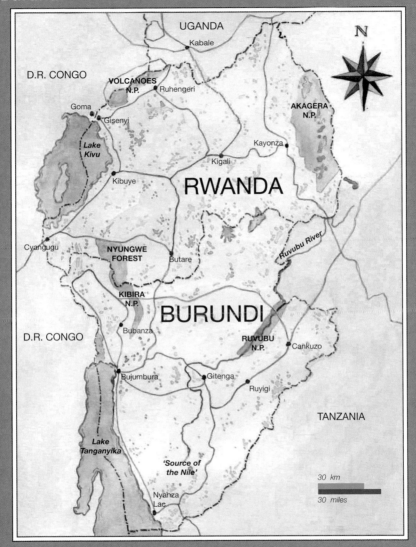

This country is characterized by rolling hills, and was a former Belgian colony along with Rwanda, previously united as Ruanda-Urundi. Although the country covers only 10,747-square-miles (26,834-km²) it has a population of close to 7 million, making this one of the most densely populated countries in the world. Kirundi is the prominent language spoken; French is also widely understood. The currency is the Franc.

BURUNDI

Burundi, one of the poorest and most densely populated countries in Africa, is a hilly country with altitudes ranging from 2,600 to 9,000 feet (790 to 2,745 m). The weather in Bujumbura and along the shores of Lake Tanganyika is warm and humid, with average temperatures ranging from 64 to 89°F (18 to 32°C); frost sometimes occurs at night in the highlands. Dry seasons are June to September and December to January; the principal rainy season is February to May.

The three major ethnic groups in the country are the Hutu, Tutsi and Twa (Pygmy). Historically, the Hutus were primarily farmers and today comprise more than half the population; their Bantu-speaking ancestors came to Burundi over 800 years ago. The Tutsi were historically a pastoral tribe and presently comprise less than a quarter of the population; they came to the region a few hundred years after the Hutus. The Pygmy (Twa), who were the original inhabitants, presently comprise less than 2% of the population.

For centuries, the region that is now Burundi had a feudal social structure headed by a king. Although Europeans explored the region as early as 1858, Burundi did not come under European administration until it became part of German West Africa in the 1890s.

In 1916, Belgian troops occupied the country, and the League of Nations mandated it to Belgium as part of the Territory of Ruanda-Urundi in 1923. Ruanda-Urundi became a U.N. Trust Territory under the administration of Belgium after World War II, and in 1962 became the independent country of Burundi.

French and Kirundi are the official languages, and Swahili is also spoken. At the top hotels, restaurants and shops, some English-speaking staff are usually available to assist travelers; otherwise, very little English is spoken in the country. Most of the people are Catholic.

There are only two large cities in the country — Bujumbura and Gitega. Over 90% of the population is subsistence farmers. Burundi's major exports include coffee, tea, cotton and food crops, and coffee provides 80 to 90% of Burundi's foreign exchange earnings.

As of this writing, security is not good for travel here, and about the only international tourists visiting Burundi are "country counters" who usually just stay in Bujumbura for a short time, and "overlanders" crossing the continent. Please get a current update on the situation before making arrangements to travel there.

🐾 WILDLIFE AND WILDLIFE AREAS

The National Institute for the Conservation of Nature (INCN) has created several parks and nature reserves. Most of the parks and reserves lack access roads, camping sites and other facilities. Hunting is forbidden throughout the country.

Burundi's premier wildlife attraction is chimpanzees, along with crested mangabeys and red colobus monkeys. Other wildlife includes buffalo, several species of antelope, hyena, serval and a variety of bird life. Over 400 species of fish inhabit Lake Tanganyika, more than almost any other body of water in the world. Hippo and crocs are present in Lake Tanganyika and both the Rusizi and Ruvubu Rivers. The combination of varying altitude and water creates a wide range of microclimates, giving rise to a great variety of flora.

Rusizi Nature Reserve (Reserve Geree De La Rusizi)

Entrances to this 35-square-mile (90-km^2) reserve are located 9 to 16 miles (15 to 23 km) northwest of Bujumbura. The park has hippo, crocs, and a variety of bird life.

Kibira National Park (Parc National De La Kibira)

Kibira National Park and the Kibira Forest are the best areas in Burundi to look for chimpanzees, red colobus monkeys and crested mangabeys. This 155-square-mile (400-km^2) park is situated 30 miles (48 km) or more to the north and northeast of Bujumbura and has a network of over 100 miles (160 km) of tracks (poor roads).

Ruvubu National Park (Parc National De La Ruvubu)

Ruvubu National Park is 193 square miles (500 km^2) in size and covers a strip of land from one to six miles (1.5 to 10 km) wide along both sides of the Ruvubu River in eastern Burundi. Wildlife in the Ruvubu Basin and Parc National de la Ruvubu includes hippo, crocs, buffalo, leopard, antelope, monkeys and some lion. More than 425 bird species have been recorded. The closest road access to the park is 134 miles (216 km) from Bujumbura. The park has about 30 miles (50 km) of tracks.

Lake Rwihinda Nature Reserve (Reserve Naturelle Geree Du Lac Rwihinda)

The Lake Rwihinda Nature Reserve and the other lakes in the northern part of the country, located approximately 125 miles (202 km) from Bujumbura, are called the "Lakes of the Birds" and include Lakes Cohoha, Rweru, Kanzigiri and Gacamirinda. They are a bird-watcher's paradise and can be explored by canoe.

Bujumbura

Founded in 1896 by the Germans, Bujumbura is the capital city, major port and commercial center of Burundi. The city has very good French and Greek restaurants. A fun restaurant and bar on Lake Tanganyika is Cercle Nautique, which also offers sailing, boating and fishing and has an abundance of hippo for entertainment.

There is a public beach called Saga, near Club du Lac Tanganyika (beware of crocodiles and hippo).

The ethnological Musée Vivant features a traditional Burundian village and daily traditional drum shows. The Parc du Reptiles is next door. The Musée du Géologie du Burundi has a good fossil collection. Jane Goodall operates a chimpanzee orphanage.

ACCOMMODATION — DELUXE: • **Club du Lac Tanganyika**, situated just outside of town on Lake Tanganyika, has a swimming pool and 60 air-conditioned rooms with en suite facilities.

FIRST CLASS: • **Novotel** has 110 air-conditioned rooms and 10 suites with en suite facilities, restaurant, bar, swimming pool, business center, exercise room and tennis courts. • **Sun City Hotel** offers 25 rooms with air-conditioning and is centrally located. • **Ubuntu Residence** has 18 rooms with en suite bathrooms, a swimming pool, restaurant and some of the rooms have kitchenettes. • **Clos de Limba** has 12 rooms with en suite facilities and a swimming pool.

TOURIST CLASS: • **Village Hotel** has 10 rooms with en suite facilities and a swimming pool. • **Amahoro Hotel** has 50 rooms with en suite facilities.

INLAND

The people outside Bujumbura seldom see tourists. Try to visit a village on market day to get a feeling of daily life in Burundi (be sure to check security in the area first).

Enroute to Gitega, you will pass Muramvya, the ancient city of the king and royal capital, and an active market at Bugarama.

Gitega, the former colonial capital, is situated on the central plateau in the middle of the country and is the second largest city. Sights include the National Museum, fine arts school, and beer market.

The artistic center of Giheta, seven miles (11 km) from Gitega, sells wood carvings, leather goods, baskets and ceramics. The southernmost possible source of the Nile is four miles (6 km) from the village of Rutovu and about 60 miles (97 km) from Gitega.

Democratic Republic of the Congo

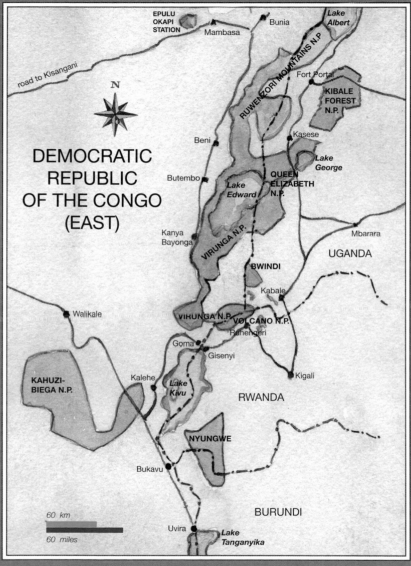

D.R. Congo is the third largest country in Africa with a surface area of 905,567-square-miles (2,345,410-km²). Most of the country lies within the Congo Basin (the world's second largest rainforest after the Amazon) below 980 ft (300 m). In the extreme east of the country the Albertine Rift gives rise to the Ruwenzori Mountains and the Virunga Volcano chain. As a former Belgian colony, French is the official language of D.R. Congo, although there are over 200 ethnic groups with their own language. The currency is the Franc Congolais.

DEMOCRATIC REPUBLIC OF THE CONGO

The Democratic Republic of the Congo (D.R. Congo), formerly the Republic of Zaire, is the third largest country in Africa. The name Zaire came from the Kikongo word *nzadi*, meaning "river." The Congo River, the tenth longest river in the world, winds 2,880 miles (4,600 km) through the Congo basin, the world's second largest drainage basin (the Amazon is the largest), and finally empties into the Atlantic Ocean.

Kivu Province, the most beautiful region of the D.R. Congo, holds the country's most exciting attractions. This province is situated along the western borders of Rwanda and Uganda in the region of the great lakes: Lakes Tanganyika, Kivu, Edward and Albert. This is an important agricultural area with large tobacco, coffee, tea and banana plantations. The only paved road in the Kivu Province runs north from Goma to the Kabasha Escarpment.

Due to the altitude, much of the region has an agreeable Mediterranean-type climate. In general, the best time to visit the eastern D.R. Congo is during the dry seasons from December to February and mid-June to August.

Of the 200 or so tribal or ethnic groups in the D.R. Congo, four-fifths are Bantu. Physically, tribal groups range from the tall nomadic herders from the north to the smaller Mbuti hunter-gatherers in the densely forested regions. About 80% of the population is Christian, with the balance embracing Muslim or traditional native beliefs.

The Congo remained virtually unknown until Henry Morton Stanley traveled from East Africa to the mouth of the Congo River (1874–1877). Belgian King Leopold II claimed the so-called Congo Free State as his personal property until he ceded it to Belgium in 1907. It was then renamed the Belgian Congo. Zaire achieved independence on June 30, 1960.

As of this writing, the country is considered unsafe for travel. Please get a current update on the situation before considering a visit there. Virtually all of the accommodations outside of the larger cities are closed. Please check for a current security update before considering venturing there.

The D.R. Congo is a country of gigantic untapped resources. Fifty percent of the land is arable and scarcely 2% is under cultivation or used as pasture. Much of the arable land, however, is covered in dense forest, and the D.R. Congo is still covered by one of the largest blocks of tropical forest in the world. Much of the soil in the Congo Basin is of very low nutrient content and would make exceedingly poor farmland. The country holds 13% of the world's hydroelectric potential. Copper accounts for about half of the country's exports, followed by petroleum, diamonds, gold and coffee.

🐾 WILDLIFE AND WILDLIFE AREAS

Eight reserves cover 15% of the country's area. Over 1,000 species of birds have been recorded in the country, which makes it Africa's richest, but the majority are forest-dwelling and hard to see. In addition, the D.R. Congo is also home to the rare okapi (giraffe-like ungulate), the highly elusive Congo peacock, and a number of other endemic species found nowhere else in the world.

Like Uganda and Rwanda, gorillas are a major attraction in the D.R. Congo. Should the region stabilize politically, mountain gorillas may be visited in Virunga National Park and eastern lowland gorillas in Kahuzi-Biega National Park.

THE NORTHEAST (KIVU AREA)

Goma

Goma is situated on the northern shores of Lake Kivu, one of the most beautiful lakes in Africa, with Nyiragongo and Nyamulagira (volcanoes) forming a dramatic backdrop to the north. It is the administrative center for Virunga National Park. Lake Kivu is suitable for swimming because there are no crocs or hippos. A few boats per week depart Goma for Bukavu across Lake Kivu.

ACCOMMODATION — TOURIST CLASS • **Hotel Stella Matutina Lodge** has 12 rooms with en suite facilities. • **Hotel Ihusi** has 19 rooms with en suite bathrooms. • **Hotel Ishango** has 17 en suite rooms, a two-bedroom suite and a few apartments.

North Of Goma

On the drive from Goma northward you pass over the dramatic Kabasha Escarpment to Butembo. The route from the Kabasha Escarpment to Beni is one of the most beautiful in Africa and is properly named the "Beauty Route." The road passes through many picturesque villages, and coffee, tea and banana plantations — the Africa that many of us have pictured in our minds.

Virunga National Park
(Parc National Des Virunga)

Virunga National Park, previously called Albert Park, is one of the oldest reserves in Africa (created in 1925) and is the finest wildlife reserve in the Eastern Congo. Altitudes range from 3,000 feet (915 m) on the grassy savannah to 16,794 feet (5,120 m) in the Ruwenzori Mountains, resulting in a tremendous variety of topography, flora and fauna.

Virunga is about 185 miles (300 km) long and 25 miles (40 km) wide. Unfortunately, as of this writing all of these areas within the park, and the accommodations, are either closed to tourism or considered too unstable for safe travel.

Volcanoes

The region around Goma is a highly volcanic area of constant activity. In the southern part of the park near Goma lie the active volcanoes of Nyiragongo and Nyamulagira, which do not require technical mountaineering skills to climb. If the volcanoes are active at the time of your visit, you may want to spend a night near the crater rim to enjoy the remarkable fireworks display. The best time to climb is December to January and June, when the weather is most clear. February, July and August are also good.

Nyiragongo

Nyiragongo (11,384 ft./3470 m) can be climbed in one day, if you begin climbing early in the morning. The guide and porter station is located at Kibati (6,400 ft./1950 m), 8 miles (13 km) north of Goma on the Rutshuru road. Hike four to five hours through submontane forest past lava flows to the summit. Have lunch on the crater rim while watching sulfurous gases escape from the crater below. Allow two to three hours to return to Kibati before dark.

It is better to take two days for the climb, overnighting at a hut (in poor condition) about a 30-minute walk below the summit. At dawn the next morning, hike to the crater rim and enjoy breathtaking views of Lake Kivu, Goma and the surrounding countryside.

Nyamulagira

Nyamulagira erupted in the year 2000 and several other times in recent years. If you are interested in wildlife, this is the better of the two volcanoes to climb. An armed guide accompanies each group, and porters may be hired. With luck, you may see forest elephant, chimpanzees, buffalo and duiker.

Nyamulagira (10,023 ft./3,055 m) is best climbed in three days. On the first day, you will hike about six hours through dense upland jungle, pass numerous lava flows and arrive at a basic lodge at 8,200 feet (2,500 m) altitude. Water is available at the lodge but must be purified. On day two you reach the tree line after about an hour's hike and the crater rim about an hour after passing the tree line. The crater itself is about a mile and a half (2 km) in diameter. Within the crater is a blowhole with a huge, 1,300 foot (400 m) diameter shaft. Descend into it and explore the crater, then return to the same lodge you slept in the night before. Hike down the mountain on the third day. Nyamulagira is reached via Kakomero (5,900 ft./1,800 m), 24 miles (39 km) north of Goma.

Bukima Gorilla Site

The main attraction of Bukima is visiting mountain gorillas *(Gorilla beringei beringei)*.

To reach Bukima from Uganda, drive from Ishasha to Rutshuru and turn off at the Park Headquarters at Rumangabo Station, or via Kisoro in Uganda, crossing the border at Bunagana. From Rwanda, go north on the Goma/Rutshuru road to the turnoff.

Trekkers usually spend the night, and the following day they hike for about 90 minutes through cultivated land and near small villages to the edge of the forest in which the gorillas live. From there, gorillas may be found in less than an hour, or the search could take several hours. For a description of gorillas and gorilla trekking in general, see "Bwindi Impenetrable Forest National Park" in the chapter on Uganda.

Djomba (Jomba) Gorilla Site

A juvenile mountain gorilla

At the Djomba Gorilla Site, four groups of mountain gorillas have been habituated to man's presence. Three of the groups reside in the area, but the Faida Group sometimes crosses the Rwanda border. Each group may be visited by up to eight people at a time. National Parks guides and armed guards must accompany each group.

Djomba is the base from which gorilla trekking begins. To reach Djomba (also spelled Jomba) drive about 40 miles (65 km) north from Goma past Nyiragongo and Nyamulagira volcanoes. Two miles before reaching Rutshuru, turn right and continue 19 miles (30 km) to Park Headquarters. Trekkers may visit with the gorillas for about an hour, as in Uganda and Rwanda. Buffalo and elephant are also present in the sanctuary, so keep an eye out for them.

Rwindi

Continuing north toward Rwindi are the Rutshuru Waterfalls and Maji Ya Moto hot-water springs, both near Rutshuru.

Rwindi was formerly a good game viewing region of Virunga National Park and is predominantly composed of savannah plains and swamp. Unfortunately, most of the wildlife here has either been poached or has crossed the border to Uganda. The Kabasha Escarpment rises up to 6,000 feet (1,830 m) above the plains below and provides a dramatic backdrop. The fishing village of Vitshumbi is located on the southern shores of Lake Edward. The main road from Goma to Butembo passes right through the park.

The best time to visit is during the dry season. Roads and tracks are poor in the rainy season. Park Headquarters and camping sites are located at Rwindi, 81 miles (121 km) north of Goma.

Ruwenzori Mountains

The third highest mountains in Africa (after Mts. Kilimanjaro and Kenya), the "Mountains of the Moon" are, in fact, the highest mountain chain on the continent. Permanently snow-covered at over 14,800 feet (4,500 m), these jagged peaks are almost perpetually covered in mist. For a map of the Ruwenzoris, see "Ruwenzori Mountains National Park" in the chapter on Uganda.

The mountain chain is approximately 60 miles (100 km) long and 30 miles (50 km) wide, and the highest peak, Margherita, is 16,762 feet (5,109 m) in altitude. A number of permanent glaciers and peaks challenge mountaineers. However, mountaineering skills are not needed for the hike itself — only for climbing the glaciers or peaks.

Unlike Mt. Kilimanjaro and many other mountains in east and central Africa, the Ruwenzoris are not volcanic in origin. The range forms part of the border with Uganda and can be climbed from either the D.R. Congo or Ugandan side. The trail on the D.R. Congo side of the Ruwenzoris is much steeper than the Ugandan side. Allow five days for the climb and longer if any peaks are to be attempted.

The Afro-alpine vegetation zones and Afro-alpine heathlands you pass through on the Ruwenzoris are the most amazing I have seen in the world. The nectar-filled flowers of massive lobelias and giant senecios attract jewel-like sunbirds while "Spanish moss" and ephiphytic orchids adorn gnarled tree branches. Colorful mosses look solid, but when probed with a walking stick (or your foot) often prove to cover a tangle of roots more than 6 feet (2 m) deep. Several plants that are commonly small in other parts of the world grow to gigantic proportions in the Ruwenzoris.

The Butawu Route is the only route regularly used on the D.R. Congo side of the Ruwenzoris. All other routes are so overgrown with vegetation that they are virtually impossible to climb.

On the first day, it takes five to six hours of hiking from the Park Headquarters at Mutsora (5,600 ft./1,700 m) through small fields of bananas, coffee and other crops to reach Kalonge Hut (7,015 ft./2,135 m). The hut sleeps 16 people, and there is room for tents nearby.

On the second day, you pass through areas with giant stinging nettles and bamboo forest more than 100 feet (30 m) high. Soon you come to a resting spot where offerings are left for the mountain gods. Your guide will expect you to leave something (a few coins will do).

At about 8,500 feet (2,600 m), the sides of the slick, muddy path become lined with spongy mosses and heather 25 feet (8 m) tall. After about five hours of hiking (actually the most difficult part of the climb), you reach Mahangu Hut (10,860 ft./3,310 m). The hut has room for 16 people, and there is room for camping.

The third day, you finally hike past the upper tree line at about 12,500 feet (3,800 m) and enter a zone of giant groundsels over 16 feet (5 m) high and giant lobelia over 25 feet (8 m) high. Before completing the five-hour hike to Kiondo Hut (13,780 ft./4,200 m), you hike along an open ridge with fabulous views of Lac Noir (Black Lake). Kiondo Hut has room for 12, and there is room for tents nearby.

On day four of the hike, the Butawu Route continues on to Wasuwameso Peak (14,600 ft./4,450 m) for some fabulous views of Mt. Stanley. Climbers then return to Kiondo Hut and continue on down to Kalonge Hut for the night.

Alternatively, take a fabulous hike past Lac Vert (Green Lake) and Lac Gris (Grey Lake) to Moraine Hut (14,270 ft./4,350 m) at the foot of the glaciers. The hike to Moraine Hut from Kiondo Hut takes about five hours round-trip and requires a short bit of easy rock climbing with fixed ropes. Then return to either Kiondo Hut or Mahangu Hut for the night.

If you hike to Moraine Hut, be sure to return to Kiondo Hut early. My guide insisted there was plenty of time to reach Moraine Hut and return to Kiondo Hut the afternoon of the third day. We were so late returning that we were forced to return in the dark. Had I not brought a flashlight, we might still be up there.

On the fifth day, return to Mutsora — hopefully for a hot bath and a soft bed!

Many hikers prefer camping at Grey Lake instead of using dilapidated Moraine Hut, which leaks. There is space for only one tent near Moraine Hut. Experienced mountaineers may press on to conquer the glaciers and peaks of the Ruwenzori from either location. Allow a minimum of six or seven days total for the climb if you wish to attempt any summits.

The best time to climb is from December to February; June to August is also good. To reach the Ruwenzoris, travel north from Goma through Butembo, and just before Beni turn east 28 miles (45 km) to Mutwanga. Park Headquarters is at Mutsora, about 1.5 miles (2.5 km) from Mutwanga.

A guide is required, and his fee is included in the park entrance fee; porters are available for a small fee. Both guides and porters expect cigarettes in addition to a tip. The guides know the path and where to find water enroute — but little else. All guides speak French; an English-speaking guide may not be available. Guides who speak English tend to know only a few words.

Guides are neither equipped for, nor experienced in glacier or rock climbing. Your group must be self-sufficient. There are none of the mountain rescue teams you would find in the Alps or the Rockies; needless to say, you must bring a comprehensive medical kit.

Guides and porters love to smoke and often share the huts with you. In any case, bring a tent as the huts may very well be uninhabitable. Also, bring a warm sleeping bag, pad, food, fuel and enough water to last at least two days. See "Mt. Kilimanjaro" in the chapter on Tanzania for a more extensive equipment checklist and other preparations. Mt. Kilimanjaro is higher, but the trail up the Ruwenzoris is much steeper, slicker and more difficult to negotiate.

THE SOUTHEAST

Kahuzi-biega National Park

This 2,300-square-mile (5960-km²) mountain sanctuary, located 17 miles (27 km) northwest of Bukavu, is dedicated to preserving the eastern lowland gorilla *(Gorilla beringei graueri)*. Searching for these magnificent, rare and endangered animals is recommended only for travelers in fairly good physical condition.

The search for gorillas usually takes an hour or two of hiking to altitudes from 7,000 to 8,200 feet (2,135 to 2,500 m) through dense upland jungle and bamboo forests. However, it occasionally takes three or four hours to locate the gorillas. The park also includes swamp, woodland and extensive equatorial rain forest. The highest point in the park, Mt. Kahuzi (10,853 ft./3,308 m), can be climbed in about six hours. Children under 15 years of age are not allowed to visit the gorillas.

Daytime temperatures average 50 to 65°F (10 to 18°C), and yearly average rainfall is high — about 70 inches (1,790 mm). The heaviest rainfall is in April and November. The best time to visit the park is in the dry season. Bring waterproof, lightweight hiking boots (you may have to wade through water), a sweater, waterproof cover jacket, lunch, snacks and a water bottle.

To reach the park, go north from Bukavu along the western side of Lake Kivu for 13 miles (21 km) to Miti, then turn left (west), traveling for 4 miles (6 km) to Station Tshivanga, the Park Headquarters.

Safari Resource Directory

We have endeavored to make the information that follows as current as possible. However, Africa is undergoing constant change. My reason for including the following information, much of which is likely to change, is to give you an idea of the right questions to ask — not to give you information that should be relied on as gospel. Wherever possible, a resource has been given to assist you in obtaining the most current information.

AIRPORT DEPARTURE TAXES

Ask your African tour operator, go on-line or call an airline that serves your destination, or the tourist office, embassy or consulate of the country(ies) in question, for current international and domestic airport taxes that are not included in your air ticket and must be paid with cash before departure. International airport departure taxes often must be paid in U.S. dollars or other hard currency, such as the Euro or British pounds. Be sure to have the exact amount required — often change will not be given. Domestic airport departure taxes may be required to be paid in hard currency as well, or in some cases may be payable in the local currency.

At the time of this writing, international airport departure taxes for the countries in this guide are listed below.

International Airport Departure Taxes

Country	Taxes due	Country	Taxes due
Botswana	*	Namibia	*
Burundi	$20.00	Rwanda	$20.00
Congo, D.R.	$20.00	Seychelles	$40.00 approx.
Egypt	*	South Africa	*
Ethiopia	*	Swaziland	$3.00
Kenya	*	Tanzania	$30.00
Lesotho	$30.00 approx.	Uganda	$20.00
Madagascar	$20.00	Zambia	$30.00
Malawi	$20.00	Zimbabwe	*
Mauritius	$41.00 approx.		
Mozambique	$20.00		

* Included in price of air ticket.

BANKS

Barclays and Standard Chartered Banks are located in most of these countries.

BANKING HOURS

Banks are usually open Monday through Friday mornings and early afternoons, sometimes on Saturday mornings, and closed on Sundays and holidays. Most hotels, lodges and camps are licensed to exchange foreign currency. Quite often, the best place to exchange money is at the airport upon arrival.

CREDIT CARDS

Major international credit cards are accepted by most top hotels, restaurants, lodges, permanent safari camps and shops. Visa and MasterCard are most widely accepted. American Express and Diner's Club are also accepted by most first-class hotels and many businesses. However, American Express is not often taken in more remote areas and camps. ATMs are in many locations in South Africa but are found in few other countries (except some major cities) covered in this book.

CURRENCIES

The currencies of Namibia, Lesotho and Swaziland are on a par with the South African Rand. The South African Rand may be accepted in Namibia, Lesotho and Swaziland; however, the currencies of Namibia, Lesotho and Swaziland are not accepted in South Africa.

Current rates for many African countries can usually be found on the Internet.

For U.S. dollars, bring only the newer "big faced" bills as the older bills are generally not accepted. Traveler's checks are *not* widely accepted.

CURRENCY RESTRICTIONS

A few African countries require visitors to complete currency declaration forms upon arrival; all foreign currency, travelers checks and other negotiable instruments must be recorded. These forms must be surrendered on departure. When you leave the country, the amount of currency you have with you must equal the amount with which you entered the country less the amount exchanged and recorded on your currency declaration form.

For some countries in Africa, the maximum amount of local currency that may be imported or exported is strictly enforced. Check for current restrictions by contacting the tourist offices, embassies or consulates of the countries you wish to visit.

In some countries, it is difficult (if not impossible) to exchange unused local currency back to foreign exchange (i.e., U.S. dollars). Therefore, it is best not to exchange more than you feel you will need.

The currencies used by the countries included in this guide are as follows:

Botswana	1 Pula	=	100 thebe
Burundi	1 Burundi Franc	=	100 centimes
Congo, D.R.	1 Zaire	=	100 makutas
Egypt	1 Egyptian Pound	=	100 piasers
Ethiopia	1 Birr	=	100 santim
Kenya	1 Kenya Shilling	=	100 cents
Lesotho	1 Loti	=	100 licente
Madagascar	1 Malagasy ariary	=	5 iraimbilanja
Malawi	1 Kwacha	=	100 tambala
Mauritius	1 Mauritius Rupee	=	100 cents
Namibia	1 Namibian Dollar	=	100 cents
Rwanda	1 Rwanda Franc	=	100 centimes
Seychelles	1 Seychelles Rupee	=	100 cents
South Africa	1 Rand	=	100 cents
Swaziland	1 Lilangeni	=	100 cents
Tanzania	1 Tanzania Shilling	=	100 cents
Uganda	1 Uganda Shilling	=	100 cents
Zambia	1 Kwacha	=	100 ngwee
Zimbabwe	1 Zimbabwe Dollar	=	100 cents

CUSTOMS

Australian Customs:

The Customs Information Centre: tel. (612) 6275 6666 (from outside Australia) and 1300 363 263 (from inside Australia); Monday through Friday, 8:30 a.m. to 5:00 p.m.; email: information@customs.gov.au.

Canadian Customs:

For a brochure on current Canadian customs requirements, ask for the brochure I Declare from your local customs office, which will be listed in the telephone book under "Government of Canada, Customs and Excise."

New Zealand Customs:

Custom House, Box 29, 50 Anzac Ave., Auckland; tel. 09 359 6655, fax 09 359 6735, fax from overseas: 0064 9359 6730 / call from overseas: 0064 9300 5399; www.customs.gov.az.

United Kingdom:

HM Customs and Excise, Kent House, Upper Ground, London SE1 9PS.

U.S. Customs:

For current information on products made from endangered species of wildlife that are not allowed to be imported, contact Traffic (U.S.A.), World Wildlife Fund, 1250 24th St. NW, Washington, DC 20037, tel. (202) 293-4800, and ask for the leaflet "Buyer Beware" for current restrictions.

DIPLOMATIC REPRESENTATIVES OF AFRICAN COUNTRIES

Check the websites of the countries you plan to visit for the most current information.

In Australia:

Kenya: Level 3, Manpower Building 33/35 Ainslie Avenue Canberra ACT 2601, Australia; tel. (02)62 474788 or 62 474722, fax (02) 62 576613; Monday through Friday, hours 9:00 a.m. to 4:00 p.m.; email: khc-canberra@kenya.asn.au.

Mauritius: 2 Beale Crescent Deakin, Canberra ACT 2600, Australia; tel. (02) 62 81 1203 or 62 82 4436, fax (02) 62 82 3235; Monday through Friday, hours 8:45 a.m. to 3:15 p.m.; email: mhccan@cyberone.com.au.

Seychelles: 12th Floor West Clock, Wisma, Selangor Dredging, 142C Jalan Ampang, 50450 Kuala Lumpur, Malaysia; tel. (60-3)21305726 or (60-3)21635727, fax (60-3)21635729.

Zimbabwe: High Commissioner, 11 Culogoa Circuit, O'Malley, ACT 2606, Canberra, Australia; tel. (02) 62862700 or (02) 6286 2281 or (02) 62862303, fax (02) 62901680; email: zimbabwe1@iimetro.com.au.

In Canada:

Burundi: 325 Dalhousie Street, Suite 815, Ottawa, Ontario, Canada, K1N 7G2; tel. (613) 789-0414 or 789-7042, fax (613) 789-9537.

Congo, Democratic Republic of: 18 Range Rd., Ottawa, Ontario, Canada, K1N 8J3; tel. (613) 230-6391, fax (613) 230-1945.

Kenya: High Commission for the Republic of Kenya, 415 Laurier Avenue East, Ottawa, Ontario, Canada, K1N 6R4; tel. (613) 563-1773, fax (613) 233-6599; email: kenrep@on.aibn.com.

Malawi: 7 Clemow Ave., Ottawa, Canada, K1S 2A9; tel. (613) 236-8931, fax (613) 236-1054; email: Malawi-highcommission@sympatico.ca.

Rwanda: 121 Sherwood Dr., Ottawa, Ontario, Canada, K1Y 3V1; tel. (613) 569-5420/2224, fax (613) 569-5421/5423; email: embarwa@sympatico.ca.

South Africa: High Commission of the Republic of South Africa, 15 Sussex Dr., Ottawa, Ontario, Canada, K1M 1M8; tel. (613) 744-0330, fax (613) 741-1639, email: safrica@ottawa.net.

Swaziland: 130 Albert St., Suite 1204, Ottawa, Ontario, Canada, K1P 5G4; tel. (613) 567-1480, fax (613) 567-1058; email: shc@direct-internet.net.

Tanzania: 50 Range Rd., Ottawa, Ontario, Canada, K1N 8J4; tel. (613) 232-1509, fax (613) 232-5184; email: tzottowa@synapse.net.

Uganda: 231 Coburg St., Ottawa, Ontario, Canada, K1N 8J2; tel. (613) 789-7797, fax (613) 789-8909.

Zimbabwe: 332 Somerset St. West, Ottawa, Ontario, Canada, K2P 0J9; tel. (613) 237-4388/9, fax (613) 563-8269; email: zimembassy@bellnet.ca.

High Commissions in the United Kingdom:

Botswana: 6 Stratford Place, London, England, W1C 1AY; tel. (020) 7499-0031, fax (020) 7495-8595.

Burundi: Square Marie-Louise, 46, 1000 Brussels; tel. (00 322) 230-5-35, fax (00 322) 230-78 83.

Congo, Democratic Republic of: 38 Holne Chase, London, England, N2 0QQ; tel. (020) 8458-0254, fax (020) 8458-0254.

Kenya: 45 Portland Place, London, England, W1N 4AS; tel. (020) 763-62371/5, fax (020) 732-36717.

Lesotho: 7 Chesham Place, Belgravia, London, England, SW1 8HN; tel. (020) 7235-5686, fax (020) 7235 5023; Monday through Friday, 09:00–16:00; email: lesotholondonhighcom@compuserve.com.

Malawi: 33 Grosvenor St., London, England, W1K 4QT; tel. (020) 7491-4172/7, fax (020) 7491-9916.

Mauritius: 32/33 Elvaston Place, London, England, SW7 5NW; tel. (020) 7581-0294-8, fax (020) 7823-8437; email: Londonmhc@btinternet.com.

Namibia: 6 Chandos St., London W1M 9LU, England; tel. (020) 7636-6244, fax (020) 7637-5694; email: Namibia.hicom@btconnect.com.

Rwanda: 58-59 Trafalgar Square, London, England, WC2N 5DX; tel. (020) 7930-2570, fax (020) 7930-2572; email: ambarwanda@compuserve.com.

Seychelles: Box 4PE Eros House, 2nd Floor, 111 Baker Street London, United Kingdom, England, W1M 1FE; tel. (020) 7224-1660, fax (020) 7487-5756.

South Africa: South Africa House, Trafalgar Square, London, England, WC2N 5DP; tel. +44 (0) 20-7451-7299, fax +44 (0) 20-7451-7283; email: general@southafricahouse.com.

Swaziland: 20 Buckingham Gate, London, England, SW1E 6LB; tel. (020) 7630-6611, fax (020) 7630-6564.

Tanzania: 43 Hertford St., London, England, W1Y 7DB; tel. (020) 7499-8951, fax (020) 7491-9321; email: tanzarep@tanzania-online.gov.uk.

Uganda: 58-59 Trafalgar Square, London, England, WC2N 5DX; tel. (020) 7839-5783, fax (020) 7839-8925.

Zambia: 2 Palace Gate, Kensington, London, England, W8 5NG; tel. (020) 7589-6655, fax (020) 7581-1353.

Zimbabwe: 429 Strand, London, England, WC2R 0JR; tel. (020) 7836-7755, fax (020) 7379-1167; email: zimlondon@callnetuk.com.

In The United States:

Botswana: Intelsat Building, Suite 7M, 3400 International Dr. NW, Washington, DC 20008; tel. (202) 244-4990/1, fax (202) 244-4164.

Burundi: Suite 212, 2233 Wisconsin Ave. NW, Washington, DC 20007; tel. (202) 342-2574, fax (202) 342-2578.

Congo, Democratic Republic of: 1800 New Hampshire NW, Washington, DC 20009; tel. (202) 234-7690/1, fax (202) 232-0748.

Kenya: 2249 R St. NW, Washington, DC 20008; tel. (202) 387-6101, fax (202) 462-3829.

Lesotho: 2511 Massachusetts Ave. NW, Washington, DC 20008; tel. (202) 797-5533, fax (202) 234-6815; email: lesotho@afrika.com.

Malawi: 2408 Massachusetts Ave., Washington, DC 20008; tel. (202) 797-1007, fax (202) 265-0976.

Mauritius: 4301 Connecticut Ave. NW, Suite 441, Washington, DC 20008; tel. (202)244-1491/2, fax (202)966-0983; email: Mauritius.embassy@prodigy.net.

Namibia: 1605 New Hampshire Ave. NW, Washington DC 20009; tel. (202) 986-0540, fax (202) 986-0443.

Rwanda: 1714 New Hampshire Ave. NW, Washington, DC 20009; tel. (202) 232-2882, fax (202) 234-4544.

Seychelles: Embassy of the Republic of the Seychelles and Tourist Office, 800 2nd Ave. # 400C, New York, NY 10017; tel. (212) 972-1785, fax (212) 972-1786.

South Africa: 4301 Connecticut Ave. NW, Suite 220, Washington, DC 20008; tel. (202) 232-4400, fax (202) 244-9417.

Swaziland: 3400 International Dr. NW, Suite 3M, Washington, DC 20008-3006; tel. (202) 362-6683, fax (202) 244-8059.

Tanzania: 2139 R St. NW, Washington, DC 20008; tel. (202) 939-6125, fax (202) 797-7408.

Uganda: 5911 16th St. NW, Washington, DC 20011; tel. (202) 726-7100, fax (202) 726-1727; email: info@ugandaembassyus.org.

Zambia: 2419 Massachusetts Ave. NW, Washington, DC 20008; tel. (202) 265-9717, fax (202) 265-9718.

Zimbabwe: 1608 New Hampshire Ave. NW, Washington, DC 20009; tel. (202) 332-7100, fax (202) 483-9326; email: info@zimbabweembassy.us.

Missions to the United Nations or Consulates in New York:

Botswana: 103 East 37th St., New York, NY 10017; tel. (212) 889-2277, fax (212) 725-5061.

Burundi: 336 East 45th St., 12th Floor, New York, NY 10017; tel. (212) 499-0001, fax (212) 499-0006.

Congo, Democratic Republic of: 14 East 65th St., New York, NY 10021; tel. (212) 744-7840/1/2, fax (212) 744-7975; email: Cogun@undp.org.

Kenya: 866 United Nations Plaza, Suite 486, New York, NY 10017; tel. (212) 421-4740/1/2/3, fax (212) 486-1985; email: Kenya@nyct.net.

Lesotho: 204 East 39th St., New York, NY 10016; tel. (212) 661-1690, fax (212) 682-4388; email: Lesotho@un.int.

Mauritius: 211 East 43rd St., Suite 1502, New York, NY 10017; tel. (212) 949-0190/1, fax (212) 697-3829; email: Mauritius@un.int.

Malawi: 600 3rd Ave., 30th Floor, New York, NY 10016; tel. (212) 949-0180, fax (212) 599-5021; email: malawi@un.it.

Namibia: 135 East 36th St., New York, NY 10016; tel. (212) 685-2003, fax (212) 685-1561; email: Namibia@un.int.

Rwanda: 124 East 39th St., New York, NY 10016; tel. (212) 679-9010, fax (212) 679-9133; email: rwaun@undp.org.

Seychelles: 800 Second Ave., Suite 400-C, New York, NY 10017; tel. (212) 972-1785, fax (212) 972-1786; email: Seychelles@un.int.

South Africa: 333 East 38th St., New York, NY 10016; tel. (212) 213-4880, fax (212) 213-0102; email: sacg@southafrica-newyork.net.

Swaziland: 408 East 50th St., New York, NY 10022; tel. (212) 371-8910, fax (212) 754-2755; email: Swaziland@un.int.

Tanzania: 205 East 42nd St., 15th Floor, New York, NY 10017; tel. (212) 972-9160/9123, fax (212) 682-5232; email: Tanzania@un.int.

Uganda: Uganda House, 336 East 45th St., New York, NY 10017; tel. (212) 949-0110, fax (212) 687-4517; email: Uganda@un.int.

Zambia: 800 Second Ave., 9th Floor, New York, NY 10017; tel. (212) 758-1110, fax (212) 758-1319; email: Zambia@un.int.

Zimbabwe: 128 East 56th St., New York, NY 10022; tel. (212) 980-5084, fax (212) 308-6705; email: Zimbabwe@un.int.

DIPLOMATIC REPRESENTATIVES IN AFRICA

United States of America

Botswana: United States Embassy, P.O. Box 90, Gaborone, Botswana; tel. (267 31) 395-3982/3/4, fax (267 31) 395-6947; email: consulargaboro@state.gov.

Burundi: United States Embassy, B.P. 1720 Ave. Des Etats-Unis, Bujumbura, Burundi; tel. (257) 223454, fax (257) 222926.

Congo: B.P. 697, 310 Ave. des Aviateurs, Kinshasa, Congo; tel. (243 88) 43608, fax (243 88) 41036.

Egypt: United States Embassy Cairo, 8 Kamal El Din Salah Street, Garden City, Cairo, Egypt; tel. (202 2) 2797-3300, fax (202 2) 2797-3602; email: CairoWebMaster@state.gov.

Ethiopia: United States Embassy, Entoto Street, P.O. Box 1014, Addis Ababa, Ethiopia; tel. (251 11) 124-2424, fax (251 11) 124-2435; email: pasaddis@state.gov.

Kenya: United States Embassy, United Nations Avenue, P.O. Box 606 Village Market Nairobi, Kenya 00621; tel. (254 20) 3636000, fax (254 20) 3633410.

Lesotho: United States Embassy, P.O. Box 333, Maseru 100, Lesotho; tel. (266 22) 312-666, fax (266 22) 310-116; email: infomaseru@state.gov.

Madagascar: United States Embassy, 14-16 Rue Raintovo, Antsahavola — Antananarivo 101, Madagascar; tel. (261-20) 22 212-57, 212-73 209-56, fax (261-20) 22 345-39.

Malawi: United States Embassy, P.O. Box 30016, 16 Jomo Kenyatta Road, Lilongwe 3, Malawi; tel. (265) 773 166, fax (265) 770 471.

Mauritius: United States Embassy, Rogers Bldg., Fourth Floor, John Kennedy Ave., P.O. Box 544, Port Louis, Mauritius; tel. (230) 202-4400, fax (230) 208-9534; email: usembass@intnet.mu.

Mozambique: United States Embassy, Avenida Kenneth Kaunda 193, Caixa Postal 783, Maputo, Mozambique; tel. (258-21) 49-27-97, fax (258-21) 49-01-14.

Namibia: United States Embassy, Ausplan Bldg., 14 Lossen St., Private Bag 12029, Windhoek, Namibia; tel. (264) 61 295 8500, fax (264) 61 295 8603.

Rwanda: United States Embassy, Blvd. de la Révolution, B.P. 28, Kigali, Rwanda; tel. (250) 505 601, 505 602, 505 603 / Ext 3315, fax (250) 507 143, 57 2128; email: irckigali@state.gov.

Seychelles: U.S. Consular Agency, Victoria House, 1st Floor, Room 112, P.O. Box 251, Victoria, Seychelles; tel. (248) 22 22 56, fax (248) 22 51 59; email: usoffice@seychelles.net.

South Africa: United States Embassy, P.O. Box 9536, 877 Pretorius St., Pretoria, South Africa; tel. (27 12) 431 4000, fax (27 12) 342 2299.
Johannesburg Consulate: P.O. Box 1762, Houghton 2041, 1 River St, Killarney, Johannesburg, South Africa; tel. (27 11) 644 8000, fax (27 11) 646 6916.
Cape Town Consulate: PostNet Suite 50, Private Bag x26, Tokai 7966, 2 Reddam Ave., Westlake 7945, South Africa; tel. (27 21) 702-7300, fax (27 21) 702-7493.

Swaziland: United States Embassy, 2350 Mbabane Place, P.O. Box 199, Mbabane, Swaziland; tel. (268) 404-6441/5, fax (268) 404-5959.

Tanzania: United States Embassy, 686 Old Bagamoyo Road, Msasani, P.O. Box 9123, Dar es Salaam, Tanzania; tel. (255 22) 266 8001 / Ext 4122, fax (255 51) 266 8247; email: DRSacs@state.gov.

Uganda: United States Embassy, 1577 Gaba Road, Kansanga, P.O. Box 7007, Kampala, Uganda; tel. (256 41) 259 791, fax (256 41) 258 451; email: Kampalauscitizen@state.gov.

Zambia: United States Embassy, Independence & United National Aves., P.O. Box 31617, Lusaka, Zambia; tel. (260 1) 250 955, fax (260 1) 252 225; email: ConsularLusaka@state.gov.

Zimbabwe: United States Embassy, 172 Herbert Chitepo Ave., P.O. Box 3340, Harare, Zimbabwe; tel. (263 4) 250593/4, fax (263 4) 796488; email: consularharare@state.gov.

Canada

Botswana: Consulate of Canada, Vision Hire Bldg., Queens Road, P.O. Box 882, Gaborone, Botswana; tel. (267) 3904 411, fax (267) 3904 411.

Congo: The Embassy of Canada, 17 Avenue Pumbu, Commune de la Gombe, P.O. Box 8341, Kinshasa, Democratic Republic of Congo; tel. (243) 89895 0310/0311/0312, fax (243) 81301 6515; email: knsha@international.gc.ca.

Egypt: The Embassy of Canada, 26 Kamel El Shenawy St., Garden City, P.O. Box 1667, Cairo, Egypt; tel. (20 2) 2791 8700, fax (20 2) 2791 8860; email: cairo@international.gc.ca.

Ethiopia: The Embassy of Canada, Old Airport Area, Nefas Silk Lafto Sub City, Kebele 04, House No. 122, Addis Ababa, Ethiopia; tel (251 11) 371 3022, fax (251 11) 371 3033; email: addis@international.gc.ca.

Kenya: The High Commission of Canada, Limuru Road, Gigiri, P.O. Box 1013, 00621 Nairobi, Kenya; tel. (254 20) 366 3000, fax (254 20) 366 3900; email: nrobi@international.gc.ca.

Madagascar: The Consulate of Canada, c/o Madagascar Minerals S.A., Villa 3H, Lot II-J-169, Ivandry, Antananarivo, Madagascar; tel. (261 20) 22 425 59, fax (261 20) 22 425 06; email: consulat.canada@dts.mg.

Mauritius: The Consulate of Canada, 18 Jules Koenig Street, P.O. Box 209, Port Louis, Mauritius; tel. (230) 212-5500, fax (230) 208-3391; email: canada@intnet.mu.

Mozambique: The High Commission of Canada, Avenida Kenneth Kaunda, No. 1138, P.O. Box 1578, Maputo, Mozambique; tel. (258 21) 492 623, fax (258 21) 492 667; email: mputo@international.gc.ca.

Seychelles: The High Commission of Canada, 38 Mirambo St., Garden Ave., P.O. Box 1022, Victoria, Mahe, Seychelles; tel. (248) 225 225, fax (248) 225 127.

South Africa: The High Commission of Canada, Private Bag X13, 1103 Arcadia St., Hatfield 0028, Pretoria.; tel. (27 12) 422 3000, fax (27 12) 422 3052; email: pret@international.gc.ca.

South Africa Johannesburg: Canadian High Commission, P.O. Box 1394, Parklands, 2121 Johannesburg, South Africa; tel. (27 11) 442 3130, fax (27 11) 442 3325; email: jobrg@international.gc.ca.

Tanzania: The High Commission of Canada, 38 Mirambo St., P.O. Box 1022, Dar es Salaam, Tanzania; tel. (255 22) 216 3300, fax (255 22) 211 6897; email: dslam@international.gc.ca.

Uganda: The Consulate of Canada, IPS Building, Plot 14, Parliament Ave., P.O. Box 20115, Kampala, Uganda; tel. (256 41) 258141, fax (256 41) 349484; email: canada.consulate@utlonline.co.ug.

Zambia: The High Commission of Canada, 5199 United Nations Ave., P.O. Box 31313, Lusaka, Zambia 10101; tel. (260 1) 250 833, fax (260 1) 254 176; email: Isaka@international.gc.ca.

Zimbabwe: The Embassy of Canada, 45 Baines Ave., P.O. Box 1430, Harare, Zimbabwe; tel. (263 4) 252181/5, fax (263 4) 252186; email: hrare@international.gc.ca.

United Kingdom

Botswana: British High Commission, Private Bag 0023, Plot No. 1079-1084, Queens Road, Main Mall, Gaborone, Botswana; tel. (267) 3952841, fax (267) 3956105; email: bhc@botsnet.bw.

Burundi: British Liaison Office, Building Old East, Parcelle No. 1-2, Place de l'independence, Bujumbura, Burundi. Permanent staff in Kigali, Rwanda; tel. (257) 22 246 478, fax (257) 22 246 479; email: belo@cni.cbinf.com.

Congo: British Embassy, 83 Avenue du Roi Baudouin, Kinshasa, Gombe, Congo; tel. (243 81) 715 0761, fax (243 81) 346 4291; email: ambrit@ic.cd.

Ethiopia: British Embassy, Comoros Street, P.O. Box 858, Addis Ababa, Ethiopia; tel. (251 11) 661 2354, fax (251 11) 661 0588; email: BritishEmbassy.AddisAbaba@fco.gov.uk.

Kenya: British High Commission, Upper Hill Road, P.O. Box 30465, Nairobi, Kenya; tel. (254 20) 284 4000, fax (254 20) 284 4033.

Lesotho: British Honorary Consul, Sentinel Park, United Nations Road, Maseru, Lesotho; tel. (266 22) 313929, fax (266 22) 310254; email: pmb@leo.co.ls.

Madagascar: British Honorary Consul, BP 12193, Ankorandrano, Antananarivo 101, Madagscar; tel. (261 20) 24 521 80, fax (261 20) 24 263 29; email: ricana@wanadoo.mg.

Malawi: British High Commission, P.O. Box 30042, Lilongwe 3, Malawi; tel. (265) 772400, fax (265) 772657; email: bhclilongwe@fco.gov.uk.

Mauritius: British High Commission, Les Cascades Building, Edith Cavell Street, P.O. Box 1063, Port Louis, Mauritius; tel. (230) 202 9400, fax (230) 202 9408; email: bhc@bow.intnet.mu.

Mozambique: British High Commission, Av Vladimir I Lenine 310, Caixa Postal 55, Maputo, Mozambique; tel. (258 21) 356000, fax (258 21) 356060; email: bhc@consular@tvcabo.co.mz.

Namibia: British High Commission, 116 Robert Mugabe Ave., P.O. Box 22202, Windhoek, Namibia; tel. (264 61) 274800, fax (264 61) 228895; email: general. windhoek@fco.gov.uk.

Rwanda: British Embassy, Parcelle No. 1131, Boulevard de l'Umuganda, Kacyiru-Sud, BP 576, Kigali, Rwanda; tel. (250) 584098, fax (250) 582044; email: embassy.kigali@fco.gov.uk.

Seychelles: British High Commission, Oliaji Trade Centre, Francis Rachel Street, P.O. Box 161, Victoria, Mahe, Seychelles; tel. (248) 283 666, fax (248) 283 657; email: bhcvictoria@fco.gov.uk.

South Africa: Dunkeld Corner, 275 Jan Smuts Av., Dunkeld West 2196, Johannesburg 2001; tel. (27 11) 327 0015, fax (27 21) 425 1427
South Africa Cape Town: British Consulate General, 15th Floor, Southern Life Center, 8 Riebeek Street, Cape Town 8001. South Africa British High Commission, 255 Hill St., Arcadia 0002, Pretoria, South Africa; tel. (27 21) 425 3670, fax (27 21) 425 1427.

Swaziland: British Honorary Consul, P.O. Box A41, Eveni, Mbabane, H103 Swaziland; tel. (268) 551 6247, fax same; email: nonbritcon@realnet.co.sz.

Tanzania: British High Commission, Umoja House, Garden Ave., P.O. Box 9200, Dar es Salaam, Tanzania; tel. (255 22) 211 0101, fax (255 22) 211 0102; email: bhc.dar@fco.gov.uk.

Uganda: British High Commission, 4 Windsor Loop, P.O. Box 7070, Kampala, Uganda; tel. (256 31) 2312000 or (256 41) 257304; email: Consular.kampala@fco.gov.uk.

Zambia: British High Commission, 5210 Independence Ave., P.O. Box 50050, Lusaka, Zambia; tel. (260 1) 251133, fax (260 1) 253798; email: BHC-Lusaka@fco.gov.uk.

Zimbabwe: British Embassy, Corner House, Samora Machel Ave., Leopold Takawira St., P.O. Box 4490, Harare, Zimbabwe; tel. (263 4) 772990 or 774700, fax (263 4) 774617.

DUTY-FREE ALLOWANCES

Contact the nearest tourist office or embassy for current, duty-free import allowances for the country(ies) that you intend to visit. The duty-free allowances vary; however, the following may be used as a general guideline: 1 to 2 liters (approximately 1 to 2 qt./33.8–67.4 fl. oz.) of spirits, one carton (200) of cigarettes or 100 cigars.

ELECTRICITY

Electric current is 220 to 240-volt AC 50 Hz. Adapters: Three-prong square or round plugs are most commonly used (plugs not drawn to size).

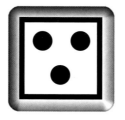 

GETTING TO AFRICA

By Air:

Most travelers from North America flying to the countries listed in this guide must pass through Europe, with the exception of South African Airways, which flies New York-JFK and Washington-Dulles to Johannesburg, South Africa and Delta from Atlanta and New York to Johannesburg and Cape Town. Airfares and air routings to Africa change continuously. For special discount air fares, please call The Africa Adventure Company at 1-800-882-9453 (U.S.A. and Canada) or (954) 491-8877, fax (954) 491-9060, email safari@AfricanAdventure.com or visit the World Wide Web pages at http://www.AfricanAdventure.com. In any case, I strongly suggest you book your air with the tour operator with which you are booking your land arrangements; if there is an air schedule change or cancellation it will appear on their airline computer screens and they can work to get you back on track and adjust your land arrangements accordingly — otherwise you may show up at an airport only to find there is no flight!

By Road:

From Egypt to Sudan and Ethiopia to Kenya and southward; trans-Sahara through Algeria, Niger, Nigeria or Chad, Cameroon, Central Africa Republic, Democratic Republic of the Congo, Rwanda or Uganda and eastern and southern Africa. Allow several months because the roads are very bad.

By Ship:
Some cruise ships stop along the coasts of Kenya, Tanzania and South Africa and at Mauritius and the Seychelles.

GETTING AROUND AFRICA
See each country's map for details on major roads, railroad lines and waterways.

By Air:
Capitals and major tourist centers are served by air. There is regularly scheduled commercial air service to the following destinations within Africa (there is also scheduled air charter service to most parks and reserves):
Botswana: Gaborone, Maun, Francistown and Kasane.
Burundi: Bujumbura.
Congo, Democratic Republic of: Kinshasa.
Kenya: Kisumu, Malindi, Mombasa, Lamu and Nairobi.
Lesotho: Maseru
Malawi: Blantyre, Lilongwe, Mzuzu.
Mauritius: Plaisance International Airport.
Namibia: Windhoek, Luderitz, Swakopmund and Walvis Bay.
Rwanda: Kigali.
Seychelles: Mahe and Praslin.
South Africa: Bloemfontein, Cape Town, Durban, Eastgate (Hoedspruit), East London, George, Johannesburg, Kimberley, Nelspruit, Port Elizabeth, Richards Bay, Mpumalanga (replaced Skukuza), Umtata and Upington.
Tanzania: Kilimanjaro International, Dar es Salaam and Zanzibar.
Uganda: Entebbe.
Zambia: Lusaka, Livingstone (Victoria Falls), Mfuwe (South Luangwa National Park) and Ndola.
Zimbabwe: Bulawayo, Harare, Hwange, Kariba and Victoria Falls.

By Road:
Major roads are tarmac (paved) and are excellent in Namibia, South Africa, Botswana and Rwanda. Most major roads are tarmac in fair condition in Kenya, Tanzania, Uganda, Zambia, Malawi and Swaziland. Burundi, Lesotho and the D.R. Congo have very few tarmac roads. Many dirt roads (except in Namibia) are difficult and many are impassable in the rainy season (especially the D.R. Congo), often requiring 4wd vehicles.

Gas (petrol) and diesel are readily available in the main towns and cities of Botswana, Kenya, Lesotho, Malawi, Mauritius, Namibia, South Africa and

Swaziland; may be difficult to obtain in Burundi, Rwanda, parts of Tanzania, Zambia and Zimbabwe; and they are very difficult to obtain in the D.R. Congo.

Taxis are available in the larger cities and at international airports. Service taxis travel when all seats are taken and are an inexpensive but uncomfortable means of long-distance travel. Local buses are very crowded, uncomfortable and are recommended for only the hardiest of travelers. Pickup trucks (matatus in East Africa) often crammed with 20 passengers, luggage, produce, chickens, etc., and are used throughout the continent. Be sure to agree on the price before setting off.

By Rail:

The Blue Train and Rovos Rail rate as two of the most luxurious trains in the world. The Blue Train runs from Cape Town to Pretoria and vice versa while Rovos Rail runs from Pretoria to Cape Town, Victoria Falls, Durban, Windhoek and Swakopmund (Namibia) and Dar es Salaam (Tanzania). Please see the chapter on South Africa for further details. The so-called "Lunatic Express" from Nairobi to Mombasa in Kenya, as of this writing, is in poor condition. Otherwise, with the exception of South Africa, regular train travel is slow and not recommended except for those who are on an extremely low budget or who have plenty of time to spare. Train travel is possible from Arusha (Tanzania) through Zambia, Zimbabwe and Botswana to Cape Town, South Africa.

By Boat:

Steamer service on Lake Tanganyika serves Bujumbura (Burundi), Kigoma (Tanzania), Mpulungu (Zambia) and Kalemie (D.R. Congo) about once a week; steamers on Lake Victoria service Kisumu (Kenya), Musoma and Mwanza (Tanzania) and Kampala-Port Bell (Uganda); steamers circumnavigate Lake Malawi.

HEALTH

Malarial risk exists in all of the countries included in this guidebook (except for Lesotho and much of South Africa), so be sure to take your malaria pills (unless advised by your doctor not to take them) as prescribed before, during and after your trip. Contact your doctor, an immunologist or the Centers for Disease Control and Prevention in Atlanta (toll-free tel. 1-888-232-3228, fax 1-888-232-3299, Web site: www.cdc.gov) or the appropriate source in your own country for the best prophylaxis for your itinerary. Use an insect repellent. Wear long-sleeve shirts and slacks for further protection, especially at sunset and during the evening.

Bilharzia is a disease that infests most lakes and rivers on the continent but can be easily cured. Do not walk barefoot along the shore or wade or swim in a stream, river or lake unless you know for certain it is free of bilharzia. Bilharzia does not exist in salt water or in fast flowing rivers or along shorelines that have waves. A species of snail is involved in the reproductive cycle of bilharzia, and the snails are more often found near reeds and in slow-moving water. If you feel you may have contracted the disease, go to your doctor for a blood test. If diagnosed in its early stages, it is easily cured.

Wear a hat and bring sun-block to protect yourself from the tropical sun. Drink plenty of fluids and limit alcohol consumption at high altitudes. In hot weather, do not drink alcohol and limit the consumption of coffee and tea unless you drink plenty of water.

For further information, U.S. citizens can obtain a copy of "Health Information for International Travel" from the U.S. Government Printing Office, Washington, DC 20402.

INOCULATIONS

See "Visa and Inoculations Requirements" on page 655.

INSURANCE

Travel insurance packages often include a combination of emergency evacuation, medical, baggage, and trip cancellation. I feel that it is imperative that all travelers to Africa cover themselves fully with an insurance package from a reputable provider. Many tour operators require guests to be fully insured, or to at least have emergency evacuation insurance as a requirement for joining a safari. The peace of mind afforded by such insurance far outweighs the cost. Ask your Africa travel specialist for information on relatively inexpensive group-rate insurance.

MAPS

Before going on safari, obtain good maps for each country you intend to visit. This will increase your awareness of the areas you want to see and enhance your enjoyment of the trip. For a free catalog of difficult-to-find country maps, regional maps and mountain maps, see the catalog at the end of this book or contact The Africa Adventure Company, 5353 N. Federal Highway, Suite 300, Fort Lauderdale, FL 33308, tel. (954) 491-8877 or 1-800-882-9453 or view the catalog at www.AfricanAdventure.com. It is best to purchase maps before arriving in Africa, because they may not be readily available upon your arrival.

METRIC SYSTEM OF WEIGHTS AND MEASURES

The metric system is used in Africa. The U.S. equivalents are listed in the following conversion chart.

MEASUREMENT CONVERSIONS

1 inch	=	2.54 centimeters (cm)
1 foot	=	0.305 meter (m)
1 mile	=	1.60 kilometers (km)
1 square mile	=	2.59 square kilometers (km²)
1 quart liquid	=	0.946 liter (l)
1 ounce	=	28 grams (g)
1 pound	=	0.454 kilogram (kg)
1 cm	=	0.39 inch (in.)
1 m	=	3.28 feet (ft.)
1 km	=	0.62 mile (mi.)
1 acre	=	0.4 hectares
1 km²	=	0.3861 square mile (sq. mi.)
1 l	=	1.057 quarts (qt.)
1 g	=	0.035 ounce (oz.)
1 kg	=	2.2 pounds (lb.)

TEMPERATURE CONVERSIONS

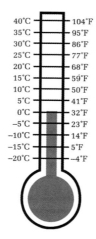

TEMPERATURE CONVERSION FORMULAS
To convert degrees Centigrade into degrees Fahrenheit:
Multiply Centigrade by 1.8 and add 32.
To convert degrees Fahrenheit into degrees Centigrade:
Subtract 32 from Fahrenheit and divide by 1.8.

MONEY

One way to obtain additional funds is to have money sent by telegraph international money order (Western Union), telexed through a bank or sent via international courier (i.e., DHL). Do not count on finding ATM machines, except in South Africa and in some major cities in other countries. Traveler's checks are not widely accepted except at most airport banks.

PASSPORT OFFICES

To obtain a passport in the United States, contact your local post office for the passport office nearest you. Then call the passport office to be sure you will have everything on hand that will be required (www.travel.state.gov/).

SEMINARS ON AFRICA

Contact the Africa Adventure Company to arrange a seminar by Mark Nolting, author of this guidebook. Tel. (954) 491-8877 or 1-800-882-9453, fax (954) 491-9060, email: safari@AfricanAdventure.com.

SHOPPING

If you like bartering, bring clothing (new denims and T-shirts are great) or pens to trade for souvenirs. This works particularly well at roadside stands and in small villages in East and Central Africa, although the villagers are becoming more discerning in their tastes.

SOME SHOPPING IDEAS

Botswana: Baskets, wood carvings, pottery, tapestries and rugs. There are curio shops in many safari camps, hotels and lodges.

Burundi: Crafts available in numerous shops.

Congo, Democratic Republic of: Wood carvings, malachite, copper goods, semiprecious stones and baskets.

Ethiopia: Traditional clothes and textiles, weavings, carvings, ethnic artifacts, wooden headrests, spices/coffee, silver and gold jewelry and paintings with both modern and religious influences.

Kenya: Makonde and Akomba ebony wood carvings, soapstone carvings, colorful kangas and kikois (cloth wraps) and beaded belts. In Mombasa, Zanzibar chests, gold and silverwork, brasswork, Arab jewelry and antiques.

Lesotho: Basotho woven carpets are known worldwide, tapestry weavings and conical straw hats.

Malawi: Wood carvings, woven baskets.

Mauritius: Intricately detailed, handmade model sailing ships of camphor or teak, pareos (colorful light cotton wraps), knitwear, textiles, T-shirts, Mauritian dolls, tea, rum, and spices.

Mozambique: Wood carvings, colorful paintings, silverware, cashew nuts and island sarongs.

Namibia: Semiprecious stones and jewelry, karakul wool products, wood carvings, ostrich eggshell necklaces and beadwork.

Seychelles: Coco-de-mer nuts (may be purchased with a government permit that is not difficult to obtain), batik prints, spices for Creole cooking and locally produced jewelry, weavings and basketry.

South Africa: Diamonds, gold, wood carvings, dried flowers, wire art, wildlife paintings and sculpture, and wine.

Swaziland: Beautiful handwoven tapestries, baskets, earthenware and stoneware, and mouth-blown handcrafted glass animals and tableware.

Tanzania: Makonde carvings, meerschaum pipes and tanzanite.

Uganda: Wood carvings.

Zambia: Wood carvings, statuettes, semiprecious stones and copper souvenirs.

Zimbabwe: Carvings in wood, stone and Zimbabwe's unique verdite, intricate baskets, wildlife paintings and sculpture, ceramic ware, and crocheted garments.

SHOPPING HOURS

Shops are usually open Monday through Friday from 8:00 or 9:00 a.m. until 5:00 to 6:00 p.m. and from 9:00 a.m. until 1:00 p.m. on Saturdays. Shops in the coastal cities of Kenya and Tanzania often close midday for siesta. Use the shopping hours given above as a general guideline; exact times can vary within the respective country.

THEFT

The number one rule in preventing theft on vacation is to leave all unnecessary valuables at home. What you must bring, lock in room safes or safety deposit boxes when not in use. Carry all valuables in your carry-on luggage — do not put any valuables in your checked luggage. Theft in Africa is generally no worse than in Europe or the United States, but consider leaving showy gold watches and jewelry at home. One difference is that Africans are poorer and may steal things that most American or European thieves would consider worthless. Be careful in all African cities (like most large cities in North America) and do not go walking around the streets at night.

TIME ZONES

EST = Eastern Standard Time (east coast of the United States)
GMT = Greenwich Mean Time (Greenwich, England)

EST + 3/GMT – 2
Cape Verde

EST + 4/GMT – 1
Guinea-Bissau

EST + 5/GMT
Algeria
Ascension
Burkina-Faso
The Gambia
Ghana
Guinea
Ivory Coast
Liberia
Mali
Mauritania
Morocco
St. Helena
São Tomé & Principe
Senegal
Sierra Leone
Togo
Tristan de Cunha

EST + 6/GMT + 1
Angola
Benin
Cameroon
Central African Republic
Chad
Congo
Democratic Republic
  of the Congo (western)
Equatorial Guinea
Gabon
Niger
Nigeria
Tunisia

EST + 7/GMT + 2
Botswana
Burundi
Democratic Republic of
  the Congo (eastern)
Egypt
Lesotho
Libya
Malawi

Mozambique
Namibia
Rwanda
South Africa
Sudan
Swaziland
Zambia
Zimbabwe

EST + 8/GMT + 3
Comoros
Djibouti
Eritrea
Ethiopia
Kenya
Madagascar
Somalia
Tanzania
Uganda

EST + 9/GMT + 4
Mauritius
Reunion
Seychelles

TIPPING

A 10% tip is recommended at restaurants for good service where a service charge is not included in the bill. For advice on what tips are appropriate for guides, safari camps and lodges, ask the Africa specialist booking your safari.

TOURIST INFORMATION

In addition to the addresses below, information may also be available through embassies or consulates of the countries in question. See "Diplomatic Representatives" above. Check the respective Web sites for current contact information.

Offices in Africa

Botswana: Department of Tourism, P / Bag 0047, Gaborone, Botswana; tel. (267) 395-3024, fax (267) 390-8675; email: botswanatourism@gov.bw.

Burundi: National Office of Tourism, Liberty Ave., B.P. 902, Bujumbura 257 Burundi, tel. (257) 222023, fax (257) 229390.

Congo, Democratic Republic of: 15 Ave des Clinques, B.P. 12348, Kinshasa-Gombe, Congo tel. (243) 30235, fax (243) 32668.

Kenya: Kenya-Re Towers, Ragati Road, P.O. Box 30630 — 00100 Nairobi, Kenya, tel. (254) 20-271-1262, fax (254) 020-271-9925.

Lesotho: National Tourist Board, P.O. Box 1378, Maseru 100, Lesotho; tel. (266)223-12238, fax (266)223-10189.

Malawi: P.O. Box 402, Blantyre, Malawi; tel. (265) 620 300, fax (265) 620 947.

Mauritius: Mauritius Tourism Promotion Authority, 11th Floor, Air Mauritius Centre, 5, President John Kennedy Street, Port-Louis, Mauritius; tel. (+230) 210-1545, fax (+230) 212-5142.

Namibia: Ministry of Environment & Tourism, Directory of Tourism, Private Bag 13306, Windhoek, Levinson arcade, Capital Centre, Namibia; tel. (+264) 61 284-2178.

Rwanda: Office Rwandaise du Tourisme et des Parcs Nationaux (ORTPN), The Rwanda Tourism Board, Boulevard de la Révolution n° 1, PO Box 905, Kigali, Rwanda; tel (250) 576514 or 573396, fax (250) 576515.

Seychelles: P.O. Box 47, Independence House, Victoria, Mahe, Seychelles; tel. (248) 225 313, fax (248) 224 035.

South Africa: Tourism Board, Private Bag X10012, Sandton 2146, Bojanala House, 12 Rivonia Road, Illovo Johannesburg 2196, South Africa; tel. (27 11) 778 8000, fax (27 11) 778 8001; email: info@southafrica.net.

Swaziland: Government Tourist Office, P.O. Box 451, Mbabane, Swaziland; tel. (268) 42531.

Tanzania: Tanzania Tourist Board, P.O. Box 2485, Dar es Salaam, Tanzania; tel. (255) 022 2111244, fax (255) 022 2116420.

Uganda: IPS Building, Parliament Avenue 14, P.O. Box 7211, Kampala, Uganda; tel. (256) 41 242 196, fax (256) 41 242 188.

Zambia: Century House, Cairo Road, P.O. Box 30017, Lusaka, Zambia; tel. (260) 1 229 087, fax (260) 1 225 174; email: zntb@zamnet.zm.

Zimbabwe: Tourist Development Corporation (ZTDC) P.O. Box 8052, Harare, Zimbabwe; tel. (263) 793 666, fax (263) 793 669.

Offices in Australia

South Africa: Level 6, 285 Clarence St., Sydney, NSW 2000 Australia; tel. (61) 2 9261 3424, fax (61) 2 9261 3414; email: info@satour.com.au.

Offices in Canada

South Africa: (two offices) Suite 1001, 20 Eglington Ave. West, Toronto, Ontario, M4R 1K8; tel. (416) 283 0563, fax (416) 283 5465.

Suite 205, 4117 Lawrence Ave. East, Scarborough, Ontario M1E 2S2.

Offices in the United Kingdom

Botswana: Botswana High Commission; 6 Stratford Place, London, England, W1N 9AE; tel. 020 7499 0031, fax (44) 207 409-782.

Democratic Republic of Congo: Embassy of the Democratic Republic of the Congo; 38 Holne Chase, London, England, N2 0QQ; tel. +44-20-72789825, fax +44-20-72788497.

Kenya: Kenya High Commission; 45 Portland Place, London, England, W1N 4AS; tel. (020) 7636 2371, fax 020 7323 6717.

Lesotho: High Commission for the Kingdom of Lesotho; 7 Chesham Place, Belgravia, London, England, SW1 8HN; tel. 020 7235 5686, fax 020 7235 5023; email: lhc@lesotholondon.org.uk.

Malawi: High Commission for the Republic of Malawi; 33 Grosvenor St., London, England, W1K 4QT; tel. 020 7491 4172, fax 020 7491 9916.

Mauritius: Mauritius High Commission; 32/33 Elvaston Place, London, England, SW7 5NW; tel. 020 7581 0294, fax 020 7823 8437; email: londonmhc@btinternet.com.

Namibia: High Commission for the Republic of Namibia; 6 Chandos Street, London, England, W1G 9LU; tel. (020) 7636 6244, fax 020 7636 2969.

Rwanda: Embassy of the Republic of Rwanda; 58/59 Trafalgar Square, London, England, WC2N 5DW; tel. 020 7930 2570, fax 020 7930 2572.

Seychelles: High Commission for the Seychelles; 2nd Floor, Eros House, 111 Baker Street, London, England, W1U 6RP; tel. 020 7224 1670, fax 020 7487 5756.

South Africa: South African High Commission; South Africa House, Trafalgar Square, London, England, WC2N 5DP; tel. +44 (0) 20 7451 7299, fax +44 (0) 20 7451 7283.

Swaziland: Kingdom of Swaziland High Commission; 20 Buckingham Gate, London, England, SW1E 6LB; tel. 020 7630 6611, fax 020 7630 6564.

Tanzania: High Commission for the United Republic of Tanzania; 43 Hertford Street, London, England, W1Y 7DB; tel. 020 7499 8951, fax (020) 7491 9321.

Uganda: Uganda High Commission; Consular & Tourism Department, 58/59 Trafalgar Square, London, England, WC2N 5DX; tel. 020 7839 5783, fax 020 7839 8925.

Zambia: High Commission for the Republic of Zambia; 2 Palace Gate, Kensington, London, England, W8 5NG; tel. 020 7589 6655, fax 020 7581 1353.

Zimbabwe: High Commission for the Republic of Zimbabwe; Zimbabwe House, 429 The Strand, London, England, WC2R OJR; tel. 020 7836 7755, fax 020 7379 1167.

Offices in the United States

Kenya: 2249 R St. NW, Washington, DC 20008; tel. (202) 387-6101, fax (202) 462-3829.

Mauritius: 8 Haven Ave., Port Washington, NY 11050; tel. (516) 944-3763, fax (516) 944-8458.

Seychelles: 235 East 40th St. #24A, New York, NY 10016; tel. (212) 687-9766, fax (212) 922-9177.

South Africa (two locations): Office of Tourism. 9841 Airport Blvd., Suite 1524, Los Angeles, CA 90045; tel. (213) 641-8444 or (800) 782-9772, fax (213) 641-5812. Suite 2040, 500 Fifth Ave., New York, NY 10110; tel. (212) 730-2929 or (800) 822-5368, fax (212) 764-1980.

Tanzania: 205 East 42nd St., Room 1300, New York, NY 10017; tel. (202) 939-6129, fax (202) 797-7408.

Zambia: 2419 Massachusetts Ave. NW, Washington, DC 20008; tel. (202) 265-9717, fax (202) 332-0826.

Zimbabwe: Tourist Office, 1270 Avenue of the Americas, Suite 412, New York, NY 10020; tel. (800) 421-2381 or (212) 332-1090, fax (212) 332-1091.

TRAVELER'S CHECKS

American Express, Thomas Cook's, MasterCard and Visa traveler's checks are accepted at most banks and currency exchanges in international airports but in few other locations and therefore are not as useful as cash in hard currencies (U.S. Dollar, British Pound, Euro, etc.). Stay away from lesser-known companies; you may have difficulty cashing them.

VACCINATIONS

Check with the tourist offices or embassies of the countries you wish to visit for current requirements. If you plan to visit one or more countries in endemic zones (i.e., in Africa, South America, Central America or Asia), be sure to mention this when requesting vaccination requirements. Many countries do not require any vaccinations if you are only visiting the country directly from the United States, Canada or Western Europe; but, if you are also visiting countries in endemic zones, there may very well be additional requirements.

Then check with your doctor, and preferably an immunologist, or call your local health department or the Centers for Disease Control in Atlanta, GA (toll-free tel. 1-888-232-3228, toll-free fax 1-888-232-3299, Web site: www.cdc.gov) for information. They will probably recommend some vaccinations in addition to those required by the country you will be visiting.

Make sure you carry with you the International Certificate of Vaccinations showing the vaccinations you have received.

Malarial prophylaxis (pills) is highly recommended for all the countries included in this guide, except for Lesotho and parts of South Africa.

◢ VISA AND INOCULATION REQUIREMENTS

Travelers from most countries must obtain visas to enter some of the countries included in this guide. You may apply for visas with the closest diplomatic representative or through a visa service well in advance (but not so early that the visas will expire before or soon after your journey ends) and check for all current requirements (see "Diplomatic Representatives" on pages 636–639),

Travelers must obtain visas (either before travel or on arrival) and have proof that they have received certain inoculations for entry into some African countries.

Visa and Inoculation Requirements

Travelers must obtain visas and have proof that they have received certain inoculations for entry into some African countries.

● VISA REQUIREMENTS   INOCULATIONS

COUNTRY	U.S.	CANADA	U.K.	
Botswana	No	No	No	Yellow fever**
Egypt	Yes	Yes	Yes	Yellow fever**
Ethiopia	Yes	Yes	Yes	Yellow fever
Kenya***	Yes	Yes	Yes	Yellow fever**
Lesotho	No	No	No	Yellow fever**
Madagascar	Yes	Yes	Yes	Yellow fever**
Malawi	No	No	No	Yellow fever**
Mozambique	Yes	Yes	Yes	Yellow fever**
Namibia	No	No	No	Yellow fever**
Rwanda	No	No	No	Yellow fever
South Africa*	No	No	No	Yellow fever**
Swaziland	No	No	No	Yellow fever**
Tanzania***	Yes	Yes	Yes	Yellow fever
Zanzibar (Tanzania)				Yellow fever
Uganda	Yes	Yes	Yes	Yellow fever
Zambia***	Yes	Yes	Yes	Yellow fever**
Zimbabwe***	Yes	Yes	Yes	Yellow fever**

Notes:

1. Some optional vaccinations include: (a) hepatitis A, (b) hepatitis B, (c) typhoid, (d) tetanus, (e) meningitis, (f) oral polio.

2. Anti-malaria: It is not mandatory but is strongly urged. Anti-malaria is a tablet, not an inoculation. Malaria exists in almost all of the countries listed above.

3. Cholera: The cholera vaccination is not a guaranteed inoculation against infection, and most countries do not require a cholera vaccination for direct travel from the United States. Check with your local doctor and with embassies of the respective countries. Some require proof of a cholera vaccination even if you are arriving directly from the United States.

4. **Yellow fever: Only if arriving from infected area (i.e., Nigeria).

5. ***: Visa may be obtained on arrival by paying a visa fee.

6. Complete necessary visa forms and return with your valid passport (valid for at least six months after travel dates) to the embassy or consulate concerned or use a visa service.

7. *South Africa: Yellow fever vaccination is required if arriving from Kenya, Tanzania or Uganda. Visitors must have at least two consecutive blank pages in their passport.

WILDLIFE ASSOCIATIONS

African Wildlife Foundation, 1400 16th St. NW, Suite 120, Washington, DC 20036; tel. (202) 939-3333.

The African Wildlife Foundation (AWF) is one of the leading international conservation organizations working in Africa. It is also one of the most experienced U.S.-based conservation organizations dedicated solely to Africa. AWF works with people — its supporters worldwide and its partners in Africa (local, national, and international partners, including communities, government at all levels, NGO's, research and training institutions, and donor agencies) — to craft and deliver creative solutions for the long-term well-being of Africa's remarkable species, their habitats and the people who depend upon them. AWF has been working with the people of Africa since 1961. Most of its staff is based in Africa, spread between eight countries, working at a grass-roots level with park managers and communities to safeguard wildlife and wilderness areas. AWF focuses on the big picture while achieving concrete results, helping African nations design successful long-term strategies for conserving their magnificent natural treasures. For more information on AWF and its programs, visit www.AWF.org.

Big Cat Trust is a partnership with National Geographic and world-famous film makers Beverly and Dereck Joubert. The emergency fund has been created to avert the complete loss of the Maasai lions in and around Amboseli National Park, Kenya. The decline of the lion population in this region has reached critical status. Website: www.thebigcattrust.com.

Birdlife International has conservation partnerships with many African countries. www.birdlife.net Email: birdlife@birdlife.org.uk.

Born Free Foundation is based in Nairobi and oversees a number of important projects aimed at conserving habitats, protecting wildlife and working with local communities that live beside wildlife areas. Kenya Representative: c/o Alice Owen, 3 Grove House, Foundry Lane, Horsham, RH13 5PL, United Kingdom; website: www.bornfree.org.uk.

David Sheldrick Wildlife Trust was established in 1977 in Kenya and has been involved in a variety of activities to conserve wildlife, most notable is its work with elephant and rhino orphans. USA Representative: One Indiana Square, Suite 2800 Indianapolis, IN 46204-2079; website: www.sheldrick wildlifetrust.org.

Dian Fossey Gorilla Fund, 45 Inverness Dr. East, Englewood, CO 80112-5480; tel. (303) 790-2345. website: www.gorillafund.org.

East African Wildlife Society, One of the most effective conservation agencies in Kenya, Tanzania and Uganda. USA Representative: c/o P Bakker, 175 West 79th Street, New York, NY 10024. website: www.eawildlife.org.

Endangered Wildlife Trust, c/o Mike Delvin, 346 Smith Ridge Road, New Canaan, CT 06840; tel. (203) 966-1981. website: www.ewt.org.za

International Fund for Animal Welfare works worldwide. Within Southern and East Africa they have campaigns to protect elephants as well as other species and local conservation organizations. International Office: 290 Summer Street, Yarmouth Port, MA 02675; tel. (800) 932-4329. website: www.ifaw.org.

Maasailand Preservation Trust works in conjunction with Ol Donyo Wuas and 4,500 Maasai shareholders. Lions are regularly killed by the locals for preying on their livestock. The outreach program pays compensation for cattle losses due to predators and positive results are the rise in the lion population. Website: www.oldonyowuas.com/thetrust; Kenya Representative: Richard Bonham, email Bonham@swiftkenya.com.

Mauritius Wildlife Foundation, 4th floor, Ken Lee Building, Edith Cavell St., Port Louis, Mauritius; tel. (230) 211-1749, fax (230) 211-1789.

Save the Rhino Trust, P.O. Box 2159, Swakopmund, Namibia; tel. and fax (64) 403829; email: srtrhino@iafrica.com.na.

The Save the Rhino Trust (SRT) mission is to "actively promote and maintain the welfare of the people by adopting policies aimed at the maintenance of ecosystems, essential ecological processes and biological diversity of Namibia and utilization of living natural resources on a sustainable basis for the benefit of all Namibians both present and future."

Wilderness Safaris Wildlife Trust

The Wilderness Safaris Wildlife Trust seeks to make a difference in Africa, to its wildlife and its people. These projects address the needs of existing wildlife populations, seek solutions to save threatened species and provide education and training for local people and their communities. Since its formation, the Trust has supported a wide variety of wildlife management, research and education projects in southern Africa. Financial and educational empowerment of local communities so that they benefit from the wildlife on their doorsteps is vital, and as such, broad-based and comprehensive initiatives are the bedrock of the Trust, providing skills, knowledge and education necessary to communities to value and manage their wildlife populations. A portion of each guest's fare while staying in Wilderness Safaris camps and lodges is allocated to this trust, and 100% of these funds go to Trust-approved projects.

For American taxpayers, donations to the Trust can be tax-deductible through a 501c facility. This facility levies a 5% administration fee. Please email Laura Mass of the Resources First Foundation at lmass@resourcesfirstfoundation.org <mailto:lmass@resourcesfirstfoundation.org> or call her on 207-221-2753 for details. For more details about the Trust or donations, please call Trust Secretary Mari dos Santos in Johannesburg, South Africa, tel: +27 11 807 1800.

Safari Glossary

Ablution block: A building that contains showers, toilets and sinks, most often with separate facilities for men and women.

Acacia: Common, dry-country trees and shrubs armed with spines or curved thorns; they also have tiny, feathery leaflets.

Adaptation: The ability, through structural or functional characteristics, to improve the survival rate of an animal or plant in a particular habitat.

Aloe: A succulent plant of the lily family with thick, pointed leaves and spikes of red or yellow flowers.

Arboreal: Living in trees.

Avifauna: The birdlife of a region.

Banda: A basic shelter or hut, often constructed of reeds, bamboo, grass, etc.

Boma: A place of shelter, a fortified place, enclosure, community (East Africa).

Browse: To feed on leaves.

Calving season: A period during which the young of a particular species are born. Not all species have calving seasons. Most calving seasons occur shortly after the rainy season begins. Calving seasons can also differ for the same species from one park or reserve to another.

Camp: Camping sites; also refers to lodging in chalets, bungalows or tents in a remote location.

Canopy: The uppermost layer of a tree.

Caravan: A camping trailer.

Carnivore: An animal that lives by consuming the flesh of other animals.

Carrion: The remains of dead animals.

Crepuscular: Active at dusk or dawn.

Diurnal: Active during the day.

Endangered: An animal that is threatened with extinction.

Endemic: Native and restricted to a particular area.

Estrus: A state of sexual readiness in a female mammal when she is capable of conceiving.

Gestation: The duration of pregnancy.

Grazer: An animal that eats grass.

G.R.: An abbreviation for "Game Reserve".

Habitat: An animal's or plant's surroundings that offers everything it needs to live.

Habituated: An animal that has been introduced to and has accepted the presence of human beings.

Herbivore: An animal that consumes plant matter for food.

Hide: A camouflaged structure from which one can view wildlife without being seen.

Home range: An area familiar to (utilized by) an adult animal but not marked or defended as a territory.

Kopje (pronounced kopee): Rock formations that protrude from the savannah, usually caused by wind erosion (southern Africa).

Koppie: Same as kopje (East Africa).

Kraal: Same as boma (southern Africa).

Mammal: A warm-blooded animal that produces milk for its young.

Migratory: A species or population that moves seasonally to an area with predictably better food/grazing or water.

Midden: Usually, an accumulation of dung deposited in the same spot as a scent-marking behavior.

Mokoro: A traditional-style canoe made of synthetic materials, which is used for exploring the shallow waters of the Okavango Delta.

Nocturnal: Active during the night.

N.P.: An abbreviation for "National Park".

Omnivore: An animal that eats both plant and animal matter.

Pan: A shallow depression that seasonally fills with rainwater.

Predator: An animal that hunts and kills other animals for food.

Prey: An animal hunted by a predator for food.

Pride: A group or family of lions.

Rondavel: An African-style structure for accommodation.

Ruminant: A mammal with a complex stomach which therefore chews the cud.

Rutting: The behavioral pattern exhibited by the male of the species during a time period when mating is most prevalent, e.g., impala, wildebeest.

Sala: An additional private lounge area located off a tent's deck and features comfortable seating for relaxing.

Savannah: An open, grassy landscape with widely scattered trees.

Scavenger: An animal that lives off of carrion or the remains of animals killed by predators or which is dead from other causes.

Species: A group of plants or animals with specific characteristics in common, including the ability to reproduce among themselves.

Spoor: A track (i.e., footprint) or trail made by animals.

Symbiosis: An association of two different organisms in a relationship that may benefit one or both partners.

Tarmac: An asphalt-paved road.

Termitarium: A mound constructed by termite colonies.

Territory: An area occupied, scent-marked and defended from rivals of the same species.

Toilet, long-drop: A permanent bush toilet or "outhouse" in which a toilet seat has been placed over a hole that is dug about 6 feet (2m) deep.

Toilet, safari or short-drop: A temporary bush toilet, usually a toilet tent used on mobile tented safaris in which a toilet seat is placed over a hole that has been dug about 3 feet (1m) deep.

Tracking: Following and observing animal spoor by foot.

Tribe: A group of people united by traditional ties.

Troop: A group of apes or monkeys.

Ungulate: A hooved animal.

Veld: Southern African term for open land.

Wallow: The art of keeping cool and wet, usually in a muddy pool (i.e., rhinoceros, buffalo and hippopotamus).

LATIN/SCIENTIFIC NAMES OF MAMMALS AND REPTILES

Mammals

Aardvark (antbear)	*Orycteropus afer*
Aardwolf	*Proteles cristata*
Antelope, roan	*Hippotragus equinus*
Antelope, sable	*Hippotragus niger*
Baboon [olive]	*Papio cynocephalus anubis*
Baboon, [chacma]	*Papio cynocephalus ursinus*
Baboon, sacred	*Papio hamadryas*
Bat, epauletted fruit	*Epomophorus* (6 species)
Bat, yellow-winged	*Lavia frons*
Blesbok/Bontebuck	*Damaliscus dorcas*
Bongo	*Tragelaphus euryceros*
Buffalo, African	*Syncerus caffer*
Bushbaby, greater	*Galago crassicaudatus*
Bushbaby, lesser	*Galago senegalensis*
Bushbuck	*Tragelaphus scriptus*
Bushpig	*Potamochoerus larvatus*
Caracal	*Felis caracal*
Cat, African wild	*Felis sylvestris*
Cheetah	*Acinonyx jubatus*
Chimpanzee	*Pan troglodytes*
Civet, African	*Civettictis civetta*
Colobus, black-and-white	*Colobus guereza or guereza*
Colobus, Zanzibar red	*Procolobus kirkii*
Dikdik, Kirk's	*Madoqua kirki*
Dog, African wild	*Lycaon pictus*
Dolphin, bottle-nosed	*Tursiops truncatus*
Duiker, blue	*Cephalophus monticola*
Duiker, grey (bush)	*Sylvicapra grimmia*
Duiker, red/forest	*Cephalophus natalensis/harveyi*
Eland, (Patterson's)	*Taurotragus (Tragelaphus) oryx*
Elephant, African	*Loxodonta africana*
Fox, bat-eared	*Otocyon megalotis*
Fox, Cape	*Vulpes chama*
Gazelle, Grant's	*Gazella granti*
Gazelle, Thomson's	*Gazella rufifrons* (see oryx, southern)
Gemsbok	
Gelada	*Theropithecus gelada*
Genet, large-spotted and small-spotted	*Genetta tigrina/genetta*
Gerenuk	*Litocranius walleri*
Giraffe, Maasai	*Giraffa camelopardalis tippelskirchi*
Giraffe, reticulated	*Giraffa camelopardalis reticulata*
Giraffe, Rothschild's	*Giraffa camelopardalis rothschildi*
Giraffe, southern	*Giraffa camelopardalis camelopardalis*
Gorilla, lowland (Western)	*Gorilla gorilla gorilla*
Gorilla, Grauer's	*Gorilla beringei graueri*
Gorilla, mountain (Eastern)	*Gorilla beringei beringei*
Hare, African	*Lepus capensis*
Hare, scrub	*Lepus saxatilis*
Hare, spring	*Pedetes capensis*
Hartebeest, Lichtenstein's	*Sigmoceros lichensteini*
Hartebeest, red (Kongoni)	*Alcelaphus buselaphus*
Hedgehog	*Atelerix albiventris*
Hippopotamus	*Hippopotamus amphibius*
Hog, giant forest	*Hylochoerus meinertzhageni*
Hyena, brown	*Hyaena brunnea*
Hyena, spotted	*Crocuta crocuta*
Hyena, striped	*Hyaena hyaena*
Hyrax, bush	*Heterohyrax brucei*
Hyrax, rock	*Procavia capensis*
Hyrax, tree	*Dendrohyrax arboreus*
Impala	*Aepyceros melampus*
Jackal, black-backed	*Canis mesomelas*
Jackal, golden	*Canis aureus*
Jackal, side-striped	*Canis adustus*
Klipspringer	*Oreotragus oreotragus*
Kob	*Kobus kob*
Kongoni	*Alcelaphus buselaphus*
Kudu, greater	*Tragelaphus strepsiceros*
Kudu, lesser	*Tragelaphus imberbis*
Lechwe	*Kobus leche*

Leopard	*Panthera pardus*
Lion	*Panthera leo*
Mangabey, crested	*Cercocebus galeritus*
Mangabey, gray-cheeked	*Cercocebus albigenia*
Meercat (Suricate)	*Suricata suricata*
Mongoose, banded	*Mungos mungo*
Mongoose, dwarf	*Helogale parvula*
Mongoose, Egyptian	*Herpestes ichneumon*
Mongoose, slender	*Galerella sanguinea*
Mongoose, slender	*Herpestes san-guineus*
Mongoose, water (marsh)	*Atilax paludinosus*
Mongoose, white-tailed	*Ichneumia albicauda*
Mongoose, yellow	*Cynictis penicillata*
Monkey, blue	*Cercopithecus nictitans*
Monkey, de Brazza's	*Cercopithecus neglectus*
Monkey, L'Hoest's	*Cercopithecus l'hoesti*
Monkey, Patas	*Erythrocebus patas*
Monkey, vervet	*Cercopithecus aethiops*
Monkey, Syke's or Samango	*Cercopithecus mitis/albogularis*
Mouse, striped	*Rhabdomys pumilo*
Nyala	*Tragelaphus angasi*
Oribi	*Ourebia ourebi*
Oryx, fringe-eared	*Oryx beisa*
Oryx (Gemsbok)	*Oryx gazella*
Otter, Cape clawless	*Aonyx capensis*
Otter, spotted-necked	*Lutra maculicollis*
Pangolin, Temminck's ground	*Manis temmincki*
Porcupine (southern or northern African)	*Hystrix africaeaustralis/cristata*
Puku	*Kobus vardoni*
Ratel (Honey Badger)	*Mellivora capensis*
Reedbuck, bohor	*Redunca redunca*
Reedbuck, common	*Redunca arundinum*
Reedbuck, mountain	*Redunca fulvorufula*

Rhinoceros, black	*Diceros bicornis*
Rhinoceros, white	*Ceratotherium simum*
Seal, Cape fur	*Arctocephalus pusillus*
Serval	*Leptailurus serval*
Shrew, elephant (Sengi)	*Elephantulus* (10 species)
Sitatunga	*Tragelaphus spekei*
Springbok	*Antidorcas marsupialis*
Springhare	*Pedetes capensis*
Steenbok	*Raphicerus campestris*
Squirrel, ground	*Geosciurus inauris*
Topi	*Damaliscus korrigum*
Tsessebe	*Damaliscus lunatus*
Warthog	*Phacochoerus africanus*
Waterbuck, common	*Kobus ellipsiprymnus ellipsiprymnus*
Waterbuck, Defassa	*Kobus ellipsiprymnus defassa*
Weasel, striped	*Poecilogale albinucha*
Wildebeest, common (gnu)	*Connochaetes taurinus*
Wildebeest, black	*Connochaetes gnou*
Wolf, Ethiopian	*Canis simensis*
Zebra, Burchell's (plains)	*Equus burchelli*
Zebra, Grevy's	*Equus grevyi*
Zebra, Cape mountain	*Equus zebra zebra*
Zebra, Hartmann's mountain	*Equus zebra hartmannae*
Zorilla	*Ictonyx striatus*

Reptiles

Chameleon, flap-necked	*Chamaelo dilepis*
Crocodile, Nile	*Crocodylus niloticus*
Monitor, Nile	*Varanus niloticus*
Python, African Rock	*Python sebae*

Suggested Reading

GENERAL/WILDLIFE/AFRICA

Africa, John Reader, 2001 (USA: National Geographic)
Africa, Michael Poliza, 2006 (USA: teNeues Publishing Company)
Africa, A Continent Revealed, Rene Gordon, 1997 (U.K.: New Holland)
Africa, A Biography of the Continent, John Reader, 1998 (USA: Penguin)
Africa, An Artists Journal, Kim Donaldson, 2001 (U.K.: Pavilion; USA: Watson Guptil)
Africa in History, Basil Davidson, 2001 (U.K.: Phoenix Press)
Africa, Timeless Soul, Wilby, 1996 (U.K.: Pan MacMillian)
Africa, Biography of the Continent, John Reader, 1998 (U.K.: Penguin)
African Ceremonies, Carol Beckwith and Angela Fisher, 1999 (USA: Harry N. Abrams)
African Elephants, Daryl and Sharna Balfour, 1997 (South Africa: Struik)
African Folklore, Best of, A. Savoury, 1972 (South Africa: Struik)
African Game Trails, T. Roosevelt, 1983 (USA: St. Martins Press)
African Insect Life, A. Skaiffe, John Ledger and Anthony Barnister, revised 1997 (South Africa: Struik)
African Laughter, Doris Lessing, 1992 (U.K.: Flamingo)
African Magic, Heidi Holland, 2001 (U.K.: Viking/Allen Lane)
African Nights, K. Gallmann, 1995 (U.K.: Penguin Books)
African Predators, Gus Mills, 2001 (South Africa: Struik)
African Trilogy, P. Matthiessen, 2000 (U.K.: Harvill Press)
Africa's Big Five, William Taylor and Gerald Hinde, 2001 (South Africa: Struik)
Africa's Elephant, A Biography, Martin Meredith, 2001 (U.K.: Hodder & Stoughton)
Africa's Top Wildlife Countries, Mark Nolting, 2008 (USA: Global Travel)
Behaviour Guide to African Animals, Richard Estes, 1995 (South Africa: Russel Friedman Books; USA: University California Press)
Birds of Kenya & Tanzania, Zimmerman, Turner and Pearson, 1996 (U.K.: A & C Black)
Birds of the Indian Ocean Islands, I. Sinclair and O. Langrand, 1998 (South Africa: Struik)

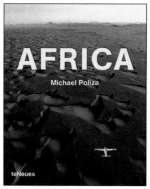

By Michael Poliza
ISBN: 978-3-8327-9127-8

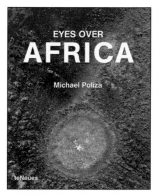

By Michael Poliza
ISBN: 978-3-8327-9209-1

Creatures of Habit, Peter Apps and Richard du Toit, 2000 (South Africa: Struik)
Elephant Memories, Cynthia Moss, 1999 (USA: Chicago University Press)
Elephants for Africa, Randall Moore, 2000 (South Africa: Abu Publications)
Eyes Over Africa, Michael Poliza, 2007 (USA: teNeues Publishing Company)
Field Guide to the Larger Mammals of Southern Africa, Chris and Tilde Stuart, 1996
   (South Africa: Struik)
Field Guide to the Mammals of Southern Africa, Chris and Tilde Stuart, 1996 (South
   Africa: Struik)
Field Guide to the Reptiles of East Africa, S. Spawls, K. Howell, R. Drews and J. Ashe,
   2002 (U.K.: Academic Press)
Gorilla: Struggle for Survival in the Virungas, Michael Nichols, 1989 (USA: Aperture
   Press)
The Guide's Guide to Guiding, Garth Thompson, 2001 (South Africa: Russel Friedman
   Books)
I Dreamed of Africa, K. Gallman, 1991 (USA: Penguin Books)
Island Africa: The Evolution of Africa's Rare Animals and Plants, Jonathan Kingdon, 1990
   (U.K.: William Collins)
The Kingdon Field Guide to African Mammals, Jonathan Kingdon, 1997 (U.K.:
   Academic Press)
Last Edens of Africa, Francois Odendaal, 1999 (South Africa: Southern Books)
Malaria, A Layman's Guide, Martine Maurel, 2001 (South Africa: Struik)
Mountain Gorillas–Biology, Conservation, and Coexistence, Gene Eckhart and Annette
   Lanjouw, 2008 (USA: University Press)
Night of the Lions, K. Gallman, 2000 (U.K.: Penguin Books)
North of South, Shiva Naipaul, 1994 (U.K.: Penguin)
Once We Were Hunters: A Journey with Africa's Indigenous People, P. Weinberg, 2001
   (South Africa: David Philip)
Origins Reconsidered, R. E. Leakey and R. Lewin, 1992 (USA· Doubleday) (O/P)
Pyramids of Life, John Reader and Harvey Croze, 2000 (U.K.: Collins)
Roberts Birds of Southern Africa, Gordon Maclean, 1993 (South Africa: Voelcker Trust)
Running Wild, John McNutt and Lesley Boggs, 1996 (South Africa: Southern Books
   Publishers)
Safari Companion, A Guide to Watching African Mammals, Richard D. Estes, 2001
   (South Africa: Russel Friedman Books; USA: Chelsea Green Publishing)
Scramble for Africa, 1876–1912, T. Pakenham, 1992 (USA: Avon Books; U.K.: Phoenix
   Press)
Smithers Mammals of Southern Africa, Peter Apps, 1996 (South Africa: Southern Books)
Southern, Central, and East African Mammals, A Photographic Guide Chris and Tilde
   Stuart, 2000 (South Africa: Struik)
The African Adventurers, Peter Capstick, 1992 (USA: St. Martins Press)
The Behavior Guide to African Mammals, Richard Despard Estes, 1991 (South Africa:
   Russel Friedman Books; USA: University of California Press)
The Blue Nile, Alan Moorehead, 1983 (U.K.: Penguin)
The End of the Game, Peter Beard, 1996 (USA: Chronicle Books; U.K.: Thames & Hudson)
The Great Migration, Harvey Croze, 1999 (U.K.: Harvill Press)
The Kingdon Field Guide to African Mammals, Jonathan Kingdon, 1997 (U.K.: Harcourt
   Brace)
The Tree Where Man Was Born, Peter Matthiessen, 1997 (USA: Dutton)
The White Nile, Alan Moorehead, 1973 (U.K.: Penguin)
Through a Window, J. Goodall, 2000 (U.K.: Phoenix Press)
Time With Leopards, Dale Hancock, 2000 (South Africa: Black Eagle Publications)
Vanishing Africa, Kate Klippensteen, 2002 (USA: Abbeville Press)
Whatever You Do, Don't Run, Chris Roche, 2006 (South Africa: Tafelberg Publishers)
When Elephants Weep, Emotional Lives of Animals, Jeffrey Masson, 1996 (U.K.: Vintage)

Wild Africa, Patrick Morris, et al., 2001 (U.K.: BBC Books)
Wildest Africa, Paul Tingay, 1999 (U.K.: New Holland)

SOUTHERN AFRICA
Complete Book of South African Birds, Peter Ginn, revised 1996 (South Africa: Struik)
Complete Book of South African Mammals, Gus Mills and Lex Hes, 1997 (South Africa: Struik)
Discovering Southern Africa, Thomas V. Bulpin, 2000 (South Africa: Tafelberg Publishers)
Field Guide to Mammals of Southern Africa, Chris and Tilde Stuart, 1991 (South Africa: Struik)
Field Guide to Snakes and Reptiles of Southern Africa, Bill Branch, 1992 (South Africa: Struik)
Guide to Nests & Eggs of Southern African Birds, Warwick Tarboton, 2001 (South Africa: Struik)
I'd Rather Be On Safari, Gary Clark, 2001 (USA: Baranski)
Illustrated Guide to Game Parks and Nature Reserves of Southern Africa, 1999 (South Africa: Readers Digest)
In the Footsteps of Eve, Lee Berger, 2001 (USA: National Geographic)
Living Deserts of Southern Africa, Barry Lovegrove, 1993 (South Africa: Fernwood Press)
Long Walk to Freedom, Nelson Mandela, 1995 (U.K.: Abacus, Little Brown)
Lost World of the Kalahari, Laurens van der Post, 2001 (U.K.: Vintage)
Majestic Southern Africa, Land of Beauty and Splendour, Thomas V. Bulpin 1999 (South Africa: Readers Digest)
National Parks & Other Wild Places of Southern Africa, Nigel Dennis, 2000 (South Africa: Struik)
Newman's Birds of Southern Africa, Kenneth Newman, 2002 (South Africa: Struik)
Peoples of the South, Derek De La Harpe, 2001 (South Africa: Sunbird)
Raconteur Road, Shots into Africa, Obie Oberholzer, 2000 (South Africa: David Phillip Publishers)
Sasol Birds of Southern Africa, Ian Sinclair, 2002 (South Africa: Struik)
Smithers Mammals of Southern Africa: A Field Guide, R. H. N. Smithers, 1999 (South Africa: Struik)
Southern Africa Revealed, Elaine Hurford, 2000 (South Africa: Struik)
Southern African Trees: A Photographic Guide, Piet van Wyk, 1993 (South Africa: Struik)
Tracing the Rainbow, Art & Life in Southern Africa, S. Eisenhofer, 2001 (Germany: Arnoldsche)
Trees of Southern Africa, Keith Coates Palgrave, 1977 (South Africa: Struik)
Walk with a White Bushman, Laurens van der Post, 2002 (U.K.: Vintage)
Wildlife of Southern Africa: A Field Guide, V. Carruthers, 1997 (South Africa: Southern Books)
Zambezi River of the Gods, Jan and Fiona Teede, 1990 (South Africa: Russel Friedman Books)

BOTSWANA
Chobe, Africa's Untamed Wilderness, Daryl and Sharna Balfour, 1999 (South Africa: Struik)
Common Birds of Botswana, Kenneth Newman, 1998 (South Africa: Southern)
Cry of the Kalahari, Mark and Delia Owens, 1984 (USA: Houghton Mifflin)
Hunting with Moon, The Lions of Savuti, Derek and Beverley Joubert, 1998 (USA: National Geographic)
Miracle Rivers, The Chobe & Okavango Rivers of Botswana, Peter and Beverly Pickford, 1999 (South Africa: Struik)
Okavango: Sea of Land, A. Bannister, 1996 (South Africa: Struik)
Okavango: Africa's Wetland Wilderness, A. Bailey, 2000 (South Africa: Struik)
Okavango, African's Last Eden, Frans Lanting, 1993 (USA: Chronicle U.S.)

Suggested Reading

Okavango: Jewel of the Kalahari, Karen Ross, 2003 (USA: Macmillan)
Panoramic Journey through Botswana, Alfred le Maitre, 2000 (South Africa: Struik)
Plants of the Okavango Delta, Karen and William Ellcry, 1997 (South Africa: Tsaro)
Prides: The Lions of Moremi, C. Harvey and P. Kat, 2000 (South Africa: Struik)
Running Wild, John McNutt and Lesley Boggs, 1996 (South Africa: Southern Book
  Publishers)
Shell Field Guide to the Common Trees of the Okavango Delta, Veronica Roodt, 1993
  (Botswana: Shell)
Shell Field Guide to the Wildflowers of the Okavango Delta, Veronica Roodt, 1993
  (Botswana: Shell)
The Africa Diaries, Derek and Beverley Joubert, 2000 (USA: National Geographic)
The Bushmen, P. Johnson, A. Bannister and A. Wallenburgh, 1999 (South Africa: Struik)
The Heart of the Hunter, Laurens van der Post, 2002 (U.K.: Vintage)
The Kalahari: Survival in a Thirstland Wilderness, Joyce Knight, 1999 (South Africa:
  Struik)
The Lions and Elephants of the Chobe, Bruce Aitken, 1986 (South Africa: Stramill)
This is Botswana, Peter Joyce, 2000 (South Africa: Struik)
Wildlife of the Okavango: Common Animals and Plants, D. Butchart, 2000 (South Africa:
  Struik)

ZAMBIA and ZIMBABWE
African Laughter, Doris Lessing, 1992 (U.K.: Harper Collins)
Bitter Harvest, Ian Smith, 2001 (U.K.: Collins)
Don't Let's Go the Dogs Tonight, An African Childhood, Alexander Fuller, 2001 (USA:
  Random House)
Eye of the Elephant, Mark and Delia Owens, 1992 (USA: Houghton Mifflin)
Hwange, Retreat of the Elephants, Nick Greaves, 1996 (South Africa: Struik)
Kakuli, Norman Carr, 1995 (U.K.: Corporate Brochure Company) (O/P)
Luangwa, Zambia's Treasure, Mike Coppinger, 2000 (South Africa: Inyathi Publishers)
Mukiwa, Peter Godwin, 1996 (U.K.: Picador)
The Leopard Hunts in Darkness (and other series), Wilbur Smith, 1992 (U.K.: Macmillan)
The Spirit of the Zambezi, Jeff and Veronica Stutchbury, 1991 (U.K.: Corporate Brochure
  Company)
This is Zimbabwe, Gerald Cubitt and Peter Joyce, 1992 (South Africa: Struik)
Zambezi — A Journey of a River, Michael Main, 1990 (South Africa: Southern Book
  Publishers) (O/P)
Zambezi — The River of the Gods, Jan and Fiona Teede, 1991 (U.K.: Andre Deutsch)
Zambezi, L. Watermeyer, J. Dabbs and Y. Christian, 1988 (Zimbabwe: Albida Samara Pvt. Ltd.)
Zambia Landscapes, David Rodgers, 2001 (South Africa: Struik)
Zambia Tapestries, David Rodgers, 2001 (South Africa: Struik)

MALAWI
Malawi, Lake of Stars, Vera Garland, 1998 (Malawi: Central Africana)

NAMIBIA
Desert Adventure, Paul Augustinus, 1997 (South Africa: Acorn Books)
Desertscapes of Namibia, Jean Du Plessis, 2002 (South Africa: Struik)
Etosha, A Visual Souvenir, Daryl and Sharna Balfour, 1998 (South Africa: Struik)
Heat, Dust and Dreams, Exploration People & Environment Kaokoland & Damaraland,
  Mary Rice, 2001 (South Africa: Struik)
Himba — Nomads of Namibia, Margaret Jacobson, 1991 (South Africa: Struik)
Namibia African Adventurers Guide, W. and S. Olivier, 1999 (South Africa: New Holland)

Namibia, Africa's Harsh Paradise, A. Bannister and P. Johnson, 1978 (South Africa: Struik)
Panoramic Journey through Namibia, Alfred le Maitre, 2000 (South Africa: Struik)
Sands of Silence, On Safari in Namibia, P. Capstick, 1991 (USA & U.K.: St. Martins Press)
Scenic Namibia, Thomas Dreschler, 2000 (South Africa: Tafelberg)
Sheltering Desert, Henno Martin, 1996 (South Africa: Ad Donker)
Skeleton Coast, a Journey through the Namib Desert, Benedict Allen, 1997 (U.K.: BBC)
Skeleton Coast, Amy Schoeman, 1999 (South Africa: Southern Book Publishers)
This is Namibia, Gerald Cubitt and Peter Joyce, 2000 (U.K. & South Africa: New Holland)

SOUTH AFRICA

Cape Floral Kingdom, Colin Paterson-Jones, 2000 (South Africa: Struik)
History of South Africa, Frank Welsh, Revised and Updated 2000 (U.K.: HarperCollins)
Kruger National Park, Wonders of an African Eden, Nigel Dennis, 1997 (USA: BHB International; South Africa and U.K.: New Holland)
Long Walk to Freedom, Nelson Mandela, 1995 (U.K.: Abacus, Little Brown)
Magnificent Natural Heritage of South Africa, Johann Knobel, 1999 (South Africa: Sunbird)
Magnificent South Africa, Elaine Hurford and Peter Joyce, 1996 (South Africa: Struik)
My Traitor's Heart, Rian Malan, 2000 (USA: Moon Publications)
Presenting South Africa, Peter Joyce, 1999 (South Africa: Struik)
Rock Paintings of South Africa, Stephen Townley Bassett, 2002 (South Africa: David Philip)
Somewhere over the Rainbow, Travels in South Africa, Gavin Bell, 2001 (U.K.: Abacus, Little Brown)
The Covenant, James A. Michener, 1980 (USA: Random House)
The Heart of the Hunter (series), Laurens van der Post, 1987 (U.K.: Vintage)
The Washing of the Spears: The Rise and Fall of the Zulu Nation, Donald R. Morris, 1995 (U.K.: Pimlico)
This is South Africa, Peter Borchert, 2000 (South Africa: Struik)
Twentieth Century South Africa, William Beinart, 2002 (U.K.: Oxford University Press)
When the Lion Feeds (series), Wilbur Smith, 1986 (U.K.: Macmillan)
Wild South Africa, Lex Hes and Alan Mountain, 1998 (U.K.: New Holland)
Wildlife of the Cape Peninsula: Common Animals and Plants, D. Butchart, 2001 (South Africa: Struik)
Wildlife of the Lowveld: Common Animals and Plants, D. Butchart, 2001 (South Africa: Struik)
World That Made Mandela, L. Callinicos, 2001 (South Africa: STE Publishers)

EAST AFRICA

A Guide to the Seashores of Eastern Africa, M.D. Richmond (Ed.), 1997, (Sweden: Sida; Zanzibar: Sea Trust)
A Primates Memoir, Love, Death and Baboons in East Africa, Robert Sapolsky, 2001 (U.K.: Jonathan Cape)
Africa's Great Rift Valley, Nigel Pavitt, 2001 (USA: Harry N. Abrams)
African Trilogy, Peter Matthiessen, 1999 (U.K.: Harvill Press)
Among the Man-eaters, Stalking the Mysterious Lions of Tsavo, Philip Caputo, 2002 (USA: National Geographic)
Birds of Kenya & Tanzania, D. Zimmerman, D. Turner and D. Pearson, 1996 (U.K.: A & C Black; South Africa: Russel Friedman Books)
Field Guide to the Birds of East Africa, Terry Stevenson and John Fanshawe, 2002 (U.K.: Academic Press)

Field Guide to the Reptiles of East Africa, Stephen Spawls, 2002 (U.K.: Academic Press)
Guide to Mt. Kenya and Kilimanjaro, edited by Iain Allen, 1981 (Kenya: Mountain Club)
Helm Field Guide to Birds of Kenya and Tanzania, Dale Zimmerman and Donald A.
   Turner, 1999 (U.K.: Croom Helm)
Illustrated Checklist, Birds of East Africa, B. von Perlo, 1995 (U.K.: Collins)
In the Shadow of Kilimanjaro, Rick Ridgeway, 2000 (U.K.: Bloomsbury)
Pink Africa, Nigel Collar, 2000 (U.K.: Harvill Press)
Portraits in the Wild: Animal Behavior in East Africa, Second Edition, Cynthia Moss, 1982
   (USA: University of Chicago Press) (O/P)
Safari Guide to Common Birds of East Africa, D. Hosking, 1996 (U.K.: Collins)
Safari Guide to Larger Mammals of East Africa, D. Hosking, 1996 (U.K.: Collins).
White Hunters, Golden Age of African Safaris, Brian Herne, 1999 (USA: Henry Holt)

KENYA

Big Cat Diary, Brian Jackson and Jonathan Scott, 1996 (U.K.: BBC)
Birds of Kenya & Tanzania, D. Zimmerman, D. Turner and D. Pearson, 1996 (U.K.: A & C
   Black; South Africa: Russel Friedman Books)
Born Free Trilogy, Joy Adamson, 2000 (U.K.: Macmillan)
Elephant Memories, Portraits in the Wild, Cynthia Moss, 1999 (USA: Chicago University
   Press)
F/G Birds of Kenya & Northern Tanzania, Dale A. Zimmerman, Donald A. Turner and
   David J. Pearson, 1999 (U.K.: A & C Black; South Africa: Russel Friedman Books)
Flame Trees of Thika: Memories of an African Childhood, Elspeth Huxley, 1998 (U.K.:
   Pimlico)
I Dreamed of Africa, Kuki Gallman, 1991 (U.K.: Penguin)
Illustrated Checklist Birds of East Africa, B. von Perlo, 1995 (U.K.: Collins)
Journey Through Kenya, M. Amin, D. Willetts and B. Tetley, 1982 (U.K.: Camerapix)
Kenya Pioneers, Errol Trzebinski, 1991 (U.K.: Mandarin)
Kenya the Beautiful, Brett Michael, 1997 (USA: BHB International; South Africa: Struik)
Kingdom of Lions, Jonathan Scott, 1992 (U.K.: Kyle Cathie; South Africa: Russel Friedman
   Books)
Out in the Midday Sun, Elspeth Huxley, 2000 (U.K.: Pimlico)
Out of Africa, Isak Dinesen, 1989 (U.K.: Penguin Books)
Samburu, Nigel Pavitt, 2002 (U.K.: Kyle Kathie)
The Great Safari — The Lives of George and Joy Adamson, William Morrow, 1993 (USA:
   Adrian House) (O/P)
The Ukimwe Road: From Kenya to Zimbabwe, Dervla Murphy, 1995 (U.K.: Flamingo)
Wildlife Wars, Battle to Save Africa's Elephants, Richard Leakey, 2001 (U.K.: Macmillan)
Vanishing Africa, The Samburu of Kenya, Kate Klippensteen, 2002 (USA: Abbeville Press)

TANZANIA

Cheetahs of the Serengeti Plains, T.M. Caro, 1994 (USA: University Chicago Press)
Golden Shadows, Flying Hooves, George B. Schaller, 1989 (USA: University of Chicago
   Press)
In the Dust of Kilimanjaro, David Western, 2000 (USA: Island Press)
Journal of Discovery of the Source of the Nile, John Hanning Speke, 1996 (USA: Dover
   Publications)
Kilimanjaro, A Journey to the roof of Africa, Audrey Salkeld, 2002 (USA: National
   Geographic)
Kilimanjaro: The White Roof of Africa, Harald Lange, 1985 (USA: Mountaineers Books)
   Large photo book (O/P)
Mara Serengeti, A Photographer's Paradise, Jonathan Scott, 2000 (U.K.: Newpro U.K. Ltd)

Ngorongoro Great Game Park, Chris Stuart, 1995 (South Africa: Struik)
Serengeti Lions, Predator Prey Relationships, G. B. Schaller, 1976 (USA: University of Chicago Press)
Serengeti: Natural Order on the African Plain, Mitsuaki Iwago, 1996 (USA: Chronicle Books)
Serengeti Shall Not Die, Bernard and Michael Grzimek, 1960 (U.K.: Hamish Hamilton)
Snows of Kilimanjaro, Ernest Hemingway, 1994 (U.K.: Arrow)
Tanzania, Portrait of a Nation, Paul Joynson-Hicks, 1998 (U.K.: Quiller Press)
The Chimpanzees of Gombe, Patterns of Behavior, Jane Goodall, 1986 (USA: Harvard University Press) Chimpanzee research.
Thorns to Kilimanjaro, Ian McCallum, 2000 (South Africa: David Philip Publishers)

RWANDA
Across the Red River, Rwanda, Burundi and the Heart of Darkness, Christian Jennings, 1999 (U.K.: Indigo Paperbacks)
Gorillas in the Mist, Dian Fossey, 2001 (U.K.: Phoenix Press)
In the Kingdom of Gorillas, Bill Weber and Amy Veder, 2002 (U.K.: Aurum Press)
Lake Regions of Central Africa, Richard Burton, 2001 (USA: Narrative Press)
Mountain Gorillas–Biology, Conservation, and Coexistence, Gene Eckhart and Annette Lanjouw, 2008 (USA: University Press)

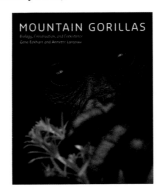

UGANDA
Bonobo, The Forgotten Ape, Frans De Waal, 1997 (USA: University of California Press)
Ecology of an African Rain Forest, Thomas Struhsaker, 1998 (USA: University of Florida Press)
Forest of Memories, Tales from the Heart of Africa, Donald McIntosh, 2001 (U.K.: Little Brown)
Guide to the Ruwenzori, H. A. Osmaston and D. Pasteur, 1972 (U.K.: West Col Productions)
Mountain Gorillas–Biology, Conservation, and Coexistence, Gene Eckhart and Annette Lanjouw, 2008 (USA: University Press)
Rwenzori Mountain National Park, Uganda, H. A. Osmaston and Joy Tukahirwa, 1999 (Uganda: Makerere University Press)
Uganda, Ian Leggett, 2001 (U.K.. Oxfam)
Uganda/Rwenzori, David Pluth, 1997 (Switzerland: Little Wolf)
Uganda: Pearl of Africa, Paul Joynson-Hicks, 1994 (U.K.: Quiller Press)

CONGO

Congo Journey, Redmond O'Henlon, 1996 (U.K.: Hamish Hamilton)
The Forest People, Colin Turnbull, 1994 (U.K.: Pocket Books) On pygmies of the Ituri
Forest.
The Mountain People, Colin Turnbull, 1987 (U.K.: Pocket Books)
The Road from Leopold to Kabila, A Peoples History. George Nzongola-Ntalaja, 2002
(U.K.: Zed Books)
Facing the Congo, Jeffrey Taylor, 2001 (U.K.: Little Brown)
Travels in the White Mans Grave, Memoirs from West & Central Africa. Donald McIntosh,
2001 (U.K.: Abacus)
In the Footsteps of Mr. Kurtz, Living on the Brink of Disaster in the Congo, Michaela
Wrong, 2001 (U.K.: Fourth Estate)
King Leopold's Ghost, Story of Greed & Heroism in Colonial Africa, Adam Hochschild,
2000 (U.K.: Macmillan)

CUSTOMS

Culture and Customs of Botswana, by James Denbow and Pherry C. Thebe 2006 (USA
Greenwood Press)
Culture and Customs of Zimbabwe, by Oyekan Owomoyela 2002 (USA Greenwood Press)

CUISINE

A Taste of Africa: Traditional & Modern African Cooking, by Dorinda Hufner, 2002 (USA:
Ten Speed Press, Berkeley)
The Soul of a New Cuisine: A Discovery of the Foods and Flavors of Africa, by Marcus
Samuellson, 2006 (USA: Willow Creek)
South African Cape Malay Cooking, by Sonia Allison, 1997 (England: Absolute Press)
Modern South African Cuisine, by Garth Stroebel, 2005 (South Africa: Struik (C.) Pty.Ltd)
The South African Illustrated Cookbook, by Lehla Eldridge, 2002 (South Africa: Struik)
*Flavors of Africa Cookbook: Spicy African Cooking-From Indigenous Recipes to Those
Influenced by Asian and European Settlers,* by Dave Dewitt, 1998 (USA: Prima
Lifestyles)
The African Kitchen: A day in the life of a Safari Chef, by Josie Stow, 2004 (USA: Interlink
Pub Group Inc)
Zainabu's African Cookbook: With Food and Stories, by Zainabu Kpaka Kallon, 2003
(USA: Citadel Press)

ARTS AND CRAFTS

Art and Craft in Africa: Everyday Life Ritual Court Art, by Laure Meyer, 2005 (France:
Terrail Pierre)
Art and Craft of Southern Africa: Treasures in Transition, by Rhoda Levinsohn, 1984
(USA: Delta Books)
Hands-On Africa: Art Activities for All Ages Featuring Sub-Saharan Africa, by Yvonne
Merrill, 2006 (USA: Kits Publishing)
African Beads: A Book and Craft Kit by Metropolitan Museum of Art, 1999 (USA: Simon
& Schuster)
Colors of Africa, by Duncan Clarke, 2000–09 (London: Thunder Bay Press) (CA)
Craft Art in South Africa, by Elbe Coetsee, 2003 (Struik Publishers)
Women and Art in South Africa, by Marion Arnold and Brenda Schmahmann, 1996 (U.K.:
Macmillan)
The Scramble for Art in Central Africa, by Enid Schildkrout and Curtis Keim, 1998 (USA:
Cambridge University Press)

DVDs

Duma (2006) Warner Bros Ent; Director: Carroll Ballard
Explore the Wildlife Kingdom Series: Wildebeest-the Great African Migration (2006) Reel Productions
Explore the Wildlife Kingdom Series: Lions — Kings of Africa (2005)
Geldof in Africa by Bob Geldof (2006) Weasel Disc Records
I Dreamed of Africa (2000) Director: Hugh Hudson
Out of Africa (1985) Director: Sydney Pollack
Kilimanjaro — To the Roof of Africa (2002) Director: David Breashears
As Close As You Dare — Africa; Documentary (2007) Crowe World Media

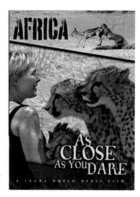

Immerse yourself in the dangers, beauty, and humor of the African wilderness! As Close As You Dare — Africa was shot on location in Zimbabwe, Botswana, and Namibia. It follows the extraordinary adventures of American artist, Becci Crowe, as she returns to the African bush. Accompanied by professional Wildlife Guide, Ivan Carter, and her husband, Mark Crowe, this film immerses you in startlingly close encounters with wildlife and a rare opportunity to interact with a disappearing culture, the San Bushmen. Inspired by the sheer beauty and dynamic interface of raw nature, Becci's art takes shape and materializes during the film. Get close — As Close As You Dare!

Strongly recommended for anyone interested in walking safaris and African cultures.

List price $19.95. Available from the Africa Adventure Company for $9.95, www.AfricanAdventure.com; 800-882-9453, 954-491-8877.

Acknowledgments

The completion and accuracy of this guide would not have been possible without the assistance of many people. Many thanks to all who have contributed to this project, including the following:

To all the guides in the field that have shared their in depth knowledge of wildlife in Africa, and to our clients who have provided us with comprehensive trip reports on their African adventures.

Special thanks to Dawn Scheepmaker, Colin Bell, Dave van Smeerdijck, Kim Nixon, Keith Vincent, Chris Badger, Tessa Redman, Dave and Linda Bennett, Phil Ward, Yasmin Ravenscroft, Mike Myers, Tim Farrell, Russel Friedman, Yvonne Christian, David Evans, Duncan Butchart, Matthew Copham, John Coppinger, Nick Murray, Desiree Murray, Craig Sholley, Gene Eckhart, Steve Turner, Joseph Birori, Tony Hickey, Neil and Brenda Digby-Clark (Namibia chapter), Peter Jackson, Rita Bachmann, Andy Biggs, Abby Lazar, Becci and Mark Crowe, Shakir, Taqi and Abbas Moledina for their assistance; to Sarah Taylor for her many hours of work on this update; to my staff at The Africa Adventure Company including Bill Rivard, Irene Groden, Kathryn Berry, Karen Liza, Cinthia Liza, Andre Steynberg, Milissa Rubino, JoAnna Price, Elena Theodosieu, Louise Steynberg, Kyle Witton, Antony Gray, Janet Kenny, Judy Vince, Lynne Glasgow, Saskia de Gouveia and Szilvia Hegyi; and especially to my wife, Alison, for her assistance on the entire project.

About Mark Nolting,
Author and Africa Expert

Mark Nolting wanted adventure. He found it as an Olympic sportscaster, international businessman, oil engineer and Hollywood actor. But it wasn't until he traveled through Africa that he found the excitement he was looking for.

Mark Nolting heads up The Africa Adventure Company, Ft. Lauderdale, Florida. He is the author of two award-winning books, *Africa's Top Wildlife Countries* and the *African Safari Journal*.

Known as the "Travel Expert of Africa" in the industry, Nolting and his experienced staff arrange safaris for travelers who want to experience the beauty and drama of Africa in exciting ways.

It all began in 1975. Nolting graduated from Florida State University the previous year with a degree in business administration and minors in chemistry, physics, math and biology. For a year and a half, he worked for a south Florida marketing firm, but the call of the wild beckoned.

"One morning," said Nolting, "I just woke up and realized I wanted to travel around the world. And I decided, if I don't go, I'll always regret it, and if I don't go now, I never will."

Two weeks later, he departed for Luxembourg. During the 1976 Winter Olympics in Innsbruck, Austria, he worked for ABC Sports. Next he found a job in middle management with the world's third-largest mail order catalog house, located in Germany.

But Nolting wasn't trying to become a European businessman. He was out to see the world. Although his itinerary called for him to head for India, Nepal and the Far East, he took a six-month detour through Africa and traveled across the Sahara Desert and on through central and east Africa. He toured several parks and reserves and fell in love with the "safari experience."

Then he found his way to the Mideast and was fast-tracked through a program for oil-drilling engineers. He eventually came back to the United States — Los Angeles. It occurred to Nolting that he'd never tried acting, so he decided to give it a shot and wound up working for four years.

Yet the yearning for more in-depth travel through Africa was still with him. He couldn't shake the memory of the wildlife and the spectacular terrain he had seen there. And so, once again, he was off, heading for Africa with a purpose in mind.

He returned to Africa and traveled for two years through 16 countries, from Cairo to Cape Town, gathering material for his books and establishing contacts with safari companies and tour guides. On his return to the United States in 1985, he wrote his books and established The Africa Adventure Company.

In July 1992 he married Alison Wright, whom he had met a few years previously at a safari camp she was running in Zimbabwe. In July 1993, they had their first child, Miles William Nolting, and in 1996, their second child, Nicholas Hamilton Nolting.

His many visits have included touring the antiquities of Egypt and scuba diving off the Sinai Peninsula; crossing Lake Nasser and the deserts of Sudan; experiencing the multitude of lodge safaris and authentic African mobile tented safaris in the wildlife reserves of Kenya and Tanzania; climbing Mt. Kenya, Mt. Kilimanjaro in Tanzania and the Ruwenzoris in the Democratic Republic of the Congo; visiting the beautiful Kenyan coast; gorilla trekking and mountain climbing in Rwanda; hunting with Pygmies, gorilla trekking and game viewing in the Democratic Republic of the Congo; and taking the ferry from Bujumbura (Burundi) to Kigoma (Tanzania) and visiting the tribes in the Omo River Valley and the rock-hewn churches and other antiquities in Ethiopia.

In southern Africa his adventures have included walking safaris from bush camp to bush camp and day and night game drives in Zambia; 1- and 7-day, white-water, rafting safaris (Class 5) on the Zambezi River; viewing Victoria Falls at different times of the year; kayak safaris upstream of Victoria Falls; several canoeing safaris on the lower Zambezi River; walking with top professional guides and game viewing by boat and open vehicle on day and night game drives in Zimbabwe; flying safaris to the major reserves of Botswana; mokoro safaris in the Okavango Delta; a fly-in safari to the Skeleton Coast and visiting Etosha Pan and other parks in Namibia; driving the Garden Route, sightseeing in Cape Town and visiting the private reserves and parks in South Africa; pony trekking in Lesotho; traveling through Swaziland; holidaying in the beautiful island countries of Mauritius and the Seychelles; and visiting some of the most primitive tribes in the world in Ethiopia, along with castles and fourteenth century rock-hewn churches in the north.

Mark continues to travel to Africa yearly to update information and explore new areas, and especially enjoys taking his family with him on safari. Hard-to-find information on Africa is always at his fingertips, and he loves to take the time to talk to people about the many adventures that can be found on the continent.

— The Publishers

Bush Tails

"We have been back from our safari for about 10 days now and I've been busy sorting through the 1,000 pictures that we took but I wanted to relay to you and your co-workers that we had the most amazing time of our life! Our safari was incredible, it exceeded our expectations on every level.

The staff at the camps were outstanding, we were met at each and every arrival point promptly, professionally and courteously. We were so well taken care of and had such a tremendous time. We loved our guide "Duxe" at **Vumbura** and "Ester" at **Victoria Falls**, she is amazing. Your guidelines were perfect, we felt very prepared for Safari. Everything went so smoothly, I cannot wait to go back again and the girls loved it as well. We will share your services with all of our friends to be sure and cannot say enough thank you's to everyone there for the trip of a lifetime!

P.S. The animals were amazing too, plenty of them, up close and personal, we were not disappointed! Regards,"

—*JULIA AND SCOTT HUDSON, TEXAS*

"Dear Andre and Staff of the Africa Adventure Company,

My whole trip can be summed up by one word — AMAZING!! It has been over three months, yet I don't think a single day has gone by that I have not thought about it. I feel so fortunate to have experienced Africa for the first time the way I did. The days were so perfectly planned to highlight the many aspects of **Tanzania** — the beautiful landscapes, the varied people, and of course the fascinating wildlife. I have so many memories, emotions, and the photos to go along! I have been on many trips before and have taken a lot of photographs but nothing like the magnitude of the photos I took on this trip. The joke has become that there must not have been an elephant that I did not take a picture of. I think I could have a whole album just of elephants. Who knew they were so photogenic!

A huge thank you to you, Andre, for working with me in selecting the best itinerary and being so patient and understanding with my many, many questions and concerns. The trip ran without a hitch from the time I left Newark, N.J. through my return. Every detail was considered which made for anxiety-free travel. I thoroughly enjoyed the variety of places we stayed, each having its own special African quality. The reserve and every park were beautiful and unique unto themselves. And I can't say enough great things about our guides Firoz Rafiq Nathoo and Omar Hussein Seif. They were so professional, knowledgeable as well as insightful to the needs and interests of the group. And that's not to mention fun. They were the best! The trip was more than I ever expected — just truly AMAZING.

Thank you so much. I have truly been touched and hope this was just my very first trip to Africa. Most Sincerely,"

— *JoAnn Patton, New Jersey*

"We wanted to send a huge Thank You to Africa Adventure for our safari in June of this year.

Our trip was everything we could hope for & more. Our guide Brookes was outstanding in every way. He is bright & funny. He did a great job in meeting the desires, needs & safety of our group.

We saw more wildlife than we had a right to see on one safari.

This was my [Lou's] dream trip. Cheri has always longed to go to Alaska, now she is willing to skip Alaska for another trip to Africa.

Sorry we are so slow in sending our thanks; we took over 3,300 digital photos & printed approximately 600 for our album. Cheri & I have been busy showing our photos to family, friends & co-workers. Thanks much."

— *Lou & Cheri Firehammer, Missouri*

"We have now finally gotten somewhat used to being home from our most wonderful trip through **Kenya** and **Tanzania**…and all three of us want to thank the both of you for all the assistance you gave us in making it truly a "trip of a lifetime". It could have not worked out better…all the arrangements, trip transfers, lodging, guides, meals and of course sights were the best possible!!

One person who stands out was our guide for 8 days while in Tanzania… Omar Seif outdid himself in making sure we were comfortable, well taken care of and learned more than we could have possibly imagined about African wildlife…his command of the English language, superb knowledge of every thing African, wit and charm, maintenance of our vehicle and willingness to stay out late, leave early, sidetrack if we wanted to and just wonderful nature contributed immeasurably to the success of our trip. I would appreciate your passing this on to his company…

Within a few hours of our arrival in Samburu we had already begun to realize that we were truly in Africa…we had seen elephants, zebras, giraffes, gazelles, baboons and we had just gotten started. All of our accommodations were outstanding… We truly enjoyed Samburu, Little Governors and, of course, Tortillis…what a place to end a fantastic journey!!

Anyway we are now culling through many, many pictures and will try and get some of the better ones off to you as soon as possible.

Thank you so much again for all of your work in putting this trip together for us."

— *BOB YOUNG, RUTH HARGIS AND LARRY RUBOTTOM, CALIFORNIA*

"One New Year's resolution that I'm still trying to keep is to catch up on some important thank you's. The Treesh family had a wonderful experience on our safari to **South Africa** and **Zambia** last June/July, in no small part because of your patience, helpful advice and support! We reminisce about the trip at least once a week, and each of the kids has told me several times that we have to go back to Africa before they go off to college… it is gratifying to know that we were able to create such happy memories and strong desires to return as a family. Madeleine is even willing to try a tent for our next safari (though I daresay it will have to be a permanent tented camp — baby steps). So, I wanted to finally say "Thank you, thank you, thank you" from all of us, and to let you know that we will return to Africa soon. I hope my thanks rings even more sincerely as it is coming with a strong promise to use The Africa Adventure Company to assist us for the next trip.

Thank you again, and I look forward to working with you again in the not-too-distant future. Warm regards."

— *KEVIN TREESH AND THE TREESH FAMILY, CONNECTICUT*

"Hello Alison, The 3 of us (Jeff, Dan and Judy Kaine) returned from our **Kenya** safari about 1 month ago and I haven't had a chance to drop you a note until now. First of all, the trip was spectacular. I don't think your company could have done a better job. All of our accommodations were excellent and people couldn't have been nicer! Our guides were also consistently good. There is a new manager at Larsen's Camp who is certainly a pleasant fellow. Everyone seems to think that the place is getting better all of the time.

The game watching at Samburu was fantastic and I have enclosed one of our favorite pictures with this email. Next to Loldia house which was also extremely nice and the staff was great. Low key but very nice. I thoroughly enjoyed going to the school, infirmary and one of the local villages.

The Mara — what can you say — you have obviously been there multiple times. Ballooning was worthwhile despite the expense. Having your own guide also is very worthwhile. Encourage people to visit the Maasai or Samburu people, also a great experience. Our last stop was Lamu which was a nice exotic way to end the trip. I suspect many people might think that two days was not enough but I live in Sarasota so we are all used to spending time on the beach. I thought it was fine. Overall, a spectacular time. Kudos to you and your staff!"

— *JEFF KAINE, FLORIDA*

"Janet and I got back from our trip yesterday and I wanted to write you as soon as I could to let you know that we had, litcrally, the time of our lives. There were moments on the trip that were transforming, and some that will stay with me for the rest of my life — such as sleeping out in the middle of the pan under the stars on our last night at **San Camp**. We saw all the wildlife we wanted to see (with the exception of a rhino, which I know is almost impossible). I was astonished at how close we were able to get to all the animals.

Everything went perfectly. All the connections connected. And most importantly, the itinerary you and Andre put together could not have been better. We saw all (or at least most) of the features **Botswana** has to offer. At all the camps we were asked by our guides what our itinerary was, and when we told them they always had the same response — that we couldn't have done better.

So thank you very much. You have made a lifelong dream of mine a reality, one that was better than I had expected and in fact was better than I had hoped. Most sincerely,"

— *BILL AND JANET BACKS, ILLINOIS*

"Well, we certainly had the adventure of our lives! This was the most exciting adventure we've done so far, and it all went off without a single hitch because of the great attention to detail and follow-up that you all did in helping us plan our safari to **Kenya** and **Tanzania**. From the first interaction with your rep. on our arrival at the Nairobi airport, to the driver who brought us to the airport at the end of our trip, everyone was there for us. Our 3 personal guides — Clemence in the Serengeti and Eric in Amboseli, and Edwin in the Maasai Mara were all excellent. They were very knowledgeable not only about the animals and flora we sighted, but also about the history of the country and the local peoples. They took us almost anywhere we wanted to see, and many places we had no concept we'd be seeing, They kept us safe and made us feel safe at all times, and helped us to feel the genuine warmth, friendliness and welcoming attitude of all the African people we met, including our 2 visits to Maasai bomas. We fell in love with the country and hope to return in the future. The accommodations were fantastic, and the food was unexpectedly excellent everywhere we stayed.

And a special thank you for getting us into the Giraffe Manor on our first day in Africa — that was a major delight and a wonderful way to begin our adventure.

We will be sure to recommend you to anyone we know who's planning a trip to Africa. Carol's sending you some pictures and a personal note.

Thanks once again for an excellent and very thorough job well done."

— *ALAN AND CAROL MAGNER, PENNSYLVANIA*

"I am writing to give you feedback from our recent safari to **South Africa, Zimbabwe** and **Botswana**...Firstly I would like to say that the whole trip was very well organized and everything that had been planned went more smoothly than I had expected. This resulted in a relaxing and stress free vacation for all the family — myself especially. I would like to thank you for making the arrangements which resulted in a truly fantastic experience.

I feel that overall The Africa Adventure Company did a very good job of addressing our request for 'a bit of everything' in our safari experience. The whole trip went very well and was enjoyed by all of the **family**. I was impressed by the professional way in which our trip was organized, especially with the amount of traveling involved and the logistics of this. It all worked very well and the timing was excellent. Both Alison and myself have said we will be visiting South Africa and surrounding countries again in the future for another vacation. The kids enjoyed it immensely, though it was tiring for all of us.

I would again like to thank you for organizing the trip for us and will be recommending your services to some of my colleagues who wish to have the same type of experiences. I have attached a couple of photos from our trip for the competition."

— *JEFF AND ALISON KNIGHT AND FAMILY, UNITED KINGDOM*

"This summer's safari was the BEST, MOST AMAZING family vacation!

As you know, our family had always dreamed to taking an African safari — but were unsure about where to go, how old the boys should be to truly appreciate the experience and how to organize a trip so that we could relax and enjoy the sights and sounds of Africa. After our discussions, we put our "trip of a lifetime" in your team's hands — and the result was more than we could have ever imagined!!!

Thank you and the members of your team for all the hard work that went into our trip. The advice on where to go and what time of year was perfect. The camps you suggested were amazing and offered our **family** an opportunity to see and experience wildlife in their habitat. The people we met on our trip were wonderful and your selection of Matt Copham as our guide was perfect for our family.

Please thank everyone at The Africa Adventure Company for making this safari a Trip of a Lifetime!"

— *DAVE BOSSUNG, INDIANA*

"We wanted to thank you for arranging our trip to **Zimbabwe** and **Botswana**. It was incredible! Victoria Falls, Duma Tau, Tubu Tree, and Mombo were all wonderful places. And all the people were extremely friendly and gracious. In every phase of our trip, we were met punctually and with a smile. The camp staff and guides were absolutely fantastic. And the camp facilities were very well done and comfortable. Mombo was especially nice! The food was great, too! And then there was the wildlife. It exceeded our expectations. Every game drive was a new and exciting experience. We had close encounters with herds of elephants, zebra, antelopes, and hippo. We watched troops of baboons play and herds of giraffe gallop across the plains. We watched lions and hyenas feed on a kill (at one time, there were over 30 hyenas at the dinner table!). We saw an amazing number of birds of every shape and color. It was a trip of a lifetime that we will definitely be doing again! Thank you!"

— *MARK CAREY, OHIO*

"Africa is amazing. Thank you for arranging such a wonderful safari. We agree with Nolting's assessment that the Maasai Mara is undoubtedly the finest wildlife area in **Kenya**. The **Ngorongoro** lived up to its reputation too. We very much enjoyed the hike with our Maasai guide up the Olmoti Crater. It felt good to mix game drives with other activities like hiking, canoeing, and oh yes the ballooning. We loved the ballooning. The Selous was a wonderful change of pace and very relaxing. **Rwanda** and the gorillas were beyond words.

From our experience, we strongly advocate having **private guides**. Our two guides in Kenya (Anthony and Joseph) were outstanding and our guide in Tanzania, Selemoni, was experienced, knowledgeable and a very kind person. They taught us so much and we learned not only about the animals but also about the people. The camp staff at Tarangire spoiled us while the Selous staff went out of their way to make our stay memorable.

We saw so many animals in many different situations. Lions mating, killing, walking together, and resting. A cheetah mom with five cubs hunting for their supper...she is a very good mom. **Gorillas**, magnificent and so very much like us. Elephants in all situations, including a charge. We have many unique and special memories that it is hard to capture them in this email. We are reviewing and culling 3,000 or so pictures and will send special ones shortly.

The trip was nearly flawless...We want to especially thank Saskia for her efforts to contact the Embassy's at the last minute and for her good work on our trip. Thank you!"

— *STEVEN AND ROBERTA SHAW, NEW MEXICO*

"We've just returned from out latest African Adventure. We've been to many camps in various countries in Africa, but this last trip was a whole new level of excitement. In addition to Game drive at Chitabe Trails in **Botswana**; Shumba Camp in Kafue NP **Zambia**, Ruckomechi Camp in **Zimbabwe**, and Vundu Camp in Mana Pools NP Zimbabwe, we did night drives in the first 3 camps, boat game drives on the Zambezi River, a **canoe trip** down the Zambezi, and walking safaris in Mana Pools at Vundu Camp in Zimbabwe.

Vundu Camp showed us the 'real African Safari'. We drove around Mana Pools NP and when we saw an interesting animal in the distance, we parked the car (cars are not allowed off the roads in Zimbabwe NPs). I grabbed the camera gear, the guide grabbed his rifle, and **we walked**. The result was a fantastic experience. When we returned home and told our family and friends that when we saw tracks from 5 lions, we got out of the car and tracked them down, they said we must be crazy. Our guide, Nick Murray, kept us safe… The photos of the lions were fabulous. For 4 mornings, I was up and out of camp by 5:30 in search of African wild dogs. It took a lot of walking, but we found their den and were rewarded with excellent photos of 10 adults. The photos of the Bull Elephants standing on their hind legs to reach up to eat the apple peel Acacia trees could only be obtained after a walk. Walking felt like a real safari. Zimbabwe is the place to go for anyone serious about photography. The scenery, the animals and above all else the light was fabulous. The haze in the air from the smoke generated from the burning across the river in Zambia provided extraordinary light. And I captured it. One night at sunset we had red light. I got a photo of a baboon in red light. How cool was that! This baboon looks fabulous…

Thanks again, not only for making our arrangements, but for that piece of your mind that put us in position to have the safari of my lifetime. I seem to remember that I've said that already after the first and the second safari you booked for us. Can't wait for # 4."

— *Gene and Teri Covey, New Hampshire*

"We had a wonderful trip. I went to be amazed and I was!

The quality of the lodging was more than we expected. Our favorite was the tented camp experience. The food was always good, the coffee excellent and the staff was accommodating and helpful.

As an Interior Designer, I was interested in the construction and detailing both of the exterior and interior of all the lodges. My experience will undoubtedly influence some of my future designs.

All the guides knew their business, were great drivers, and answered most of our questions. Firoz, our primary guide, was particularly outstanding. We had asked for a guide who was proficient in many things including birds, reptiles, plants and animals because we are interested in everything and Peter is a biologist. Firoz was the perfect choice for us. He was also willing to stop to watch any bird or animal and share information about them.

Firoz offered to identify a few birds from our photos that we may have trouble naming. I am hopeful that our email with photos reached him so he can reply.

We are most appreciative of the planning Africa Adventure did in making this a most memorable trip!"
— *LINDA BRITT AND PETER YINGLING, ARIZONA*

"I just wanted to let you know that our trip was absolutely wonderful! I am already thinking and planning my next trip! It really could not have been better! Both Mark and Nic were absolutely spectacular! The guides are really the key to the quality of the trip — and they were truly the best. Is it too soon to try and book Nic and Mark for 2009?!!"
— *SARAH GERTMENIAN, CALIFORNIA*

"We're back, exhausted and ready to go again. The safari through **Kenya** and **Tanzania** far exceeded our expectations. The lodges were beautiful, the food delicious and the guides friendly and extremely knowledgeable. And the animals — WOW. We saw at least 4 leopards, dozens of lions, lots of hippopotami, a few rhinoceros, hundreds of elephants and about a million zebra, wildebeest and gazelles. And some of the lions and elephants were up close and personal.

You can use us as a reference any time. The experience was absolutely wonderful. And we can hardly wait to go again."
— *JOHN AND SHIRLEY CHARLES, FLORIDA*

"Hello, Mark and Company,

I'm sure you hear this quite regularly from clients, about what an extraordinary time we had in Africa, and what a marvelous job you all did in making it such a sweet success. Half-way through the trip, after making several connections in tiny airstrips, being shuttled through various and sundry queues, and always, at every stop, being greeted by name by a pleasant and helpful someone who was looking out just for us, it dawned on me what a bargain we made by using your company to manage the logistics. I know from painful experience how it can go really wrong, and how much of the pleasure of a trip can be lost by confusion, arguments, and missteps. It was smooth sailing all the way...

...The great time we had in **Mana Pools** with Nick Murray. Nick is a real pro, and we had a wonderful time with him at Vundu Camp. A lovely spot. Being able to walk around with Nick and get really personal with the wild animals was breathtaking; both awesome and scary. We loved it. And the canoe trips on the Zambezi were everything you promised. Tom caught a great tiger fish our last afternoon and we had it for dinner that night. The staff prepared it over coals, burnt to a crisp, head and scales still on. It was delicious.

I realize I could go on for pages, now that I am well into remembering the stories. Thank you for everything you all did to make this such a splendid adventure. When we go back, we'll be in touch to help with the plans!"

— *NANCY WINSHIP AND TOM FISH, WASHINGTON*

"I cannot begin to describe how pleased we were with the adventure you put together for us. It met all of our expectations and satisfied our desire to combine safari life with enhanced cultural immersion and activities. There were too many highlights to mention but several stand out.

The experience at Greystoke Camp in Mahale Mountain Park was one of them. We found the **chimpanzees** two of the three days and it was a wonderful experience. The camp guide who led our 'slow' group was particularly considerate of the need to rest frequently and climb slowly. He always took the opportunity during rest breaks to give us lessons in chimp behavior and the local flora. As a result we were never bored and when we found the chimps were able to enjoy the experience fully because we were rested and knowledgeable about what the animals were doing and eating. Also the Park Ranger who accompanied us was very helpful.

Our experience with **Taita Discovery Center** was another standout. Our community participation consisted of Susie teaching at Kitege village Primary School and I worked on the construction of their new school. We also got envolved with the other villages and schools in the Kasigau area. On Sunday of our week, which was our day off, we visited Tsavo East for a wonderful game drive. The interaction with the local villagers and participation in their everyday lives is exactly what we were looking for and thoroughly enjoyed it. Shopping for construction materials in the hardware store in Voi was great fun as well as very enlightening as to life in area commerce center. Our driver/guide Joel Korir was outstanding and contributed to our overall enjoyment.

All of the Safari Camps were comfortable and enjoyable. The game drives were quite successful in each area. As this was our **fourth trip** to Africa we knew what to expect during the game drives. We like to be out at first light and each camp accommodated that with picnic breakfasts and where possible, early evening sundowners. That is always a treat. We observed many animals in each area and inadvertently got caught in the middle of a cheetah hunt several times. Again the game drives were successful, interesting and fun thanks to the efforts of all the local guides...

It was a wonderful adventure in all respects and you are to be commended for putting it together the way you did. Everything worked as planned. There were no hitches the entire trip. The information and detail you provided was complete and set everything out in a manner that made it easy to just enjoy ourselves. Thank you for your efforts on our behalf. We will contact you when we are ready to start putting together our next Africa adventure."

— *JIM AND SUSIE DOYLE, WASHINGTON*

"...I don't know how we got lucky enough to have our own **private guide** in **Tanzania** but I am so thankful that happened and appreciate that you worked it out for us. Even more important, the fact that you set us up with Robert. He is truly an amazing guide and an amazing person. We hit it off immediately and by the second day both Paula and I felt we had not only a guide, but a friend. His sense of humor and personality are a winning combination. Of course, his knowledge of the area and the animals and birds and the history of the country is unsurpassed! There was not a question we asked that he couldn't answer...and we asked a lot. Not just answers, but reference books and stories. He kept us thoroughly entertained even when we weren't viewing amazing scenery and wildlife. What a guy! He had so many good things to say about Africa Adventure Company as well. We knew we had made the right choice because all the planning went so well but everything that happened surpassed my expectations. Robert was the diamond in the crown of the trip.

After two weeks I was (almost) ready to come home as it is a sometimes overwhelming experience but I do miss Africa and I really want to come back. I am telling all my friends about The Africa Adventure Company (AAC) and my pictures alone have impressed everyone. I think we were very lucky to see some of the things we saw but I also really believe that Robert made a difference as well. I know he has been doing this for a number of years but he is so enthusiastic. We were excited every day with the adventure and we knew how happy he was for us and he really did make it special.

Again, thank you so much for the trip of a lifetime (both Tanzania and Kenya...Joseph was a doll too) and if, no when, I decide to see more of Africa it will definitely be with AAC."

— *JONI HOLLIS, CALIFORNIA*

"I just wanted to thank you for an awesome safari experience! My brother and I had a really great time and thoroughly enjoyed every minute of our trip to Africa. Both safari lodges that we stayed at were really nice, and the food they served was really good. At Makalolo Camp we saw a young pride of lions feasting on a buffalo on our first night. We also saw a rhino and many elephants as well. We even got a rare glimpse of an aardwolf...

At **Mana Pools** the scenery was fantastic, and we got to see a pack of wild dogs. We even did a half day canoe safari and saw tons of hippos and crocs. It was very cool, but also very nerve-wracking.

I can't wait to do my next safari in Africa in the future and would recommend you to anyone I know who wants to go on safari. Thanks again for an awesome trip! Thanks again for everything!"

— *DARRYL LUKE, ILLINOIS*

"Dear Mr. Nolting,

I have been home almost three weeks from my Galloping Gnu safari, although somehow it seems more like three months. Our trip was so wonderful in so many ways, I promised myself I would write to you thank you for the many things Joni and I experienced.

First of all, I would like to commend you on your choice of guides…All accommodations were excellent. My personal favorite was Kikoti. It was a lovely compromise of being in pampered accommodations while still being out in the wild and hearing the animals and birds all around us. By the way, I think the meals at Kikoti were the best of the trip. The staff there was especially nice and accommodating, and I felt very sad and shed a tear when we left the camp.

I would also like to commend The Africa Adventure Company (AAC) for its support to the local citizens in Africa, specifically the Maasai tribe in Ngorongoro. Your generous payment allowing us a total-access visit is to be commended.

I truly had no expectations about this trip. If I had, they would have all been exceeded. I have shared my photographs with many friends, and they are amazed. I have nothing but the highest praise for your company and its employees. We have strongly recommended AAC to all of our friends, and if we return (I think we promised that we would), it will certainly be with AAC."

— *PAULA S. HOUCK, CALIFORNIA*

"We had a wonderful time. Our first desire was to see and photograph animals, however, the people of **Tanzania** were so memorable and impressive that in some ways that was the trip highlight!! Our guide was terrific. Omari Mnyangala was our guide… and his knowledge of everything, his pleasant demeanor, and driving abilities were excellent.

The wildlife parks were great. We especially liked Tarangire and the elephants. Kikoti camp was our favorite. The remote location was interesting and the room was beautiful. We also stayed at Migration Camp. The room there was very nice and the dining experience was lovely. You could only HEAR the hippos because there was a lot of forest between the pool and the camp. I got a glimpse of one as he walked up a hill one morning but we did not see the hippos there except for that. We would highly recommend the permanent tented camps above the lodges. At Kikoti we saw a herd of elephants walk right by our room. Mountain Village Lodge was lovely and the dining service there was excellent. Gibbs Farm was OUTSTANDING and we wished we could have stayed longer there. We had a tour of the grounds with Moses and he was great! The mobile tented camp experience was enjoyable because of the great staff of people. We were the last ones to use the present tents and drop toilets!! The staff again made it fun.

We saw all the animals we wanted to see, leopards in trees, cheetah, lions, hyenas, etc. The only elusive one was the rhino, but it was a little windy and Omari said they don't like that. On another try to see them, it rained and we decided to turn back and not risk the deep mud near the water. The Maasai people were beautiful and so very interesting. Also the trips through the small towns were amazing. All the people walking — walking — walking!! We also visited the Tloma Primary School which was eye-opening and amazing. Such adorable and happy children. We would like to send them some things.

Thanks again for the wonderful adventure!! I will surely recommend you to anyone who will listen and wants info.!!"

— *Marcee and Dennis Perelman, Colorado*

"Sorry for the delay in dropping you a line about my recent trip to **Kenya** and **Rwanda**. I had to jump back in at full speed at work virtually from the day I got back — and that's always a bit of a challenge for me after a trip to Africa.

The trip was great. I had an especially amazing time in Rwanda. Not just the gorilla trek — which was incredible to say the least — but also with some locals I managed to spend time with at Gorilla Nest and in Kigali — primarily as a result of the fact that I had my driver/guide more or less to myself the entire time I was in Rwanda. He was a really good guy — Arthur, and I found the people of Rwanda in general to be extremely warm and friendly and eager to make me feel welcome in their country. And the country itself is quite beautiful.

I very much enjoyed my time at Elsa's Kopje and Meru — that park has tremendous potential it seems to me and everyone associated with that operation is top notch.

My week in the Maasi Mara...was just fantastic. It's funny, there are certain things I didn't like about the Mara — mainly the crowds — but on the other hand — I saw stuff there that was truly amazing and that I'm not sure you'd easily see anywhere else — a lion taking down a wildebeest — a cheetah taking down a young impala — a leopard getting bit in the face by a snake — a topi being born and 10 minutes later taken by a lion. How can you not go back to a place like that even if you do have to share many of the experiences with 10 other vehicles?

In any event, my passion for Africa continues to grow. Thanks again for everything. You guys at The Africa Adventure Company do a great job of making things smooth and life easy while I'm in Africa. I'm sure we will work together again."

— WALT TURNER, CALIFORNIA

"George and I are finally back home in New York. But memories continue to linger as it usually happens after an extraordinary holiday trip. We can't stop reminiscing about the beautiful landscapes we saw in Moremi Game Reserve, the enthralling magic of its prolific wildlife, and the wonderful people we met at the **mobile tented camp**. (How could we ever forget the thrill of five leopard sightings in six days, the joy of leisurely observing a pride of lions with many cubs, the excitement of following an impressively big male lion at night, the privilege of observing the daily survival of predators and preys in accordance to natural laws, etc., etc.)

Matusadona and the **Mana Pools National Parks**, the enthralling magic of their prolific wildlife, and the wonderful people we met at the Rhino Lodge Safari Camp and the Vundu Campsite. (How could we ever forget the excitement of **tracking black rhino by foot** in the wilderness of Matusadona, the jolting surprise of Mvura's visit to the Rhino Lodge with her baby calf, the marvels of **canoeing** along the Zambezi River enjoying its paradisiacal wonders, the joy of leisurely admiring large elephant herds crossing the river, the thrill of tracking and finding a pack of wild dogs with pups.)

George and I want to thank you again for your endless kindness, thoughtfulness and generosity. The Africa Adventure Company (AAC) should be very proud of you because you have what it takes to enhance people's lives. Dave Carson's passion and enthusiasm are contagious. We admired his great sense of humor and 'joie de vivre' — not to mention your encyclopedic knowledge of African flora and fauna. We admired Mark's love for every form of life — his passion and enthusiasm are contagious. This was our **sixth African safari** and I can safely say that Dave Carson and Mark McAdam are indeed the BEST naturalists and safari guides we have ever had. In my humblest estimation, both of you have few or no peers in your line of work. We anticipated that AAC's 'Call of the Wild' signature safari would be full of surprises, but I think Dave and Mark were the best surprises."

— KEMBELL HUYKE AND GEORGE MULLANE, NEW YORK

"We returned home on Monday and our trip was fabulous. We all had some anxieties about this trip but they were certainly unfounded. From the time we landed in Nairobi until the end of our trip we felt very well taken care of and secure. The transfers by road and air all went smoothly and staff without exception was accommodating and pleasant. Our guides were all knowledgeable, personable and made every effort to satisfy what we wanted to see. With regard to specifics on the accommodations and game parks this is my assessment: **Tarangire** Treetops was perfection and I didn't picture something so wonderful. An added bonus while we were there was a bull elephant who took up residence in the camp. Great fun despite the fact that he happened to like to hang out during the day under our tent. Game drives at this park were also top notch for variety, close proximity and sheer numbers.

So glad our final stop was Little Governors and the Maasai Mara. What a great camp! And the wildlife was spectacular. We saw the migration and the crossing and many big cats. I could go on and on about the wonders of this place. Oh. Norfolk was very lovely and nice to return to before leaving…Assante (sp?) to all of you at Africa Adventure I will be sure to pass your names on to friends. Pictures to follow in a few days."

— RANDI ZOOT, ILLINOIS

"I'm finally getting caught up and want to fire off an email to tell you what a great trip we had. Rovos Rail was simply wonderful. We especially enjoyed the service and the food and wine! The daily excursions were great! One minor suggestion to them would be for an exercise car with a couple of tread mills etc. to work off the wonderful food! We got a kick out of taking a photo of Mr. Vos (owner of Rovos Rail) himself cleaning up trash along the railroad tracks! He sure sets an example for his employees!!

The animal viewing safaris, food & wine and service at MALA MALA were also excellent! I took over 500 photos and am getting them into a photo book!

All six of us agreed it truly was 'The trip of a lifetime.' Thanks for the great organization and the abundant information you provided for us! I will surely recommend the trip! Saludos,"

— GERALD C. NIELSEN, CALIFORNIA

"I knew this trip would be the greatest of my entire existence…and it was. **Uganda** and **Rwanda** are truly breathtaking places to experience.

It's hard to put into words the experience of seeing the chimpanzees and gorillas in person. There is nothing I could say that would even come close to putting that into words.

My guide Emmanuel "Emmy" was professional, knowledgeable and absolutely wonderful!!! I felt comfortable with him from the start and he always put my safety first.

I will return to Uganda and Rwanda in two years time. I will definitely want Emmanuel to be my Guide/Driver again!

Thank you Andre for helping me during my planning stages of this magnificent experience. You have been very patient, kind and truly professional. I will call you when the time is right for me to go back to Uganda and Rwanda... the adventure continues..."

— *RAEMONDE BEZENAR, CANADA*

"I'm finally settling down following an amazing two weeks in Africa. My expectations of our African Adventure were far exceeded, due singularly to you and your company's gifted and talented efforts. Nothing was overlooked. Everything was on time. There were no missteps.

Sure, we saw 40+ mammals and 140+ bird species; however, the experience far exceeded those incredible moments. Which brings us to Omari. His 25 years of experience was a gift for us. We learned so much and saw beyond the expected. His insights, manner, and style, were so contagious and enhanced our trip ten fold.

Omari brought us to an AIDS orphanage, to schools where we gave away inflatable soccer balls from America. We had dinner with him as often as possible to learn as much as possible and had the pleasure of meeting his family. Thank you so very much for assigning this talented guide for our safari. We always will remember his beautiful smile and gentle manner.

We fully understand why The Africa Adventure Company is constantly rated one of the top companies in the safari business. You all worked so diligently, communicated so well, and gave us memories which will influence our future years and provide memories that will last forever.

And Kyle, you are the best, the very best. Thank you for your skill, professionalism, and the gift of AFRICA that you gave to my friend Morrie and me. All the best!"

— *JACK HEFFERNAN, MAINE*

"We are very pleased with our vacation. The safari that you planned was fabulous. Even though this was my **third trip** to the continent, it was the best viewing of leopards, rhinos and cheetahs that I have seen. At Phinda alone, we saw 17 different cheetahs. I researched Phinda for a conservation project when I was in college and it was wonderful to see that the translocation of animals has been most successful in this area.

The accommodations every where were superb and service gracious and hospitable. I cannot say enough about this adventure. The highlight for me was riding an African elephant under starry skies and ambling into a male lion who quickly removed himself from the path of the pachyderms. We loved the elephants so much that we took three game rides on them. It was very difficult to return to work and I decided to cut back a couple days a month. It was a very good decision."

— *MARIANNE TUCKER AND PATRICK CLOONAN, CALIFORNIA*

"I want to thank you, Alison and Africa Adventure for an unbelievable trip to Africa this past June and July. A week in **Egypt** and a week in **Kenya** turned out to be the perfect combination for our group.

Talk about different cultures. Our first safari camp was at Tortillis in Amboseli National Park. The individual tent camps were by far the best we experienced in Kenya. Sitting in the foothills of Mt. Kilimanjaro made for wonderful views and pictures. The Maasai village we visited there shows how a tribe can be happy without any of the things in our modern world we take for granted. Next we were off to Little Governors Camp in the Maasai Mara. The cceded our wildest expectations. Fred was our guide for ttle Governors and he was the best. Of all the people we ere the only group that actually saw and photographed t, we saw it. Antelope, too many to count, elephants prides of lions, some which numbered up to 15 was the and rhino's horns were both enormous. But watching nas feed on fresh kills always made our drives fasci- reed watching a cheetah almost run down a Thomson e service at both safaris was outstanding and the food at Little Governors was wide ranging and absolutely delicious."

— *GLENN AND MARY STECH, VALERIE MITCHELL AND SCOTT AND SUSAN STRATTON, ILLINOIS*

"Dear Africa Adventure Company—

I'm finally getting around to letting you know that my trip to Africa was amazing...Kyle did an excellent job of setting up my itinerary and everyone I spoke with at your company was great — professional, friendly and so helpful. Everything on my trip went very smoothly. Each of the places I stayed was lovely and all of my transfers were on time, friendly and efficient. Most of my transfers were like mini tours with knowledgeable drivers happy to share their stories and local information with me. Your local contacts are doing a great job taking care of your travelers. A particular highlight was my tour of **Victoria Falls** with Esther. She was so knowledgeable and made the experience very memorable — not just amazing views of the falls, but a background on the history, geology and cultural features of the falls. I never expected a private tour — what a treat to spend that time with Esther.

...The staff and guides at **Djuma** were so fantastic. Their warmth and willingness to share their stories of the animals, their families, and their experiences added so much to the game drives and at meal times...it was the best.

Muchenje was also a wonderful place and it was great to get the different perspectives from the two parks. At **Sabi Sands** we saw leopards everyday, got very close and saw lots of small groups of different animals. At **Chobe** we saw large groups of elephants, hippos, stalking lions and I especially enjoyed seeing the animals at the river's edge from the boat. Even though there was quite a lot of rain during my trip, it never slowed us down or seemed to affect our ability to see animals. We also did see tons of baby animals...I recommend that you continue to work with parks and guides that are concerned about any impacts they may be having on the wildlife.

Thank you for all your efforts to make sure my trip went smoothly. I have been passing out your cards and recommending you to everyone who asks about the details of my trip... Thanks again."

— *Lynne Barre, Washington*

"The **Tanzania** itinerary was excellent — not only as planned with you but with some additional items such as the Olmoti Crater hike and visit to the Maasai Village which were pleasant surprises. The internal flight from Serengeti to Arusha was a great idea. After getting bumped and jostled for 10 days, avoiding the 7 hour drive back to Arusha was a delightful relief.

We had a very good briefing at the outset and everything took place as scheduled. The Toyota Land Cruiser performed amazingly well without any beak-downs — I didn't know vehicles could take such a beating day in and day out. The raised roof was a nice feature — many of the vehicles we saw had open roofs. We loved the fact that we had a vehicle designed for 6 or 7 clients but there were only 4 of us — it really made for ample room to maneuver in game viewing and photographing.

Our guide, Rassul, was first class. He is an excellent driver and a very nice, gentle man whom we came to feel quite close to. In particular, his patient, relatively slow style was very successful in finding game. In most cases, we were the ones to discover game that others would charge over to see. He clearly was the primary factor in a very successful safari, for we saw every significant animal there was to see: lions, cheetahs, leopards, elephants, giraffe, rhinos, hippos, ostrich, cape buffalo, wildebeest, zebra, gazelle, baboons, colobus monkeys, warthogs, a variety of antelope e.g. Hartebeest, Waterbuck etc. and a great variety of birds. We were also privileged to have a very good sighting of a cerval — somewhat of a rarity according to Rassul.

The Serena lodges were all excellent — friendly staff, comfortable rooms with great views (in Ngorongoro and Serengeti) and very nice food. I particularly liked the extensive breakfast buffets with eggs to order. We decided that Ngorongoro Serena had the best food.

Kikoti camp was a particularly nice change from the lodges. The huts themselves are quite unique; and Jenny and her staff were very pleasant and accommodating. Also, we were delighted with the "add-ons" they provided including a late afternoon nature walk, a Maasai dance performance and a night game drive.

All in all, it could not have been a better experience. Thank you from all of us for making it possible with your thoughtful planning and arrangements. Best regards,"

— *DAN TRACY, MARYLAND*

"Well, I am back and still jet-lagged, but I wanted to write and thank you and The Africa Adventure Company for the amazing and wonderful experience you provided for us in Africa! This was my fourth visit to the Dark Continent and by far the best — the excellent planning and organization which your company provided ensured that everything went smoothly — quite a feat in Africa. I especially appreciated the wonderful little surprises that awaited us, courtesy of The Africa Adventure Company, at each location…

Our visit to **Djuma** exceeded our expectations as well. A friendly and helpful staff catered to our every need and we appreciated the complimentary drinks throughout our stay. One of the biggest thrills of the trip for me was the sighting of a leopard on our first game drive. He had just finished a big meal of impala and he snoozed and posed in the grass for us for about 45 minutes. I must have taken 50 photos! The food at Djuma was delicious…We were fortunate enough to be there for one of their evening dinners in the bush — a bonfire, candles and lanterns everywhere, and an interesting, tasty meal.

As you had assured us, **Victoria Falls** felt completely safe. And Esther was a gem! Thank you so much for sending her to us and providing that fascinating tour of the Falls. She was such a delight — her demeanor reminded me of a favorite teacher or a beloved aunt…

Of course we were floored when we arrived at **Chobe Chilwero** and thought we had entered an episode of "Lifestyles of the Rich and Famous"! What a fabulous way to end a vacation! The accommodations, the food, the service — all were amazing. The manager was knowledgeable and entertaining and his wife was the epitome of grace and courtesy. We loved the wildlife — a highlight here occurred during our boat ride when we encountered 2 hippos in the midst of a romantic interlude. Lots of roaring in each other's faces which gave us some great shots of wide-open hippo jaws!

Truly, this was the trip of a lifetime!…Again, many, many thanks for your hard work and the excellent care you took of us throughout the trip. Although I had planned for this to be my last trip to Africa, Jeremy and I are already talking about a possible trip to Kenya with Africa Adventure in a couple of years. So, I hope to be talking with you again!"

— *SHANNON BORREGO, FLORIDA*

"Jambo Mark & Alison,

It's been several months since I arrived back from my amazing journey through Africa. I was part of the Kim Smith Group that traveled to **Kenya and Tanzania**. I was also part of a small group that ventured to **Zimbabwe** prior to joining up with our official "Lucky Ladies 13" at the Norfolk in Nairobi.

Although I know that Kim forwarded an email on behalf of our entire group, I wanted to send along my accolades as well...Since reliving the trip through pictures recently, I find myself wanting to let you know how awe struck I was during our safari. Not only was it my first trip outside the US (other than Mexico or the Caribbean), it was also my first helicopter ride, my first charter airplane ride, and my first stamped passport. Thank you for allowing me to experience all of this with great accommodations, incredible cuisines, first rate staff and rangers, amongst the spectacular terrain and wildlife. It was indeed a trip of a lifetime!

I hope to explore much more of Africa in years to come! Thank you again for making it all happen!"

— *LAURI SPECTOR, FLORIDA*

"In response to your kind letter, we would like to offer an informal review of our recently concluded travel arranged through The Africa Adventure Company...

The safaris in both **Botswana** and **Zimbabwe** far exceeded our expectations, which were quite lofty. We saw all the game that we so looked forward to seeing, with the exception of cheetah which we saw only in captivity at the De Wildt Cheetah Center in South Africa. Among the many highlights were extended periods viewing leopards at Moremi Reserve, an encounter with three rare black rhino in Matusadona NP, an opportunity to study a pack of wild dogs in Mana Pools NP, and lunch with some 14–16 elephant in the Khwai concession in the Okavango Delta. For Becky, the chance to interact with the resident warthogs, her favorite animals, at the Khwai campsite was an unexpected delight.

Our guide Nic Polenakis possessed an infectious enthusiasm that carried us along with him over the trails and paths in Botswana. Both his obvious love for and understanding of the land and its denizen, along with his interest in us, made for a completely enjoyable experience. We understand why many of his guiding clients are repeat visitors, as indeed we intend to be.

Mark McAdam was a complete professional and we benefited from his qualifications as a registered Professional Guide and River Guide with the

Zimbabwean National Parks Authority and his 15 years of guiding experience. Richard Taylor, who accompanied us on safari in Zimbabwe, impressed us with both his personality and his enthusiasm in videotaping our adventures.

We doubt we would have seen the black rhino had not Mark kept us on foot and moving through the brush, then sliding over elephant dung to reach a suitable vantage point to view the rhino...

As for mobile tenting, we could not agree more that this is where unspoiled Africa exists, where the special privilege of absorbing the awesome, majestic grandeur of the African landscapes and its wildlife is still possible. Now, of course, we can't imagine going on safari any other way.

We have been wholeheartedly enthusiastic in referring friends to The Africa Adventure Company. Thank you for a memorable trip!"

— *Becky and Scott Osborne, Tennessee*

"...Terry and I had a fantastic Africa adventure!

First, everything went really smooth from the beginning to the end, all the local representatives in **Kenya** and **Tanzania** were excellent. Selemani is a very experimented guide, very knowledgeable and good personality, we enjoyed the Serengeti the most in Tanzania, and Migration Camp certainly makes the experience even greater, our tent was very comfortable and the service excellent! And we have seen all the animals we could have wish, lion's families, leopard, elephant, hyena, cheetah, zebra, etc...

Then we met with Preston at the border who drove us to Amboseli. Preston is also a very interesting man, very educated, he told us about his "wild life" school for children in his village and a lot of projects...we had a great time, especially at Tortillis Camp, what a special place!!! And again the staff was remarkable! Although Kilimanjaro was "very" shy...

We enjoyed the 2 flights to reach the Maasai Mara, it was fun to see the land so well from the sky, it's such a beautiful country.

There, Henry was waiting for us, also a very special person, Henry is a Maasai and doing so much for help education in his community, I would say he has being our best guide for making every moment so exciting, always looking for the most rare animal that we did not see before. The Mara was a great continuation of the Serengeti where landscape and animals were the most beautiful. Governor II camp was very nice, and the staff outstanding, the cook made some special dishes just for us and all of them were very, very helpful... and gracious!

Would we go back? Definitely YES, especially in Kenya, we felt comfortable in all aspects, with the country and people...

Thank you so much for your great help, all your advice was right on! Our best regards."

— *Terry and Marie Heilman, Arizona*

Accommodations, Places and People Index

Map Index

CHARTS –

Photo Credits

Thanks to all the Africa camps and companies, guides and Africa Adventure Company travelers.

Front Cover
African Continent
Elephants – Colin Bell
Lions – Alison Nolting
Vehicle with cheetah –
 Wilderness Safaris
Zebras – Michael Poliza
Lodge – Singita Boulders

Spine – Wilderness Safaris

Back Cover – Nigel Robey

Call of the Wild:
Pg 11 Matthew Copham
Pg 13 Alison Nolting
Pg 14 Colin Bell
Pg 17 Dana Allen
Pg 19 Becci Crowe
Pg 20 Nic Polenakis
Pg 22 Mike Myers
Pg 24–25 Andy Biggs
Pg 28 Rick Harvey – Bushlife
Pg 29 Nic Polenakis
Pg 31 Gene Eckhart
Pg 33 David Carson
Pg 34 Londolozi
Pg 36 upper – Ranger Safaris
 Lower – Capture Africa
Pg 38 Gene Eckhart
Pg 40 Andre Steynberg
Pg 42 upper – Terri Jakway
 Lower – Susan Stowers
Pg 44 upper – Wilderness Safaris
 Middle – Dana Allen –
 Wilderness Safaris
 Lower – Selous Safari
 Company
Pg 47 upper – Becci Crowe
 Lower – Cheli & Peacock
Pg 48 Nigel Robey
Pg 50 Nigel Robey
Pg 51 Ranger Safaris
Pg 52 Colin Bell
Pg 53 Colin Bell
Pg 55 Dana Allen – Wilderness
 Safaris
Pg 58 Mike Myers
Pg 59 Dana Allen
Pg 61 Iva Spitzer
Pg 63 Nic Polenakis
Pg 66 Warren Yu

Pg 67 Nigel Robey
Pg 70 upper – Gene Eckhart
 Lower – Gene Eckhart
Pg 71 Steve Turner
Pg 75 Jami Graham
Pg 76 Alison Nolting
Pg 84 Mark Crowe
Pg 93 Matthew Copham
Pg 94 Dana Allen – Wilderness
 Safaris
Pg 100 Steve Turner
Pg 102 upper – Alison Nolting
 Lower – Abby Lazar
Pg 103 Abby Lazar
Pg 104 upper – Abby Lazar
 Lower – Abby Lazar
Pg 106 Abby Lazar
Pg 107 upper – Abby Lazar
 Lower – Steve Turner

Botswana:
Pg 109 Colin Bell
Pg 112 Matthew Copham
Pg 113 Matthew Copham
Pg 114 Judith Kaine
Pg 115 upper – Wilderness
 Safaris
 Lower – Wilderness Safaris
Pg 116 Beverly Joubert
Pg 119 Mike Myers
Pg 120 upper – Capture Africa
 Middle – Matthew Copham
 Lower – Brian van Nierkerk –
 Wilderness Safaris
Pg 121 Gerald Grant
Pg 122 Matthew Copham
Pg 123 Matthew Copham
Pg 124 upper – Skip Shipman
 Lower – Gene Covey
Pg 125 Dana Allen – Wilderness
 Safaris
Pg 126 upper – Wilderness
 Safaris
 Middle – Wilderness Safaris
 Lower – Mike Myers –
 Wilderness Safaris
Pg 127 Michael Poliza –
 Wilderness Safaris
Pg 129 Matthew Copham
Pg 130 upper – Mike Myor
 Lower – Marilou Angelo
Pg 131 Wilderness Safaris

Pg 132 upper – Sanctuary Lodges
 Middle – David Hamman –
 Wilderness Safaris
 Lower – Capture Africa
Pg 133 Dana Allen – Wilderness
 Safaris
Pg 135 upper – Matthew Copham
 Lower – Colin Bell
Pg 136 upper – Colin Bell
 Lower – Wilderness Safaris
Pg 137 Lincoln Jong
Pg 139 Mike Myers
Pg 141 Saskia de Gouveia
Pg 143 Dana Allen – Wilderness
 Safaris
Pg 144 upper – Matthew Copham
 Lower – Uncharted Africa
Pg 145 Uncharted Africa
Pg 148 upper – Mashatu Game
 Reserve
 Middle – Mashatu Game
 Rooorvo
 Lower – Adventure Mashatu
Pg 149 Scott Knierem
Pg 150 upper – Mashatu Game
 Reserve
 Lower – Mashatu Game
 Reserve

Zimbabwe:
Pg 153 Dave Christiansen
Pg 156 Colin Bell
Pg 157 Maurice Scheetz
Pg 159 upper – Rick Cassidy
 Lower – Bob Peck
Pg 160 upper – Bob Peck
 Lower – Grant Gerald
Pg 163 Wild Horizons
Pg 164 upper – Victoria Falls
 Safari Lodge
 Middle – Victoria Falls Safari
 Lodge
 Lower – Victoria Falls Hotel
Pg 168 upper – Wilderness
 Safaris
 Lower – Dana Allen –
 Wilderness Safaris
Pg 169 Wilderness Safaris
Pg 170 Dana Allen – Wilderness
 Safaris
Pg 171 African Bush Camps
Pg 172 upper – Amalinda Camp
 Lower – Amalinda Camp

Photo Credits

Pg 303 upper – Grande Roche
Middle – Le Quartier Francais
Lower – Le Quartier Francais
Pg 306 upper – Bushmans Kloof
Lower – Bushmans Kloof
Pg 307 Lorraine Lutgen
Pg 308 Lorraine Lutgen
Pg 310 upper – Grootbos Nature
Reserve
Lower – Grootbos Nature
Reserve
Pg 311 Grootbos – Dyer Island
Cruises
Pg 312 Grootbos – Dyer Island
Cruises
Pg 313 Lorraine Lutgen
Pg 314 upper – The Plettenberg
Lower – The Plettenberg
Pg 316 Pezula Resort
Pg 317 Shamwari
Pg 318 CC Africa
Pg 319 upper – CC Africa
Lower – CC Africa
Pg 321 Zimbali Lodge
Pg 322 Caroline Culbert –
Wilderness Safaris
Pg 325 upper – CC Africa
Middle – Abby Lazar
Lower – CC Africa
Pg 326 upper – CC Africa
Middle – CC Africa
Lower – CC Africa
Pg 328 upper – Wilderness
Safaris
Lower – Wilderness Safaris
Pg 329 upper – Dean Morton –
Wilderness Safaris
Lower – Wilderness Safaris

Tanzania:
Pg 333 Gene Covey
Pg 336 Gene Covey
Pg 337 Karma Kumlin-Diers
Pg 338 upper – Marcee & Dennis
Perelman
Lower – Ronald Davis
Pg 341 Serena Hotels
Pg 342 Hatari Lodge
Pg 343 Hatari Lodge
Pg 344 Gene Covey
Pg 345 Ndarakwai Ranch
Pg 347 Lynn Glasgow
Pg 348 upper – Andre Steynberg
Lower – Asilia Lodges
Pg 349 upper – Andre Steynberg
Lower – Elewana Afrika
Pg 351 upper – Kyle Witten
Lower – Serena Safari Lodges
Pg 352 CC Africa

Pg 353 Alison Nolting
Pg 354 upper   Alison Nolting
Lower – Alison Nolting
Pg 355 Alison Nolting
Pg 357 Middle – Craig Emden
Pg 358 CC Africa
Pg 359 Tom Saville
Pg 360 Andre Steynberg
Pg 361 Mark Nolting
Pg 362 Serena Safari Lodges
Pg 364 Warren Yu
Pg 365 Lincoln Jong
Pg 366 Gene Covey
Pg 368 Lower – Marilou Angelo
Pg 369 Ranger Safaris
Pg 370 upper – Sayari – Asilia
Lodges and Camps
Middle – Serena Safari
Lodges
Lower – Elewana Afrika
Pg 372 upper – Suyan – Asilia
Lodges and Camps
Lower – Ranger Safaris
Pg 373 upper – Singita Grumeti
Reserves
Middle – Singita Grumeti
Reserves
Lower – Singita Grumeti
Reserves
Pg 375 Ranger Safaris
Pg 376 Ranger Safaris
Pg 377 Ranger Safaris
Pg 379 Megan Hearthway
Pg 382 Megan Hearthway
Pg 391 Steven Steiner
Pg 392 Sand Rivers Selous
Pg 393 upper – Sand Rivers
Selous
Lower – Lukula Selous
Pg 394 Selous Safari Company
Pg 395 upper – Retreat Safari Ltd.
Middle – Nomad Tanzania
Lower – Selous Safari
Company
Pg 396 Ranger Safaris
Pg 397 Ruaha River Lodge –
Foxes African Safaris
Pg 399 Ranger Safaris
Pg 400 Fire Light Expeditions
Pg 401 Ranger Safaris
Pg 403 Nomad Tanzania – Paul
Joynson-Hicks
Pg 404 upper – Nomad Tanzania
Lower – Ranger Safaris
Pg 405 upper – Nomad Tanzania
Lower – Nomad Tanzania
Pg 407 upper – Foxes African
Safaris
Lower – Serena Hotels

Pg 409 upper – Gary Balfour –
ARP
Lower – Gary Balfour – ARP
Pg 410 upper – Andre Steynberg
Lower – Asilia Lodges
Pg 411 upper – Asilia Lodges
Lower – Chumbe Island – Hal
Thompson
Pg 412 upper – Chumbe Island –
Hal Thompson
Middle – CC Africa
Lower – CC Africa
Pg 413 CC Africa

Kenya
Pg 415 Karma Kumlin-Diers
Pg 418 Alison Nolting
Pg 419 John Norvell
Pg 420 Gene Covey
Pg 421 Cad Dennehy
Pg 422 upper – Kathy Berry
Lower – Warren Yu
Pg 423 upper – Origins Safaris
Lower – Serena Hotels
Pg 424 upper – Ngong House
Lower – House of Waine
Pg 425 Tortilis Camp
Pg 427 Tortilis Camp
Pg 428 upper – Colin Bell
Middle – Colin Bell
Lower – Colin Dell
Pg 429 upper – Colin Bell
Lower – Campi ya Kanzi
Pg 431 upper – Steve Turner
Lower – Finch Hattons
Pg 432 Steve Turner
Pg 433 Origins Safaris
Pg 434 Brian Stanszewski
Pg 436 Steve Turner – Origins
Safaris
Pg 437 upper – Gene Covey
Lower – Warren Yu
Pg 438 upper – Heritage
Management Ltd
Middle – Governor's Camp
Lower – Heritage
Management Ltd
Pg 439 CC Africa
Pg 440 upper – Elephant Pepper
Camp
Lower – Ol Seki Mara Camp
Pg 443 upper – Rusinga Island
Lodge – Origins
Lower – Rusinga Island
Lodge – Origins
Pg 445 Cheli & Peacock
Pg 448 upper – Serena Lodges
Lower – Serena Lodges
Pg 450 upper – Elsa's Kopje
Lower – Elsa's Kopje

Ethiopia
Pg 545 (chapter cover) Steve Turner
Pg 547 Abby Lazar
Pg 548 upper – Abby Lazar
Lower – Abby Lazar
Pg 549 Abby Lazar
Pg 550 upper – Mark Nolting
Lower – Steve Turner
Pg 551 upper – Steve Turner
Lower – Steve Turner
Pg 553 Steve Turner
Pg 555 upper – Steve Turner
Lower – Steve Turner
Pg 556 Steve Turner
Pg 557 upper – Abby Lazar
Lower – Abby Lazar
Pg 558 upper – Steve Turner
Middle – Abby Lazar
Lower – Steve Turner

Pg 559 Steve Turner
Pg 560 upper – Steve Turner
Lower – Steve Turner
Pg 561 upper – Steve Turner
Lower – Mark Nolting
Pg 562 upper – Mark Nolting
Lower – Mark Nolting
Pg 563 upper – Abby Lazar
Middle – Mark Nolting
Lower – Mark Nolting
Pg 564 upper – Mark Nolting
Middle – Mark Nolting
Lower – Mark Nolting
Pg 565 upper – Mark Nolting
Middle – Mark Nolting
Lower – Mark Nolting
Pg 566 upper – Mark Nolting
Lower – Mark Nolting
Pg 567 upper – Mark Nolting
Lower – Mark Nolting

Pg 568 Mark Nolting
Pg 569 upper – Mark Nolting
Lower – Mark Nolting

Malawi
Pg 595 upper – Dana Allen – Wildeness Safaris
Lower – Dana Allen – Wilderness Safaris
Pg 599 upper – Dana Allen – Wilderness Safaris
Lower – Dana Allen – Wildeness Safaris

Democratic Republic of the Congo
Pg 629 Abby Lazar

Praise for
African Safari Journal

As someone who has visited Africa over 40 times, I can say without hesitation that the *African Safari Journal* is the best single resource one can have with them on what is sure to be an adventure of a lifetime. Its easy-to-read style and wide variety of information make it a "must have" for anyone on safari!

— RON MAGILL COMMUNICATIONS & MEDIA MIAMI METROZOO

Mark Nolting has done it again! Clearing out the clutter from the safari experience, making sense of what is good and what is bad, getting prepared once you have decided are all often overlooked and sometimes overwhelming aspects of the safari. Thanks to *African Safari Journal* it's all done for you, and all that is left is to engulf yourself in our continent's pleasures.

— DERECK JOUBERT, EXPLORER IN RESIDENCE AT THE
NATIONAL GEOGRAPHIC SOCIETY, CONSERVATIONIST, FILMMAKER

If *Africa's Top Wildlife Countries* is the first book to grab when planning your safari, then the *African Safari Journal* is the first book to grab when you're headed to the airport to go on your safari! Nolting has got you covered from planning your safari, to living it, and reliving it again through the notes in your own personal safari journal. Packed full of information, maps, hundreds of color illustrations, and space for your own notes, it's the only book you'll ever need while on safari!

— GENE ECKHART — PROFESSIONAL PHOTOGRAPHER AND AUTHOR OF
"MOUNTAIN GORILLAS: BIOLOGY, CONSERVATION AND COEXISTENCE"

Mark Nolting's *African Safari Journal* has accompanied our family on each of our sojourns to Africa. Incorporating an abbreviated guide to the African bush, a planner and a personal journal in a compact format, the *African Safari Journal* has been an indispensable tool accompanying our travels. Upon return, it remains a keepsake of treasured memories and mementos secreted within its pages.

— TERRI WILLIAMS-JAKWAY WHITE BEAR LAKE, MN

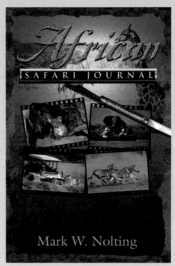
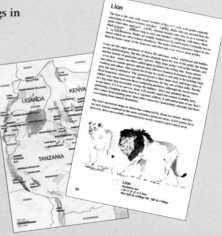

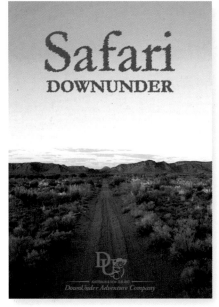

AUSTRALIA & NEW ZEALAND
DownUnder Adventure Company

Adventure
If there is adventure in your soul, live it on a safari DownUnder!

Wildlife
Our experienced private guides will get you up close to the wildlife.

Marine Life
Encounter spectacular marine life from a boat or helicopter.

Off the Beaten Track
Escape to the peace and quite of these two beautiful and diverse countries, leaving the tourist crowds far behind.

Families
Create fun and exciting experiences that leave your family with memories that last a lifetime.

Culture and Art
Immerse yourself in ancient cultures and art.

Indulgence
Relax and rejuvenate in the magnificent lodges and day spas.

New World Wine
Enjoy the excellent New World wines of Australia and New Zealand.

For more information and to receive a brochure
Call **Louise Steynberg** at **1-800-882-9453** or **954-491-8877**
email: info@SafariDownUnder.com

www.SafariDownUnder.com

Dear Adventurer:

The Africa Adventure Company is your passport to the safari of your dreams. Our team is managed and directed by Mark and Alison Nolting, two people whose combined experience and knowledge of Africa is unsurpassed in the safari business.

Mark is the author of *Africa's Top Wildlife Countries*, an award-winning guide book that is considered by the travel industry as the quintessential guide for planning a safari, and the *African Safari Journal*, a diary, phrase book and wildlife guide, all in one. He has received the **Conde Nast Traveler** magazine award as one of the World's Top African Travel Specialists several years in a row. Born and raised in Zimbabwe, Alison managed a safari camp for several years hosting guests in the bush and worked in the Africa travel industry in England before joining Mark in 1991.

So how do you know which safari is right for you? Private or group? East Africa or Southern Africa? A luxury itinerary with premier camps and lodges or camping out in the bush with mobile tents? This is where our passionate staff and years of experience set us apart. We are here to guide you through all the choices.

We offer a refreshing assortment of over 150 unique and exciting itineraries that can only beckon your travel spirit to Africa. Many can be adapted to your personal specifications. Taking into consideration your needs and desires, we take your dream of the "perfect day on safari" and make it a reality.

As we constantly receive reports from our guides and operators on the ground and trip reports from thousands of returning clients, we are kept current as to where the best wildlife is being seen and which safari camps and lodges are providing the best accommodations, food and service NOW — allowing us to present the absolute best safari options for you. No amount of research on the Internet can provide this information.

We encourage you to contact us so that we may send you our easy-to-use SAFARI PLANNER and assist you in planning your African journey. Our personalized service will exceed your expectations!

Cordially,

Mark and Alison Nolting

The Africa Adventure Company • 5353 N. Federal Hwy., Suite 300, Ft. Lauderdale, FL 33308
Tel: 800.882.9453 or 954.491.8877; Fax: 954.491.9060 • Email: safari@AfricanAdventure.com
Website: www.AfricanAdventure.com

P.S.: Please read a sampling of trip reports from our clients in "Bush Tails" (pp. 676–695)

10 GREAT REASONS TO TRAVEL WITH THE AFRICA ADVENTURE COMPANY

1. **We wrote THE definitive guide book on safaris to Africa**
   The President of our company, Mark Nolting, has written the quintessential book on traveling to Africa, *Africa's Top Wildlife Countries* — a testament to our level of expertise.

2. **One of the world's top African Travel Specialists**
   We have been recognized as one of the World's Top African Travel Specialists for the past several years by Conde Nast Traveler. This is only one of many prestigious magazines that have recommended our high-quality safaris.

3. **We are committed to sustainable tourism and eco-conservation**
   For over 20 years we have promoted local ground operators and guides, camps and lodges that see the merits of low-impact travel and the survival of habitats. Equally as important are the camps and lodges featured in our programs that support local communities, wildlife projects and low utilization of energy resources.

4. **Our safari consultants have the highest level of experience**
   Our travel consultants have an average of over 10 years experience in African travel — a level unmatched in the industry. Many of our staff were born and raised in Africa.

5. **Over 70% of our business is repeat or referral**
   Our repeat/referral rate is the envy of the industry. Exceed people's expectations and they will come back time and time again. We have a number of clients that have taken over 10 safaris with us!

6. **Great Value — BETTER safaris FOR LESS!**
   As one of the larger "Africa only" tour operators in the world, we command great discounts. In addition, we spend much less on advertising than our competitors, as many people find us through the books we have written. These savings are passed on to you in the form of a higher quality safari for less.

7. **Relationships built during 22 years in the African safari business**
   With more than two decades in this business, we have fostered close relationships with safari guides and owners of camps, lodges, and local safari companies. Our "extended family" in Africa is a priceless asset, as they will do everything possible to make your travel experience special!

8. **More than 150 safari itineraries!**
   Many safari companies offer a few set itineraries. Take it or leave it. We offer a wide selection of safari options, with trips to over 20 countries. Why compromise? Take the trip of your dreams!

9. **Our own air department offers competitive rates and convenient "one-stop shopping"**
   Our IATA/ARC in-house air department offers great discounted airfares. More importantly, book your air with us and we will be there to assist you if your flights are changed or cancelled. It is no fun arriving at an airport in Africa with no flight to catch — and having to fend for yourself!

10. **24-hour emergency hotline**
    In case of a travel emergency, we can be reached 24/7 by your family here at home, or by you, while on safari.

The Africa Adventure Company specializes in adventures to the following countries:

Botswana	Malawi	South Africa
Egypt	Mauritius	Swaziland
Ethiopia	Mozambique	Tanzania
Kenya	Namibia	Uganda
Jordan	Rwanda	Zambia
Madagascar	Seychelles	Zimbabwe

We know that an African safari is an investment of time, money, and your dreams

The
Africa Adventure
Company

*"For a Safari
of a Lifetime"*

Tel: 800.882.9453
Tel: 954.491.8877
Fax: 954.491.9060

5353 North Federal Highway, Suite 300
Fort Lauderdale, Florida 33308 U.S.A.

safari@africanadventure.com
Look for us on the web!
www.AfricanAdventure.com

The
Africa Adventure
Company

*"For a Safari
of a Lifetime"*

Tel: 800.882.9453
Tel: 954.491.8877
Fax: 954.491.9060

5353 North Federal Highway, Suite 300
Fort Lauderdale, Florida 33308 U.S.A.

safari@africanadventure.com
Look for us on the web!
www.AfricanAdventure.com

The
Africa Adventure
Company

*"For a Safari
of a Lifetime"*

Tel: 800.882.9453
Tel: 954.491.8877
Fax: 954.491.9060

5353 North Federal Highway, Suite 300
Fort Lauderdale, Florida 33308 U.S.A.

safari@africanadventure.com
Look for us on the web!
www.AfricanAdventure.com

The
Africa Adventure
Company

*"For a Safari
of a Lifetime"*

Tel: 800.882.9453
Tel: 954.491.8877
Fax: 954 491.9060

5353 North Federal Highway, Suite 300
Fort Lauderdale, Florida 33308 U.S.A.

safari@africanadventure.com
Look for us on the web!
www.AfricanAdventure.com

Mark Nolting, author of
Africa's Top Wildlife Countries - 7th edition
ISBN: 978-0-939895-12-0
US $29.95

and the

African Safari Journal - 5th edition
ISBN: 978-0-939895-11-3
US $19.95

Available at bookstores and from
The Africa Adventure Company

Mark Nolting, author of
Africa's Top Wildlife Countries - 7th edition
ISBN: 978-0-939895-12-0
US $29.95

and the

African Safari Journal - 5th edition
ISBN: 978-0-939895-11-3
US $19.95

Available at bookstores and from
The Africa Adventure Company

Mark Nolting, author of
Africa's Top Wildlife Countries - 7th edition
ISBN: 978-0-939895-12-0
US $29.95

and the

African Safari Journal - 5th edition
ISBN: 978-0-939895-11-3
US $19.95

Available at bookstores and from
The Africa Adventure Company

Mark Nolting, author of
Africa's Top Wildlife Countries - 7th edition
ISBN: 978-0-939895-12-0
US $29.95

and the

African Safari Journal - 5th edition
ISBN: 978-0-939895-11-3
US $19.95

Available at bookstores and from
The Africa Adventure Company

PLEASE GIVE THESE TO ANYONE INTERESTED IN TRAVELING TO AFRICA